Don Heist

W9-CNX-800

Linda Bezemer
c/o M Scott Quad
Bloomington, In

Don Hewetson   1195
Briscoe 1023
337-8534

75.95
F9

To my parents

INTRODUCTORY

PSYCHOLOGY

Jonathan L. Freedman
Columbia University

▲ ADDISON-WESLEY PUBLISHING COMPANY

Reading, Massachusetts   Menlo Park, California   London   Amsterdam   Don Mills, Ontario   Sydney

Copyright © 1978 by Addison-Wesley Publishing Company, Inc. Philippines copyright 1978 by Addison-Wesley Publishing Company, Inc.

All rights reserved. No part of this publication may be reproduced, stored in a retrieval system, or transmitted, in any form or by any means, electronic, mechanical, photo-copying, recording, or otherwise, without the prior written permission of the publisher. Printed in the United States of America. Published simultaneously in Canada. Library of Congress Catalog Card No. 76-15461.

ISBN 0-201-05788-3
ABCDEFGHIJ-RN-7987

DESIGN AND ILLUSTRATIONS BY ROBERT A. ROSE

ACKNOWLEDGMENTS

Cover photograph copyright by the California Institute of Technology and Carnegie Institution of Washington. Reproduced by permission from the Hale Observatories.

Figures

2.2 Bourne, L. E., and B. R. Ekstrand (1973). *Psychology: Its Principles and Meanings*, 2d ed. Hinsdale, Ill.: Dryden. Copyright © 1976 by Holt, Rinehart and Winston. Reprinted by permission of Holt, Rinehart and Winston. **3.6** Miller, N. E., and A. Banuazizi (1968). Instrumental learning by curarized rats of a visceral response, intestinal or cardiac. *J. Comp. physiol. Psychol.* 65:1-7. Copyright 1968 by the American Psychological Association. Reprinted by permission. **4.8** Bower, G. H. (1972). Mental imagery and associative learning. In L. Gregg (ed.), *Cognition in Learning and Memory*. New York: Wiley. Reprinted by permission. **4.10** Landauer, T. K. (1969). Reinforcement as consolidation. *Psychol. Rev.* 76:92-6. Copyright 1969 by the American Psychological Association. Reprinted by permission. **4.12** Peterson, L. R., and M. J. Peterson (1959). Short-term retention of individual verbal items. *J. exp. Psychol.* 84:472-81. Copyright 1959 by the American Psychological Association. Reprinted by permission. **5.1** Van Osterman, G. F. (1952). *Manual of Foreign Languages*, 4th ed. New York: Central Book Company. Reprinted by permission of Clark Boardman Company, Ltd. **7.5** Harrell, T. W., and M. S. Harrell (1945). Army General Classification Test scores for civilian occupations. *Educational and Psychological Measurement* 5:229-39. Reprinted by permission. **9.1** Clark, R. (1959). Some time correlated schedules and their effects on behavior. *J. exp. Anal. Behav.* 2:1-22. Copyright © 1959 by the Society for the Experimental Analysis of Behavior, Inc. **9.7** Lowell, E. L. (1952). The effect of need for achievement on learning and speed of performance. *J. Psychol.* 33:31-40. Reprinted by permission of The Journal Press. **9.8** Zajonc, R. B. (1968). Attitudinal effects of mere exposure. *J. Pers. soc. Psychol.* 9:1-29. Copyright 1968 by the American Psychological Association. Reprinted by permission. **10.5** Lazarus, R. S., E. M. Opton, Jr., M. S. Nomikus, and N. O. Rankin (1965). The principle of short-circuiting of threat: further evidence. *J. pers.* 33:622-35. Copyright 1965 by Duke University Press. **10.7** Schlosberg, H. (1952). The description of facial expressions in terms of two dimensions. *J. exp. Psychol.* 44:229-37. Copyright 1952 by the American Psychological Association. Reprinted by permission. **11.1** Kleitman, N. (1960). Patterns of dreaming. *Sci. Amer.* 203:82-8. Copyright © 1960 by Scientific American, Inc. All rights reserved. Adapted by permission of William C. Dement. **12.3** Hilgard, J. (1932). Learning and maturation in preschool children. *J. genet Psychol.* 71:36-56. Reprinted by permission of The Journal Press. **12.6** Hess, E. H. (1959). Imprinting. *Science* 130:133-41. Reprinted by permission of the American Association for the Advancement of Science. **12.10** Harlow, H. F., and R. R. Zimmerman (1959). Affectional responses in the infant monkey. *Science* 130:431-2. Reprinted by permission of the publisher and H. F. Harlow, University of Wisconsin Primate Laboratory. **13.1** Tanner, J. M., R. H. Whitehouse, and M. L. Takaishi (1966). Standards from birth to

Continued on page A32

Preface

Introductory psychology should be one of the most fascinating, stimulating courses in college. It deals with the one topic that interests just about everyone—how people think and behave, what we feel and why, and how we function. Yet it seems as if all too often introductory psychology is disappointing. Students think that many of the topics are irrelevant to their own lives and wonder why they must be covered. They also feel that they have been exposed to too many separate topics without ever understanding how they relate to each other. These are real difficulties, but I sincerely think they can be overcome and I wrote this book as a partial solution. Naturally, a successful course depends primarily on the teacher, but I hope this text will provide a framework within which psychology can be taught in a rigorous, thorough manner while communicating the great excitement of the field.

The most important theme or principle of the book is that the topics of psychology are closely interrelated, that it is impossible to understand any single topic without knowing a great deal about other areas in the field. Thus, this book provides full coverage of all of psychology, but whenever possible shows how each topic relates to others. This not only makes each topic more interesting, but also gives readers a broader view and helps them make connections that are important to a full understanding of the field. For example, the book begins with a chapter on perception, often a difficult topic for students. The chapter provides a thorough discussion of perception, but also shows how perception is related to other fields in psychology by pointing out that contrast effects occur in social judgments, that adaptation level is applicable to many areas, that figure-ground relationships are useful in understanding attribution theory, that perception in general may be considered a cognitive process much like thinking and memory, and so on. Similar connections are drawn in other chapters. Thus, the so-called basic topics of psychology are presented as important in their own right, but also as critical in helping us understand issues and principles in other areas.

A second important characteristic of the book derives from the fact that I am a social psychologist, though I have also worked in experimental areas such as concept formation and memory. Although the text covers all the topics of psychology, it has a more social emphasis than other books. This shows up in somewhat more coverage of social psychology than is usually found in introductory texts, but more importantly in the examples that are used in other chapters.

The connections that are made are often to topics in social psychology, to how people interact or react in social situations. I believe that this makes all of the book more relevant and interesting for most students. It shows them how the basic topics are related to their daily lives, and makes even complex principles of experimental psychology easier to understand and appreciate.

In addition, there are two unique chapters in the book. One deals with sexual behavior, sex roles, and adult development. Most texts devote a chapter to child development and a few pages to development throughout the rest of life, but the latter is a very active research area at the moment. The other unique chapter covers environmental psychology, my own specialty and an especially dynamic, growing field. Both of these chapters deal with extremely important issues and will be of great interest to students.

A special feature of the text that is not found in any other is a series of interviews with prominent people who use psychology in their work. These are not psychologists, but people in other fields who, in a sense, practice what we teach. Psychologists study hunger and obesity—Jean Nidetch organized Weight Watchers; we talk about and study sex roles and changing attitudes—Betty Friedan's *The Feminine Mystique* started the modern feminist movement; environmental psychologists study the effects of crowding and architecture on people—Philip Johnson is one of the world's leading architects. I talked with advertising executive Jerry della Femina; police commissioner Robert diGrazia, director Abe Burrows, novelist Judith Rossner, and others about how they work and how psychology enters into what they do. Besides teaching us about the uses of psychology in the real world, the interviews by these outstanding people make fascinating reading. They were tremendously fun to do—I hope they are as enjoyable to read.

Finally, I believe that how material is presented is very important. Psychology need not be dry. Textbooks, no matter how long, need not read like encyclopedias. Accordingly, I have tried to write in a light, easy, conversational manner so that the student will find the book easy to read and to understand.

Introductory psychology must cover the field, show how the various topics relate to each other, and keep the student's interest high. I hope this book has done this. ■

New York, New York   J. L. F.
October 1977

Acknowledgments

Many people have worked on this book and I am very grateful to them. First, at Addison-Wesley, Roger Drumm and Stuart Johnson, psychology editors, encouraged me with their confidence and advice; Karen Guardino handled endless details and made my life easier; and Tom Begner, who was in charge of the whole operation throughout, helped me with ideas, toughmindedness, and friendship. The production department turned out an exciting, original book. Two people deserve very special thanks. Melissa Hodgson is the best copyeditor I have met or hope to meet and absolutely lovely to work with besides. Kathe Golden was superb as developmental editor. She improved the book in countless ways—criticizing, suggesting additions and deletions, organizing, reorganizing, scheduling interviews, providing ideas, and doing just about everything possible to help with the book. I am enormously grateful to her. Indeed, from beginning to end I have enjoyed and profited from working with all of the people at Addison-Wesley.

Other people also helped. Robert Krauss and Philip Shaver read and commented on various chapters; Steve Woods wrote a draft for part of the physiological chapter; and the following people read all or part of the book: Thurston L. Cosner, Cuyahoga Community College; Dr. Jane Cross, Cardinal Glennon Memorial Hospital for Children; Jane Dallinger; Nancy W. Denney, University of Kansas; John C. Hallock, Lakeland Community College; Winfred F. Hill, Northwestern University; Richard M. Lerner, Pennsylvania State University; Michael J. Scavio, California State University—Fullerton; David J. Schneider, The University of Texas—San Antonio; Jerry S. Wiggins, University of British Columbia; Richard A. Kasschau, University of Houston; James M. Royer, University of Massachusetts; and Leslie E. Wong, Fort Steilacoom Community College. I thank them all. Finally, I am especially thankful to Rona Abramovitch, who provided advice on the developmental chapters and many other sections of the book, assistance in finding references, encouragement, and much more. ∎

Contents

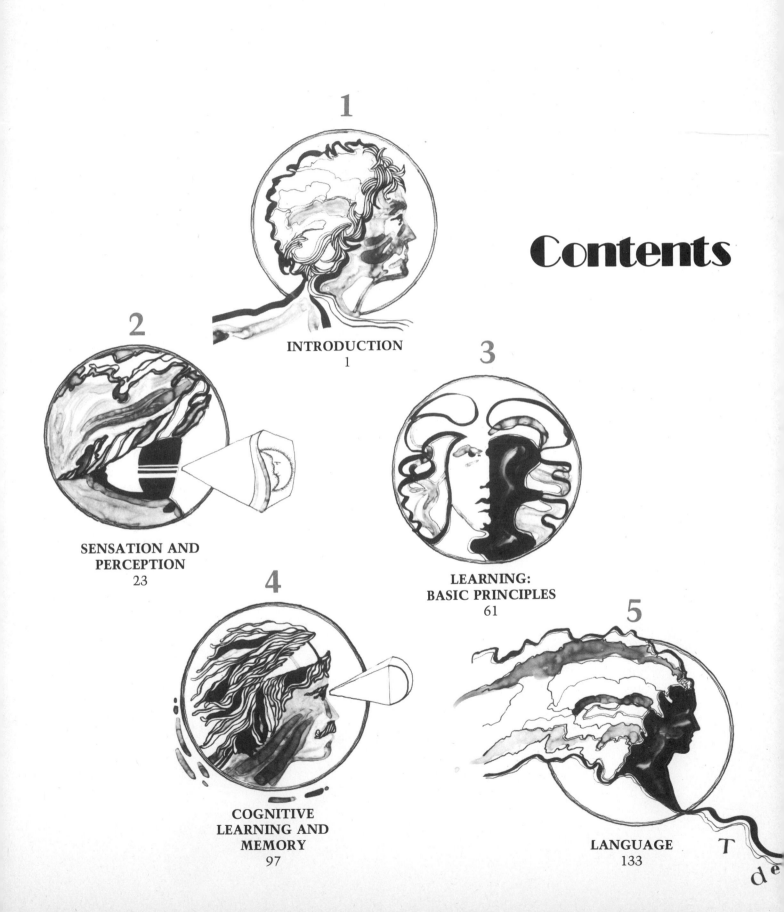

1

INTRODUCTION
1

2

SENSATION AND
PERCEPTION
23

3

LEARNING:
BASIC PRINCIPLES
61

4

COGNITIVE
LEARNING AND
MEMORY
97

5

LANGUAGE
133

6

THINKING
161

7

PSYCHOLOGICAL
TESTING AND
INTELLIGENCE
195

9

MOTIVATION
251

8

BIOLOGICAL BASIS
OF BEHAVIOR
221

10

EMOTIONS
283

12

DEVELOPMENTAL
PSYCHOLOGY
347

11

STATES OF
CONSCIOUSNESS
315

13
SEX AND
ADULT DEVELOPMENT
379

14
PERSONALITY
419

15
PSYCHOPATHOLOGY
455

16
TREATMENT OF
PSYCHOPATHOLOGY
493

17
SOCIAL
PSYCHOLOGY
527

18
SOCIAL
INFLUENCE
559

19
ENVIRONMENTAL
PSYCHOLOGY
589

Contents

CHAPTER 1 INTRODUCTION 1

The major fields of psychology / 3

Who are psychologists and what do they do? / 7

General approaches to psychology / 8

Psychology as a scientific discipline / 11

Key issues / 19

Organization of the text / 20

CHAPTER 2 SENSATION AND PERCEPTION 23

The real versus the perceived world / 25

SENSATION / 26

The sense organs / 27

    BOX 2.1 VISUAL FEATURE DETECTORS 30

PERCEPTION / 36

Psychophysics / 36

    BOX 2.2 THE PSYCHOPHYSICS OF AIRPLANE NOISE 37

Contrast and adaptation / 38

Distance and depth perception / 40

Constancies / 42

    BOX 2.3 THE MOON ILLUSION 42

    BOX 2.4 THE ILLUSION OF MOVEMENT 44

Rules of organization / 45

    BOX 2.5 CAMOUFLAGE: THE ART OF MISLEADING 46

    BOX 2.6 RULES OF ORGANIZATION IN OTHER PSYCHOLOGICAL PHENOMENA 50

The role of innate mechanisms and learning / 51

Other factors affecting perception / 53

    BOX 2.7 TIME PERCEPTION 54

    BOX 2.8 HOW RELIABLE IS EYEWITNESS TESTIMONY? 56

CHAPTER 3 LEARNING: BASIC PRINCIPLES 61

Learning: a definition / 62

Classical conditioning / 63

    BOX 3.1 CONDITIONING HUMANS 64

Operant conditioning / 67

    BOX 3.2 SKINNER, THE SKINNER BOX, AND WALDEN TWO 68

    BOX 3.3 CHIMPS AND CHIPS: SECONDARY REINFORCERS 71

    BOX 3.4 PLEASURE CENTERS IN THE BRAIN 73

    BOX 3.5 SCHEDULES OF REINFORCEMENT 76

    BOX 3.6 SUPERSTITIOUS BEHAVIOR 80

Classical and operant conditioning compared / 83

    BOX 3.7 LEARNED HELPLESSNESS AND DEPRESSION 84

Imitation / 85

Two basic principles of learning / 87

    BOX 3.8 APPLICATIONS OF LEARNING TO MENTAL DISORDERS 90

Innate versus learned behavior / 92

CHAPTER 4 COGNITIVE LEARNING AND MEMORY 97

    BOX 4.1 DO OTHER ANIMALS LEARN COGNITIONS? 99

The basic process of cognitive learning—contiguity / 100

Factors affecting cognitive learning / 101

    BOX 4.2 NONVERBAL ASSOCIATIONS 105

    BOX 4.3 EIDETIC IMAGERY 108

The memory system / 109

    BOX 4.4 MNEMONIC TRICKS 111

    INTERVIEW: Harry Lorayne 112

    BOX 4.5 MEMORY CONSOLIDATION AND ELECTRIC SHOCK THERAPY 116

Why we forget / 118

    BOX 4.6 INTERFERENCE VERSUS DECAY 120

Memory retrieval / 122

Applications of learning research to education / 127

CHAPTER 5 LANGUAGE 133

The importance of language / 135

Elements of language / 135

    BOX 5.1 MEANING AND CONTEXT 138

    BOX 5.2 AMBIGUOUS SENTENCES 141

How language develops / 141

How language is acquired / 146

Can other animals acquire language? / 149

Language and thought / 152

    BOX 5.3 AVOIDING SEXUAL STEREOTYPES IN LANGUAGE 153

Nonverbal communication / 154

    BOX 5.4 NONVERBAL COMMUNICATION AND LIE DETECTION 156

Language in perspective / 157

CHAPTER 6 THINKING 161

Thinking defined / 162

Concept formation / 163

    BOX 6.1 DEFINING A SIMPLE CONCEPT 165

Problem solving / 170

Learning to learn / 176

Insight—the "Eureka" phenomenon / 178

Creative thinking / 180

Limits of the mind / 182

    INTERVIEW: Judith Rossner 183

    BOX 6.2 MENTAL ARITHMETIC TRICKS 186

CHAPTER 7 PSYCHOLOGICAL TESTING AND INTELLIGENCE 195

The theory of testing / 197

Factors determining the usefulness of a test / 197

Intelligence and intelligence tests / 199

    BOX 7.1 THE EFFECT OF BEING LABELED SMART OR DUMB 206

The role of heredity and environment in intelligence / 211

Mental retardation / 214

The mentally gifted / 216

CHAPTER 8   BIOLOGICAL BASIS OF BEHAVIOR   221

BOX 8.1   BIOLOGICAL EFFECTS—SOME EXAMPLES   222

The neuron / 222

Organization of the nervous system / 224

Central nervous system / 225

BOX 8.2   FINDING YOUR WAY AROUND A BODY   228

BOX 8.3   AROUSAL AND THE RETICULAR FORMATION   229

BOX 8.4   LOCALIZATION OF MEMORY   232

Peripheral nervous system / 235

Endocrine glands / 238

BOX 8.5   MENSTRUAL CYCLES   238

Behavior genetics / 242

CHAPTER 9   MOTIVATION   251

Learning versus performance / 252

Motivation defined / 252

Theories of motivation / 253

Basic physiological motives / 255

How motives operate—the example of hunger / 257

BOX 9.1   MOTIVATION AND PERFORMANCE   259

INTERVIEW: *Jean Nidetch   262*

Other basic motives / 265

BOX 9.2   CONFLICTING MOTIVES—APPROACH-AVOIDANCE   268

Learned motives / 270

BOX 9.3   A HIERARCHY OF NEEDS AND MOTIVES   274

CHAPTER 10   EMOTIONS   283

Definition of emotions / 284

Theories of emotion / 285

BOX 10.1   BRAIN FUNCTION AND EMOTIONS—THE LIMBIC SYSTEM   286

BOX 10.2   PREFRONTAL LOBOTOMIES   288

Expressing and identifying emotions / 294

BOX 10.3   CONTROLLING YOUR EMOTIONS   297

Emotion and behavior: aggression / 298

BOX 10.4   FREE EXPRESSION OF EMOTIONS   299

INTERVIEW: *Robert J. DiGrazia and Carl Velleca   306*

The effects of emotions / 310

CHAPTER 11   STATES OF CONSCIOUSNESS   315

Sleep / 317

Dreams / 322

BOX 11.1   THE CONTENT OF DREAMS   324

BOX 11.2   AGGRESSION IN DREAMS   327

Hypnosis / 328

BOX 11.3   AN EXAMPLE OF POST-HYPNOTIC SUGGESTION   330

Meditation / 334

Mystical experiences / 337

Psychoactive drugs / 338

CHAPTER 12   DEVELOPMENTAL PSYCHOLOGY   347

Physical growth and skills / 348

BOX 12.1   MULTIPLE BIRTHS   352

Perceptual development / 354

Piaget's stages of cognitive development / 356

Erikson's stages of social development and personality / 362

BOX 12.2   STYLES OF DISCIPLINE   369

BOX 12.3   GUILT AND HAPPINESS   370

Identification / 371

Moral development / 372

Further development / 375

CHAPTER 13   SEX AND ADULT DEVELOPMENT   379

Adolescence and sexual behavior / 380

Current sexual attitudes and behavior / 382

  BOX 13.1   SEX THERAPY   384

Sexual deviance / 385

Sex roles / 388

  BOX 13.2   TRANSSEXUALISM   389

  BOX 13.3   METHODOLOGICAL ERRORS PRODUCE SEX DIFFERENCES   392

  INTERVIEW: *Betty Friedan   394*

Adult development / 400

  BOX 13.4   WORKING WOMEN   404

  BOX 13.5   ALTERNATIVES TO TRADITIONAL MARRIAGE   406

  BOX 13.6   MARRIAGE AND HAPPINESS   409

  BOX 13.7   FACTORS IN HAPPINESS   411

CHAPTER 14   PERSONALITY   419

Theories of personality / 421

Constitutional or physiological theories / 421

Psychoanalytic theories / 423

Social learning theory / 434

Humanistic psychology and self-actualization / 437

  BOX 14.1   DOES PERSONALITY EXIST?   438

Comparison of the personality theories / 440

Personality assessment / 442

  BOX 14.2   JURY SELECTION   447

Some specific personality traits / 448

CHAPTER 15   PSYCHOPATHOLOGY   455

Mental health—a definition / 456

Types of psychopathology / 460

Neuroses / 460

  BOX 15.1   NERVOUS BREAKDOWNS   461

Personality disorders / 465

  BOX 15.2   THE INSANITY PLEA   468

Psychoses / 470

  BOX 15.3   MULTIPLE PERSONALITIES   475

Causes of psychopathology / 479

  BOX 15.4   PSYCHOSOMATIC CONDITIONS   486

Prevalence of psychopathology / 488

CHAPTER 16   TREATMENT OF PSYCHOPATHOLOGY   493

  BOX 16.1   THE CONCEPT OF MENTAL ILLNESS   495

Who does therapy? / 496

  BOX 16.2   CLINICAL PSYCHOLOGISTS, PSYCHIATRISTS, AND PSYCHOANALYSTS   497

Types of treatment / 497

Organic techniques / 498

Psychological techniques / 501

  BOX 16.3   REINFORCEMENT AND TOKEN ECONOMIES   510

  BOX 16.4   THE ETHICS OF BEHAVIOR CONTROL   511

  BOX 16.5   OTHER KINDS OF TREATMENT AND THERAPY   512

Evaluation of therapies / 519

  BOX 16.6   HALFWAY HOUSES   521

CHAPTER 17   **SOCIAL PSYCHOLOGY**   527

Social concerns / 528

Social perception and attribution theory / 532

Affiliation / 536

  BOX 17.1   BIRTH ORDER AND AFFILIATION   538

  BOX 17.2   OBJECTIVE SELF-AWARENESS   541

Social facilitation / 542

Competition versus cooperation / 543

Groups / 545

  INTERVIEW: *Abe Burrows   546*

  BOX 17.3   CROWDS AS ATTENTION-GETTERS   550

CHAPTER 18   **SOCIAL INFLUENCE**   559

Increasing compliance and obedience / 562

Altruism, equity, and social justice / 565

Bystander intervention / 567

  BOX 18.1   BRAINWASHING   568

Attitudes / 569

Theoretical approaches to attitudes / 570

Changing attitudes / 574

  INTERVIEW: *Jerry Della Femina   576*

  BOX 18.2   ATTITUDES AND BEHAVIOR   580

  BOX 18.3   THE EFFECT OF TOO MUCH REWARD   583

  BOX 18.4   SELF-PERCEPTION EXPLANATION OF DISSONANCE RESULTS   584

CHAPTER 19   **ENVIRONMENTAL PSYCHOLOGY**   589

Noise / 590

Personal space / 594

Crowding / 598

  BOX 19.1   THE PACE OF LIFE   601

  INTERVIEW: *Philip Johnson   607*

Life in the city / 612

APPENDIX   A1

BIBLIOGRAPHY   A9

GLOSSARY   A33

AUTHOR INDEX   A48

SUBJECT INDEX   A54

There are few things more exciting to me . . . than a psychological reason.
Henry James, The Art of Fiction

1 Introduction

The major fields of psychology ▪ *Who are psychologists and what do they do?* ▪ *General approaches to psychology* ▪ *Psychology as a scientific discipline* ▪ *Key issues* ▪ *Organization of the text*

P sychology is the systematic study of how animals, and particularly humans, function. It deals with how they perceive, think, learn, behave, and deal with the environment. It tries to describe and explain every aspect of human activity—simple and complex, external and internal, observable and inferrable. Certain physical mechanisms and reactions are left mainly to the fields of biology, physiology, and medicine; and the complex workings of whole societies are primarily the domain of sociologists and anthropologists. But with these few exceptions, any question that can reasonably be asked about human beings falls within the field of psychology.

Consider some examples . . .

Stanley Schachter is investigating why people smoke. He proposes that smokers are addicted to nicotine, making them similar to heroin or any other drug addicts.

James Olds studied how mechanisms in the brain affect learning. He discovered that there may be "pleasure centers" in the brain that make the animal feel good whenever they are stimulated.

Albert Bandura applies principles of learning to a wide range of problems in personality and social behavior. He has shown that techniques of learning can be used to relieve people of their fear of snakes and other so-called phobias.

William Dement studied the relationships between sleep and dreams and showed that dreams occur mostly during one level or stage of sleep. He also demonstrated that depriving people of dreams can have serious effects on their behavior.

Stanley Milgram asked people to give electric shocks to others as part of an experiment on learning. Most people dutifully gave shocks, including some that were potentially lethal, to someone with a known heart condition.

Allen and Beatrice Gardner have shown that it is possible to teach a chimpanzee quite a lot of sign language. Chimps cannot talk, but their chimp, Washoe, has mastered a great many signs and combines them in new ways.

Roger Sperry split the connections between the two halves of the brain and found that each side functioned separately. There is also some evidence that the left side of our brain tends to be logical and scientific, while the right side is more imaginative and creative.

Mark Lepper showed that paying too much can undermine someone's interest in doing something. The large reward made people uninterested in doing the activity unless they were paid, even though they used to do it freely because they enjoyed it.

John Calhoun observed rats that were placed in a large cage and allowed to reproduce. When the cage got very crowded, the animals began acting disturbed—overly aggressive, sexually promiscuous, and socially deviant.

William Michelson, on the other hand, has shown that crowding is not especially harmful to people. Living in high-rise housing in the middle of a big city has no negative effects compared to living in individual homes outside the central city.

Others have studied hypnosis, meditation, the effects of drugs, the development of language, how we solve problems, our response to people who stand too close to us, how we communicate without words, how we remember, and why we forget. There is work on what motivates us, how emotions are produced, what causes certain personalities to develop, why people and animals are aggressive but also altruistic, why some people become disturbed, and how they can be treated.

Psychology is a vast field, and, as we shall see, discoveries and research in each of its subparts are usually related to work in other areas. The organism, whether it be a rat or a person, is an integrated entity and only by understanding all aspects of it can we fully understand any one part.

THE MAJOR FIELDS OF PSYCHOLOGY

The science of psychology is generally divided into a number of separate fields, but to a great extent these overlap. Psychologists often work in several different areas, and findings in one area may be directly relevant to problems in another. Therefore, the divisions that follow are offered mainly as a convenient way of organizing psychology and giving some idea of its scope.

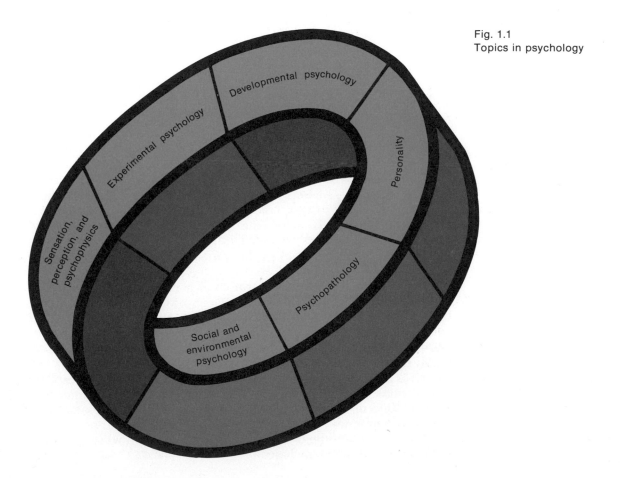

Fig. 1.1
Topics in psychology

Sensation, Perception, and Psychophysics

How do we see color? How can we manage to stand in a room full of people, with twenty conversations going at once, and follow one conversation? Why does a six-foot person look about the same height ten feet away as a hundred feet away? And why does this same person look taller when surrounded by short children than when surrounded by basketball players? And how do the answers to these questions relate to social phenomena, such as the fact that people who seem smart in high school may seem less smart in college?

This area deals with how the organism receives and interprets information about the world. It attempts to describe how the sense organs work, what stimuli they respond to, how this stimulation is translated in the brain into our perceptual experiences, and the relationship between psychological and physical stimulation. This area relies heavily on extremely sophisticated equipment and physiological techniques, and much of its data are self-reports by the subjects of what they are experiencing. It is probably the oldest area of modern psychology, dating back to Weber, Fechner, Wundt, and Helmholtz in the middle of the nineteenth century.

Experimental Psychology

What principles control learning? Why do we forget? How do we manage to recall one piece of information from our huge memories? What are emotions and why are we sometimes uncertain what emotion we are experiencing? How do we solve problems? How do children learn to speak grammatically when even their parents are seldom able to state the correct rules of grammar? Does our language affect the way we think? And how are the answers to some of these questions related to other fields such as the treatment of mental disturbance and the development of personality?

This broad area of psychology includes the separate topics of learning; memory; higher mental processes such as concept formation and problem solving; motivation; and emotions. Psycholinguistics—which deals with the development and structure of language—is sometimes included in experimental psychology and sometimes in social psychology, but probably belongs more closely to the former.

At least until recently experimental psychology was the dominant area in American psychology. More effort was spent studying these questions and developing these principles than in any other area. As a modern field it dates back to Ivan Pavlov's work with dogs and John Watson's behaviorism, and has been greatly influenced by Clark Hull, Edward Tolman, and B. F. Skinner. In recent years the emphasis has shifted somewhat from traditional problems in learning to questions of information processing and other mental functions, and the field of motivation has become even more physiologically oriented than it was before. Nevertheless, experimental psychology remains, in a sense, the core field of psychology upon which all other fields are to some extent based.

Developmental or Child Psychology

Can you speed up your child's development by encouragement or training? Why does a young child think that if you pour water from a short wide glass into a narrow tall glass, there is more water in the second glass than in the first? How do children develop morality? Why do adolescents so often seem to be going through a crisis? How do sex roles develop? What are the sexual habits of Americans now? What are the crises during adulthood?

Developmental psychology focuses on the maturation process— how children develop into adults, and how experiences in childhood affect this development. Since topics such as language, thinking, personality, and social behavior are themselves separate areas of concern, the study of their development naturally overlaps these other areas very closely. Indeed, much of the work in developmental psychology is done by people who are primarily concerned with these specific topics and choose to study them using children as subjects. However, the true developmental investigation involves age as a variable, and compares children of different ages in order to see how a particular function or behavior changes over time. Jean Piaget's work on cognitive development in childhood, Sigmund Freud's, Erik Erikson's, and John Bowlby's contributions to personality development, and the work of Robert Sears and Eleanor Maccoby on the influence of childhood experience on adult development are landmarks in this field. Because work in this area generally involves long-term observations of the same subjects, sometimes over a space of ten or twenty years, it is particularly difficult. For this reason, in recent years there has been relatively little work of this sort done and most developmental psychologists have focused on the short-term changes that occur in intellectual or moral behavior or on specific perceptual or intellectual behaviors in very early childhood. There have also been ingenious and exciting studies of perception in very young infants that potentially could reveal a great deal about the innate properties of our perceptual processes.

Personality

Is there such a thing as a personality trait? What role do physiological and physical structure play—are fat people always jolly? Do we acquire our personality or is it determined more by inherent qualities? How do principles of learning explain the development of personality? Are there authoritarian kinds of people? Can you distinguish people in terms of levels of anxiety? Is there a kind of person who takes advantage of others and always does well in bargaining situations?

This area concerns the description and development of the individual's enduring style and preferences in behavior. It also concerns the interrelationship among various parts of the individual's structure, and the interdynamics of how the person functions. Hans Eysenck and William Sheldon proposed physical or organic theories of personality. Early contributions in the development of personality were made by Sigmund Freud and his followers such as Carl Jung and Alfred Adler, but more recently psychologists such as Walter Mischel and Neal Miller have applied principles of learning and social functioning to the study of personality. There has also been some questioning of the traditional concept of personality, with greater emphasis on situational variables affecting behavior rather than the individual's own style.

Psychopathology, Clinical Psychology, or Abnormal Psychology

What does it mean to be mentally disturbed? How can you tell disturbed people from "normal" or healthy ones? Isn't everyone neurotic to some extent? What are the rates of mental disturbance? Is there a physical cause of mental disturbance? How is psychotherapy supposed to work? Does it work? What about drugs and electric shock—how do they work and do they help? Can techniques of learning be effective with mental disturbance?

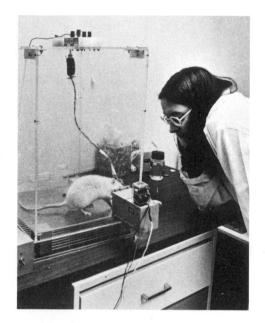

Deviations and disturbances in normal development are the subject of abnormal psychology. Studies concentrate on mental disturbances such as neuroses, phobias, and psychoses, attempting to answer the question of why they occur and how they can be treated. This field is very closely related to those of development and personality, since many of the same mechanisms are involved. In recent years there has been a tendency to drop the term *abnormal* and also the traditional concept of *mental illness*, both of which imply judgment, and consider these problems to be deviations in development. Traditional approaches such as Freud's theory of psychoanalysis and David Rapaport's theories on ego psychology are still important, but there has also been a great deal of work by social learning theorists such as Albert Bandura and Joseph Wolpe, who attempt to apply principles of learning to the treatment of these conditions. There are also a wide variety of humanistic therapies, including those developed by Carl Rogers and Fritz Perls. Many people who work in this area also do clinical practice themselves, treating individuals who suffer from various forms of mental disorder.

Psychologists play a number of different roles in our society. At top, a physiologist observes a rat pressing a lever in order to receive stimulation to the "pleasure centers" in its brain; at bottom, a therapist uses the technique of behavior modification to treat a severely disturbed child.

Social and Environmental Psychology

How can you change someone's attitude? Why does advertising work? Do people behave differently when they are in groups than when they are alone? What makes people like or love each other? Why do people obey orders even though they know what they are doing is wrong? How does noise affect us? Are cities unhealthy places to live? Is it bad to be crowded?

The topics of social psychology include social behavior—how individuals act in social situations, how they are affected by groups, and how groups themselves function—and all forms of interpersonal behavior such as liking and aggression. Recently the field of environmental psychology has begun to develop, concentrating on people's reactions to their environment. These are both relatively new fields in modern psychology. Although social psychology as a discipline dates back to the early twentieth century, its development as an organized field came largely during and after the Second World War. At that time Kurt Lewin and Carl Hovland, and somewhat later Leon Festinger and Stanley Schachter, made major contributions that have had lasting influence on the field.

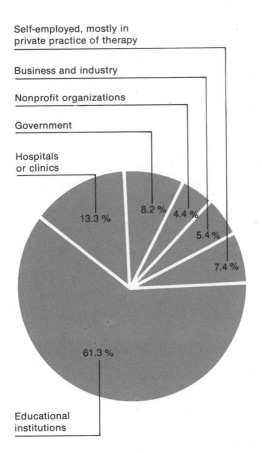

Self-employed, mostly in
private practice of therapy

Business and industry

Nonprofit organizations

Government

Hospitals
or clinics

13.3 %   8.2 % 4.4 %

5.4 %

7.4 %

61.3 %

Fig. 1.2
Where psychologists work

Educational
institutions

WHO ARE PSYCHOLOGISTS AND WHAT DO THEY DO?

There are approximately 35,000 people in the United States with
Ph.D.'s in psychology and quite a few more with Master's degrees. Of
these, 20.5 percent are women, and only 2 percent belong to minority
groups (including blacks, American Indians, and Asians—there are no
figures available for the number of psychologists of Spanish, Puerto
Rican, and Mexican descent). Although women and minority group
members are clearly underrepresented, there has been some improvement in this respect in recent years.

Detailed figures for what psychologists do and where they work
are available only for Ph.D.-level psychologists. These are given in
Figs. 1.2 and 1.3. As you can see, most psychologists teach and/or do
research in educational institutions, and the next largest number do
therapy, work with mental patients, or offer consulting services of
various kinds. Actually, many psychologists perform several of these
roles. They work for colleges, but also consult with government and
industry and do some therapy; or they work in hospitals seeing
patients, but also do research and perform some administrative services; and so on.

Fig. 1.3
What psychologists do

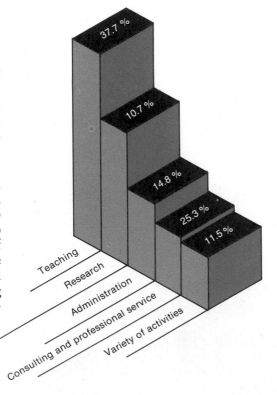

37.7 %

10.7 %

14.8 %

25.3 %

11.5 %

Teaching

Research

Administration

Consulting and professional service

Variety of activities

GENERAL APPROACHES TO PSYCHOLOGY

Throughout this book we will be discussing theories that involve specific topics and issues; some deal with very broad problems, some with quite limited ones. In each case, the theory is an attempt to explain a set of results—to say why a particular phenomenon occurs, why certain variables have the effects they do, or why variables are related to each other. Some of these theories will be discussed in several chapters because they apply to a variety of situations, while others will be dealt with in only one place because they relate to only one issue. In all cases, the theories are crucial for a full understanding of the topics.

In addition to specific theories, there are a few broad approaches to almost any problem in psychology. These do not attempt to explain a particular set of results, but are a means of conceptualizing the whole field. A psychologist who accepts one such approach probably sees most issues and attacks most problems somewhat differently from a psychologist who accepts another approach. Because the various approaches have such important influences on psychology and psychologists, let us describe them briefly now.

Physiological-Biological Approach

Some psychologists concentrate their research on the physiological mechanisms that affect behavior. Clearly, everything an organism does must be controlled by some physical process in its body; therefore, discovering the relationships between the physiology and behavior will help us understand why the organism behaves the way it does. For example, we have discovered how reinforcement leads to learning, but physiological psychologist James Olds studied mechanisms in the brain that produced the reinforcement. In addition, we can discover many principles that describe how we remember information, but the particular memories must be stored somewhere in the brain. Physiological psychologists study memory by looking for the physical mechanism by which memories are

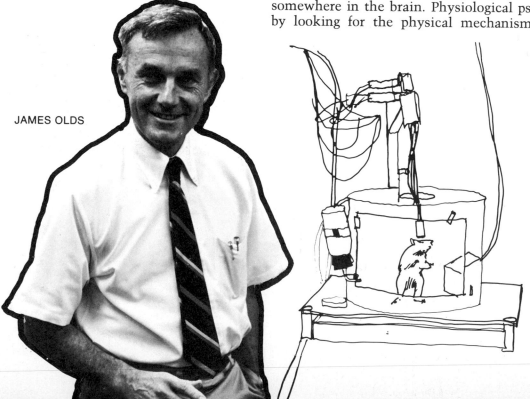

JAMES OLDS

stored. They employ a similar approach in many other areas: they study vision by investigating the physical apparatus that enables us to see; they study hunger by looking at the relationship between various physical conditions and how much people eat and by exploring the physical causes of eating; and so on. In each case, the approach is to study the underlying physical mechanism that controls the behavior.

In addition to searching for physical mechanisms, researchers investigate the contribution of inherited characteristics. To what extent do such factors affect intelligence, mental disorder, aggressiveness, or any other behavior?

Much of this work has been done by people who are not trained as psychologists. Often they are physiologists, biologists, or medical researchers. A physiological psychologist usually combines expertise in physiology with an interest in behavior. Thus, there is a concern not just with discovering a particular physical mechanism but also with relating it to specific behavior. As we shall see, the physiological approach has been important in many different areas of psychology including perception, learning, memory, motivation, emotions, and psychopathology.

Behavioral Approach

As its name implies, this approach focuses on behavior—activities of an animal that can be observed directly—rather than on internal activity. Running a maze, talking, answering questions, and sweating are observable behaviors and are the subject of studies by behavioral psychologists. Anger, thoughts about baseball, or a sinking feeling in your stomach are not behaviors, cannot be observed directly, and therefore are usually not studied by behaviorists. Behaviorism is sometimes called *stimulus-response* or *S-R* psychology because it deals with how an organism responds to a stimulus without considering what goes on inside the organism. It is also called "black box" psychology, because the behaviorist thinks of the animal as a black box, closed and unknowable. The behaviorist exposes the black box to various stimuli and observes how the box responds. The behavorist develops laws and rules about how stimuli and responses are related, but says little about what happens *inside* the box. Naturally, most behaviorists know that something is going on inside, but they tend to limit themselves to observable behavior because it is more objective and scientific. Internal changes are important only in so far as they produce changes in behavior, and any internal change should produce some change in behavior. Therefore the behaviorist need not study the internal processes, because they will show up in behavior.

This approach, which was advocated by John Watson in the early twentieth century and was more recently expounded by B. F. Skinner and Neal Miller, has been extremely influential in American psychology. It is probably accurate to say that for many years it was the dominant approach and stimulated a vast amount of research, especially on learning and reinforcement. In recent years, principles discovered by behavioral psychologists have been applied in a wide variety of fields including education and psychotherapy. However, behaviorism is no longer as dominant as it once was and in general has been greatly influenced by the cognitive viewpoint, which we will describe next.

B. F. SKINNER

GEORGE A. MILLER

Cognitive Approach

The cognitive approach to psychology emphasizes the role of thought in determining behavior. Cognitions refer to thoughts, beliefs, connections among events, memories, expectations, and other mental activity. Psychologists with a cognitive viewpoint look for the mental processes that control the behavior being studied. What is the animal or person thinking? What does it know about the situation? What knowledge does it have? How does memory affect its behavior? What mental processes are involved in interpreting the situation? These are the kinds of questions that are asked. Whereas a behaviorist studies observable behavior, a cognitive psychologist focuses on what is going on inside the brain. For example, imagine a dog that has been given food every time his master opens a particular cupboard in the kitchen. After a while, the dog salivates, wags its tail, and stands near its dish whenever the cupboard is opened. A behaviorist might say that that dog has learned to perform those actions when the cupboard is opened, while a cognitive psychologist might wonder what information the dog has acquired and might say that the dog has learned that when the cupboard opens he will be fed. This is an important distinction because the cognitive psychologist assumes that the dog understands the connection between the cupboard being opened and the food, whereas the behaviorist, more conservatively, makes no such assumption. As we shall discuss in Chapter 4, early cognitive psychologists such as Edward Tolman argued with early behaviorists such as Clark Hull about whether animals really know anything.

When we turn to people, there is obviously little doubt that they do have thoughts and do acquire information. Nevertheless, the behaviorist still tends to minimize the role of cognitions and to concentrate on the relationships between external events and behavior. In contrast, the cognitive psychologist stresses the role of thought, pointing out that people must interpret external events and are not passive receivers. The cognitive approach is especially influential in American psychology at the moment. The work of Ulrich Neisser on perception; research by people such as Gordon Bower, Noam Chomsky, and George Miller on memory, language, and information processing; and even work in social psychology by Stanley Schachter, Harold Kelley, and Edward E. Jones are affected by this cognitive emphasis. For example, as we shall see in Chapter 10, emotions such as anger are explained most fully by a combination of physiological, cognitive, and social factors. Similarly, a child learns a language in part by the principles of learning described by behaviorists; but the child's cognitive abilities and potentials also play a crucial role. Cognitive psychologists do not deny the importance of basic principles of learning, but they feel that mental functions are also very important.

Humanistic Approach

The physiological, behavioral, and cognitive approaches we have described tend to consider humans as a species and to search for principles and laws that apply to all people. The humanistic approach does not disagree with this perspective but it emphasizes the individual as a unique person rather than merely as a representative of the species. Thus the term *humanism.* According to the humanists, people, unlike other animals, are free to act and must take responsibility for their actions. Moreover, they have a goal, which is to achieve what psychologist Abraham Maslow calls *self-actualization*—the full and complete expression of their own potential. Each of us is different, we all must be encouraged to express ourselves, and we must recognize that what is right for one person may not be right for another.

Unlike behaviorism, which concentrates on observable behavior, humanistic psychology focuses on subjective experience (experience as we interpret it mentally or feel it emotionally). The important thing for each of us is what we *feel*, with behavior being merely the external reflection of internal responses. Thus, humanistic psychology is to some extent the opposite of behaviorism—it deals with internal events rather than external behavior, concentrates on individuals rather than general principles, and treats the person as free to act rather than responding more or less automatically to a stimulus.

The humanistic approach has influenced work on personality, development, and especially psychotherapy. Although it has not generated a great deal of scientific research, this approach has made the crucial point that people are individuals and must be treated accordingly. In addition, humanists tend to be concerned with actual problems in the real world rather than abstract issues, and that concern, too, has had an impact on the field.

ABRAHAM MASLOW

PSYCHOLOGY AS A SCIENTIFIC DISCIPLINE

One question that people often ask psychologists is why there has to be a scientific field devoted to studying something that everyone already knows so much about. It is certainly true that an unusual characteristic of the field of psychology, one that makes it troublesome as well as exciting for students, is that everyone is to some extent an expert in psychology. Most of us have no direct experience with chemical reactions, laser beams, the actions of drugs, genetics, or even the internal workings of our bodies. We come to the fields of chemistry, physics, medicine, and biology with few preconceptions; we are ready to be told "the truth." In contrast, we all have lots of experience with the subject matter of psychology. We spend our lives interacting with other people, observing them and ourselves, and naturally have gathered all sorts of information about how we and others function. If we did not have this information, we would be unable to get along in the world at all. We know that when we go from a dark room into the sunlight or the other way around our eyes take a while to "get used" to the change; that we like activities for which we are rewarded; and that the longer we have gone without eating, the hungrier we are and the more we will eat. We also have learned that people usually like other people who are similar to them, that we get angry and aggressive when someone annoys us, that we have dreams that we cannot remember clearly, and that we are often influenced by advertisements and political campaigns. And on and on. Anyone who is in college has naturally learned a great deal about human behavior without ever studying it scientifically. This knowledge gives students of psychology a big headstart because much of what they will encounter in the course is already familiar, sounds right, and can be fitted into their own experience.

However, personal experience also causes trouble because not everything we *think* we know about human behavior is correct. Systematic research often shows that common assumptions about how we act are wrong—that intuitions and day-to-day observations lead to false conclusions. Indeed, that is why there needs to be systematic study of psychology. We must discover which of our intuitions are correct, and also, of course, learn other facts about ourselves that do not appear in intuitions at all.

Consider some statements: four sixty-watt bulbs make a room seem twice as bright as two sixty-watt bulbs; rewarding a child every time he makes his bed will produce longer-lasting learning than rewarding him only half the time; we can tell when we're afraid from certain recognizable physical reactions of the body; schizophrenics have split personalities like Jekyll and Hyde; some people dream all the time and others dream very little; and paying a Democrat a lot of money to make a speech in favor of a Republican will be more likely to make her change her own mind than if you pay her less. You may agree with all, some, or none of these statements. They are all plausible descriptions of human behavior, *but they are all false.* This does not mean that our personal observations are always wrong—it does mean that systematic study is necessary to find out when they are right. And that is what psychology provides.

Systematic Research

All of which leads back to our original description of psychology as a *systematic* investigation of behavior. The key word here, of course, is systematic. What does it mean? Imagine a physicist walking along the street, carefully noticing certain natural phenomena. He sees a brick fall off a building, a stone fall from a ledge, an apple drop from a tree. Over many days he watches lots of objects of various sizes and shapes fall from various heights. On the basis of these observations, he concludes that all objects fall at the same speed. He has discovered the law of freely falling bodies. But surely we would not base a science on these observations. No physicist would suggest that these kinds of casual observations were scientifically valid. They may be excellent sources of ideas, but they are not scientific data. The reason is that they have not been collected systematically, under controlled conditions that could be repeated. It is necessary for the physicist to measure carefully the speed of falling objects, to weigh and measure the objects, and so on. Once this systematic research is done we begin to trust the findings.

This is obvious in physics, which is a highly advanced, precise science with a long tradition of careful research. It is equally true of psychology. Just as we should not and would not trust the casual observations of the physicist, we should not trust unsystematic observations of human behavior. If someone meets many different men and women over the course of a year, notices how they behave, and then concludes that women are more passive than men but better at writing, we should not put much faith in these conclusions. We should ask how the person measured passivity and verbal ability; whether he saw a representative group of men and women; whether his judgments were biased; and so on. In contrast, if the investigator designed a study, selected some men and women, gave them standardized tests, and got the same results, we should begin to believe him. This would be systematic research.

The emphasis on systematic collection of data does not imply that casual observations are always wrong or useless. Often they are right, and even when they are wrong they might be useful in giving us ideas and hunches. But they are not scientific data we can rely on. When data come from systematic research, we know how they were collected, could in theory collect the same kind of data again, and could check to be certain that the results come out the same way a second time. We can also perform statistics on the data to see just how much confidence we should have in the results (see Appendix). Thus, psychology as a scientific discipline differs from everyday psychology primarily in the systematic way in which we gather data. This is the beginning and the essence of psychology as a science. Therefore, the methods of gathering data are of the utmost importance because they provide the basis for our conclusions about human behavior.

Research Methods

Psychologists employ many different methods for collecting data. They do studies in laboratories and in natural settings, using animals and humans as subjects; and they measure responses with sophisticated electronic and mechanical equipment, by observing, and also by simply asking people to respond. Some research is done on individuals, some on groups. Some requires a great many different subjects (the participants in the research), while other work is based on very few subjects or even just one or two individuals. And, of course, there is an enormous variety of specific techniques. But all of the research falls into two general classes—experimental and correlational. Let us describe each of these types of research and then turn to some special variations and procedures.

The experiment In an *experiment*, the investigator asks, "If this factor varies, how does it affect this other factor?" If I increase the heat in the test tube, what happens to the color of the chemical? If I give this medicine, what happens to the illness? If I increase the person's level of fear, how does it affect his desire to be with other people? The questions involve cause and effect—what effect does this change have on this behavior or response? As we shall see, correlational studies also ask for relationships between factors, but do not discover clear causative links. Thus, the one great strength of an experiment is that it enables you to make a statement about what caused something to happen.

Although there is virtually unlimited variation in the details of experiments, they all have essentially the same basic design. In an experiment, we want to compare two or more situations that are identical to each other in every way except the one variation we are studying (see Table 1.1.). Then, if the two situations produce different results, we can be sure that the difference was produced by that one variation. If more than one thing varies, we can never be sure what produced the difference. To take a simple medical example first, if you want to test the effect of a new drug on the flu, you give the drug to some people and not to others. However, even in this simple study,

Table 1.1
DESIGN OF AN EXPERIMENT

Condition	Factors in situation
Control	*A, B, C, D, . . . N*
Experimental	*A, B, C, D, . . . N + X*

In an experiment, all conditions should be identical except for the one factor being investigated. Then, if the conditions produce different results, that difference must be due to the extra factor.

you must be careful to make the groups exactly comparable except for the drug. You would not simply give a pill to some people and not to others, because there is always the possibility that taking a pill has some psychological effect on the illness (called the *placebo effect*) or that those receiving the pill are less likely to take other drugs on their own, which would hurt your results. So, you give everyone a pill, but half of the people get a pill that contains the new drug and half get a pill containing some other substance that is known to have no effect (a *placebo*); and you do not tell the people which kind of pill they have taken. Only then can you be certain that the situations are identical except for the drug; and only then can you be certain that whatever effects you get are due to the drug.

This is a simple example, but often it requires great ingenuity to be sure that the conditions are comparable. Consider the question of how fear affects affiliation, wanting to be with other people. The design is simple—you want to make other people more afraid than others, and measure their tendency to affiliate. But how do you accomplish this? You could pour smoke into the room, have someone yell fire, and give the subjects the impression that the building was burning down. This would probably make them quite afraid, and you could compare them to other subjects who did not think the place was on fire. Aside from the ethical and practical problems, this would not be a suitable procedure because too many factors differ in the two situations. Being in a burning building not only arouses fear, but also introduces many elements that are lacking in the no-fire condition—such as a strong desire to scream for help and run as fast as you can out of the building. You have varied fear level, but you have varied too much. Another possibility would be to expose some subjects to an apparently dangerous snake and others to a harmless snake. Finding ourselves in a room with a huge rattler would make most of us afraid, while a garter snake should be less frightening. In this procedure all subjects are exposed to a snake, making the situations certainly more similar than in the fire, no-fire conditions. However, snakes are probably a poor choice for varying fear. In the first place, some people are terrified of all snakes; in the second, a dangerous snake evokes all sorts of feelings, including running and screaming, that are not usually evoked by a harmless snake. A final practical, but critical difficulty, is that subjects would be terribly suspicious about finding snakes crawling around the laboratory.

The procedure selected by Stanley Schachter (see Chapter 17) is to tell some subjects that they will receive severe electric shocks while others expect mild shocks. They all expect shocks, they are all slightly alarmed, but those in the severe shock conditions almost surely are more worried. Moreover, this is a plausible thing for a psychologist to be doing, so suspicion is relatively low. You may be able to conceive of an even better way of varying fear while keeping conditions comparable. The point is that great care must be taken in selecting a procedure in order to rule out other variables that you are not concerned with.

The great strength of the experiment is that it provides maximum control over the variables, and allows us to make statements about causation. For those reasons, psychologists usually prefer experimental research whenever it is possible. However, there are many times when an experiment is not practical or possible, when it is inappropriate to the particular question being studied. Then psychologists usually employ the other major type of research, a correlational study.

Correlational studies In an experiment we are looking for the effect of one variable on another. In *correlational research,* we are searching instead for associations among variables. The basic question in correlational studies is what variable goes with what other variable. If there is a lot of *A*, is there also a lot of *B*? For example, taller people tend to be heavier, so we say that height and weight are correlated. This does not mean that height *causes* weight or vice versa—just that more of one usually goes along with more of the other. When two variables do go together—when higher scores on one are associated with higher scores on the other, or the reverse of that—we say they are *correlated,* and we can compute the exact degree of correlation statistically (see Table 1.2).

First, let us see what correlation means. If we measure the incomes and educational levels of people in neighborhoods we can plot these data on a graph such as the one in Fig. 1.4, usually called a *scatter plot.* Each neighborhood is represented by one circle that shows its income level on the horizontal axis and education on the vertical. On the plot you can see that neighborhoods with higher incomes also have higher educational levels. This is called a *positive correlation,* because an increase in one variable goes along with the same increase in another. In contrast, as shown in Fig. 1.5, income and crime rate, while also strongly related, go in reverse directions—higher income is related to lower crime rate. This is a *negative correlation*—an increase in one is associated with a decrease in the other. And income and weight are unrelated—they have no correlation—because when one variable increases the other does not consistently either increase or decrease (Fig. 1.6). Correlations range from -1.0 to $+1.0$, from perfectly negative to perfectly positive.

Table 1.2
DESIGN OF A CORRELATIONAL STUDY

Measure factor *A*	Measure factor *B*
A_1	B_1
A_2	B_2
A_3	B_3
A_4	B_4
$\vdots$	$\vdots$
A_n	B_n

In a correlational study, two or more factors are measured on the same people or situations. Then we observe whether the scores on the factors tend to be associated—that is, when a score on *A* is high, the score on *B* tends to be high; when *A* is low, *B* is low.

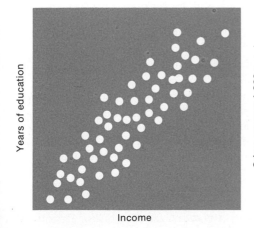

Fig. 1.4
Positive correlation—income and education

Average educational level and income for neighborhoods are positively correlated. Higher income is strongly correlated with more years of education.

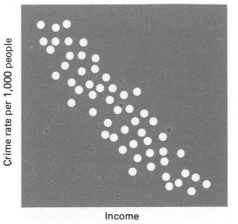

Fig. 1.5
Negative correlation—income and crime

Average income and crime rate in neighborhoods are negatively correlated. High-income areas have lower crime rates.

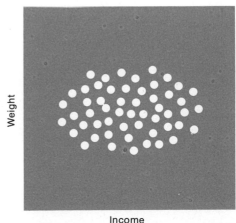

Fig. 1.6
Uncorrelated data

Average income and average adult weight are unrelated. There is no correlation.

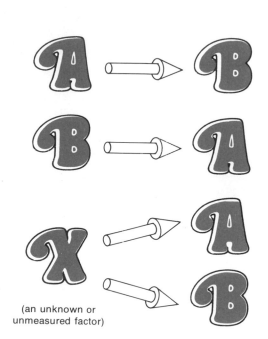

(an unknown or unmeasured factor)

Fig. 1.7
Causation in correlations

Causation in correlations generally cannot be determined. If the two factors are correlated, A may be causing B; B may be causing A; and, most important, some other factor or factors (X) may be affecting both A and B similarly.

Correlational studies are often done when we want to look at factors that we cannot control, such as poverty, age, or birth order. Obviously, no psychologist can affect these variables directly—we cannot go out and make some people rich and others poor, some young and others old. Instead, we find people who happen to have particular incomes and are certain ages. We also do correlational studies when we want to look at a great many variables at once. For example, in investigating crime, we might conduct correlational studies in order to see which factors seem related to crime rate and which are not related. In various studies, measures of income level and neighborhood crowding were correlated with measures of juvenile delinquency. Obviously none of these factors can be controlled by the experimenter; also, you want to look at data based on thousands of individuals rather than on just a few. The results were that income level was the major factor relating to crime, with crowding being unimportant. Now this did not necessarily mean that low income *caused* crime—only that it was *related*, with poorer people committing more crimes than people with more money. But the correlation is a first step, and already tells us that income is probably more critical than crowding.

Although you cannot make definite statements about causality from correlations, obviously you can decide what is and what is not plausible. In the crime example, you can probably assume that the crime is not causing the poverty—that is, people are not poor because they commit crimes. The opposite is much more likely. However, there is still the possibility that some factor not included in the study is related to both crime and poverty. Perhaps people are poor and commit crimes because there is something wrong with them, or because society discriminated against them, or almost anything else. Correlations give you hunches about causation, but almost never allow you to draw firm conclusions about what caused the relationship to occur (see Fig. 1.7).

Observational research Observation is the oldest, most natural way of studying behavior. We all watch what is going on around us, how people and animals behave, and how they are affected by various factors. Yet over the past twenty or thirty years detailed observations have been used surprisingly little by research psychologists. *Ethologists*, people who study the behavior of animals in natural settings, rely almost exclusively on observation. But many psychologists have felt that this procedure was not scientific enough for their purposes. This is because it is extremely difficult to make accurate, reliable observations of behavior and because most of the older work that used observations was not well controlled.

However, recently there has been renewed interest in observational research with people in natural settings. Much of this work involves children. Canadian psychologists such as Rona Abramovitch and Fred Strayer are using observational methods to study dominance, attention, and spacing (1976). In addition, a group of British psychologists including N. Blurton Jones, Peter Smith, and William C. McGrew have conducted a number of fascinating observational studies of children in natural situations. For example, Jones (1972) observed interactions among two- and four-year-old children. Although it is generally accepted that boys are more aggressive than girls, the careful observation in this work indicates that this may not be totally correct. Jones suggests that it is important to make a distinction between aggressive behavior, in which the goal is to hurt the other person, and what he calls rough-and-tumble behavior, which is playful. There is no question that boys engage in more rough-and-tumble play, but this study found no difference between boys and girls in aggressiveness. Obviously this is an important finding and, if it is supported by additional work, may change our views of sex differences in aggressiveness. The more general point is that systematic observations in natural settings may tell us a great deal about human behavior that we could not learn by measuring behavior in the laboratory.

Survey research A special kind of research involves collecting data by asking people questions about their beliefs, attitudes, and feelings. When this is done by distributing questionnaires, going door-to-door, or telephoning it is called *survey research.* The purpose is to describe the current state of people's opinions on whatever you are studying. The Gallup and Roper polls are famous for assessing how people are likely to vote in political elections, but they also gather information on a wide variety of other items such as preferences among commercial products or opinions on the environment and birth control. Because the survey is usually intended to reflect the opinions of the whole country, or at least a large portion of the country (all voters, for example), it is essential that those you survey be representative of the rest—they must include the same percentage of men and women, whites and nonwhites, old and young, rich and poor as the total population. This is a difficult achievement, and is one of the main jobs of a good polling agency.

The other big problem is to be certain that the questions are not biased in any way. To find out how people feel about pollution, you would not ask, "Don't you think too much money is being spent on antipollution?" because the question clearly implies that the asker thinks so and this might cause the person to agree. Instead, you ask something like "Do you think we are spending too much, too little, or about the right amount to alleviate pollution?" This is a less biased question. Often, pollsters ask several different questions on the same topic to minimize the chance of bias being introduced by a single, poorly worded question.

The remarkable fact is that surveys can often give a good estimate of the national feeling even though they are based on as few as 1,500 or 1,800 responses. The Nielsen ratings of TV watching are relied on by all TV stations, and various checks on the validity of the Nielsen surveys have shown that they are quite accurate in assessing what people are watching. While we may not want our TV programs to depend so much on a popularity contest, the surveys can be accurate if done correctly.

Research with nonhumans Although most psychologists are ultimately interested primarily in human behavior, a considerable amount of research is done with other animals. There are several reasons for this. First, it is much easier to do certain kinds of research with animals other than humans. Any problem dealing with strong stimulation, pain, severe deprivation, long-term control of the environment, or physiological preparations automatically raises logistical and ethical questions that are more difficult to deal with when human subjects are involved. Any time the research requires exposing the subject to unpleasantness or in any substantial way changing its life, it is difficult or impossible with human subjects except under very special circumstances. In addition, research that involves a great deal of time or more than one generation is obviously much easier with other animals. We can watch ten generations of rats, but no one psychologist lives long enough to watch that many generations of humans.

By using other animals as subjects, psychologists can study problems with the hope of discovering basic principles that will also apply to humans. There are limitations to this method; not everything that applies to rats, pigeons, or even chimpanzees is applicable to humans. But in general, the more basic and simple the behavior, the more likely it is that generalizations from one species to another will be legitimate. Many of the factors governing perception, learning, and motivation operate for humans as well as other animals. When more complex problems such as personality, the development of intelligence, and social interactions are involved, work with animals is less useful in discovering how humans behave. Yet even with these complex areas, systematic work with other animals at least provides suggestions that can then be followed up in research on humans.

Still another reason for studying other animals is that discovering how other animals behave puts human behavior in a broader perspective that allows us to evaluate and perceive our own behavior more clearly. Both the similarities and differences between humans and other species are important. Understanding other animals gives us insight into human behavior even if the principles governing our behavior are sometimes different. For example, if we knew completely the principles of learning in rats and found that some operated with humans but there were some differences, we would be in a good position to speculate about the causes of these differences. The findings with rats would give us a foundation on which to build our understanding of human learning. Indeed, this is what has happened in psychology. In this text, Chapter 3 covers much of learning that is applicable to both humans and other animals, while Chapter 4 deals with principles and problems of learning that are more typical of humans. There is little question that our understanding of the phenomena in Chapter 4 is fuller because of the research on other animals described in Chapter 3.

Nevertheless, it is important to recognize that species are different from each other. It is always dangerous to generalize from one animal to another without testing to be certain that the generalization is valid. In the final analysis it is usually necessary to test principles derived from research on other animals directly with human subjects. That is the only way to be certain how humans behave. Therefore, although we shall mention many animal experiments throughout this book, as much as possible we shall rely on research with human subjects.

Copyright © 1973 by Sam Gross

KEY ISSUES

Certain issues run through most fields of psychology, cutting across many theories and involving almost all phenomena. They concern the relative contribution of innate characteristics and experience; and the relationship among motives, learning, and cognitions.

Innate versus Acquired Characteristics

Are men naturally more aggressive than women? Is schizophrenia inherited? What role does heredity play in intelligence? These questions involve the role of innate characteristics, those features an organism is born with that determine its behavior throughout its life. Some of these features are apparent at birth—shape, number of arms and eyes, sense organs, and so on—and some appear automatically as the organism matures—some perceptual processes, and limitations of height, size, and probably of intelligence, strength, and resistance to disease. In general, an animal cannot exceed certain limits set by these inherited characteristics, and except in the case of severely unhealthy conditions, it will also be above some minimum. A giraffe that reaches maturity will never be smaller than an ant. No human being is shorter than one foot, or taller than twelve feet, and none can fly.

However, within these limits the animal's experience plays a major role. Many characteristics emerge from an interaction of innate factors and experience. What an animal learns and is exposed to shapes its behavior, defines its qualities, and determines where on the possible continuum each characteristic falls for that animal.

The roles of innate and acquired characteristics are relatively simple and uncontroversial as long as the question involves primarily physical characteristics. The complex question is how these two factors affect more psychological qualities such as perception, musical ability, intelligence, mental adjustment, social interactions, and personality. As we shall see throughout this text, the two factors generally interact to determine these characteristics, and the more complex the behavior, the greater the role of experience.

Motives, Learning, and Cognitions

Behavior that is not innately controlled or automatically regulated is determined by a complex interaction of factors. Motives involve the desire or need for an object or goal; learning involves the acquisition of a response to a stimulus; and, as mentioned earlier, cognition refers to thoughts, beliefs, memories, and other mental activity.

The role of each of these varies considerably depending on the particular behavior that is involved. Eating a steak that is placed in front of you is probably determined largely by motives (are you hungry) but also to some extent by learning (you know that it is a steak, that it is edible, that it tastes good, and that the knife and fork are used in a particular way), and less so by cognitions (but you may have the cognition that you are too fat so should not eat the whole thing). At the other extreme, solving a new puzzle requires mainly cognitions but also some motivation (you have to want to solve it) and a

B.C. by permission of Johnny Hart and Field Enterprises, Inc.

considerable amount of learning (you probably must recognize similarities to other puzzles). As we shall see, the question of the relative roles of these three basic mechanisms, as well as the way they interact, comes up in practically every area of psychology.

ORGANIZATION OF THE TEXT

This book tries to give a full picture of human behavior. Like other books, it presents the facts about basic processes such as perception, learning, and thinking, but it gives considerably more weight to more complex phenomena such as personality, social behavior, language, and sexual behavior. The book is organized with the relatively basic processes covered first (how the eye works, rules of learning) and the relatively complex processes later (social behavior, treating schizophrenia). This does not mean that the early topics are easier or the principles governing them simpler to discover. It means only that processes such as perception and learning are so basic to human functioning that it is necessary to deal with them first in order to understand more complicated processes such as social interaction and personality. With this in mind, we have attempted wherever possible to point out how these basic processes relate to more complex ones.

To sum up, psychology is a field of interactions and interrelationships. Every process is related to virtually every other one, and the only way to approach the study of human behavior is to recognize this. Social psychologists can no more ignore the work of learning theorists than learning theorists can ignore work on motivation. Naturally, some processes are more basic than others, and some are more closely related than others, but all are related in some way. Throughout this text we shall attempt to explore these interrelationships and what they tell us about the complex phenomenon called human behavior. ■

Summary

1. Because of the vast scope of psychology, it is convenient to organize the study into logically related areas. Major topics include sensation and perception; experimental psychology; developmental psychology; personality; psychopathology, clinical psychology, or abnormal psychology; and social and environmental psychology.

2. Broad approaches to psychology include the following: (a) the physiological-biological, which studies the physiological and genetic mechanisms that affect behavior; (b) the behavioral, which concentrates on the observable (external) activities of an organism, especially learning; (c) the cognitive, which looks for the mental processes that control the behavior being studied; and (d) the humanistic, which emphasizes the individual as a unique person.

3. Psychology is the systematic study of how animals, particularly human beings, function. It is a scientific discipline in that information is gathered and studied systematically. This is in contrast to the everyday observations we all make about human behavior.

4. Research methods fall into two general groups—experimental and correlational. In experimental research, we look for *causative relationships* between two variables. In correlational research, we look for *associations* among variables (if there is a lot of *A*, will there also be a lot of *B*). When two variables go together, we say they are *correlated*. Correlational studies are done in order to study factors that we cannot control (such as poverty) or when we want to look at many variables at once.

5. Recently there has been renewed interest in observational research, or systematic observation of people in natural settings. This method is particularly useful with children.

6. Survey research consists of gathering data to describe people's opinions on a particular topic. Two necessities with this type of research are getting a representative sample of the population and ensuring that the questions are not biased.

7. Although psychologists are ultimately interested in human behavior, much research must be conducted on nonhumans because of ethical, logistical, or time problems. Animal research is useful in that simple behaviors can be generalized from nonhumans to humans, and the differences between human and nonhuman behaviors can provide a foundation for better understanding human behavior.

8. Early psychologists raised certain key issues about human behavior that are still being investigated today. Those that will be discussed throughout this text are the effect of innate characteristics versus those acquired through experience; and how motives, learning, and cognitions interact.

RECOMMENDED READING

American Psychological Association. *A Career in Psychology.* Washington, D.C.: American Psychological Association, 1970. For those who are considering pursuing a career in psychology.

Boring, E. G. *A History of Experimental Psychology,* 2d ed. New York: Appleton-Century-Crofts, 1950. Although it covers only the early period, this book provides the best history of the beginning of modern psychology.

Deese, J. *Psychology as Science and Art.* New York: Harcourt Brace Jovanovich, 1972. A short, interesting book about how psychology works.

Hinde, R. *Animal Behavior.* New York: McGraw-Hill, 1970. One of the very best ethologists describes his work and that of others.

Nordby, V. J., and C. S. Hall. *A Guide to Psychologists and Their Concepts.* San Francisco: Freeman, 1974. This provides a brief description of the lives and work of the most important psychologists. An informal, easy-to-read book with a page or two on each person.

Schultz, D. P. *A History of Modern Psychology.* New York: Academic, 1975. An up-to-date history of psychology. It may not have the style of Boring's earlier book, but it covers the modern period.

Whether beautiful or ugly or just conveniently at hand, the world of experience is produced by the man who experiences it.
Ulrich Neisser, Cognitive Psychology

2 Sensation and Perception

The real versus the perceived world ■ *Sensation* ■ *The sense organs* ■ *Perception* ■ *Psychophysics* ■ *Contrast and adaptation* ■ *Distance and depth perception* ■ *Constancies* ■ *Rules of organization* ■ *The role of innate mechanisms and learning*

A witness in a trial testifies that he saw a man rush into the bank, raise a gun, and say in a deep, gruff voice, "Put your hands up." The man is described as tall, dark-haired, light-skinned, and attractive, with no special distinguishing features. Some time after the holdup, the witness was shown a police lineup of seven men, each of whom said the words "Put your hands up." Out of this lineup, the witness picked the defendant as the man he had seen in the bank. At the trial the witness again identifies the defendant by pointing at him where he sits in the courtroom. This seems like very strong evidence, the jury is noticeably impressed, and things look bad for the defendant. Yet the jury should not be so impressed, and a smart defense attorney should be able to cast considerable doubt on this testimony. We shall see later some of the points the attorney should make, but the general issue is that perceptions, especially under stressful circumstances, are not as accurate and reliable as we might think. People tend to see what they expect to see, to be influenced by many subtle factors in the situation, to distort their perceptions in line with later information, and so on. We know the world through our sense organs and perceptual mechanisms, but our perceptions are not perfect reflections of the world outside us; this has important implications for many areas, including the legal situations described above.

When you walk into a room full of people, you are immediately exposed to a vast variety of stimuli. Yet you instantly perceive the whole scene in an ordered, organized way even if you have never been in the room before. You do not see blobs of shapes and colors resembling a child's finger painting. Instead, you see the room, tables, chairs, lamps, people, and any other objects present. People do not blend into each other, one person's arm seeming to be part of someone else's back; they are distinct, whole people who have clearly defined boundaries. Nor do you hear a mass of indecipherable sounds. You hear the rattling of dishes, the clinking of glasses, the music and voices separately. Moreover, you can easily distinguish one voice from another and, if you want, can follow one conversation and ignore others. With little or no effort on your part the whole scene falls into place. Your sensory and perceptual mechanisms receive, translate, and organize the stimulation and enable you to know what is going on. How this is accomplished—the rules and processes by which the mechanism operates—is the subject of this chapter.

It is fitting that we deal first with the question of *how* we know the world around us. All our behaviors, actions, and thoughts depend to a great extent on the stimuli that impinge on us and our experience of them. Obviously we could take no deliberate action, we could barely be said to be alive, if we did not have some contact with the world outside ourselves. Psychological functioning—responding to and dealing with the world—is wholly dependent on the processes of *sensation* (receiving stimulation through our sense organs) and *perception* (becoming aware of and interpreting that stimulation). And as we shall see, more complex psychological phenomena such as child development, personality, and social behavior are affected by and also follow many of the rules of perception. Therefore, not only is it important and interesting to know about perception for its own sake, but it is also essential to understand perception if we are to comprehend fully other psychological processes.

THE REAL VERSUS THE PERCEIVED WORLD

One of the most influential recent books in psychology has been Ulric Neisser's *Cognitive Psychology*, published in 1967. Neisser's major purpose was to argue that perception is, at least in part, a cognitive process—that what we experience of the world is due to mental processes that change and interpret the sensory stimulation we receive. As he described it, "Whether beautiful or ugly or just conveniently at hand, the world of experience is produced by the man who experiences it." Also, "The central assertion is that seeing, hearing, and remembering are all acts of *construction,* which may make more or less use of stimulus information depending on circumstances." This view that perception depends on or rather consists of cognitive processes similar to memory and thinking has reshaped the field of perception and stimulated much of the current research.

Most people tend to put complete trust in their own perceptions and to assume that they correspond exactly to the real world. If we see a magician saw a woman in half or turn a pink scarf into a blue pigeon, we assume we have been deceived because that is what magic is all about. But if we see a lake, hear a scream, or touch a hot stove, we almost always believe that we are experiencing what is there. This is not correct. Distorted perception is not limited to magic shows— our perceptions are never exact replicas of the external world. If they were, perception would still be terribly complicated but would have relatively little psychological significance. The fact is, however, that every sense organ responds to only a limited sample of the available stimulation and further distortion is introduced by various perceptual mechanisms. The world is defined for us by sensation and perception and every animal, indeed every individual, experiences the world differently.

Dramatic illustrations of perceptual distortion are provided by optical illusions such as those shown in Fig. 2.1, which cause most people to see something different from what is there. But optical illusions, although forceful demonstrations of the difference between the real and perceived world, are merely special instances of what occurs in all perception. Human perception is not a passive process in which all stimuli are treated equally and turned into images identical to the source of the stimulation. Rather, our perception is selective and active. Our conscious centers receive some kinds of stimuli and not others; we respond more to some than to others; and we distort, interpret, and organize all stimulation in clear and predictable ways. The psychological study of perception is mainly an attempt to describe these distortions and explain how and why they occur.

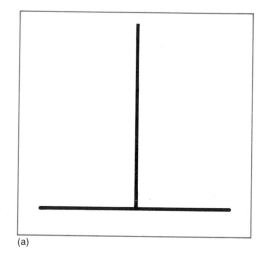

(a)

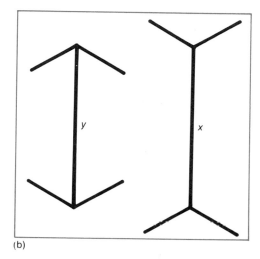

(b)

Fig. 2.1
Optical illusions

In (a), the vertical line seems longer, although it is exactly the same length as the horizontal line, while in (b) the Mueller-Lyer illusion makes line *x* look longer than line *y*; no matter how these two lines are viewed—upside down, sideways, from far and near— the illusion persists, despite the fact that the two lines are equal in length. (c) Connect the dots to make two horizontal lines. You will find that the Hering illusion makes the lines look bowed when actually they are parallel. (But if you hold the book up to eye level and look at the lines, the illusion disappears.)

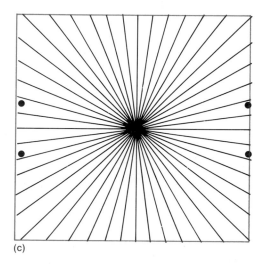

(c)

To answer the broad question of how we experience our surroundings, we must first understand sensation—how the sense organs work, the stimuli to which they respond, and how they transmit the information they receive. Second we must understand perception—the rules and mechanisms by which this information is processed, organized, and interpreted. Throughout our discussion of these phenomena, we shall frequently use vision as an example because it is the sense that has been studied the most and the one on which people generally rely most heavily.

Sensation

Folklore suggests that our senses are very poor compared to those of other animals. Cats can see in the dark, deer can hear a footstep miles away, and dogs can smell a week-old scent, whereas we supposedly respond only to the strongest, most obvious stimulation. While some animals do see, hear, or smell more keenly than humans, human sense organs are actually remarkably sensitive. However, they are highly selective—exceptionally sensitive to certain stimuli and not at all to stimuli outside that limited range.

The human eye responds to one photon of light energy—the smallest amount possible. On a dark, clear night a person with normal eyesight can see a candle flame thirty miles away (Galanter, 1962). But the eye does not respond to all *types* of energy. Figure 2.2 shows the complete range of electromagnetic radiation, and you can see what a minuscule percentage is called light and is visible to us. Obviously, the world would appear very different if we could see the infrared energy emitted by hot stoves, the beams of radio stations reflecting from clouds, or bursts of gamma rays in the atmosphere.

Like the eye, the human ear is very sensitive to a limited range of stimuli. A person with normal hearing can detect the tick of a watch twenty feet away in a quiet room or the sound of a pin dropped twelve feet away on a wooden floor. No wonder even a faucet dripping three rooms away or a radio on in the house next door can keep us awake.

The ear responds to vibrations of the air, which, like light energy, travel in waves that vary in length, or frequency. The human ear responds only to frequencies between 20 and 20,000 cycles per second (cps, now more commonly called hertz or Hz). Other animals respond to higher and lower frequencies. Bats and dolphins, for example, can hear sound frequencies above 100,000 Hz; and dogs respond to whistles well above the 20,000 Hz that humans can hear. A person who fans herself slowly with a piece of cardboard can feel air hitting her face and see the fan moving, but she cannot hear the air vibrating because the frequency is much too low. If we were sensitive to other frequencies, we would be bombarded with sounds from every moving object. We would hear dogs wagging their tails, tall buildings swaying in the wind, and the constant, very rapid vibration of window panes and other such rigid objects. We would be able to say "I heard him nod yes" or "he waved goodbye loudly."

Although we tend to rely on them less than on vision and hearing, our organs of taste, smell, and touch are also very sensitive. We can taste one teaspoon of saccharine dissolved in six gallons of water, smell a single drop of perfume diffused through a three-room apartment, and feel the wing of a fly falling on our cheek from a distance of

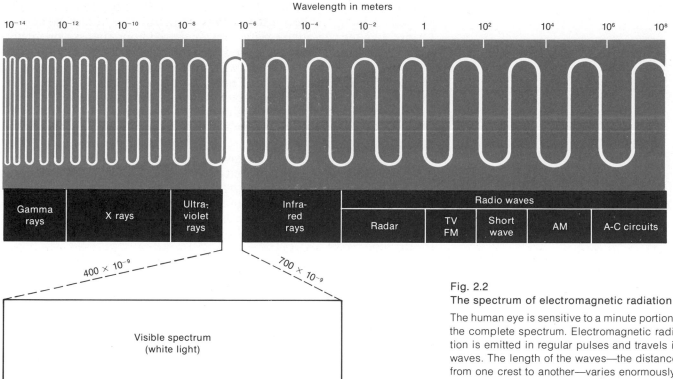

Wavelength in meters

| 10^{-14} | 10^{-12} | 10^{-10} | 10^{-8} | 10^{-6} | 10^{-4} | 10^{-2} | 1 | 10^2 | 10^4 | 10^6 | 10^8 |

| Gamma rays | X rays | Ultra-violet rays | Infra-red rays | Radio waves |||||
| | | | | Radar | TV FM | Short wave | AM | A-C circuits |

400×10^{-9} 700×10^{-9}

Visible spectrum
(white light)

400   500   600   700

Wavelength in nanometers

Fig. 2.2
The spectrum of electromagnetic radiation

The human eye is sensitive to a minute portion of the complete spectrum. Electromagnetic radiation is emitted in regular pulses and travels in waves. The length of the waves—the distance from one crest to another—varies enormously. Shorter waves are less than a trillionth of an inch long, and longer ones are more than fifteen miles long. We see only waves between approximately 380 (violet) and 750 (red) nanometers, which is less than one-trillionth of the total range. We are blind to waves above and below these levels. (From Bourne and Ekstrand, 1973)

one centimeter. In addition, our *kinesthetic sense* can tell us when we are less than one degree from perfectly vertical and can detect practically any movement of the body.

THE SENSE ORGANS

In order to understand fully the psychological process of perception, it is necessary to know as much as possible about how the sense organs work. Let us consider each of the senses in turn.

The Eye

The physiology of vision

The physical mechanism that allows us to see is shown schematically in Fig. 2.3. Light strikes the *cornea*, a transparent, rounded covering that provides protection and also helps to bend and focus the rays. The light then passes through the *pupil*, which is an opening in the *iris*, the colored portion of the eye. When there is a lot of light, the iris closes; with little light, it opens. This adjustment is automatic— over a wide range of intensities the size of the iris adjusts to admit the right amount of light. After passing through the pupil, the light is

Fig. 2.3
Schematic of the eye

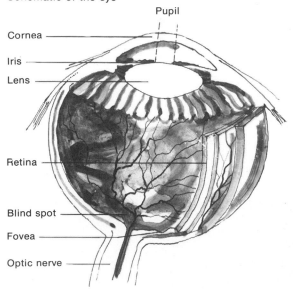

Pupil
Cornea
Iris
Lens
Retina
Blind spot
Fovea
Optic nerve

focused by the *lens*. The lens has great flexibility and range, and actually changes shape automatically to bring near or distant objects into focus on the appropriate area of the back of the eye or *retina*. When the focused light strikes the retina, "seeing" actually begins. The retina contains about 125 million *rods* and about 6.5 million *cones*. The cones are scattered around the retina but are concentrated primarily in the *fovea*, a recessed portion of the retina. Cones are the receptors for color vision and require a considerable amount of light to respond. The rods, which appear in all areas of the retina except the fovea, are extremely sensitive and function mainly in dim light. They record all colors as shades of gray. The point at which the optic nerve is connected to the retina contains neither rods nor cones and is called the *blind spot* (see Fig. 2.4). Both of the "seeing" elements contain chemicals that respond to light—*rhodopsin* in the rods and *iodopsin* in the cones. When struck by light, these chemicals generate minute amounts of chemical and electrical energy.

Fig. 2.4
Blind-spot demonstration

Close your left eye, hold the book at arm's length, and focus on the X. Move the book slowly toward you. At some point the cat's face should disappear. Repeat by focusing the other eye on the cat and the X will disappear.

This energy moves along the *optic nerve*, through the *optic chiasma* and the *lateral geniculate body* (the visual center of the thalamus), and, through a system of crossing over of fibers (see Fig. 2.5), finally reaches the *occipital lobe* of the cerebral cortex in the brain. We do not know how the brain translates these impulses into images, but we do know that the experience of sight occurs in the brain.

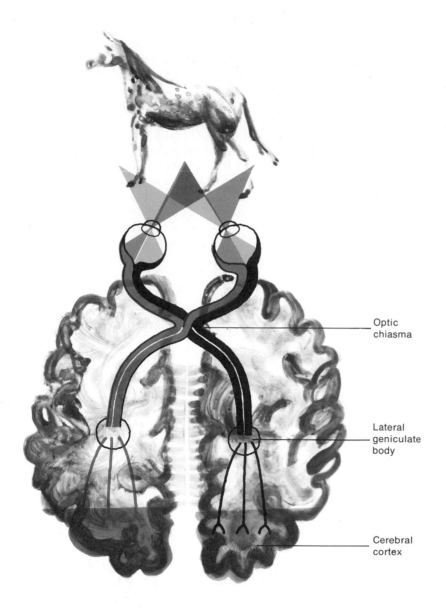

Optic
chiasma

Lateral
geniculate
body

Cerebral
cortex

Fig. 2.5
Crossover of visual images

The left half of each retina transmits to the left side of the brain, and the right half transmits to the right side of the brain. However, everything to the left of where your eyes are focusing (called the left *visual field*) strikes the right side of the retina, while the right visual field strikes the left side of the retina. Thus both eyes transmit information to both sides of the brain.

Color vision

The spectrum. Although the human eye is sensitive only to wavelengths ranging from 380 to 750 nanometers (nm), this small part of the spectrum provides a remarkable variety of visual experience (see Plate A*). Our perceptual process translates the various frequencies into the color spectrum, which ranges from red to orange, yellow, green, blue, indigo, and violet. A convenient way to remember the order of the spectrum is that the initial letters of the colors spell the name ROY G. BIV. (We shall discuss such memory aids in more detail in Chapter 4.)

* The color plates can be found between pages 30 and 31.

VISUAL FEATURE DETECTORS

Modern techniques make it possible to record the electrical response of a single cell, or *neuron*. Using these procedures, Hubel and Wiesel (1965) demonstrated that certain neurons in the brain are activated by highly specific types of visual stimulation. Some cells become active when the eye is exposed to a vertical line, others when we see lines with other orientations. Moreover, some of these cells respond only to vertical lines in a particular part of the visual field, while other, more complex cells respond to vertical lines wherever they appear. Although this mapping is far from complete, it appears that the brain contains many types of cells of this sort, each responding only to its special type of stimulation.

This discovery provides the beginning of an explanation for how the brain translates the separate points of stimulation on the retina into a full picture of the visual field. The rods and cones on the retina respond to whatever light hits them without regard to specific patterns of stimulation. However, when the impulses from the retina reach the brain, they are coded by a series of cells that respond differentially to various patterns. Lower-level cells code the pattern, others code its location, and still more complex ones (what Hubel and Wiesel call *hypercomplex* cells) code the length and width of the pattern. Presumably, there must be even more complex systems that combine separate features to produce our perceptions of intricate patterns; but these higher-level cells or mechanisms have not yet been discovered.

The color circle. The spectrum ranges from low to high frequencies, but psychologically the two ends of the range appear quite similar. As shown in Plate A, when the colors of the spectrum are arranged in a circle, violet and red seem quite close even though they are the furthest apart in wavelength. Colors that are opposite each other on the circle are called *complementary* colors because equal portions of them will cancel each other and produce gray. When all the colors are mixed together, they eliminate color entirely and you see white. Similarly, when light is reflected from a colorless background, either white or gray, it contains all of the colors of the spectrum.

These colors are so familiar that it is difficult to imagine others. However, individual differences in sensitivity to various frequencies probably produce many individual variations on the standard color spectrum. Some animals see no colors, only varying intensities of light (grays), and some see quite different colors than we do. In addition, people who are partially colorblind see some colors and not others and may not even know that their vision differs from that of most people. To test your color vision, try to identify the numbers hidden in the squares in Plate B.

Afterimages. An interesting aspect of color vision is that we sometimes "see" colors without external stimulation. If you stare at a bright circle of light for a few minutes and then close your eyes, you will still see a circle of light. If the bright light is red and if, instead of closing your eyes, you look at a gray sheet of paper, you may continue to see a red circle for a short time. This is called a *positive afterimage* and is probably caused by a continuation of the neural activity produced by the initial stimulation.

If you continue to stare at the gray paper, the red circle will turn slightly bluish-green. Similarly, a yellow circle would become purple,

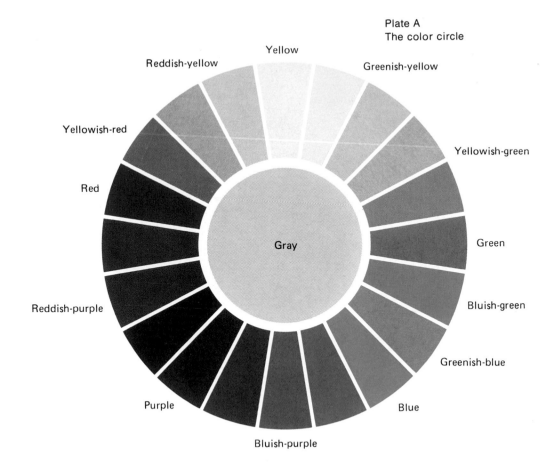

Plate A
The color circle

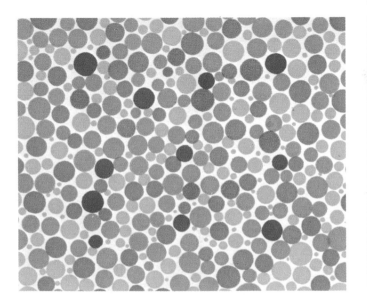
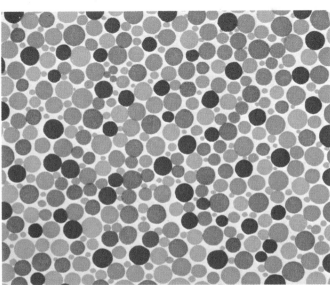

Plate B
Tests for colorblindness
People with certain types of colorblindness would have difficulty reading the 75 and 47 shown in these squares, although people with normal vision would have no trouble. (Reproduced by permission of American Optical.)

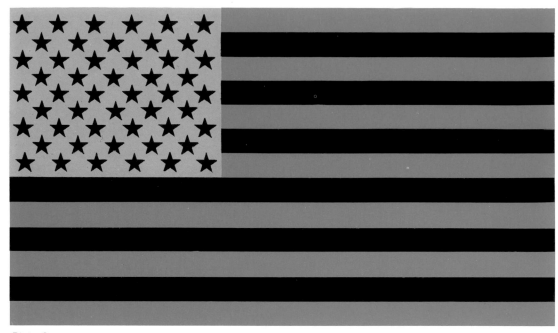

Plate C
The negative afterimage
Stare at the bottom right-hand corner of the orange square for about thirty seconds. Then quickly look from there to a neutral-color surface. You should see a familiar picture.

Plate D
Natural camouflage
The tiger's stripes and coloring make it almost seem to disappear into the tall yellow grass. (Reproduced by permission of Diane Wayman.)

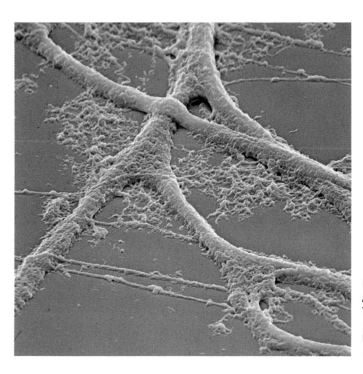

Plate E
An isolated nerve cell, highly magnified
The diameter of the nerve cell body is less than .01 millimeter thick. (From Lennart Nilsson, *Behold Man*. Boston: Little, Brown, 1974. Reproduced by permission.)

Plate F
A detail of the cerebral cortex, highly magnified
In humans and other higher species, the surface of the brain is convoluted in order to accommodate the myriad cells of the cerebral cortex. In lower species the surface of the brain is much smoother. In this photo, the membranes covering the brain have been removed and the naked surface of the cerebral cortex is seen together with some small openings for vessels. (From Lennart Nilsson, *Behold Man*. Boston: Little, Brown, 1974. Reproduced by permission.)

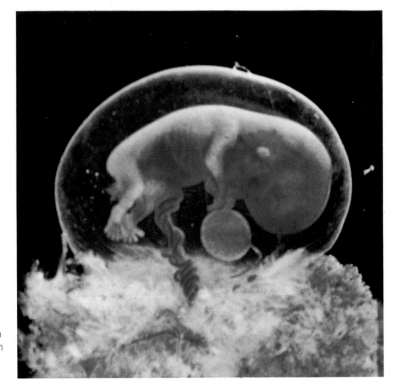

Plate G
The human fetus at eight weeks in amniotic sac
The fetus is only eight millimeters (⅓ inch) long from crown to rump and weighs 1/1000 of an ounce. (From Robert Rugh and Landrum Shettles, *From Conception to Birth*. New York: Harper & Row, 1971. Reproduced by permission.)

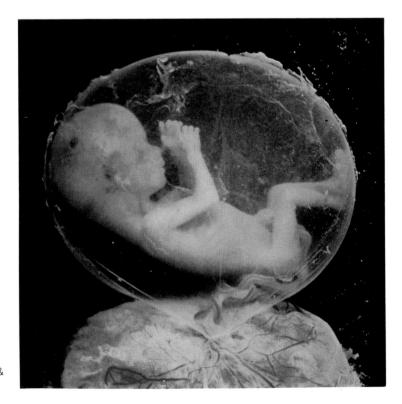

Plate H
The human fetus at twelve weeks in amniotic sac
The fetus is 150 millimeters (3 inches) long from crown to rump and weighs ½ ounce. (From Robert Rugh and Landrum Shettles, *From Conception to Birth*. New York: Harper & Row, 1971. Reproduced by permission.)

orange would become greenish-blue, and so forth. This is the *negative afterimage*, so-called because the afterimage corresponds to the complement (or opposite) of the original color (see Plate C). The negative afterimage occurs because those elements in the eye that are sensitive to the color being shown become fatigued after a time. When the eye is then exposed to light of all frequencies (that is, when the observer stares at the gray paper), these fatigued elements respond less strongly than those that are sensitive to their complement. If the red elements are tired, the green ones will predominate and the circle will look green. This can produce dramatic effects.

Theories of color vision. Many theories attempt to explain how the human eye sees color and why afterimages occur. The *Young-Helmholtz theory*, proposed in the nineteenth century, suggested that there are three different types of cones in the retina, each of which produces one of three basic colors—red, green, or blue. Other colors are produced by appropriate combinations of activity in these three types of cones. Thus, we experience red when only the red cones are stimulated, orange when the red cones are strongly stimulated and the green cones slightly stimulated, yellow when the red and green cones are equally stimulated, and so on. When all the cones are equally stimulated, we experience white.

The *opponent-process theory* was proposed by Weald Hering in 1870 and modified in 1957 by Hurvich and Jameson. This theory also assumes the existence of three types of cones: two of which each produce two color experiences—red and green or yellow and blue— while a third type produces only white. Stimulation of one of the colors of a particular cone opposes or cancels the other color of that cone. When the red-green cone is stimulated by a green light, we experience green and the color red is canceled. When the red-green cone is stimulated by both red and green light, they cancel each other and eliminate the experience of color. If the eye is stimulated by light of all frequencies, both kinds of color cones are canceled and we experience white.

Each of these theories explains much about color vision, but neither is fully adequate. The Young-Helmholtz theory does not account convincingly for yellow, for example. It claims that yellow is caused by equal stimulation of the red and green cones, but people can perceive yellow in parts of the retina where they cannot see either red or green. Also, some people are blind to red and green but not to yellow. On a more intuitive level, as Hochberg (1964) has pointed out, "while it is easy to accept that aqua is a combination of blue and green and violet a mix of red and blue, it strains credulity to consider yellow a greenish red." The opponent-process theory, on the other hand, accounts more easily for negative afterimages. When the red half of a red-green cone is fatigued, the red part of the cone works less strongly, and the person sees green. This explains very neatly why a negative afterimage is always the complementary color—it is simply the other half of the dual-purpose cone.

Physiological research by MacNichol (1964) as well as others has provided convincing evidence for the existence of three types of cones in the retina. These cones respond to the light of frequencies corresponding roughly to blue, green, and red, which seems to offer direct

JULIAN HOCHBERG

support for the Young-Helmholtz theory. Yet other work (DeValois and Jacobs, 1968) showed that the lateral geniculate body, a major vision center between the retina and cerebellum, has cells that respond in an opponent manner to either red-green or blue-yellow light.

A resolution suggested by MacNichol (1964) is that the retina does contain the three kinds of cones proposed by Young and Helmholtz, while some other part of the visual system has cells that respond in the opponent manner described by Hering. In some way, information from the retina is translated from the three-color to the opponent-process system. This would, of course, make the mechanism of color vision considerably more complex than either theory proposed, but such a complex theory may be necessary to account for all of the phenomena of color vision.

The Ear

The physical mechanism that allows us to hear is shown in Fig. 2.6. The ear perceives sounds in three dimensions: loudness, pitch, and timbre. *Loudness* refers to the magnitude or intensity of the sensation produced (a whisper versus a shout); *pitch,* to the highness or lowness of the sound (middle C versus high G); and *timbre,* to the tonal quality of the sound (the tone of a violin versus that of a trumpet). Several theories attempt to explain how loudness and pitch are determined.

Determination of loudness is fairly simple. The ear is sensitive to a vast range of sound intensities, the strongest being many million times louder than the weakest. Some of the hair cells on the organ of Corti are less sensitive than the others, and are activated only be strong vibrations (Thompson, 1967). There is general agreement that perceived loudness (measured in decibels, or dB) is determined by the total number of hair cells, especially the number of less sensitive hair cells, that are stimulated enough to "fire."

Determination of pitch or frequency of sounds is considerably more complicated. The ear is sensitive to vibrations ranging from about 20 to 20,000 Hz. One hypothesis, called *place theory,* was originated by Helmholtz in the nineteenth century and proposes that pitch is determined by the part of the basilar membrane that is stimulated. Work by Von Békésy (Von Békésy and Rosenblith, 1951)—for which he received the Nobel Prize in 1961—indicated that sounds with high frequencies produce more stimulation in certain parts of the basilar membrane than in others. But Von Békésy also found that low-frequency tones caused the whole membrane to respond about equally. Thus, place theory can account for perception of high frequencies but not for perception of low ones.

An alternative explanation, called *frequency theory,* proposes that our ability to hear pitch is determined by the frequency of the impulses within the auditory nerve. According to this view, a higher frequency vibration produces a greater frequency of electrical stimulation in the nerve. Indeed, the activity of the auditory nerve does correspond closely to the frequency of vibrations—up to about 4,000 Hz. However, a single neuron cannot conduct more than about 700 impulses per second, so an additional theory was needed to account for response above that level.

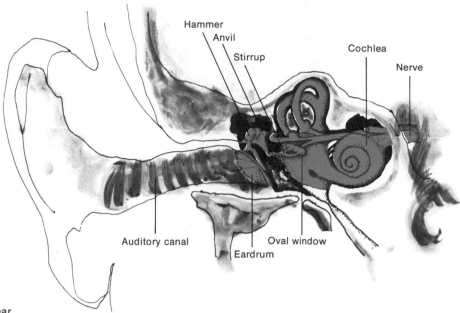

Fig. 2.6
Schematic of the ear

The hearing process starts in the *outer ear,* which carries the vibrations along the *auditory canal,* at the end of which they hit the *eardrum.* This acts like a diaphragm in a loudspeaker, vibrating in response to the sound waves. In turn, the vibrating eardrum causes the small bones of the inner ear—the *hammer, anvil,* and *stirrup* (also known as *ossicles*)—to vibrate.

The hammer, which is attached to the eardrum, vibrates first; it then transmits the vibration to the anvil, which passes it along to the stirrup. The stirrup is attached to the *oval window,* a membrane much like the eardrum. As the window vibrates, pressure waves are transmitted to the *basilar membrane* (not shown) of the *cochlea,* where they are translated into neural impulses by the *hair cells* on the *organ of Corti* (not shown), which sends impulses along the auditory nerve to the brain.

This need led to *volley theory* (Wever, 1949), which suggests that nerve fibers are divided into groups that "fire" at different times. For example, when a vibration of 2,000 Hz reaches the ear, different neurons fire at slightly different times, producing a total of 2,000 impulses each second traveling along the auditory nerve. The brain thus receives bursts of stimulation at a frequency of 2,000 per second, equivalent to the original stimulation. However, limits to the capacity and responsivity of the neurons prevent this theory from explaining how frequencies much above 4,000 Hz could be carried.

The ultimate explanation for how frequencies are transmitted is probably a combination of place and volley theories, with place theory explaining the perception of high frequencies and volley theory accounting more easily for low and intermediate tones.

Smell

The sense of smell is relatively unimportant in humans. Although it tends to add richness to our experiences and is certainly closely related to the sense of taste, we rely on smell much less than do other animals. Although we can perceive the odor of chemicals when they are diluted as much as one part in 30 billion, our sense of smell is generally much weaker than that of dogs and other animals.

Moreover, there are great individual differences in sensitivity to particular odors. We all adapt very quickly to background odors, no longer noticing that they are there. You probably have had the experience of entering a room and immediately smelling something, when the occupants of the room, who are used to the odor, were unaware of it. Similarly, when you go from the city to the country or vice versa, you are suddenly aware of the smell in the air, whereas you seldom notice the smell of the air where you live.

At the moment we know little about the mechanism of smell. We cannot even devise a classification of various smells comparable to what we have for colors or tastes. We do know that the smell receptors are located in the mucous membrane of the upper nose, and that they transmit directly to the olfactory bulb of the brain, which in turn is connected with the olfactory cortex. But the precise connections and interconnections of nerves and other parts of the brain have not been firmly established.

Taste

Just as all colors are composed of three primary colors, the enormous variety of tastes consists of combinations of four basic sensations— sweetness, sourness, saltiness, and bitterness. Our taste receptor cells are arranged in groups on the approximately ten thousand taste buds that are located primarily on the edges and back of the tongue, with a few scattered on the soft palate, pharynx, and even the larynx. The taste cells appear to vary in their sensitivity to the four basic tastes, responding more to certain tastes than to others. For example, the taste cells at the tip of the tongue respond more to sugar and salt than to sourness or bitterness; while in the back of the tongue, sensitivity to salt is quite low. So if you have to swallow a very salty pill and want to avoid the taste, throw it far back in the throat to miss the salt receptors; and if you want to relish a delicious candy fully, keep it at the tip of your tongue as long as possible.

While the taste receptors are sensitive to only four basic tastes, our enjoyment of food depends on much more than just the taste buds. The odors, texture, and even temperature of the food play an important role. Something that tastes good hot may be unpleasant cold and vice versa. And if you hold your nose so that you cannot smell the food you will find that most tastes are greatly reduced, which is why foul-tasting medicines are often taken this way.

Recent research has begun to isolate some of the chemicals involved in taste. For example, a chemical that can be derived from the artichoke appears to be part of the reaction that produces the sensation of sweetness. If you put this chemical on your tongue, everything tastes sweet—even a sour lemon. You can perform a weak version of this experiment by eating an artichoke and then seeing if other foods tend to taste sweeter afterwards.

Touch

What is usually thought of as the sense of touch actually includes sensitivity to a variety of stimuli. Receptors in the skin respond to temperature, pressure, and pain. We can tell when a hot or cold object touches us, although (as with many senses) we are more sensitive to changes in temperature than to the absolute temperature. If our skin happens to be cool, things seem hotter than if our skin is normal temperature. In other words, our skin sensors tell us when something is hotter or colder than our skin, not how hot or cold it is in terms of some absolute scale.

A fascinating phenomenon that we do not fully understand is the sensation of being tickled. Almost everyone is ticklish to some extent, and it is clear that tickling is produced by relatively light touching of the skin. Usually the touching cannot be too light, however, or it ceases to be ticklish. Moreover—and this is especially difficult to understand—it is almost impossible to tickle yourself. It feels entirely different when you touch yourself than when someone else touches you. This is probably due partly to the sensation of touching from both areas; for example, you feel your hand on your face and also your face being touched. Naturally, when someone else touches you, you feel only one sensation. You have probably felt this difference by touching a part of your body when it was anesthetized. To most people this feels very strange, unlike touching someone else's body, when you get no feedback. Why these differences occur is unclear—it is one of the many questions about the sense of touch that remain to be answered.

Kinesthetic Sense

Our *kinesthetic* and *proprioceptive* senses tell us about our bodies' relation to the outside world. The kinesthetic sense receives sensory data from the body's muscles, and the proprioceptive sense receives information from the body's skeletal joints. From these data, the brain assembles a picture of the body's position in space.

Of all of our senses, we probably take these most for granted. Indeed, although we can imagine being blind or deaf, it is difficult to conceive of being unable to tell whether we are upright, whether we are moving, or where our hands are at any given moment. In fact, we are extremely good at distinguishing the vertical—a deviation of even 1 percent is easily noticed. Similarly, we can tell whether or not our bodies are accelerating (except when the acceleration is extremely gradual). Sitting in a plane or standing in an elevator, it may be difficult to tell whether we are moving; but we almost always know when the plane or elevator is accelerating. As with touch, we are more sensitive to changes than to steady states. Our perception of uprightness and motion depends largely on information received from the *semicircular canals* and *vestibular sacs* in the inner ear. The canals are filled with fluid that responds to movement of the head, especially rotation. Feedback from the movement of the fluid tells us when we are moving, but, as with a glass full of water, the fluid does not move around if the motion of the body is steady. Thus, we can tell if our head is moving and our body is not, or whether we are accelerating, but not whether we are moving if there is no acceleration or deceleration. The vestibular sacs are constructed so that normal feedback occurs when we are upright, and any deviation produces different pressure and tells us just how far we are leaning.

To demonstrate how accurate your body image can make your actions, try these simple experiments. With your eyes closed, extend your arm straight out to one side. Then, with one motion, bring your index finger in to touch the tip of your nose. Extend both arms out from your sides and bring them together so your index fingers touch. Place the index finger of your left hand on the underside of a table top and then place the index finger of your right hand at the same point on the top of the table. Note how close your fingers are to the goal each time, even though you could not see where you were placing them (based on Hochberg, 1964).

Perception

Perception refers to the actual experience of the world. It begins with the actions of the sense organs, but eventually takes place in the brain. Sensory mechanisms respond to only certain segments of available stimulation and to some extent they shape and distort even these. When the information from the sensory mechanisms reaches the brain, still more shaping and distortion occur, and eventually perception. Although we understand little of the specific process by which the brain interprets and organizes the information, we do know some of the rules by which it operates.

PSYCHOPHYSICS

One of the most obvious examples of how we distort reality is the lack of identity between the *strength* of a physical stimulus and our *perception* of it. If one person starts to whistle in a quiet library he or she shatters the silence. But a second person joining the whistling will not double the disturbance. Similarly, when a single bulb is lit in a dark room we see a blaze of light, but a second bulb does not double the amount of light we perceive.

The study of the relationship between physical stimuli and psychological experience is known as *psychophysics.* The basic procedure of psychophysics is to establish thresholds, which are essentially measures of perceptual sensitivity. An *absolute threshold* is the point at which a person can reliably tell if a stimulus is present. If the light, sound, smell, or other stimulus is any weaker, the person cannot consistently perceive it. A *difference threshold* is the point at which a person can reliably distinguish between two stimuli. A person with normal sight can easily see that a 150-watt bulb is brighter than one of 100 watts. She can also distinguish between a 100- and a 105-watt bulb. But at some point the difference between the intensities of light emitted by the two bulbs becomes so small that she cannot reliably say which is brighter. The difference threshold is the smallest change that enables her to perceive a *just noticeable difference* (j.n.d.).

However, the determination of both absolute and difference thresholds is actually extremely complex because an individual's response to a stimulus depends on many aspects of the situation in addition to the strength of the stimulus and the ability of the person to perceive it.

THE PSYCHOPHYSICS OF AIRPLANE NOISE

A practical application of psychophysics involves the issue of how airplane noise affects people who live near airports. This issue has been especially important in recent years because of controversy over the supersonic Concorde. Critics of the plane showed that it produced between two and four times as much noise in takeoffs and landings as other jets. However, the questions arose as to how the amount of noise measured in purely physical terms related to psychological perception of loudness; and then, how loudness related to discomfort or annoyance. For example, a plane that was twice as loud might be perceived as only 10 percent louder and perhaps only 5 percent more annoying.

These questions have not yet been answered fully, and the problem clearly requires complex psychophysical techniques. Eugene Galanter has been exploring the relationship between noise of planes and how annoying people find them. In a series of studies, subjects listen to recordings of planes and then rate annoyance in a variety of ways. One procedure consists of giving the subjects a standard noise and calling that 100. Then other noises are given and the subject says how they compare to the standard by assigning them a number smaller or greater than 100, giving us a mathematical scale of noise annoyance. In addition, Galanter has been trying to compare the annoyance produced by noise to annoyance caused by other sources. For example, an annoyance number of 100 is assigned to having one's bike stolen. Subjects are then asked to assign numbers to other incidents and various noises depending on how much more or less annoying they are than having a bike stolen. Such studies give us an idea of how airplane noises relate to other unpleasant events that occur in people's lives.

These techniques do not provide definitive answers to the question of whether we should encourage or even allow loud planes to land at our airports. But the information from this research should help us make this kind of decision more rationally.

EUGENE
GALANTER

As our example of the two bulbs in a dark room makes clear, the effect of a difference in size varies depending on the magnitude of the stimuli employed. We can easily see the difference between one and two bulbs in a dark room, but we would have difficulty seeing the difference between 100 and 101 bulbs. Although the *absolute amount* of light added by each bulb is always the same, the *psychological difference* is not. When light is very dim, the addition of a small amount of light is noticeable. Thus, if the only light available were a 6-watt bulb, we would notice the difference between it and a 6.1-watt bulb. But with a 600-watt bulb, the smallest humanly detectable difference would be about 10 watts. In both cases, the difference we could detect would be 1/60th of the light intensity already present, but as the initial intensity increased, the absolute size of the difference would increase proportionately. The *Weber-Fechner law* of psychophysics states that, for any of the senses, *the just noticeable difference in intensity is always the same proportion of the existing stimulus.* The necessary proportion differs for various kinds of stimulation. Table 2.1 lists some proportions that have been fairly well established.

This proportional relationship is not confined to sensory stimulation, but seems to hold for a wide variety of psychological judgments as well. A glass of beer that costs 75 cents is noticeably more expensive than one that costs 50 cents. However, a pair of jeans that costs $8.75 might be barely distinguishable from one that costs $8.50. And surely there is no noticeable difference between a car that costs $3,000 and one that costs 25 cents less. In each case, 25 cents is involved, but its psychological importance decreases as the total amount of money involved increases. The absolute amount of money has remained the same in all cases, but the proportion it represents has changed drastically.

The psychophysical law is a clear illustration of the difference between physical stimulation and psychological perception. Two bulbs produce twice as much light as one, but do not appear twice as bright; on the piano, middle C has a frequency of 256 Hz and the C one octave higher is 512 Hz, but it does not sound twice as high. The human perceptual system does not merely accept external stimulation, but rather interprets it. And it is these interpretations, rather than the physical stimuli themselves, that describe our world for us.

Table 2.1
SOME OF WEBER'S PROPORTIONS

Stimulus	Proportion
Pitch	1/333
Brightness	1/60
Lifted weights	1/53
Loudness	1/11
Smell of rubber	1/10
Skin pressure	1/7
Taste, saline	1/5

Notice that humans are remarkably good at distinguishing pitch; a difference of 1/333rd is much smaller than the difference between two adjacent notes on the piano. They are relatively poor, however, at distinguishing differences in saltiness.

Source: Boring, Langfeld, and Weld, 1948.

CONTRAST AND ADAPTATION

Our perception of a stimulus is determined in part by comparison with other stimuli. This is called the *contrast effect.* Figures 2.7 and 2.8 show two impressive examples of this contrast effect in terms of size. Similar effects occur with colors. A white circle appears blue against a yellow background and yellow against a blue background. In general, any stimulus, whether of light, smell, taste, sound, or touch, is perceived more intensely against a "weak" (low intensity) background than against a "strong" (high intensity) background.

Contrast effects are closely related to a more general phenomenon known as *adaptation*, which refers to the fact that our perceptions are usually relative to what we are used to at a particular moment. Everyone is familiar with the effect of walking into a building on a sunny day—even if the rooms are well lighted, they appear dark temporarily because they are so much less bright than the outside. Conversely, after watching a movie in a dark theater, we think the lobby is very bright even if it is not particularly well lighted. This phenomenon is due not only to the contrast effect but also to actual physical changes in the sensitivity of the sense organs. After continual exposure to a stimulus, our senses become less sensitive to that stimulus and eventually cease to respond to it. Someone who has been in bright light for an hour will not be able to see well, if at all, in a dimly lit room because the active chemical in the rods in the retina, which do most of the seeing in dim light, has been exhausted from prolonged exposure to bright light and requires time to recover sensitivity. After you have been in a dark room for a while, however, you begin to see objects that were not visible at the beginning. This is called *dark adaptation*. Similarly, after someone has been in total darkness for several hours, his eyes may be as much as a hundred thousand times as sensitive to light as someone who has been in bright sunlight. Going from a dark room to full sunlight requires adaptation of the cones, which have become too sensitive to deal with the sudden high level of stimulation. The same kinds of phenomena occur with other kinds of visual stimulation and with many other senses. We adapt to noise level, particular odors, particular colors, and temperature, to name some of the most important kinds of sensory adaptations.

Adaptation and contrast effects, like many of the other principles discussed in this chapter, occur in many kinds of behaviors and judgments. We evaluate other people largely by comparing them to some standard to which we have grown accustomed. Someone who seems very smart in high school may appear less smart in college, where the general level of intelligence is usually higher. Someone who is perceived as bright and cheerful in one group may, by contrast, appear drab in another. A friend who is cheerful and talkative most of the time may seem depressed or sad when he talks a little less, but a friend who rarely talks would be considered almost euphoric if she talked that much. Indeed, one of the most important theories in social psychology, the theory of social comparison, deals in detail with how we make judgments about ourselves and others by using comparisons (see Chapter 17).

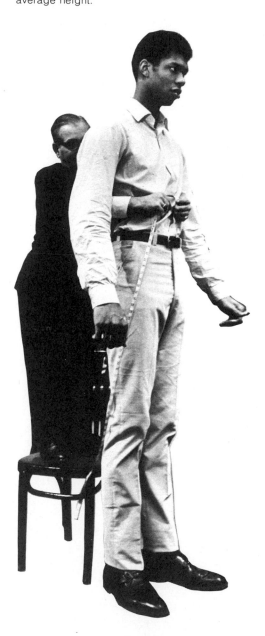

Fig. 2.7
Contrast effect
Kareem Abdul Jabbar looks tall on a basketball court, but he looks even taller next to someone of average height.

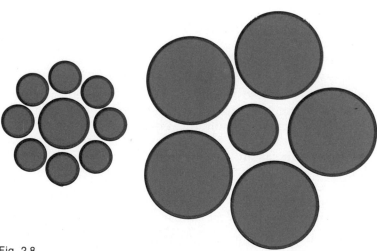

Fig. 2.8
Contrast effect
The middle circle on the right looks smaller than the one on the left, but they are exactly the same size.

DISTANCE AND DEPTH PERCEPTION

Perception of depth and distance plays a critical role in all sorts of human activities, from reaching for a glass to driving a car. It is also essential for size constancy and, to some extent, for shape constancy. Finally, it adds dimension and richness to our surroundings; without depth perception the world would be literally and figuratively flat. Depth perception depends on cues (stimuli or bits of information)— some that involve both eyes (*binocular cues*) and some that involve only one eye (*monocular cues*).

Binocular Cues

The most important binocular basis for judging distance is *retinal disparity*, which is the difference between the images seen by the right eye and those seen by the left eye. Since the eyes are several inches apart, each views a scene somewhat differently. Try this experiment: hold a pencil at arm's length and look past it, first closing one eye and then the other. The pencil appears to move in relation to the scene behind it. Now move the pencil closer to your eyes, say six inches, and repeat the procedure. The pencil appears to move much more than it did before. Figure 2.9 shows how retinal disparity decreases as the distance from our eyes to the object increases.

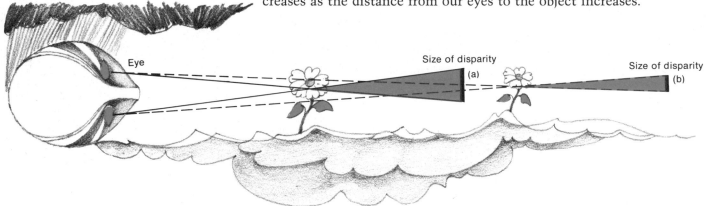

Eye   Size of disparity (a)   Size of disparity (b)

Fig. 2.9
Retinal disparity as cue to depth perception

When the eyes focus on a close object, the angle (a) between the two eyes is greater than when the object is further away (angle b). This difference is used as a cue to distance.

Retinal disparity is also a primary basis of depth perception. Although images hitting the retina are two-dimensional, we see the world as possessing depth and solidity. This perception of depth is produced by the difference in the images the two eyes receive. Three-dimensional movies are based on this principle. To see a 3-D movie, the viewer wears polarized glasses that allow slightly different images to enter each eye.

A second type of binocular cue is *convergence*—the angle necessary to focus both eyes on an object so that the disparate images fuse. The acuteness of the angle increases as the object moves closer and thus provides a clue to its distance. To demonstrate convergence to yourself, focus on a pencil held at arm's length and move the pencil toward you. As you do this, you can feel your eyes straining to focus. Eventually, of course, your eyes cross. Convergence is the principle by which some photographic and military range finders operate—the angle at which the two images converge indicates the distance of the object. The farther apart the two lenses are, the greater will be the difference in the convergence angle and the more accurate will be the estimates of distance. Because human eyes are only a few inches apart, convergence helps in estimating distances of only seventy feet or less.

Monocular Cues

The simplest of the monocular cues used in judging depth and distance is the relative position of objects in the visual field. If one object is *superimposed* on another, it is necessarily closer and is seen as such. Other monocular cues are *clearness, brightness, pattern of shadow, texture gradient,* and *linear perspective.*

Our perceptual process takes into account that distance usually makes outlines and details less clear and objects less bright. Therefore, the clearer and brighter an object is, the closer we perceive it to be. The pattern of light and shadow is another important cue to distance. On any three-dimensional object, prominent features catch the light, while indentations are usually in shadow. Accordingly, we perceive darker areas as being deeper or farther away. Gradients in texture also affect our impression of distance; the finer textures appear to be farther away and coarser ones closer. Finally, linear perspective makes equally spaced objects appear closer together as they become more distant. We can see this clearly when we look down railroad tracks, which appear to converge in the distance. Figure 2.10 shows a few of these monocular cues.

Distance is portrayed in painting by rules of perspective based on the principles of depth perception we have just described. However, some painting, including early Western, Oriental, and much of African painting, does not employ perspective. European art before the tenth century rarely portrayed depth at all. The paintings appeared flat, with all figures at equal distances from the viewer. In some cultures, arbitrary rules are used to illustrate distance. For example, Japanese painting places objects that are supposed to be further away higher on the canvas.

Fig. 2.10
Monocular cues

Clearness, brightness, pattern of shadow, texture gradient, and linear perspective are all helping us to perceive distance in this one photograph.

Fig. 2.11
Hogarth print on perspective

"Whosoever maketh a design without the knowledge of perspective will be liable to such absurdities as are shown . . ."

CONSTANCIES

One of the most important and to some extent mysterious aspects of perception is that we interpret sensory input as changing less than it actually does. Even though the physical stimuli reaching our sense organs may change markedly, we recognize familiar objects, shapes, colors, and other stimuli and perceive them as unchanged. We impose certain rules on the world and view it as constant, despite variations in the input from our sense organs. These regularities are called *perceptual constancies.*

Size Constancy

Our tendency to perceive familiar objects as more or less always the same size regardless of their spatial relationship to us is called *size constancy.* Imagine, for example, walking down the street and seeing a woman several hundred yards away. She comes closer and finally passes you. What happens to your perception of the woman? Does she appear to change from an ant into a giant? No, she appears to be about the same size no matter how far apart you are. At two hundred yards, you may be uncertain whether she is 5 feet 1 inch or 5 feet 9 inches tall, but you do not think she is only a few inches tall. Moreover, this size constancy is not a deliberate intellectual function. We do not say to ourselves, "That is a woman and no matter how small she may

BOX 2.3

THE MOON ILLUSION

A striking example of how various constancies and rules of depth perception produce distortions is the *moon illusion.* A full moon appears much larger when it is close to the horizon than when it is higher in the sky—despite the fact that the image on the retina and the moon

itself remain the same size. This effect is so strong that even people who are familiar with it are usually amazed at how big the moon appears when it is just over the horizon.

One explanation of the illusion is that when the moon is low in the sky it is seen in relation to the horizon and trees, houses, and hills. In comparison to these much smaller objects, the moon appears

look to me, I know that she is about 5½ feet tall." The woman actually does look the right height.

People judge size on the basis of distance and the size of the image on the retina. The smaller the image, the smaller the object. Also, the farther away something is, the smaller will be its image. Therefore, if two objects produce an image of the same size on the retina and one is twice as far away as the other, it is perceived as being twice as large. Of course, because accurate perception of size depends to some extent on the accurate perception of distance, we need to

B.C. by permission of Johnny Hart and Field Enterprises, Inc.

larger. But careful research by Kaufman and Rock (1962) indicates that the major cause is that the moon on the horizon is "behind" all the objects on the earth and is also seen against the textured terrain, both of which make it seem very far away. When it is overhead there is nothing with which to compare it, and so it seems closer. The farther away it appears, the larger it is seen to be.

Both explanations are supported by demonstrations that eliminate the moon illusion by removing the ordinary cues. For example, E. G. Boring (1943) showed that if you view the moon upside down through your thumb and forefinger or through a small window that removes the surrounding objects, the illusion is lost.

Fig. 2.12
The Ames room

The Ames room (a) creates a drastic distortion of the actual heights of these three people, shown in (b). The observer is fooled because, although it looks normal, the room is constructed so that its ceiling is much lower on the right than on the left, none of the angles are right angles, and all the ordinary cues to distance and size are missing or distorted, causing the observer's perceptual system to interpret reality wrongly.

know how far away something is to make the correct translation of retinal image into perceived size. Fortunately, human beings are very good at judging distance.

At times size constancy leads to serious errors in perception. For instance, it is probably the basis behind the Mueller-Lyer illusion shown in Fig. 2.1. Perhaps the most impressive illusion based on perspective distortions is illustrated in Fig. 2.12.

(a)

(b)

BOX 2.4

THE ILLUSION OF MOVEMENT

Visual illusion is the basis for motion pictures, television, and neon signs that appear to move. The *phi phenomenon* is the perception of movement caused by two objects or two lights that are close to each other appearing successively with only a brief interval between their appearances (Wertheimer, 1912). A row of arrows on a neon sign appears to move when the arrows light in rapid succession. If a dot of light is flashed on a screen and then a second dot is flashed close by, we tend to perceive one dot that moves rather than two separate dots. This occurs for practically any object or light as long as the distance between the two appearances is small and, most important, the time interval is less than .03 seconds. If the time interval is greater, we perceive two separate objects. A motion picture consists of a series of separate images that appear on the screen in rapid succession. When the timing is just right and the images change position slightly, we perceive motion. The effect is probably due to the fact that this rapid succession of images approximates what happens when an object actually does move. In each case, two slightly different parts of the retina are stimulated in quick succession. Because the retina receives similar information in both cases, we tend to perceive both the illusion *and reality* as movement.

Another illusion of movement occurs when a small source of light is presented in a dark room with no background for comparison. The light appears to move, usually erratically and unpredictably. This *autokinetic phenomenon* is not fully understood, but it is probably caused in part by the tiring or satiation of the area of the retina that is receiving the light (Bruell and Albee, 1955). This illusion caused a serious problem for pilots during World War II. In night flights, a pilot was supposed to keep in formation by watching the tail light of the plane ahead of him. But pilots perceived the lights to be moving and often became disoriented. The problem was solved by the use of flashing lights, which eliminate the effect. Today, all planes have flashing rather than fixed lights.

(a)

(b)

Shape Constancy

The perceived shape of an object does not change because we view it from a different perspective. When we look at a door opening and closing, for example, we do not perceive it as changing from a rectangle to a trapezoid, but rather as remaining a rectangle (see Fig. 2.13).

Brightness and Color Constancies

Similarly, we tend to see objects as having fairly constant brightness. A sheet of white paper looks just about as white in bright sunlight as it does in a dim room. Coal is seen as black and sugar as white regardless of the amount of light available. If there is a shadow on a paper, we still see it as a white paper with a shadow on it rather than as a white and gray paper. This constancy applies to colors as well as to brightness. Although a background color does affect the perceived shade somewhat, tomatoes are seen as red and canaries as yellow within a wide range of light intensities.

RULES OF ORGANIZATION

The retina and other sense organs are bombarded by a vast array of stimuli. Yet we perceive the world as a fairly well-ordered place. One of the most important functions of the perceptual process is to create order out of this chaotic stimulation. To accomplish this, the perceptual mechanism follows certain rules of organization. Much of the credit for discovering and describing these rules belongs to Kurt

Fig. 2.13
Shape constancy

A closed door is obviously rectangular (a). As it opens toward us (b), the image on our retina corresponds to a trapezoid, with the edge closest to us being longer than the one farther away. Yet we still perceive it as a rectangle.

Koffka (1925) and other members of the Gestalt school of psychology. *Gestalt* is a German word meaning "shape," "whole," or "form." The school of Gestalt psychology was so named because it stressed the tendency to perceive the world in terms of whole structures rather than bits and pieces. For example, people perceive an entire scene rather than the separate colors and lights of a visual stimulus, and they hear a melody rather than the pitch and intensity of each individual tone.

Box 2.5

CAMOUFLAGE: THE ART OF MISLEADING

Camouflage uses an observer's perceptual tendencies to mislead her. Just as illusions produce false perceptions, so does camouflage produce one perception and conceal another.

Gestalt organizing principles play an important role in camouflage. For example, the principles of continuation and good form are employed to conceal familiar shapes in Fig. (a). Triangles and squares are better forms than the number 4, so the

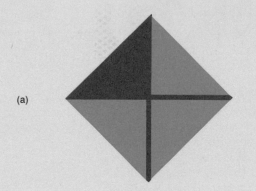

(a)

(b)

4 can be disguised by embedding it in the geometric shapes. Continuation tends to carry the lines of the numeral beyond the point at which it might be recognized. Try to find the hidden numeral in Fig. (b), outlining it with a pen so that it stands out. In both cases, note why the numbers were difficult to recognize and the rules of organization that were involved.

The figure-ground relationship is par-

ticularly critical in camouflage. The form to be hidden must not be the figure or it will be seen easily. Therefore, it is disguised as the ground. This is the principle behind most natural camouflage (see color Plate D). Animals blend with their surroundings by not being distinctive: yellow lions against tall, yellow grass; bright birds in lush, green forests, and drab birds in less colorful areas.

Color is often the key factor—the camouflage depends on an animal's being the same color as the background. The chameleon and various marine animals actually change their colors to blend in, whereas other animals simply have coloring that makes them merge with the ground. This phenomenon led the United States Air Force to employ colorblind people to "see through" camouflage in World War II. Because they did not see the colors, they were less likely to be misled by camouflage that used protective coloring.

Figure-Ground

Probably the most basic rule of organization is that some part of the visual field (the figure) is seen to stand out against the rest of the field (the ground). This *figure-ground relationship* occurs in almost any visual scene. Familiar objects or shapes are seen as figures, and the relatively undifferentiated surroundings are seen as the ground. A plane against a background of sky or a tree in an open field are typical examples. The phenomenon also occurs with other senses. For example, we hear a person call for help against a much louder background of traffic noise.

Even when the shapes and objects in our visual field are not familiar ones, we still tend to organize them into figure and ground. The diagrams in Fig. 2.14 illustrate this principle. And sometimes the figure and ground relationship can reverse, revealing different shapes under the two conditions. The important point is that our perception of the world is greatly influenced by which part of the field we see as the figure and which as the ground. In general, we make sense of the world by seeing important objects and consistent shapes as figures, because these are the stimuli with which we have to deal most often.

(a)

(b)

Fig. 2.14
Figure-ground

In (a), you can see either a white vase against a black background or the silhouettes of two black faces against a white background. In (b), you can see either white or black creatures.

Rules of Grouping

In addition to perceiving the world in terms of figures and grounds, we tend to perceive stimuli as being part of some kind of structure, form, or "Gestalt." They fall into a pattern rather than remaining as isolated bits.

The primary rules by which this structuring occurs are illustrated in Fig. 2.15. In (a) and (b), we can see that stimuli are grouped according to *similarity*. In (a), most people would perceive three horizontal lines made up of circles and *x*'s. In (b), we would perceive three vertical lines. Yet obviously both formations are identical: each has three rows—two of circles and one of *x*'s—and could easily be perceived as either vertical or horizontal lines. The similarity of the items in a line determines the groupings that we perceive. Note that in (c), where each line contains both *x*'s and circles, we are much less likely to group the stimuli in lines. Instead we might see a diamond formation of *x*'s with a cross of circles through it. Or we could see a 3×3 square with no further differentiation into groups.

Figure 2.15(d) shows the effect of *proximity* (closeness) on grouping. Instead of seeing six lines, most people would see a single line on the left, then two groups of two lines each, and, finally, a single line on the right. The four lines in the middle tend to be seen as two groups of two because the members of each pair are close together.

The third principle is the tendency to perceive the *continuation* of a line, a curve, or any kind of shape. A straight line is ordinarily seen as remaining straight, a curved line follows the direction of the curve, and so on. In Fig. 2.15(e), for example, we see a line starting at the upper left and running *through* an irregular figure, not a line branching at the point marked *x*. This tendency toward continuation is one of the bases for most kinds of camouflage. We conceal a shape by encouraging the eye to perceive the continuation of various lines that distract the viewer from the true form of the hidden object.

The final principle of organization, *good figure*, is more complicated and, in a sense, is a combination of all the other principles. People tend to organize stimuli into recognizable shapes or figures. As such, good figure is closely related to figure-ground since recognizable shapes emerge as the figure. If no familiar form is visible, we look for symmetrical shapes. For example, Fig. 2.15(f) is identical to Fig. 2.15(d) except that small extensions have been added to the lines. Yet these extensions cause us to see three rectangles instead of just groups of lines, so we organize the drawing entirely differently. Note that the principle of proximity becomes secondary to the tendency to find symmetrical shapes. When good figure is combined with continuation, the effects are particularly strong. For example, most people see a circle in Fig. 2.15(g) and a triangle in Fig. 2.15(h), despite the fact that neither form is complete and both are disjointed by many interfering lines and shapes. This tendency to see a complete figure even if there are gaps in it is sometimes called *closure*.

The term *good figure* comes from the idea that some figures are "better" than others. This is a rather vague notion, but perhaps it refers to those figures that most people are able to organize fairly easily into recognizable shapes. However, there are no comprehensive rules for deciding whether a particular shape is a good figure. Several experiments have assessed simplicity by drawing a figure on graph paper and asking subjects to guess whether each successive square on the sheet is empty or filled. Presumably, the simpler the shape, the more quickly the subject will recognize regularities in it and be able

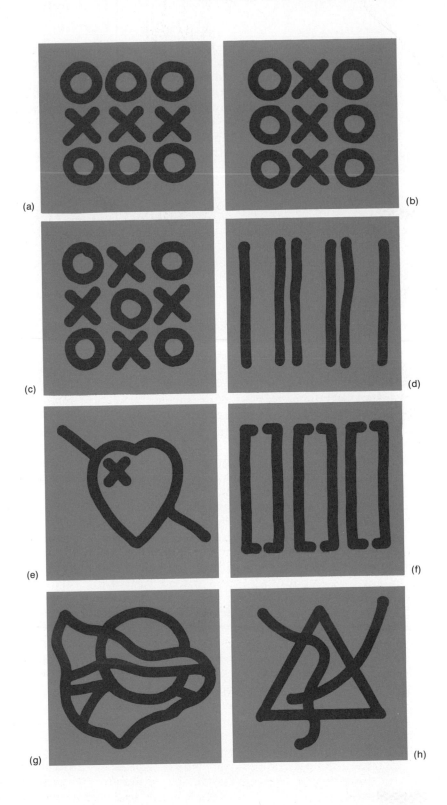

Figure 2.15

to guess accurately (Attneave, 1974). But there is more to good figure than simplicity. It probably depends on some combination of simplicity, predictability, and the individual's familiarity with the particular figure. The numeral 5 may not be as simple as a square, but it is more likely to emerge as a recognizable shape than an equally complex form that is unfamiliar (for example, an upside-down 5). In other words, this basic principle of perceptual organization depends on both the physical aspects of the structure and the person's experience.

Box 2.6

RULES OF ORGANIZATION IN OTHER PSYCHOLOGICAL PHENOMENA

Although the Gestalt rules of organization have been applied primarily to vision, they also apply to some extent to other modes of perception. For example, the rules of proximity, similarity, and continuation play an important role in the perception of sound. If you hear someone say "They are frying chickens" you might not know whether people are frying some chickens or whether these particular chickens are for frying. We shall discuss this kind of ambiguous sentence at greater length in Chapter 5. For now, the important point is that how the sentence is uttered will tend to favor one meaning or the other. The sequence "man eating . . . shark" sounds quite different from "man . . . eating shark." Say them out loud and you will hear that proximity causes words to be perceived together, just as it does with visual stimuli.

The role of similarity is even clearer. If you are listening to a conversation and another voice chimes in, you have a very strong tendency to perceive all sounds of the same frequency and quality as belonging together. You do not confuse one voice with another and lose the thread of the conversation. To some extent this is also an example of continuation—the original sound is followed even if you cannot hear it temporarily because of an interrupting sound.

Organizing principles also operate in perceptions involving other people. Continuation and good-figure cause us to fill in missing bits of information in our social perceptions. If we see a football quarterback fade back and raise his arm, we will assume he is going to pass and will see the scene in the usual way (including perhaps even the ball itself) even if the whole play is a fake. In magic, the basis of many tricks is to cause the observer to follow one action and to make usual assumptions while something entirely different is happening. And a student who is seen smiling and nodding in class is usually perceived by the teacher as interested and paying attention. The fact that the student's eyes are closed and she is sleeping may be missed because it does not fit the normal pattern.

In social behavior the rule of figure-ground is especially important. Whenever you are in a social situation, one of the most critical questions is whether you are standing out and being noticed or blending into the background. Depending on your purpose and how you are feeling, you may prefer to be the figure or the ground; but in all instances your behavior and how you are treated will depend on which you are. An especially dramatic example occurs whenever someone is different from those around him. The person who is different or deviant almost always stands out and accordingly becomes the focus of attention. A black person in a white group experiences this, as does a white person in a black group. Indeed, all of us at one time or another find ourselves surrounded by people who are different from us, and we become the deviant and the figure against a ground of other people. Thus, the rules of organization of stimuli apply to many areas of human behavior, not only to the physical modes of perception.

THE ROLE OF INNATE MECHANISMS AND LEARNING

Innate Perceptual Mechanisms

As we discussed in Chapter 1, a major theme in psychology is the interaction of heredity and learning. This interplay is particularly evident in the area of perception.

It seems clear that some perceptual mechanisms are entirely or largely innate. The individual is born with them and requires no experience to operate them. For example, a great many animals appear to have some *depth perception* as soon as they can open their eyes.

The existence of depth perception in very young animals has been demonstrated by Gibson and Walk (1960) and others by the use of an apparatus known as the *visual cliff.* As shown in Fig. 2.16, the subject is placed on a shelf that appears to drop off to the floor on one side. If the subject has depth perception, it will discriminate between the two sides of the shelf.

The procedure is so simple that almost any kind of animal can be observed—chicken, monkey, rat, lamb, or human baby. Results indicate that by the time they are old enough to be tested, all these species have depth perception (Gibson and Walk, 1960; Fantz, 1957). Lambs only one day old can move around and avoid the cliff. Children do not move around until they are between six and fourteen months old, but at that age all the children tested demonstrated depth perception.

In addition, several experiments (McKenzie and Day, 1972) confirmed that infants as young as six weeks can fix their gaze on objects, provided the objects are only ten or twelve inches away. However, these results also indicate that infants, viewing objects of the same size at different distances, primarily detect the differences in distance rather than the constancy in the objects' size. Thus, depth perception is probably innate, but size constancy appears to be quite limited at an early age and improves with time.

Infants also have various perceptual preferences. They react to change more than to static stimuli (Haith, 1966) and to patterns more than to solid fields (Fantz, 1957). Shown a triangle, infants focus on certain lines or angles rather than the empty area in the center (Salapatek and Kessen, 1966), and they focus on the line dividing a half-white, half-black circle (Kessen, Salapatek, and Haith, 1965). There are undoubtedly many other specific preferences in infancy, but these few make it clear that many aspects of human perceptual processes are present at birth.

The Role of Experience

Although some aspects of perception are innate, many of them depend on experience to develop or are sharpened and extended by experience. Even depth perception, which is functioning very early, becomes more acute as the child grows older. And the appearance of almost all of the constancies and organizing rules are in part a function of the individual's exposure to appropriate stimulation.

Fig. 2.16
The visual cliff

Although the shelf appears to drop off on one side, actually, just below the shelf there is a sheet of glass that gives off a minimum of reflection. On the "deep" side, a pattern is placed on the floor several feet below the glass to enhance the perception of depth. On the "shallow" side, the pattern is immediately beneath the glass. When a subject is placed on the shelf, the experimenter can observe whether it avoids the deep side of the apparatus.

Probably the most basic constancy of all is *object constancy*—perception of an object as retaining its identity even if it vanishes for a moment. As we shall see in Chapter 12, this ability develops with age and experience: an infant who watches a car go behind a house and emerge on the other side does not necessarily think it is the same car. We do not fully understand the mechanism by which this tendency eventually emerges, but we do know that infants lack it. As with most human behavior, some experience and maturation is necessary for the individual to develop this basic perceptual constancy.

Cultural differences We can see the effect of experience when we consider how differently people from different cultures perceive similar situations. For example, the Bambuti pygmies live among vegetation so dense that they rarely have an opportunity to see an object at a distance greater than a few yards. Anthropologist Colin Turnbull reports (1961) that the Bambuti pygmies appear to lack size constancy when distances are great and there are no familiar objects for comparison purposes. In a graphic account, Turnbull describes the response of a pygmy named Kenge to an open plain, something he was seeing for the first time in his life:

> Kenge looked over the plains and down to where a herd of about a hundred buffalo were grazing some miles away. He asked me what kind of insects they were, and I told him they were buffalo, twice as big as the forest buffalo known to him. He laughed loudly and told me not to tell such stupid stories, and asked me again what kind of insects they were. He then talked to himself, for want of more intelligent company, and tried to liken the buffalo to the various beetles and ants with which he was familiar.
>
> He was still doing this when we got into the car and drove down to where the animals were grazing. He watched them getting larger and larger, and though he was as courageous as any Pygmy, he moved over and sat close to me and muttered that it was witchcraft. . . . Finally, when he realized that they were real buffalo he was no longer afraid, but what puzzled him still was why they had been so small, and grown larger, or whether it had been some kind of trickery.

Similarly, people of different cultures vary in the extent to which they see geometric optical illusions (Segall, Campbell, and Herskovits, 1966). The Zulus, for example, live in circular huts with rounded doorways and no windows. They plow their land in curved rather than straight furrows, and most of their possessions are rounded rather than rectangular. As you might expect, they are relatively unaffected by optical illusions such as the Mueller-Lyer or rotating trapezoid, which depend on the perception of rectangles or straight lines. Other tribes, living in huts with rectangular doors and windows, see these optical illusions to the same extent that we do.

Adaptability Because their perception depends in part on experience, humans can adapt extremely well to changes in the environment. Young chickens who are fitted with lenses that displace their visual field slightly to one side never learn to compensate for this distortion.

No matter how long they wear the lenses, they continue to peck at the place where the grain appears to be, even though they never hit it (Hess, 1956). Similarly, when the eyeball of a frog is surgically inverted so that it sees objects on the right as if they were on the left, the frog will jump to the left when a fly is dangled on its right, and it will never learn to correct this. But when humans are given lenses that turn the world upside down or transpose left and right, they learn to compensate. Moreover, after a while, the world actually appears correct to them—in some way, their perceptual system has corrected the distortion and the world is seen as right side up. Some subjects adapt so well that they can ride a motorcycle while wearing inverting glasses (Kohler, 1962).

OTHER FACTORS AFFECTING PERCEPTION

Attention

Perceptual mechanisms and rules operate more or less automatically. Individuals do not intentionally turn them on, nor can they ordinarily turn them off. On the other hand, people's perceptions are greatly affected by their internal state. Physical factors such as fatigue, fever, and the effect of many different drugs alter perceptions. But perhaps the most important psychological determinant of perception is attention. This phenomenon is more complex than one might imagine. In the first place, obviously we perceive only those stimuli to which we are exposed. If we look in one direction, we see objects in that direction and not those behind us. Similarly, if we pay attention to one object by touching it, we feel its texture while we do not feel that of another object we do not touch. Thus, at the simplest level, attention operates by determining which stimuli impinge on our sense organs.

This is by no means a trivial effect. As we shall discuss in more detail in the chapters on learning (Chapter 3) and thinking (Chapter 6), individuals can learn to attend to certain characteristics and ignore others. This kind of learning can play a major role in the ability to discriminate among stimuli, and in the capacity to solve complex problems. Indeed, one basis of efficient and creative thinking is attention to the critical aspects of a problem and the ability to distinguish them from irrelevant characteristics.

But there is more to attention than simply where one looks or what one touches. Some parts of the visual, auditory, or other sensory fields stand out, are noticed more, and are more likely to be remembered. This is due partly to the stimuli themselves. As we have already discussed in connection with the figure-ground relationship, familiar and well-formed objects tend to stand out, as does something that is different from its surroundings, like a cat among five dogs. And when we are accustomed to seeing or hearing certain stimuli, a novel one elicits a stronger response than the familiar ones. For example, if someone is shown four white circles and then three white circles and a white square, the square receives a stronger response than when the person has not previously seen all circles. In other words, not only is the square different from the other three figures, but also the person is

BOX 2.7

TIME PERCEPTION

Just as we perceive concrete objects, we also perceive the passage of time. If someone asks you how long you have been sitting in class, you can give some impression of how long it has been. If you close your eyes and try to say how long a minute takes, you will probably be inaccurate but you will certainly give an answer that is closer to one minute than to ten seconds. And we also perceive longer time periods, such as the length of time since last summer or since we met someone we love. We do not understand exactly *how* we perceive time, but we do know some of the factors that affect it.

Time perception seems to depend in part on our perception of what happens during the period. The more separate events we perceive, the longer the time seems to us. This is true even of simple events such as brief sounds—the more we hear in a given period, the longer we judge the period (Ornstein, 1969). The explanation seems to be that we must process any information we have received. On the other hand, if too much information is received (for example, the stimuli are so complex that we cannot really process them), we tend to ignore it and judge the time period as somewhat shorter (Hogan, 1975).

This view of time perception deals with retrospective judgments—those made after the interval has passed. The comparable judgments in everyday life might be how long an evening seemed in which you did a lot of things as against one in which you just sat and listened to music. Presumably, you will remember the evening in which you did a lot of things as being longer.

A somewhat different kind of judgment is how quickly time seems to be passing at the present. We have all experienced evenings that seem to drag forever because we are bored, and others that seem to race by because we are busy or having a good time. Although there is no research on this issue, intuitively it appears that this kind of perception is exactly the opposite of retrospective judgments—the more that is happening, the quicker time seems to pass. However, time passes more slowly if we are bored not because of information processing but because when there is nothing going on we pay more attention to time, check our watch constantly, and wonder whether the evening (or the lecture) will ever be over. It is the *focus* on time that makes it seem to pass slowly, not our perceptions in terms of how much information we have processed. In other words, the two types of time perception may be based on entirely different processes—information processing when we look back, but attention and boredom while we are in the period.

used to seeing circles and the square is novel (Berlyne, 1951). In short, a stimulus that is different from its surroundings or different from what is expected will stand out.

Beyond these stimulus characteristics, individuals themselves seem to be able to affect their own perceptions by deliberately paying attention to certain aspects of the perceptual field. It is this aspect of attention that is most fascinating and difficult to understand. Even though all stimuli impinge on the sense organs, we can choose to notice some more than others. We can focus our attention on letters rather than numbers, the temperature of an object rather than its texture, the sound in a room rather than its appearance, and so on. In each case, the stimuli to which we attend are perceived more clearly and are more likely to be remembered.

Experiments have demonstrated that we can also pay more attention to sounds that are coming in one ear than to those coming in the other. For example, Donald Broadbent (1958) played different messages to the left and right ears and told subjects to pay attention primarily to one or the other. He found that they understood and remembered the material from the "primary" ear much better than the material from the other. Similarly, George Sperling (1960) flashed a set of numbers on a screen and told subjects to attend to a particular corner. Even though they were told to fix their eyes on the center of the screen and were therefore presumably exposed equally to the whole set of numbers, subjects could remember many more from the selected corner than from the rest of the field.

However, we cannot entirely turn off our perceptions. Short of looking away, closing our eyes, or covering our ears, we cannot screen out stimuli completely. Even though we are paying attention to our left ear and ignoring our right, we do perceive some information from the right. For example, if both ears are receiving the same message at slightly different times, eventually the listener notices the similarity (Treisman, 1964). And we all have a strong tendency to recognize our own names even when they are presented to the ear we are supposedly ignoring (Moray, 1959).

R.C. by permission of Johnny Hart and Field Enterprises, Inc.

Motivation and Set

An individual's motivation or values and her expectations (*set*) also affect perception. Some early research appeared to demonstrate that values produce an actual change in perception. Poor subjects presumably value money more than rich subjects do, and some experiments showed that coins were actually seen to be larger by the poor (Bruner and Goodman, 1947). This is very impressive, since it involves a sizable distortion of familiar objects. However, subsequent research (Carter and Schooler, 1949; Klein, Schlesinger, and Meister, 1951) has failed to confirm this result, and most psychologists today doubt that people's values can directly affect their perceptions.

However, motivation and values can alter the individual's *interpretation* of an ambiguous stimulus and affect his focus of attention. A poor person may be more likely to interpret a small round object on the ground as a coin than a bottle top, and he may also be more motivated than a richer person to look for lost coins by glancing down. Thus, he would be more likely to perceive the ambiguous object as a coin and also more likely to see an actual coin.

BOX 2.8

HOW RELIABLE IS EYEWITNESS TESTIMONY?

We have seen that our perceptions are not perfect reflections of the world outside us. Many factors including perceptual constancies, rules of organization, attention, motivation, and set tend to influence our perception of people, objects, situations, and even how we see ourselves. This fact has important implications in many areas, particularly in social interactions. Now let us reconsider our hypothetical case involving an eyewitness at a trial. The witness testified that he saw a man rush into the bank, raise a gun, and say in a deep, gruff voice, "Put your hands up," and later, identified the defendant as the man he had seen in the bank. Should we assume his perceptions—made under very stressful circumstances—are accurate?

In fact, our eyewitness could easily have picked out the wrong man. For one thing, considerable time had passed before he looked at the police lineup, and the passage of time tends to distort our memory of initial perceptions. The quality of the police lineup would also be an important factor. For example, if the suspect is the only tall man in a lineup of short men, the witness might be more likely to pick him out. Since he has a particular set (he is looking for a *tall* man) he might choose this tall man because he stands out from the others. Suppose, however, that the police are more careful in selecting men for the lineup. They find six men who are tall, dark-haired, light-skinned, and have deep, gruff voices and no distinguishing features. But one crucial factor is missing—only the accused is attractive. Again the witness might tend to select the accused because he holds the expectation of seeing an attractive man and the suspect stands out in this important way.

A similar error actually did occur in a court case in North Carolina. A defendant accused of kidnapping another man was identified from a police lineup, convicted, and sentenced to a life term. In a television interview later the accused pointed out that the witness had described a dark-haired, dark-complexioned man as the kidnapper, and that in the lineup the accused was the *only* man with dark hair and a dark complexion!

Prejudices and preconceptions can affect the judgment of an eyewitness by producing perceptual distortions. For example, if the witness in our trial is prejudiced against blacks, he might actually "see" a black man holding the gun. This kind of distortion can occur with virtually any other type of preconception; so, in assessing the validity of a witness's testimony, it is essential to find out if he has any biases that might be relevant to what he says he saw.

Another difficulty with eyewitness testimony is the tendency to be consistent. There is evidence that once a witness has identified someone under unfair circumstances (such as a lineup), he will continue to identify the same person in part just to be consistent. Moreover, a witness whose perceptions or memories are biased by slanted questions (such as "What was the defendant doing at that time?" when it has not yet been determined that the defendant was even there) will give biased testimony much later and will, in fact, remember perceiving the situation as it was described in the biased question (Miller and Loftus, 1976). For example, asking someone "Do you remember where the red car was standing?" when in truth there was no red car, will cause the person later to remember seeing a red car. The question suggests that a red car was there, and the witness distorts her perceptions or memories of her perceptions in line with this suggestion. Thus, it is especially important to avoid biasing a witness immediately after the event because these biases tend to persist. The problem is that the jury is rarely aware of the existence of the biasing incident if it occurs long before the trial. This is a strong argument for keeping careful, explicit records of everything that happens to every witness so that biases of this sort can be caught.

The effect of set is similar to the operation of motivation. Look at each row in Fig. 2.17 while covering the other row with your hand. In row (a) you probably perceived numbers, including the number 13; in row (b) you probably perceived letters, including the letter B. Yet the figure you saw as 13 is identical to the one seen as B. Because you have a set to see numbers in list (a) and letters in list (b), you perceive the figure differently.

This effect of set also occurs in social situations and all too often results in inaccurate and biased perceptions. For example, a person who is prejudiced against blacks and thinks they are violent will sometimes perceive a black-white interaction in terms of this expectation. If a black person stumbles and falls against a white person in a crowded subway, an unbiased observer might perceive just what has happened but a prejudiced onlooker might perceive the black to be shoving or even attacking the white person. The same is true of any other prejudice or strong expectation whether it involves blacks, whites, women, men, or any other social group. ■

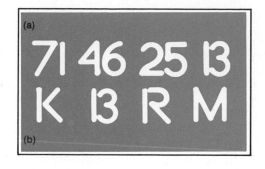

Figure 2.17

Summary

1. Our perceptions are not perfect representations of the world outside us; rather, we actively select, distort, and interpret sensory impressions.

2. Human sense organs are highly selective and remarkably sensitive.

3. The human eye functions much like a camera. Light strikes the cornea, passes through the pupil, and is focused by the lens. The focused light strikes the retina, which contains receptors called rods and cones. When struck by light, chemicals in the rods and cones generate electrical energy, which moves along the optic nerve to the brain.

4. The human eye translates various frequencies of light into the color spectrum, which ranges from red to orange, yellow, green, blue, indigo, and violet. Colors that are opposite each other on the color circle are called complementary colors.

5. The Young-Helmholtz theory of color vision assumes the existence of three different types of cones, each of which produces one color—red, green, or blue. The opponent-process theory also assumes there are three types of cones but suggests that two types produce two color experiences—red-green and yellow-blue—while the third produces only white.

6. The process of hearing begins when sound waves strike the outer ear. The vibrations are carried along the auditory canal to the eardrum, which vibrates like a loudspeaker. In turn, the eardrum causes the bones of the inner ear to vibrate; pressure from these vibrations is translated into neural impulses that move along the auditory nerve to the brain.

7. Loudness is determined by the number of hair cells on the organ of Corti that "fire." Place theory accounts for perception of high frequencies, and volley theory accounts for low and intermediate tones.

8. Smell and taste are closely related. Smell receptors are located in the mucous membrane of the upper nose and transmit to the olfactory bulb of the brain. Taste receptors for the four basic taste sensations—sweetness, sourness, saltiness, and bitterness—are arranged on taste buds located primarily on the edges and back of the tongue.

9. Receptors in the skin are responsible for sensitivity to temperature, pressure, and pain—the stimuli involved in the sense of touch.

10. Our kinesthetic and proprioceptive senses tell us our body's position in space.

11. Psychophysics studies the relationship between physical stimuli and psychological experience. An absolute threshold is the point at which a person can reliably tell if a stimulus is *present*. A difference threshold is the point at which a person can reliably *distinguish* between two stimuli.

12. Contrast effects refer to changes in perception that occur when we compare one stimulus with another, as when a white circle appears blue against a yellow background. Adaptation involves a change in the sensitivity of the sense organs after they have been exposed to a particular level of stimulation.

13. Perception of distance and depth depend on both binocular and monocular cues. Binocular cues include retinal disparity, which is the difference between the images seen by the right eye and those seen by the left eye, and convergence, which is the angle necessary to focus both eyes on an object so the different images from each eye fuse. Monocular cues include clearness, brightness, pattern of shadow, texture, gradient, and linear perspective.

14. Our tendency to view objects, shapes, colors, and other stimuli as unchanging despite variations in the physical stimuli on our sense organs is known as perceptual constancy. The primary constancies include size constancy, brightness and color constancies, and shape constancy.

15. Our perceptual mechanism creates order out of the bombardment of stimuli on our senses by following rules of organization. We perceive the world in terms of figures and grounds, and we also tend to interpret stimuli as being part of some kind of form, or "Gestalt." We group stimuli according to similarity, proximity, continuation, and good figure.

16. As in many areas of psychology, both innate mechanisms and experience affect perception. The perception of depth is probably present at birth, but size constancy appears to be greatly affected by experience, as does object constancy.

17. Other factors affecting perception include our attention to stimuli and our expectations.

RECOMMENDED READING

Gregory, R. L. *Eye and Brain.* New York: McGraw-Hill, 1966. Paperback. A very well written, amusing introduction to the field.

Gibson, E. *Principles of Perceptual Learning.* New York: Appleton-Century-Crofts, 1969. A provocative book by one of the outstanding figures in the field. Not easy reading, but worth it.

Held, R., and W. R. Richards, Eds. *Recent Progress in Perception—Readings from the Scientific American.* San Francisco: Freeman, 1976. Self-explanatory. These articles are up to date and generally well written. Not highly technical.

Hochberg, J. E. *Perception,* 2d ed. Englewood Cliffs, N.J.: Prentice-Hall, 1977. An excellent and thoughtful introduction.

Kahneman, D. *Attention and Effort.* Englewood Cliffs, N.J.: Prentice-Hall, 1973. The problem of attention getting the attention it deserves. A difficult book that does not have all the answers but at least asks the right questions.

Neisser, U. *Cognitive Psychology.* New York: Appleton-Century-Crofts, 1967. A classic work of great importance. Discusses perception as a cognitive process.

We live and learn, but not the wiser grow.
John Poole, Paul Pry

Though a man be wise
It is no shame for him to live and learn.
Sophocles, Antigone

3 Learning: Basic Principles

Learning: a definition ■ *Classical conditioning* ■ *Oper-*
ant conditioning ■ *Reinforcement* ■ *Classical and op-*
erant conditioning compared ■ *Imitation* ■ *Two basic*
principles of learning ■ *Innate versus learned behavior*

earning is essential for our survival and growth. This may seem obvious, but it is not true for all organisms. A tree has all its functions built in. Some trees bend with the wind more than others, some are more resistant to fire than others, but none learns to avoid the wind or get away from fire. Simple animals also inherit most or all of their functions. Although even a worm can acquire new responses, virtually all of its behavior is predetermined by built-in patterns. It does what it was born to do, no more, no less.

How different it is with higher animals and particularly with humans. A newborn child knows nothing about the world and has few innate behavior patterns. It cries and thrashes about when uncomfortable, it has some perceptual skills and a few physical reflexes, but that is about all. Clearly the infant has no chance of surviving on its own. Even if it were fully grown, its few built-in behavior patterns would not enable it to live in our complex society. People survive by acquiring vast numbers of new behaviors and countless pieces of new information. This learning continues throughout life. As adults we face new situations and problems every day and learn to deal with them. We manage to drive a new car, operate strange machines, play new sports, find our way around an unfamiliar city, and so on through the process of learning. And perhaps equally important, we are able to apply what we already know to new situations so that we do not have to start learning all over again.

Our ability to learn gives us enormous flexibility in our dealings with the world. A tree must endure its environment; we can adapt to the environment and make the most of it. By learning new behaviors we each maximize our chance of survival and our mastery over the world. Thus learning is one of the key phenomena in psychology. As we shall see, it plays a crucial role in all aspects of human behavior from perception to social interaction, from motivation to mental disorders. In order to understand any of these phenomena fully, it is essential to know the basic principles of learning.

LEARNING: A DEFINITION

Although most of us have a general idea of what we mean by "learning," it is helpful to agree on a specific, clear definition of the term. We can define learning as a *relatively permanent change in behavior caused by experience or practice.* There are three parts to this definition. First, after you learn something, *you behave differently* from before. After Sally has learned to talk, her actions change. If you learn the material in this course, your answers on the final exam will be different than if you had not taken the course. After five tennis lessons, you play better than before the lessons (if you have learned anything).

Second, *the change must be fairly permanent,* or at least consistent. This distinguishes changes due to learning from those caused by temporary physiological or external influences. A person's behavior often changes markedly in reaction to LSD or alcohol (see Chapter 11) or because of fatigue, hypnosis, or meditation. And, as we mentioned in Chapter 2, we adapt to particular levels of stimulation and this can affect our behavior. But such changes are temporary—we have not acquired a new behavior pattern.

Third, *the new behavior must be due to experience or practice.* This distinguishes learning from behavioral changes caused by illness, injury, or maturation. A broken leg causes you to limp—a major change in behavior but not due to learning. The increase in sexual behavior that occurs at puberty is due in part to the maturation of the sexual organs and the presence of sex hormones. Although it is not always easy to determine whether a particular change is due to maturation, learning, or a combination of the two, we assume that maturation occurs regardless of the individual's experiences while learning depends entirely on those experiences.

Though all learning falls under this general definition, different types of learning involve somewhat different mechanisms and functions. In this chapter we shall focus on classical conditioning, operant conditioning, and imitation. In the next chapter we shall discuss cognitive learning, through which we acquire conceptual and verbal material, and the role of memory.

CLASSICAL CONDITIONING

History

Early in the twentieth century Ivan Pavlov, the Nobel-Prize winning Russian physiologist, largely by accident discovered *classical conditioning.* Pavlov was studying the physiology of digestion by putting a small amount of food on a dog's tongue and measuring the amount of salivation (see Fig. 3.1). Pavlov noticed that after a while the dog began salivating as soon as it saw the food or even when the experimenter entered the room. (Just like the dog, we often salivate at the sight of a big steak or pucker our lips before biting into a sour lemon.)

Fig. 3.1
Pavlov's classical conditioning apparatus

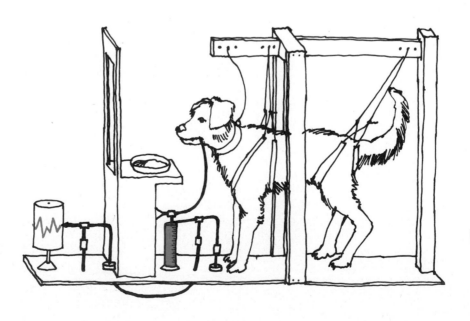

Fig. 3.2
Steps in classical conditioning

Before conditioning:

CS (e.g. bell) → No response

US (e.g. food) → UR (salivating)

After pairing CS and US continuously:

CS → CR (salivating)

US → UR

Before conditioning, the US (food) elicits the UR (salivating), but the CS (any neutral stimulus such as a bell) does not. After the CS and US have been paired a number of times, the CS alone also elicits salivation—the conditioned response.

Intrigued by this behavior, Pavlov decided that although salivating at the *taste* of food was an automatic, innate response, salivating at the *sight* of food must have been learned. Furthermore, he guessed that if dogs could learn to salivate at the sight of food, they could also learn to salivate in response to any other stimulus. Eventually he taught dogs to salivate at the sound of a bell, the click of a metronome, the flash of a light, and a wide variety of other stimuli by consistently following each stimulus with a taste of food.

Elements of Classical Conditioning

Classical conditioning, as this kind of learning is called, always involves four elements: the *unconditioned stimulus* (US), which automatically without any learning produces the *unconditioned response* (UR), and the *conditioned stimulus* (CS), which initially produces no response but after being paired often enough with the US produces the *conditioned response* (CR), which is similar or identical to the UR (see Fig. 3.2). For Pavlov's dogs, food was the US and caused salivation (the UR) whenever it was placed on the tongue. The CS was a bell, which originally had no effect but after being rung just before food was given several times also caused salivation (the CR).

Humans also learn to salivate at the sound of a dinner bell or the sight of food and to flinch at the sight of a gun being fired before

BOX 3.1

CONDITIONING HUMANS

Classical conditioning techniques have been applied to humans in a wide variety of situations. (See Chapter 16 for a discussion of their use in the treatment of mental illness.) Probably the first dramatic demonstration was provided by John B. Watson, the founder of modern behaviorism. He and Rosalie Rayner (1920) conditioned Albert, an eleven-month-old baby, to be afraid of rats by making a loud noise whenever the baby touched or saw a toy rat (see figure at right). Although initially Albert had no fear of the rat, after five days he shrank back and whimpered whenever it appeared. Moreover, his fear became generalized to other furry objects, including a toy rabbit, a fur coat, and a Santa Claus mask. Many psychologists today would question the ethics of this experiment, but it does show the power of the conditioning technique.

A more practical and beneficial application of classical conditioning is often used in the treatment of bedwetting. A simple device attached to the bed rings a bell at the first sign of wetness on the sheets. This has three effects. First, it wakes the child so he can go into the bathroom rather than soak the bed. Second, it conditions the child to associate the pressure in his bladder with the bell and the response of waking up. Eventually, the pressure alone is sufficient to awaken him and he no longer wets. Third, the sound of the loud bell is probably unpleasant in itself, so it punishes the act of wetting the bed, and thus helps to prevent it.

Similar techniques have been used to treat a variety of conditions from smoking to sexual deviancy. As we shall discuss in Chapter 16, there is considerable controversy about the use and success rate of these procedures. But there is no question that classical conditioning and other techniques derived from research on learning have had a major impact on the practice of therapy.

hearing the noise, and may be conditioned to react to something with fear. And we all have both positive and negative responses to people that are based to some extent on classical conditioning. If you have had a very pleasant experience with someone, you may find that your heart beats faster whenever you see that person; if you had a negative experience, you may react with fear or disgust. This phenomenon plays some role in the development of prejudice, which is essentially a negative response to a whole group of people. If you have had unpleasant experiences with a few members of a group, you may develop a negative conditioned response of fear to everyone who belongs to that group. There is, of course, much more to prejudice than this, but such conditioning is one factor in its development.

Sequence and Timing

How well a conditioned response is learned depends in part on the interval between the occurrence of the conditioned stimulus and the occurrence of the unconditioned stimulus (the CS–US interval). The standard procedure is for the CS to come just before the US, and the

Fear conditioning

At first, the baby has no fear of the rat (a). When a loud noise is sounded at the same time as the baby sees the animal (b), the baby develops a conditioned response of fear to the animal (c). The baby may also generalize this fear to other furry or hairy objects (d).

timing is crucial. Sounding a bell and presenting food two hours later will not produce conditioning. Indeed, as shown in Fig. 3.3, classical conditioning will usually not occur if the interval is more than a few seconds.

Fig. 3.3

Classical conditioning and timing of CS and US

The optimal interval for many conditions is .5 second, with the CS preceding the US. If CS occurs at the same time as or after the US, little or no conditioning occurs.

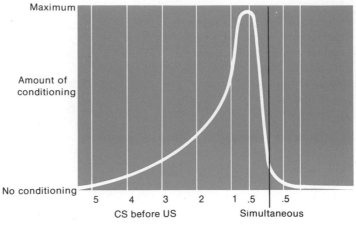

The optimal interval for conditioning (that is, the interval that produces the strongest learning) varies considerably for different responses and different species. Skeletal responses such as the blink of an eye tend to have shorter optimal intervals than autonomic responses such as the galvanic skin response (skin moisture). However, for some reason, the optimal interval for many different responses is half a second. Figure 3.3 shows a typical relationship between interval and amount of conditioning. As you can see, learning is best at about .5 seconds and gets weaker with longer or shorter intervals. Little or no conditioning occurs if the usual order is reversed, with the CS following the US, so-called *backward conditioning*. Apparently the CS must signal the appearance of the US to produce conditioning, and obviously it cannot do this if the CS comes second.

Extinction and Spontaneous Recovery

In classical conditioning the subject learns to respond to the CS even when the US is not presented. Each time the US fails to appear, however, the strength of the conditioned response becomes weaker, or *extinguishes*. The number of trials necessary to produce total extinction varies considerably. Often only a few unreinforced trials are sufficient. For example, Pavlov's dogs extinguished after only nine trials in which they saw the food but were not given any. However, there are some cases in which a well-learned conditioned response takes a great many trials to extinguish. Solomon and Wynne (1954) showed that the conditioned response of fear lasted for thousands of trials and never fully extinguished.

Even when a response appears to have extinguished it may not have disappeared entirely. If there is a rest period during which neither CS nor US is presented, an extinguished conditioned response often regains strength. If the CS is then presented by itself, the conditioned response appears stronger than it was before the rest period (see Fig. 3.4). This is called *spontaneous recovery* and indicates that the connection between the CS and US has not been lost completely.

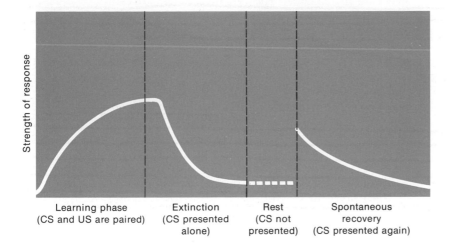

Strength of response

Learning phase
(CS and US are paired)

Extinction
(CS presented
alone)

Rest
(CS not
presented)

Spontaneous
recovery
(CS presented again)

Fig. 3.4
Extinction and spontaneous recovery

As it is paired with the US, the neutral stimulus (CS) elicits a stronger and stronger response (CR). When the US is no longer presented, the strength of the CR declines (the CR is extinguished). But after a pause during which neither CS nor US is presented, the response to the CS recovers somewhat.

OPERANT CONDITIONING

Classical conditioning is a fascinating and powerful type of learning. However, it is limited to responses that are automatically elicited by some stimulus. Dogs learn to salivate to any stimulus that is paired with food; people learn to be afraid of any stimulus that is followed by pain. But clearly dogs and people learn vast numbers of responses and behaviors that are never elicited automatically by any stimulus. Dogs learn to run into the kitchen when they hear a can of food being opened, people learn to turn off the electricity to avoid shocks, and so on. In order to explain how these kinds of behaviors are learned, psychologists studied another kind of learning that is called *operant* or *instrumental conditioning*. As the name implies, in this kind of learning you must do something—take an action, operate on the environment—in order to acquire a new behavior pattern; and what you learn is a behavior that is instrumental in achieving some result.

Reinforcement

The central element in operant conditioning, indeed one of the most important concepts in psychology, is *reinforcement*. This is defined as *any stimulus or event that increases the likelihood that a response will occur again in the future*. There are two types of reinforcement—positive and negative. *Positive reinforcement* involves giving a pleasant, desirable, or positive stimulus after a response. A rat presses a lever and gets a food pellet; a baby cries and gets a bottle; or a student studies and gets a high mark—all have been positively reinforced and the lever pressing, crying, and studying will be more likely to occur again. *Negative reinforcement* involves the termination of an unpleasant, undesirable, or negative stimulus after a response. A rat that is being shocked presses a lever and the shock ceases; a baby who is feeling hunger pangs sucks on a bottle and the pangs stop; a student who has a headache takes an aspirin and the pain subsides—all have been negatively reinforced and the lever pressing, bottle sucking, and aspirin taking will recur in future. This is sometimes called escape or avoidance training because the animal escapes from (or avoids entirely) an unpleasant stimulus by means of a behavior that in turn is negatively reinforced and becomes more probable. The term "negative" does not mean that negative reinforcement makes the response less likely. On the contrary, it is important to remember that both positive and negative reinforcement make the response *more* likely.

You can also make responses *less* likely by the appropriate use of either pleasant or unpleasant stimuli. When a response is followed by an unpleasant stimulus, we usually call this *punishment* and the response becomes less probable. A rat who presses a lever and gets shocked; a baby who throws its food and gets spanked; a person who drinks too much and gets a headache are all punished and learn not to perform these acts. You can also reduce the likelihood of a response by removing a pleasant stimulus following the response. A child who misbehaves at dinner and has his dessert taken away will learn not to misbehave at dinner.

BOX 3.2

SKINNER, THE SKINNER BOX, AND WALDEN TWO

The person most closely associated with operant conditioning is B. F. Skinner (1938 etc.). Most of his research is conducted in an experimental chamber he devised called the *Skinner box*. This chamber can be set up differently for different experiments, but it provides a way to present stimuli, give reinforcements, and allow the animal to make a specified response. For example, in an experiment with rats, the Skinner box might have a lever, a light, a food tray, and an electric grid. When a rat is first put into the box, it usually wanders around, sniffs corners, explores the food tray, and more or less accidentally presses the lever, which produces a food pellet in the tray. The rat eats the food and probably wanders around the cage some more, eventually returning and pressing the lever again. A second pellet appears, the rat eats it, and the process begins again. However, each time the rat tends to return to the lever more quickly, and before long it is pressing the lever very rapidly. At that point, we say that it has "learned" to press the lever.

The Skinner box can also be used to teach by punishment. The floor of the box is usually made of metal and can be electrified in order to give the animal a shock. If a shock is given when the rat puts its front legs against the wall of the box, it will soon learn not to perform that particular behavior. And it will also learn any behavior that removes the unpleasant stimulus (negative reinforcement). For example, if an animal that is being shocked can turn the current off by pressing a lever, it will learn to press the lever.

Skinner is also famous for his book *Walden Two*, which is a description of a utopian society based on learning principles. The basic idea is that children can be rasied in such a way that they are ideal members of society. They are not aggressive, they are highly productive, they form good relationships with others, and they cooperate rather than compete. Moreover, with appropriate training, the right number of children become interested in and skilled at each of the various jobs required. Instead of everyone

Thus, giving positive or removing negative stimuli (both a form of reward) *increases* the likelihood of the behavior; while giving negative or removing positive stimuli (both a form of punishment) decreases the likelihood.

Positive reinforcement versus punishment Both positive reinforcement (giving rewards) and punishment are effective techniques for teaching. However, they have somewhat different effects and should generally be used for different purposes. Positive reinforcement is especially useful when you want to *encourage* a particular response—you want the dog to come when called or a child to pick up her toys so you give them appropriate rewards when they do. Moreover, positive reinforcement tends to produce a good feeling in the person who receives it. Punishment, on the other hand, is particularly effective in *preventing* behavior—a dog who is slapped for chewing on the furniture or a child who is not allowed to go out to play because she has strewn her toys all over her room will learn not to perform those acts. But it is important to remember that just as positive reinforcement produces a good feeling, punishment produces the opposite. Children who are punished obviously do not like it. They feel bad, may become angry, and certainly may develop negative feelings toward the person who punishes them.

The Skinner box, courtesy of B. F. Skinner

wanting to be a doctor or lawyer, and some wanting these positions who are not qualified, everything works out perfectly because of the way children are taught. The method is naturally based on operant conditioning, with certain behaviors reinforced and others not reinforced.

Clearly, this is a utopian vision that most people would consider impossible and perhaps undesirable at the moment. Although we do understand a great deal about operant conditioning, we do not yet know exactly how to raise children so that they are always cooperative and never aggressive. Even if we had full control over how a child was raised, it seems unlikely that psychologists would be able to produce this result with any consistency. Nevertheless, Skinner's idea that child rearing and the structure of society could be made more rational and could be based, at least in part, on established principles of learning is certainly provocative. Indeed, one small community has been set up more or less according to the notions in *Walden Two*. Its success or lack of it is still uncertain.

The practical difficulty is that although you want your child to love you and be happy, you must wait until the correct act is committed if you are to use only positive reinforcement. This difficulty becomes especially crucial when the undesirable act is dangerous. A dog that chews not on the furniture but on visitors cannot be allowed to continue terrifying your friends, and a child who rushes across busy streets cannot be allowed to continue this behavior because she might get killed.

The solution is probably to combine the two techniques. Although both methods are effective, positive reinforcement is generally preferable, and punishment should probably be used primarily when the behavior is highly undesirable or even dangerous. After punishing a child for bad actions, reward her for doing right. Also, be sure to give the punishment out of love and in a kindly way rather than angrily, because it then will probably be more effective and produce fewer negative side effects (Parke and Walters, 1967).

Using the techniques we have discussed in this section, there is almost no limit to what can be taught by means of operant conditioning. Pigeons, hardly the brightest of creatures, have been taught to dance, play ping pong, and even guide a rocket by pecking at keys (Skinner, 1960). And obviously people can learn extremely complicated behaviors if they are reinforced appropriately. However, it is important to remember that the one limitation is that the animal must be *able* to perform the behavior. No amount of training can teach dogs to talk or pigeons to read books; similarly, you can teach people to wave their arms very fast, but you cannot teach them to fly. This is an obvious point, but it is sometimes overlooked because operant conditioning is such a powerful technique for learning.

Primary versus secondary reinforcers There are two types of reinforcers, primary and secondary. *Primary reinforcers* are stimuli or events that satisfy basic physiological needs such as the needs for food, water, air, and sex. There are equivalent stimuli that might be called primary punishers, such as pain and extremes of temperature. Primary reinforcers are effective without any learning or experience on the part of the individual.

Secondary reinforcers are stimuli that the individual learns through experience to associate with either positive or negative outcomes. They are what society and the world teach us to consider important for our satisfaction. Secondary reinforcement occurs when some initially neutral stimulus that is paired with a primary reinforcer eventually takes on the quality of the reinforcer and becomes a secondary reinforcer. In classical conditioning, a tone that is consistently followed by food elicits salivation. The tone can also take the place of the food (the US) in producing classical conditioning. If another stimulus such as a bell is followed by the tone, the bell will eventually produce salivation. In operant conditioning, a stimulus that has acquired reinforcing properties through association with a primary reinforcer can be used to teach an animal a particular behavior. For example, a rat that has learned that it can obtain food by pressing a lever every time a tone sounds will press the lever rapidly in order to get the food. Even if the food is omitted, the rat will continue to press the lever at the sound of the tone. Moreover, a well-conditioned rat will actually learn a new behavior—say, pulling a string—if that behavior is followed by the tone alone. The tone has become a secondary reinforcer.

Secondary reinforcers of this kind play an important role in human behavior. As infants, we learned to associate our mother's face with food, comfort, warmth, and so on—all the basic, primary reinforcers we needed. After a while, our mother's face alone became a reinforcer. We became eager to see our mother's face, as long as it was smiling and not angry.

CHIMPS AND CHIPS: SECONDARY REINFORCERS

Just as humans work for the secondary reinforcer money, chimpanzees have been taught to work for poker chips that could eventually be exchanged for food. In a series of studies, J. B. Wolfe (1936) first gave chimps grapes from a machine and then gave them the grapes only when they inserted poker chips into the machine. Next he gave the poker chips only for certain activities, such as lifting weights. The chimps worked hard to get the chips, even when they could not use them in the machine until many hours or days later. As soon as the machine was made available, they flocked to it and inserted their chips to get the grapes. Some animals even began to hoard the chips. These misers slaved away at the weights until they accumulated vast numbers of chips, far more than they could use in the foreseeable future. The chips themselves seemed to give these chimps pleasure—they ran their fingers through them, played with them, and acted just as human misers might with a pile of gold coins.

BOX 3.3

Perhaps more important, we learned that a smile is positively reinforcing as opposed to an angry or neutral expression, and we extended this association to other people. As we go through life, there are few stimuli more reinforcing than a smile. Smiles elicit other smiles, we feel pleased when people smile at us, we tell jokes to get people to smile, and much of our behavior can be controlled by people either smiling or not smiling at us. This is true even if the smile is not followed by any particular primary reinforcer.

More generally, we learned that having people like us and approve of us is positively reinforcing. Having someone say something complimentary to us or about us is a secondary reinforcer. Although a compliment has never satisfied any biological need, it has always been associated with primary reinforcers that do satisfy basic needs. Thus, a kind word is always rewarding and a major motivation among most adults is to get other people to like them and approve of them. Money is a similar kind of secondary reinforcer. Although it has no inherent value, we learn and perform tasks in order to earn it.

Much of human motivation and behavior is shaped by secondary reinforcers rather than by primary reinforcers. Almost all animals share the same basic biological needs. Humans are unique in that an enormous range of learned needs and reinforcers probably plays a more important role in determining their behavior than do the few innate needs.

Theories of reinforcement Although the effects of the various types of reinforcement are quite straightforward, the question remains: What determines whether an event is positively reinforcing, negatively reinforcing, or neutral? There is no definitive answer to this question yet, but various theories have been proposed. The simplest, called *drive-reduction* theory (Hull, 1943; Miller, 1959), is based on the fact that physiological needs usually produce an arousal state called *drive.* According to this theory, anything that reduces an organism's drive, and hence its physiological needs, is positively reinforcing.

There is little question that satisfying physiological needs such as hunger and thirst is positively reinforcing. However, events that do not reduce such needs also seem to reinforce behavior. Rats learn when reinforced with saccharine, which tastes sweet but satisfies no physiological need (Sheffield and Roby, 1950). It has also been demonstrated that sexual arousal is reinforcing, even if consummation is prevented. In one study (Sheffield et al., 1951), male rats were allowed to get near sexually receptive females, but their courtship was interrupted so that the males did not ejaculate. Although this may sound unpleasant, and certainly prevented the satisfaction of the sexual impulse, the males acted as if they had been reinforced. They performed behaviors in order to get near the females again. In addition, many animals—and almost all people—learn complex behaviors simply out of curiosity. Animals enjoy exploring a new cage or playing with a puzzle. Since no drive is satisfied by eating saccharine, being near sexually receptive females, or exploring a cage, it seems apparent that drive-reduction theory cannot account for all positive reinforcement.

A supplementary possibility is that all animals have an optimal level of arousal. This ideal state may not be *total* relaxation and satisfaction of *all* needs, but rather some minimal level of arousal. Anything that returns the animal to that level will be reinforcing. Feeding a very hungry animal will lower its drives to the optimal level. But for a relaxed, quiet animal, exposure to new stimuli, such as sexually receptive partners and even sweet tastes, is just *arousing* enough to produce the optimal level. Thus, these stimuli too should be reinforcing.

This is a complex and appealing notion, but does not explain how new stimuli always seem to produce just the right amount of arousal, regardless of the prior state of the animal. It seems more likely that the new stimuli are reinforcing in themselves, and thus independent of the animal's arousal state. Nevertheless, the basic idea that total relaxation is not the ideal state is very useful, particularly in the context of drive-reduction theory, which seems to suggest that it is the ideal state.

PLEASURE CENTERS IN THE BRAIN

Most of the reinforcements we have discussed involve either physiological needs, learned needs, or the avoidance of discomfort. Reinforcement often consists of reducing these drives—or perhaps producing some minimal level of arousal. However, physical pleasure manages to be both reinforcing and motivating at the same time. For example, eating something delicious is pleasurable even if you are not particularly hungry. Although the reinforcement could be said to be the reduction of the specific appetite for that food, it seems more likely that the pleasure is produced by the taste of the food and is rewarding by itself. To put it another way, if someone suddenly put a marvelous chocolate in your mouth, without your expecting it or having your appetite for chocolate aroused, you would probably still enjoy the taste. Thus, pleasure seems to be a pure reinforcement and the pursuit of pleasure itself can be considered one of the most important motives.

We know very little about why some stimulation is pleasurable and other stimulation is not, nor do we understand the physiological mechanisms involved. Some of them seem to be innate. Children prefer sweet tastes and dislike bitter tastes almost from birth. They like to have their bodies rubbed gently, particularly certain areas, but the pressure must be neither too hard nor too soft. There are probably good reasons for many of these preferences in terms of survival and adjustment, but they do not seem to be associated with specific needs or motives other than pleasure.

Although we know little about why touching one spot or tasting one food is more pleasurable than another, there is considerable evidence that stimulating certain areas of the brain produces intense sensations of pleasure. If a tiny electrode is introduced into certain regions of a rat's brain and a small electric charge is passed through it, the rat acts as if the experience were intensely rewarding (Olds and Milner, 1954). It will cross painful barriers, press levers, and even learn complex mazes to receive the stimulation. Rats will run faster and cross more painful grids to get this stimulation than to get food, even if they are extremely hungry. In addition, the speed and duration of response to this brain stimulation is remarkable. Rats have been observed to press a bar 2,000 times an hour for twenty-four hours straight, as long as they are given the "pleasurable" stimulation. Characterization of the experience as pleasurable is, of course, based on assumptions about what the rat is feeling. It does behave as if the stimulation were rewarding, but whether it corresponds to what we think of as pleasure is uncertain. On the other hand, people who have had analogous parts of their brains stimulated directly in connection with surgery or specific conditions such as Parkinson's disease have sometimes reported keenly pleasurable sensations. Whatever the subjective experience, it is clear that stimulation of certain parts of the brain can reinforce behavior and cause the individual to take actions in order to receive it. This line of research may enable us to understand more fully the interrelationship between the experience of pleasure and reinforcement in general.

BOX 3.4

Although each theory we have discussed explains some aspects of reinforcement, neither of them provides a complete explanation. Certainly many reinforcers depend on reducing a drive, and in most situations drive reduction is reinforcing. On the other hand, we sometimes are reinforced when we become more, not less, aroused. Sexual stimulation, curiosity, and probably excitement in general are reinforcing even though drives are increased rather than decreased. Sometimes this seems to fit the notion of an optimal level of stimulation, but often the arousal is quite high, far above the level that, under other circumstances and with other drives, we would find unpleasant. We do know that reducing drive, increasing drive, and even finding just the right level of drive are all reinforcing under some circumstances, but it appears that a complete understanding of reinforcement will depend on all these ideas plus others not yet formulated. For the moment, we do know that certain events are consistently reinforcing. If an event acts as a reinforcer in one situation, it almost always will act as a reinforcer in other situations. Therefore, despite the fact that we lack a full theoretical understanding of reinforcement, we are able to identify reinforcements and use them to produce learning.

Factors Affecting Conditioning

Timing of reinforcement Like classical conditioning, successful operant conditioning depends on the proper timing of reinforcement. The less delay there is between the behavior and the reinforcement, the more effective the conditioning will be. However, the time interval can be much longer than in classical conditioning where, as noted in Fig. 3.3, it is usually restricted to a few seconds.

Whether or not an animal will learn a behavior when reinforcement is delayed depends on the situation and on the animal being conditioned. It is sometimes possible to teach rats a response when reinforcement is delayed for up to twenty minutes, but it is a very difficult task. Pigeons and rats rarely learn if the reinforcement is delayed for more than thirty seconds (see Fig. 3.5). The problem is that the animal must associate the reward with the behavior. If the rat presses a lever and food appears immediately, it will have little difficulty making the connection. But if the food does not come for some time, the rat will not connect the lever with the food. During that interval the rat probably has performed all sorts of behaviors—scratched itself, rubbed against the side of the box, sniffed in a corner, turned around a few times, pressed the bar, and so on. In addition, after pressing the bar, perhaps it looked around, took a walk, and in general continued doing what rats do. When the food arrives, the rat does not associate any of its actions with the arrival of the food. Thus the closer the reinforcement comes to the behavior, the less chance there is of other behavior intervening and the more likely the animal is to draw the connection.

This is a highly cognitive way of explaining the problem of delayed reinforcement. Most behaviorists would not agree that the animal "knows" that the behavior and the reward go together. Rather, a behaviorist would explain operant conditioning in terms of

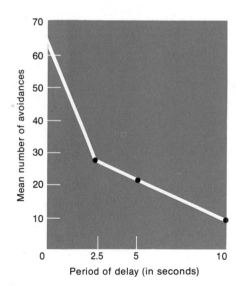

Fig. 3.5
Delay of reinforcement and conditioning

The longer the interval between a response and reinforcement, the weaker the operant conditioning.

the behavior and the reward occurring in rapid enough succession so that the immediate memory of the behavior overlaps with the reinforcement. Unless there is this overlap, no conditioning will occur. Since the trace fades rapidly, the longer the delay, the weaker the conditioning; after a certain time, none will be produced. This formation makes no assumptions about the animal's beliefs or knowledge—learning is seen as an automatic process that occurs whenever the behavior and reinforcement overlap.

In contrast to other animals, people often learn when reinforcement is delayed beyond thirty seconds. We perform behaviors to get reinforcements that are delayed many hours, days, or even years. In fact, this ability to put off reinforcement is one of the basic differences between humans and most other animals, and is one of the most important aspects of the socialization process. A child must learn to delay the gratification of his needs under many circumstances. He cannot relieve the pressure on his bladder whenever he wants; that particular reinforcement must be sought only at certain times and in certain places. Learning restraint is essential if he is to function in adult society.

Moreover, we often can increase our rewards by delaying them. A child's choice between a cookie now or a hot fudge sundae later is repeated in adulthood with similar choices as well as much more important ones. We must choose between spending our money on small pleasures or saving for larger ones, going to the movies tonight or studying so that we have a chance to get into medical school. People not only are able to put off reinforcements, they must do so.

Nevertheless, we must not lose sight of the great difficulty in learning when reinforcement is delayed. Even for humans, learning is much simpler and more efficient when the action is followed immediately by the reinforcement. Children learn much better when they are rewarded soon after the behavior, and even adults learn better when there are at least partial reinforcements along the way to bigger goals. The student who is aiming for medical school needs to be reinforced by good grades and other kinds of encouragement while she is pursuing this relatively distant reinforcement. Thus, although we can learn with considerable delay of reinforcements, for most people, in most situations, shorter delays are much more successful and clearly preferable.

Humans often wait many years for reinforcement.

Amount of reinforcement Reinforcements vary in how often they occur and how large they are when they do occur, and both affect the speed of learning. A rat gets a hundred reinforcements of one pellet each or twenty reinforcements of five pellets each. You may win five dollars at a slot machine ten days in a row, or fifty dollars once. The greater the number of reinforced trials, the more likely it is that the behavior will occur again. In cognitive terms, this is because you are more certain that the behavior will be followed by reinforcement. Regardless of how much you win, if you have won ten times in a row, you expect to win the next time; if you have won once, your expectation of winning should be much weaker. In noncognitive terms, the association between the act and the result becomes more firmly established the more trials that are reinforced.

Larger reinforcements teach the response more quickly. After two big wins, you are more likely to play slot machines than after two small wins. In addition, the larger the reinforcement, the more intensely the behavior will be performed. A rat will press a bar harder after getting large food pellets than after getting small ones. You will be more enthusiastic about slot machines and maybe even pull the handle harder or insert coins faster after winning a lot than after winning a little. And, of course, the size of the reinforcements is determined by its quality as well as its quantity. Rats are reinforced more effectively with sweet than with sour food; monkeys respond faster to bananas than to lettuce; humans prefer ice cream to cereal, a movie to a lecture, a good movie to a bad one. The more often you are reinforced for a behavior and the larger and better the reinforcement, the stronger the conditioning.

BOX 3.5

SCHEDULES OF REINFORCEMENT

Partial reinforcement can be given on many different schedules, varying in frequency, regularity, and whether the reinforcement depends on the passage of time or the animal's responses. The four major types of schedules and their characteristic effects on an animal's response are shown in Figs. (a)–(d). In this type of research, responses are usually measured by a *cumulative recorder*, which keeps a running count of the responses made. The steeper the line, the faster the animal is responding at that point.

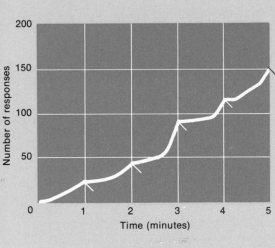

(a)

Fixed interval (FI)

Reinforcement is given for the first correct response after a set time period. The FI schedule usually causes an animal to respond slowly just after a reinforcement and increase its speed of response sharply just before a reinforcement is due, producing a scalloped pattern. (Figs. (a)–(d) from *Introduction to Modern Behaviorism*, 2d. ed., by Howard Rachlin. W. H. Freeman and Company. Copyright © 1976.

(b)

Fixed ratio (FR)

Reinforcement is given after a certain number of responses, regardless of how long they take. The FR schedule tends to produce a very high rate of responding until the reinforcement is earned, followed by a rest. Note that with this schedule, the faster the animal responds, the more reinforcements it receives, whereas with the FI schedule the animal can do nothing to speed up its reinforcements. Therefore, the FR schedule ordinarily results in a much higher rate of responding.

Extinction and partial reinforcement Operant learning extinguishes in a manner similar to classical conditioning. Just as a response that is reinforced increases in probability, a response that is not reinforced decreases in probability. A rat that has learned to press a bar because that response is followed by food will eventually stop pressing the bar if the food does not appear. If operant conditioning is produced by giving a reinforcement every time the response occurs, any trial on which reinforcement is not given is an extinction trial and will reduce the strength of the conditioning. The speed of extinction depends on many factors, including the number of reinforced trials that have occurred, the type of response, the specific situation, and even the species of the animal. But generally, when learning has been based on reinforcement on every trial, extinction is quite rapid.

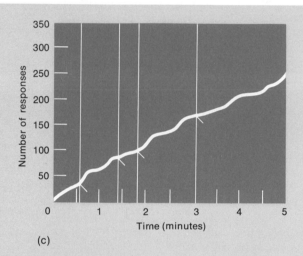

(c)

Variable interval (VI)

In this schedule, reinforcements are given at random times, even though the average number of reinforcements for each time period is fixed. Because there is no fixed pattern in the VI schedule, the animal responds at a fairly steady rate.

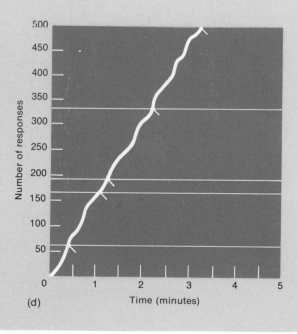

(d)

Variable ratio (VR)

The *average* rate of reinforcement is based on the number of responses, but the number of responses between reinforcements varies. Again, this schedule produces a steady rate of responding, but, as with the FR schedule, the rate is high because the faster the animal responds, the more reinforcements it receives.

A slot machine operates on a VR schedule and thus leads players to push money in as fast as they can. The faster they play, the more reinforcements they receive. Of course, the faster they play, the more money they lose also, because the machine is programmed to pay off less than people put in.

However, life rarely involves reinforcements every time a particular response occurs. Even if the behavior is "correct," much of the time it will not lead to reinforcement. Putting a dime in a pay phone usually is rewarded with a dial tone, but the result may be dead silence—and a lost dime. A specific technique for golf, studying, or dating may sometimes be followed by success and sometimes by failure.

A great deal of research has been done on *schedules of reinforcement* (see Box 3.5). It has been found that animals can learn a behavior even when they are not reinforced on every trial. They learn it less rapidly the less frequently they are reinforced, but eventually they do learn it, just as if they were reinforced 100 percent of the time.

The remarkable finding of this research is that partial reinforcement makes the behavior more resistant to extinction. Learning under continuous reinforcement schedules extinguishes quite rapidly when the reinforcement is no longer given; but learning due to partial reinforcement (say, one random reinforcement in ten trials) takes much longer to extinguish. Imagine that you buy coffee from a particular machine every day. Over a two-month period, your dime produces coffee every time. Then one day you put a dime in and nothing happens except that your dime is returned. Probably your reaction, after you have perhaps kicked the machine, will be to try the dime again. If you do not get coffee the second time, you might conceivably try a third time, but that would probably be your limit, at least for that day. And if you came back the next day and a dime still produced no coffee, you probably would not even bother to try a second dime.

Now imagine that over the two-month period, the machine produced coffee only about one time in three. You would put a dime in and wait to see if the machine worked; if it did not, you would press the coin return, get the dime back, and put it in again. Each day, if you inserted the dime often enough, you would eventually get a cup of coffee. Having had this kind of experience with the machine, on the day that it was actually broken you would probably keep trying it much longer than you would if the machine had operated properly all along. Since it had often taken three or four trials to get coffee, you might try as many as ten times before giving up. And the next day you would start all over. Probably you would try for a number of days before abandoning the machine entirely. Just as in laboratory demonstrations, partial reinforcement, although not so pleasant or agreeable as continuous reinforcement, does lead to increased resistance to extinction.

Partial-reinforcement schedules are so effective primarily because they make it difficult to know when extinction trials have begun. If the behavior is reinforced 100 percent of the time, you know that something has changed as soon as the reinforcement is omitted. You may keep trying for a while, but soon you realize that reinforcement is simply not coming anymore. In contrast, partial reinforcement involves many trials in which reinforcement is not given. Although eventually it becomes clear that the situation has changed and reinforcement is no longer being given, it will take much longer. Thus, learning under partial reinforcement is more resistant to extinction because the distinction between reinforced and nonreinforced trials is less clear.

If a parent wants to teach a child something as rapidly as possible, the parent should use continuous reinforcement. Every time the child says a word or makes her bed, the parent should give her a hug or a cookie or whatever reinforcement seems most effective. But most of the time parents want their children to learn a behavior so well that it will not be extinguished when reinforcements are not given or when no one is there to give them. Accordingly, a parent should not reward a child every time she says a word or makes her bed, but should give rewards only periodically. Probably the most effective technique is to start with continuous reinforcement and shift gradually to random partial reinforcement. The child may learn the behavior somewhat more slowly but will more likely continue it when reinforcements are not forthcoming. Thus the child will be more independent of her parents in these behaviors—she will be able to behave on her own without expecting constant reinforcement. Of course, some reinforcement is necessary to maintain any behavior, but it is much less crucial when the learning has occurred under a partial-reinforcement schedule.

Gambling casinos make practical use of the long-term effect of partial reinforcement on behavior. Slot machines in particular are intriguing to many people because of their reinforcement schedule. Although they are adjusted so that eventually you lose money, every once in a while the machines reinforce you with a win. You see three bells line up in the window, lights flash, a bell rings, and, best of all, lots of coins spew out of the machine. You may have inserted two hundred coins and are now receiving only one hundred, but you feel wonderful and are strongly reinforced. In fact, most machines are set to give frequent small reinforcements of two or three coins as well as occasional jackpots. The most effective slot machines give just enough reinforcement to keep you interested and at the same time maintain the house advantage.

Shaping behavior As we noted earlier, an animal can be taught only behavior of which it is physically capable. However, this does not limit learning to behavior that the animal normally performs on its own. By *shaping* the animal's behavior, also called the process of *successive approximations*, operant-conditioning methods can be used to teach entirely new behavior patterns that are not ordinarily in an animal's repertoire.

The technique involves reinforcing behaviors that gradually approximate the desired behavior, until the animal is performing the desired behavior. The process of shaping resembles the game in which someone looks for an object and is told "hot" when he gets closer and "cold" when he gets further away. Eventually he zeroes in on the right object.

Human behavior can also be shaped. For example, teaching a deaf child to speak involves first reinforcing sounds that only faintly resemble normal speech. Once these are learned, reinforcements are given for sounds that are a little closer to normal, and so on. If you waited until the child spontaneously uttered perfect words, you

BOX 3.6

SUPERSTITIOUS BEHAVIOR

As we have discussed, an action that is followed by reinforcement is more likely to be learned. If a pigeon is given food whenever it scratches its head, it will learn to scratch its head. However, any reward is preceded by many actions besides the one that is deliberately being reinforced. While the experimenter may be rewarding the animal every time it scratches its head, on the first trial there is no way for the animal to know that. Therefore, the rewards reinforce all the bird's recent actions equally. Over a long series of trials in which reward is given only for head-scratching, the pigeon should learn to scratch its head and the other actions should be extinguished since they do not lead to reward. But if the animal happens to perform an action in several of the trials, it will tend to learn that act as well as the head-scratching, even when that chance act had nothing to do with the reinforcement. This is called *superstitious behavior*.

For example, in one study (Skinner, 1948) pigeons were given food at regular intervals regardless of their behavior. Most of the pigeons developed clearly defined behavior patterns that they performed as if the reward depended on them. One bird made two or three counterclockwise turns about the cage before each reinforcement; another thrust its head repeatedly into the corners of the cage; and two acted like pendulums, extending their heads forward and swinging from right to left with a sharp movement followed by a slower return. None of this behavior was necessary to get the reward, but as long as the birds kept performing these actions the reward arrived, so they had no reason to abandon them. Presumably, if the pigeons omitted the action on a number of trials and the reward came anyway, they would eventually give up the behavior. But an eager pigeon might never be so careless as to stop its superstitious behavior.

might wait indefinitely; you would certainly give very few reinforcements and progress would be terribly slow. With shaping you can give lots of reinforcements and gradually but steadily teach the child to talk.

Students often shape a teacher's behavior either deliberately or unintentionally. Imagine a teacher who does not tell jokes, but every once in a while makes a slightly funny remark. The class may laugh at anything that is remotely amusing, so the teacher receives reinforcement in the form of laughter. She may then begin to make amusing remarks more often. After a while, these no longer elicit as much laughter, but perhaps an occasional joke will creep into the lectures and these receive laughter. This will cause more and more jokes and eventually the lectures will include jokes and other attempts at humor that were not originally in the teacher's normal repertoire. Naturally, this works only if the teacher is potentially funny—it might be disastrous if the jokes are less amusing than the original lectures. Once again, almost anything can be produced by shaping but it must be within the capacity of the individual.

Superstitious behavior and athletes

Some superstitious stars (left to right): The Dallas Cowboys' Ralph Neely, who put so much stock in staying at a motel before game days that he continued the practice even after the Cowboys abandoned it; Muhammad Ali, who unleashed a black cat during his weigh-in for the Ken Norton fight; Phil Esposito, who insists that his uniform and equipment be laid out a specific way before each game; Manny Mota, who follows each base hit with a bath at exactly 3 P.M. the following day; and Pele, who is unusually preoccupied with the number 10.

Humans are also likely to engage in superstitious behavior. Athletes, for example, are especially susceptible. Race driver Mario Andretti signs thousands of autographs, but will not use a green pen. Golfer Gary Player wears black clothes because he feels the color gives him strength. Bobby Orr, the great hockey star, must touch every player on the shoulder before each game. And another hockey player, Phil Esposito, wears a black shirt backwards while playing, avoids having any hockey sticks crossed in the dressing room, and lays his clothes out in a complex way before putting them on before a game.

Often these habits develop following a particularly successful or unsuccessful performance. For example, Esposito wears his shirt backwards because he happened to wear it that way during a game in which he scored three goals. Some habits may indirectly affect performance. Orr's touching his teammates probably has nothing to do with the outcome of the game, but it may give him and the team a sense of fellowship that could improve morale. And if the color of a shirt makes the player feel better, it may improve his play. Thus, what starts as a superstition may eventually have some positive effect, which would reinforce the behavior.

The common cold leads to all sorts of superstitious behaviors. An old joke goes that careful treatment, rest, and staying out of drafts will cause a cold to go away in seven days, while doing nothing will make it last a week. In fact, medicine has no treatment that shortens the course of a cold, although some drugs relieve the symptoms somewhat. Yet people take dozens of different medicines and all sorts of other treatments for colds and have great confidence in their favorite remedies. If they continue the treatment, whatever it is, for about a week, the cold will indeed disappear, so they are continually reinforced using their own method.

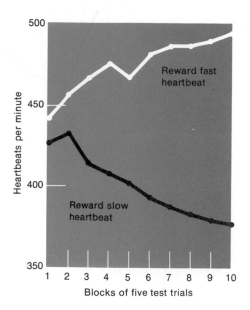

Fig. 3.6
Operant conditioning of heart rate

Heart rate can be increased or decreased by rewarding either fast or slow beats. (From Miller and Banuazizi, 1968)

NEAL E. MILLER

Types of Responses

Physiological responses Although we have stressed that conditioning affects only behavior in the individual's repertoire, recent research suggests that the behavior need not be under that individual's deliberate control. It now appears that certain internal responses that we would not ordinarily expect to be affected by learning can be conditioned.

For example, the body responds almost instantly and automatically to an injection of insulin, a drug used in the treatment of diabetes. Too much insulin produces a strong physiological shock. It has been shown that when an overdose of insulin is repeatedly paired with a neutral stimulus, the neutral stimulus alone will eventually elicit the shock. Sawrey, Conger, and Turrell (1956) exposed rats to a bright light and then injected them with insulin, and the rats developed a conditioned response to the light. Then when the rats were shown the light and injected with a harmless saline solution, they reacted almost as strongly as when they had been injected with insulin. In other words, through traditional procedures of classical conditioning, a complex physiological response was evoked by a neutral stimulus.

Similar findings have begun to appear in work involving operant conditioning. We have said that any behavior an animal is physically capable of performing can be learned through operant conditioning. Until recently, this was assumed to mean only behaviors that are ordinarily under the animal's conscious control. It now appears possible, however, that operant conditioning can even extend to those responses we usually think of as automatic. Neal Miller (1969) has demonstrated that rats can be taught to control many internal physiological reactions, such as blood pressure, intestinal contractions, and even heart rate (see Fig. 3.6). Although there is still some question about the reliability of these findings (Miller, 1973), they suggests vast possibilities for human learning.

The finding that internal responses can be conditioned to neutral stimuli is consistent with a phenomenon that is frequently observed in the treatment of illness. People often respond as positively to a neutral substance as they do to a potent medicine. This effect of *placebos* (neutral chemicals) sometimes makes it difficult to tell whether a new drug is actually effective. Apparently, if someone believes that a drug will help them, it often will. If you take a pill for a headache and think it is an aspirin, it will probably help somewhat even if it happens to have no relation whatsoever to headaches. People claim that fancy headache remedies are superior to aspirin, that foul-tasting tonics cure colds, and so on—and perhaps they do, if the people have been conditioned to believe in them enough. This does not mean that all conditions can be cured just by thinking a drug will work, nor that drugs do not have specific effects. But it does demonstrate the strength of the conditioning process. Because of this, testing of new drugs must be done "blind"—that is, the patient must not know what drug she has taken. Then if those who take the real drug improve more than those who take a neutral substance, you can be sure that it is the drug that works and not just the patient's learned response.

This work on the conditioning of physiological responses suggests that we can establish much more control over our internal processes than most of us have. This will come as no surprise to Yogis and members of other religions who have long asserted that they can control virtually all of their physiological functions. As we shall see in Chapter 6, science is just beginning to explore this possibility systematically.

Motor skills and practice It is important to realize that we often learn what behavior to perform in a particular circumstance without being able to perform it correctly. This is particularly true of behaviors that involve complex actions or intricate coordination. When you learn to drive a car with a standard shift, you may quickly learn that you have to press the clutch down before shifting and then gradually release the clutch while increasing pressure on the gas pedal. Knowing this is easy, but doing it smoothly takes a lot of practice—as anyone who has caused a car to lurch and buck down a street knows. The correct form in tennis is easy to learn by operant conditioning or imitation, but it takes years of practice for most of us to master it even partially.

One of the characteristics of motor learning is that as we progress we sometimes reach *plateaus*, periods during which no apparent progress occurs. The usual pattern in learning tennis or the piano is that you make rapid progress at first, then seem to slow down to a crawl, and then start making progress again. The reason for this is that with complex skills of this kind you master certain aspects of the behavior faster than others. First you learn a relatively easy part of the skill and make great progress. Then, until you begin to learn the next aspect, nothing seems to happen. After you master that you make progress again until you reach the next difficult part, and so on. This can be extremely frustrating when you expect to continue learning at the same rate throughout. If you realize that everyone goes through these plateaus, you may be encouraged to keep practicing until your next spurt of progress appears.

CLASSICAL AND OPERANT CONDITIONING COMPARED

Classical and operant conditioning have many similarities, and a few important differences as well. They both depend on a particular sequence and the occurrence of a crucial event. In classical conditioning, the stimulus to be conditioned must precede or coincide with the unconditioned stimulus, and the latter must occur for conditioning to be produced. In operant conditioning, the sequence is a behavior followed by reinforcement, the latter being necessary for learning. In both, any substantial alteration in the sequence prevents conditioning; and elimination of the US or reinforcement leads to extinction. In both kinds of learning, higher-order conditioning can occur with a previously neutral stimulus producing learning. And, as we shall see in the next section, classical and operant conditioning are subject to the basic phenomena of generalization and discrimination.

The major difference between classical and operant conditioning involves the action of the subject. In classical conditioning, the subject is a *passive* participant—the stimuli are presented and eventually the response (CR) is elicited by a stimulus (CS) that did not elicit it before. In operant conditioning, the subject must take an *active* role, performing the behavior in order for it to be reinforced. In addition, the range of behaviors that can be learned is much broader in operant conditioning since it includes any action the subject can make voluntarily (and perhaps even involuntarily). Classical conditioning is generally limited to behaviors that are automatically elicited by some stimulus.

Despite the few differences just listed, it should be apparent that both types of learning obey many of the same laws, and may not in fact be entirely distinct phenomena. The differences may be ones of emphasis rather than basic principles.

BOX 3.7

LEARNED HELPLESSNESS AND DEPRESSION

Usually when we talk of learning we are referring to someone acquiring a new behavior, strengthening an old one, or associating an action with a new situation. But it is also possible to learn *not* to act. You can teach rats to run slowly by feeding them only when they take a long time to reach the goal box (Logan, 1956), and presumably a pigeon could be taught not to peck at a light or even to stand quietly in the corner. In fact, much of a child's socialization process consists of learning not to perform certain acts, or to perform them only under specific, limited conditions.

A special case of learning not to act apparently occurs when an animal is faced with an unpleasant situation from which it is powerless to escape. A rat is confronted with an impossible discrimination problem, a dog is given an electric shock no matter what it does, a person is given problems to solve that have no solution. In all these cases, the individual eventually ceases to struggle; according to Martin Seligman (1975), it learns that it is helpless. Faced with inescapable pain or frustration, the individual not only stops fighting it but also learns not to struggle in other situations. This *learned helplessness* causes the individual to accept unpleasant situations passively rather than try to escape. He becomes essentially paralyzed in the face of even minor frustrations that he would ordinarily be able to handle.

A series of experiments by Seligman and others has shown that these effects do appear in a wide variety of situations. The rat that faced the impossible discrimination problem performed poorly on later discrimination problems (Bainbridge, 1973). The dog that had been exposed to inescapable shock never learned to escape from a later situation where escape required only a simple response that other dogs learned easily (Overmier and Seligman, 1967). And people who are given insoluble problems work less hard on subsequent soluble ones (Hiroto and Seligman, 1975).

Seligman (1975) has suggested that learned helplessness is the basis of the mental condition called depression, in which the individual typically becomes passive, lacking in initiative, and unable to deal with life's frustrations. This analysis is still controversial and there is little convincing evidence to support it. However, the idea that individuals can learn not to struggle because they have been faced with a series of situations beyond their control is plausible. Some members of society—the poor, the oppressed, the unlucky—face many inescapable hardships. Such people are bound to learn that they cannot cope with some aspects of the world. Then when they are in a situation in which effort could help them, they are less likely to act than others who have not learned to be helpless. And this pattern understandably could play some role in the appearance of depression.

© Punch (Rothco)

IMITATION

A third major process by which learning occurs is *imitation*. Without the pairing of a conditioned stimulus with an unconditioned stimulus, without the reinforcement of a particular behavior, an animal can learn simply by *observing* the behavior of another animal. If a rat, a monkey, or a child watches another member of the same species (or even of a different species) find a piece of food under one box and not another, the observer will learn to choose the box that was reinforced even though he himself did not get the reinforcement. As one moves up the developmental scale, the effects of imitation get stronger until they peak at the human level. Many of a child's actions, gestures, habits, and even values are acquired by observing what his parents and peers do and then trying to copy them. This is not meant to minimize the great importance of both classical and operant conditioning in human development, but merely to emphasize the role of imitation, which is so often given less attention than it deserves.

The major difference between imitation and the other kinds of learning is in its efficiency. Although operant conditioning is a strong technique, it ordinarily requires several reinforced trials. In contrast, imitation is fast and easy. Imagine how long it would take to learn a vocabulary by operant-conditioning techniques. The child would have to utter a vast number of sounds, be reinforced for some of them, and eventually learn which ones make words. Imitation provides a shortcut. The child hears her parents say a word and tries to repeat it. Naturally these repetitions are not perfect the first time, but the imitation gives her a head start. Moreover, she does not have to be reinforced by someone else every time she says a word correctly. The child can often tell when she is correct, and thus in a sense teaches herself. In fact, it might be said that she provides her own reinforcements because getting it correct is rewarding. Just why this is so is not clear, but it probably gives the child a sense of mastery and is also associated with those times that the parent does reward her for being right. In other words, the child learns that it is good to imitate correctly and when she succeeds in doing this, she is reinforced.

The fact that imitation plays a role in learning has been accepted for many years (Miller and Dollard, 1941). However, not until recently has it been studied in detail and given the attention it deserves. Previous research had demonstrated that many animals learn rapidly by imitating each other, but Albert Bandura concentrated on humans. In a famous study by Bandura, Ross, and Ross (1961), children watched adults act either aggressively or nonaggressively. The aggressive adults kicked a doll, shouted at it, said "Hit it down, punch it," and behaved quite savagely. When the children were allowed to play in the same room, those who had watched the aggressive models were much more aggressive than the others. Indeed, they imitated the adults' behavior very closely, even to the point of saying the same words. Similar research has been conducted for a wide variety of behaviors, and the results demonstrate that, theoretically at least, the only criteria of learning by imitation are that the behavior must be observed and the observer must be capable of performing it.

Various factors affect the extent to which humans will imitate behavior. If a child is rewarded for imitating in one situation, imita-

Fig. 3.7
Imitation of aggressive behavior

Children who watch an adult act aggressively behave the same way themselves. Photos from Bandura, Ross, and Ross, 1961.

tion will increase in other situations (Durrell and Weisberg, 1973). High-status models are imitated more than low-status models. Models who are more similar to the observer, who are liked more, who are more powerful, and who are themselves rewarded for their actions are also more likely to be imitated (Bandura, Ross, and Ross, 1963). As might be expected, the more difficult and novel the behavior, the less closely it will be copied; but the research on aggression illustrates that unusual behaviors are imitated as long as they are easy for the subject.

In general, imitation appears to follow many of the rules of other types of learning. Repetition, difficulty of behavior, strength of the response, and extinction all operate in imitation as they do in operant conditioning. The strength and efficiency of imitation as a learning tool, particularly for humans, is that it eliminates the trial and error that would otherwise be necessary. When one individual has been taught a specific behavior, it can be passed on to others quickly and simply.

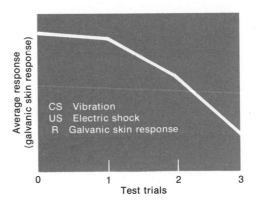

TWO BASIC PRINCIPLES OF LEARNING

Throughout this chapter we have been talking as if learning were precise and specific, as if the animal learned exactly one well-defined response to exactly one stimulus situation. Although discussions of learning are usually put in these terms, it is by no means an accurate description of the phenomenon. A dog that learns to salivate when a bell is rung before food is presented will salivate not only to that particular bell, but also to other bells and to quite different sounds. It will probably salivate to other aspects of the situation, such as the experimenter entering the room, a click of a microswitch that might precede the ringing of the bell, the sight of the food, and so on. A rat that learns to press a lever whenever a red light is flashed will press the lever at the sight of other lights, and will press other kinds of levers than the one on which it learned. But with sufficient training, both animals can be taught to narrow their responses so that they react only to a particular stimulus and not to others. The dog can learn to salivate only to a certain bell and not to any other bells or any other factors in the situation. The rat can be taught to press the lever only to a red light of a particular intensity, and to press only that certain lever. The tendency to respond to stimuli similar to the one on which the learning occurred is called *stimulus generalization*. The narrowing of the response is called *discrimination*. These two processes are essential aspects of all kinds of learning.

Stimulus Generalization

As in the example above, when a response has been learned to a particular stimulus, the response will also be elicited by other, similar stimuli. This *stimulus generalization* follows the rule that the more dissimilar the new stimuli are to the original one, the less likely the response is to occur and the weaker it will be if it does occur. The resulting curve of response is called the *generalization gradient* (see Fig. 3.8).

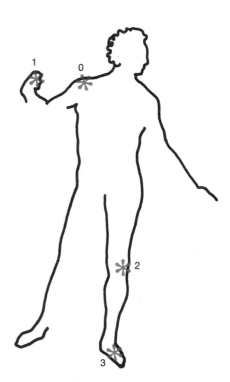

Fig. 3.8
Stimulus generalization

A man was conditioned to respond to stimulation of a point near his shoulder. Then other points on his body were stimulated. He responded most strongly to the initial point and less and less strongly as the point stimulated was further from his shoulder. The resulting curve of response is called the generalization gradient. (After Bass and Hull, 1934)

Note that this tendency to generalize does not have to be taught. Whenever anything is learned, the animal naturally will generalize to other stimuli according to this simple rule. This applies to every animal that has been involved in learning studies—from worms to rats, dogs to humans.

Generalization can occur along any dimension to which the animal can respond. Pigeons tend to notice light frequency especially, so that is usually the critical factor determining generalization for them. People who learned to respond to a particular light would probably generalize on the basis of many dimensions—frequency, intensity, size, shape, and anything else that seemed important. In fact, we perceive similarity among stimuli on the basis of an almost limitless number of characteristics. A child who was bitten by an English sheep dog might generalize her fear according to physical appearance (and be afraid of all large, shaggy animals), the type of animal (and be afraid of all dogs), the concept of animal (and be afraid of all animals), the concept of pets (and be afraid of cats, dogs, canaries, and tropical fish), or anything else that is distinctive about sheep dogs. It is even conceivable that she would generalize quite specifically to the name of the breed of dog and be afraid of anything that is English or has to do with sheep. Some of these generalizations seem sensible, some do not; but all are possible.

Generalizations to the characteristics of other people are especially important. A child who is fed and comforted by his parents tends to develop strong positive reactions to them. This positive response can generalize to all other people or to people with certain characteristics. As we shall see in Chapter 12, Erikson suggests that early positive feelings toward the parents can produce positive feelings toward people and the world in general (what he calls basic trust). The generalization can be more specific, however, with the child generalizing his positive feelings toward his mother to all other women, or to all people with the same hair color, skin, accent, or anything else. Negative feelings also may generalize. This is particularly apparent with prejudices that are based on unpleasant interactions with one member of a group. The individual learns to dislike or fear a particular black, white, Protestant, Jew, Russian, or Italian and generalizes to other members of that group. It would be just as sensible to generalize along dimensions such as hair color, lefthandedness, height, or shape of the head, but we have also learned that ethnicity is "more important" than these other characteristics and we tend to generalize according to the most important qualities.

Although, as in the case of prejudice, it sometimes leads to mistakes, stimulus generalization is absolutely essential to the learning process. Because we constantly find ourselves in different situations and are confronted by different stimuli, we need to be able to apply our past experiences to current situations. Otherwise, we might learn to stop our car only at a red light of a particular frequency and intensity but would drive through a slightly different red light. Our mother's smile might be reinforcing, but if she smiled in a slightly different way, it would not be. We would have to learn not only every single word separately, but every minor variation in pronunciation and accent. In contrast to this chaotic state, the actual situation is orderly. Once we have learned a response to a particular stimulus, we can generalize that response to all similar stimuli. Minor variations and even fairly major ones can be ignored—the learning still applies.

Discrimination

It is extremely useful to generalize from learning to insert a dime in one coke machine to inserting it in other machines, but you must know not to put a dime in a pay phone when you want a coke. If you love German shepherds, you must know not to give a friendly pat to a bear or timberwolf, and also that you should treat your own shepherd differently from shepherds trained as attack dogs. It is fine to learn to appreciate a smile on anyone's face, but a baby should learn to recognize his own mother and to respond to her differently from others. If one person reinforces you for caressing them, you must not caress everyone you see. Thus, just as stimulus generalization is crucial to learning, so is *discrimination*. It is necessary to distinguish among stimuli and to respond only to certain ones.

Discriminations are learned in two ways—by *differential reinforcement* and by continued experience with the reinforced stimulus. In differential reinforcement, responding to one stimulus, called the *discriminative stimulus*, is reinforced while responding to another is not. After a while, the response becomes stronger to the reinforced stimulus and weaker to the other. Thus, even if the two stimuli are extremely similar, the subject will eventually learn to discriminate between them. Figure 3.9 is an illustration of this process of discrimination.

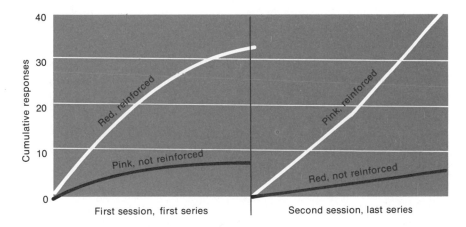

Fig. 3.9
Discrimination learning

A twelve-month old boy is first reinforced for responding to a red light and not a pink light and then, at a second session, the pink light is reinforced. The boy learns both discriminations—responding more to the light that is reinforced. (After Simmons and Lipsitt, 1961)

Continued experience with a reinforced stimulus means that as the stimulus becomes more and more familiar, the animal learns to discriminate it from similar stimuli. The *generalization gradient* tends to get steeper—that is, the response is elicited only by increasingly similar stimuli and drops off in strength more and more sharply. The animal apparently learns to recognize the critical element of the situation, the discriminative stimulus. Other stimuli sharing that

Box 3.8

APPLICATIONS OF LEARNING TO MENTAL DISORDERS

As we shall discuss in detail in Chapter 16, behavioral psychologists view mental disorders as a form of *maladaptive learning*. The person has learned to behave or react in ways that are destructive or limiting, and the solution accordingly is to extinguish the original learning and replace it with new responses. For example, many people suffer from *phobias*, unreasonable fears that focus on particular objects or situations. Some common phobias are fear of snakes, fear of flying, fear of enclosed spaces, and fear of heights. Obviously someone who was terrified of being in an enclosed space would have a lot of difficulty managing in our society. Elevators, trains, busses, and crowded rooms would all arouse the fear and make day-to-day living a constant strain. But behavior therapists argue that a fear of enclosed spaces, for example, was learned just as any other behavior or response would be. The person may have been locked in a closet as a punishment when she was very young, and this experience terrified her and caused her to develop a conditioned response of fear to closets. This generalized, perhaps strengthened by other negative experiences involving small spaces, to all enclosed areas and the phobia emerged.

Given this explanation of the cause of the phobia, the behavior therapist treats it by using standard learning techniques designed to make the person unlearn (extinguish) the original response and to learn new, more *adaptive* responses. Various procedures are employed, which we shall describe in Chapter 16. But one method is to work back along the *stimulus generalization gradient*, extinguishing the fear as you go. That is, the person is most afraid of closets (the original stimulus), less afraid of elevators, still less of crowded rooms, and presumably still less of small, uncrowded rooms. Each person will have a different gradient, but every phobic is more afraid of some situations than others. The therapist begins with a situation that arouses only a little fear. The phobic person is told to imagine or actually put herself in this situation, say a moderate-size room that makes her feel slightly uncomfortable. While there, she is taught to eliminate any fear she might feel by relaxing fully, realizing that it is not dangerous, and spending time in the room until she feels totally comfortable. Once this is done, she proceeds to the next step on the gradient—perhaps a slightly smaller room. The procedure is repeated until she feels comfortable there, and so on until she can actually enter a dark closet and stay there without experiencing fear. Since the phobia was learned originally, it can be unlearned in this way. Similar techniques are used for a wide variety of mental and behavioral disorders including the standard psychiatric disorders, sexual deviances, and criminal behavior.

A controversial but important application of learning research is the use of operant techniques with mental patients. In particular, some hospital wards have

element elicit the response; however, stimuli that are similar in other respects except that they do not contain the critical element do not elicit the response.

Humans are capable of exceedingly fine discriminations. The socialization process whereby a child is taught to behave "properly" consists in large part of learning complex and fine discriminations. We must learn not only a vast array of behaviors, but also exactly when they are appropriate and when they are not. The rules of society generally do not tell us that certain behaviors are right and others wrong, but rather under what circumstances a behavior is acceptable and when it is not. Violence is generally condemned, but it is quite

been turned into so-called *token economies*, in which patients are given actual tokens when they perform certain behaviors. For example, they might get a token for making their bed, for cleaning their room, for being quiet at dinner, for not fighting, or for anything else. These tokens have value because they can be exchanged for privileges such as going to the movies, being allowed to use the grounds freely, or visiting home. The idea is that each desired behavior is reinforced immediately and tangibly with a token, and the patient therefore is conditioned to perform that behavior rather than behaviors that are punished by the loss of tokens. Although reinforcement of various behaviors goes on constantly in hospitals in terms of nurses and doctors giving verbal approval or disapproval or giving and taking privileges, these reinforcements are usually given quite haphazardly and inconsistently. In the token economy, the reinforcement is consistent and concrete—the patient knows immediately that he is rewarded and he has the token in his hand to prove it.

Although we cannot yet be certain how effective token economies are in the long term, they clearly have substantial effects on the behavior of mental patients. The wards become better organized and pleasanter for all concerned, and the patients cause less trouble, take better care of themselves and their surroundings, and probably become more accessible to other forms of therapy.

The argument against these techniques is that the patients are being treated as if they were children or even animals. Giving an adult a token for making her bed is demeaning; she feels humiliated, and this makes her mental condition even worse. Moreover, behavior control, or behavior modification as this is sometimes called, has somewhat the quality of a fascistic thought control that makes the patients automotons rather than people.

While there is some truth in these arguments, it should also be recognized that mental hospitals are never very pleasant places to be. Many hospitalized people are likely to be treated like children anyway, particularly if they are not behaving in socially acceptable ways. If the token economy can make them behave better, they will immediately be treated better by others and will feel better because they have more, not less, control over what happens to them. True, the procedure forces them to follow certain rules and procedures, but at least it does not use inconsistent and arbitrary punishments to achieve this. In other words, making the reinforcements consistent and systematic should increase their effectiveness; and since the reinforcements are there anyway, the system is no worse than it was before.

This is a complex argument that will not be resolved until these new techniques are fully understood and their effectiveness carefully evaluated. Nevertheless, the learning theory approach to the treatment of various disorders appears to be very promising and is being used more and more widely.

allowable and even commendable in a football game, in the defense of one's family, or in a war protecting freedom. Sexual behavior is condemned if it is done in public, with an unwilling person, and in many other situations, but it is acceptable at other times, in other places, and with other people. Nor are stealing, lying, or cheating always wrong—to some extent, the evaluation of actions depends on the particular circumstances. One of the most difficult problems for everyone is to generalize enough so that learning is useful but to discriminate enough so that the behavior is still appropriate. It is not enough to learn a response—you must learn exactly when to give it and when not to.

INNATE VERSUS LEARNED BEHAVIOR

All animals are born into the world with a complex set of characteristics. These characteristics play a major role in determining how the animal will function throughout its life. A newborn dog is clearly different from a newborn cat, a monkey from a human, a woman from a man, and indeed every individual from every other individual. These innate characteristics affect all aspects of the animal's life, from simple physical processes to complex mental ones, and from how it perceives the world to how it behaves in a wide variety of situations.

Yet these innate qualities are far from the whole story. Much of the animal's behavior will be affected by its experiences and in particular by what it learns. The importance of learning in determining behavior increases as we ascend the developmental scale. Although worms have been shown to be capable of some learning, most of their behavior is entirely under the control of their innate characteristics. Similarly, the behavior of one rat is very much like that of another. This may be an unfair statement to make from our human vantage point, but variations among rats are relatively small compared to those among higher animals. Some rats are more active than others; some smarter, some hungrier; some learn to perform certain acts to get food or avoid danger while others learn other acts. But they all have most of their behavior patterns already established at birth. As a rat matures, it will find food, eat, mate, build a nest, raise its young, and fight in pretty much the same way as every other rat.

The uniformity of rat behavior does not mean that rats cannot learn. On the contrary, they learn certain kinds of behaviors very quickly. As we have seen, rats and pigeons can be taught a great variety of actions. But all this learning occurs within a relatively narrow range of possible behaviors, and tends to involve how and when to carry out innate behaviors, rather than the learning of new behaviors.

In contrast, human beings can learn an enormous variety of behaviors. A newborn infant has relatively few instinctive behavior patterns. It cries when hungry or uncomfortable, displays some inborn physical reflexes, and has certain perceptual tendencies (as we saw in Chapter 2). As the child matures, various other innate capacities develop, including more complex perceptual mechanisms and physical acts, such as walking. These innate capacities and maturational developments are, of course, extremely important in determining the person's behavior. But they are mainly limiting factors, the framework within which the person can develop, rather than a complete set of behavior patterns. That is acquired only by learning. Surely one of the wonders of nature is that the helpless human infant, with so few built-in behavioral mechanisms, matures into the complex human adult. And each infant turns into a unique individual with her own personality, ideas, thoughts, talents, concerns, and style.

There has been considerable discussion of the relative importance of innate and acquired characteristics. Most psychologists now agree that human behavior is a product of the interaction of heredity and learning and that the more important question is how each functions. A reasonable approach seems to be to think of innate characteristics as the framework within which an individual can develop according to his experiences. For example, as we saw in the chapter on perception, all human beings see electromagnetic waves between 400 and 750 millimicrons, they are born with or soon develop size constancy within a distance of about ten feet, and they have an innate tendency to perceive the world in terms of figure and ground. No amount of experience or learning will enable people to see ultraviolet or infrared light, nor will it remove size constancy or figure-ground relations. But within the limits imposed by the perceptual organs, human perception is greatly influenced by learning. Some people develop size constancy for great distances, while others do not; some perceive optical illusions such as the Mueller-Lyer and the vertical-horizontal, while others do not. But all of us learn to recognize certain objects and shapes, to judge the size of particular objects accurately, and to identify letters and symbols that are used in communications. The innate physical characteristics and tendencies of our perceptual system determine the limits and general direction of our perceptions, but learning accounts for the variability in perception from one person to another and from one culture to another. We shall return to the question of the relationship between innate and acquired characteristics several times throughout the book. The important point to remember is that human behavior is a joint product of innate and acquired characteristics and cannot be discussed realistically in terms of only one or the other. ∎

Summary

1. Learning can be defined as a relatively permanent change in behavior caused by experience or practice.

2. Classical conditioning involves four elements: the unconditioned stimulus (US), which automatically produces the unconditioned response (UR), and the conditioned stimulus (CS), which after being paired often enough with the US produces the conditioned response (CR).

3. Extinction—the elimination of a conditioned response—occurs when CS and US are not paired. Spontaneous recovery occurs when an apparently extinguished conditioned response regains strength after a period of no trials.

4. Operant conditioning requires the subject to *operate* on the environment in order to acquire a new behavior. The behavior is learned through reinforcement, an event that increases the likelihood that a response will occur in the future.

5. Drive-reduction theory states that anything that reduces an organism's drive is positively reinforcing. The idea of an optimal level of arousal explains why arousal is sometimes positively reinforcing. Every animal has an optimal level of arousal. An

animal in a relaxed state (below optimal level) may be brought back to its optimal level by exposure to arousing stimuli.

6. A conditioned, or secondary reinforcer is an initially neutral stimulus that acquires some of the properties of a primary reinforcer and can serve as a reinforcer. Much of human motivation and behavior is shaped by conditioned reinforcers.

7. Successful operant conditioning depends on the proper timing of reinforcement. Humans can learn even when reinforcement is delayed for a long time because they are able to make connections between events and anticipate the future.

8. The greater the number of reinforced trials, the better a response will be learned; similarly, larger reinforcements teach a response more quickly. However, partial reinforcement makes a behavior more resistant to extinction than continuous reinforcement.

9. By means of the process of shaping, an animal can be taught behavior patterns that are not ordinarily in its repertoire. Shaping involves reinforcing successive behaviors that gradually approximate the desired behavior, until the animal is performing the desired behavior.

10. Research on operant conditioning of physiological processes suggests that humans and other animals can be conditioned to establish more control over internal bodily processes than they do ordinarily.

11. A third type of learning, imitation, involves observing a behavior and then repeating it. Imitation is extremely efficient because it eliminates the need for trial and error required by both classical and operant conditioning.

12. The tendency to respond to stimuli similar to the one on which the learning occurred is called stimulus generalization. The narrowing of a response so that the individual reacts only to particular stimuli is called discrimination. Generalization is essential to learning because it enables us to apply our past experiences to current situations; discrimination is necessary because it allows us to distinguish among stimuli and respond only to appropriate ones.

13. Innate characteristics and experience both play a part in behavior, but the role of learning increases as we ascend the developmental scale.

RECOMMENDED READING

Bandura, A. L. *Social Learning Theory*. Englewood Cliffs, N.J.: Prentice-Hall, 1977. Probably the best description of the application of learning theory to social and developmental psychology. This approach is also extremely influential in the fields of personality and psychotherapy.

Hilgard, E. R., and G. H. Bower. *Theories of Learning*, 4th ed. Englewood Cliffs, N.J.: Prentice-Hall, 1975. Still the best survey of the various theories.

Rachlin, H. *Introduction to Modern Behaviorism*. San Francisco: Freeman, 1970. The behaviorist, Skinnerian approach presented in a clear, forthright manner. Not easy reading, but this is difficult material.

Skinner, B. F. *Walden Two*. New York: Macmillan, 1948. A fictional account of how principles of learning can produce a "perfect" world.

Memory is the treasury and guardian of all things.
Cicero, De Oratore

Memory is like a purse—if it be over-full that it cannot shut, all will drop out of it.
Fuller, Holy and Profane States

4 Cognitive Learning and Memory

The basic process of cognitive learning—contiguity ■ Factors affecting cognitive learning ■ Stimulus materials ■ Ease of forming associations ■ Situational factors ■ The memory system ■ How is learning stored? ■ Why we forget ■ Memory retrieval ■ Applications of learning research to education

f you turn the television on and see a familiar face, you usually know immediately whose it is, where you have seen it before, and so on. When you are asked a particular question on an organic chemistry exam, you often know the answer right away. After reading the previous chapters, you know that Pavlov discovered classical conditioning and Skinner did research in operant conditioning. You may never have been rewarded or punished in connection with any of these responses, and yet you have acquired all this information. Even though you have millions of pieces of information stored in your memory, you usually can find just the right one for each occasion. How do you manage this? Why do you learn some information and not other seemingly similar information? Why, a year or a week after or even during an exam, do you forget something you knew before? And how do you find the piece of information you need?

These questions involve *cognitive learning* and *memory*, the processes by which we acquire and recall beliefs, connections among events, expectations, and information in general. When cognitive learning takes place, we have learned not only to perform a behavior in response to a stimulus, but something new about the situation as well. When we learn to put a coin in a soft-drink machine because we have gotten something to drink by doing so in the past, we have acquired the behavior that was reinforced. But we also learn the new cognition (or fact) that the coin usually produces a soft drink; and we fully expect to get one each time we insert the right coin.

Humans have an unmatched ability to acquire, store, retrieve, and use cognitive information. This ability plays an exceedingly important role in our lives, affecting virtually all our behavior. In this chapter we shall first discuss the principle by which cognitive learning operates and some of the factors that affect how easily a particular

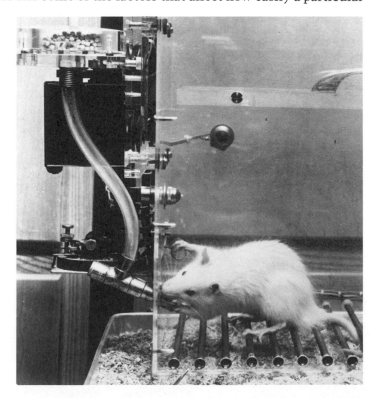

BOX 4.1

DO OTHER ANIMALS LEARN COGNITIONS?

For many years, the question of whether animals learned anything other than new behaviors was a burning controversy among psychologists. Hull, Skinner, and other behaviorists held that a pigeon that was reinforced for pecking a green disk learned simply to peck the green disk and had no expectation about getting food; a dog that heard a bell and then received food learned simply to salivate at the sound of the bell but did not expect the food to arrive; and so on. In contrast, Tolman and others argued that this explanation was too mechanistic; they maintained that animals formed connections and expectations under many circumstances. The pigeon and the dog both knew that food usually appeared—they not only learned the behavior but also developed some expectations and understanding of the situation.

Animal Expectation

Although this controversy is not settled, a number of experiments strongly indicate that some animals under some circumstances do learn something about the situation in addition to the relevant behavior. They form expectations, learn the location of objects, and so on. For example, Tinklepaugh (1928) conducted an experiment that involved giving monkeys a choice between two baskets, one of which had food under it. When the monkey picked the correct basket it found a banana, one of its favorite foods. Once the animal had learned to choose the correct basket, the experimenter substituted lettuce, a less favored food, for the banana. If the animal had learned to pick the correct basket solely because it was reinforced and had formed no expectations, the lettuce would be reinforcing. But if the animal expected a favorite food and received a less good one, it would be upset—and it was. When the monkey found lettuce under the box rather than a banana, it usually searched around as if it were looking for something and then threw a tan-

trum. Other research (Elliott, 1928) has supported Tinklepaugh's findings that non-human animals also form expectations.

Latent Learning

Other evidence for cognitive learning in animals includes the phenomenon of *latent learning*, which is learning that does not immediately affect behavior. The animal continues to act just as it did before the experience until the appropriate situation occurs. Then the learning—previously hidden, or latent—appears in the form of changed behavior. Latent learning occurs often with humans. For example, if you are a passenger in a car and do not have to find your way, when you drive later to the same place, you may know the directions. We accumulate lots of information without being aware that we have it; when it is needed, it will appear.

Other animals also demonstrate latent learning. They can learn the locations of objects and acquire other kinds of information about a situation. Tolman and Honzik (1930) demonstrated that rats become familiar with a complex maze even though their performance does not improve until they are rewarded. One group of rats ran through a maze ten times without receiving any reinforcement and was then rewarded with food on the next seven trials; another group was rewarded on all trials. The second group performed better than the first during the first ten trials, but once rewards were given to the first group, it performed as well as the second group almost immediately. In other words, the rats in the first group were learning about the maze during the first ten unrewarded trials, but did not change their behavior until they were reinforced.

Despite this evidence, the existence of cognitive learning in other animals is uncertain. Since we cannot ask them directly yet (but maybe a talking chimp will tell us—see Chapter 5), we can only infer it—and some behaviorists have offered arguments against cognitive interpretations of the research.

piece of information is learned. Second, we shall deal with the process of storing that information in our memory system. Third, we shall look at some of the reasons why we forget, and fourth, we shall look at the mechanism by which information is retrieved from our memory system. And finally, we shall consider some of the ways in which research on learning is applied to education.

THE BASIC PROCESS OF COGNITIVE LEARNING—CONTIGUITY

We learn most information by forming associations among any stimuli that appear together at the same time. When you see CONTIGUITY-ASSOCIATION-COGNITIVE LEARNING, these stimuli tend to become connected in your mind, even though they may be totally unrelated except for this one appearance together. Once stimuli have appeared together, an association is formed; that is, one stimulus will tend to make us think of the other. "Contiguity" will make us think of "association" and "cognitive learning"; and "cognitive learning" will make us think of "association" and "contiguity." Moreover, since all of these stimuli appeared in a paragraph in this book, in a psychology course, in this school, each word will also make you think of "psychology," the name of the school, the teacher, and so on. All things that appear together become associated, but the closer together they appear, the stronger the association.

Learning by contiguity is simple, flexible, and automatic. Unlike classical conditioning, which requires an unconditioned stimulus, and operant conditioning, which requires reinforcement, learning by contiguity simply happens. Indeed, the learning occurs whether or not you want it to. Look for a moment at the pair of words shown in Fig. 4.1. Even if you just glance at them you will remember them, and making an effort not to will probably not interfere with the association. This one exposure to these two simple words forms an association with no effort on your part and with no reinforcement. In fact, you may remember this pair for years even if you do not think about them at all in between.

Figure 4.1

Semantic versus Episodic Memory

Endel Tulving (1972) has made an important distinction between two types of memory he calls semantic and episodic. *Semantic memory* involves knowledge about what words mean, what items go with what other items, associations between any two pieces of information, and all complex ideas. *Episodic memory* concerns only knowledge of temporal events—when or in what circumstances something occurred. For example, if you remember that you recently heard the name Tulving, that the phone rang ten minutes ago, or that you entered college two years ago, that is episodic memory. In contrast, if you know that Tulving studies memory, that the phone rang four times, or that you got accepted to six colleges and decided to go to the present one because it offered you the best scholarship, that is semantic memory. Much of the experimental work on memory involves episodic memory because people are shown a list of words and asked to remember them. If you saw a list containing eggplant, giraffe, and ocean and could then recall these words later, you obviously did not learn the words themselves—you knew the words and their meanings long ago. You learned only that the words had appeared on the list, which is temporal knowledge. At the moment we do not know much about the differences between how these two types of memory operate, but the distinction between them seems real and should be taken into account in thinking about memory and learning in general.

FACTORS AFFECTING COGNITIVE LEARNING

Although it is clear that we form associations almost instantly and effortlessly simply by contiguity, we do not fully understand why this happens. It appears to be a mechanism built into our cognitive structure that operates regardless of any attempts by us to turn it either "on" or "off." The process is by no means uniform. Sometimes it works better than at other times; sometimes we learn and remember information and sometimes we do not. And even though we do not understand exactly why the basic mechanism works, we do know many of the factors that determine when and how well it operates. Some of these factors involve the type of stimulus material, some involve the ease with which associations are formed, and some are concerned with how the material is presented.

Stimulus Materials

Some kinds of stimuli are easier to learn than others; we tend to remember them better and for a longer time and in general to deal with them with greater facility. The three most important characteristics of the material that determine how easily it is learned are its familiarity, its distinctiveness, and how compactly it is presented.

Familiarity Semantic memory usually involves forming new associations among previously learned stimuli, but sometimes the stimulus to be learned is either entirely new or unfamiliar. Other things being equal, the more familiar the material, the easier it is to learn and to form new associations with. A brief exposure to "angry-eggplant" forms a strong, easily remembered association. "Eggplant" is not a particularly common word, but it is familiar to most readers. On the other hand, the pair "angry-cepes" is much harder to learn because most of us are not familiar with "cepes," a rare kind of mushroom. We can learn the colors of the spectrum quite easily because red, orange, yellow, and the rest are already familiar to us. We would have a much harder time learning them in a foreign language or if they were uncommon colors such as ocher, sienna, or fuchsia. To see for yourself the effect of familiarity, try to learn the two lists in Fig. 4.2.

There are various reasons why familiar material is easier to form into new associations. When faced with new material we must learn to recognize the new stimulus before we can form associations with it. This extra task naturally makes the learning more difficult. In addition, familiar material already has meaning for us, and therefore

Fig. 4.2
The effect of familiarity on learning

Study list A for thirty seconds and then immediately write down as many items from the list as you can. Repeat this process for list B. You should remember many more items from list B because they are more familiar.

A		B	
urn	onyx	table	shoe
awl	sternum	elephant	wall
lemur	gingko	hammer	boat
folio	oraler	page	sparrow
vega	stere	road	worm
ulna	jackdaw	arm	sun
emu	epee	pencil	box
stylus	freon	radio	clock
etui	augur	pin	glass
mural	gnu	stove	pipe

has two advantages: it has distinctive features, and it brings with it prior associations, both of which factors, as we shall see, facilitate learning.

Distinctiveness We learn material that is unusual, different from its surroundings, powerful, or in any other way *distinctive* more easily than material that does not have distinctive qualities. When you are introduced to a large group of people, you probably remember only a few names. If one person is seven feet tall, has an unusual name, or is very attractive, you are more likely to remember that person's name. Similarly, you remember a beautiful, handsome, or ugly face better than a plain one.

The effect of distinctiveness is easy to demonstrate. Look for a moment at the list in Fig. 4.3. Then look away and write down as many items on the list as you can remember. You will probably remember "CF" very easily, because it is the only letter pair in a list

Fig. 4.3
The effect of distinctiveness

54	68	19	CF	73
46	27	53	95	80

Who in this picture would you be most likely to remember? Why?

of numbers. Also, you are more likely to remember the first and last numbers on the list, because their position makes them stand out. Whenever people learn a list, they tend to remember items at the beginning and end more easily than those in the middle.

Distinctive material is learned more easily for two reasons. First, we pay more attention to it, and the more attention we pay to material, the more likely we are to remember it. Second, the more different something is from the items around it, the less likely we are to confuse it with those other items.

However, what is distinctive in one situation may not be in another. The word *tiger* would not be distinctive among a list of animals, but would stand out in a list of trees. As we mentioned in our discussion of contrast effects in perception, seven-foot Kareem Abdul Jabbar will appear taller and be more distinctive when he is not surrounded by other basketball players. Distinctiveness is not inherent in a particular stimulus—distinctiveness depends on comparison with the surrounding stimuli and the individual's experience and expectations.

Compactness of material Study the letters in line A of Fig. 4.4 for ten seconds and then write down as many as you can remember. Now repeat the process with the same letters arranged into words, as shown on line B. You will probably discover that you remember five or six letters from line A and perhaps all the words from line B. Although people differ somewhat in their ability to memorize in a short time, most of us can recall approximately seven units. George Miller (1962) called this the "magic number seven" because regardless of the type of material to be learned or who is trying to learn it, generally between five and nine pieces of information are recalled—or, as Miller put it, seven plus or minus two.

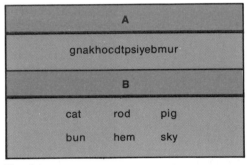

Fig. 4.4
Chunking and memory

Despite this limitation, note that you remembered a great deal more *information* from line B than from line A. Even if you remembered seven units from each list, you actually recalled three times as many letters when they were formed into words as when they were separate. In both cases you were remembering the information in units, but in line B, the units, or *chunks,* were larger. Up to a point, the size of a chunk does not seem to affect how many are remembered. However, there is some limit. Using himself as a subject, Herb Simon (1974) found that he could recall seven one- or two-syllable words, six three-syllable words, but only four two-word phrases and only three longer phrases. Nevertheless, there is no question that the larger the chunks, the more information an individual can learn.

This principle can be a help in learning telephone numbers. For many years the number for the New York weather service was 767-2676. This is not a particularly difficult number to learn, but many people made it even easier by transforming it into POPCORN.

Another way of chunking is to arrange letters in some form of sequence. For example, although the sequence D, E, F, G does not have the same level of meaningfulness as a word, we can remember it better than single letters because we have to recall only the first letter of the chunk and the fact that it is in alphabetical sequence. Thus, providing *any* organization or meaning that combines separate units into larger chunks of information increases the ease with which they can be remembered.

Ease of Forming Associations

Closely related to the specific stimulus characteristics we just discussed are qualities of the stimulus material that involve the ease with which associations are formed. The stronger the associations, the more likely it is that the information will be learned well and remembered later. Sometimes you may remember a particular name because it is highly distinctive (for example, Jabbar or Katmandu) but have difficulty forming an association with it and therefore will not remember anything about that name. You may know that Katmandu is a city, but forget that it is the capital of Nepal. The most important factors determining the ease of forming associations are the existence of prior associations, the meaningfulness of the material, and the use of imagery.

Prior associations All stimuli we have seen before tend to bring with them associations that have already been formed. We cannot look at *eggplant* without thinking of vegetables, eggs, plants, the color purple, and various other things. Even words we have never seen before may arouse associations based on former experiences. For example, it is difficult to construct a nonsense syllable (three letters that can be pronounced) that does not have some associations. Try it. Almost any combination (jix, mip, baf) is somewhat similar to, and therefore makes us think of, some word or part of a word (jinx, pip, baffle). Indeed, it is probably safe to say that nothing we encounter in life is entirely free of some associations, no matter how weak or distant.

When we are trying to form a connection between two words, any prior association between those words will make the new association easier. If the words are already somewhat associated, they will be much easier to learn than if they are not. This is most obvious in a common form of learning called *paired-associate learning,* in which pairs of words are presented and the individual must learn to give the second half of the pair when the first half is shown. This is essentially the task facing anyone who is trying to learn the definition of a word ("loquacious" means talkative), someone's name (that face is called Sam), or the date of an important event (World War II ended in 1945). In each case, one stimulus must be paired with another. When the two halves of the pair have something in common or are connected in some way, they are easier to learn than if they are totally unrelated. This is illustrated in Fig. 4.5.

Meaningfulness Closely related to the other factors determining the ease of forming associations is the *meaningfulness* of the material to be learned. By definition, a stimulus that carries meaning must be familiar to the individual. Either she has seen that particular stimulus before, or she associates it immediately with stimuli that she has seen. The word *eggplant* has more meaning to most Americans than the word *cepes* simply because the former is familiar and the latter not. Thus, meaningful material is easier to learn because it is more familiar, does not have to be learned by itself, carries with it more associations, and is easier to distinguish from other material.

One way to add meaning to a set of items is to organize them according to a logical scheme. This can be done by dividing them into groups that have similar meanings, functions, forms, or any other characteristic. For example, the following words are difficult to re-

A	B
strong – light	big – small
tall – good	warm – hot
bean – chair	corn – cob
house – sing	book – read
horse – lamp	dog – cat
grass – slow	sky – blue
lake – tree	car – truck
rose – red	thin – fat
man – run	bird – fly
shirt – talk	sugar – sweet

Fig. 4.5
Paired-associate learning

Study lists A and B for 30 seconds, reading each pair aloud once. Then turn to p. 131 and try to supply the second half of each pair. You probably remembered many more items from list B because the pairs already are associated in English. But you probably remembered "rose-red" from list A, since it is a strongly associated pair.

BOX 4.2

NONVERBAL ASSOCIATIONS

Although the research on learning by contiguity tends to concentrate on verbal stimuli, people form associations among all kinds of stimuli. Obviously, visual and auditory stimuli are involved in associative learning. We learn the names that go with faces, who lives in what house, and the melodies of many songs. Although we are probably less aware of them, odors, tastes, textures, and touches also evoke very strong associations. The odor of Chinese food is strongly associated with the taste of that food, and probably with particular restaurants and evenings—as is the taste of it when you finally get to eat it. Many people associate the feel of grass under bare feet with being in the country, a memorable picnic spot, various words, and so on. And in his novel *Remembrance of Things Past*, Marcel Proust describes how a sip of tea and the taste of a bit of cake looses a flood of childhood memories:

Many years had elapsed during which nothing of Combray had any existence for me, when one day in winter, as I came home, my mother, seeing that I was cold, offered me some tea, a thing I did not ordinarily take. She sent out for those short, plump little cakes called petites madeleines and soon I raised to my lips a spoonful of the tea in which I had soaked a morsel of the cake. No sooner had the warm liquid, and the crumbs with it, touched my palate than a shudder ran through my whole body, and I stopped, intent upon the extraordinary changes that were taking place. An exquisite pleasure had invaded my senses, but individual, detached, with no suggestion of its origin. In that moment all the flowers in our garden and in Mr. Swann's park and the good folk of the village and their little dwellings and the parish church and the whole of Combray sprang into being, town and gardens alike, from my cup of tea.

People who have tried to free associate in psychotherapy or any other situation know that almost any stimulus is capable of bringing up all sorts of unlikely associations that have been formed in the past. Thus, despite the fact that this chapter deals mainly with verbal associations, keep in mind that the same rules and principles apply to all cognitive learning and to associations involving all kinds of stimuli.

member as they are listed: rat, kangaroo, carrot, bear, spinach, chair, potatoes, desk, bed. But divided into three groups as shown below, they will be easier to learn. Because the members of each group are associated, recalling one member of the set will probably bring the others to mind.

Animals	Vegetables	Furniture
rat	carrot	chair
kangaroo	spinach	desk
bear	potatoes	bed

Tying all of the items together in a story is an even more effective means of organization:

A rat munching on a carrot is being carried by a kangaroo while a bear eating a huge head of spinach sits on a chair and peels potatoes at a desk. The rat is so frightened it has to go to bed.

This or any other simple story provides meaning to the previously unrelated list and greatly facilitates learning.

A	
true	our
to	it
inclinations	sort
them	required
that	interpreters
art	be
are	there
believe	but
the	I
understand	dreams
of	is
and	

B
I believe it to be true that dreams are the true interpreters of our inclinations; but there is art required to sort and understand them.
Montaigne, *Essays*

Fig. 4.6
The effect of meaningfulness on memory
Study list A for two minutes and try to recall as many words as you can. Then look at B for the same length of time. Organized into a meaningful paragraph, the words are much easier to remember.

The effect of meaningfulness is scarcely noticeable when we are learning individual stimuli or pairs, but it has a dramatic and important effect on the learning of larger bodies of information. See, for example, the special case illustrated in Fig. 4.6. Forming individual words into connected groups facilitates learning; and this is even more apparent when the associations among the words form a coherent meaningful whole.

Imagery Making up a story incorporating a list of words facilitates learning the list. This effect is even stronger if you try to visualize the story by forming images of it in your mind. The more imagery is involved, the better the learning. To remember *angry artichoke,* for example, you might picture a big artichoke with a face that has an angry expression on it. The effect of forming such images is extremely powerful. In a series of studies (Bower, 1972), subjects were shown paired-associate lists and half the subjects were told to form a bizarre and detailed mental image of each pair. For example, for *giraffe-onion*

GORDON BOWER

Figure 4.7

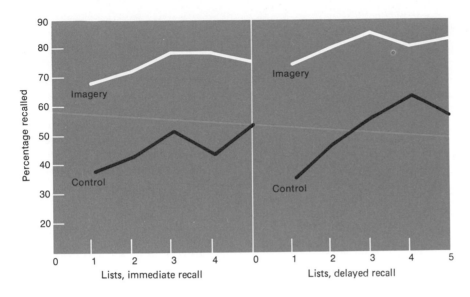

Fig. 4.8
Immediate and delayed recall of five lists by subjects who used imagery and controls who did not. (From Bower, 1972)

Fig. 4.9
The effect of imagery

Study list A for two minutes without using any imagery and try to recall as many words as you can. Repeat for list B, but make up a story employing vivid imagery whenever possible. You should recall more items from list B.

they might picture an image like the one shown in Fig. 4.7. The other half of the subjects were given no instructions about using images to learn the word pairs. The results of the experiment indicate that the subjects who used imagery recalled more than twice as many word pairs as those who did not (see Fig. 4.8). You can see for yourself the effects of imagery by using it to learn one of the lists in Fig. 4.9 and not the other.

We do not know for certain why forming images has such a powerful effect. We do know that we are able to remember purely visual stimuli extremely well. In one study (Standing, Conezio, and Haber, 1970), subjects saw 2,560 slides for only ten seconds each, yet recognized 90 percent of them later. And we all recognize thousands of faces with great accuracy. Producing images translates verbal material into visual material, which is easier to remember. It probably helps to reduce confusion, since the association that is formed is unique and unlikely to be confused with any other. It also provides a meaningful (though sometimes bizarre) context within which to embed the association, thus providing other clues to the correct stimulus. For example, if you can remember that the giraffe is crying, you will probably remember that the onion is causing it.

Situational Factors

Various aspects of the context in which information is presented affect how well it is learned. We have already seen that more distinctive material is learned more easily, and that to some extent distinctiveness depends on the particular context. The state of mind and body of the person trying to learn also plays an important role. If you

A	B
book – dragon	tree – moon
ship – street	hammer – bear
cat – window	bed – spider
clock – ocean	milk – car
scissors – carpet	paper – chair
robin – pepper	house – mountain
toy – rose	ear – glass
foot – snake	man – lake
chicken – suit	card – butter
gun – window	dress – wolf

BOX 4.3

EIDETIC IMAGERY

Eidetic imagery, also known as photographic memory, is the ability to look briefly at a picture or a page of type and retain a clear image of it in the mind. People with this ability can examine their retained image for some minutes afterwards, as though it were a photograph. Thus they can recall details they did not consciously notice during the viewing—a feat that would be impossible for other people. For example, an eidetic imagist who glanced at the photograph could later tell you what all the signs said. Someone who does not have eidetic imagery would have a general impression of the scene, but would be unable to give such exact details. An eidetic imagist can look at a page of fifty numbers for a few minutes and then recall all of them perfectly—in any order. And some imagists could "read back" a whole page of this text from memory.

Eidetic imagery is most prevalent in young children; the ability generally fades away as a person grows older. However, this is a less serious loss than might be supposed. Eidetic imagery is impressive, but it is seldom a great benefit to those who possess it. For some reason, people with eidetic imagery cannot use the information contained in the image as readily as material learned in the usual way and they cannot form it into new associations. Thus, an eidetic imagist could repeat a list of new words and definitions immediately after glancing at it, but could not use those same words in an essay question that required abstract thinking.

are tired, uninterested, or drunk you will almost certainly learn less well than if you are alert and paying attention. The most important situational factors have to do with how often material is presented and the timing of the presentations.

Repetition and distribution of practice Repetition improves all kinds of learning. In classical conditioning, the more often a tone is paired with food, the stronger is the conditioned response to the tone. In operant conditioning, the more times lever-pressing is reinforced by food, the stronger the animal's tendency to press the lever. Similarly, in learning by contiguity, the more often two stimuli are paired, the stronger the association between them.

In addition, in most kinds of learning, the longer the interval between repetitions (up to a limit), the greater the increase in learning. For example, in conditioning a person to blink his eye when a tone is sounded, conditioning trials given every 90 seconds were more effective than those given every 30 seconds, which were in turn more effective than those given every 9 seconds (Spence and Norris, 1950). A similar effect occurs when a pair of stimuli are presented at intervals ranging from 10 to 170 seconds. As shown in Fig. 4.10, the longer the interval between presentations, the better the pair was remembered (Landauer, 1969).

Timing A separate issue is how the learning of a large amount of related material is affected by the timing of its presentation. If you want to learn a hundred chemical reactions or the dates of fifty crucial events in English history or the names and capitals of all the countries of Africa, should you study the material over a short period of time or space it out? Everyone has heard that it is bad to cram for an exam, and in fact most research supports this view. In general, studying over a long time (*spaced or distributed practice*) is more efficient than studying the same material in a short time (*massed practice*), even if the same amount of time is spent studying. In other words, it is better to study the chemical reactions for one hour a day for a week than for seven hours on one day. This explains why it is so difficult to learn the names of a whole group of people whom you have just met for the first time. You have to form many new associations between faces and names, and there is usually a great deal of confusion among both names and faces. In contrast, it is relatively easy to learn ten new names if they are spaced over many days. And if you already know everyone in a group it is quite easy to learn the name of one new person.

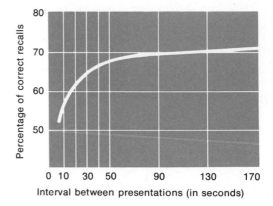

Fig. 4.10
Intertrial interval and recall

A pair of nonsense syllables is presented twice at various intervals ranging from 10 to 170 seconds. Varying numbers of other pairs are presented in between the two presentations. As the figure shows, the longer the interval between presentations, the better the paired syllables are remembered twenty minutes after the last presentation. (From Landauer, 1969)

THE MEMORY SYSTEM

We have seen that cognitive learning occurs by the process of forming associations among stimuli that appear contiguously, and we have discussed some of the factors that make this learning easier or harder. But the process of learning also involves a complex system by which the information is incorporated into our memories. When we see a pair of words together, we do form an association between them right away, but this association and the pair itself do not immediately embed themselves indelibly in our memories. On the contrary, there are at least three stages to our memory system, and information must pass through all of them in order to be remembered for more than a few seconds. First, the stimuli enter a purely sensory store or register; next they go into short-term memory; and finally, they reach long-term memory, which is the only stage at which we retain the information for any appreciable time. At each stage, the information will be lost if it does not proceed to the next. And each stage has certain properties and functions that contribute to the total memory system. A diagram of the memory process is shown in Fig. 4.11.

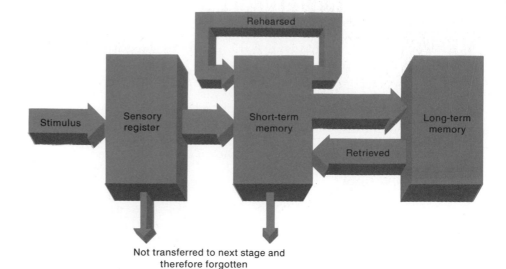

Fig. 4.11
The memory process

The Sensory Register

If you are driving a car and approach a curve, the stimulus of the curve reaches your retina, is processed by the visual system, and eventually reaches your brain. For a moment, the perception of the curve remains in what is often called a *sensory register.* The contents of the register constantly change as new stimuli arrive. Nothing remains in it for more than a brief interval—less than a second. But while the perception of the curve is in the sensory register, you can respond to it directly and turn the wheel of the car so you make the curve. Once the information leaves the sensory register, it is lost unless it enters short-term or long-term memory.

Evidence for the existence of sensory registers comes from the work by George Sperling (1960) that was discussed in Chapter 2. In this research, Sperling shows subjects groups of letters and asks them to recall as many as they can. The letters are shown for a very brief time, usually about one-twentieth of a second, which is less time than it would take the subjects to move their eyes. Whether six, nine, or more letters are shown, the subjects can report only four or five letters. Sperling next showed nine letters in three rows of three each and immediately afterward sounded a tone that was high, medium, or low. The subjects were then supposed to report only the letters in the row corresponding to the tone they heard (top row for the high tone, and so on). The results are remarkable. Subjects can report almost perfectly. Even though they could tell us only four or five from the whole display, they can report all three from any row. How can this be? If they knew all three, they must have known all nine because they did not know which row to focus on until after the letters had disappeared. The answer seems to be that all the letters are available in the sensory register for a very short time. When the signal occurs, they are still there and the subjects can transfer them to memory and retain them, but they can only retain four or five, not all of them. The signal tells them which to retain, and so they can report those perfectly. Other research supports this interpretation. If the signal is delayed as much as one second, the subjects do no better than you

MNEMONIC TRICKS

Mnemonists (*nih-mon'-ists*) are people who develop amazing memories. Although some of them have powerful memories naturally, most use mnemonic tricks, or techniques that assist memory. We have already described a number of these techniques—organizing material into larger, more meaningful chunks; forming associations with familiar material; and forming mental images that relate items.

Mnemonists are particularly dependent on imagery—the technique of making up strange pictorial stories to improve memory. First, they memorize a list of key words that indicate numerical order. For example, a mnemonist might learn a rhyming set such as *one-bun, two-shoe, three-tree, four-door,* and so on. Then, when he performs on stage, he asks the audience to shout out words so he can demonstrate his "fantastic" memory. Taking each word in sequence, he forms a mental image between it and his previously memorized key word. For example, if the first word from the audience were *telephone,* he might form the image of a *telephone* in a *bun* looking like a frankfurter. If the second word were *garage,* he would form an association between *garage* and *shoe* (his second keyword). Finally, to recall the words in order, he would simply think of his key word, which would bring to mind the mental image he has formed and the correct answer. You might try this for yourself. Learn the following ten key words and then have somebody give you ten words to remember. You will find that you can remember all ten words and can easily repeat them in order.

One is a bun,
Two is a shoe,
Three is a tree,
Four is a door,
Five is a hive,
Six are sticks,
Seven is heaven,
Eight is a gate,
Nine is a line,
Ten is a hen.

Mnemonists also visualize a familiar scene and "place" objects within it. The Russian psychologist Luria (1968) described how a mnemonist used a street for this purpose. "Frequently he would take a mental walk along that street—Gorky Street in Moscow—beginning at Mayakovsky Square, and slowly make his way down, 'distributing' his images at houses, gates, and store windows." Then, to recall the list, he would take the walk again, "picking up" the objects he had left.

There are many other mnemonic tricks. For example, rhymes make difficult material much easier to remember—"Thirty days hath September . . ." enables us to remember how many days each month has. Similarly, you probably remember the colors in the spectrum, if you have read Chapter 2, by recalling the name that keys them.

BOX 4.4

would expect from their overall performance. After one second, they can remember four or five from the total list, and only one or two from each row. The sensory register has faded and they must now rely on memory.

Other evidence for the existence of a sensory register distinct from short-term memory comes from Michael Posner's ingenious letter-matching experiments (Posner, 1969; Posner et al., 1969). In this research, subjects are shown two letters and asked to say whether they are the same (for example, both A's) or different. There are three kinds of trials: two identical letters (A A), two different forms of the same letter (A a), or two different letters. The finding of interest to us

INTERVIEW

Harry Lorayne is the world's foremost memory specialist. He is the best-selling author of many books on memory; The Memory Book was at the top of all national best-seller lists for over nine months. A more recent title is Remembering People. Mr. Lorayne is the founder and president of the Harry Lorayne School of Memory. He is relaxed, easy to talk with, and rather impish in the way he smiles and jokes—a real performer, and very likable. He says that his memory is inherently no better than anyone else's but that he has trained it. Other people, using his techniques, also have great memories. In his most famous demonstration, he is introduced once to everyone in a large audience (up to five hundred people) and then calls off all the names correctly! Although Mr. Lorayne is not a psychologist, you will find as you read the interview that his techniques and principles are remarkably similar to those derived from experimental psychology.

HARRY LORAYNE

If I cannot picture it, I cannot remember it.

Q: Can you say anything about the method you use or how you approach remembering them if someone reads off a bunch of numbers?

A: The most difficult things in the world to remember for the average person are anything that's abstract—numbers, letters of the alphabet, and names. What's a name—a conglomeration of sound. Numbers are designs, they're like quicksilver—the more you grasp them as far as memory is concerned, the further away they spurt. How do I go

about it? Well, to condense thirty-five years of my knowledge into one quick answer, what I do with numbers is make them meaningful. I cannot remember numbers any better than you can; they have no meaning. Four doesn't mean anything except it's higher than three and lower than five. There's no way I can picture it, and if I cannot picture it I cannot remember it.

Q: So how do you go about picturing it?

A: I have given each digit a sound. There are ten digits and

also ten basic consonant sounds in English, like puh, vuh, cuh, and so on, and I gave one of the ten sounds to each digit. To make it simple, one to me has always represented the sound tuh or duh; two was always nuh as in Nancy, three was always M, and so forth. Once I do that, the problem is simple. Give me a two-digit number.

Q: Thirty-four.

A: Thirty-four to me is "mayor." Now I can picture a mayor.

Q: In each case you make a word out of it.

A: Yes, or a phrase. For example, the word dentist to me is 12101. There are five consonant sounds that represent five digits. I can picture a dentist—that's easy— but I cannot picture 12101.

Q: That's terrific. You've taken five meaningless digits and made one simple word.

A: My systems also enable you to remember dentist associated with anything else. A number always has to be remembered with something else. For example, 12101 might be someone's address. All memory breaks down to entities of two. Obvious examples are names and faces. If you know just the name, what good does it do you? If I call you Mr. Smith because you walked in with him and I call him Mr. Freedman, whom am I impressing? Nobody.

Q: Right. It's like the old joke about knowing lots of dates— 1947, 1851, 1468. I have no idea what happened on them, but they are dates.

A: Exactly. It's meaningless. To remember the two items I must force my mind to concentrate on that information for a split second and form an image.

Q: And is it usually images you think of, actual visual images?

A: Yes, which is nothing new. Aristotle wrote two books on memory and the first sentence in one of them was, "In order to think we must speculate with images." Forming images is part of what I call the "slap in the face principle." Aristotle was a teacher and when he made a point, do you know what he did? He slapped the student very hard in the face. The student never forgot the point. That's what I apply except I make it painless.

Q: How do you do it painlessly?

A: Silly pictures. If I want to remember a cigarette and a shoe, it's difficult because these are two everyday items. It's the simple, ordinary, everyday things that people tend to forget. It's the obscene, violent, bombastic, and novel they remember. To think of cigarettes and shoes I picture myself wearing gigantic lighted cigarettes instead of shoes. That's a silly picture and I'll never forget it. In other words, what I'm saying is grab your mind by the scruff of the neck and make it *aware*. It's what I call "original awareness";

force information to register *in the first place*. When most people say they forget things, I say they don't remember them in the first place. You've got to make it register originally.

Q: Do you see much of this being done in advertising?

A: Some people do it. The Hawaiian Punch commercial is a good example. "Do you want a Hawaiian punch?" Bang. There's action and they use the name. *Time* magazine asked me what I would do with Peugeot a couple of years ago when we were having the gas shortage. They were trying to get across the point that Peugeot doesn't use much gas. I said, have a full-page ad of a gas station. On the top say "Joe's"— the name of the gas station is Joe's. Show Joe leaning against this gas pump and there are cobwebs all over because he hasn't been selling any gas. Two words: "Poor Joe." Why? Poor Joe sounds like Peugeot. One of the problems is nobody can pronounce the goddamn thing. Poor Joe was the closest I could think of that had meaning and would help you remember the pronunciation of the car. Poor Joe—Peugeot. The gas station has cobwebs, you don't need much gas with a Peugeot.

Q: Terrific ad. Let me ask you another question. What do you do with strange words, foreign words, or nonsense syllables?

A: If I have any philosophy at all in my work, it's simple: take any intangible thing and make it tangible. That's what I teach with foreign words and names. Here's an example. I was in Portugal a few years ago and I happen to be a clam lover. They have the greatest clams in the world and serve them a thousand at a time. Anyway, the first time I was in a restaurant and ordered clams I happened to be with a Portuguese man who spoke English. Nobody in this particular area speaks English, so I asked my friend how to say clams. He said, the word is *amezuis*. This sounds like a complete conglomeration of sounds to me.

Q: And nothing like clams.

A: No connection at all. What I did was saw a picture in my mind, I visualized a gigantic clam walking towards me—it just came out of the sea and was dripping wet, filthy, and dirty. So I looked at the clam and said, "What a mezz you is!"

Q: That's great. I'll never forget it.

Comment

Harry Lorayne is able to remember vast amounts of information and can teach others to do so. It is clear that he uses principles that have been well documented by psychological research. Two obvious examples are his emphasis on giving meaning to the material and his use of imagery. Another principle that he uses but did not mention specifically is the condensation of many units into one--what we have called chunking. He does this ingeniously by transforming five individual digits into one word--dentist. Thus, it seems as if his methods are clever adaptations of principles we have been discussing.

Do you think his "slap in the face" principle explains why imagery is so helpful to memory? How would you apply Mr. Lorayne's methods to remembering what name goes with what face when you meet people at a party? By the way, remember that he can recall the names of hundreds of people after meeting them only once.

is that it takes less time to give the correct answer when the letters are identical than when they are different forms of the same letter. According to Posner, this indicates that with identical letters the subject simply notes that the sensory register contains two identical forms; while with different forms, the subject must use stored information to label each letter by its name and then note that the names are the same. The extra time needed to give an answer is due to this consultation of memory.

Thus, the sensory register contains only perceptual information and not information that has been learned earlier. We respond directly and rapidly to information in the sensory register, but the information remains only briefly. If it is to be retained, it must move to the actual memory system.

Short-Term Memory

The sensory register is where we receive information. Information that is not lost almost immediately then goes to *short-term memory*. When you see a curve in the road you can turn the wheel of the car immediately, but you may not remember it at all a few seconds later because it has left your sensory register and not gone into short-term memory. By repeating to yourself that there was a curve, you can make it enter short-term memory and will be able to recall it for at least a few seconds.

Short-term memory is also involved when we want to deal directly with old information. For example, if someone asks you for your phone number, you bring that information into short-term memory and then supply it. Or if you are asked for the names of three kinds of big cats, you may bring from your memory store all the names of cats and then read off lion, tiger, and leopard. In other words, short-term memory contains the information we are dealing with at any given moment.

The capacity of short-term memory is limited to about seven units. As we mentioned earlier, we have immediate memory for about seven numbers, letters, words, or anything else (the magic number seven). We can deal directly with about this much information and no more—although, of course, by passing information into and out of short-term memory we work with vast amounts of information in a short time.

Information does not stay in short-term memory for long. If you do not repeat the information to yourself or aloud (called *rehearsing*) your ability to recall it declines very sharply. In one study (Peterson and Peterson, 1959), subjects were shown three letters and then instructed to count backward by threes so that they could not repeat the letters to themselves. At various intervals, they were asked to reproduce the original three letters. As you can see in Fig. 4.12, their memory of the letters declined sharply. After only eighteen seconds, in fact, there was practically no recall at all. This might be hard to believe, so try the same experiment yourself. You will find that you have great difficulty remembering the three letters. The explanation seems to be that once information leaves short-term memory, it is forgotten unless it goes into the final stage, which we call long-term memory.

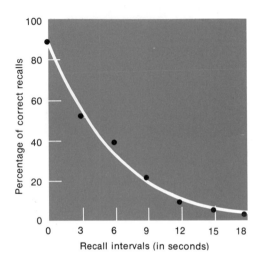

Fig. 4.12
Short-term recall of three letters after counting backward by threes (From Peterson and Peterson, 1959)

Long-Term Memory

Once information enters *long-term memory*, it can stay there indefinitely. Exactly what occurs when information goes from short- to long-term memory is unknown—perhaps a chemical change that produces a lasting memory. Whatever the process, it is clear that the information becomes established, or, as it is usually termed, *consolidated.*

Several sources of evidence support the idea of two kinds of memories and consolidation. Perhaps the most conclusive evidence comes from experiments in which a person is presented with information to which he is not paying attention. (See Chapter 2 for a discussion of this research as it relates to attention.) For example, a subject wearing earphones hears one story in his left ear and a different one in his right ear and is told to pay careful attention only to the story entering his right ear (Broadbent, 1962). If he follows these instructions, he will be able to repeat with great accuracy the story he hears with his right ear, and will recall almost nothing about the other story. On the other hand, if the sound to both ears is turned off and he is asked immediately what he just heard in his left ear, he will be able to report it with considerable accuracy. Apparently, the information entering both ears goes into short-term memory and can be retrieved briefly. But only the information entering the ear to which the subject is paying attention goes from short-term to long-term memory.

Similar phenomena occur often in our daily lives. When you drive a car, you generally pay attention to the traffic and barely notice signs and other landmarks. At the end of the drive, you probably could not recall whether you had passed a red barn or had seen a particular billboard. But if you were asked immediately after passing the red barn, you would probably remember seeing it. All of the information about the scenery goes into the sensory register; some goes into short-term memory; but most of it fails to reach long-term memory and is forgotten. However, some information about your drive is transferred to long-term memory. This tends to be important information, such as landmarks that tell you where to turn or an impressive incident such as a near accident or a fire along the road. And we also remember lots of trivial bits of information that get into long-term memory more or less by chance. You may forget almost everything about the drive except a particular tree or one stretch of road that, for reasons we cannot specify, just happens to be stored in your long-term memory.

The three types of memory compose a highly efficient system that allows us to deal with the current situation by means of sensory and short-term memory but preserves the space in long-term memory for relatively important information. This system may be the reason why we always seem to be able to store more information. If every bit of information were treated equally, even our huge storage might eventually be filled up and we would be unable to store new information without displacing the old. Moreover, the endless bits of trivia might make it more difficult to find the information we really need. As it is, we store what seems more important (although we all seem to remember vast amounts of trivia, too) and discard the rest.

How Is Learning Stored?

But where and how is the information stored? Although psychologists now know quite a bit about how memory operates, they have only begun to investigate the actual mechanism by which it is accomplished. For many years psychologists searched like gold prospectors for the *engram*, a hypothetical structure constituting a memory. Since our memories must exist somewhere, it was believed that there must be electrical currents, pathways, or some other physical entity that contains the information. It is now reasonably clear that the first two possibilities are not correct. The brain does not have specific electrical circuits or paths for each piece of information. However, there is some evidence that learning is stored as chemical changes in brain cells.

Learning as chemical changes in the brain We know that some cells in the body carry vast amounts of information. The genes contain

Box 4.5

MEMORY CONSOLIDATION AND ELECTRIC SHOCK THERAPY

The effects of electric shock therapy provide additional evidence that memories are consolidated, and that the process of consolidation takes some time. Strong electric shocks are sometimes applied to the heads of patients suffering from severe depression (see Chapter 17 for a discussion of this treatment). One major effect of this treatment is some memory loss. The patients totally forget all or most of the events that immediately preceded the shock. They also lose some long-term memories, but this loss is much less severe and is more selective. Experiments with animals confirm that these results are not limited to humans. Whatever the mechanism by which memories are stored, the shock obviously destroys those memories that have not yet been consolidated but has relatively little effect on memories that have had more time to become fixed (Glickman, 1961; McGaugh, 1966).

The process is even more complicated, however, because some memories that are lost immediately after shock treatment recover spontaneously or can be retrieved with clues. For example, if someone forgets that her doctor is named Reynolds, she might remember it if she is told that it starts with an "R" or is a brand of aluminum foil. And this recovery of seemingly lost memories holds for both recent and long-term information. In addition, animals that have learned a response and are shocked immediately afterwards relearn the response more quickly than animals that have not received the initial training (Geller and Jarvik, 1968; Miller and Springer, 1973). This indicates that the shocked animals retained some memory of the training even though it did not show up right after the shock.

Various explanations of this recovery phenomenon have been offered. One clear possibility is that the shock only weakens some of the memories, and these recover or are recoverable. Another explanation is that the short-term memory is destroyed, but the information has already begun to enter long-term memory and has been partially consolidated there. And it has recently been suggested (Miller and Springer, 1973) that the shock interferes not only with consolidation but also with retrieval, so that the memory is still there but cannot be retrieved. In any case, the fact that recent memories are lost more than older ones indicates that consolidation does take place and that some time is needed for it to be completed.

information in the form of minor variations in the chemical structure of the DNA (deoxyribonucleic acid) molecules that determine the makeup of the entire organism. Because DNA is capable of coding huge amounts of information, it is possible that RNA (ribonucleic acid), a close relative of DNA, may be capable of such coding also. And because RNA exists in the brain, perhaps RNA plays a role in memory.

This idea is still highly speculative because research has provided only inconsistent support. Flexner and Flexner (1967) injected mice with chemicals that block the formation of RNA, and the animals learned less well and forgot what they had already learned. Barondes (1970) got similar results. Also, injecting rats with RNA has been found to improve learning (Siegel, 1967; Davidson and Cook, 1970). And research by Ungar (1973) suggests that specific memory molecules exist. However, other experiments (Cohen and Barondes, 1967) have failed to confirm these results, so there is considerable skepticism about them. A more consistent finding is that the relevant RNA in the brain undergoes appreciable chemical changes following learning (Hyden and Lange, 1970). This suggests that RNA is somehow involved in memory, even though it may not be the sole location of the memory.

Chemical transfer of learning—the worm returns Startling but more questionable evidence has been provided by experiments in which brain cells from an animal that has learned something are transferred to another animal, resulting in some transfer of the learning. In a series of studies, James McConnell (1962) classically conditioned planaria (primitive worms) and then injected some of their cells containing RNA into other planaria. Those receiving the injection learned the conditioned response more quickly than those who were not injected. Similar results have been reported by investigators in Denmark (Fjerdingstad, Nissen, and Roigaard-Petersen, 1965) and the United States (Jacobson et al., 1965) using rats. Moreover, Jacobson's group reported the same effect when RNA was taken from hamsters and given to rats. These results suggest that the learning was contained in the RNA molecules and was passed along to other organisms.

Imagine the implications if this finding were proved accurate! We would no longer have to study any subject. There could be educational drugstores containing bottles of pills labeled French, Latin, Italian, Psychology, Geology, Physics, and so on. We would merely have to take the pills to know all the information. Of course, if the only way to produce the pills were to extract RNA from the brain cells of the experts, there could be some tough legal and moral problems. Brilliant experts might well prefer to keep their own brain cells rather than pass them on.

Unfortunately for those who dislike studying, there has been great difficulty in duplicating these results and there is now considerable doubt about their validity. Many of the original experiments contained errors in design or execution, and more controlled work has not found the same effects. A paper by twenty-three investigators summarizing research in this area reported unanimously negative results (Byrne et al., 1966). However, findings continue to be mixed and the controversy continues (Cartwright, 1970, got positive results; Cherkin, 1970, negative ones). Thus, although the transfer of learning by ingesting or absorbing RNA cells should still be considered a possibility, it is not now accepted by most psychologists.

Despite these negative findings, it is still generally believed that RNA is involved in some way in the storage of learning or at least that this storage is chemical in nature. However, we have a long way to go before we understand the physiological or chemical mechanisms by which the storage of learning is accomplished.

WHY WE FORGET

Although human memory is extremely efficient and has an enormous capacity, we do forget huge amounts of information, including some that is presumably in long-term memory. You may remember the first telephone number you ever had, but you have certainly forgotten lots of other numbers. You may not remember your first-grade teacher's name, the capital of North Dakota, the formula for the volume of a sphere, a friend's address, or the losing candidate for vice-president in 1972. Moreover, sometimes you temporarily forget your present phone number or even the name of your best friend. Information you knew perfectly well before you entered a room to take an exam may suddenly slip from your mind when a question is asked. Why is information that has been learned forgotten either temporarily or completely? The three major reasons that have been suggested as causes of forgetting are decay, interference, and retrieval failure.

Copyright © 1975 by permission of Bernard Schoenbaum and Saturday Review

Decay

The simplest explanation for forgetting is that with the passage of time information gets weaker and weaker until it disappears. Just as unused muscles eventually atrophy, so unused memories decay until they can no longer be recalled.

It is likely that the process of decay plays a role in the loss of short-term memory. It probably also plays a role in the loss of information that has reached long-term memory but that has not been very well learned. If you cram for an examination and memorize a long list of dates, names, and events, the information must reach long-term memory in order for you to use it on the exam. However, if you do not continue to use the information, you will begin to lose it immediately after the test. Eventually most of it will disappear. We may remember the dates 1066, 1492, and 1789 and what happened in those years from high-school history courses, but most of us forget crucial dates such as 1215, 1453, 1517, and even 1865. It seems likely that this kind of forgetting is due largely to the fact that the material was not learned well originally.

If memory is stored chemically it may be that the chemical change is not entirely stable. It lasts for a while, but eventually breaks down and the memory is lost. Decay, however, is not the whole story. We often remember information that we have not used for many years but do not remember other similar information. If decay were the only process causing forgetting, all information that was equally well learned should be equally well forgotten. Yet this is not the case.

Interference

In order to remember accurately, we must distinguish one word, figure, image, or other stimulus from every other one. When one item is substituted for or confused with another, it is called *interference*, and this naturally tends to weaken or even remove the memory. For example, when you first study physiology you may learn about the hypothalamus, the pituitary, and the thyroid glands. The names of these three organs are quite different, and each has a different function, so it is fairly easy to remember this information. As you study more, you will learn about the pineal, thalamus, and hippocampus. Unfortunately, these three organs have names and functions somewhat similar to the previous ones. Because this new information and the old are so similar, they will tend to become confused and you will remember the original information less well. You may no longer be certain whether it is the hypothalamus, the hippocampus, or the thalamus that controls eating; or whether the name of the organ is the hypothalamus or the hippothalamus. Add to this the words thyroid, thymus, hypothyroid, and hydrocephalic, all of which are somewhat related to physiology, and you will have more and more difficulty keeping everything straight.

Over many years, you receive so much new information that there is interference with virtually everything you have learned. Certain associations are so strong that they last indefinitely despite interference, and some are so unique that new material creates little interference. But in most cases, memories are weakened by new associations that create confusion among stimuli.

Box 4.6

INTERFERENCE VERSUS DECAY

The difference between interference and decay has been studied in experiments by Underwood (1973), Wickelgren (1965), and many others. The basic method is for all subjects to learn a list of words or word pairs. Some subjects then learn a second list that is similar to the first, some learn a dissimilar list, and some perform an unrelated activity. Finally, all subjects are asked to recall the original list. Those who learn a dissimilar list remember the first list less well than those who perform an unrelated activity; and those who learn a similar list remember the most poorly of all. Clearly, the memory loss is due to interference.

But even the group that performs the unrelated task remembers the first list less well than they did immediately after they had learned it. Was this due to decay or to interference from other sources? In a study to test this, subjects had to learn a list and then either go to sleep or continue their normal daily activities (Jenkins and Dallenbach, 1924). As shown in the figure, subjects who slept after learning the list forgot less of it than did those who remained awake. Apparently, normal daily activities, even if they are not directly related to the original learning, produce some interference. This does not eliminate the possibility that some decay occurred (note that even the sleeping subjects forgot some of the items) but it does show that interference plays a major role in forgetting.

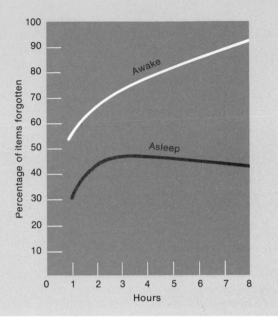

Proactive and retroactive interference We usually distinguish between two types of interference—*proactive,* in which new material is harder to learn because of its similarity to old information; and *retroactive,* in which old information is harder to remember because of new information. The mechanism is the same in both types, and almost always works in both directions. It is harder to learn that optometrists give eye tests if you have already learned that ophthalmologists are eye surgeons (proactive interference); but you are also more likely to forget the definition of ophthalmologist when you try to learn about optometrists (retroactive interference).

As you can see from the preceding examples, the more similar the stimuli are to other stimuli, the more interference will occur. We are more likely to confuse optometrists with ophthalmologists than with dermatologists or giraffes. The similarity can occur along any dimension—spelling, sound, function, appearance, and so on. But in all cases, the more similarity, the more interference and the greater the effect on memory.

Retrieval Failure

Still another reason we forget is that we are unable to find the information even though it is still stored in the brain. This distinction between loss of memory and failure of retrieval is quite important because different processes are involved. In the former, the memory is no longer in storage, it is lost; in the latter, the memory is there, but for some reason you cannot bring it into short-term memory.

Tip-of-the-tongue phenomenon The difference between memory storage and retrieval is illustrated nicely by those occasions on which you know that you have a particular piece of information but cannot quite recall it. The information is there somewhere—it is on the *tip of your tongue.* You know the name of the famous psychologist who worked with pigeons and boxes—you were just talking about him yesterday—but you cannot remember it. It's not Shinman or Kindler. No, it starts with S, you're pretty sure of that. Is it Swindler, Singer, Sinder, Skindler . . . no, but ah, finally, Skinner.

Systematic research on the tip-of-the-tongue phenomenon (Brown and McNeill, 1966) indicates that people usually remember certain aspects of the word even though they cannot produce the whole thing. Generally, we remember the first letter of the answer. The next most common piece of information is the approximate length of the word—the number of syllables and even how long they are. And there may also be some memory of other letters in the word, such as a key consonant (the k in Skinner). When we try to recall the word, the other, incorrect answers tend to resemble the right one in terms of sound rather than meaning. We would try Shindler and Skinman rather than words that have related meanings but do not sound similar to the one we are looking for, like Miller or Tolman. This suggests that the difficulty in retrieval involves the specific sound and structure of the word, rather than its meaning.

Research by Freedman and Landauer (1966) showed that people who were given clues such as the first letter or last syllable of the answer often suddenly got the right answer. Try this yourself. If you cannot think of a word you are sure you know, try first to think of the first letter or have someone give you the first letter. You will probably find that the correct answer pops into your head soon after you know the beginning letter. Apparently, the retrieval system needs a clue to get it working again.

Motivated forgetting Another possible reason for retrieval failure is that we do not want to remember a particular piece of information. Everyone has unpleasant experiences and associations. A word or image might remind us of a painful accident, of an unhappy love affair, or of fears, anxieties, or conflicts within us. Sometimes we would rather not remember this kind of information and, by a mechanism that we do not fully understand, we manage not to retrieve it. We shall discuss this idea of motivated forgetting in more detail when we consider Freud's psychoanalytic theory in Chapter 16.

At the moment we do not know very much about why the retrieval system fails, but it does seem clear that not remembering is often due to problems with retrieval rather than storage. In fact, the retrieval process is perhaps even more important than the ability to store information in the first place, and therefore a great deal of attention is being paid to it by psychologists. Having discussed reasons for forgetting—decay, interference, and retrieval failure—let us now turn to a consideration of memory retrieval, one of the most basic processes in mental functioning.

MEMORY RETRIEVAL

In an important lawsuit, a major corporation was charged with destroying the index that made it possible to retrieve information stored on computer tapes. This was a serious situation because, although the information was still there, there was no way to retrieve it without the index. Imagine what it would be like if human beings had no memory retrieval system! No matter how great our capacity to store information, it would be useless if we could not find the information when we needed it. It would be like having a library of a million books with no index, card catalogue, or titles on the books. To find anything we would have to spend so long randomly searching that it would hardly be worthwhile.

Fortunately, the human memory system is not only large but amazingly accessible. By some process that we are far from understanding completely, we can usually reach into our enormous store of information and pluck out the one small bit we need, and we can do this with remarkable accuracy and efficiency. Asked to give the capital of the United States, most Americans can tell you immediately what it is. We can give our telephone number, the name of our school, our textbook, the name of a famous psychologist who worked on learning in pigeons, the score of a recent basketball game, and practically anything else that we have at one time learned well, and we accomplish this retrieval in a matter of seconds or less. Even if we have not thought about a particular piece of information for years, we are often able to retrieve it just as quickly as if we had thought about it last week or even an hour ago. This ability to retrieve diverse bits of information long after they have been learned and with almost no delay is one of our most remarkable capabilities.

Before discussing the little we know about how this retrieval is accomplished, it is important to make clear the distinction between memory storage and retrieval. Although this may seem like a somewhat arbitrary distinction (since you cannot know if it is stored unless eventually it is retrieved), different processes are involved. This is shown clearly by the difference between recall and recognition tests of memory.

Recall versus Recognition

Look at questions 1 and 2. Which is easier to answer?

1. Which worm was experimented on in studies of the chemical transmission of memory?
2. The worm that has been used in experiments on the chemical transmission of memory is the:

   a) earthworm   c) planaria
   b) prentaxia   d) asparagus

Most people would choose question 2 (the correct answer is c). The fact is, it is much easier to *recognize* the right answer from a group than to recall or produce it ourselves. This is true in part because the answer has been narrowed down to four choices, so just by guessing you still have a 25 percent chance of being right—recall would require that you select the correct response from thousands of possibilities. But another reason a multiple-choice question is easier to answer is that even if there were a large number of choices and many of them were similar (produria, plenaxura, plenabitude, planaria, and so on), you are relieved of the additional task of retrieving the exact word yourself. And as we have discussed, this aspect of the retrieval process sometimes breaks down even if you do have the correct piece of information in your memory.

Recognition is exceedingly powerful and accurate, particularly if the individual has to decide only whether a particular item has been seen before. When you meet someone, you probably know if you have seen her before, even if you do not know her name or when you saw her. Although, as we discussed earlier, most of us can recall only about seven items after a brief exposure, we can recognize hundreds after seeing them only once (Shepard, 1967).

Models of Human Memory Retrieval

We do not yet know enough about how the human mind functions to propose detailed models of information retrieval. At the moment, the best we can do is suggest the types of processes that are probably involved and eliminate those that are probably not. The first step is to describe how information is stored in memory, and then we can begin to understand how it is retrieved.

Organization of memory It seems highly likely that the information in our memory is not stored in an entirely aimless, random way. Rather, it is probably organized according to fairly specific rules and principles. One reason for believing this is that we almost always tend to organize our world instead of leaving it unorganized. As we discussed in Chapter 2, our perceptions are organized according to various principles; and as we shall see in Chapter 6, we form concepts of all sorts of things and organize our thoughts to coincide with these concepts. In addition, the way in which we recall information suggests that it is stored in an organized manner. If you are asked to give the names of some animals, you can usually reel off lots of animal names almost without pausing between them, and the same would hold for any familiar category. This implies that somewhere in memory you have grouped together the names of animals into one category. In contrast, if someone asks you to name animals that are taller than they are long or have shaggy hair, you will probably take a lot longer to find examples—presumably because this is not a typical way of categorizing animals and therefore they are not organized that way in your memory. These are by no means definitive arguments that memory is organized in a particular way, but they do support the idea.

Various specific suggestions have been made as to how memory is organized. Many of them are based on the assumption that the organization is built around noun categories and that memory is hierarchical, with larger categories over smaller ones that are over

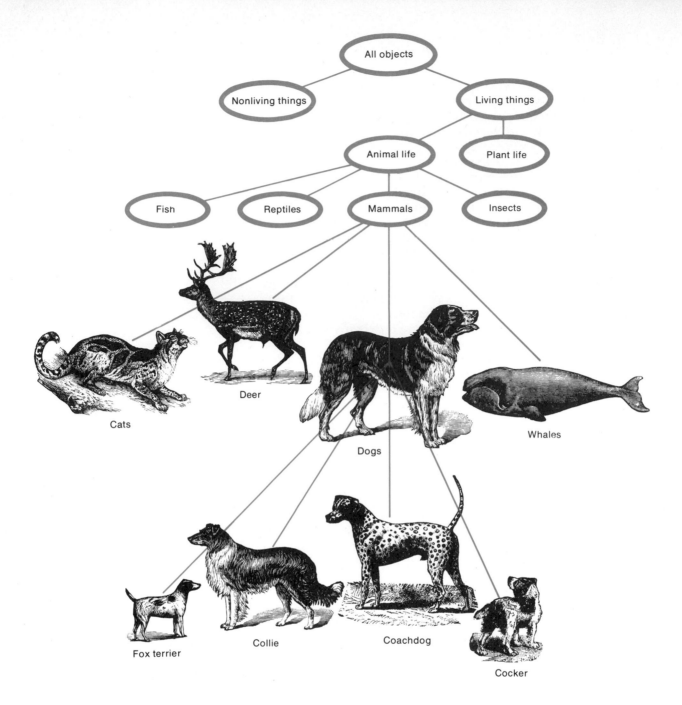

Fig. 4.13
Hierarchical model of memory

Smaller categories are grouped under larger ones. To discover if a word (for example, collie) is a member of a category (for example, living things), you find the word and search the hierarchy. (After Collins and Quillian, 1969)

still smaller ones. An example of such a model is shown in Fig. 4.13. In this organization (Collins and Quillian, 1969), each of the larger categories includes all the smaller ones under it. For example, living things includes animals, which include mammals, which include dogs. Although not shown in the figure, the organization probably includes information about the entries at each level. That is, along with "animals" are some descriptive words such as "move around," "reproduce," and so on; and along with dogs would be characteristics that are common to all dogs.

Despite its complexity, this organization is clearly an oversimplification of the actual situation. Each person will differ in the number of category levels—a biologist, for example, would include many more levels and more sophisticated types of categories for this particular set of words. In addition, there are probably categories based on characteristics other than noun classes—functional or descriptive categories. For example, we may have a category of edible items. Or we might classify objects according to size, so that elephants, redwood trees, dams, King Kong, and other large objects will be stored together. In other words, there are probably many different types of organizations, with many items in more than one category, and with categories overlapping rather than being neatly hierarchical as in the figure. The point is that even if this hierarchical structure is correct, it almost certainly does not account for the full plan of organization of human memory.

Retrieval Processes

Having some idea of the organization of memory, we can then proceed to consider how memory retrieval occurs. In particular, psychologists have distinguished between two types of processes: sequential ones, in which one step follows another; and parallel ones, in which two or more steps occur simultaneously. There is no reason to believe that retrieval is dependent on only one of these types of processes, but we can ask whether both are involved and, if so, when each operates.

Sequential processing—random search The simplest mechanism for memory retrieval would be a random sequential search. This search begins at some point in the memory store and looks aimlessly, with no order, considering one item at a time, until it finds the correct piece of information. For example, to find the name of the losing vice-presidential candidate in 1976, you would simply take items one at a time as they appeared. So, you might start with candidate, since that was what you were asked, then have asparagus, Shakespeare, island, zoo, witness, France, and so on until you happen to find Dole, the correct answer. In each case, you take the information that comes with the item to see if it is correct. This could be done very rapidly, perhaps hundreds or even thousands of items a minute, but would still be terribly inefficient. For each question you would have to search through vast amounts of information before getting the right answer. Even if the search were not *entirely* random, but progressed from one item to others associated with it, the search would be long. Although we may occasionally resort to more or less random searches, it seems unlikely that our retrieval could be so fast and accurate if it depended to any great extent on this kind of process.

Directed search Another type of sequential processing is based on the model of organization we discussed previously. According to this model, we find information by searching along organized pathways in the hierarchy. Thus, to find out whether a collie was a dog, we would find the item collie, and then search along various connecting pathways to find out whether we eventually found the item dog. In this case, collie is directly under dog and so we quickly are able to answer yes. If the question were whether a collie was an animal, we would have to search further—first to dog, then to animal. Again the search is along these existing pathways, but the distance traveled is further. Therefore, it should take somewhat longer to answer this second

ELIZABETH LOFTUS

question. Sure enough, it does take slightly longer to say that a collie is an animal than that it is a dog; or more generally to say that something is or is not a member of a larger category than a smaller category (Collins and Quillian, 1969; Meyer, 1970; Landauer and Freedman, 1968). The differences are very small, but they do seem to be consistent. Thus, the evidence supports the idea that memory is organized according to some kind of hierarchical structure and that memory retrieval involves a search along pathways within that structure.

Simultaneous processing Although some kind of directed, successive search process probably does occur in certain types of memory retrieval, there is also evidence that a simultaneous process is used. This is especially relevant when people are asked to produce or recall a word rather than simply decide whether or not something is a member of a category. In one study (Freedman and Loftus, 1974) subjects were asked to produce a member of a familiar category that began with a particular letter (for example, a country beginning with *H* or an animal beginning with *Z*). Try some of these items in Fig. 4.14 and try to note how rapidly you got the right answer. There are two findings of interest. First, people are very good at this task. No matter how obscure the answers, the typical subjects gave the right answer very rapidly. Second, neither the size of the category nor the number of possible correct items made much difference. People gave the name of a dog beginning with *C* as quickly as they gave an animal beginning with *C* even though there are many more animals and obviously many more items that are correct. If it were necessary to search through the category using successive steps, the size of the category should affect retrieval time. Because it does not, it seems likely that some kind of simultaneous process is involved—perhaps a search through many different categories at once, or a search that begins in several different places within a category and considers items at the

Fig. 4.14
Memory retrieval items

Category	Beginning letter	Answer	Time
animal	Z	_____	_____
country	H	_____	_____
planet	P	_____	_____
ocean	I	_____	_____
island	M	_____	_____
tree	E	_____	_____
fruit	K	_____	_____
dog	A	_____	_____
lake	S	_____	_____
city	R	_____	_____

same time. We do not know precisely what process is involved, but this work indicates that the simple hierarchical model with a sequential search along pathways is not sufficient by itself. It does seem to play a role in certain kinds of retrieval, but other processes are also involved.

We are still at the beginning stages of understanding memory retrieval. We have evidence that some organization of memory is likely, that random sequential search is rarely used, that search along hierarchical pathways probably does occur, and that some kind of simultaneous processing is involved. But we do not know the specific mechanisms by which retrieval is accomplished, nor exactly what determines which of the mechanisms operates under any given circumstances. This is perhaps one of the most fascinating questions left for psychologists because in a sense it asks how the human mind functions.

APPLICATIONS OF LEARNING RESEARCH TO EDUCATION

As we have seen, much of the emphasis of research on learning has been on the factors that facilitate or inhibit learning. Even though there is still considerable controversy about exactly how and why these factors operate, there is general agreement as to their effect. We know that repetition, partial reinforcement, distinctiveness, chunking, and distributed practice have important, predictable effects on how well material is learned. Therefore, it is understandable that great attention has been paid to applying this knowledge to education, in an effort to teach material more efficiently and effectively. Two methods that are based on various principles of learning are programmed instruction and computer-assisted instruction.

Programmed Instruction

When a teacher writes a textbook or delivers a lecture, she is trying to impart as much information as possible to the student. She tries to organize the material and make it clear and easily understood. However, she does not ordinarily worry too much about how the student is going to study the material. That is left up to the student.

A programmed textbook or teaching machine also presents the material in a clear and organized fashion. But the program is designed so that the student will study the material efficiently and effectively. It forces the student to learn the material as he moves from one section to the next; it gives immediate reinforcement when he is right and, in some cases, additional training when he is wrong.

The basic method of most programmed instruction is to present a small bit of information and then make the student do something active to demonstrate that he has learned it. For example, each unit may contain a series of short statements followed by either a question or a statement with a word left out, and the student is required to respond with the crucial word or phrase. After he has given his response, he is shown the correct answer and thus receives immediate feedback as to whether he was right. Because the material is presented in such small units, the student gives mostly correct responses so he receives many positive reinforcements.

Other programs, in particular those designed to be controlled by a computer, apply the same basic principles but have many variations or *branches*. In this kind of program, a student who makes errors is given more training on the material he has missed, while a student who gets all the answers correct is given new material to learn. Each student learns at his own pace and is drilled only when he needs it. In a sense, this is a method of forcing the student to respond actively to the material and to receive additional training when he is not learning it.

Computer-Assisted Instruction

Computer-assisted instruction (CAI) is very similar to programmed instruction; both apply the same principles of learning to education. However, the computer, because of its enormous capacity, can handle extremely complex programs. A complicated programmed textbook could conceivably have two or three branches, but a computer could easily handle dozens or even hundreds of program variations. In computer-assisted instruction, the student is shown the material and communicates her answer to the computer. The computer tells her if she is correct or not, and, if she is not, gives her the correct answer. Then, on the basis of the student's performance, the computer chooses the next material to present.

Communication between the subject and the computer can be accomplished in a variety of ways. An elaborate system was used by Richard Atkinson and Patrick Suppes of Stanford University in a long-term project conducted during the 1960's. Each student sat in front of a console containing a cathode-ray tube, a typewriter, and a screen. The computer would show pictures on the screen and write questions or information on the cathode-ray tube, and the student responded either by typing her answer or by indicating her choice of answers on the tube with a special light-pen. Simpler devices have used just a typewriter, with both computer and student typing material. Still other systems have attempted to have a computer communicate by asking questions over a telephone, with the student responding by pressing the appropriate button on a push-button phone. However the communication is accomplished, computers have been shown to be enormously effective because they can adjust the program to optimize each student's learning.

Computer-assisted instruction may sound at first like part of a nightmarish futuristic society with disembodied machines running the schools and humans being phased out. However, it is far more likely that computers will aid teachers rather than replace them. The teacher will still be present, especially to help students who need guidance and to provide some instruction, but the computer could relieve the teacher of many burdens and free him to devote time to these other tasks.

The computer is particularly helpful in arousing the interest and holding the attention of young or disadvantaged students. It makes learning fun because the student sits in front of a strange-looking machine that does all sorts of tricks. This makes the experience more like a game. And holding the attention of the learner and increasing her motivation greatly improves performance. Although this aspect of the computer is probably less important in teaching college students, even at this level it can help maintain interest.

Perhaps the major advantage of a computer is that it can drill the student, a task that most teachers do not have either the time or the patience to perform. No teacher is able to sit with thirty students for an hour a day and teach each to read. At best, a teacher can drill an entire class at the same time. But the computer can give individualized instruction to each student, remembering exactly what her performance was the preceding day, month, or year, and tailoring the instruction to her needs. In addition, the computer is always attentive, always gives immediate feedback, is never frustrated by a slow learner, and treats all students equally and fairly.

It seems clear that computer-assisted instruction should be most useful in teaching basic skills such as reading and arithmetic to young children, especially those who are culturally deprived. A project at Stanford University has in fact demonstrated that underprivileged children taught by computers and teachers learned arithmetic and reading much faster than students who were taught only by teachers. Unfortunately, the federal government has greatly reduced its support for research on these techniques and therefore the development of computer-assisted instruction has slowed down considerably. Nevertheless, it does seem to hold tremendous promise for the future. ■

RICHARD C. ATKINSON

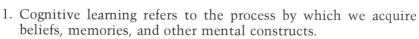

Summary

1. Cognitive learning refers to the process by which we acquire beliefs, memories, and other mental constructs.

2. We learn much information by contiguity—forming associations among stimuli that appear together at the same time. Learning by contiguity is simple and automatic. It does not require an unconditioned stimulus, as in classical conditioning, nor reinforcement, as in operant conditioning.

3. Stimulus materials that are familiar and/or distinctive are learned more easily than materials that are unfamiliar or do not

stand out. Organizing separate units into larger chunks—called chunking—enables us to remember them more easily.

4. Forming associations is easier if prior associations exist among the stimuli to be learned, if the stimuli are meaningful (and therefore familiar), and if we use imagery to form a visual association among them.

5. As in other kinds of learning, repetition increases learning by association. The timing of presentations also affects how easily material is learned. Practicing something over a period of time (distributed practice) is more efficient than practicing or studying intensely over a short period of time (massed practice).

6. In order to be retained, information must be incorporated into the memory system. Information passes through three stages: the sensory register, short-term memory, and, finally, long-term memory.

7. The sensory register is a sensory store where perceptions are registered for less than a second. If the information is not lost after this second, it moves into short-term memory, which has a capacity of around seven units of information. Information can be recalled from short-term memory for at least a few seconds and information from long-term memory moves into short-term memory when we want to deal with it directly. Information that reaches long-term memory has been consolidated by rehearsal and can remain there indefinitely.

8. Forgetting can be accounted for by decay, interference, and retrieval failure.

9. Information in short-term memory probably decays because it has not been fully learned; similarly, information in long-term memory that has not been learned well is also probably lost by decay.

10. Interference involves substituting or confusing a new item of information with an old item. This tends to weaken the memory of the original information. In proactive interference, new material is harder to learn because it is similar to old information; in retroactive interference, old information is harder to remember because of new information.

11. Memories can become distorted by assimilation—altering memories to fit previously learned information.

12. Research suggests that both successive scanning and directed search play a role in memory retrieval. Scanning is probably important in retrieval from short-term memory, whereas direct processes are dominant in retrieval from long-term memory. Psychologists are only beginning to understand the specific mechanisms by which memory retrieval occurs.

13. Learning research is being applied to education to facilitate more efficient and effective teaching. Programmed learning organizes the material to be studied, provides immediate feedback, and enables students to work at their own pace. Computer-assisted instruction is especially successful with disadvantaged children because the machine arouses interest and increases motivation.

RECOMMENDED READING

Klatsky, R. *Human Memory.* San Francisco: Freeman, 1975. An upper-level undergraduate or graduate text that covers the field of memory in detail.

Loftus, E. F., and G. R. Loftus. *Human Memory.* New York: Wiley, 1976. Another book that gives an up-to-date summary of what we know about memory. Well written and clear.

Luria, A. R. *The Mind of a Mnemonist.* New York: Basic Books, 1968. A fascinating account that tells us a lot about how memory might work.

Norman, D. A., Ed. *Models of Human Memory.* New York: Academic, 1970. A difficult book that presents theoretical accounts of how memory operates.

Posner, M. I. *Cognition: An Introduction.* Glenview, Illinois: Scott, Foresman, 1973. An introduction to the field by one of the most important psychologists active in it right now.

A	B
strong –	big –
tall –	warm –
bean –	corn –
house –	book –
horse –	dog –
grass –	sky –
lake –	car –
rose –	thin –
man –	bird –
shirt –	sugar –

Try to supply the pairs to these words from Fig. 4.5. Did you remember more from list B than from list A?

"Then you should say what you mean," the March Hare went on.
"I do," Alice hastily replied; "at least—at least I mean what I say—that's the same thing, you know."
"Not the same thing a bit!" said the Hatter. "Why, you might just as well say 'I see what I eat' is the same thing as 'I eat what I see!'"
Lewis Carroll,
Alice's Adventures in Wonderland

5 Language

The importance of language ■ *Elements of language* ■ *How language develops* ■ *How language is acquired* ■ *Can other animals acquire language?* ■ *Language and thought* ■ *Nonverbal communication* ■ *Language in perspective*

P eople who travel to a country where no one speaks their language really appreciate how important language is in almost all aspects of our lives. If you cannot speak the language, the simplest things become enormously difficult. How do you find the post office, bathroom, or nearest bar when you cannot ask someone? Imagine trying to tell someone that you like them when you cannot say it in words. Romantic fiction tells us that all we need to do is gaze into their eyes and they will know. As we shall see, this does help, but in fact it is not so easy. And communicating ideas, values, attitudes, or other complex thoughts is virtually impossible without language. In a sense, someone who does not have language cannot participate fully in human society.

The development of language may be the most remarkable human accomplishment. It is almost certainly the one that distinguishes us most from all other species. To be sure, other animals communicate, using songs, cries, grunts, facial expressions, and bodily gestures to convey information. Some animals, such as the rhesus monkey, the chimpanzee, and the porpoise, even use a fairly extensive series of verbal communications (see Table 5.1). But only human beings have developed the highly complex, systematic capability of language.

Language is closely related to the process we call thinking. We shall discuss this relationship briefly in this chapter, but our primary focus will be on the elements of language and language acquisition. In Chapter 6 we will take up the question of what thinking is, how people form concepts, the processes involved in problem solving, and intellectual creativity.

Table 5.1
RHESUS CALLS

Call	Description	Situational context
Roar	Long, fairly loud noise	Made by a very confident animal, when threatening another of inferior rank
Pant-threat	Like a roar, but divided into "syllables"	Made by a less confident animal, who wants support in making an attack
Bark	Like the single bark of a dog	Made by a threatening animal who is not aggressive enough to move forward
Growl	Like a bark, but quieter, shriller, and broken into short units	Made by a mildly alarmed animal
Shrill bark	Not described	Alarm call
Screech	Involves an abrupt pitch change, up then down	Made when threatening a higher-ranked animal
Geckering screech	Like a screech, but broken into syllables	Made when threatened by another animal
Scream	Shorter than a screech and without a rise and fall	Made when losing a fight and being bitten
Squeak	Short, very high noise	Made by a defeated and exhausted animal at the end of a fight

Source: Marler and Hamilton, 1966; after Rowell and Hinde, 1962.

THE IMPORTANCE OF LANGUAGE

Human language is characterized by the use of symbols—sounds, letters, or signs that stand for something else. By manipulating these symbols we can describe the world around us, express our thoughts and feelings, and communicate complex ideas. Language provides us with a history. We can describe and preserve in memory what came before. In short, because we have language we can accumulate a degree of knowledge, experience, and self-awareness unmatched by the most intelligent of other animals.

Moreover, language plays a key role in much of human learning. Other animals learn primarily by the slow process of trial and error, and to some extent by imitation. Anyone who has tried to teach a rat to press a lever to get food knows how tedious this can be. A talented, patient experimenter can shape the rat's behavior so that it presses the bar consistently after hundreds of reinforcements, but it takes many hours or even days.

How different the process is with humans. To teach the same behavior to a person, all we have to do is say "Press the lever to get food." No trial and error is necessary; humans learn what to do simply by hearing or reading instructions. Much complex learning can be accomplished in this manner, and the instructions can be as long and complicated as necessary to impart all of the information.

Obviously, verbal instructions do not always produce perfect performance. Particularly if the behavior is complicated, some practice is necessary. Most of us did not drive a car perfectly the first time we tried, even though we had been told exactly what to do, had read instruction booklets, and had watched others drive. Similarly, an instructor and books can teach you how to hold a tennis racket, where to aim the ball, and the basic principles of the game, but only practice will enable you to play well. In short, it is important to keep the role of language in perspective. Language is vital to complex human learning and speeds up the process greatly, but it does not ordinarily eliminate the need for practice, particularly when physical skills are involved.

ELEMENTS OF LANGUAGE

Phonemes

The most basic elements of a language are *phonemes*—the elementary sounds made by a speaker. In fact, each phoneme represents a range of sounds that are perceived and used as one sound in a language. A New Yorker and a Texan pronounce an *r* quite differently, but it is still heard as the same sound.

English has approximately forty-five phonemes, while other languages have as many as eighty-five different phonemes or as few as twelve (see Fig. 5.1). Someone who has never learned a foreign language may find it difficult to imagine that there are many possible sounds that are not included in English. Yet even familiar languages such as German and French have phonemes that do not exist in English—for instance, the gutteral *h* in German and the rolled *r* in French. Less familiar languages have a large number of exotic and

Devanāgarī (Indian, Hindustani)
48 Phonemes:

    10 vowels: a ā i ī u ū ṛ ṝ ḷ ḹ
     4 diphthongs: e ai o au
     4 gutterals: ka kha ga gha ṅa
     5 palatals: ca cha ja jha ña
     5 cerebrals: ṭa ṭha ḍa ḍha na
     5 dentals: ta tha da dha na
     5 labials: pa pha ba bha ma
     4 semivowels: ya ra la va
     4 sibilants and aspirates: śa ṣa sa h
     1 rare lingual: ḻa

Hawaiian
12 phonemes

a, e, i, o, u, h, k, l, m, n, p, w

Fig. 5.1
Phonemes in other languages—Devanāgarī
(48) versus Hawaiian (12)

We have not tried to specify exactly how each phoneme sounds, but they are all distinct to native speakers. Despite the dramatic difference between Hawaiian and Devanāgarī in number of phonemes, there is no apparent difference in the ability of the languages to communicate. Both Hawaiians and Hindustanis can express any message they want in their own language. (After von Osterman, 1952)

not-so-exotic phonemes that we do not use, such as the clicking noises used by Bantu and Kung Bushmen. One description of the Bushman's click is that it resembles the sound you might make if you swallowed a lifesaver whole, by mistake, producing a small air bubble that popped. Perhaps this explains why it is usually written as !—"surprise."

Phonemes generally have no meaning by themselves. An occasional phoneme may have some meaning because it happens to constitute a whole word (for example, *a* and *I* in English), but these are exceptions. This is a crucial point that distinguishes a language from more primitive means of communication. The rhesus monkey may have nine different sounds that convey information, but each sound has a particular meaning all by itself; it does not need to be combined with any other sound. A particular grunt might mean "danger" while another might mean "I give up." But each of the nine sounds has one and only one specific meaning and together they can deliver only nine different messages. In contrast, phonemes in a language carry no information on their own; instead they are building blocks that combine to make meaningful units.

Morphemes

Morphemes are the smallest meaningful units of a language. They are divided into two types: *free* morphemens can stand alone; *bound* morphemes must be combined with other morphemes to form words. In the sentence *The porpoises are swimming*, both kinds of morphemes appear. *The, porpoises,* and *swim* are meaningful units that can stand alone in English. The *s* at the end of *porpoise* and the *ing* at the end of *swim* are also meaningful units, the *s* forming a plural and the *ing* changing the form of the verb, but neither *s* nor *ing* appears by itself in English communication. The forty-five phonemes in English can be combined into vast numbers of morphemes (considerably more than a hundred thousand meaningful units), which can in turn be combined into many hundreds of thousands of words.

Curiously, every language has rules about how its phonemes are combined and where certain combinations are allowed to appear. For example, an English morpheme can begin with any single consonant, but of the 380 possible pairs of consonants (eliminating the possibility of the same consonants appearing twice and counting *y* as a semivowel), fewer than a hundred are used. Combinations of three consonants are almost never employed at the beginning of a morpheme. People who speak the language correctly follow these rules even though they might not be able to formulate them. Figure 5.2 lists a number of words that will be unfamiliar to almost everyone. Nevertheless, you should be able to distinguish those that are possible words in English from those that are not possible because the latter use unacceptable combinations.

Yes	No		Yes	No
	sgronic			noctule
	ladkin			scazon
	menald			jrovance
	uleatol			trochite
	leamer			chalder
	tebuier			lexfent
	waramge			gfadite
	inlepk			fribble
	fhezing			schmester
	jowter			branner

Fig. 5.2
Acceptable and unacceptable English morphemes

Half of these are real (though rare) English words; the other half are not English words, and could not be because they violate the rules of combining phonemes. Try to guess which are which. The answers are elsewhere on this page.

These relatively simple rules have nothing to do with the meaning of the morpheme. Indeed, the meaning of most morphemes is entirely arbitrary. There is no rule or logic by which you could decide that *house* means a building in which people live, while *horse* means the four-footed animal that people ride. Nor is there any way of deducing that adding an *s* makes a noun plural and adding *ed* makes a verb past tense. Although at some point in the history of the language there may have been reasons why certain morphemes were associated with certain meanings, there are no general rules for these associations. This is in sharp contrast to the meaning of sentences. Some sentences may be somewhat ambiguous, but in all cases the meaning (or possible meanings) can be derived from a relatively small body of rules that govern sentence construction.

Grammar

Grammar is the set of rules that govern construction and allow us to understand the meaning of a sentence. There are two types of grammatical rules: those governing variations or *inflections* in the words

Answers to Fig. 5.2
The following are the real words: ladkin, menald, leamer, jowter, noctule, scazon, trochite, chalder, fribble, and branner.

themselves, and those governing the *order* of the words. Some examples of inflections are tenses of verbs and cases of pronouns and nouns. "The gazelle runs" means something different from "the gazelle ran" because the verb's tense changed. Similarly, "He saw me" clearly means that the other person did the seeing.

Similarly, meaning depends on rules of order. The typical sequence in English is subject, verb, object. Whichever noun comes first is the subject, and the one that follows the verb is the object. "The gazelle saw the lion" means that the gazelle did the seeing, while the reverse order carries the opposite meaning.

Languages vary considerably in their reliance on the two types of grammatical rules. While English has few inflections and relies largely on word order, Russian is heavily inflected and the order of the words is almost without meaning. The subject can come almost anywhere in a Russian sentence. But regardless of which rules are

Box 5.1

MEANING AND CONTEXT

Although the meaning of a sentence is determined by the assigned meaning of the words and the grammatical rules of the language, the social and cognitive context often plays an important role. Words and sentences have different meanings and totally different significance depending on when they are uttered and who says them. A nice example of this is provided by the words *boy* and *girl*. *Boy* usually refers to a young male. If it is applied to someone over the age of, say, thirty, the term is usually insulting, as in "Thanks, boy" to a waiter or "Take it easy, boy" to someone who is lower in status. The traditional southern use of the term to refer to any black male is clearly meant to imply that the person addressed is of lower status (perhaps this usage is decreasing). On the other hand, saying "Atta boy" when someone hits a home run is complimentary and acceptable.

The significance that is attached to the word *girl* is even more complex and subtle. It is often used to refer to any female, as in "That's a pretty girl," or "The girls are getting together for bridge." Until recently, such phrases were generally not meant nor taken to be insulting. However, the feminist movement has made us aware that such usage tends to imply that women are somehow inferior or less adult than men. Even if this is not intended deliberately, it may have that effect. We do not usually call a thirty-year-old man a boy, and therefore calling a woman of that age a girl makes her sound less mature and responsible than the man. This may be true even when the person making the statement is trying to be extremely complimentary. If you doubt this, compare the sentences "You're a great woman," and "You're a great girl." Clearly, they have different meanings when applied to a grown female. As we shall discuss in more detail in Chapter 13, these kinds of linguistic habits often reflect and reinforce underlying attitudes and values that are unfair and discriminatory.

The meaning of a phrase sometimes depends on who says it. We are all familiar with the fact that members of an ethnic group can use words to describe themselves that would be extremely insulting if used by nonmembers. And to continue the previous example, it is less demeaning for a woman to refer to herself or other women as girls than for a man to. But even this usage may reinforce negative attitudes about the group that she herself may share.

Another example of the way in which meaning is subtly changed by characteristics of the speaker is that some words are considered less appropriate for some

used, people who speak a language well derive the meaning of a sentence from their knowledge of these rules.

Transformational grammar Most of us are not able to state the full set of rules we use, even though we have learned them very well and use them efficiently. We are usually unaware of both the intricacies and the simplicities of our grammar. Linguists, however, devote themselves to studying the nature and structure of language. Linguists such as Noam Chomsky (1968) make a distinction between the *surface structure* of a sentence, which is simply the sequence and form of the morphemes, and what they call the *deep structure,* which is the underlying or intended meaning of the sentence. The question is how someone derives the intended meaning from the actual sentence, or put another way, how a person finds the deep structure from the surface structure. The answer is that the person follows rules,

NOAM CHOMSKY

people than for others. Most people have no difficulty identifying phrases that are "feminine" or "masculine." In our society certain words and phrases are generally associated with one sex more than the other, and when used by the "wrong" sex sound inappropriate. When a woman uses a "masculine" phrase, she may sound harsh or unnatural to some listeners; when a man uses a feminine phrase, he may sound weak or effeminate.

Naturally, there is enormous variation in these linguistic habits from one group to another in our society, and the habits change rapidly. Cursing used to be considered vulgar when women did it, but tough and forceful when men did it. This feeling may persist to some extent, but obviously it has altered quite a bit over the last ten years. The term *Negro* used to be considered the most appropriate and respectful way to refer to *blacks,* which is now the preferred word. All of this is arbitrary, of course, and ideally terminology should not be more appropriate to one sex or one group of people than to another. But these distinctions do exist in our society, and they may have substantial effects on our interpretation of phrases and our reaction to them.

What role does context play in the meaning of the two signs in this cartoon?

Drawing by Levin; © 1976 The New Yorker Magazine, Inc.

which we call grammar. A complete set of rules is called a *transformational grammar* because it enables us to transform the surface into the deep structure. It is actually just one possible model or theory of the rules a person would need in order to understand all the sentences in her language. The construction of transformational grammars is extremely difficult. No one has yet produced a perfect grammar, one which actually does allow any legitimate sentence to be understood.

The distinction between surface and deep structure, and the idea of a transformational grammar, are important because sentences with identical surface structure often have different or ambiguous meanings, while sentences with quite different structures can have the same meaning. "The porpoise ate the fish" has a different surface form but means the same (has the same deep structure) as "The fish was eaten by the porpoise." Transformational rules relating to the passive voice explain why the meanings are the same. The sentence, "They are jumping gazelles," however, is ambiguous. It could mean that the gazelles are jumping, or that they are the type of gazelles that jump, or that some other creatures are jumping onto or over gazelles. Another ambiguous example is illustrated in Fig. 5.3. Out of context, it is not clear for any of these examples which deep structure is intended and which transformation is appropriate. Therefore the rules enable us to specify the possible meanings but not to choose between them. In short, even a complete grammar cannot avoid some ambiguity. But this does not distract from the fact that in almost all cases the exact meaning of a sentence can be derived from a knowledge of grammar and the meaning of the morphemes, and that even in the ambiguous cases the most likely meanings can be derived.

Fig. 5.3
Ambiguous sentences

The meaning depends on the deep structure. In the phrase "man eating shark," do you see a shark that eats people or a person eating shark meat?

AMBIGUOUS SENTENCES

To get an idea of the great complexity of language, consider the following:

"He is too hot to eat." This may seem clear at first glance (the man is so hot he does not feel like eating), but add "said the cannibal," and another meaning becomes clear. If the sentence were, "The chicken is too hot to eat," the two meanings would be even more obvious.

Some ambiguous sentences have many possible meanings. Consider the following (based on a suggestion by Jacobs and Rosenbaum, 1968):

"He was told to stop smoking on the train."

There are at least six possible meanings of this sentence. Some of them may be somewhat more likely than others, but they are all plausible interpretations of a seemingly normal sentence. Before looking at the answers, try to find them all.

1. He was smoking on the train and was told to stop (anywhere).
2. He was smoking and was told (on the train) to stop.
3. He was smoking and was told to stop (but only on the train).
4. He was told to stop others from smoking (but only on the train).
5. He was told (on the train) to stop others from smoking.
6. He was told to stop others who were smoking on the train.

The languages of the world differ in a great many respects, but they all have the essential features we have just described:

1. Every language starts with a small number of phonemes, basic sounds that do not have any meaning by themselves.
2. These phonemes are combined (within certain limitations) into tens and sometimes hundreds of thousands of morphemes, units that have arbitrary meanings.
3. These meaningful units are combined according to grammatical rules into sentences, the meanings of which can be derived from a knowledge of the grammar.

It is possible to discuss the essential design features of a language in considerably more detail than this (for example, Hockett, 1958), but these three features seem to be the most basic and universal. Without any one of them, a means of communication simply could not have the enormous flexibility and variety that characterize human language.

HOW LANGUAGE DEVELOPS

How does a person acquire a language? We will answer this question in two parts: first with a description of the stages by which language appears; and second with a discussion of the possible mechanisms underlying its acquisition. Throughout this consideration of the development of language, it is important to remember that language is a universal human attribute. As we have mentioned, every human society has language, and every human being who is exposed to language (and is not severely retarded mentally) will develop the ability to use that language. Thus, descriptions and explanations of language development must take this universality into account.

The Appearance of Speech

All infants make pretty much the same noises. They cry, scream, and utter various grunts, gurgles, and cooing sounds. Sometime before the age of six months, however, the noises they make begin to sound more and more like speech. This babbling, as it is usually called, does not consist of real words, but it has some of the sounds that will eventually be used in words. Even at this stage, babies all over the world are alike—the babbling of a Japanese baby is indistinguishable from that of an American baby (Atkinson, MacWhinney, and Stoel, 1970). As the months go by, however, the babbling begins to change, and narrows somewhat according to the particular language to which the child is exposed. Sounds that do not appear in the language are babbled less and less often; those that are common in the language appear more frequently. During this period (four to eight months), the child utters its first distinguishable words. These almost always involve consonants that are relatively easy to pronounce, beginning with *p, m, d, t,* or *b*. Within a year, the child builds up a small vocabulary that it can use more or less accurately. He will say "Mama" when his mother enters the room; "Dada" for his father; "milk" or something resembling it; and so on. Up to this point the child has been working mainly to develop speech and a small set of morphemes. Then, sometime during the second year of life, a real language begins to emerge. For the first time, the child constructs and utters combinations of words—two-word and sometimes three-word sentences. From this stage onward, complex language development occurs—which is why so much research has been devoted to this period.

The study of children's speech is extremely complicated. Essentially, it consists of recording verbatim what children say, over as long a period and in as varied situations as possible. Some investigators have simply taped everything that was said when the child was in the room. Others have taken random samples over a longer period of time. And some have transcribed a selected set of childhood utterances. In all cases, the basic data consist of the record of spontaneous utterances by the child during a particular period of life. There have been a number of studies of this sort made with English-speaking American children (Bloom, 1970; Brown and Bellugi, 1964); Swedish-speaking children (Rydin, 1971); Spanish-speaking children (Tolbert, 1971); and also children speaking Samoan (Kernan, 1969), French, German, Hebrew, Japanese, Korean, Luo, Russian, and by now probably several other languages. Thanks to these studies, generalizations about the development of children's speech can be based on a broad sampling of diverse languages. Whatever conclusions are drawn need not be limited to just one language or even one family of languages.

Children's Grammar

How does a child learn to use language? As we mentioned earlier, the rules of grammar are the key element in a language. In seeking answers to this question, therefore, most investigators look at the extent to which children use grammar in their utterances, and just what kind of grammar they use.

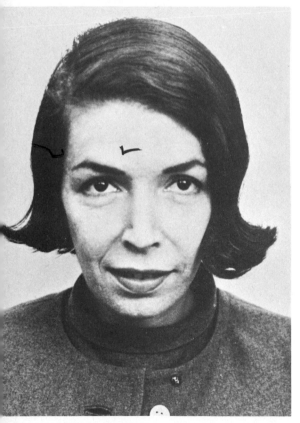

LOIS M. BLOOM

There are a number of current descriptions of how grammar is acquired in early childhood. Although none of them is fully adequate or fully accepted by experts in the field, they have contributed greatly to our understanding in recent years.

Telegraphic speech At a purely descriptive level, the first sentences young children produce resemble simplified adult sentences. They are simplified in much the same way that an adult would construct a telegram. Unnecessary descriptive words, prepositions, articles, conjunctions, most pronouns, and auxiliary verbs are omitted. If an adult wanted to send a telegram that conveyed the message, "I've arrived in London, the weather is good, and I will return to the United States on Tuesday," the telegram would probably read, "Arrived London, weather good, return States Tuesday." In much the same way, a two-year-old child who wants to tell his parents that he would like to go outside and ride his bicycle will say, "Go out, ride bicycle" or perhaps, "Want go out ride bicycle." This kind of telegraphic speech appears to be a universal characteristic of early language. It also appears when children try to imitate adult speech. For example, Brown and Fraser (1963) asked six children between the ages of two and three to imitate thirteen simple English sentences. Some of the results are shown in Table 5.2.

Table 5.2
CHILDREN'S IMITATIONS OF ADULT SPEECH

	Eve, 25½ months	Adam, 28½ months	Helen, 30 months	Ian, 31½ months	Jimmy, 32 months	June, 35½ months
1. I showed you the book.	I show book.	(I show) book.	I showed you the book.	I show you the book.	C	Show you the book.
2. I am very tall.	(My) tall.	I (very) tall.	I very tall.	I'm very tall.	Very tall.	I very tall.
3. It goes in a big box.	Big box.	Big box.	In big box.	It goes in the box.	C	C
4. Read the book.	Read book.	Read book.	—	Read (a) book.	Read a book.	C
5. I am drawing a dog.	Drawing dog.	I draw dog.	I drawing dog.	Dog.	C	C
6. I will read the book.	Read book.	I will read book.	I read the book.	I read the book.	C	C
7. I can see a cow.	See cow.	I want see cow.	C	Cow.	C	C
8. I will not do that again.	Do—again.	I will that again.	I do that.	I again.	C	C
9. I do not want an apple.	I do—apple.	I do—a apple.	—	I do not want —apple.	I don't want a apple.	I don't want apple.
10. Do I like to read books?	To read book?	I read books?	I read books?	I—read book?	C	C
11. Is it a car?	'T car?	Is it—car?	Car?	That a car?	Is it car?	C
12. Where does it go?	Where go?	Go?	Does it go?	Where do it go?	C	C
13. Where shall I go?	Go?	—	—	C	C	C

In telegraphic speech, the older the child, the more of the sentence is repeated. At all stages, however, the dropped words and morphemes are those that would ordinarily be omitted from a telegram because they carry the least essential information. Note that the order of the sentence is almost always retained, and that suffixes such as *ed* at the end of verbs are almost always dropped.
C, correct imitation; —, no intelligible imitation obtained.
Source: Brown and Fraser, 1963.

Although telegraphic speech is a fairly accurate characterization of children's utterances, it tells us little or nothing about their understanding of grammar. Obviously, they use simplified language and it makes sense that they would omit nonessential words, but how do you know *which* are nonessential? Are they following any specific grammatical rules? If so, to what extent are these rules similar to those of adults?

Pivot grammar One of the earliest descriptions of childhood grammar was proposed by Martin Braine in 1963. At about the same time, Roger Brown (Brown and Fraser, 1963; Brown and Bellugi, 1964) and Miller and Ervin (1964) suggested quite similar ideas. The basic theory is that two-word sentences constructed by children consist of two classes of words: *pivot words,* which are few in number and are used very frequently, and *open words,* which are much more numerous and occur much less frequently. Different children have different pivot words, but according to this description, each child consistently uses certain words as pivots and others as open words.

For example, Steven, one of the children studied, used the words *want, see, more,* and *there* as pivots, while Gregory used *more* and *see* but added *pretty, my,* and *bye-bye.* The point is that each child selects certain words that represent basic concepts in his world and uses them constantly in connection with all other words. Table 5.3 lists some of the utterances according to class and type of sentence. According to the theory, pivots almost never occur alone. They appear only in two-word sentences and each particular pivot almost always occurs in the same position, either first or second. In contrast, open words often appear by themselves, and in two-word sentences can appear in either position. For example, Gregory might say, "see boy, see sock, see boat, see mommy" but would never say just "see" nor would he say "boy see" or "mommy see." He would, however, say just "mommy" or "boy."

ROGER BROWN

Table 5.3
EXAMPLES OF PIVOT GRAMMAR FROM BRAINE'S STUDY

	Pivot and open	Open and pivot	Open and open
Gregory	See: boy, sock		Mommy sleep
	Pretty: boat, fan	Push it	
	My: Mommy, milk	Move it	
	Bye-bye: man, hot		
	More: taxi, melon		
Andrew	All: broke, fix	Boot off	Dry pants
	I: see, sit	Water off	
	More: car, sing	Mail come	
	Other: bib, milk	Mama come	
Steven	Want: baby, get	Bunny do	Find bear
	See: ball, Stevie	Want do	
	More: ball, book		
	There: ball, high		

Adapted from Brown, 1973, p. 92; based on Braine, 1963.

The importance of this description of children's speech is that it involves some kind of grammar. Sentences are constructed systematically according to certain rules, just as are adult sentences. On the other hand—and this is most important—these rules do not correspond to any in adult language. Thus, pivot grammar is not a first step toward understanding the complex grammar of the language. Rather it is an entirely different set of rules that must be entirely replaced.

In recent years the whole concept of pivot grammar has come under attack; and most linguists do not accept it now as an adequate or even accurate description of children's speech. Research by Bloom (1970), Bowerman (1970), Brown (1973), and many others has demonstrated that pivot grammar fails on several points. Most crucial is that at the purely descriptive level, pivot grammar is not a very good representation of what young children say. There are almost certainly certain words that they use more than others, but these words do not occur in fixed positions nor do they occur only in combination with one of the less frequent words. Thus, all that can be said now is that children do have words they use frequently and words they use less frequently, and that the frequent words have a tendency to appear in the initial position in two-word sentences. This is far from the original notion of pivot grammar, and does not, in fact, assume anything about rules of construction or elementary grammar.

Figure 5.4

Early grammar A number of authors (Bloom, 1970; Schlesinger, 1971) have suggested that children have a much greater understanding of adult grammar than that proposed in early pivot-grammar descriptions. According to these authors, children's sentences are intended to convey complex structural meanings even though they are quite simply constructed. Just as some adult sentences with identical surface structure have different deep structures (intended meanings), so a child's simple sentences may have entirely different meanings in different contexts. To take one of Bloom's examples, "Mommy sock" can mean "That is Mommy's sock," "Mommy is putting the sock on Katherine," and probably various other things as well (see Fig. 5.4). Indeed, the alert adult understands these varying meanings, and will often expand the child's sentence into a more normal adult sentence. When the child says, "Mommy sock," the mother might say, "Yes, it's my sock" or, in the other context, "Yes, Mommy is putting the sock on your foot." Of course, it is difficult to be certain that the child really intends these "adult" meanings, but the child's reactions to these expansions imply that the child does.

This view of the development of language in children holds that the earliest grammar is an extremely simplified form of adult grammar. It varies from child to child and presumably also from culture to culture. Different children adopt different parts of adult grammar, but it seems likely that they are modeling their sentence construction after adult grammar rather than following rules that are unique to young children. In support of this view, researchers have noted that English-speaking children almost always start forming sentences in approximately the word order required by adult grammar.

It is clear that we are just beginning to describe and understand the stages of language development in children. The relatively simple notion of telegraphic speech is reasonably accurate, but it is purely descriptive and leaves out much of the detail and complexity with which children produce utterances. The idea of pivot grammar was appealing because it was simple and yet assumed that young children have some awareness of grammar. However, this theory has turned out to be an inaccurate description of the utterances themselves, and contains misleading assumptions about the limitations of childhood grammar and its lack of correspondence to adult grammar. It now appears that even two- and three-year-old children have a rudimentary grammar that is a simplified form of adult grammar, and it seems likely that children attempt to convey a wide variety of messages with relatively simple constructions. This view eliminates the discontinuity between children's and adult's rules that was proposed by pivot grammar. However, we still do not know in detail how children begin to use and master adult grammar.

HOW LANGUAGE IS ACQUIRED

Language is one of the most complex human achievements. The rules of grammar of any language are so intricate that even trained linguists have a great deal of difficulty stating them all clearly. Yet almost every person who is exposed to the language from birth masters it well enough to express and understand virtually any message. Not everyone speaks perfectly grammatically, but the basic rules are known so well that errors rarely interfere with comprehension. What are the mechanisms by which this mastery is achieved?

There are two somewhat different views of language acquisition. The first is that children learn a language just as they learn to tie their shoes, eat with a fork, multiply numbers, or anything else. This *learning view* (exemplified by Skinner, 1957) assumes that other than a certain necessary level of intellectual capacity all the normal principles of learning can account for the development of language.

The *cognitive view*, advanced by Noam Chomsky (1968) and others, is that the ability to use language is qualitatively different from other skills. According to these theorists, language demands such a high level of intellectual complexity and organization that learning principles alone cannot account for language acquisition. Indeed, they argue that the capacity to master a language is built into the human system and that, like depth perception, language stems from our innate cognitive structure. The child must be exposed to language in order to develop it, but the child's inherent intellectual capacity is a prerequisite for this development. Moreover, language itself is a reflection of this innate intellectual organization. Although there have been fierce arguments between these two opposing camps, it seems to us that the positions are more complementary than contradictory and that the eventual answer to how language is acquired will be in terms of both learning and innate characteristics.

The Role of Learning

Children are not born with a vocabulary, nor with a knowledge of grammatical rules. They must hear the word "dog" in order to learn it, and must also notice somehow that it is associated with a four-footed animal with various characteristics. As we have said, all infants make pretty much the same noises and babble much the same sounds, but by the age of three they are speaking only the one or two languages to which they have been exposed. The child in an English-speaking family does not amaze and terrify her parents by speaking Japanese. Only in fantasies such as *The Exorcist* do children speak languages they have never heard before. In short, children evidently rely on the ordinary processes of learning to acquire a vocabulary.

Imitation is a particularly powerful mechanism in acquiring new words. Although children are often rewarded and encouraged when they say their first few words, they do not receive direct reinforcement often enough to account for the very large vocabulary they eventually build up. Instead, they hear their parents and others use thousands of different words and learn to say many of them by imitation. Once they have mastered the sound of the word, they may then be reinforced directly by parental praise, or indirectly because they have made themselves understood and gain reinforcement in that way.

Acquisition of grammar is more complex. Obviously, the child must learn the meanings of specific words, but how does he develop the complex rules for constructing sentences and using words? Is the child selectively reinforced for using correct grammar? Does the parent reward the child for saying "I want the milk" rather than "Want milk?" There is no evidence that parents are bothered by such ungrammatical or incomplete statements, nor that they systematically correct the child who makes them. Brown (1973) asserts that parents correct wrong facts, mispronunciations, naughty words, and verb forms such as "digged" or "runned" (which show that the child has learned the general rule for making a past tense but not the more complicated exceptions for common irregular verbs). But most errors are not corrected.

One explanation for this reported lack of correction is that the parent has no trouble understanding the child. As Brown says, "Why the dog won't eat?" is translated into "Why won't the dog eat?" in the parent's mind. Because grammatical errors do not interfere with comprehension to any appreciable extent, there is little reason for the parent to worry about them, or indeed even to notice them. There is still far too little evidence on the extent to which corrections or systematic reinforcements are given. Nonetheless, it seems unlikely that parents provide enough consistent reinforcement to explain the child's progression from rudimentary talk to the highly complex grammar of adults. Occasional reinforcements and corrections certainly occur and are helpful, but some other mechanism probably plays a greater role in the acquisition of grammar.

A Cognitive Explanation of Acquiring Grammar

The specific nature of this other mechanism is unclear. In all formulations, however, it differs from the simple learning model in that the child's intellectual capacity plays a more active part. Rather than being simply the passive recipient of training, either by deliberate reinforcement or by imitation of specific phrases, the child is assumed to discover the grammatical structures of adult speech. This is not the same as saying that children merely express an innate structure when they reach the appropriate age. Such a notion is implausible. Obviously, the English-speaking child cannot have one innate set of rules and the German speaker another. Thus, when Chomsky and others talk about innate structures they are not referring to specific grammatical rules but rather to an *intellectual capacity* that is expressed in the form of language.

According to this view, the child listens to a vast number of adult utterances and abstracts from them the rules of grammar. Just as there seems to be a natural inclination to imitate all other kinds of adult behavior, so there may be a strong tendency to imitate "correct" speech. The child does not need to speak grammatically in order to be understood and is not punished for speaking ungrammatically. Nonetheless, she may need to communicate better and grammar would be helpful. Or she may simply want to speak the same way as her parents (this tendency to imitate may be innate or might itself be learned through reinforcements). Whatever the reason, the child tries to discover the rules by which her parents construct sentences, and she then tries to use these rules herself.

Concept Formation and Grammar

The process of forming grammatical concepts is obviously very complicated and involves many different kinds of mechanisms. At first, the child probably memorizes specific phrases and usages. This is a beginning, but it will not enable him to construct entirely new sentences of his own. That requires a process through which the child abstracts the essential principles of grammatical construction. For example, after hearing hundreds of sentences, the child may notice one critical element in all of them—the noun precedes the verb. Later he notices other rules (concepts) that are common to all or most sentences. Then, by applying these rules and using memorized phrases as well, the child begins to construct original sentences. As the child gains experience, the sentences conform more and more to standard grammar and increase in length and complexity. Some structures will be heard so rarely that the child will not have an opportunity to extract a rule governing them. We all know the correct sequence of words in an English sentence and the use of the past tense; few of us, and presumably no young children, have mastered the pluperfect subjunctive. A child's concept-formation ability improves with age; certain concepts that are difficult at one age become

easy a bit later. Just as in other kinds of concept formation, the abstracting of grammatical rules will depend on the complexity of the rule, the stage of development of the child, and the number of instances to which he has been exposed.

Critical Periods

It is possible that there are one or more critical periods in the acquisition of language. Perhaps a young child has a strong tendency to abstract these grammatical rules, whereas older children and adults, while presumably capable of forming the concepts, simply do not devote themselves to this kind of concept formation. Thus, a child learning her first language acquires the grammatical rules seemingly without effort and with little or no systematic reinforcement. In contrast, an adult learning a second language has much more difficulty with the grammatical rules and depends on systematic reinforcement in order to learn them at all. When a language is learned after childhood, even people who are perfectly fluent in it often make grammatical errors that would not appear in the speech of a twelve-year-old native speaker (for example, the use of articles—"I like to play the baseball"). These errors are ones that do not interfere with comprehension (presumably, the speaker would soon learn to correct them if they did). They reflect a misunderstanding of grammatical rules that are rarely spelled out in language courses—rules that adult learners do not seem to be able to pick up simply through experience.

On the other hand, there does not seem to be a critical period during which a young child must be exposed to language in order to learn it. Children who have never been exposed to language are still able to master a language once given the opportunity. The case of Isabel (Davis, 1940, 1947), who was kept secluded by a deaf-mute mother for six and a half years, illustrates this point. One week after Isabel was finally exposed to language she was able to vocalize; within two years she was speaking approximately normally for her age group. As with most human skills, once a capacity develops it does not seem to disappear just because the typical or normal period of development has passed. However, the critical period for language development may be much later (around twelve), and after that age acquiring a language, while still possible, may be much more difficult.

To sum up, language acquisition appears to depend on a combination of learning by the usual mechanisms of reinforcement and imitation, plus the child's active attempts to abstract essential grammatical rules by a process akin to concept formation (see Chapter 6). The capacity to learn these rules is obviously a critical element in the development of language. Any human or animal that did not have that capacity would be unable to acquire a language in the usual way and would probably never be able to master one fully.

CAN OTHER ANIMALS ACQUIRE LANGUAGE?

Animals other than humans have not developed communications comparable to human language. But is it possible that other animals have the capacity to learn a language if they are adequately taught?

Obviously, this is a fascinating notion. The idea of communicating directly with another species has long been a part of human folklore and children's fantasies. But on a scientific level, the question of whether animals can learn a language is important primarily because it relates to the controversy between the cognitive and the learning approaches to language. If language is dependent on and is actually an outgrowth of the intellectual structure of the human mind, there is the strong supposition that only humans are capable of using language. Therefore, Chomsky and other psycholinguists have argued that only humans can learn a language, while most behaviorists feel that with sufficient patience it should be possible to teach an animal some sort of language. Although the two schools of thought clearly differ on this point, it is not really a crucial test of the two theories. If a chimpanzee can master a simple language all it would mean is that the chimp's intellectual capacity and brain structure are more similar to ours than we thought. It would not necessarily imply that our intellectual structure is unimportant in our own mastery of language. Thus, teaching an animal language is an impressive demonstration of the power of learning techniques, but it is not evidence that language is developed entirely through learning.

On the other hand, the question of whether other animals can learn a language is fascinating in its own right, aside from its value as a test of the two theories of language development. Accordingly, whatever one's position on the theoretical dispute, we must consider training an animal to use language a dramatic accomplishment.

The Case of Gua

For many years it appeared that other animals simply could not master a language. A number of attempts were made to teach chimpanzees (probably the brightest other species with the possible exception of the porpoise and gorilla), but these attempts always ended in failure. The Kellogs (1933) raised a female chimpanzee, Gua, along with their own child, Donald. Gua was treated very much as one of the family and presumably was exposed to many of the same experiences as Donald. Though Gua learned to recognize and respond to about seventy words, she never spoke a word herself, while Donald developed a normal mastery of English. Other, similar attempts produced about the same results. The chimps recognized a fairly large number of utterances from their masters, but did not use language themselves. Clearly dogs, cats, horses, and many other animals can respond to verbal commands, and well-trained elephants know more than twenty different words. Therefore, up to this point the chimpanzees had accomplished only slightly more than other species, and certainly had not demonstrated the true knowledge of language.

The Achievement of Washoe

However, the status of animal language has been altered dramatically in recent years by the accomplishments of Allen and Beatrice Gardner (1971) and their chimpanzee, Washoe. The Gardners decided that trying to teach chimpanzees to talk was hopeless because chimpanzees have great difficulty in the instrumental use of their voices. Instead, they began to teach Washoe American Sign Language,

Fig. 5.5
Washoe and her mentor

developed for use by deaf-mutes, which clearly was within a chimpanzee's manipulative capacities. American Sign Language uses complex hand gestures that stand for words, and has its own grammar that is similar to but distinguishable from English.

Over several years, Washoe has learned at least 130 signs that she both understands and uses herself. This has been demonstrated in controlled tests, in which objects or pictures of objects are shown to Washoe and she makes the appropriate sign. Although she is not perfect, she typically gets about fifty right out of one hundred and her errors are usually mistaking one animal for another or one object for one that is quite similar to it. If she were responding by chance, she would only get one or two right out of a hundred since many different items are shown and she knows so many different signs. But it is important to remember that this accomplishment is only quantitatively superior to that of many other animals who learn the meaning of words or signals. The critical difference is that Washoe not only understands but uses these signs.

However, the truly significant achievement is that Washoe spontaneously produces combinations of signs that she has never "heard" before. Since the construction of sentences is the essence of language, this is a great step forward in animal language. Washoe knows how to say "open," "door," and "window." Sometimes, entirely on her own, she will make the sign phrase for open-window and open-door. The Gardners have counted 294 different two-sign combinations that Washoe uses, and she probably has made others. Some of these she may have learned directly from the Gardners, but they assure us that many of them were produced by Washoe on her own. Thus, this chimpanzee has mastered 130 meaningful signs and uses them in sentences of two or more signs in order to communicate. Moreover, as she has grown older and more experienced, Washoe has begun producing longer sign combinations. And other chimps have also learned many signs.

Whether this constitutes the complete mastery of language is debatable, since Washoe and the others still seem to have little awareness of or use of grammar. On the other hand, they can understand and produce a wide variety of messages—much greater than any other nonhuman animal in recorded history.

Fig. 5.6
Lana at the keyboard

Other Successful Techniques

While the Gardners decided to use sign language because it was within the physical capacity of the chimp, Premack (1971) chose something even easier. He tried to teach a chimpanzee to use plastic tokens varying in size, shape, color, and texture to indicate meaning. Although there is some question about the accomplishments of Premack's chimp Sara, it is clear that she has learned to recognize a large number of tokens and to combine them in primitive sentences. And other chimps have also reached this level of achievement. Perhaps the most spectacular success has been achieved by a chimp named Lana, who communicates by manipulating symbols on a computerized keyboard. According to her teachers at the Yerkes Primate Laboratory, Lana has learned to ask for the names of new objects. If further research supports these observations, Lana may turn out to be the first nonhuman to demonstrate abstract thought.

In short, using various methods of communication, different chimpanzees and an occasional gorilla have managed to communicate at about the level of a somewhat slow four-year-old child. This may not be the limit of the chimps' abilities—perhaps more intensive or more ingenious training will carry them further—but it is certainly a substantial step beyond what has been done before. If nothing else, it demonstrates the enormous importance of learning in the acquisition of language, and opens up the possibility that someday we will be able to communicate at least on a minimal level with other species. This research does not, however, contradict the idea that a human child participates actively in the acquisition of language, not only learning and imitating what she hears, but also abstracting grammatical principles from the utterances of others.

LANGUAGE AND THOUGHT

The relationship between language and thought has been the subject of much speculation. One hypothesis, proposed by Benjamin Whorf (1956), is that the words and structures peculiar to any language actually determine, to some extent, how and what speakers of that language think. Since much of our thought seems to be in words, it may follow that the words available to us will limit and shape the contents of our thoughts. This has generally been called the *Whorf hypothesis*, since Whorf was the first to propose it. This fascinating possibility has been extremely difficult to test definitively. There is little question that people with different languages think and perceive somewhat differently. For example, Arabs are said to have 6,000 ways of naming camels, and the Hanuwoo, natives of the Philippines, 92 names for varieties of rice. Eskimos have 20 or 30 words to describe different types of snow, an avid skier may have 5 or 6, and most of us have only 2 or 3. Coinciding with these differences in vocabulary are differences in sensitivity to variations in the objects. For example, an Eskimo will notice minor differences in the snow that most of us would ignore entirely. Skiers are well aware of the difference between powder and corn snow, while city cab-drivers generally notice only how slippery the snow is and whether it is piling up. But these observations do not necessarily support the Whorf hypothesis, be-

AVOIDING SEXUAL STEREOTYPES IN LANGUAGE

As we will discuss in Chapter 13 on sex and adult development, traditional male and female sex roles are being challenged in many ways. The women's movement, economic conditions, education, and other factors are weakening sexual stereotypes and opening the way for greater freedom of choice for both sexes. Among other areas being affected is language itself. Women have pointed out that many common terms in English seem to be biased in favor of males and support old views of women. As a result, publishers, newspapers, magazines, and so on have begun to offer nonsexist alternatives in usage. The idea seems to be that getting rid of stereotypes in language will help us get rid of stereotyped thinking.

The following examples of nonsexist alternatives are taken from a guide published by the Houghton Mifflin Company.

Objective: To present occupations and achievements as available to and suitable for males and females alike.

a) Avoid modifiers that suggest an exception to the rule.

    Do not say: woman doctor, female lawyer, or male nurse
    Say: doctor, lawyer, nurse

b) Do not offer descriptions for one sex that you would not offer for the other. Instead, treat descriptions uniformly, mentioning only those facts relevant to the achievement.

    Do not say: Mrs. Joan Abbot, brilliant scientist and mother of four; Dr. Zoe Griffin, attractive dentist; Stan Larsen, father of two
    Say: Joan Abbot, brilliant scientist; Dr. Zoe Griffin; Stan Larsen

Objective: To describe males and females as individual people with separate identities.

    Do not say: Mr. Albert Crane and his wife Elizabeth
    Say: Albert and Elizabeth Crane

Objective: To include both sexes in the pronoun construction when appropriate.

    Do not say: the reader . . . he; the voter . . . he; the secretary . . . she

This is probably the most difficult problem because we are so accustomed to using "he" as the general term and because English provides no general alternative ("it" cannot be used for people).

    Some solutions: a) avoid pronouns.
    Do not say: The teacher sent her students
    Say: The teacher sent the students or sent students.
    b) Use passive or plural.
    The students were sent by the teacher; teachers send their students
    c) Use second person singular.
    Do not say: The shopper will find her grocery bill.
    Say: You will find your grocery bill.
    d) Finally, you can use both pronouns or alternate.

Objective: To use a universal or neutral rather than masculine term for an occupation or title.

    Do not say: chairman, real estate man, anchorman
    Say: moderator or chairperson; real estate agent, newscaster

Note: These examples are based on *Avoiding Stereotypes*, Houghton-Mifflin, 1975. Some of the examples and wording have been changed.

cause a simple alternative explanation is available. Instead of the vocabulary affecting the perception of snow, it might be the other way around. An Eskimo is much more concerned and familiar with the various qualities of snow and therefore constructs words that describe snow in great detail. The words do not govern the perceptions—the concern and perceptions govern the vocabulary. This is almost certainly true of skiers, who quickly learn terms such as "corn" and "powder" but presumably have no difficulty distinguishing between corn and powder snow even before they hear the words. The words may not be available, but the perceptions are.

Although some early work produced results that seemed to support Whorf's hypothesis, later research did not. At the present time there is little evidence that language has any *direct* effect on perception or thought.

Language and Memory

On the other hand, there is no question that language does affect thinking indirectly, primarily by making it easier to remember some objects than others. When a simple word is available to describe an object, that object will be remembered more easily than if no word is in the person's vocabulary. The perception of the object will not differ, and it will still be possible to describe the object even if no single word exists, but remembering and thinking about the object will be harder.

This is a simple instance of the familiar effect of chunking on memory. If you know a lot about dogs, you can name twenty or thirty varieties and will instantly recognize them. If you are shown pictures of a St. Bernard, collie, German shepherd, Great Pyrenees, Doberman, Scottie, Welsh terrier, and others, you will assign the appropriate (and familiar) name to each. If you are asked later which kinds of dogs you saw, you will probably be able to name most if not all of them. But if you do not know the names, you will have difficulty remembering many of the dogs even though you can tell them apart quite easily. The description "a large, white, long-haired, snub-nosed dog with a long, bushy, curved tail" is much harder to remember than "Great Pyrenees" because many more bits of information are involved in the former. Thus, although language does not seem to affect perception directly, it does have substantial effects on ease of memory and therefore to some extent probably does govern what we think about.

NONVERBAL COMMUNICATION

Although we tend to think of verbal language as the means by which people communicate, there are many nonverbal ways in which we and other animals transmit information. Some of these cues are obvious and simple to understand, while others are exceedingly subtle. If you are walking down the street and encounter a dog that bares its fangs, growls, and lunges forward against its leash, you will have little difficulty in understanding that it is being unfriendly. It might take an expert to know whether the dog is simply warning you or is about to attack, but you certainly get the general idea. Similarly, if a person shakes his fist at you, you can be pretty sure he is angry or at least upset. And as we shall discuss in Chapter 10, we can identify a wide variety of emotions from facial expressions alone. In fact, there are several nonverbal ways in which humans communicate.

Paralanguage

One common form of nonverbal communication, called *paralanguage*, involves aspects of speech other than the actual words. The pitch, tempo, loudness, hesitations, and so on that occur in any verbal exchange carry considerable amounts of information. Each of us has a characteristic way of speaking that reflects some combination of our personality, background, and present emotional state. In addition, variations in our speech contribute to and perhaps even alter the meaning of the message. Inflections at the end of a sentence can turn a simple declarative statement into a question. (Read aloud the statement "you want to be a doctor" as if it had either a period or question mark at the end of it; note the entirely different rhythm and inflection in the two readings.) Sarcasm is indicated almost entirely by tone rather than words, and the same is often true of deep feelings such as passion, love, and hatred. Anyone can learn the lines in a play, but only a great actor can say them so as to convey precisely the right emotional meaning.

Although we have been using intonation as our major example, paralanguage includes pauses, hesitations, and all sorts of other noises that also impart meaning to a sentence. Researchers are just beginning to explore the enormous variety of paralinguistic utterances and to construct reliable rating instruments. Just as in learning the vocabulary of a language, it is necessary to learn the vocabulary of paralinguistics and gestures. However, the problem is even more complicated, because words generally have strictly defined meanings that all people share, whereas nonverbal signs are often ambiguous and vary from person to person and situation to situation. In the exercise in Fig. 5.7, for example, you will find that the meaning of a sentence often depends in large part on the nonverbal cues that accompany it. Indeed, one of the most difficult problems in writing is to communicate exactly what you mean when you are not there to provide nonverbal cues. To make up for this, writers often describe nonverbal cues directly by telling us how a speech was delivered ("he said sarcastically") or what the person was doing ("he said, looking out the window and not meeting her gaze"). Although it is possible to

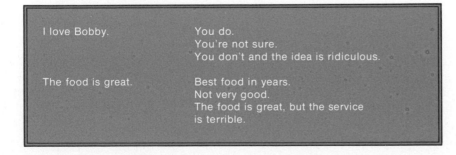

| I love Bobby. | You do. You're not sure. You don't and the idea is ridiculous. |
| The food is great. | Best food in years. Not very good. The food is great, but the service is terrible. |

Fig. 5.7
Intonation and meaning
Say each sentence aloud trying to give the indicated meaning by changes in intonation and timing.

communicate fairly well using only words, we rely on nonverbal cues to clarify much of what we say and to interpret what someone else is trying to tell us.

Gestures

People use a variety of bodily gestures to communicate. Some of these may have fairly stylized and consistent meanings. Tapping with your finger on a table usually means you are restless or bored; licking your lips usually means you are tense; and, of course, nodding your head up and down indicates agreement while shaking your head from side to side shows the opposite. These are fairly obvious examples, but even these are not entirely consistent among people and certainly not across cultures. While it is clear that subtle gestures do carry a great deal of information (Birdwhistell, 1970; Condon and Ogston, 1967), it is impossible to make generalized statements as to exactly what every gesture and body movement means. An open palm is not always an invitation; sitting with legs crossed does not always imply defensiveness. No one has constructed a gestural vocabulary and, indeed, no one could, because the meaning of a gesture varies greatly from person to person and situation to situation.

Box 5·4

NONVERBAL COMMUNICATION AND LIE DETECTION

It is sometimes suggested that nonverbal cues carry more information or more accurate information than do verbal cues. This is obviously not true in general. However, nonverbal communication does supplement verbal communication by providing additional information about emotions and eliminating some ambiguities.

A fascinating aspect of this issue is the relationship between nonverbal cues and honesty or credibility. Many people believe that you can tell when someone is lying by watching that person's hands and face—that his gestures will give him away. But research by Robert Krauss (Krauss, Geller, and Olson, 1976) indicates that, in fact, the opposite is true. Nonverbal cues make someone seem more sincere and honest. Subjects were less good at detecting lying when they both saw and heard someone than when they only heard his voice; the nonverbal cues covered up the lie rather than revealing it. On the other hand, there is evidence that a particular paralinguistic cue is helpful in detecting lying. The average pitch of the voice is higher when someone is lying than when she is telling the truth: Thus, lie detection could be based on an analysis of voice frequency without regard to content (Ekman, Friesen, and Sherer, 1977; Streeter et al., 1977).

ROBERT M. KRAUSS

Distance

People also communicate by how close they stand to someone else. If someone of the opposite sex stands very close to you at a party even though there is lots of room, you will probably sense that this person is interested in you. If another person backs away from you slightly, you may feel that he is being "distant" or "stand-offish." We shall discuss this concept of personal space in more detail in the chapter on environmental psychology. For now, we can note that personal spacing of this kind is a nonverbal and also nongestural means of imparting emotional information.

Eye Contact

You are speaking to someone when you suddenly get the idea that she is totally uninterested in what you are saying. She answers your questions, nods at the appropriate times, and yet you have the strong impression that what you say couldn't matter less. If this happens, it is likely that she is communicating disinterest by means of eye contact—or more accurately, lack of eye contact. When someone looks you in the eye, you feel that she is interested in you and is paying attention. When she does not look you straight in the eye, you usually get the impression that she is uninterested (Weisbrod, 1965). In addition, eye contact serves to indicate and regulate the beginning and end of speaking. Someone who is talking usually looks away as she begins in order to prevent an immediate response from the listener, and then looks up when she is about to finish talking (Kendon, 1967).

Besides controlling the flow of conversation and indicating interest or lack of it, eye contact communicates certain kinds of messages. Under the right circumstances, it can indicate personal interest. Meeting someone's gaze (or, as it is sometimes described, staring into someone's eyes) tells the person you are attracted to him. Under other conditions, however, eye contact is threatening. In a series of studies, experimenters standing on a street corner stared or did not stare at people who were driving or walking past. People who were stared at drove or walked through the intersection faster than those who were not stared at. Apparently, being stared at is challenging, and people try to avoid it unless the other person is obviously trying to be friendly, as at a party or other social situation (Ellsworth, Carlsmith, and Henson, 1972). Moreover, staring causes subjects to be less aggressive to the person who is staring at them, again presumably because the staring is seen as threatening (Ellsworth and Carlsmith, 1973). It is interesting to note that eye contact and standing close both have these contradictory meanings—either personal interest or threat. Both forms of nonverbal communication carry the information that the person is more involved emotionally, but whether the involvement is positive or negative depends on the particular context.

What do the nonverbal cues in this photograph show about the relationship among these three girls?

PHOEBE ELLSWORTH

LANGUAGE IN PERSPECTIVE

In recent years there has been a great deal of interest in the kinds of nonverbal, nonlinguistic means of communication described above. A great deal of work has demonstrated that gestures, paralinguistic variations, facial expressions, and such amplify language and sometimes replace it. They often eliminate ambiguities in language, and can also give subtle nuances that are difficult or impossible to communicate directly with words. It is important to realize how much information is transmitted in face-to-face exchanges without the use of language.

However, it is also clear that a vast majority of our communication is by means of language. This becomes obvious when we consider the importance of written messages in our lives. A picture may be worth a thousand words, but we tend to rely on the words to communicate. This is true of the complex material that makes up our cultural and scientific heritage—history, literature, science, technology. It is also true of everyday communications such as personal letters, road signs, and business transactions. Even in face-to-face situations it is largely language that is used to transmit information and to carry on social interactions. T. S. Eliot's Sweeney says, "You gotta use words when you talk to me," and surely someone who cannot use words, who does not have command of a language, or who speaks a different language from those around him, is extremely limited in his ability to interact with other people. Language requires the most complex, intricate, and advanced mental powers. It might be said that someone who does not have language is, in a truly basic respect, not fully human.

■

Summary

1. Language is a complex, systematic system of symbols that humans use as a primary means of communication. Language also plays a key role in learning by reducing the need for trial and error.

2. The building blocks of a language, called phonemes, are basic sounds that have no meanings by themselves. Phonemes can be combined into vast numbers of morphemes, units that have arbitrary meanings. Morphemes, in turn, are combined into sentences according to a set of rules we call grammar.

3. Language development begins in infancy with the development of speech and the acquisition of a small set of morphemes. Acquisition of complex language occurs when the child begins to learn to use grammar.

4. We are just beginning to understand the stages of language development in children. Telegraphic speech is a useful description of children's utterances. Recent research suggests that the earliest grammar is a very simplified form of adult grammar.

5. Language is probably acquired both by learning (the learning view) and through innate characteristics (the cognitive view). Imitation is particularly important in acquiring vocabulary. The process of acquiring grammatical concepts is more complex. First the child probably memorizes specific phrases and usages; after much exposure to language he begins to abstract the principles of grammar that enable him to construct sentences of his own. The fact that adults have much more difficulty learning a second language after childhood suggests that there are critical periods in the acquisition of language.

6. Primate research has demonstrated the enormous importance of learning in the acquisition of language and raises the possibility that some higher animals may have the capacity for abstract thought. But this research does not contradict the idea that the human child participates actively in the language acquisition process.

7. While there is little evidence to suggest that language has any direct effect on perception or thought, it is certain that language does affect the ease with which we remember. Thus language to some extent probably affects what we think about.

8. Verbal language is the major means of communication, but humans also transmit information nonverbally. Paralanguage, gestures, eye contact, and physical distance amplify language, give subtle nuances, and often eliminate ambiguities, thus enriching the communication.

RECOMMENDED READING

Brown, R. *A First Language: The Early Stages.* Cambridge, Mass.: Harvard, 1973. Roger Brown is one of the finest writers in the field. This book describes what we know about how language develops in early childhood.

Chomsky, N. *Language and Mind.* New York: Harcourt Brace Jovanovich, 1968. Chomsky has had an enormous effect on the study of language and many other areas of psychology. This book presents some of his views.

Hinde, R. A. *Non-Verbal Communication.* New York: Cambridge, 1972. A book of readings edited by one of the most active people in the field. Fascinating reading.

Slobin, D. I. *Psycholinguistics.* Glenview, Ill.: Scott, Foresman, 1971. Probably the best introduction to the field available at the moment.

The power of thought—the magic of the mind.
Lord Byron, Corsair

Man is but a reed, the weakest in nature, but he is a thinking reed.
Blaise Pascal, Thoughts

6 Thinking

Thinking defined ▪ *Concept formation* ▪ *Heuristics: strategies for concept formation* ▪ *Problem solving* ▪ *Information processing and computer models* ▪ *Learning to learn* ▪ *Insight—the "Eureka" phenomenon* ▪ *Creative thinking* ▪ *Limits of the mind*

n January 1971, Dougal Robertson, an ex-farmer and expert seaman from Scotland, embarked with his family on a circumnavigation of the world. A few days out to sea their craft, a fifty-year-old, forty-three-foot schooner, was attacked by killer whales. It sank in less than sixty seconds. In a nine-foot dinghy with no charts, no compass, and enough food and water for only three days, the family faced sharks, savage storms, and starvation. Using the debris collected from the sunken vessel and their own resourcefulness, they were able to fashion tools that would help them survive: a metal piece from a pressure cooker became a weight for a fishing line; plastic from a luff wire was attached to an oar to fashion a sail; a piece of wood was whittled into a spearhead for catching fish and turtles. They sustained themselves on fish and turtle meat, turtle eggs, and fresh rainwater. In all, they spent thirty-seven days alone on the ocean under conditions of incredible hardship. Yet Robertson, his wife, and their four boys survived!

Dougal Robertson's thoughts on the twentieth day:

> *I knew from hard-won experience that where the land may be kindly to man, the sea was as impartial as the sky and that, in an environment where every other living creature had adapted and perfected its means of survival over millions of years, our chances of surviving among them lay in our ability to adapt our past experience to present circumstances. Our ability to fashion tools, to help each other physically and psychologically and to use knowledge as a weapon of offense as well as defense, these were the attributes that would allow us to live from the sea. (Robertson, 1973)*

The abilities Robertson describes are central to the process we call thinking. While most of us are probably not as resourceful as the Robertson family or the sixteen Uruguayans who survived for seventy-one days after their plane crashed in the high Andes, we can all use the vast store of information at our disposal to deal with problems that confront us. Moreover, we can use that information creatively, adapting it and the environment to the problem at hand. This ability to reorganize, change, and manipulate materials, whether they be pieces of information or objects in the world, is the essence of thinking and the highest achievement of the human mind. In this chapter we will discuss thinking in its varied and complex aspects: concept formation, problem solving, and creativity. We will also talk about the limits of the mind and consider the question of whether supernormal powers (often called extrasensory perception) exist.

THINKING DEFINED

Thinking is difficult to define precisely. People often define thinking broadly, using it to refer to any kind of mental process, including everything from random associations and images to spectacular acts of creativity. This definition is too all-inclusive for our purposes. To distinguish thinking from the kinds of processes already discussed in earlier chapters, we shall limit our definition to such complex mental processes as *concept formation, mental rehearsal of alternatives, and problem solving, as well as all forms of intellectual creativity.* Although these functions are sometimes called *higher mental processes,* it is important to remember that the mechanisms discussed in Chapter 4, particularly the retrieval of information, are also exceedingly complex and crucial to man's intellectual activities. The distinction between higher and lower mental processes is for convenience only, and does not imply that different mechanisms are involved.

CONCEPT FORMATION

Concepts identify similarities among a number of different stimuli or situations; concepts may be simple or complex, concrete or theoretical. The ability to form concepts is basic to complex thinking. Look at the problems in Fig. 6.1. The answer to set 1 is simple; set 2 is a little more complicated; and by the time you get to set 5, you are looking for a concept that is exceedingly difficult to find. Although these concept-formation problems may seem unconnected to real-life situations, they do illustrate the process that enables us to function effectively.

Concept formation consists of learning that certain objects belong to the same group and then learning to discriminate one class of objects from another. For example, we learn the concept of the letter *G*, of a car, of a house, and so on. We are then able to identify all *G*'s—in script, italic, or whatever form they appear. And we know that a Ford we see on the street is a car, even though it looks different from our own Chevrolet. Conversely, we learn that *G*'s are not the

Fig. 6.1
Concept-formation problems

Discover the element or elements that distinguish the A's from the B's in each set. The answers are given on p. 165.

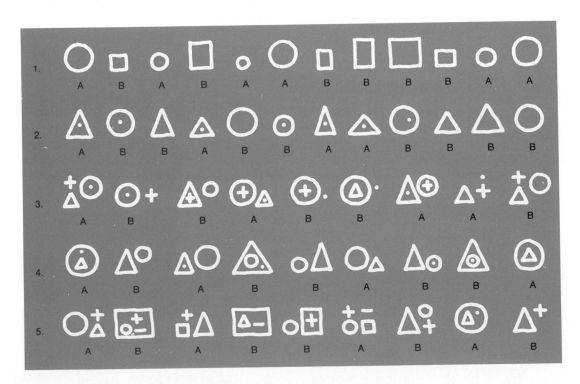

set 1

set 2

set 3

Figure 6.2

same as *R*'s and that cars are different from trucks. Look at Fig. 6.2; all the drawings in set 1 are obviously *G*'s; all but one of the animals in set 2 are cats; and four of the faces in set 3 are perceived as smiling, even though the smiles are all different. We also form concepts involving abstract ideas such as love, peace, or justice. Although peace is obviously not as definite as a house, it does contain certain specific elements—the absence of war, mutual restraint and consideration, and so on.

The Importance of Concept Formation

One reason concepts are so important is that they enable us to treat similar objects and situations in the same way. As we discussed in Chapter 3, stimulus generalization—the tendency to respond similarly to similar stimuli—is essential if we are to use what we have learned. Without such generalization, a young child who burned herself by touching a hot stove would not learn to avoid other hot stoves. Stimulus generalization is the basis of the transfer of training—it allows us to use information learned in one situation in other appropriate situations.

But how do we decide that the two situations are similar? Concepts are a major factor in defining similarity. Once we know what a stove is, we can generalize to other stoves. The crucial problem is how to distinguish a stove from a refrigerator, a desk, or a tree. For instance, all stoves get hot, are used for cooking or heating rooms, and have certain other recognizable characteristics. Once the concept is formed, objects within the class can be responded to similarly (stoves may be hot, so watch out) and objects outside the class can be treated differently (refrigerators will not burn you). Until concepts are formed, generalization will be haphazard, with responses made to inappropriate objects and often not made to appropriate ones. Clearly, concept formation is one of the bases of our understanding of how the world operates. Only by grouping objects together can we find any regularities and consistencies.

Types of Concepts

There are two basic types of concepts. The simplest and most common is called a *conjunctive concept*. In this type of concept, a class is defined by *several characteristics that must all be present* for an object to fit the class. For example, a mitten is an article of clothing worn on the hand that has a separate thumb but no separate fingers. If it had separate fingers, it would be a glove; if it were not designed for the hand, it could be a sock or a hat. A boat is a vehicle that operates only in water and has sides. All three elements are necessary: if it were not a vehicle, it might be a whale; if it did not operate only in water, it could be a car or plane; and if it did not have sides, it might be a raft or a log. These are simple conjunctive concepts. To gain some idea of the difficulty of defining a concept fully, you might try to give all the characteristics of flowers, humans, or music.

A special type of conjunctive concept is one that relies on the *relation among qualities* rather than on the qualities themselves. In Fig. 6.1, set 4, all the *A*'s have triangles and circles. But the presence of these objects is not sufficient to define the concept because some of

DEFINING A SIMPLE CONCEPT

Seemingly simple concepts are often quite complex. For example, before reading further try to give the distinguishing characteristics of a table (the kind you write or eat on) so that someone who had no idea what you were talking about could recognize a table when she saw one.

The Oxford unabridged dictionary says a table is "a flat, relatively thin piece of wood, metal, stone, or other material." The definition then continues for many pages, giving special meanings, derivations, and so on. Clearly this basic definition is only a beginning, and the additional detail does not help much. Yes, a table usually is flat and relatively thin, but this does not apply to all tables and certainly does not allow us to distinguish a table from, say, a writing tablet, a manhole cover, a cutting board, or the cover of this book. Figure (a), not a table, is included in the definition, while Fig. (b), a fancy table, is not.

So we have to add that a table has legs, or sits on a platform, or is thick enough so that it provides its own base. But now we cannot distinguish a table from other pieces of furniture, such as the stove in Fig. (c). Clearly, we must include the *function* to make a useful definition: a table is used for writing, eating, holding objects, working, and so on. To distinguish it from a desk, we might add that it does not have a kneehole and is not ordinarily used primarily for office work. But since the difference between a desk and a table is often arbitrary, these qualifications may begin to exclude some tables from our definition. Thus, even everyday concepts that *seem* very simple are often exceedingly complex.

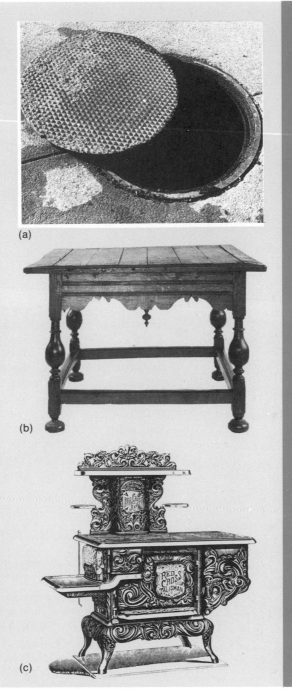

(a)

(b)

(c)

BOX 6.1

the *B*'s have them too. In this case, the concept depends on the relationship between the triangles and circles—all the *A*'s have triangles that are *smaller* than the circles and this is not true of any of the *B*'s.

A *disjunctive concept* is defined in terms of one characteristic *or* another. That is, the class of objects must contain one of a group of qualities—it need not contain all. An example of a disjunctive con-

Answers to Fig. 6.1
1. A = circle   2. A = triangle with dot   3. A = triangle, dot, and cross   4. A = triangle and circle, but triangle smaller   5. A = a large circle or a small square

EARL HUNT

cept is a strike in baseball. A strike can occur when a ball is pitched across the plate between the armpit and knee of the batter, and the batter does not swing; or when the batter swings and misses the ball; or when the batter hits a foul ball and there are fewer than two strikes against him; or when the batter attempts to bunt and hits a foul ball, regardless of the number of previous strikes. Set 5 in Fig. 6.1 illustrated a disjunctive concept. Even if you managed to figure it out, you probably saw that disjunctive concepts are much more difficult than conjunctive ones, and research has supported this impression (Hunt and Hovland, 1960; Wells, 1963). There are three reasons for the difficulty of disjunctive concepts. First, people generally expect concepts to be conjunctive rather than disjunctive. Second, disjunctive concepts involve at least two alternative characteristics, and so the trial-and-error solution tends to involve more comparisons. Third, our normal ability to get a general impression of a concept is hampered because, in a sense, two different kinds of objects are being included in the same category. In fact, it can be argued that a disjunctive concept is actually two different concepts joined together arbitrarily or by some more abstract principle.

Theories of Concept Formation

We form a concept by determining the element or elements that distinguish one group of objects or events from others, but just how we accomplish this is not entirely understood. Much of the time, we are told only part of what constitutes a concept. For example, a child is not usually told what makes a dog a dog. Her parents may tell her that a dog is an animal, that it has four legs, that it is usually hairy, and so on. She probably will be shown pictures of a number of animals that are called dogs and a number of others that are not dogs. But when a two- or three-year-old sees sheep for the first time, she is likely to say "dog," because her parents probably omitted some crucial characteristics. As far as the child knows, any four-legged, hairy animal is a dog.

After a while, the child begins to notice the differences, and to form a concept of her own. Many times she will make incorrect inferences. For example, she may decide that all dogs have long hair, because she has seen only Scotch terriers, poodles, and collies. Great danes and chihuahuas will confuse her. Eventually she learns most of the characteristics that make an animal a dog and can distinguish dogs from practically any other beast. How does she accomplish this?

There are four major approaches to understanding concept formation: association theory, hypothesis testing theory, perceptual or Gestalt approach, and the information-processing approach. Although they are by no means mutually exclusive, they all focus on certain important aspects of the process and all have stimulated considerable research. In addition, they are also applied to the study of more complex thinking such as problem solving, which we shall discuss later in this chapter.

Association theory Concept formation may be seen as a problem in discrimination learning, with the essential elements of the concept (the discriminative stimuli) being acquired through the forming of associations. This formulation is thus called *association theory* (Restle, 1955; Bourne and Restle, 1959). The proponents of this theory reason that each time we see a representative of the concept (called a positive instance), we are exposed to all of its stimulus characteristics and thus tend to form associations between the concept-name and all of these qualities. Some characteristics will be present in some positive instances and some in others, but only the essential elements will be present in all and these will therefore form the strongest associations. When we have seen enough positive instances, we will have learned the essential elements of the concept simply by this process of selective strengthening of associations.

In other words, the process is identical to that of discrimination learning. You learn what elements are important and what unimportant just as a pigeon learns to peck a blue disk and not a red one to get food. Clearly this theory does not view concept formation (or any other kind of thinking) as distinct from learning. Concept formation may be harder and more complex than learning to press a lever to get food, but the mechanisms are seen as similar.

Hypothesis-testing theory In contrast to the somewhat mechanistic view of association theory, concept formation may be seen as a process of *testing a series of hypotheses*. According to this theory, we form hypotheses about the concept on the basis of the examples we have seen, and we test these hypotheses with new information. For example, a child sees an object and is told that it is a book. He decides that all small, heavy objects are books and when he sees an iron he says "book." The parents say "No, that's not a book, this is a book," and leaf through the pages of a book with him. So the child drops his first guess and decides that a book must have pages with printing on them. When he sees a newspaper, he says book and is told no, it's a newspaper, and is shown a paperback novel. He then decides a book must have a cover as well as pages and print. Next he identifies a magazine as a book—and on it goes. Naturally, the process may take a long time unless the parent is deliberately trying to teach this particular concept; but with each piece of information, the child either confirms or rejects his hypothesis. He is not simply forming associations, but rather focusing on specific characteristics of the positive instances and testing to see if they are essential.

It seems clear that both association and hypothesis testing play a role in concept formation. Indeed, many of the proponents of the hypothesis-testing theory first worked on association theory and consider them similar approaches to the problem (for example, Restle, 1962; Bower and Trabasso, 1964).

Perceptual or Gestalt approach In addition to the gradual strengthening of associations and deliberate testing of hypotheses, humans can to some extent "short-circuit" the tedious process of concept formation by gaining a general perceptual impression of the class of objects. A child who has seen only one horse might form a good enough impression of the animal so that she would be unlikely to confuse it with either an elephant or a car. The child probably would not be able to list the critical elements to which she is responding, but she would have some general idea of "horse." She would have to sharpen the concept further in order to distinguish a horse from a cow, but the ability to perceive form would greatly facilitate the task of concept formation.

Figure 6.3

This ability to notice the form or pattern of an object comes easily to people but is exceedingly difficult for computers. Much time and effort have been spent trying to develop computers that can recognize printed or written letters. Complex optical scanning devices can now read and recognize standard printed numbers and some letters, but no one has been able to design a machine that can read even handwritten zip codes reliably. Yet it is a trivial matter for literate people to recognize that all the symbols in Fig. 6.3 are 4's.

Information-processing approach The information-processing approach to concept formation in a sense combines all of the others. Concept formation is viewed as a problem in dealing with and interpreting information, and all kinds of mechanisms may be involved. The individual must first receive the relevant information, recognize the various characteristics, organize them in some way, and then abstract the essential elements from the larger array. Information-processing theory attempts to apply models of how a computer works or how a computer might deal with information to human thinking. Many of the elements in an information-processing model are similar to those already discussed, but the model attempts to give a complete description of the process—including all the assumptions about human functioning that are necessary to explain how we form concepts. Thus, an information-processing model would assume that people have certain perceptual tendencies and certain limits on their memory, that they form associations according to certain rules, and that they are capable of testing hypotheses. By means of the appropriate combination of these elements, the model attempts to describe in detail the process of concept formation. It is possible to test the model by giving a computer appropriate instructions and seeing if it gives the same results in a concept-formation problem as a person does. Any errors can lead to changes in the model; the new assumptions are then tested, and so on (for example, Hunt, Marin, and Stone, 1966). As we shall see, this approach has had considerable impact on research on thinking, particularly on more complex problem solving.

These four approaches to concept formation are by no means mutually exclusive. Though each of the first three tends to emphasize particular aspects of the process, it seems almost certain that they are all involved in the actual formation of concepts. The particular mechanism that is used, as well as the relative efficiency of each, depends largely on the specific concept, how it is presented, and probably the age of the person as well.

Heuristics: Strategies for Concept Formation

Probably the most important contribution of the information-processing approach has been its emphasis on *heuristics*—strategies that people employ in thinking. When they try to solve a complex problem or discover a concept, people do not start randomly. They focus on certain aspects of the problem, try certain classes of solutions, play certain hunches. All such problem-solving strategies are called heuristics, and they are one of the keys to understanding human thinking.

For example, in solving a concept formation problem, many people will first try solutions based on only one factor and only if all of these fail will they move on to more complex solutions. Certainly, in most cases, conjunctive concepts will be tried before disjunctive ones. The particular strategies used will differ for different situations, different people, and different kinds of materials. But the choice of heuristic will always play a major role in how quickly the problem is solved. Some specific heuristics that people use are focusing and scanning, which are quite general approaches to concept formation, and exercising preferences for certain types of material. Each of these is discussed below.

Focusing If you already know the major characteristic of a concept or are dealing with a relatively simple concept, you can try to find the remaining elements by comparing two very similar instances, one of which is positive (fits the concept) and one that is negative (does not fit). Then, by noticing the few ways in which the similar instances differ, you can discover the crucial elements. This technique is known as *conservative focusing* (Bruner, Goodnow, and Austin, 1956).

Look again at Fig. 6.1, set 3. Compare the first and last items and you will notice that they differ in only one respect—the absence of a dot—which therefore must be a critical element. A comparison of the fourth and fifth instances reveals the second critical element (a triangle). By using this procedure rather than the long process of trial and error, you can solve the problem very quickly. However, conservative focusing is effective only if you already have a general idea of the concept. Clearly, the way to discover the essential characteristics that make something a dog is *not* to compare a dog with a wolf. That might tell you that a dog has different kinds of teeth from a wolf, but it will not tell you how to distinguish a dog from thousands of other kinds of animals. Before concentrating on relatively minor features, you have to know that a dog has four legs, hair, lives on land, and so on. Only when you know these basic features would you want to concentrate on the difference between a dog and a wolf.

Scanning An entirely different strategy consists of forming a hypothesis and then testing it by *scanning* all of the relevant instances. For example, you may decide that the correct answer is a large circle. To test this, you first scan all of the positive instances to be certain that they contain large circles, and then you scan the negative instances to see if any of them is also a large circle. If all the positive instances have the key element and none of the negative ones has it, clearly your hypothesis is correct.

This strategy does not produce new hypotheses (as focusing does) but rather tests an idea that has already developed. A combination of the two methods would use conservative focusing to form a hypothesis about what element is important (shapes of the figures) and then test this hypothesis by scanning (see if all positive instances have circles and negative ones do not). It seems likely that most people use a combination of these two techniques plus other, less organized methods for discovering concepts.

Preferences As part of their heuristic strategies, people do not treat all material equally. They have preferences among both stimuli and concepts, and these preferences can facilitate or interfere with concept formation, or even determine the nature of the concept that is formed. In general, for example, people notice the concrete qualities of objects more than form or quality. The concept of buildings or birds is usually recognized more quickly than the concept of roughness or redness, and these in turn are easier than concepts of number (Heidbreder, 1947). However, the characteristics people pay attention to change somewhat with age. Young children have considerable difficulty with functional concepts, such as tools, vehicles, and dwellings, even when they involve concrete objects. But as people get older, they find it easier to form concepts of either the function or meaning of an object, even if the concept itself is quite abstract—for example, the concept of weapons. Indeed, one of the most reliable indicators of brain damage in adults is an inability to recognize abstract concepts.

PROBLEM SOLVING

Concept formation is a special case of a more general kind of thinking that is usually called *problem solving*. A problem exists whenever you are trying to achieve a goal, initial attempts have failed, a variety of alternative approaches remain, and the goal can in fact be reached. In addition, for thinking to be involved, the choice among the alternatives must be based on something more than just chance—you must have some information or at least a strategy that might be helpful.

Acquiring a concept is obviously one kind of problem solving, but the mind is capable of much more complex activity than this. Throughout their lives, humans and other animals are faced with problems that must be solved. These can be simple or extremely difficult. And, of course, the degree of difficulty depends in part on who is trying to solve the problem. A chicken that wants to get to the other side of a fence has to figure out how to accomplish this. Although this is a trivial problem for man, it is surprisingly difficult for chickens—and most other animals.

The theoretical approaches to problem solving are essentially the same as those that deal with concept formation—the building up of associations, the testing of hypotheses, the organization or reorgani-

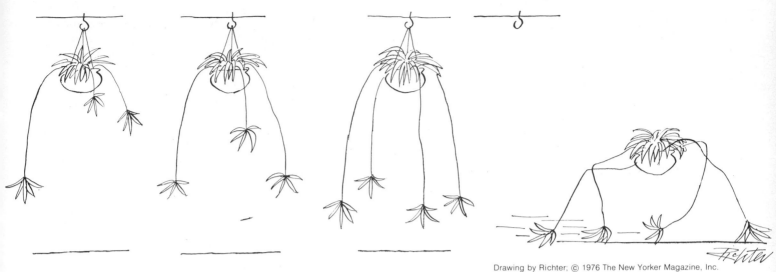

Drawing by Richter; © 1976 The New Yorker Magazine, Inc.

zation of perceptions, and information processing. After we see how these theories apply to problem solving, we will discuss two fascinating phenomena—learning to learn, and insight.

Association Theory—Trial and Error

Association theory sees problem solving as a series of more or less random attempts to reach a solution. When one behavior fails, certain associations are weakened; when one succeeds, others are strengthened. Eventually, the subject learns to solve the problem because the appropriate associations are powerful enough to produce the correct response.

In a classic study by Thorndike (1898), cats were put in "puzzle boxes" that could be opened only by manipulating a latch, bolt, bar, or loop. Figure 6.4, for example, shows a puzzle box that can be opened by stepping on a pedal. The cats in these studies were hungry and wanted very much to get out of the box. They clawed,

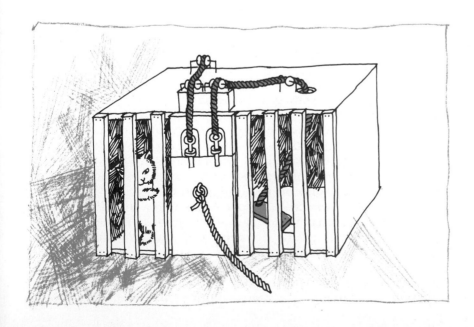

Fig. 6.4
Thorndike's puzzle box

kicked, whined, jumped, and bit at everything in sight. This activity usually led the cat to make the correct response and open the box. But the solution was achieved only by accident, and generally after much random activity. The cats demonstrated no understanding of the mechanism, nor even an awareness that some specific behavior was necessary to let them out. Nonetheless, they got better and better at solving a particular puzzle. Photographs of the cats show that they performed any behavior that was followed by success, whether or not the behavior had anything to do with the solution. A cat that had accidentally backed against the bar apparently did not learn that the bar was important. Instead, the cat learned to back up in the box and usually hit the bar and opened the box. This superstitious behavior shows that the solution was due to the strengthening of successful behaviors rather than any awareness of the correct solution.

Although this view of problem solving may appear to apply only to less intelligent animals, even humans sometimes resort to trial-and-error learning of this sort. For example, many of us resort to this approach when faced with a broken piece of machinery or electrical apparatus. When a television set suddenly stops working, the typical response of most of us with little electrical knowledge is to fiddle with every button available—to push, pull, twist, and turn every knob, and, occasionally, to slam the set on its side. If the TV still does not work, we might check the antenna and plug. Although our behavior is not entirely random (we are at least concentrating on the television set and trying procedures that could conceivably solve the problem), we are actually in much the same situation as the cat in the puzzle box. Evidently, both cats and humans resort to trial and error when they have no information on which to base a different type of solution.

Hypothesis-Testing Theory

Hypothesis-testing theory takes quite a different view of problem solving. It holds that individuals do not merely try random behaviors until one works; instead, they test one or more hypotheses on each trial. If the hypotheses fail, they are systematically discarded and new ones are tried. Rather than relying on sheer luck and perseverance, problem solvers attempt to understand the situation and act accordingly.

An electrician working on the broken TV would presumably test a series of hypotheses. Perhaps it is the tuner and this tube should be replaced; perhaps it is the picture tube and that can be tested; and so on. The approach is more deliberate and systematic, and each failure eliminates certain possibilities and may suggest others. In practice, the difference between a purely associative trial and error and hypothesis testing probably depends on the extent of knowledge of the problem. Even someone totally ignorant of electrical systems could devise hypotheses about the TV, but these would consist in essence of random attempts to fix it. That is, the hypothesis testing might not differ substantially from pure trial and error except that it might be more likely to be systematic. Nevertheless, the mental process involved is quite different. In association theory, there is no direct attempt to understand the problem or find a specific solution—the animal is simply trying various behaviors. In hypothesis-testing theory, mental activity is directed at discovering how to solve the problem and little emphasis is placed on the gradual strengthening of associations.

The Perceptual Approach

The *Gestalt* or *perceptual approach* to problem solving emphasizes the necessity of reorganizing (or at least correctly organizing) the perceptual aspects of the situation. Productive people have available a great deal of information and experience. They usually know many procedures for solving problems, are skilled at manipulating certain material, and, most important of all, can retrieve from their memories items appropriate to the present situation. Yet, paradoxically, past experience can interfere with the solution of a new problem. People tend to perceive problems in terms of previous, similar situations. Thus they will begin by trying solutions that were successful in the past, even though these may be inappropriate to their present task.

Rigid thinking It is natural for someone facing a new problem to try a technique that worked in the past, and usually it is effective. Difficulties arise when a new problem *appears* similar to a previous one but is actually different in important respects. When this occurs, old solutions will be either inefficient or totally useless. The individual must recognize that the problem has changed substantially, that the old solution will not work, and thus a new approach is necessary.

Before reading any further, try to solve the problems in Fig. 6.5. After solving the first two or three, you probably realized that a standard technique worked for all of them. Once you discovered this technique, the remaining problems were quickly solved. However, if you used this technique to solve problem 5, you were acting in a somewhat rigid manner. Although the method does work, a much simpler, faster solution is available: just add the contents of the two smaller containers to the larger one. Using the more complicated solution is inefficient because a simpler method works. This illustrates how past experience can produce a *set* or tendency to use the same method that interferes with performance on later tasks.

Figure 6.6 also illustrates this phenomenon. Try working out the problem before reading further or looking at the solution. The problem is difficult for most people because, based on their past experi-

Fig. 6.5
Water-jar problems

Using only jars A, B, and C, how can you end up with exactly the desired amount of water? (You may fill and empty any or all of the jars as often as necessary.) Answers are given elsewhere on this page.

	Size of jars (oz.)			Desired amount (oz.)
	A	B	C	
1.	8	24	3	10
2.	6	15	2	5
3.	7	35	12	4
4.	2	19	8	1
5.	6	27	5	11

Fig. 6.6
The nine-circle problem

Connect all of the circles with four straight lines, without lifting your pen from the paper or going through any circle more than once. The solution is give on p. 193.

Answers to Fig. 6.5

1. Fill B and pour it into A, leaving 16 oz.; then pour B twice into C, leaving 10 oz. in B. 2–5 are solved the same way, but 5 can be solved more quickly by simply filling A and C and then pouring both into B.

SAM GLUCKSBERG

ence with squares, they assume that the lines they draw must stay within the nine-dot square. Holding to this assumption makes the problem unsolvable. Only by drawing lines beyond the perimeter of the square can the problem be solved. It is remarkable how strongly most people feel bound by the limits of the square even though no limits are mentioned in the instructions.

The tendency to treat objects or forms in rigid ways has been referred to by Karl Duncker (1945) as *functional fixedness.* Duncker suggested that creative thinking often consists of using familiar objects (and we would add information) in entirely new ways to meet new demands. Conversely, the inability to solve new problems may be due to the individual's rigid use of objects in old ways.

Duncker studied this phenomenon by presenting people with problems that could be solved only by breaking through this functional fixedness. One such problem is illustrated in Fig. 6.7; try it for yourself before reading further. The difficulty is that the boxes are presented as containers, and most subjects continue to think of them in that context. This functional fixedness is reduced somewhat when the subjects are given the objects separately; that is, the candles, matches, and tacks are not *in* the boxes (Glucksberg, 1962). This puts less emphasis on the "container" function of the boxes, making it easier for the subjects to think of using them in a different way.

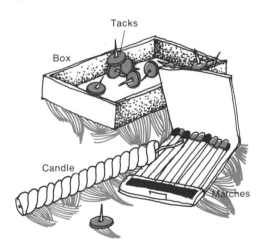

Fig. 6.7
The functional-fixedness problem

Subjects are given scissors, pencils, and boxes of candles, matches, and thumbtacks. The task is to mount the candles on the wall. The boxes are the key elements because the solution uses the boxes as platforms for the candles. (After Duncker, 1945)

In real life, people often break through functional fixedness to solve problems. Almost everyone is familiar with the idea of using a dime as a screwdriver and a penny as an effective but dangerous replacement for a burnt-out fuse. Indeed, as we shall see later in this chapter, the ability to think of unusual uses for familiar objects is sometimes considered to be one of the crucial elements of creativity.

Information Processing and Computer Models

The information-processing approach to problem solving tries to incorporate all the elements of other theories. Thus, a complete model would involve perceptual tendencies, sets, gradual learning through associations, hypothesis testing, limits of memory, and so on. Every

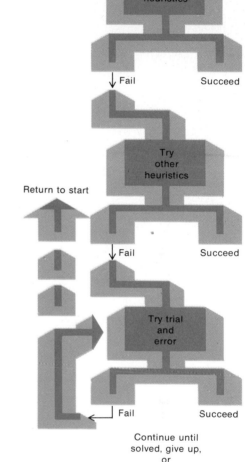

element in human thinking that plays a role in problem solving would be included in the model. At the moment, this is largely an ideal goal that has not been fulfilled. Although this approach is very flexible and allows us to use computers to test the models, we simply do not yet know enough about human problem solving to allow us to construct such a complete model.

Flow charts One way to study problem solving from this viewpoint is to devise what is called a *flow chart,* which outlines the steps that the individual takes in working on a problem (see Fig. 6.8 for an example). Built into this chart are certain heuristics that the individual is assumed to employ, as well as her responses to the success and failure of each attempt. Such a chart can then be translated into computer language and the computer can be given appropriate problems to solve. If a computer and a person produce the same solutions to the problem, it is assumed that to some extent the flow chart and the more complex program are accurate reflections of how the person actually solves these problems. If there are differences between the machine's solutions and the person's, the program can be changed to eliminate them. In this way, working back and forth between people and computers, a more comprehensive model of human problem solving can be constructed.

Computer simulations Attempts to program a computer to operate like a person are called *computer simulations,* in that the machine acts *as if* it were a person. The first important simulation of human thinking was devised by Newell and Simon in 1956. Called the Logic Theorist, it was able to solve many complex mathematical problems including thirty-eight of the theorems in the classic book on mathematics by Whitehead and Russell, *Principia Mathematica.* Another program, the General Problem Solver (Newell, Shaw, and Simon, 1960), dealt effectively with a wider range of problems. However, both these models and more recent ones are only rough approximations of human thinking. Though they can solve many problems on their own, there is little evidence that they solve them in the same way as humans. But this is potentially a powerful technique for studying human thinking and is expected to prove increasingly effective in coming years.

Chess programs There has been extensive work on writing a computer program that can play chess. Every move in chess involves a vast number of alternatives—there are millions of possibilities in just

Fig. 6.8
Flow diagram of a possible model of problem solving

If old solutions fail, try to find new ones relying on heuristics. If this fails, use trial and error. Eventually give up or return to beginning and try to gain better understanding of problem.

the first two moves by each player, and approximately ten billion possible moves in a game. Neither humans nor computers can trace the consequences of every possible move. Instead, they must both employ heuristics, and that is what the computer programs have concentrated on. At the moment, no computer chess program can beat Bobby Fischer or even lesser champions, but it can compete well against average and moderately strong players. On the other hand, a checkers-playing program has actually beaten some world-champion checkers players.

LEARNING TO LEARN

We have said that trial and error is a slow way to solve a problem, and often the correct solution cannot be repeated because the individual is not aware exactly how or why the problem was solved in the first place. However, trial-and-error solutions can lead to more efficient and more generalized problem solving. This occurs because the individual learns not only to solve a particular problem, but also how to solve other, similar problems. Even if the solver does not fully understand the solution, he may learn what aspect of the puzzle is important and what to give most attention to. In other words, through a series of solutions to a set of problems, he learns to pay attention to certain characteristics more than to others.

Lawrence (1950) demonstrated that rats can be taught to focus on certain aspects of a stimulus and ignore others. In this study, the rats had to learn a complex discrimination that was based on either the color of the stimulus or the presence of a chain. After continued exposure to discriminations involving one dimension, they were much faster at solving other discriminations that involved the same kind of stimulus even though the solution was different.

A similar effect occurs in learning a concept in which the correct solution is changed. We all have learned the concept that a red traffic light means stop and a green light means go. Imagine that suddenly a red traffic light meant go and a green light meant stop. That would take a little getting used to, but we would understand the concept fairly quickly because we have learned to pay attention to a particular aspect of the situation—the color of the lights—and ignore other aspects. This kind of change is called a *reversal shift* (Kendler and Kendler, 1962).

In contrast, if the system were changed so that the intensity of the light gave the signal, it would probably be much more difficult to figure out the concept because we have learned to pay attention to the color, not the intensity. When entirely new characteristics (such as the intensity of the light) define the concept, the change is called a *nonreversal* shift, and this kind of concept is generally much harder to learn than a reversal shift.

Experience can facilitate problem solving even when the critical characteristics of the solution change. Harlow (1949) studied what he called "learning to think" by giving monkeys a series of discrimination problems involving a wide range of stimuli. In each problem, two stimuli were presented; one was rewarded consistently and the other was not. For example, the monkey was shown a bottle cap and a soap

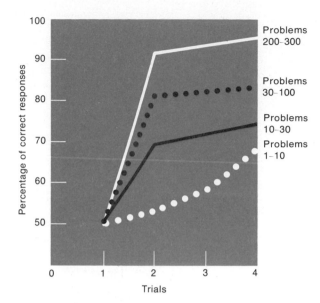

dish, and if he chose the cap, he was given some food. On the next trial, the same two stimuli were shown and the same one was rewarded. Once this problem was mastered, with the monkey choosing correctly every time, a new problem with entirely different stimuli was given.

The second trial for each new problem should be simple. If the guess on the first trial was right, the monkey should continue to make the same choice; if it was wrong, the other stimulus should be picked. Though this may sound easy, it gave the monkeys considerable difficulty at first. On the early problems, the monkeys guessed right only half the time on the second trials. But they learned rapidly. By the time they had solved twenty-five problems, they were guessing right on 70 percent of the second trials; after one hundred problems it was up to 80 percent; and by three hundred problems they were right 95 percent of the time on the second trials (see Fig. 6.9). Even though the stimulus materials were totally different for every new problem and there was no way to know from previous problems which stimulus would be correct, the monkeys' performance improved dramatically.

This result suggests that the monkeys were learning a great deal about the situation during their trial-and-error solving of each problem. They were learning what was expected of them, that the stimuli in front of them were crucial, that the stimulus that was right on the first trial would be right on the other trials, and so on. In other words, they learned to pay attention to the important aspects of the situation (to the stimuli, not to what the experimenter was doing or the smells in the room) and they also learned what kinds of problems they were dealing with.

This process certainly operates with people also. The brain teasers and mathematical tricks in this chapter are much easier if you have worked on other problems of this type. The solutions to the other problems will not work on these, but you have probably learned general ideas, strategies, or heuristics that often lead to a solution. In any enterprise or activity, there always seem to be some people who

Fig. 6.9
Learning to learn

On the first few two-choice problems, the monkeys find the solution slowly. As they work on more problems, they solve them faster and faster, even though no specific information is provided by the earlier problems. (After Harlow, 1949)

are marvelous troubleshooters. Whatever goes wrong, they seem able to pinpoint the trouble faster than anyone else. They can solve the problem even though it is a brand-new difficulty that never occurred before. The explanation of this knack is probably that they have learned what to look for, what cues are important, and what strategies they should try. This does not assure a solution, but it greatly increases the chances of one.

INSIGHT—THE "EUREKA" PHENOMENON

Building up the correct associations through trial and error, hypothesis testing, and perceptual or functional reorganization are all important elements in problem solving. However, they do not explain fully one of the most fascinating phenomena of thinking—*insight*. This somewhat mysterious event occurs as you are working on a problem. Suddenly you realize the critical elements, you see to the core of the problem, and your behavior, which might have been rather aimless and haphazard up to this point, becomes sharply directed toward the correct solution. If you solved the nine-dot problem in Fig. 6.6, it probably struck you suddenly that you could go beyond the boundaries of the square. If so, that realization was an insight. Without it, you might never have solved the problem; with it, the solution is easy.

The Gestalt psychologist Wolfgang Kohler studied insight by giving animals problems that were almost impossible to solve by trial and error. In one demonstration (Kohler, 1925), Sultan, his brightest chimpanzee, was in a cage and wanted to get a piece of fruit that was on the floor outside. But the fruit was too far away for Sultan to reach by hand or with a short stick he had in the cage. Lying outside the cage was a longer stick, which Sultan could reach with the stick he already had. In solving this problem, Sultan gives a clear demonstra-

Fig. 6.10
Eureka!

tion of trial-and-error tactics followed by insight. First he tries to reach the fruit with the smaller stick but fails. Then he tears a piece of wire from the roof, and tries that. Next he spends some time sitting still and looking around the cage and at the fruit. Suddenly the light dawns. He quickly grasps the smaller stick, uses it to pull the longer stick toward him, and then uses the longer stick to reach the fruit. This last sequence is very rapid, with no pauses. Obviously, Sultan attained insight.

A humorous anecdote about this kind of research concerned a chimpanzee who was given the problem of reaching a banana suspended from the ceiling. The chimp had available two sticks, neither of which was long enough to reach the banana. However, the two sticks could be fitted together to make one long stick, which could then knock down the banana. Most chimps faced with this problem would try first one stick, then the other, and suddenly catch on to the idea of fitting the sticks together; they would then reach the banana. This particular chimp, however, found an even easier solution. The experimenter happened to be standing directly under the banana, so the chimp scurried up the experimenter and grabbed the banana without having to bother with the sticks. Instances of insightful problem solving such as these are strong evidence that animals are capable of complex, creative, and productive mental activity.

Most problem solving by humans involves at least some insight. The experience of working on a problem for a long time and suddenly discovering the essential elements is exciting and highly rewarding. Supposedly, when Archimedes discovered the principle of displacement of water as he was taking a bath, he was so delighted by his insight that he ran naked down the streets shouting, "Eureka, I've found it!" While few of us have achieved such spectacular insight, everyone has experienced the sensation at one time or another.

The phenomenon of insight often occurs when we are trying to solve a brain teaser—a problem that is deliberately constructed so that the trial-and-error approach will either fail or be extremely tedious. Some problems of this type are given in Fig. 6.11. Try to solve them, paying particular attention to how you do so and just when the insight occurs. Unless you are already familiar with the problem, you will probably make a number of unsuccessful attempts and then, quite suddenly, see how to find the answer.

Unfortunately, psychologists do not understand the mechanism by which insight occurs. However, they do know some of the characteristics and consequences of a solution achieved by insight. With trial and error progress is necessarily gradual and slow. When insight has been achieved, behavior becomes more directed and ordinarily a solution is found fairly quickly. Of course, there are times even after insight has been achieved when the solution is still elusive. Nevertheless, the individual focuses her behavior along the lines dictated by her insight rather than acting in a random manner. Moreover, when a solution is achieved through insight, it almost always is easy to repeat. Because the individual understands the problem and has solved it in a deductive, logical way, she should have no trouble solving it again. In contrast, when a problem is solved through trial and error, the individual often has no understanding of how the solution was achieved or even, sometimes, what the solution was.

Fig. 6.11
Brain teasers. See p. 193 for answers.

Brain Teasers

1. Three men go to a hotel and are told that a room costs $30. Each one gives the room clerk $10. After they are in their room, the clerk discovers that the correct price of the room is $25, so he gives $5 to the bellboy to return to the guests. The bellboy goes to their room, gives each of them $1, and keeps $2 for himself. That means that each man has paid $9 for a total of $27, and the bellboy has $2, for a grand total of $29. What happened to the other dollar from the original $30?

2. A man buys a horse for $20 and sells it for $30. Some time later he buys it back for $40 and sells it for $50. How much money did he make on the whole deal?

3. Assuming that the earth is totally flat, where on earth can you walk 10 miles south, 10 miles east, and 10 miles north and arrive back at the place you started from? One answer is relatively easy, but where else can you do it?

4. Arrange ten pennies as shown in the photo below. Change the diagram so that it is a triangle with the point at the top by moving only three coins.

5. You have nine coins and know that one of them is counterfeit and weighs more than the others. How can you tell which is the counterfeit coin with only two weighings on a balance scale?

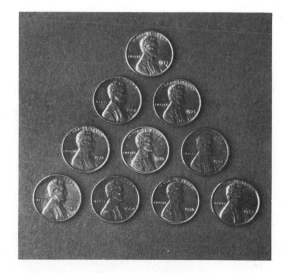

CREATIVE THINKING

Although we all agree that some people are more creative than others, we probably disagree considerably on what we mean by the term *creative. Creativity* refers to an original way of perceiving the world or interpreting experience for others. It is also the ability to solve problems in new and original ways. Thus artists and sculptors, composers and writers, and performers such as musicians, actors, dancers, and singers are considered creative. And scientists and inventors, educators, architects, and businesspeople are also considered creative, even though the types of thinking they use and the products of their thinking may differ greatly from those of people in the arts. It could be argued that they all share flexibility and originality. This is true for both artistic creativity, in which the situations are perceptual or emotional, and for scientific creativity, which involves rational solutions to problems. Whether the same kind of ability is involved in both pursuits is unclear. More important is the fact that creativity can exist in any kind of endeavor, from the purely artistic to the scientific, the practical, or the manual. Any situation that an individual faces can be perceived and dealt with in creative ways.

It is important to distinguish between creativity and originality. Not everything that is new or different is creative. Creative thoughts and perceptions are also meaningful, in terms of clarifying or solving a situation. For example, if you were trapped on a mountain with no food or water, a number of solutions might come to mind. Catching

This photo shows one inventor's ideas about how to find relief from noisy children. Would you consider this solution creative or merely original?

LIVING MADE EASY.

GLASS COVERS FOR NOISY CHILDREN.

rain in your clothes and blankets and wringing them out, digging up tender roots of trees, licking the dew off leaves, and eating insects might all be considered reasonably creative ideas. But chewing on rocks, eating dirt, or working up a rain dance, while original, do not solve the problem and therefore would not be considered creative.

Similarly, artistic creativity should be distinguished from mere originality. Poetry, music, painting, sculpture, and the other art forms often involve new ways of looking at old objects or combining familiar sounds, but not all new visions are creative. Obviously, a series of random sounds or words is likely to produce an original combination of elements, but this does not constitute art. It is not easy to decide what is creative and what only new. In art, this is largely a personal judgment—what one person likes, another will find ridiculous. But with actual problem solving, it is easier to decide. Something new that works is creative; if it fails, it is not useful and therefore not creative in the usual sense. Yet even here, an idea that fails might be brilliantly innovative and eventually prove useful in another context, so that definitive judgments are still difficult.

Testing Creativity

As we shall see in the next chapter, intelligence (IQ) tests attempt to measure a person's ability to solve problems, learn material, remember, and think logically. These abilities, taken collectively, are sometimes called *convergent thinking*. Creativity is thought to involve different kinds of abilities, including forming unusual associations, constructing original arguments, and making up new conclusions that do not necessarily stem from the available facts. These types of abilities, usually termed *divergent thinking*, are measured by creativity tests. It should be noted that there is little or no relationship between someone's intelligence (IQ) and creativity (Wallach and Kogan, 1965a; Getzels and Jackson, 1962). In fact, highly creative individuals may be found at almost any level of intelligence.

One kind of creativity test known as the Remote Association Test (RAT) is designed specifically to measure the ability to form or recognize unusual associations (see Fig. 6.12). Another kind of creativity test is designed to assess the individual's ability to produce a wide variety of new associations to the same stimulus. In the RAT test the job is to find one particular association, while in these other tests it is to produce many different associations. Getzels and Jackson (1962) simply measured the number of different meanings an individual could produce for a common word such as "duck," or "run." Since an unabridged dictionary devotes several pages to the word "run," to some extent this does test the person's ingenuity and creativity. A slightly different form of this test was devised by Guilford in 1954 and has been used quite widely. It requires the individual to name as many uses as possible for a common object. Each use must be entirely different, but there are no other limitations. Thus, for a paper clip, holding together papers, envelopes, and postcards would all count as one use; but hanging a picture from a nail would count as a separate use. It is surprising how many discrete uses can be found for common objects. To test yourself, try listing all the uses you can think of for a brick.

What fourth word is associated with each of the three words in a set?
SAMPLE: wheel-electric-high
ANSWER: chair

a. knob-open-way
b. shake-right-some
c. top-high-rack
d. surprise-line-birthday
e. sky-moon-sea
f. rat-blue-cottage

Fig. 6.12
Tests of creativity

The Remote Association Test (RAT), devised by Sarnoff Mednick in 1962, presents three words and the task is to find a fourth word that has some meaningful or familiar association with the other three. Answers are given below.

Answers to RAT
a. door b. hand c. hat d. party e. blue f. cheese

(a)

(b)
Think of titles for this story

A missionary has been captured by cannibals in Africa. He is in a pot and about to be boiled when a princess of the tribe obtains a promise for his release if he will become her mate. He refuses and is boiled to death.

Common titles
African death
Eaten by savages
The african missionary
In darkest africa
Boiled by savages

Original titles
Stewed parson
A hot price for freedom
Chaste in haste
A mate worse than death
Goil or boil

(c)
Complete this drawing

Ordinary response   Creative response

(d)
Think of an image that is symbolically equivalent

Empty bookcases

Stimulus image

An empty mind

A deserted room

Random subjects

The vacant eyes of an idiot

An abandoned beehive

Creative subjects

Usual responses
The sun
Two igloos
Three people sitting on a table
Table with glasses on it
Raindrops

Unusual responses

Lollipop bursting into pieces
Two haystacks on a flying carpet
Three mice eating a piece of cheese
A foot and toes
Worms hanging

Fig. 6.13
Creativity tests

Answers are scored for originality. ((a) After Wallach and Kogan, 1967; (b) from Guilford, 1959; (c) after Barron, 1958.)

Many other creativity tests have been devised, a few more of which are shown in Fig. 6.13. In general, there is relatively little evidence to support the idea that these tests measure a distinct characteristic or that they have high correlations with other measures of creativity. Nevertheless, these tests are useful attempts to assess this important but mysterious quality that we call creativity.

LIMITS OF THE MIND

In addition to remembering and retrieving information, learning, forming concepts, and solving problems, the mind appears to be capable of a wide variety of other functions. We will now examine several of these functions, ranging from demonstrable skills to controversial possibilities.

Mathematical Prodigies

A few individuals are capable of mental feats so far beyond what most people can do that they seem almost to involve different mental processes. There are documented cases of people who can perform

INTERVIEW

Judith Rossner is a serious writer who is best known as the author of the enormously successful novel Looking for Mr. Goodbar. *The idea for the book came from a newspaper account of the murder of a young woman by a man she picked up in a singles bar. In the novel, Ms. Rossner focuses on the question of whether this woman was somehow responsible for her own death. Her new novel,* Attachments, *deals with an even more unusual topic—the lives of Siamese twins and the women they marry. In the interview we talked about the creative process involved in producing a novel.*

Q. Let's talk about the creative process. How do you go about getting an idea, and then when you have the idea, somehow producing something from it?

A: Well, I don't think it's copping out to say you don't *get* an idea. I think that there's a wellspring that to some extent is beyond our control. Inspiration is striking all the time and I guess one of the differences between the creative person and the noncreative person is that the creative person is more open to the well when it gushes. I'd like to think of a better metaphor. Let's take the businessman who wakes up in the morning and cuts off his dreams and goes into an office; whereas the writer stays home and tries to get back in touch with the fantasy life which is the source of fiction or any creative art.

JUDITH ROSSNER

A writer is like a still. The very raw stuff goes in, and if the writer is talented something smooth and palatable comes out.

Q: Are you saying that part of it is that everyone has ideas but that creative people recognize them more? They sort of say, "Now *that's* an idea!" whereas other people would just ignore it?

A: Well I guess in the sense that there's a leap of confidence involved from "I have had a dream" to "Hey, that's interesting, I should set it down." Actually, the question of what's interesting comes later on. I think that the

ability to recognize what's interesting in what one does is terribly important in terms of self-editing, although *not* necessarily in terms of creating. In point of fact, many people who have the will to be creative are constantly destroying their own work. I have a friend who is quite brilliant, but who edits herself out of existence. She looks at something and starts worrying about whether it's going to be interesting. Much the better part is to allow everything to come up.

Q: To sort of suspend judgment while you're producing and then you can be critical later.

A: Yes, the intellect can sharpen your work and improve it.

Q: One of the ideas that Freud had, and even more so the ego psychologists, is regression in the service of the ego, which is sort of what you were mentioning before. Letting your dreams come . . .

A: Letting yourself be back in touch, leaving yourself in that vulnerable position. I have a friend who complained to me that if he called me up about 11:30 or 12:00 in the morning, which is the time I normally stop work or take a break, we immediately get mired in these extremely heavy conversations. That's because I'm way down there someplace. I'm all regressed.

Q: It's sort of "Don't talk to me about ordinary things, I'm being creative!"

A: Right. Well, it's even more automatic than that. It's closer to the old joke about two psychiatrists meeting in the elevator and one says hello and the other says what did you mean by that. Nothing seems insignificant when you're working at that level.

Q: Let me ask you another side of it. You have these creative ideas, but then you have to get them down on paper and it has to be expressed in words. That's the point at which many people who are creative just can't function. How does it work? What happens when you're actually producing the words? Do they flow into your mind, or do you have to sit and think out each sentence?

A: Sometimes they flow. Sometimes they tumble in unbidden. Right now I'm not planning to start my new book until I come back from a trip in six weeks or so. But without my wanting it, some things are beginning to come into my mind about that book. But I also think that can be an excuse. Many people *wait* for that time, wait for that stuff, and I do think that it's very important for anyone who's serious about writing not to wait but to force oneself to set aside time.

Q: Discipline.

A: Oh, absolutely. The thing is that you're more likely to have that stuff flow into your mind if you have set aside a time. You can't say, "I will write no matter what," but you can say, "I will not do anything else."

Q: Or, "I will sit near the typewriter at least."

A: *At* the typewriter. *At* the desk and do nothing else.

Q: But in the meantime, now you say the next six or eight weeks, you have a plan for a book; it's percolating, gestating.

A: Yes, exactly.

Q: You had a quote about that process that you mentioned to me.

A: Oh, that wonderful Flaubert line. I was once describing to someone when I was finishing this last book, *Attachment*, how I am more open, my defenses are down when I'm creating. And this friend said, well I should think your kids would be like a kind of balance to keep you from sinking too far into it. It wasn't true, but I couldn't explain why. And then in Flaubert's letter he was explaining himself to his lover, a poet whom he saw once or twice a year because to see her more would have interfered with his work. And he said, "I am like a pan of milk. In order for the cream to rise to the top, I must not be disturbed."

Also, one day I was reading the copyedited manuscript of my new book and I thought, "What cost me such effort in this book?" I'd look at this light dialogue and these casual scenes and I could not understand why I was in such a state of anguish during the writing of those scenes. And I realized—and I think it's more than a literary metaphor—that a writer is like a still. The very raw stuff goes in, and if the writer is talented something smooth and palatable comes out. And that it's because the writer is the still herself, or himself, that it's such agony.

Q: All the churning goes on inside and what comes out may or may not be any good.

A: It may be Jack Daniels or it may be rotgut.

Q: I'm sure other people have asked you this, but with *Goodbar*, here's this incident that millions of people read about and then you made up a story about it. The incident is a small part of it. It need not have happened. But probably thousands of people thought about, well why did this happen. How did you start thinking about making a novel out of it?

A: Well, in the case of Goodbar, the woman was murdered close to my old neighborhood. I remember being interested, but it wasn't even in the *Times* very much at first. And then about three weeks later I was in a very bad automobile accident and I was in bed for a month or two afterward. And during this time the murderer of this woman was caught, and that rearoused my interest in the case. I think my entry into it from a psychological viewpoint was one that wouldn't be obvious. The issue for me in my automobile accident, which pertained to the issue for me as I started working on the book, was whether I caused it—the extent to which I was responsible for my own fate—and similarly, did this woman create her own death? I was going to do a magazine article on it, but the idea was vetoed by the legal department of the magazine, because at that time the murderer was still alive and there was concern with jeopardizing his right to a fair trial. So when I heard this I remember saying, well it's just as well because I'm really a lousy journalist and I'm a good storyteller, and I'll just throw out the real story—which I didn't know too much about anyway—and I'll do it as fiction.

Comment

Psychologists have always been fascinated by the creative process, but to a great extent it remains a mystery. There does seem to be a distinction between logical, rational intelligence and creative ability. As Judith Rossner points out, the critical, analytic use of intelligence can often interfere with creativity by judging too harshly or preventing original ideas from appearing. She suggests that to be creative you must allow all kinds of fantasies, dreams, and unstructured ideas to enter your mind and you must take them seriously. After you have used this material, you can and should use your intelligence to pick what is good and discard what is bad.

However, the creative process goes on in part without any effort on the part of the person. In her terms, the writer is a still that bubbles and boils and distills material, and then the creative work emerges. Perhaps this is similar to how insight emerges in the problem-solving process—we cannot force insight to occur, but we can leave ourselves open to it. We can also focus on the right aspects of the problem, or in creative writing, on the fantasies and ideas that are most likely to be useful. Creative people seem to use their own lives, ideas, personality, and experiences to interpret and understand a particular story or event. By adding themselves to the story, they make it unique. Yet, as Ms. Rossner says, discipline is also necessary—you cannot just sit around hoping for inspiration to strike, but must work at it just as you work at anything else.

extremely complex mathematical calculations entirely in their heads and in an amazingly short time. Whereas most of us have difficulty doing mental multiplications much larger than 28 times 31 and would have great difficulty multiplying 56 times 87, these people can multiply four- or five-digit numbers in their heads in seconds, and can find the cube root of a nine-digit number almost instantly—something that most people cannot do in many minutes with paper and pencil.

Such feats cannot be dismissed as simple tricks or cleverness. For example, Zerah Colburn, a prodigy who lived in the early 1800s, performed the following calculations: raised 8 to the 16th power and produced the correct answer, 281,474,976,710,656, in a few seconds; found the cube root of 268,336,125 almost instantly; and could multiply two four-digit numbers with almost no delay. Johann Dase, perhaps the most rapid of these prodigies, multiplied 79,532,853 by 93,758,479 correctly in fifty-four seconds, and found the square root of a one hundred-digit number in fifty-two minutes. All of these calculations are done without pencil and paper, so just the feat of memory involved is fantastic—imagine even remembering a hundred-digit number, much less finding its square root.

Most of these prodigies do seem to use some tricks in their calculations, and they certainly must have phenomenal memories. Many have memorized the multiplication tables up to 99 times 99 and some of them even beyond that. The use of some simple rules gives them control of the table up to 1,000. In addition, they are so familiar with numbers that they recognize aspects of the problem that most of us would not see. For example, in finding the cube root of 188,132,517, George Bidder realized immediately that the answer had three digits, and that the left-hand number must be 5 since 6^3 was too large (216). Also, he happened to remember that the only two-digit number whose cube ends in 17 is 73 and therefore the answer had to

Box 6.2

MENTAL ARITHMETIC TRICKS

Sometimes the explanation of seemingly mysterious arithmetic powers is a simple trick that anyone could use. Many of these tricks are familiar to mathematicians and others who use numbers in their work.

Squaring a two-digit number ending in 5 (for example, 65) is difficult by the usual process. Instead, multiply the first digit by the next higher digit and attach the number 25. For example, to find 65^2, we would multiply 6×7 and get 42. So the answer would be 4,225. For 55, it would be $5 \times 6 = 30$, plus $25 = 3,025$.

To multiply any two-digit number by 11 is fairly easy without tricks. To make it even easier, merely insert the sum of the two digits between them. For example, 54×11: $5 + 4 = 9 = 594$; 34×11: $3 + 4 = 7 = 374$. If the two digits add to more than 9, carry the 1 to the first digit. For example, in 76×11, $7 + 6 = 13$. The answer would then be 7 13 6, so simply carry the 1 to the 7 to get 836.

A more complicated trick involves compound interest. How long would it take for money to double if you invest it at 5 percent compounded annually? To calculate this would normally require raising 1.05 to a power until it equaled 2. Instead, simply divide the rate of interest (5 percent) into 73, and you will arrive at a very close approximation (in this case, 14.6 years). This works for any rate of interest compounded annually.

be 573. Thus, these amazing feats do involve some tricks and certainly depend on phenomenal memories.

Nevertheless, this does not by any means constitute a full explanation. Some of the answers come so fast that the process could scarcely involve a series of mental calculations. And there are other people who can name the day of the week of any date in history. Since they give this information almost instantly, it seems implausible that they are employing a complex system of tricks. Moreover, no obvious calculations could produce the result. In fact, an expensive calculator is now available that provides this information, but only for a short span of years and only if additional information is given, such as the present date and day of the week. This marvel of the transistor age is far inferior to the mental wizards at this particular task.

Surprisingly, many of these prodigies are not particularly intelligent in other respects. Some of them, the so-called *idiot-savants,* are mentally retarded in most ways despite their mathematical skill. Exactly how these prodigies do it is still unknown, but their extraordinary ability suggests that the mind may be capable of feats far beyond those with which we are familiar.

Cognitive Control over Bodily Functions

Many bodily functions are ordinarily beyond conscious control. Most of us cannot deliberately speed up our hearts, control the flow of saliva or any other internal secretions, stop our eyes from blinking at a puff of air, control the sensitivity of our skin to pain, cause goose bumps, or stop ourselves from breathing. But the distinction between bodily functions that are under conscious control and those that are not has recently been called into question. Work on the conditioning of physiological responses, discussed in Chapter 3, demonstrates that internal mechanisms can be affected by learning. These experimental results appear to be consistent with the many anecdotal accounts of people who can seemingly assert mysterious control over their bodies such as walking on hot coals without getting burned. Some observers have suggested that the walker need simply relax and move swiftly and smoothly in order to escape injury, but it seems likely that the full explanation is considerably more complicated. The trained walker may protect himself somehow by stimulating the sweat glands in his feet, or he may be able to reduce his skin's sensitivity in ways that we do not fully understand.

Research on the cognitive control of pain (Zimbardo, Rapaport, and Baron, 1969) supports the idea that people can reduce their sensitivity to pain in all or part of their bodies. Moreover, various psychological and social factors can change their perception of pain and apparently make a given level of, say, electric shock, hurt less (Nisbett and Schachter, 1966). And as we shall describe in Chapter 11, people can withstand a great deal more pain when deeply hypnotized than when awake. Similarly, yogis can slow down most of the physiological processes of their bodies. In many ways they act as though they were in a coma—their heart, pulse, and breathing rates become greatly slowed and they are unresponsive to external stimulation. Yet they are fully awake.

At the moment we do not know the limits of cognitive control over physiological mechanisms, nor do we know the process by which this control is achieved. Perhaps it is much like wiggling one's ears. Some people have this ability, others do not, even though everyone has the same muscles available to them. For someone who knows how to wiggle her ears, it is apparently a simple matter. For someone who does not, it is even difficult to try. She does not know where to start, what to tell her body to do, what muscles to contract. She concentrates very hard, and suddenly her nostrils flare, or her mouth twitches, or her face contorts—but nothing happens to her ears. And yet the potential for wiggling her ears is probably present. Similarly, the potential to control other, more complicated physiological mechanisms may lie within us, but we simply do not know how to use it.

Control of Brain Waves: Biofeedback

Electrical waves in the brain, measured by an electroencephalogram (EEG), indicate the quantity and quality of mental activity. The EEG pattern of a person when sleeping or dreaming is different from his pattern when he is awake. In addition, the waves of someone who is alert or thinking hard are different from those when he is relaxed.

Because these waves are, in a sense, a direct indication of mental activity, it is hardly surprising that people can exert some control over them. In fact, Kamiya (1969) has demonstrated that people can learn to increase or decrease the presence of certain types of brain waves. Most of his work focused on the alpha rhythm, a relatively slow type of wave that seems to occur primarily when people are calm, meditating, feeling detached, or having pleasant mental images.

Fig. 6.14
Subject undergoing biofeedback

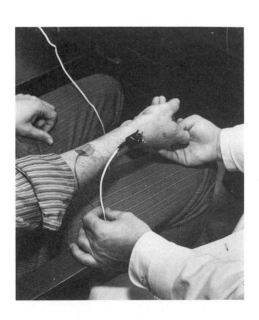

Teaching people to control these waves is fairly simple, and involves a procedure called *biofeedback*. A mechanism that measures alpha waves is attached to a subject's head and a tone is sounded whenever there is a high percentage of alpha rhythms. The subject is instructed to try to keep the tone on by doing or thinking whatever seems to cause it in the first place. The procedure is largely a matter of trial and error, but most people learn to increase the percentage of alpha rhythms dramatically.

The process is circular. Deliberate mental activity is used to control alpha rhythms, which are a reflection of mental activity. In other words, the subjects teach themselves to think in a particular way—in this case, to be relaxed and have pleasant mental images. By controlling other waves, people may be able to teach themselves to think logically or coherently, for example. The important point is not that brain waves can be controlled, but that people, by a deliberate effort, can alter their own mental processes.

As with the other phenomena discussed in this section, we do not know the limits of this kind of control nor its ultimate implications. Unfortunately, biofeedback has become something of a fad or cult. Although it is being used for the perfectly legitimate goal of helping people achieve a relaxed state, some of the claims that have been made for it are grandiose and the expectations of those using it are farfetched. There is, in fact, little evidence to indicate that biofeedback expands consciousness or provides any greater degree of control over mental processes than is possible without mechanical aids.

Extrasensory Perception

Despite the vast normal powers of the human mind, people have long been fascinated by the possibility that supernormal powers exist. People can communicate with one another much better than can members of any other species, and human inventions such as the telephone and television enable us to communicate almost instantly over vast distances. Nevertheless, the idea of being able to read other people's minds (telepathy), to communicate "brain to brain," seems endlessly intriguing. Equally appealing are the possibilities of exerting direct mental control over objects (psychokinesis) and seeing into the future (precognition). Clearly, a lot of people want to believe in the existence of these supernormal powers, which are generally referred to as *extrasensory perception* or ESP.

It is important to consider ESP in the context of our normal mental and physical strengths. Even if we accept the claims made for these powers, at best most of them are relatively weak compared to our normal abilities. They may have marvelous applications in special situations (for example, reading the mind of one's opponents in a card game or hearing a call for help from someone who is lost), but they cannot replace our usual means of communication or control. But these limitations of extrasensory perception do not seem to detract from its fascination. Anything that we cannot fully understand or that seems to go beyond the normal is both intriguing and exciting.

It is still difficult to evaluate the results of the research on ESP. Some studies conducted under apparently controlled conditions have found positive results (Rhine and Brier, 1968) but other studies have found less positive results (see Hansel, 1966, for a review of this literature). Most scientists today remain highly skeptical about the existence of ESP. There are a number of reasons for this lack of belief. Scientists tend to doubt the existence of a phenomenon that seems inexplicable in terms of what is known about the mental and physical world. While this is not an entirely legitimate reason to doubt the existence of ESP, anything that runs totally counter to what is known should be greeted skeptically but openly and the burden of proof should be on those who believe in the new phenomenon. Nevertheless, since ESP is seemingly magical and mysterious, it is understandable that scientists will continue to doubt its existence until it has been fully demonstrated.

Moreover, unlike most phenomena, there seems to be little consistency about ESP or control over it. A telepath may be able to read a mind one day and not the next; he may be better than chance but is always far from perfect; and he cannot increase his receptivity when he wants to. In other words, ESP powers are inconsistent and pretty much out of the control of the person who supposedly possesses them. Because this is so different from most human abilities, it makes us doubt the existence of ESP. If someone really can read minds or control the throw of dice, she should be able to prove it. To paraphrase the old saying, "if you're so psychic, why aren't you rich?" ■

Summary

1. A useful definition of thinking includes concept formation, mental rehearsal of alternatives, problem solving, and intellectual creativity. These functions are sometimes called higher mental processes.

2. In order to understand how the world operates we must be able to organize it in some way. We do this by forming concepts, which identify similarities among a number of different stimuli or situations. Concept formation allows us to group objects together, an ability that is essential to stimulus generalization. Because we can identify similarities, we can generalize from one situation to another and thereby use what we have learned.

3. We can identify two basic types of concepts. In a conjunctive concept, a class is defined by one or more characteristics that must all be present for an object to fit the class. In a disjunctive concept, the class of objects must contain one of a group of qualities, but it need not contain all.

4. Four approaches to concept formation have been proposed: association theory, hypothesis-testing theory, perceptual approach, and information processing. Association theory views concept formation as identical to discrimination learning, where the essential elements of the concept are acquired through the forming of associations. Hypothesis testing involves having theories or hunches about the concept and then testing to see if these hypotheses are correct. The perceptual or Gestalt idea is that people form a perceptual impression of a class of objects and

thereby to some extent short-circuit the process of concept formation. It seems certain that these three approaches are all involved in forming concepts.

5. Information processing attempts to apply computer models to describe the process of concept formation. In a sense it combines the other approaches because the model assumes that people form associations, test hypotheses, and have certain perceptual tendencies.

6. When people try to solve a problem or discover a concept, they apply problem-solving strategies called heuristics. The heuristics people employ help us to understand how they think. Development of heuristics that can be successfully applied in a wide variety of situations enables an individual to grasp concepts and solve problems more quickly and easily than by trial and error. Some specific heuristics that people use include focusing, scanning (usually in combination), and exercising preferences for certain types of material. The characteristics people pay attention to change somewhat with age.

7. Theories of problem solving are basically the same as for concept formation. Association theory involves trying random behaviors until one works; hypothesis testing is more systematic—on each trial a hypothesis is tested and if it fails it is discarded in favor of a new hypothesis. The Gestalt approach emphasizes the necessity of recognizing the differences between a new problem and a previous, similar problem and then reorganizing one's perception of the situation.

8. Relying on a problem-solving technique that worked in the past can result in rigid thinking—the tendency to treat objects or forms in rigid ways. When faced with a new problem, the individual cannot use the object in a new way and therefore cannot solve the problem.

9. Information processing and computer models—including flow charts, simulations, and chess programs—have made important contributions to the study of problem solving by describing the heuristics people use in reaching solutions.

10. Although trial-and-error solutions to problems are slow, they may lead to more generalized problem solving by teaching us to pay attention to important aspects of a stimulus. We learn what to look for and what strategies to try and thus increase our chances of finding a solution. That is, we can learn how to solve problems.

11. Insight involves the sudden recognition of the critical elements of a problem. We do not understand the mechanism by which this occurs, but we do know that when it happens, behavior that might have been haphazard becomes more sharply directed toward a solution. Research on insight with primates has demonstrated that animals are capable of complex mental activity.

12. Creative thinking consists of using familiar objects and information in entirely new ways to meet new demands. Creativity in problem solving differs from originality in that creative perceptions help to solve a problem, whereas original perceptions may

not. Creativity is characterized by abilities such as forming unusual associations, constructing original arguments, and reaching a conclusion that does not necessarily stem from the available facts. These abilities, termed divergent thinking, are measured by creativity tests.

13. Extrasensory perception refers to supernormal powers of the
human mind, including telepathy, psychokinesis, and precognition. Research results on ESP have been mixed, and most scientists remain skeptical about the existence of ESP because the
phenomenon is inexplicable in terms of what we know about the
mental and physical worlds and because ESP powers are inconsistent and not under the individual's control.

RECOMMENDED READING

Harlow, H. F. "The Formation of Learning Sets." *Psychological Review* 56:
(1949) 51–65. A short, amusing, and influential article that demonstrates how
one can learn to solve problems even though the actual solutions differ. The
effect is sometimes called "learning to learn" or "learning to think."

Kohler, W. *The Mentality of Apes.* New York: Harcourt Brace Jovanovich,
1925. How apes think and solve problems. Great reading by one of the first
men to study these issues carefully.

Newell, A., and H. A. Simon. *Human Problem Solving.* Englewood Cliffs,
N.J.; Prentice-Hall, 1972. The computer approach to problem solving. Rather
difficult and often unrelated to much of the actual work with people, but
illustrates this line of research.

Answer to Fig. 6.6

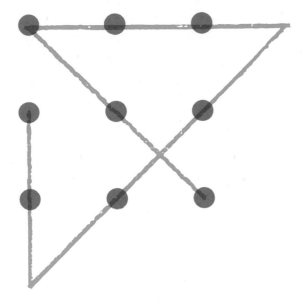

Answers to Fig. 6.11

Answers to Brain Teasers

1. The money is there, but the calculations have been totally confused by sometimes adding and sometimes subtracting. Each man paid $10 originally, *but* got back $1 so the total left to account for is $27. The hotel has $25 of that and the bellboy the other $2. You don't add the bellboy's money to the $27, you subtract it.

2. Twenty dollars. He made $10 on each transaction—the fact that it was the same horse is irrelevant. He paid a total of $60 and got a total of $80.

3. The north pole is one. Whichever way you walk first is south, east keeps you ten miles south of the pole, and ten miles north brings you back. We'll leave the other one for you to work on—.

4. Move the coins at each end of the top line to the end of the line second from the bottom, and then move the very bottom coin to the top of the diagram. The trick is to make the original top line into the two-coin line, rather than moving the three coins at the bottom. This solution and an alternative one are diagrammed at right.

5. Divide the coins into three groups of three coins each. Put one group on either side of the scale. If one side goes down, it has the counterfeit; if they balance, the remaining group contains the counterfeit. Whichever group is implicated, put one of the three coins on one side of the scale and another on the other side. If one side goes down, it holds the counterfeit coin, if they balance, the third coin is the one.

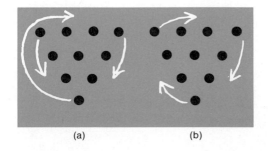

(a) (b)

The cultivation of the mind is a kind of food supplied for the soul of humanity.
Cicero, De Finibus Bonorum et Malorum

7 Psychological Testing and Intelligence

The theory of testing ▪ *Factors determining the usefulness of a test* ▪ *Intelligence and intelligence tests* ▪ *The role of heredity and environment* ▪ *Mental retardation* ▪ *The mentally gifted*

It is probably fair to say that psychological testing has aroused more controversy and had a greater impact on our lives than any other contribution of psychology. Most of us have taken psychological tests designed to tell how intelligent we are, how well we will do in school, which major we are best suited for, which career we will like, and what kind of personality we have. We take tests at all stages of our education—to get into school, to be placed in the appropriate class, to get into medical or law school, and eventually to get a job. In some other countries tests of this kind are even more crucial, determining whether someone can go to college at all. Because testing affects each of us, it is important to understand the assumptions on which tests are based in order to be able to evaluate both the strengths and limitations of psychological testing.

Psychological testing is designed to measure three broad qualities—creativity, personality, and intelligence. The preceding chapter, on thinking, took up the topic of creativity tests, and we discuss personality tests in Chapter 14. In the present chapter we shall deal with the problems and strengths of psychological testing in general, and with the concept of intelligence, tests of intelligence, the mentally retarded, and the mentally gifted.

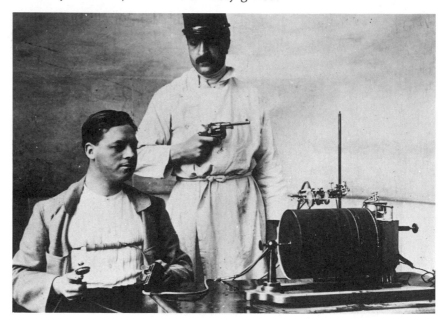

Psychological testing is not new. This 1905 photo shows a primitive setup designed to test the reactions of a man applying for work as an aviator.

To being with, testing in one form or another is as old as mankind. Contests to see who was the swiftest runner, most accurate marksman, best cook, most creative weaver, and so on must have existed as long as organized human society. All competitive sports are essentially tests of ability, and virtually all organized education uses tests to assess how much the student has learned. However, psychological testing is different because it attempts to measure not just ability and achievement but also aptitude and potential. Instead of asking how much you know about mathematics or how good you are at brain surgery, many psychological tests are designed to find out how high your *potential* is in these activities. These tests are given to someone who has no training in mathematics or surgery and therefore obviously cannot perform very well at the moment, and the test is supposed to give an indication of how well the person would perform after extensive training.

Measuring potential is obviously a much more difficult task than just assessing current ability. It involves predicting the future, always a hazardous occupation. Yet with all the difficulties involved, tests have been developed to measure potential for all sorts of activities. There are tests of verbal and mathematical aptitude, and of potential for law, medicine, piloting, psychology, or any number of specific jobs and professions. And, as we shall see, despite certain important limitations, many of these tests are quite successful.

THE THEORY OF TESTING

The basic assumption behind all psychological testing is that certain characteristics play an important role in one's ability to perform any task or develop any skill, and that measuring these characteristics will enable one to estimate how well the person will eventually be able to perform the task or learn the skill. The trick, of course, is to discover what characteristics are important and then to measure them accurately.

This idea of assessing potential before the skill has been fully learned is not new. It is common practice in athletics, dancing, and many other activities that involve physical ability. The aspiring dancer must demonstrate a certain degree of grace, coordination, strength, and agility before being accepted into a high-level ballet school. A fat, awkward candidate will probably be judged to have low potential and will be rejected. Psychologists have carried this procedure further by measuring a wider variety of qualities and, in particular, by focusing on some that are not so easily observed as physical coordination. Yet the idea is the same—find out what is important in determining potential and then measure it.

FACTORS DETERMINING THE USEFULNESS OF A TEST

The usefulness of any test is determined largely by its *reliability*, which is how consistently it produces the same result for the same person, and its *validity*, which is how well it measures what it is supposed to.

Reliability

If you want to find out how much you weigh, you might step on a scale at home and see what it registers. However, some scales, particularly ordinary bathroom scales, give different readings depending on the humidity in the room, atmospheric pressure, evenness of the floor, and even how you stand on them. You might weigh 150 one time and 155 ten minutes later because you have shifted your weight or moved the scale. Such a scale has low reliability because it gives you different answers even though you have obviously not gained weight in those ten minutes.

The reliability of psychological tests (or any other measure) is indicated by the similarity or *correlation* (see Chapter 1) between scores on one occasion and scores on another, or between the score on one half the test and the score on the other half (called *split-half reliability*). The more similar the two scores, the higher the reliability. We usually do not accept tests that have much below .8 or even .9 reliability. Unfortunately, most psychological tests do not have as high reliabilities as we would like. The problem is that performance on tests is affected by a wide variety of factors in addition to the quality being tested. How well you are feeling that day, how hard you try, how well you slept, how much you like the person giving the test, how comfortable you are, and many other irrelevant aspects of the situation tend to influence your score. In fact, virtually all of our behavior is affected by these kinds of factors and it is therefore difficult to construct highly reliable measures of any performance that depends even in part on how we are feeling. Our mood affects how fast we run, how well we paint, how well we remember organic chemistry reactions, and just about everything else.

However, some kinds of performance are more affected by extraneous factors than are others. The less effort that is involved, the less likely the response is to be affected by how hard you try. For example, intelligence tests often include items that require you to provide a piece of information, such as who wrote *Romeo and Juliet*, and also items that require you to memorize a list of numbers and repeat them back. The former involves little effort—either you know the answer or you do not. Of course, you may sometimes know it and be unable to recall it; but generally, if you have the information, you will get the answer right. In contrast, recalling numbers requires a high degree of concentration and, usually, the harder you try, the better you will do. If you do not or cannot concentrate, your score will be lower. Therefore, information tests are less affected by irrelevant, momentary factors in the situation and usually have higher reliability than digit recall. For the same reasons, multiple-choice exams that merely require you to supply the right answer are usually more reliable than essay exams that require you not only to have the information but also to organize it, construct an argument, and write a coherent essay.

A great deal of effort goes into making psychological tests reliable. Each question is checked for reliability and rejected if it does not produce consistent results. Those tests that continue to be used widely have a fairly high reliability—the scores you achieve on different days under different circumstances will be quite similar. Nevertheless, care should always be taken to administer tests in a standard way under standard conditions so as to minimize the effect of extraneous factors. One of the difficulties with the use of tests is that such care is not always taken. For example, some children taking a test of intelligence may have had a good night's rest and full breakfast while others have not, thus giving the former a distinct advantage.

Validity

Validity is even more important than reliability and harder to achieve. A test can be very reliable, producing highly consistent scores, and yet not measure the quality it is intended to measure. A bathroom scale measures weight. We know that putting a heavy weight on it makes the indicator go higher than a light weight, and we know that it usually reads zero or close to zero when there is nothing on it. But the relationship between the score and the quality being measured is much less clear with most psychological tests.

By their nature, psychological tests are designed to measure some characteristic that is not easily observed, such as aptitude for medical school, creativity, or intelligence. These are much more abstract concepts than physical qualities, we are not entirely certain what they consist of, and therefore it is much more difficult to design a test that measures them accurately.

To assess the validity of a test it is necessary to have some criterion; that is, some other measure in which you have confidence. You trust a physician's balance scale and can use it to assess the validity of a bathroom scale. If the two scales produce similar answers, you believe that the bathroom scale measures weight accurately. But against what do you compare a test of medical aptitude or intelligence? Although there are several reasonable alternatives, none of them is entirely satisfactory. For example, it seems plausible that intelligence plays an important role in school performance and we could use grade-point average as a criterion of intelligence. Then, if an intelligence test predicted how well people would do in school, we could say that the test was valid. This is reasonable up to a point, but we all know that how well someone does in school depends on a lot more than intelligence. How hard you work, what courses you take, how lenient your teachers are, and even how much they like you may contribute to your grades. So how well you do in school is not a perfect measure of your intelligence and grade-point average is not a perfect criterion against which to measure the validity of an intelligence test. The same argument holds for any other single criterion, and even applies to a criterion based on several kinds of performance. In fact, there is no perfect criterion for intelligence and therefore it is difficult to be certain that any intelligence test is entirely valid. As we shall see, much of the criticism of psychological tests in general and intelligence tests in particular has been that they are not valid measures.

With this brief introduction to psychological testing, let us now turn to a consideration of the concept of intelligence and then examine the problems and successes in measuring it.

INTELLIGENCE AND INTELLIGENCE TESTS

Just as people vary in athletic or musical abilities, so they differ widely in what has been called intellectual ability. Given a problem to solve, a concept to discover, a list of words to learn, or any other kind of intellectual material to master, some people will more or less consistently do better than others. This general ability is called *intelligence,* and is sometimes referred to simply as *g*.

Although most psychologists and lay persons think of intelligence as a single unitary characteristic, there is considerable controversy about this. We may say that someone is either intelligent or unintelligent across the board, but actually people can be above average in certain kinds of intellectual activities and below average in others. We are all familiar with people who are very good with words but bad with numbers, or vice versa. Students who have taken the scholastic aptitude tests know that they do not always do equally well on the verbal and mathematical parts of the exam. With more complex tests of intelligence that involve many different subscales and kinds of items, an individual's scores on the separate scales can differ considerably. Nevertheless, there is usually a fairly good agreement between one measure of intelligence and another. The verbal and nonverbal parts of a test usually have a correlation of at least .70, and even the subscales have quite high correlations with each other and with the total score.

Thus there are two important points about intelligence; (1) it is probably not a unitary characteristic, but it is made up of a number of different skills and potential abilities, with each individual being better in some than in others; and (2) there tends to be a fairly strong relationship among these abilities, so that someone who is very good in some will probably be quite good in the others as well, and someone who scores very low on any of them will probably score low on most of them. A low overall score does not mean that the person is equally poor in all intellectual areas—he may have some abilities that are considerably better than others. However, the evidence does seem to support the concept of general intelligence.

Individual Intelligence Tests

The Stanford-Binet The first widely used intelligence test was devised by the French psychologist Alfred Binet in 1905 and revised by Lewis Terman in 1916. The new version, known as the *Stanford-Binet* (because Terman was at Stanford University), was for many years by far the most popular test for measuring intelligence in children. The idea behind this test is that children's ability to reason and learn improves with age. A task that is impossible for a three-year-old becomes increasingly easy as the child gets older. But not all three-year-olds are equally capable. Most three-year-olds can perform only certain tasks, while some perform more and some fewer. The Stanford-Binet is administered individually. The child is presented with a series of items, each of which can be passed by about half of the children of the same age. Some of these are listed in Fig. 7.1.

With this test, Binet introduced the idea of *mental age.* If a child is at the four-year-old level, we say he has a *mental age* of four. To determine how he compares to other children, we compute his *intelligence quotient,* usually abbreviated *IQ,* which is simply his mental age divided by his chronological age (CA) multiplied by a hundred. The formula IQ = MA/CA times 100 would give this child a score of $4/3 = 1.33$ times 100 = 133. Similarly, a five-year-old with a mental age of seven has an IQ of 140, while the same child with a mental age of four would have an IQ of 80.

Note that a three-year-old operating at the four-year-old level has the same IQ as a six-year-old operating at the eight-year-old level. The assumption is that their potential is the same, despite the fact that obviously the older child is solving many more problems and operating at a higher intellectual level for the moment. A child of five with an IQ of 180 may be potentially brilliant, but he is not yet the intellectual equivalent of a twenty-year-old college student of even moderate intelligence. John Stuart Mill, one of the great geniuses of

Age 2:	Shown a board with holes into which various shapes such as square and circle can be fitted, places the correct blocks in the holes. Shown pictures of common objects such as a table or ball, correctly calls it by its name.
Age 3½:	Shown a card with a picture of a large and small object, points to the larger one when asked. Shown a picture of an animal such as a cow, can find another picture of a cow from among various animals.
Age 5:	Shown a picture of a person with some parts missing (for example, arm, leg), can tell what is missing. Asked to define simple words such as table or hat, can give correct definition.
Age 6:	Answers correctly analogies such as "a dog *walks*; a bird _____?" Defines more difficult words such as envelope. Identifies numbers by giving tester the number of blocks requested.
Age 8:	Can define more difficult words such as eyelash. Can tell how two objects such as football and apple are similar and different. Can name the days of the week and knows the correct order.

Fig. 7.1
Stanford-Binet test items

These examples are similar to those used in the Stanford-Binet test (Terman and Merrill, 1937), but are not exact duplicates.

all time, supposedly learned Greek and Latin at the age of four or five but even he did not make important contributions to human thought until he was somewhat older.

Wechsler Intelligence Tests For many years, two of the most extensively employed tests of intelligence were the Wechsler Adult Intelligence Scale (WAIS) and Wechsler Intelligence Scale for Children (WISC). To some extent they have been replaced by a wide variety of new tests, but the basic principles have been retained. Like the Stanford-Binet, the Wechsler tests are administered individually. All of these tests try to measure intelligence by assessing several different kinds of ability. For example, the Wechsler scales consist of eleven subtests divided into verbal and nonverbal (or performance) types. The adult scales are listed in Table 7.1 with a sample item or description of an item next to each. You can see that the verbal tests involve logic, reasoning, concept formation (distinguishing similarities), memory, and certain kinds of verbal information in terms of both specific facts and vocabulary. The performance tests involve the manipulation of objects, design, noticing what is absent from a picture, and the ability to use symbols. The person taking the test gets a score on each subtest, an overall score for verbal and performance, and then the total IQ score. Although, as we mentioned above, the verbal and performance scores tend to be highly related, many people do considerably better on one than on the other, and scores on specific subtests differ quite a bit, which indicates that even people of similar intelligence have different intellectual abilities.

The most important feature of the Wechsler scales is that the scoring of each subtest is based on the actual responses of a random

Table 7.1

PARAPHRASED VERBAL SCALES OF WECHSLER ADULT INTELLIGENCE TEST

Subscale	Easy item	Difficult item
Comprehension	What should you do if you see someone forget his book when he leaves his seat in a restaurant?	Why is copper often used in electrical wires?
Similarities	How are a lion and a tiger alike?	How are a parachute and a dandelion seed similar?
Vocabulary	Define: comedy, bowl	Define: abjure, stultify
Information	How many wings does a bird have?	Who wrote *Paradise Lost*?
Digit span	Repeat in order: 497 Repeat backwards: 318	Repeat in order: 62765918 Repeat backwards: 47916539
Arithmetical reasoning	Sam had three pieces of candy and Joe gave him four more. How many pieces of candy did Sam have altogether?	Sarah can get to work in forty-five minutes driving thirty miles an hour. How long will it take her if she drives fifty miles an hour?

From Wechsler, 1958.

sample of 1,700 people. Their scores, divided into seven age groups (from sixteen to sixty-four), determine the average performance on each test. For example, the average number of digits that people between the ages of twenty and twenty-four could remember is five in a forward direction and four backward for a total of nine. Therefore, a total score of nine is the average and is assigned the rating of 100. Next, the variation in the scores of the test sample is computed in terms of standard deviations (see Appendix). A score exactly one standard deviation above the mean is assigned the rating of 115 while a score one standard deviation below the mean is given a rating of 85. And each additional standard deviation above or below the mean also translates into fifteen points. Thus, a score two standard deviations above the mean on any scale would be equal to 130. In the digit span test, the standard deviation was 1.5; in other words, someone who remembered eleven rather than nine items would be about 1.3 standard deviations above the mean and would have a rating on that subtest of 120.

This standardized scoring of the tests has several advantages. First, it makes it easy to compare performance on the various subtests and on the performance and verbal halves of the scale. You can quickly determine that someone is performing at a superior level on certain tests and less well on others and you can also have a more precise measure of just how much better she is performing. In addition, you combine the scores on each subtest to get an overall IQ score. If, on average, someone scored 115 on all subtests, his IQ is 115. This score is based on how well the person did relative to others of the same age. Since, by definition, certain percentages will obtain scores 1, 2, and 3 standard deviations above and below the mean, we can be certain that an IQ score based on the Wechsler indicates where the individual falls compared to the other people. Because of the definition of a standard deviation, 13.59 percent of the scores should fall one standard deviation or more above the mean and the same percentage should fall one standard deviation or more below the mean.

Thus, a score that is one standard deviation above and equals an IQ of 115 should be obtained by only that percentage of the population. In fact, as shown in Fig. 7.2, there is some deviation from this exact figure, but it does give a close approximation of the mean of a particular IQ. Similarly, on the same basis it can be determined that only about 10 percent of the people have an IQ over 120 and only 1 percent have an IQ over 135.

Group Intelligence Tests

Because the Stanford-Binet and Wechsler scales must be administered individually, they are inefficient for testing large numbers of people. During World War I the United States Army developed tests that could be given in large groups—the Army Alpha and Beta Tests designed for literate and illiterate people respectively. During World War II the Army General Classification Tests (AGCT) and later the Armed Forces Qualification Test (AFQT) were constructed along lines quite similar to the Wechsler scales. And almost all college students are familiar with the Scholastic Aptitude Tests, which are essentially verbal and mathematical intelligence tests.

More Complex Tests

There are also much more complex tests that break intelligence down into a large number of separate factors. Thurstone (1938, 1941) used dozens of separate tests and concluded that intelligence actually consisted of seven primary abilities, including verbal comprehension, word fluency (the ability to think of words rapidly), number (simple computations), space (the ability to form visual relationships), memory, perceptual speed (the ability to recognize differences and similarities among items), and reasoning. However, it turned out that scores on these seven supposedly primary abilities were quite highly correlated and thus might all be related to what is ordinarily called general intelligence.

Guilford (1967) has proposed an even more complex model of intelligence, which hypothesizes 120 or more separate factors. Although there is some evidence for the existence of many of these factors, most psychologists continue to believe in a fairly general notion of intelligence rather than one composed of a large number of separate abilities. On the other hand, Guilford has made the important point that intelligence may have been defined too narrowly in most of

Fig. 7.2
Distribution of IQ scores

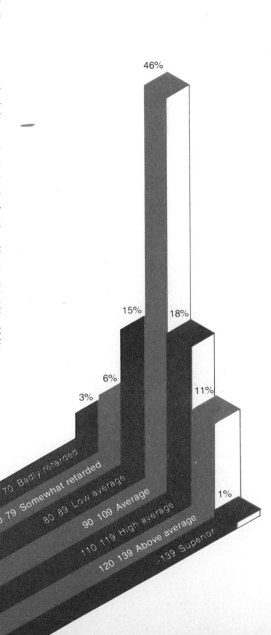

the previous tests. Creative thinking, or as he calls it *divergent thinking,* is usually excluded from intelligence tests and yet does seem to be an important part of intellectual functioning. As mentioned in Chapter 6, many tests have been devised to assess creative thinking as opposed to more logical or rational modes of thought.

Assessing Intelligence Tests

The concept of intelligence and the measurement of IQ play an important role in most of our lives. Children who score high on intelligence tests in grade school are put into advanced classes, while those who score low are often held back. Someone who is supposed to have a high IQ is treated differently by teachers, parents, and even other children. In some countries such as England and France, performance on aptitude tests determines whether you are allowed to go on to college, while in this country scores on the SAT are a major factor in whether or not you are admitted to a particular school. Although they are not strictly speaking IQ tests, the medical and law aptitude tests are merely specialized forms of intelligence tests, as are the graduate record examinations, and all of these to a large extent determine whether a student can get into a particular professional or graduate school. Since intelligence and other aptitude tests are so important, it is essential that we understand as well as possible just how good they are and what they measure. We need to answer three major questions: (1) How reliable are the tests? (2) How valid are they? and (3) How fair are they to different people and groups of people? A related issue of great interest is the role of heredity and environment in intelligence. We shall discuss this in a separate section.

Are intelligence tests reliable? The strongest aspect of most intelligence tests is that they are quite reliable. Someone taking a test at two different times within the space of a few weeks or even months will achieve approximately the same score. Similarly, subtests correlate highly with total scores, as do alternate forms of the same test. And the IQ given by one standard test such as the Stanford-Binet is consistent with that produced by another such as the Wechsler—correlations are usually above .8 and often above .9 (Anastasi, 1968; Wechsler, 1958). Thus, in general it is possible to put some reliance on an individual's score regardless of what test she has taken or when she has taken it.

One important limitation on this generally high reliability is that scores on tests given to children under the age of two are often quite different from those on tests given several years later. Whereas tests given at age seven have correlations of well over .7 with tests given at ages ten, fourteen, and even eighteen, tests given at age two have correlations of below .5 with later tests (Jensen, 1973). As shown in Fig. 7.3, reliability increases steadily with age, so that scores at ten are usually very similar to those at sixteen, eighteen, and later. The low correlations before the age of two are probably due in part to the effect of environment on intelligence (we shall discuss this later) but also to the fact that the earlier tests involve little or no language and therefore may involve different abilities.

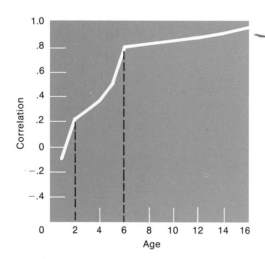

Fig. 7.3

Agreement of IQ scores obtained at early ages with those at sixteen or eighteen

Scores gotten before the age of four have little or no correlations with later scores. However, after about six, scores remain quite consistent for as long as ten years. (After Bayley and Schaefer, 1964)

The fact that intelligence scores at one age agree reasonably well with those at a later age does not by any means imply that every person's score is consistent. On the contrary, someone's score on an IQ test can change dramatically from one age to another and even from one month to the next. It is not unusual for a person to score fifteen points higher or lower when he is tested again. In other words, while the tests do have pretty good reliability, there is still a lot of room for variation. This means that one should not rely too much on any one IQ score.

There is some indication, in fact, that intelligence changes with age. Although it is difficult to be certain, most studies suggest that *actual* intelligence (intelligence compared to that of all people rather than just others in your age group) increases up to some age, which varies for different abilities, and then declines slowly (see Fig. 7.4). However, there is considerable doubt about the shape of this curve and whether any appreciable decline occurs until well over sixty or seventy. In any case, there is no need to worry about having peaked already or about beginning to decline. Even if intelligence does decline slightly as one gets older, the decrease is exceedingly gradual and largely unimportant. Moreover, any substantial decline seems to occur more in word fluency and speed rather than in more basic abilities such as reasoning and comprehension (Schaie and Strother, 1968).

With the exceptions just stated, intelligence tests tend to be highly reliable. They are not, however, perfect. Although there are few studies on this specific problem, it is obvious that momentary changes in how you are feeling can affect your scores. All of us must have experienced occasions on which we did much less well on a test than we expected to because we were extremely tired or not feeling well.

One of the major difficulties in relying on the Scholastic Aptitude Test for admission to college is that some students worry so much about their performance that their tension and fatigue interferes with their scores. Some educators are aware of this difficulty and will take it into account, but unfortunately, many educators and employers place too much trust in the scores.

Are intelligence tests valid? A much more difficult question is whether IQ tests are measuring what they are supposed to. As we mentioned above, the validity of a test is assessed by comparing the scores on the test with those on some other indicator of the characteristic supposedly being measured. In other words, testing the validity of an intelligence test requires that we have some other measure that we are confident indicates the individual's intelligence. Although there is some disagreement about this, most psychologists will agree that more intelligent people should do better in school than less intelligent people, and that therefore average grades in high school and college are reasonably good indicators of IQ. When scores on the Wechsler and Scholastic Aptitude tests are compared with performance in college, a moderately strong relationship generally appears. Neither test predicts perfectly college performance but the correlations are usually greater than .5 and are sometimes over .6. This is not an overwhelming relationship, but it does indicate that

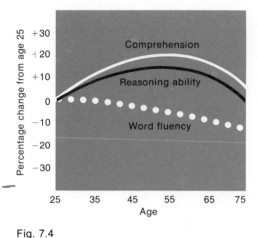

Fig. 7.4
Changes in intelligence with age

These are rough estimates, but it appears that only fluency declines appreciably. (After Schaie and Strother, 1968)

Box 7.1

THE EFFECT OF BEING LABELED SMART OR DUMB

One of the most serious difficulties with relying too heavily on IQ tests is that teachers tend to treat "bright" and "slow" children differently. Once a child has been labeled as smart because of a high IQ score, teachers will often give that child more attention, encourage him more, and generally look favorably on all that he does. Similarly, a child who is labeled slow because of a low score is sometimes ignored, discouraged, and given less good marks than he may deserve. In other words, the teacher's expectations affect how she treats the student, and this treatment in turn actually causes the student to do either better or worse depending on the original expectation.

Rosenthal (1966) has demonstrated this effect in a wide variety of circumstances. It is a serious problem in psychological research, for example, because an experimenter may produce the results he expects by treating subjects slightly differently in line with his predictions. It is especially serious when it affects the lives of students. This is one of the reasons many educators are opposed to the track system, in which students are put in separate classes according to their aptitude.

The difficulty is that someone who is put in a particular class will be treated as if she belonged there, and if the assignment was incorrect, the student will suffer. In fact, this is just one example of how any expectation or impression can affect our treatment of people; and it is a strong argument against forming such firm impressions that your behavior toward others is determined by what you expect of them rather than how they act.

ROBERT ROSENTHAL

whatever is being measured by the IQ tests plays a role in academic achievement.

Similarly, on the Stanine test to determine aptitude for pilot training, the general information scale, which is the closest to a general intelligence test, had the highest single correlation (.49) with completion of training (DuBois, 1947). This test was not specifically related to the mechanical or perceptual abilities involved in being a pilot, but it predicted even better than tests of these specific abilities. Moreover, studies of different occupational groups indicate that people with high IQ's tend to be in those professions that we would expect to require higher intelligence. For example, accountants, chemists, and engineers have a higher average score than bartenders, truck drivers, and miners (see Fig. 7.5 for some other examples). IQ does not account for all of the variation, of course; there is a great deal of overlap among the professions and there may also be other factors that cause people with high scores to go into certain professions. Nevertheless, the correlations with school performance, with specific

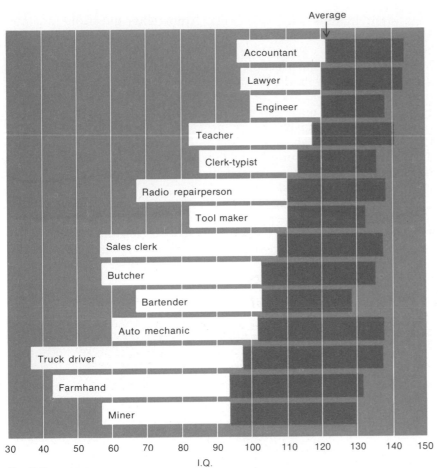

Fig. 7.5
Occupation and IQ

Although there is a wide range of IQs in every occupation (shown by width of bars), the average IQ (shown by the line between the white and the tinted halves) does differ considerably. (From Harrell and Harrell, 1945)

achievement such as the pilot training, and with occupational groups all contribute to the belief that IQ tests are reasonably valid.

Are intelligence tests fair? Most of the controversy surrounding intelligence tests revolves around the question of whether they are fair to all the people taking them. A test can be a reliable and valid measure of intelligence for some people and not for others, and can be biased toward certain groups or individuals. The major sources of bias in intelligence testing involve problems in communication, visual and auditory problems, and the use of biased materials.

Communication problems. Someone who cannot understand the question obviously cannot answer it correctly. Although it might seem fairly easy to write questions that everyone can understand, it is actually extremely difficult. Indeed, as most students are aware, teachers who write multiple-choice exams are often guilty of constructing items where both the question and the answer are highly ambiguous. Despite careful attention to this problem, intelligence tests often include such questions. Ambiguous questions are not necessarily a source of bias. If everyone has equal difficulty understanding them, this will reduce the reliability and validity of the test but will not hurt some peoples' scores more than others'. The real difficulty occurs when the language or wording used is easier for some people to understand than for others. This is clearly the case when an exam in one language is given to people who have varying degrees of mastery of that language. For some Spanish-speaking people in the United States, English is a second rather than a primary language. They may be able to communicate perfectly well in English but not have the full mastery of the language that is required for a total understanding of the test.

A less obvious source of difficulty that is sometimes overlooked occurs when someone speaks the language perfectly but uses a somewhat different dialect than the one in which the exam is written. Most intelligence tests in this country use the language of white,

Fig. 7.6

The Dove Counterbalance General Intelligence Test

This "chitlin" test was constructed by black sociologist Adrian Dove to point out the bias inherent in most intelligence tests, which use the language and idiom of the white middle class. (Copyright 1968 by Newsweek, Inc. All rights reserved. Reprinted by permission.)

1. A "handkerchief head" is: (a) a cool cat, (b) a porter, (c) an Uncle Tom, (d) a hoddi, (e) a preacher.

2. Which word is most out of place here? (a) splib, (b) blood, (c) gray, (d) spook, (e) black.

3. A "gas head" is a person who has a: (a) fast-moving car, (b) stable of "lace," (c) "process," (d) habit of stealing cars, (e) long jail record for arson.

4. "Down-home" (the South) today, for the average "soul brother" who is picking cotton from sunup until sundown, what is the average earning (take home) for one full day? (a) $.75, (b) $1.65, (c) $3.50, (d) $5, (e) $12.

5. "Bo Diddley" is a: (a) game for children, (b) down-home cheap wine, (c) down-home singer, (d) new dance, (e) Moejoe call.

6. If a pimp is up tight with a woman who gets state aid, what does he mean when he talks about "Mother's Day"? (a) second Sunday in May, (b) third Sunday in June, (c) first of every month, (d) none of these, (e) first and fifteenth of every month.

7. "Hully Gully" came from: (a) East Oakland, (b) Fillmore, (c) Watts, (d) Harlem, (e) Motor City.

8. If a man is called a "blood," then he is a (a) fighter, (b) Mexican-American, (c) Negro, (d) hungry hemophile, (e) Redman or Indian.

9. Cheap chitlings (not the kind you purchase at a frozen-food counter) will taste rubbery unless they are cooked long enough. How soon can you quit cooking them to eat and enjoy them? (a) 45 minutes, (b) two hours (c) 24 hours, (d) one week (on a low flame), (e) one hour.

10. What are the "Dixie Hummingbirds?" (a) part of the KKK, (b) a swamp disease, (c) a modern gospel group, (d) a Mississippi Negro paramilitary group, (e) Deacons.

11. If you throw the dice and seven is showing on the top, what is facing down? (a) seven, (b) snake eyes, (c) boxcars, (d) little Joes, (e) 11.

12. "Jet" is: (a) an East Oakland motorcycle club, (b) one of the gangs in "West Side Story," (c) a news and gossip magazine, (d) a way of life for the very rich.

13. T-Bone Walker got famous for playing what? (a) trombone, (b) piano, (c) "T-flute," (d) guitar, (e) "Hambone."

Those who are not "culturally deprived" will recognize the correct answers are 1. (c), 2. (c), 3. (c), 4. (d), 5. (c), 6. (e), 7. (c), 8. (c), 9. (c), 10. (c), 11. (a), 12. (c), 13. (d).

middle-class America. But people from Kentucky, Tennessee, and some other parts of the South, some blacks, and certain other groups use and understand words somewhat differently. Although this difference will probably not produce a severe decrement in their performance on the test, it can reduce their scores appreciably. Thus it is important for test items to be written in the clearest, simplest, most widely understood language and if necessary translated into the language or dialect of those taking the exam (see Fig. 7.6). Otherwise scores will be artificially reduced because of differences in comprehensibility of the language.

Visual and auditory problems.   A common cause of undeserved low test scores is a problem in either vision or hearing. Often someone will score quite low because he or she does not hear the instructions well or has some difficulty seeing the test materials. The sad thing is that people may not be aware that their sight or hearing is weak, and these low scores are therefore assumed to be accurate reflections of their ability. This is especially true of children who test poorly. Any student who scores very low on an IQ test should automatically be given tests of hearing and vision to be certain that there is no problem in perception. Indeed, any child who seems to be slow in school or to interact poorly with classmates should be checked for a possible hearing problem (problems in sight are usually noticed more easily). There are many horror stories of children who were assumed to be mentally defective or retarded when actually they were merely hard of hearing.

Which of the items in the photo on the left would not be used in tuning your car? Which of the items in the photo on the right would not be used in making a souffle? In what ways are these so-called intelligence tests biased?

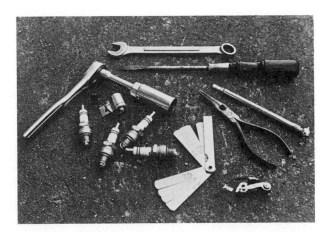

Use of biased materials.   A closely related but more subtle source of bias is the choice of materials used in the test. People who are more familiar with the material will have a clear advantage and will achieve higher scores than people who are less familiar with the material. This is not just a question of the language in which the exam is written, but specific words and materials in the language that are included in the items.

For example, a familiar type of question on an IQ test presents five items and asks the individual to select the one that does not belong. This is a test of concept formation; the person must discover similarities among the four items that go together. In solving such a problem, it is clearly necessary to understand each of the five items. Yet people differ considerably in their familiarity with even quite common objects and concepts. Figure 7.7 gives some examples of unfair test items.

Unfairness due to choice of materials is even more prevalent with tests such as the vocabulary test of the Wechsler scale, in which the individual has to define the meaning of various words. Since this is essentially a vocabulary test, the words chosen determine how high the person will score; and since different people learn different words, the test has a strong tendency to be unfair to some people. Thus, to some extent all of these tests actually measure achievement rather than aptitude and that makes them unfair to large numbers of people. Since the whole point of these tests is to discover an individual's potential—her ability rather than specific facts she has learned—any test that includes information or material that some people are more familiar with than others or have had more of a chance to learn than others is inherently unfair. It may be an excellent aptitude test for that large group of people who have been equally exposed to the material, but it is not a fair test for other groups.

Performance or nonverbal tests are generally less likely to be biased because people are equally familiar with the materials used. Assembling simple objects, noticing that an arm is missing from a picture of a man, using symbols and so on do not depend on any particular piece of information or experience. Similarly, the digit span or memory test in the verbal half of the Wechsler scale is quite free

Fig. 7.7
Examples of biased test items

1. California is to Sacramento as New York is to:

   New York City   Albany   Buffalo   Yonkers

Unfair because the correct answer depends on knowing that Sacramento is the capital of California and Albany the capital of New York. Information is necessary, not just understanding the analogy. And people who live in either state have a clear advantage over those who live elsewhere.

2. Pick the one that does not belong:

   Steinway   Baldwin   Yamaha   Wurlitzer   Franklin

Unfair because the correct answer depends on knowing that these are all names of pianos except Franklin. People with musical experience or from homes in which music is important have a clear advantage.

3. Pick the one that does not belong:

   end   tackle   guard   forward   back

Unfair because someone must know football to recognize that all of these except forward are positions on a football team. Clearly, people who are interested in sports, and especially males, would have an advantage.

4. Which of the following words is most similar in meaning to grass?

   wheat   marijuana   cabbage   heroin   amanita

Unfair because selecting marijuana as the correct answer requires knowing particular slang usage. Although this is a widely used term, some people may not know it and they will be at a disadvantage that has nothing to do with their intelligence.

1. Branch is to tree as arm is to:

  plate food sky animal

Everyone knows all of these words. Recognizing that a branch is part of a tree in much the same way that an arm is part of an animal requires no information that is not shared equally by virtually all people taking the test.

2. Pick the word that does not belong:

  sun moon ocean planet star

Again, just about everyone taking the test should know that all except ocean are terms in astronomy or objects in the universe. No special knowledge is necessary.

3. Moon is to planet as planet is to:

  sky sun earth universe

Everyone should know the terms involved and that the moon revolves around the planet. They should also recognize that planets revolve around stars. However, even here, note that some knowledge is necessary. It is almost impossible to write test items that do not involve a certain amount of basic information. The idea is to design items for which the necessary information is likely to be shared by everyone.

Try to write some test items yourself, being as careful as possible to make the correct answer depend on no information that is not universally held. You will probably see how difficult this is and therefore why so many tests are unfair to at least some people.

Fig. 7.8
Examples of bias-free test items

from bias since all children know the digits from 0 to 9. In addition, many tests have been constructed with careful attention to possible sources of bias in verbal material (for example, Cattell, 1949; Davis and Eells, 1953). Some examples of bias-free test items are given in Fig. 7.8. Theoretically it should be possible to make up items to test verbal aptitude using information that is equally available to all the people taking the exam, but in practice this turns out to be extremely difficult and it is questionable whether any verbal IQ test is entirely fair to all people to whom it is given. This does not mean that IQ tests are entirely useless nor that low test scores are necessarily due to unfamiliar material, but it does indicate that these tests should be interpreted with considerable caution.

THE ROLE OF HEREDITY AND ENVIRONMENT IN INTELLIGENCE

As we have discussed in earlier chapters, both heredity and experience play a role in almost all human behavior. In recent years, the relative importance of these two factors in accounting for intelligence has become the center of a heated controversy. One reason for this dispute is that how intelligent we are strongly influences the directions of our lives. Accordingly, there is understandable resistance to the idea that some persons are born with low intelligence and therefore will be unable to achieve certain goals regardless of training and experience.

The second reason and the source of most of the argument centers on the question of whether there are racial differences in intelligence. Such possibilities have been suggested for many years, largely by racist and nonscientific writers. But in 1969, an educational psychologist at the University of California at Berkeley named Arthur Jensen published an article in which he concluded that black people in the United States had lower intelligence than white people and that this difference was genetically determined. This conclusion understandably produced a tremendous furor and has led to a great many arguments and articles on both sides of the issue. In addition, it caused many of Jensen's critics to argue that there was little or no genetic basis for *any* differences in intelligence and at times the controversy over whether there were racial differences was translated into the question of whether heredity played any role at all in intelligence. In fact, these are two entirely different questions. Let us first discuss the question of racial differences.

Racial Differences in Intelligence

American blacks generally do score lower than whites on IQ tests. However, a vast amount of literature published in recent years has shown that these differences can probably be accounted for in terms of social background, class differences, and biases in the tests themselves. Here are some reasons for not accepting the existence of genetic differences between races in intelligence:

1. Among middle-class children, IQ differences are much smaller or disappear entirely (Lesser, Fifer, and Clark, 1965).

2. The IQ scores of blacks are considerably higher when the tests are given by blacks, when the blacks attend schools that have a majority of white students, and when blacks come from middle-class or educationally oriented homes.

3. Almost all IQ tests are constructed primarily by whites, who almost certainly introduce some biases that favor whites whether they intend to or not.

4. Both white and black American soldiers during World War II fathered illegitimate children in Germany, and all of these children were raised by white German mothers of about the same economic and social circumstances. Studies show that the children of black fathers and those of white fathers did not differ in intelligence (Eyferth, Brandt, and Wolfgang, 1960). If there were genetic differences, they would be expected to affect the intelligence of the children; the lack of such differences on IQ tests is evidence against the existence of genetic differences.

A comprehensive objective survey of all of this research was conducted by Loehlin, Lindzey, and Spuhler (1975) with reviews and input from dozens of experts from various fields. The authors conclude that there is no reason to believe that blacks or any other race are genetically inferior in terms of intelligence. While the possibility remains that there are racial differences in intelligence, or in any other quality or skill, the evidence at the moment does not warrant a belief in such differences.

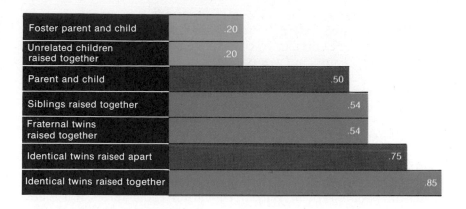

Foster parent and child	.20
Unrelated children raised together	.20
Parent and child	.50
Siblings raised together	.54
Fraternal twins raised together	.54
Identical twins raised apart	.75
Identical twins raised together	.85

Fig. 7.9

Correlations of IQ scores and relationship of people

The closer the genetic inheritance, the greater the similarity of IQ scores. But environment also has a substantial effect as shown by the difference in correlations when identical twins are raised apart or together. (After various studies such as Erlenmeyer-Kimling and Jarvik, 1963)

Genetic Factors in Intelligence

While there do not appear to be racial differences in intelligence, there is good reason to believe that heredity plays an important role. The evidence supporting this idea comes from a variety of sources, but all involve the similarity of the intelligence of people of similar heredity. Identical twins, who share identical genes, have very similar IQs; fraternal twins, whose genetic similarity is less, also have similar IQs but not as similar as those of identical twins; the IQs of siblings are less similar; and those of parents and children even less so (Newman, Freeman, and Holzinger, 1937; McNemar, 1942; Nichols, 1970; and others). Indeed, every available study of this sort reports the same pattern of results—the more similar the heredity, the more similar the intelligence (see Fig. 7.9). Estimates of the percentage of the variation in intelligence that is due to heredity range from below 40 percent to as high as 87 percent, but most psychologists would favor intermediate figures. Clearly, heredity plays an important role in determining intelligence, but just as clearly, it leaves considerable room for other factors.

It should be noted that at least one highly respected psychologist disagrees with the conclusion that heredity affects intelligence. Leon Kamin has published a scholarly work (1974) in which he reviews each of the studies on this subject. He points out methodological errors in virtually every study, and biased interpretations in many of them. Indeed, work by Cyril Burt (1958), which has produced some of the strongest data showing the effect of heredity, has recently been shown to be fraudulent. On the basis of this review, Kamin concludes that there is no convincing evidence for a genetic factor in intelligence. He does not say that there is strong evidence against it—merely that the case has not been proved. At the moment, most psychologists continue to believe that heredity plays an important role in intelligence, but perhaps Kamin's book and other work on the topic will change that view.

Environmental Factors in Intelligence

There is convincing evidence that experience can have an important effect on an individual's intelligence. Newman, Freeman, and Holzinger (1937) compared the IQs of identical twins who were raised apart from each other. Although the twins still had quite similar IQs,

The interaction of heredity and environment in shaping human development is nicely demonstrated in the case of Roger Brooks (left) and Anthony Milasi (right). These identical twins were separated at birth and raised a thousand miles apart by two culturally different families. Reunited for the first time as adults, they displayed powerful behavioral similarities that were probably genetic, such as holding a coffee cup the same way, imitating each other's speech mannerisms, and giving identical answers on sentence completion items in a psychological test. However, Roger displayed much greater emotional maturity and sensitivity, which a psychologist attributed to an environment that helped him to become independent. Anthony, on the other hand, was described as being dependent on his family and always looking for a magical, happy ending.

those who were raised in an environment that provided superior education scored considerably higher than those with less favorable environments. The number of cases is small, but IQs differed by as much as fifteen points in favor of the twin with the better education. Another bit of evidence showing the effect of environment is that fraternal twins are more similar in intelligence than nontwin siblings. Since the genetic similarity is the same for fraternal twins and siblings, the higher relationship between the twins is probably due to the fact that they are treated more similarly and exposed to more similar environments than are other siblings. Studies on the effect of home environment on foster or adopted children also indicate that experience is a very significant factor in intelligence. When homes are rated from poor to good in terms of educational advantages, it is found that children raised in the poor homes have considerably lower IQs than those raised in the average home, who are in turn below those raised in the good homes. This effect might be due to the fact that those who assigned the children to the homes tried to place the relatively bright children in the better homes. Nevertheless, it may also be due to the effect of the home life itself. Finally, differences in IQ between children who live in low and those who live in high socioeconomic conditions increase from birth to age six—again suggesting that the effect of the environment is either positive or negative (Bayley, 1965).

While none of this evidence is definitive, the accumulation does strongly suggest that intelligence is a joint function of heredity and environment. As with so many other human characteristics, genetic factors provide a set of limits within which the individual can develop, and environmental factors determine the extent to which the person achieves his or her full potential.

MENTAL RETARDATION

The intelligence scale is a continuum ranging from extremely high to extremely low. Clearly, the lower the score on the continuum, the less able the individual is to learn material, adapt his behavior to the situation, and master social, physical, and intellectual problems. People at the low end of the intelligence scale are called mentally retarded, defective, or subnormal. There is no clear dividing line between people of normal and subnormal intelligence, but the term *retarded* is usually applied to those with IQ scores below 70.

There is general agreement that between 1 percent and 3 percent of the population is to some extent retarded. Even at 1 percent this would mean that over 2,000,000 people in the United States are mentally retarded. Masland, Sarason, and Gladwyn (1958) put the figure at more than 3 percent, but concluded that only .4 percent are so retarded that they require special training and will still be unable to achieve a regular adjustment. Yet even this figure means that almost a million people in the country fall into this category.

Types and Causes of Retardation

There are substantial differences among people who are considered mentally retarded. One important distinction is between those who have obvious or known brain damage and those who do not. People who are retarded because of organic damage are sometimes called *mentally defective*. The most familiar type of mental retardation is *Down's syndrome*, also called *mongolism* because the facial features have an oriental appearance. This condition is clearly associated with a genetic abnormality, an extra chromosome, and tends to occur much more frequently in pregnancies of women over forty. In fact, the incidence of mongolism in children born to women of that age is more than ten times as great as with women under thirty. The condition is still relatively rare, but the possibility is one consideration of many older people who are thinking of having a child. Those with Down's syndrome usually have IQs between about 30 and 60, but there are instances of substantially higher intelligence. These people are generally extremely gentle, appealing, and sociable despite their low intelligence, and can often manage to live a fairly normal, though limited, life.

Other organic conditions include *microcephalus*, where there is a very small brain with an incompletely developed cerebrum; *hydrocephalus*, whose victims have very large heads caused by excess fluid that often damages brain cells; and *cretinism*, which is caused by insufficient thyroid secretions during early development.

In addition, there are diverse instances of genetic abnormalities, and of severe or mild brain damage caused by difficult birth, drugs, toxic reactions, deprivation of oxygen, and other specific causes. Also, a mother who has German measles (rubella) during the first three months of pregnancy often produces an infant who is severely retarded.

There are substantial differences among the mentally retarded in terms of their capabilities. Those at the upper end of the scale, with IQs between 50 and 70, can function moderately well in society, although there is no question that they would be considered "slow." They learn poorly, cannot handle complex intellectual tasks, and usually cannot get through high school. On the other hand, their physical skills are generally normal, and they can communicate with people, master language, and generally take care of themselves—at a very basic level.

Below the IQ level of 50, the individual's ability to function decreases considerably. These individuals rarely advance beyond the fourth-grade level, do not communicate at an adult level, and can perform only very simple tasks.

Finally, there is the severely retarded group, most of whom have obvious dramatic physical defects. The severely retarded usually have little physical control, cannot be toilet trained, communicate little if at all, and in essence require complete care and supervision in order to survive. Before the days of modern medicine almost all of these unfortunate children would have died at childbirth, and even now it is extremely difficult to keep many of them alive. They require intensive treatment throughout life and their life expectancy is always very short.

Helping the Retarded

The treatment of mental retardation clearly depends in large part on the type of deficiency involved. Organically caused retardation can sometimes be treated directly so as to remove or minimize the damage. For example, as we mentioned, cretinism is caused by insufficient thyroid secretions in early childhood. This condition can be helped considerably by early systematic doses of thyroxin. Phenylketonuria, a metabolic disorder, can be diagnosed in newborn babies and the mental retardation it produces can be avoided by a special diet. And hydrocephalics can often be helped appreciably by draining or diverting the extra fluid in the head. However, most organically caused mental retardation, whether due to genetic factors or to specific brain damage, is irreversible. Once the brain has been damaged, there seems to be no way to restore it. Thus, the treatment of most mental defectives who have brain damage must focus on helping them to cope as well as possible within the limits of their mental capacity.

When mental retardation appears to be caused wholly or in part by psychological disturbances, treatment consists of dealing with these problems directly. A child who is doing very poorly in school may be considered mentally retarded even though her potential is actually quite high. The low level of intellectual performance may be due to low motivation, rebelliousness, or any other kind of psychological problem. Helping the child deal with these psychological difficulties can often enable her to function at the level at which she is capable. Of course, in these cases the child is not really mentally retarded but is performing as if she were because of other problems. Thus, the treatment is not so much of the mental retardation but of the psychological difficulties that are seemingly producing it.

In recent years there has been a much more optimistic attitude about the capacity of the mentally retarded to learn. Except for the severely retarded and brain-damaged individuals, even quite retarded people can be taught a considerable amount with sufficient care and patience. Instead of abandoning the attempt as hopeless, many psychologists have directed their attention to devising methods of teaching retardates and recognizing the specific kinds of tasks of which they are capable. People with very low intelligence will never be able to master extremely complex tasks and material, but a large percentage will be capable of taking care of themselves and functioning in society if they are given sufficient and appropriate training.

THE MENTALLY GIFTED

Just as there are some people at the low end of the intelligence scale, there are also some at the high end. Approximately 1 percent of the population have IQs above 135 and less than a tenth of 1 percent above 150. A common stereotype of gifted children pictures them as frail, nearsighted, uncoordinated misfits who pour over books or mix strange chemicals in the basement. However, this image is far from accurate. In a massive study, Lewis Terman selected more than a thousand gifted children and followed their lives into adulthood (Terman and Oden, 1947; Oden, 1968). In direct contradiction with the stereotype, these gifted children were taller than average, walked and talked early, were above-average physical specimens, and had good health and social abilities.

A significant finding of this study was that high IQ helps but does not guarantee success in life. Many of the original group were extremely successful, were listed in *Who's Who in American Men of Science*, held high-level jobs, or received some other kind of special recognition. However, some were only moderately successful and others were extremely unsuccessful, dropping out of school or holding menial jobs. Those who were most successful had, on the average, slightly higher scores than those who were least successful but the differences were far too little to account for the major effects on their lives. Thus, even the intellectually gifted do not necessarily achieve great success—a high IQ is helpful but it is only one factor determining the course of an individual's life.

It is interesting to note that extremely bright children often have as much difficulty in school as dull ones, even though the kinds of problems are quite different. The bright child often is taught by a teacher who is less intelligent or who does not recognize the child's outstanding ability. This can cause the child to become bored and restless, and even to be considered a troublemaker. It is understandable that a teacher would become annoyed at a child who pointed out the teacher's mistakes, and yet that often occurs with exceptionally intelligent students. Thus while less intelligent children have difficulty in school because they cannot understand or learn what is being taught, highly intelligent children have difficulty because the material is too easy and they are bored and unchallenged.

One solution to both problems has been to have separate classes for slow, average, and outstanding children. But this procedure presents a number of difficulties, the foremost of which is that children are placed in one of these classes either on the teacher's recommendation or on the basis of tests, and it is then very difficult for them to move out of the class in which they are placed. A child who is in the bright class but is actually not smart enough will do poorly and experience constant failures. On the other hand, a child who is brighter than the class will be held back unnecessarily.

An alternative possibility is individualized instruction, which allows children of various ages and abilities to master material at their own pace. This is being done in many schools and may be a promising solution. ■

Summary

1. Psychological tests of intelligence and creativity attempt to measure a person's aptitude or potential rather than actual achievement.

2. Reliability and validity are the major factors in determining the usefulness of a test. Reliability refers to how consistently a test produces the same results for the test taker under different circumstances. It is determined by comparing the correlation between scores on one occasion and another or between the score on one half the test and the other half (split-half reliability). Validity—how well a test measures the quality it is intended to measure—is harder to assess because of the difficulty of finding perfect criteria against which to measure a particular quality.

3. Intelligence is defined as a general ability to master intellectual material. It is probably made up of a number of different potential abilities that tend to be closely related.

4. Intelligence tests fall into two broad categories: individual tests and group tests. The Stanford-Binet, the Wechsler Adult Intelligence Scale, and the Wechsler Intelligence Test for Children are administered individually. Group tests include, among others, the Armed Forces Qualification Test and the Scholastic Aptitude Tests.

5. The Stanford-Binet test is based on the premise that children's intellectual ability improves with age. The items are graded in terms of the ability of an average child of that age. If a child passes all items at the four-year-old level, we say she has a *mental age* of four. The child's *IQ* is a mathematical statement of how she compares in intelligence to other children (IQ = MA/CA × 100).

6. The Wechsler tests measure intelligence by assessing verbal and nonverbal (performance) types of abilities. These tests have the advantage of standardized scoring, which makes it easy to compare a person's performance on one subtest with his performance on another and to have a precise measure of how much better or worse he is performing.

7. Complex tests such as those devised by Thurstone and Guilford break intelligence down into a number of separate factors. Guilford suggests that previous tests may have defined intelligence too narrowly.

8. Intelligence-test scores tend to be highly reliable and reasonably valid, but there is controversy over whether these tests are biased in favor of certain groups of test takers. Primary sources of bias are ambiguity of the questions, difficulty with the language or dialect used on the test, visual and auditory problems, and lack of familiarity with the materials.

9. Current evidence indicates that there is probably no basis for concluding that there are genetic differences between races in intelligence. However, there is good reason to believe that heredity plays an important role in intelligence. Psychologists generally agree that the more similar the heredity, the more similar the intelligence.

10. Studies of IQs of identical twins raised in different environments provide evidence that environmental factors have an important effect on intelligence; thus, both heredity and environment play significant roles in intelligence.

11. People whose IQ scores fall below 70 on the intelligence scale are referred to as mentally retarded. There are numerous types of retardation ranging from mild to very severe, and many causes, including genetic abnormalities, and brain damage at birth caused by drugs, difficult birth, oxygen deprivation, and so on. Mildly retarded people can take care of themselves moderately well, but the severely retarded require care throughout their lives. Some forms of retardation can be helped if diagnosed early, but there is no real treatment for brain damage.

12. On the high end of the intelligence scale are the gifted—people with IQs above 135. An important study showed that gifted children walked and talked early, were above average physically,

and had good health and social abilities; another finding was that while high intelligence is useful, it does not guarantee success in life.

RECOMMENDED READING

Cronbach, L. J. *Essentials of Psychological Testing,* 3d ed. New York: Harper & Row, 1970. A high-level analysis of the problems and principles of psychological testing. Its main importance is to point out some of the pitfalls of testing.

Loehlin, J. C., G. Lindzey, and J. N. Spuhler. *Race Differences in Intelligence.* San Francisco: Freeman, 1975. A careful analysis of this complex and political problem. The authors conclude that there is no evidence for any racial differences in intelligence.

Kamin, L. J. *The Science and Politics of I.Q.* Potomic, Md.: Erlbaum Associates, 1974. A detailed analysis of virtually all of the research on the influence of heredity on intelligence. Kamin points out methodological problems with almost all the studies and concludes that there is no convincing evidence that heredity plays a role in determining intelligence.

This is the porcelain clay of humankind.
Dryden, Don Sebastian

8 Biological Basis of Behavior

The neuron ■ *Organization of the nervous system* ■
Central nervous system ■ *Spinal cord* ■ *Brain* ■
Peripheral nervous system ■ *Somatic system* ■
Autonomic nervous system ■ *Endocrine glands* ■
Behavior genetics

A tiny electric current administered to a particular part of the brain produces a sensation of great pleasure and is enormously reinforcing. Stimulating another part of the brain makes the animal insatiably hungry, while the same stimulation applied to a section very nearby makes the animal stop eating entirely. A strong electric shock to the brain can destroy memories. Too little of a chemical secreted by one gland makes us lethargic and tired all the time; too much of another chemical makes us overexcited and emotional. Variations in structures that carry hereditary characteristics can affect sex, eye color, color blindness, temperament, intelligence, and even susceptibility to mental disturbance. Although we sometimes tend to forget our physical structure and system when considering psychological phenomena, behavior is always tied closely to the biological apparatus of the body. Learning, memory, thought, language, emotions, motivation, mental disturbance and adjustment, and every other response we make are rooted in our biological makeup. Thus, in order to understand human behavior fully, we must look at its physical basis. This chapter deals with the nervous system, including the neuron, the spinal cord, the brain, and the peripheral system of nerves; with the endocrine gland system, and with the role genetics plays in human behavior.

BOX 8.1

BIOLOGICAL EFFECTS—SOME EXAMPLES

Perception Color-blindness is genetically determined. It is passed down by a recessive gene carried by the mother.

Learning Electrical stimulation of various parts of the brain is reinforcing and will produce learning.

Memory Destruction of the hippocampus seems to prevent memory storage. An electric shock to the brain can destroy memories or interfere with retrieval.

Language The language center is located in the left hemisphere. Destruction of that area makes language learning difficult or impossible.

Motivation Hunger is controlled in part by the hypothalamus. Different parts of this structure make the animal eat and stop it from eating.

Emotions The limbic system and especially the hypothalamus are involved in the arousal of emotions. In addition, various emotions are controlled by the endocrine gland system, with the adrenal gland producing the physiological state we associate with fear.

Intelligence Heredity probably plays a role. Down's syndrome, one kind of mental retardation, is certainly genetic.

Mental disturbance Susceptibility to schizophrenia and other conditions seems to be hereditary. Also, some conditions such as depression may be due in part to chemical imbalances in the brain.

Social psychology Aggressiveness and altruism may have hereditary aspects.

THE NEURON

The building block of the nervous system is the individual nerve cell or *neuron*. A typical neuron is depicted in Fig. 8.1, though this is only one of hundreds of different neuron types found within the human nervous system. A color photo of a nerve cell is shown in color Plate

E. A neuron has two parts: a central core area, called the *cell body*, that contains the nucleus of the cell; and a number of cylindrical extensions, called *nerve fibers*, leading away from the cell body. A unique property of neurons is that they are polarized anatomically, with one end being designed to receive information and the other to transmit it.

The receiving area of the neuron consists of several nerve fibers called *dendrites*, a name meaning branches of a tree. A neuron can have many dendrites, few, or even none. Dendrites in humans vary in length from as short as one millimeter to over one meter. Furthermore, a dendrite may be branched and rebranched many times.

The information-transmitting part of a neuron is called the *axon*, and each neuron has one and only one axon. The axon can be easily recognized because the cell body tapers down where it emerges. Like dendrites, axons in humans vary in length from very short to over one meter, and can be branched a great many times. The end of each branch of an axon is enlarged and is called the *axon terminal*.

To appreciate the complexity of the human brain, consider the following facts. First, every neuron has an axon that can have many branches, several hundred in some instances. Because of this, a given neuron influences the activity of a large number of other neurons. Also, a given neuron can have thousands of inputs from other neurons that influence its own activity. Finally, it has been estimated that there are between twelve and fifteen billion neurons in the human brain. Thus, the potential complexity is staggering. It is little wonder that the human brain is just beginning to be understood and that its capabilities are equal to and in many ways vastly superior to the most complex computer ever devised.

How Does a Neuron Work?

The cell membrane of the neuron is like a tiny battery. When it is activated, it produces a momentary short-circuit that causes a chemical reaction. This reaction is accompanied by an electric current that moves rapidly from the point of origin to every tip of the axon. The change of electrical activity associated with this current is called the *action potential.*

Once an action potential is produced it moves along the neuron at a rapid pace determined by various characteristics of that neuron, especially its diameter. Wider axons conduct the action potentials faster, perhaps as fast as one hundred meters (or about one football field) per second. In smaller axons the potential may move as slowly as two or three meters per second.

The synapse—where information is passed Each axon terminal lies close to a second cell, and the cleft between them, a space as small as .00002 millimeters, is called a *synapse*. It is at the synapse that information is passed from the neuron to the second cell. This is illustrated in Fig. 8.2, which shows the action potential reaching and activating the axon terminal. At the synapse, when the axon of the first neuron is activated by the action potential, the axon terminal releases a quantity of a chemical. This chemical crosses the cleft and reacts with receptors on the outer surface of the membrane of the second cell. There are two basic types of chemicals that can be

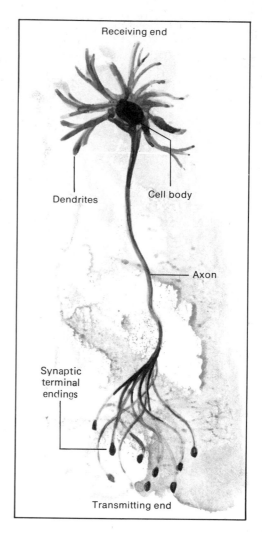

Fig. 8.1
A typical neuron, showing dendrites, axon, and cell body

The dendrites and cell body of a motor neuron exist within the central nervous system, and the axon runs out into the peripheral nervous system such that the terminal endings terminate on muscle cells.

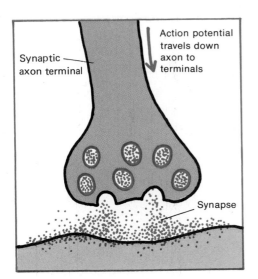

Fig. 8.2
Synaptic axon terminal

The action potential travels down the axon to the axon terminal, where it causes the release of a chemical into the synapse.

released in this manner—*excitatory* chemicals that tend to activate the second cell, and *inhibitory* chemicals that prevent it from being activated. The response of a neuron is determined by the total input arriving at any moment. If more excitatory than inhibitory inputs arrive, the neuron will be activated; while if more inhibitory inputs arrive, the neuron will be prevented from being activated.

One important characteristic of this process is that on any given occasion a neuron either fires or does not fire—there is no in-between or degree of firing. This is called the *all-or-none rule*. If the neuron receives enough excitatory chemical it produces an action potential; if it does not receive enough, it does not produce an action potential. Moreover, the action potential is always the same strength.

A second characteristic of all neurons is that immediately after producing an action potential they go into a so-called *refractory period*, during which they will not fire no matter how much excitatory chemical they receive. After this they go through a somewhat longer refractory period during which they will fire only if they receive more than the usual amount of excitation. The whole refractory period lasts a few hundredths of a second, after which the neuron returns to its normal resting state.

What Does a Neuron Do?

One function of the nervous system is to transmit information received at one part of the body to cells in other parts of the body. Information gets into the nervous system via the sensory receptors such as the retina of the eye. Each receptor is designed to detect a particular kind of energy in the environment and to translate this energy into the language of the nervous system; that is, into action potentials. When an animal is exposed to a stimulus, the sensory receptors react by transforming certain properties of the stimulus into the appropriate sequence of action potentials in the afferent or *sensory neurons* associated with that receptor. These action potentials then travel to the brain.

A second function of the nervous system is to carry commands to those parts of the body that cause responses—the muscles and glands, collectively called the *effectors*. Therefore, when a decision to respond has been made by the brain, efferent or *motor neurons* send this information to the appropriate muscles and glands via action potentials. The axon terminal in association with a muscle cell releases a chemical that causes the muscle to shorten or contract. In the case of an axon terminal in association with a gland, the released chemical causes the gland to secrete more or less of its particular chemicals. Thus, the sensory neurons carry information, while the motor neurons carry orders.

ORGANIZATION OF THE NERVOUS SYSTEM

The nervous system is composed of a vast number of neurons and nerve cell bodies combined in an immensely complex network. This network is divided into two parts—the *central nervous system*, consisting of the brain and the spinal cord; and the *peripheral nervous system*, consisting of the neurons that carry information from other parts of the body to the central nervous system and messages from the central nervous system back to the rest of the body. The peripheral system is subdivided into the *somatic nervous system*, which involves muscles, sense organs, and skin surface; and the *autonomic nervous system*, which involves internal organs and mechanisms, and plays a major role in emotional reactions. The divisions of the nervous system are illustrated in Fig. 8.3.

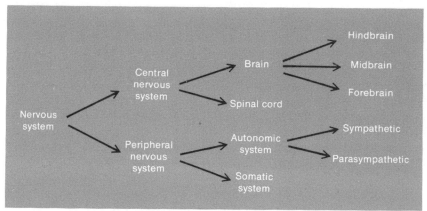

Fig. 8.3
Divisions of the nervous system

CENTRAL NERVOUS SYSTEM

Spinal Cord

If one slices through a human spinal cord, the outstanding features observed are (1) that it is divided into right and left halves, and (2) that there is an inner core of gray matter (nerve cell bodies) and an outer band of white matter (nerve fibers). The outer band of white matter is the conduit through which action potentials travel to and from the brain. It is subdivided into sensory portions, which carry information into the brain, and motor portions, which carry information from the brain.

The spines of humans, like those of all vertebrates, are segmented. As shown in Fig. 8.4, the human spinal cord is divided into thirty-one segments, each of which is connected to particular sense organs and effectors throughout the body. The number of segments for each part of the body varies from species to species. For example, giraffes have a large number of neck segments and long-tailed monkeys have a large number of tail segments.

The spinal cord receives messages from the various parts of the body and transmits them to the brain; it also carries messages from the brain to all parts of the body. Thus, it functions as a communication center much like a telephone relay complex. Messages from all over go through the spinal cord before reaching other areas.

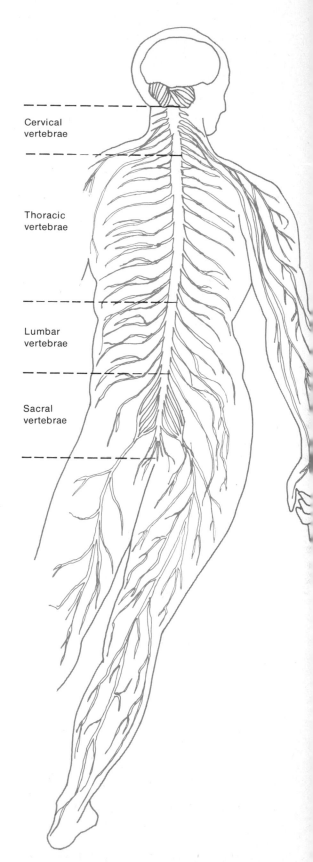

Fig. 8.4
The human spinal cord

The cord is divided into four major sections with a total of thirty-one segments.

The spinal cord also allows the body to respond to certain kinds of stimulation without involving the brain. These responses are very fast because of the time saved by eliminating transmission through the brain. Responses that involve only the spinal cord are called *spinal reflexes*. Familiar examples are the knee-jerk reflex that is often tested in doctors' offices and the pain reflex of withdrawing a hand or foot from a painful stimulus.

Although spinal reflexes are much simpler than responses that go through the brain, they are still quite complex. Consider what happens if you are walking along the beach in your bare feet and step on a sharp clam shell. Action potentials from your foot rush along the sensory nerve fibers from the toe to the spinal cord. Within the spinal cord, branches of these axons cause four separate responses: (1) The muscles of the right leg are told to flex. The result is that the joints of the right leg are all rapidly bent, and the leg is lifted up and removed from the source of the pain. (2) Extensor muscles of the right leg are told not to respond. Extensor muscles straighten the leg. Since you were stepping down when you hit the clam, you must cancel the orders that made the leg step down, because you want to bend not straighten the leg. (3) The left leg is told to straighten. (4) The left leg is told not to flex. This makes your left leg get ready to bear the weight of the body when the right leg is lifted.

All of this happens very rapidly with no conscious or deliberate effort on your part, and without your brain playing any role in it. However, while the spinal reflex is taking place, other neurons carry the message up to the brain where you experience the sensation of pain.

FOREBRAIN	Cerebral cortex	Higher mental processes—perception, memory, voluntary movement, language, thinking
	Thalamus	Integration, message center—passes sensory information to cortex, and commands from cortex
	Hypothalamus	Emotions, sleep, glandular activity—controls many emotional reactions, sex, fear, sleep, eating, drinking
	MIDBRAIN	Reflex movements of head and neck, message center
HINDBRAIN	Cerebellum	Balance, sensory input, muscle coordination
	Pons	Bridge between cortex and cerebellum
	Medulla	Essential automatic physical activity—regulates heart, blood pressure, breathing, digestion; also nausea

Brain

The brain has so many functions that it is difficult to list them all. It controls motor behavior, perception, much of emotion, and motivation, and generally keeps the body operating so that we stay alive. It is also, of course, the center of all higher processes, including thought, ideas, dreaming, concept formation, language, memory, and creativity. If asked to point to the part of the body where the real "you" is located, almost everyone points to the head—meaning the brain is the control center for almost everything and is also the center of consciousness and our sense of ourselves as individuals.

When the brain ceases to function, we are for all intents and purposes dead. Even if the heart, lungs, and other vital organs can be kept working artificially, the person is no longer alive. In fact, a court in New Jersey recently ruled that it is legal to detach mechanical life-sustaining devices if the brain is irretrievably damaged, thereby allowing someone to die.

The brain may be divided up in various ways. Probably the most convenient division that involves both structure and function is into the *hindbrain, midbrain, and forebrain*. Figure 8.5 diagrams these

Fig. 8.5
The brain

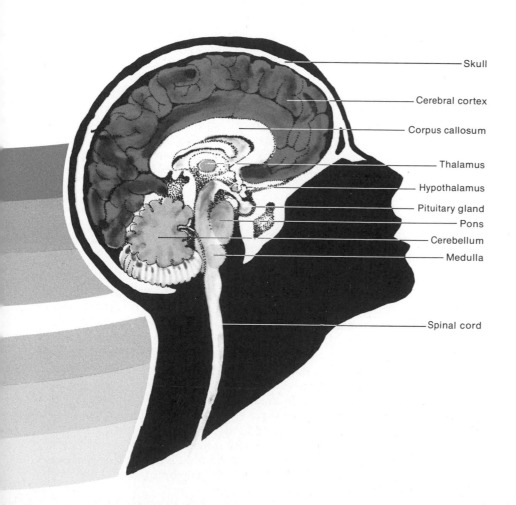

- Skull
- Cerebral cortex
- Corpus callosum
- Thalamus
- Hypothalamus
- Pituitary gland
- Pons
- Cerebellum
- Medulla
- Spinal cord

FINDING YOUR WAY AROUND A BODY

The student of psychology should be familiar with a few biological terms referring to directions or locations within the body. As a model, use the fish depicted below. The front, or head end of an animal is anterior, or rostral, and the rear end is posterior or caudal. These terms become superior and inferior respectively if the animal is normally in an upright position, such as humans. The belly side of an animal is ventral and the back side is dorsal. Finally, in the right-left dimension, a structure closer to the midline is medial and one farther from the midline is lateral. Unilateral means one-sided; bilateral means both-sided; ipsilateral means on the same side as; and contralateral means on the opposite side as. Finally, position within an appendage (such as an arm, a tentacle, a tail, or whatever) is indicated by proximal, meaning toward the origin of, and distal, meaning away from the origin of. As an example, the fingers are distal to the elbow, and the shoulder is proximal to the elbow. The right foot is contralateral to the left elbow. The right shoulderblade is anterior, dorsal, and lateral to the navel.

Unfortunately, a certain confusion exists with the orientation of humans. The reason is that the human body is curved ninety degrees so that humans walk upright while looking straight ahead. If the body were designed like that of a dog, the terms for the fish would apply exactly. However, because the long axis of the body is curved, anterior refers to the front of the face, and posterior refers to the rear end. The back of the head is therefore posterior to the face and anterior to the spinal cord. This means that the dorsal surface of the body curves around from the top of the head along the backbone, and the ventral surface curves from under the chin down through the belly.

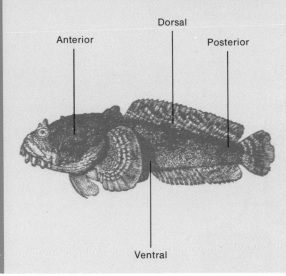

Anterior

Dorsal

Posterior

Ventral

three sections, and the accompanying chart indicates what parts of the brain are in each section. Let us now consider each separate part and its function.

Hindbrain The hindbrain controls many body activities that, although essential to maintain life, are largely automatic and generally not under our conscious control. The *medulla oblongata*, or more commonly just medulla, regulates heart rate, blood pressure, rate of digestion, breathing, and other vital functions. There is even a center within the medulla that can make you vomit when it is stimulated. This "nausea center" receives direct input from chemical receptors in the stomach as well as from areas concerned with balance. For this reason, we may get nauseous if we eat something that does not agree with us or if our sense of balance is disturbed as in seasickness. The drug dramamine fights seasickness by suppressing the nausea center and thus preventing vomiting. The medulla also contains pathways from the spinal cord to other areas of the brain, and nerve cells associated with the lower part of the face.

The next section of the hindbrain is the *pons,* a word that means bridge. It is appropriately named because it acts as a bridge between the highest part of the brain, the *cortex,* and the *cerebellum,* which is the third part of the hindbrain. The cerebellum is directly concerned with our sense of balance and also receives information from the visual, auditory, and skin receptors. In addition, the cerebellum seems to play an important role in integrating motor behavior, particularly posture, muscle tone, and perhaps coordination in general.

Midbrain The *midbrain* controls reflex movements of the head and neck triggered by visual or auditory input. For example, if you are sitting at your desk reading this book and you hear a strange sound, you will turn your head and focus your eyes appropriately to the spot from which you think the sound originated. The coordination of this movement occurs through centers within the midbrain. Finally, the midbrain is a major receiving center for the output of the cerebellum.

Forebrain When most people think of the brain, they mean the forebrain and its functions. The forebrain is involved in all of our

AROUSAL AND THE RETICULAR FORMATION

Each day our level of arousal varies over a wide range from sleep or drowsiness to extreme attention and alertness. A structure in the brain stem determines the particular level of arousal experienced at any moment of time. This area, the *ascending reticular activating system,* or ARAS, forms the most central core of the medulla, pons, and midbrain. This area became the subject of intense experimentation when it was found that a small amount of electrical stimulation applied there in a sleeping animal would cause instant awakening and arousal (Moruzzi and Magoun, 1949). The animal would sit up and look around as if something had happened. Conversely, surgical destruction of the ARAS led to permanent coma and an animal that could not be aroused (Lindsley et al, 1950).

It appears that the ARAS is involved in attention and to some extent decides what the higher parts of the brain will respond to. If two messages come in at once, the ARAS may select one as more important and somehow tell the cerebral cortex to concentrate on that one. Moreover, the ability to pay attention to one conversation in a room full of people (mentioned in Chapter 2) may depend on the capacity of the ARAS to focus attention on one stimulus and disregard others. We do not know how this system operates, but it is, of course, a mistake to think of it as a separate entity that is really making decisions. Rather, it is a control mechanism that allows the individual to respond to some stimuli more than to others, and to focus attention on urgent matters when necessary.

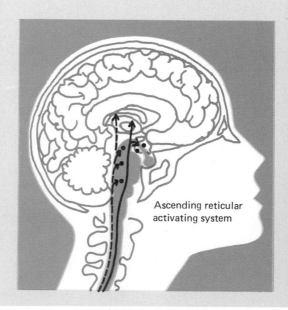

Ascending reticular activating system

BOX 8·3

higher mental processes, including language, speech, problem solving, and memory. It is also where the sensory inputs from the eyes, ears, and so on are integrated and interpreted to give us our perceptions of the world. And the forebrain plays a major role in controlling emotions and many motivations. The major parts of the forebrain are the thalamus, hypothalamus, and cerebral cortex.

Thalamus. Just in front of the midbrain lies a large area called the *thalamus*. This is the major relay center for almost all sensory information on its way to the cerebral cortex. There are also integration centers within the thalamus where information from a large number of different sources is put together and the output, which to some extent has been processed, is sent to the cerebral cortex. In more primitive vertebrates such as fish, which have no cerebral cortex, the thalamus represents the highest level of processing possible for information within the brain.

Hypothalamus. The thalamus is a relatively large section of the brain since it deals with most sensorimotor information. It is therefore very important behaviorally. Of equal importance and greater fascination for psychologists is the much smaller *hypothalamus*, a region of the brain located just below the thalamus. The hypothalamus contains centers that control whether or not an animal is sleeping or conscious, its body temperature, and when and how much it eats and drinks (see Chapter 9). Moreover, the hypothalamus plays a crucial role in controlling emotional, aggressive, and reproductive behavior. Fighting, fear, sexual attraction, and perhaps even love depend in part on activities within the hypothalamus.

In addition to these functions, the hypothalamus controls the pituitary gland. The pituitary itself has so many functions that it is sometimes referred to as the master gland of the body (see Table 8.1). However, since the pituitary is under the control of the hypothalamus, it would be more accurate to call the hypothalamus the master of the whole glandular system.

Cerebral cortex. The *cerebral cortex* is a thin sheet of nerve cell bodies, or gray matter, folded back upon itself many times (see color Plate F). The result is an irregular-shaped mass in which one-third of the total surface area is exposed and two-thirds are hidden beneath the surface. The cortex is thin, being only a few millimeters thick. The rest of this massive structure is white matter or nerve axons connecting the cerebral cortex to the brain stem and interconnecting various areas within the cerebral cortex.

The cerebral cortex is divided into left and right halves or hemispheres that are connected by a structure called the *corpus callosum*. In general, sensory inputs from the left side of the body go to the right side of the brain and vice versa. Also, the left side of the brain controls the muscles and glands on the right side of the body, while the right hemisphere controls the left side.

Each hemisphere is divided into four subunits called lobes, each of which has different functions. The structure of the cerebral cortex and some of its functions are in Fig. 8.6. The occipital lobes receive visual information from the eyes; the temporal lobes receive messages from the ears; and the frontal lobes are associated with the sense of smell. The so-called skin senses of touch, pressure, and

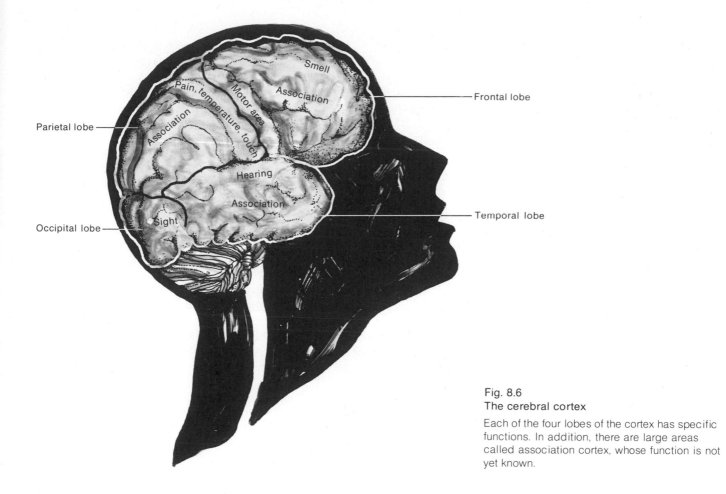

Fig. 8.6
The cerebral cortex

Each of the four lobes of the cortex has specific functions. In addition, there are large areas called association cortex, whose function is not yet known.

temperature enter the parietal lobes, where there is a tiny representation of the entire surface of the body. This is called the *sensory homunculus* meaning "little man." Its parts are not proportional to body size but to sensitivity. Those parts of the body such as the tongue, lips, fingertips, and genitals that are very sensitive to touch are represented by large areas, while less sensitive parts such as the elbows and knees have small representations.

The part of the brain that controls motor activity is located in the frontal lobe. As with the sensory centers, there is a motor homunculus whose features are proportional to the degree of control that one has over the various muscles of the body. There is a proportionately large area for the tongue and fingers and a proportionately small area for such parts of the body as the trunk. If one applies a sufficiently fine probe, a very small number of neurons in the motor cortex could be stimulated such that just a few cells of the appropriate muscle would be activated.

There are many parts of the cortex that are neither primary sensory receiving areas nor primary motor areas. The precise function of most of the other areas is unknown, however, except for a few such as Broca's speech area, located deep inside the left frontal lobe. These other areas throughout all of the lobes are called *association cortex*. Theories abound as to the possible roles that these areas play in

BOX 8.4

LOCALIZATION OF MEMORY

The localization of memory within the brain has long been debated. It has been shown many times, however, that most instances of learning other than simple classical conditioning require an intact cerebral cortex. Because of this, those researchers who have attempted to isolate memory storage have focused on the cerebral cortex. Karl Lashley (1950) worked with rats for many years and came to the conclusion that the storage of memory is a diffuse event, occurring throughout the cortex simultaneously. Lashley found that when rats had been trained to respond to a certain array of stripes, removal of any particular portion of the cerebral cortex did not seem to matter. All that mattered was the total amount of cortex removed. In fact, over 90 percent of the cerebral cortex could be removed with little deficit. Lashley therefore proposed that all areas of the cerebral cortex have the same capacity to store information and that after an experience all parts of the cerebral cortex learn simultaneously. In contrast, Wilder Penfield, a neurologist, has generated some remarkable data regarding specific locations for specific memories (1958). When people are undergoing brain surgery, they are often awake because there are no pain or other receptors located within the brain (so they feel nothing) and because it is useful for the surgeon to receive feedback from the patient during the operation. Penfield was able to stimulate certain regions of association cortex of patients being operated on for epilepsy. To his amazement, he found that a small amount of electrical activity applied to the surface of the cortex would elicit specific memories of past experiences. A patient might remember the details of a party attended while very young, details that had not been recalled for years. People tended to remember specific smells, sounds, and even emotions related to specific experiences. Penfield also found that stimulation of a nearby region would elicit an entirely different memory and that restimulation of the first would generate the first memory again. His work suggests that memory, rather than being diffuse, is localized, with each discrete locus of the cerebral cortex housing the memory of a particular past experience.

However, there is still some question that this is correct. In the first place, precise confirmation of the alleged facts of the memories of Penfield's patients is difficult. It is possible that the people are simply structuring some event from the past and inserting "facts" about details as their brain thinks they might have been. In other words, they are not giving memories but made-up stories. Further, Penfield was studying experiences that may have been learned by simple association. It may be that specific experiences are located in precise loci within the cortex and that what we call learning may be a process of gaining access to these specific experiences. And it is thus possible, as Lashley suggested, that such learning is a diffuse event, not localized in one place.

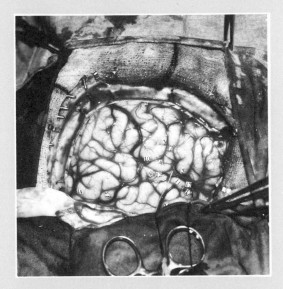

The right cerebral cortex of an epileptic patient, exposed for surgery with the patient fully conscious. The numbers indicate spots at which electrical stimulation produced positive responses—simple sensory and motor responses at spots 2, 3, 4, 7, and 8 and flashback experiences at spots 11, 12, 14, and 15.

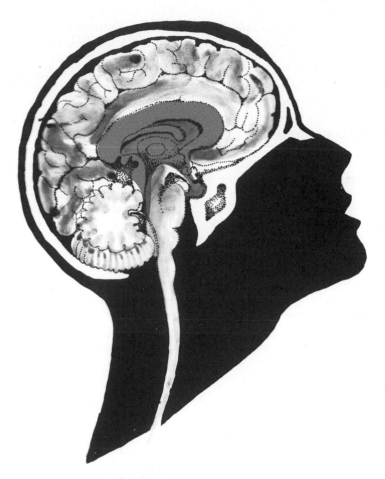

Fig. 8.7
The region of the limbic system

The area shown in color is generally considered to be the region of the limbic system, which lies beneath the cortex and surrounding the thalamus.

learning and memory, the conscious versus the subconscious, higher cognitive processes, and so on. But for the most part, these remain speculation.

Limbic system The *limbic system*, diagramed in Fig. 8.7, contains a series of structures that cut across some of the boundaries we have described. Some psychologists consider the hypothalamus part of the limbic system, and it also includes several areas in the cerebral cortex, such as the *hippocampus*. Moreover, the limbic system is closely connected with many other areas in the cerebral cortex, the thalamus, and lower areas of the brain.

There has been a great deal of research trying to determine the functions of the limbic system. As we will discuss in the chapters on emotions and motivation, it is clearly involved in emotional reactions and in turning on and off consummatory behavior such as eating. It also appears to play some role in learning and memory, since damage to the hippocampus may prevent people from forming new memories. Finally, some parts of the limbic system seem to operate as reward centers, as shown by work on electrical stimulation of the brain. Thus the limbic system is involved in a wide range of activities, including emotions, learning, and reinforcement.

Corpus callosum and split-brain phenomenon As we mentioned earlier, the two hemispheres are connected by a large bundle of axons, called the *corpus callosum*. Although this structure undoubtedly has many functions, one of them seems to be to inform one hemisphere of what the other is doing. This is necessary because each hemisphere receives sensory information only from the opposite side of the body.

Many types of experiments have demonstrated the importance of the corpus callosum in transferring information. For example, a subject can be given the simple task of stating right or wrong when a stimulus is presented. If the stimulus is presented so that the information reaches only the left hemisphere (for example, the stimulus can be placed in the right hand, or can be made to appear only in the right visual field), the subject responds very rapidly. If, on the other hand, the stimulus is presented such that it reaches only the right hemisphere, the response time is significantly longer. The increased time presumably reflects the passage of the information from the right hemisphere to the speech center in the left hemisphere.

More dramatic effects have been achieved by severing the corpus callosum, thus separating the right and left hemispheres. Although this operation was first done in experimental animals, it is not an uncommon operation for humans who suffer from a particular type of epilepsy. With this disorder, a seizure starts in one hemisphere and spreads until it encompasses most of both hemispheres. Cutting the corpus callosum prevents the spread to the opposite hemisphere and often reduces the spread within the first.

This operation produces a "split-brain" animal or person with no apparent intellectual deficit. However, such individuals seem to have two independent controllers existing in their heads simultaneously. Furthermore, neither of the two "brains" is aware of what the other is doing. For example, if a split-brain animal is taught to make one response when a stimulus is presented to its right hemisphere, it does not make that response when the stimulus is presented only to the left hemisphere. And it can be taught to make an entirely different response when the left hemisphere receives the stimulus. Moreover, the two responses will not interfere with each other.

In split-brain humans, if a stimulus is presented such that it is perceived only by the right hemisphere and the person is asked to state what the stimulus is, the person will say, "I don't know." This is because the speech center is located in the left hemisphere and has no knowledge of the stimulus (Sperry, 1970). If, however, the person is asked to find with the left hand a stimulus corresponding to a word seen only by the right hemisphere, she does very well. Normally, this split situation does not present a problem because many of the most important stimuli to humans are sights and sounds. Sounds entering both ears arrive simultaneously at each cortex, and, since the two eyes of humans see almost exactly the same images, there is rarely a problem of one eye seeing one thing and the other eye seeing something else. These situations tend to arise only in experimental situations. Nevertheless, it does seem that in some sense there are two separate cognitive entities housed within the head of split-brain people.

These split-brain experiments and other research suggest that the two hemispheres have somewhat different functions (see Fig. 8.8). We

ROGER W. SPERRY

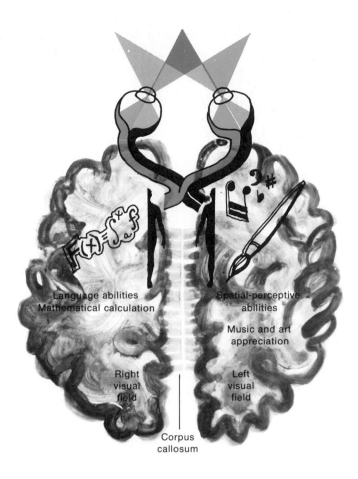

Fig. 8.8
The split-brain phenomenon

The left side of the brain controls the right side of the body while the right side of the brain controls the left side of the body. In addition, in most people the left side of the brain seems to be involved in logical functions while the right side is more creative and artistic.

know that the left hemisphere contains the center for language and speech for most people. More generally, the left hemisphere appears to control logical, deductive, and scientific thought. The ability to perform complex mathematical calculations, to solve problems requiring deductive logic, and to make rational plans seems to depend largely on the left hemisphere. In contrast, the right hemisphere is said to be the center for spatial and perceptual abilities, for the appreciation of the arts, and for inductive, creative thinking. The evidence for this distinction between the two hemispheres is not very strong at the moment, but a considerable amount of research is being done on this possibility. If it turns out to be correct, it would, among other things, lend support to the contention discussed in Chapter 7 that general intelligence and creative intelligence are separate abilities.

PERIPHERAL NERVOUS SYSTEM

We have already noted that the peripheral nervous system consists of the neurons that are not in either the spinal cord or the brain. These neurons connect the rest of the body with the central nervous system.

The peripheral system is divided into the somatic and autonomic nervous system.

Somatic System

The *somatic system* includes all the neurons that are connected with muscles, sense organs, and the skin. It deals with sensory information and controls the movement of the body. When you sit in an awkward position and your leg "falls asleep," you have temporarily blocked a nerve that is part of the somatic system. This is the system that carries most of the deliberate messages from the brain to the rest of the body. When we decide to get up, to walk, to move any part of our body, it is the somatic nervous system that transmits the orders from our brain. Moreover, somatic nerves control spinal reflexes.

Autonomic Nervous Sytem

Whereas the somatic system involves sensory data and muscles that control bodily movement, the *autonomic nervous system* controls virtually all of the internal functions and organs of the body. In particular, it is involved in automatic functions such as heartbeat, breathing, pupil dilation, stomach contractions, salivation, and sexual response. It also plays a role in controlling the actions of various glands. The autonomic system, as illustrated in Fig. 8.9, is further divided into two systems that to a large extent operate in opposition to each other—the sympathetic and parasympathetic nervous systems.

Sympathetic nervous system The sympathetic nervous system is involved in getting the body ready for action—it activates various mechanisms, heightens arousal, and generally speeds up bodily processes. When the sympathetic system is activated it is as if a bugle had been blown or an alarm bell had sounded—everything sits up and is alert. The heart beats faster, more oxygen is carried to the skeletal muscles, breathing is deeper, the pupils of the eye dilate to produce sharper vision, and the liver releases extra sugar into the blood to provide energy. All of this happens if you are suddenly frightened, if a loud noise startles you, if you are sexually aroused, or otherwise respond to an external threat or stimulation.

Parasympathetic nervous system To a great extent the *parasympathetic system* is connected to the same organs as the sympathetic, but it has an opposite effect. When the parasympathetic system is activated the body quiets down, relaxes, and generally becomes more at rest. The parasympathetic system slows the heart and breathing, contracts the pupils, stops the flow of sugar to the blood, and so on. When this system is inactive we feel tense, anxious, and excited; when the system is activated, we tend to feel calm, relaxed, and quiet.

Fig. 8.9
The autonomic nervous system

This system controls the functions of the internal organs, and many glands. The sympathetic nervous system, shown in color, generally produces arousal, while the parasympathetic nervous system, shown in white, has the reverse effect.

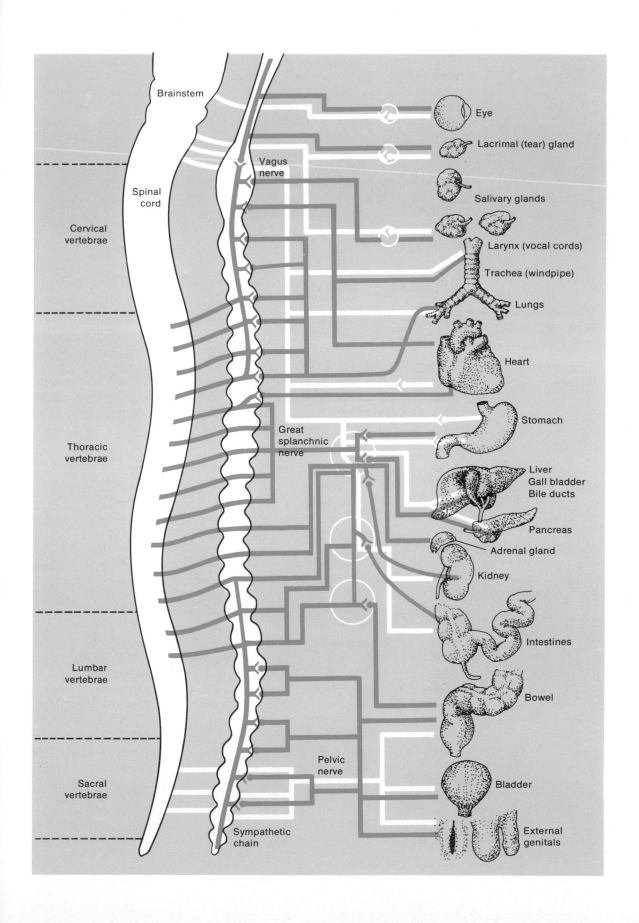

Brainstem

Spinal cord

Cervical vertebrae

Vagus nerve

Thoracic vertebrae

Great splanchnic nerve

Lumbar vertebrae

Pelvic nerve

Sacral vertebrae

Sympathetic chain

Eye

Lacrimal (tear) gland

Salivary glands

Larynx (vocal cords)

Trachea (windpipe)

Lungs

Heart

Stomach

Liver
Gall bladder
Bile ducts

Pancreas

Adrenal gland

Kidney

Intestines

Bowel

Bladder

External genitals

Whenever we are aroused, both systems are involved. The sympathetic system produces or controls the arousal itself, and the parasympathetic returns us to our normal state. This interaction of the two systems controls male sexual arousal. The sympathetic system produces all the familiar bodily reactions that we associate with sexual arousal. Ejaculation, however, is a parasympathetic response, so that system takes over and restores the body to a resting state. This is one reason that males tend to be especially quiet and tired after sex—the parasympathetic system is working. The response in females is somewhat different in that the parasympathetic is not activated immediately, and this is one reason why women are able to engage in the sexual act longer and tend to be less tired immediately after a climax.

ENDOCRINE GLANDS

The body contains a number of organs, called *glands,* that secrete chemicals with specialized purposes. Some of these glands have ducts or passages through which the substances are secreted. These glands, while very important in keeping the body functioning, are of relatively little interest to psychologists. Glands with ducts are involved in digestion (salivary glands in the mouth), keeping the eyes clean (tear ducts), skin temperature (sweat glands), and other fairly simple

BOX 8.5

MENSTRUAL CYCLES

Menstrual cycles in women are associated with changes in the levels of the sex hormones, estrogen and progesterone. Typically, estrogen levels are highest in the middle of the cycle, just at ovulation, while progesterone levels increase rapidly after ovulation. Both hormones decrease sharply just before menstruation. There is evidence that these changes in hormone level are accompanied by and probably cause changes in mood. However, as we shall see, the relationships are complex.

The traditional view, which has received some support from research, is that in general women feel less anxious, less hostile, and better about themselves and the world during the middle of the cycle, and that they feel especially bad just before menstruation (Coppen and Kessel, 1963; Bardwick, 1973). That this is related

to hormonal levels is indicated by studies on women who use contraceptive pills. The pill maintains the hormones at a constant level until just before menstruation. Sure enough, women on the pill did not show the usual mood changes (Paige, 1971; Marinari, Lesher, and Doyle, 1976); they did not have any particular low period, but they also did not experience any high period either.

On the other hand, there is evidence that not all women experience mood changes associated with the menstrual cycles. In a study of almost three hundred women, Karen Paige (1973) found that many felt depressed, irritable, tense, and restless just before menstruation but others felt none of these emotions. Those who did have distress also tended to have similar reactions in many other situations, to use more drugs, and to complain of aches, pains, and physical illnesses.

processes. Other glands do not have ducts and are accordingly referred to as ductless glands, or more generally *endocrine glands*. These are involved in a wide variety of responses that are of great psychological importance.

How the Endocrine System Works

Earlier in this chapter we discussed how the nervous system transfers information from one place in an animal to another by means of an electrical current carried in the axon. We noted that the information is passed to a second cell by means of a chemical released from the axon terminal at a synapse. The advantages of this system are that it is very fast and that the information can be directed to specific cells (if the brain wants the hand moved, it is essential that only muscles controlling the hand be activated). There are many instances, however, when information should be dispersed to a far greater number of cells and it would be inefficient to have axons going to all of the cells of the body carrying information simultaneously. The endocrine system meets this need by secreting into the blood chemicals called hormones that carry information throughout the body. This system is somewhat slower than the nervous system because it depends on the speed at which the blood circulates through the body. On the other hand, since the blood travels to virtually every area of the body, the hormone can easily affect many cells simultaneously.

That is, women who have unpleasant feelings associated with menstruation are generally anxious and nervous, and treat menstruation as if it were an illness.

Paige argues that the "raging hormones" theory of menstrual distress is inadequate because all women have the same hormonal cycle but not all experience distress. Nor does she accept the idea that women who have distress are simply neurotic. Instead, the relationship is more complex and not fully understood. One possibility is that a low level of estrogen and progesterone makes someone more emotional in general, but does not necessarily produce a negative emotional state. If the person is feeling bad for any reason (and the physical or psychological discomfort of menstruation could be such a reason), there will be a strong negative reaction. In contrast, if the person is feeling good for any reason, that emotion also would be intensified. It seems clear that hormonal levels do play a role in producing emotions but that the particular effect they have depends on the individual and her attitudes toward menstruation, physical discomfort in general, and probably many other factors.

One final point about menstrual cycles is the fascinating observation that women who spend a lot of time together tend to have cycles at the same time— that is, they menstruate in rhythm (McClintock, 1971). This is true of close friends, women who live together, residents of college dormitories, and various other groups. It is also true of female rats and probably many other species. We are not certain why this occurs, but there is some suggestion that, at least among rats, ovulating females emit an odor that somehow triggers ovulation in other females.

Fig. 8.10
The endocrine glands

The major glands are illustrated, but remember that many of them have more than one function, as described in Table 8.1.

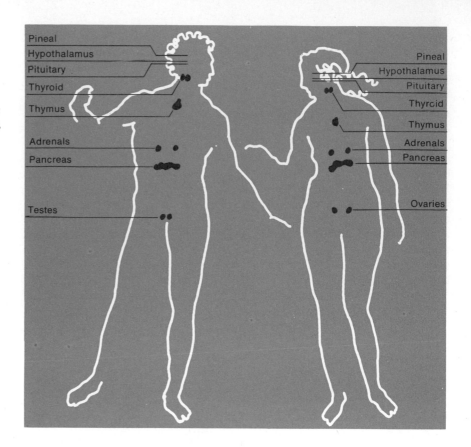

In Fig. 8.10 some of the more important endocrine glands of the body are depicted, and in Table 8.1 the major secretions of these glands are listed along with their actions. You can see there why the pituitary is called the master gland of the body. It is involved in

Table 8.1
THE ENDOCRINE SYSTEM

Endocrine organ	Hormone(s)	Major action(s)
Hypothalamus	Many hormones called releasing or inhibitory factors	These hormones go directly from the hypothalamus to the anterior pituitary where they modify the secretions of the hormones of the anterior pituitary. The hypothalamus thus totally controls the anterior pituitary.
Anterior pituitary: There are seven major hormones of the anterior pituitary, collectively called the tropic hormones. This means that they stimulate the secretions of other endocrine glands located throughout the body.	Adrenocorticotropic hormone (ACTH)	Stimulates the adrenal cortex during stress, causing the secretion of cortisol and related hormones.

Table 8.1 (cont.)
THE ENDOCRINE SYSTEM

Endocrine organ	Hormone(s)	Major action(s)
	Thyroid-stimulating hormone (TSH)	Causes the thyroid gland to secrete thyroid hormone in response to a decreased metabolic rate.
	Growth hormone	Causes the growth of many tissues including bones, muscles, and glands through the intermediary hormone, somatostatin.
	Melanocyte-stimulating hormone (MSH)	Alters the skin coloration of many animals as a protective measure.
	Follicle-stimulating hormone (FSH)	Initiates the formation of eggs and sperm in the ovaries and testes, respectively.
	Luteinizing hormone (LH)	Causes maturation of the egg or sperm. Causes ovulation in females.
	Prolactin (PRL)	Maintains maternal behavior, particularly nursing, on the part of humans.
Posterior pituitary	Antidiuretic hormone (ADH)	Prevents water loss as urine when water supplies are low in the body.
	Oxytocin	Causes milk release during nursing.
Pineal organ	Melatonin	Suppresses reproductive-related behaviors and secondary sexual characteristics. It is inhibited in many animals except during the breeding season.
Parathyroid glands	Parathormone (PTH)	Increases blood calcium if it is too low.
Thyroid gland	Thyroid hormone	Increases metabolic rate throughout the body.
	Thyrocalcitonin	Decreases blood calcium if it is too high.
Pancreas	Insulin	Enables the body to accept and use glucose for energy. It also causes fat storage.
	Glucagon	Elevates the levels of fuels (glucose or fats) in the blood if they are low.
	Somatostatin	Regulates the secretion of insulin and glucagon.
Adrenal cortex (the outer portion of the adrenal glands)	Cortisol and related steroids	Secreted during stress, it maintains blood pressure and enables the body to be more responsive.
	Mineralocorticoids (e.g., aldosterone)	Prevents the loss of sodium to the urine when sodium is low in the body.
Adrenal medulla (the inner portion of the gland)	Adrenalin (epinephrine)	Secreted in response to stress, it causes the heart to beat faster, blood pressure to go up, and elevated blood sugar, thus providing fuel for the brain.
Testes	Androgens (testosterone)	Develops and maintains male reproductive organs and male reproductive behavior.
Ovaries	Estrogens	Develops and maintains female reproductive organs and female reproductive behavior.
	Progesterone	Develops female reproductive tissues and maintains pregnancy.
Uterus	Several different hormones secreted only during pregnancy	Maintains pregnancy.

reactions to stress, and controls metabolic rate, tissue growth, momentary alterations of skin color, the production of eggs in females and sperm in males, maternal behavior, and various other functions of the system.

It should be emphasized that there is actually very little difference between the nervous and endocrine systems. Both function to transfer information to second cells by means of chemicals. In fact, many endocrine glands are comprised entirely of nerve cells. As an example of how the endocrine system operates, consider how the adrenal glands produce the fear response.

The inner core of the adrenal, called the *medulla*, secretes epinephrine (sometimes called adrenalin) and norepinephrine. *Epinephrine* produces most of the reactions we described in connection with the sympathetic nervous system. The heart beats faster, the stomach contracts, and so on. *Norepinephrine* meanwhile works in a more complex way. It causes the pituitary to stimulate the other part of the adrenal gland, the *adrenal cortex*, which in turn secretes hormones called *steroids*. These signal the liver to release sugar into the blood stream; and they also are involved in maintaining normal metabolic processes. Thus the adrenal glands, by a complicated mechanism, produce most of the responses we feel as fear. As we shall see in Chapter 10, epinephrine causes the kinds of bodily responses that are associated with emotions and it is possible to increase or decrease emotional reactions by controlling the amount of epinephrine that is present in the blood stream. Thus, giving someone an injection of epinephrine is likely to make him respond more emotionally. Similarly, people who have adrenal glands that are not functioning properly may also be overly emotional. Some people suffer from a condition involving an adrenal tumor that causes the gland to produce too much epinephrine. Because the body is constantly in a state of high arousal, the individual almost always feels emotional and tends to overreact to situations and stimuli. Removing the tumor reduces the amount of epinephrine and thereby eliminates the abnormal emotional reactions.

BEHAVIOR GENETICS

An acorn grows into an oak tree not a pine; a lamb into a sheep not a gorilla. A baby with white or black or yellow skin becomes an adult with the same color skin, and a baby girl becomes a woman not a man. These and many other physical characteristics are fixed before birth—at the time of conception. Moreover, there is good reason to believe that many traits that affect behavior, such as tendencies toward aggression, altruism, or creativity, may also be determined at least in part at conception. This determination is due to the genetic inheritance that is passed down from the parents, and the study of this process is called *genetics*, or *behavior genetics* when it involves traits affecting behavior.

The billions of individual cells within the body are alike in terms of their genetic composition. In other words, if you could analyze the components within the nucleus of each cell, you would find identical strands of specialized chemicals in all cells. These strands, called

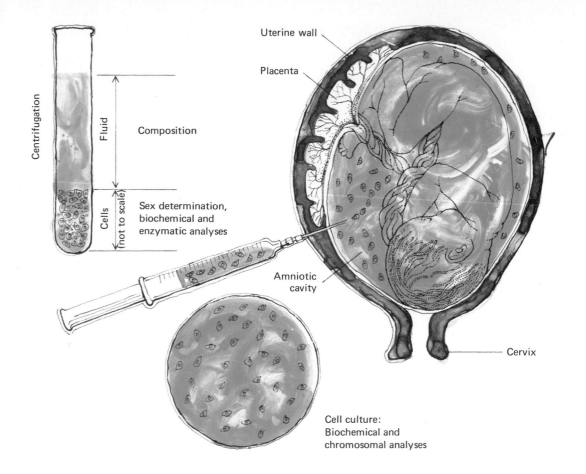

Centrifugation

Fluid

Cells (not to scale)

Composition

Sex determination, biochemical and enzymatic analyses

Uterine wall

Placenta

Amniotic cavity

Cervix

Cell culture: Biochemical and chromosomal analyses

chromosomes, consist of a complex chemical called *deoxyribonucleic acid*, or DNA. Chromosomes come in pairs, and different species of animals or plants have different numbers of pairs. Man, for example, has twenty-three pairs, or forty-six chromosomes in all.

Along the length of each chromosome are a number of areas called *genes*. The structure of the DNA in a pair of genes (one on each chromosome) determines the exact chemical nature of particular proteins within the cell. Since these proteins, called *enzymes*, control the function of the cell, ultimately it is the genes that determine how the cell functions.

Some examples of such traits that are genetically determined are eye or hair color, a tendency toward baldness, and certain kinds of mental retardation. Many traits are *monogenic*, which means that they are fully determined by one pair of genes. For example, eye color is controlled by one set of genes and, as far as we can tell, changes in any other genes have no effect. Most complex traits such as intelligence, motor coordination, and general appearance depend on the interaction of many different genes.

It is relatively easy to trace the heredity of monogenic traits. Mendel, one of the pioneers in genetic research, demonstrated that these traits follow a precise pattern. If an individual has two blue-eye genes, he will have blue eyes; if he has two brown-eye genes, he will have brown eyes. However, if one gene is for blue eyes and the other is for brown eyes, brown eyes will predominate. That gene, in this instance the one for brown eyes, is said to be *dominant* while the

Detecting hereditary diseases before birth

A technique called amniocentesis is now available that makes it possible to detect over forty severe hereditary diseases in the unborn child by about the sixteenth week of development. This technique, which permits analysis of the amniotic fluid containing cells from the body of the fetus, has important implications for the field of behavior genetics. (From Pengelley, 1974)

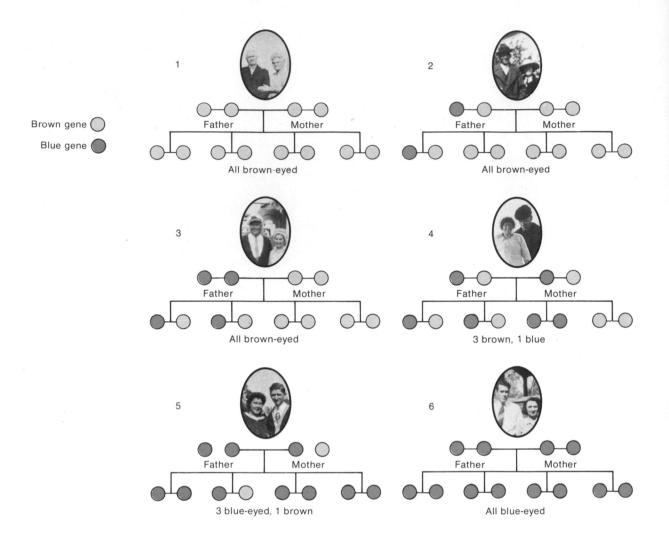

Fig. 8.11
Hereditability of eye color

Two blue genes are necessary for blue eyes, while either two brown or one brown and one blue will produce brown eyes. It is therefore possible for two parents with brown eyes to have a blue-eyed baby. Each parent must have carried both a brown and a blue gene, and by chance the baby got both blue genes. In contrast, two blue-eyed parents (who must both have two blue genes) will always produce blue-eyed offspring.

other one is called *recessive*. The implications of this for the hereditability of eye color are diagramed in Fig. 8.11.

Determining Sex

Sex is determined entirely by certain chromosomes. Along with the other twenty-two sets of chromosomes in every cell in the body, there is one pair that controls sex. In women, the two sex chromosomes are called X chromosomes because they look like an X under an electron microscope. In contrast, male cells contain one X chromosome that is identical to that found in women, plus one Y chromosome, again named for its shape (see Fig. 8.12). And this small difference between the male and female chromosomes is what produces males and females.

In the reproductive organs, certain cells, called *sperm* in men and eggs or *ova* in women, split in half and contain only twenty-three single chromosomes rather than twenty-three pairs. Since female cells began with two X chromosomes, each ova contains one X. But males began with one X and one Y, so after the split half of the sperm cells have an X and half have a Y.

During reproduction a sperm and an egg come together, forming a *zygote*, which has the full complement of forty-six chromosomes, twenty-three from each partner. This zygote, of course, divides a great many times to produce the billions of cells that eventually become a human being. The sex of this new person depends on whether the zygote contains two X chromosomes or one X and one Y; and that is determined entirely by whether the sperm that fertilized the egg had an X or a Y (because the egg always has an X). If the zygote has two X's, it is female; if it has an X and a Y, it is male. This is a simple and precise example of genetic determination, and also demonstrates the roll of chance in producing a particular individual.

Evolution

Evolution is the process by which the average genetic composition of a group of animals changes over time. Three things are necessary for evolution to occur. The first is a capacity to pass characteristics from one generation to the next. This is accomplished by the fact that the genes of one generation will determine many of the traits of the generation it produces. The second is a capacity to produce more offspring than is necessary to duplicate exactly the present population. In other words, for every two parents reproducing, an average of more than two offspring must be born in a lifetime. Virtually every animal species is capable of this. Finally, there must be a capacity for genes to change over time. This exists via what are called *mutations*, which are mistakes that occur within a DNA molecule when one cell is dividing into two cells. If this occurs in most tissues of the body, the mistake appears in only a small fraction of the animal. If, however, a mutation occurs in a reproductive organ in a cell forming a sperm or an egg, the mutation might be transmitted to the next generation. Almost all such mutations are lethal, in that an animal receiving a defective gene dies, and the rate of mutation is estimated to be extremely low. But a sufficiently large number of potentially useful mutations occur that genes do have the capacity to change over time.

Let us see how evolution works by considering the salmon. When mature, adult salmon in the ocean migrate to the precise river and streambed from which they were hatched. One female salmon may then lay 10,000 eggs and a male salmon will fertilize most of these eggs with his sperm. All of the resulting young salmon will differ from one another in very small ways. They will have a large number of genes in common, these genes defining them as salmon, but there will be tremendous variability from animal to animal. Some salmon will have slightly longer fins than others; others will be able to secrete a little more oil on the surface of the body; others may incorporate more calcium into their bones, thus making them slightly heavier; and so on. As these salmon emerge from their egg sacs in the fresh water of their stream, they encounter numerous difficulties. Sudden changes of temperature or salinity of the water kill many of them. Predators such as birds and larger fish kill others. Those that survive these dangers will eventually swim downstream toward the ocean. Many more will be killed going over rocks and some will not be able to survive in the salt water. Those that do will swim out to sea and, if they avoid predators, fishermen's nets, fisher-

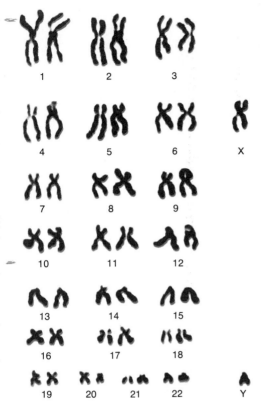

Fig. 8.12
The human chromosomes, separated into pairs.

Note the difference in size between the X (female) and the Y (male) chromosome.

men's lures, and other dangers, may return in four to five years to start the cycle anew. Out of 10,000. eggs laid, on the average two salmon will return if the population is stable. This means that 9,998, on the average, will die.

The ones that survive were presumably best able to cope with the dangers of their environment. Another way of saying this is that they were the most fit for the environment in which they had to live. Their final ability to reproduce is a statement of "survival of the fittest." This term is often misused to reflect actual combat between animals of the same species. Physical combat to death is extremely rare among animals of the same species because it endangers both animals, making it less likely that either of them will ever live to reproduce. Survival of the fittest is a more complex term, referring to the fact that some animals will be better able to meet the challenges of their environment and thus live to reproduce, whereas other animals will not survive this competition and will die, or not reproduce. By this mechanism, those traits that are best adapted to the environment will be passed along to the next generation, and those traits that were ineffective will not.

To return to the salmon, the fish with slightly shorter gills may have more easily escaped gillnets across their river and thus were better adapted than those fish with longer gills, and those salmon that could secrete more oil over the surface of their bodies might have been better able to ward off water pollution than those fish that secreted less oil. In these ways, subtle differences can influence the ability of an animal to reach the reproductive state. As the environment changes, the advantage of a particular trait may increase or decrease. This is what is meant by evolution. As a particular trait gains or loses importance, evolution is said to be occurring. For example, as humans evolved from the apes, a tail probably became less and less necessary for their particular lifestyle. Those humans without tails, in fact, may have held some advantage over those with tails such that the animals without tails survived. Over many thousands of generations, therefore, the tail disappeared. Evolution does not happen rapidly. It usually requires hundreds of generations to be evident. On the other hand, the environment of most animals does not change very rapidly either, so that a species can usually keep up with any environmental changes. There are noteworthy exceptions to this rule. One theory for the rapid decline of the dinosaurs is that they could not evolve sufficiently rapidly to overcome the climatic changes associated with the Ice Age and therefore perished. Other types of animals with genes enabling them to cope with cold temperatures were favored, leading to the increase of mammals at that time.

Natural selection is the process of survival of the fittest working, in a naturally living population. Humans can expedite evolution by enabling animals with particular traits to breed, and by preventing animals with other traits from breeding. This method of selective breeding has been used successfully to produce strains of animals that run mazes better or worse, that are attracted to light more or less, that drink more or less alcohol, or whatever. All that is necessary is to enable only those animals with a particular trait to mate in order to change the average genetic makeup of a population in favor of that trait. Animal breeders have been doing this for years, and the specific field is called *animal husbandry*. Take as an example the domestic dog. Wild dogs, or wolves, were tamed by our ancestors, and some of the dogs were selectively bred to be guard dogs, others to be hunters, others to be pointers, and so on. To do this, one simply looked at all of the available dogs, selected the male and female with the best expressions of the desired trait (such as fierceness), and mated them. The fiercest male and female were again mated from the offspring, and so on until a strain of very fierce dogs existed. This has been shown to be possible with almost any desired behavioral trait, and it demonstrates very nicely the power of evolution.

It also indicates that almost any trait can be genetically determined—at least in part. Just as intelligence is affected by heredity, so are traits that directly affect behavior such as aggressiveness, kindness, or even humor. The contribution of heredity to any of these traits in humans is unknown and may be quite small. But in theory, any behavior pattern should be affected by heredity and evolution. ■

Summary

1. Physiological psychology is concerned with finding links between the physical makeup of an organism and its behavior.

2. The basic unit for transmitting messages within the nervous system, the neuron, consists of nerve fibers (dendrites), which receive nerve impulses, and the axon, which transmits nerve impulses. Impulses are transmitted by means of a chemical change that is accompanied by electrical activity called the action potential. The action potential moves along the neuron to a space called a synapse, where information is passed from the neuron to the second cell. Excitatory and inhibitory chemicals determine whether or not the second neuron will be activated.

3. The nervous system has two major functions: (1) to transmit information received at one part of the body to cells in other parts of the body; and (2) to carry commands to those parts of the body that cause responses—the muscles and glands, called the effectors.

4. The nervous system is divided into two parts: (1) the central nervous system, which includes the brain and spinal cord; and (2) the peripheral nervous system, which includes the nerves connecting the rest of the body with the central nervous system. The peripheral nervous system is subdivided into the somatic nervous system (neurons connected with muscles, sense organs, and skin surface) and the autonomic nervous system (neurons connected with internal organs).

    The autonomic system further divides into the sympathetic nervous system, which arouses the body for action, and the parasympathetic system, which slows the body down and returns the individual to a normal state.

5. The spinal cord receives information from neurons and transmits it to the brain; it carries messages from the brain to parts of the body; and it enables the body to respond to certain kinds of stimulation without involving the brain—called spinal reflexes.

6. The brain is the control center for almost every activity of the body. A convenient division of the brain is into the hindbrain, midbrain, and forebrain. The hindbrain comprises the medulla, which regulates respiration and heart rate, the pons, a bridge between the cortex and the cerebellum, and the cerebellum itself, which is concerned with regulating motor coordination and with our sense of balance. The midbrain coordinates certain reflex movements of the head and neck, houses neurons that initiate voluntary movements, and is a receiving center for orders from the cerebellum.

7. The forebrain is the center of higher mental processes, integrates and interprets information from the sensory organs, and plays an important role in controlling emotions and motivations.

8. The thalamus, located in front of the midbrain, is the major relay center for sensory information on its way to the cerebral cortex. The hypothalamus, located just below the thalamus, controls emotional behavior, regulates activities such as eating and sleeping, and controls the pituitary gland.

9. The cerebral cortex consists of the convoluted surface of the two hemispheres of the cerebrum. Each hemisphere has four lobes that are associated with different functions. Some parts of the cortex are primary sensory receiving areas; some are primary motor areas. Other areas, called the association cortex, apparently have functions other than sensory or motor, but the exact functions are unknown.

10. The limbic system includes the hypothalamus, the hippocampus, and several areas in the cerebral cortex, and is closely connected with other areas of the brain. It is involved in a wide range of activities including emotions, learning, and reinforcement.

11. The corpus callosum, a large bundle of axons connecting the right and left hemispheres, transfers information from one hemisphere to the other. Surgical severing of the corpus callosum causes a "split-brain" individual who possesses two somewhat independent "brains." The two hemispheres apparently have different functions: the left hemisphere houses the language center and mathematical and analytic abilities; the right hemisphere is the center for spatial-perceptive abilities and appreciation of music and art.

12. The endocrine system secretes hormones into the blood stream, thus carrying information to many cells simultaneously. The endocrine glands control emotional and motivational behavior and work closely with the nervous system. The adrenal glands, which regulate emotional responses, and the pituitary gland, which has numerous functions including stimulation of other endocrine glands, are particularly important endocrine glands.

13. Genetics concerns the study of traits that are determined by heredity. Strands of DNA (deoxyribonucleic acid) called chromosomes contain areas called genes, which are responsible for determining many traits. Some charcteristics such as hair or eye color are controlled by one gene (monogenic). More complex traits such as intelligence and motor coordination depend on the

interaction of many different genes. Sex is determined entirely by a particular chromosome. Many psychological traits are also affected by heredity, but the effect may be quite small.

14. The process by which the genetic composition of a group of animals changes over time is called evolution. In the evolutionary process, traits that are best adapted to the environment tend to be passed along to the next generation and those that are ineffective are not, because individuals having these traits are less likely to survive and reproduce.

RECOMMENDED READING

Teyler, T. J. *A Primer of Psychobiology.* San Francisco: Freeman, 1975. A brief introduction to physiological psychology.

Thompson, R. F. *Physiological Psychology—Readings from Scientific American.* San Francisco: Freeman, 1972. Reprinted articles describing recent advances in the field. Interesting reading for the non-expert.

Thompson, R. T. *Introduction to Physiological Psychology.* New York: Harper & Row, 1975. A difficult but thorough and clear introduction.

What makes life dreary is the want of motive.
George Eliot, Daniel Deronda

9 Motivation

Learning versus performance ▪ *Motivation defined* ▪
Theories of motivation ▪ *Basic physiological motives* ▪
How motives operate—the example of hunger ▪ *Other
basic motives* ▪ *Maternal behavior* ▪ *The sex drive* ▪
Curiosity ▪ *Learned motives*

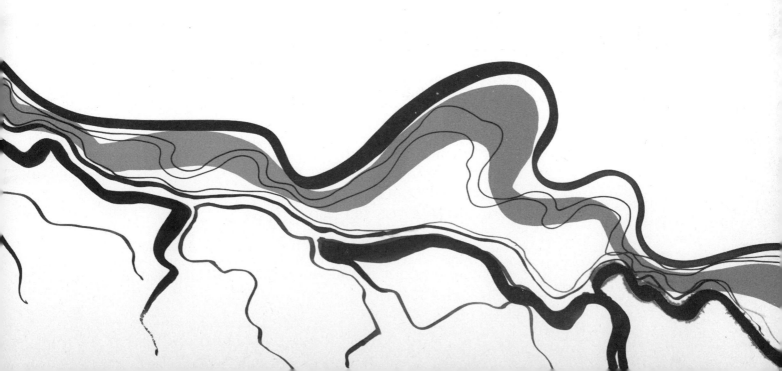

Nearly every day the newspapers carry at least one story that causes us to ask: why in the world would anybody do that? "Kidnappers Abduct Schoolchildren." "Boy Dies while Playing Russian Roulette." "Eighty-one-year-old Man to Walk across Country Backwards." In asking *why* people would do such things we are making an important assumption about human behavior—that human behavior is *motivated*. In other words, we are assuming that certain needs, drives, emotions, goals, likes, or dislikes cause the behavior to occur. To be sure, some human behavior is automatic: our knees flex when they are tapped in the right place; our pupils constrict when a bright light shines in our eyes; and much of perception occurs regardless of experiences and feelings. But the amount of human behavior determined by these automatic mechanisms is relatively small. Almost everything else we do is affected to some extent by motivation.

We can roughly divide motives into three categories: (1) motives that are closely tied to physiological needs, such as hunger; (2) motives that are basic properties of the organism but are only loosely connected to physiological processes, such as the sex drive and maternal instinct; and (3) motives that are learned, such as the human need for achievement. This chapter describes each of these types of motives and attempts to explain how some specific motives operate. The question of *what* is motivating is also explored and some theories presented that attempt to account for various motives. Motivation in humans involves a complex interplay of physiological, cognitive, social, and personality factors. The interrelationship of these factors in determining motivation is a central theme of this chapter.

LEARNING VERSUS PERFORMANCE

In Chapter 3 we described how a rat learns to press a bar to obtain food; how a pigeon pecks at a red and not a green disk; and how people learn to get a soft drink from a machine. However, it is important to realize that in such cases what has been learned is how to achieve a goal. The animal now knows to press the lever or put the coin in the soft-drink machine when it wants a drink. But the rat does not press the lever continuously nor does a person put a coin in every soft-drink machine she passes. That particular behavior will occur only when the rat is hungry or the human is thirsty.

This distinction between *learning* an act and *performing* it is very important. Most learning, and in particular human learning, consists of the capacity or ability to reach a specific goal by performing a specific action. The *motive* determines which particular piece of learning will be activated; the *learning* determines what action will be taken when the motive is aroused.

MOTIVATION DEFINED

The definition of motivation stems directly from the previous idea. Motivation involves *arousal that is connected to a specific goal*; it implies some *direction that behavior will take*. Both aspects of the definition—arousal and direction—are critical. As we shall see, without arousal the organism's behavior is not affected. Even a vital need will not affect the animals' actions unless it produces or is associated with arousal. Yet arousal alone is not motivation. Having a faster heartbeat or an increased metabolism does make all responses stronger. But it is not motivation in the usual sense. Only when arousal is associated with a goal do we call it motivation.

THEORIES OF MOTIVATION

The question of what is motivating is connected with the question of what is reinforcing. Anything we like is reinforcing and causes us to seek it; anything we dislike tends to be punishing and causes us to avoid it. Thus, each reinforcement tends to have a comparable motivation—food and hunger, water and thirst, success and the desire for achievement, and so on. Theories of motivation or reinforcement attempt to explain in general terms why particular events are rewarding or punishing, why we seek them or avoid them.

Drive-Reduction and Incentive Theories

As we discussed in Chapter 3 on learning, there are various theories of reinforcement, none of which is fully adequate. Drive-reduction theory (Hull, 1952) states that any arousal is unpleasant, we seek to reduce it, and this reduction is reinforcing. Motivation in these terms would consist entirely of seeking to reduce arousal when it exists, and of avoiding or escaping situations that produce arousal.

Incentive theory (Spence, 1956), a somewhat different version of drive-reduction theory, emphasizes the role of specific arousals (incentives) and the particular context. A juicy steak may motivate you even if you are not especially hungry; but if you are very thirsty, the steak may have no motivating effect because it does not correspond to the particular motive or incentive that has been aroused. The point is that motives are produced by an interaction of the internal state and the external situation.

Drive-reduction and incentive theories explain many kinds of motives. Hunger is uncomfortable; eating reduces the hunger and is therefore reinforcing. This holds for physiological needs for water and air, and for the avoidance of pain and extremes of temperature. However, it cannot account for motives that seem to involve increasing arousal. For example, we are often motivated to seek sexual stimulation even if our sexual desires are increased rather than reduced by the experience. Similarly, the excitement of a roller coaster or horror movie is reinforcing for many people even though their arousal level is greatly increased. The ideal theory of motivation must explain why both reduction and increase of arousal can be reinforcing.

Homeostatic Theory and Adaptation Level

One attempt to provide such an explanation states that motivation serves to maintain a particular level of arousal (Hebb, 1949). Deviations from that level produce motivation that causes you to seek a way to return to the original level. If the arousal state rises above this ideal level, you are motivated to reduce stimulation; if it drops below

D. O. HEBB

it, you are motivated to increase stimulation. This dual activity that maintains a constant level is called a *homeostatic* process, and the ideal amount of arousal is called the *adaptation level*.

There is no question that there are many homeostatic systems at work in the human body. If you run a mile at top speed, your heart speeds up, your temperature rises, and your whole system is highly aroused. Various mechanisms will reduce the speed of your heart, lower your temperature, and return the body to its usual level of arousal. This homeostatic tendency operates in a great many parts of the system, maintaining the right level of hormones and other chemicals in the blood stream, providing just the right amount of oxygen to the cells, excreting unnecessary chemicals and sometimes producing those that are necessary, and so on. Thus the notion that motivation consists of maintaining some ideal state certainly is consistent with certain workings of the organism. Without the homeostatic processes we would not survive, and it seems likely that many of our motives are ways the body has to keep the system at the right level.

This theory would explain motives that are mainly drive reducing as well as instances in which we seek increased arousal. However, it seems clear that we do not always seek to maintain a constant level of arousal. The high-pitched excitement of the roller coaster is obviously way above the level of arousal we usually like; conversely, we often seek periods of tranquility, in which there is little or no arousal. It may be that the homeostatic process operates over a relatively long time period, and that we try to maintain an average level of arousal over that period. Thus we seek highs and lows, moments of excitement and of calm, that average to some optimal level.

Yet even this is not the whole story because certain kinds of arousal are clearly pleasant and others are unpleasant. The arousal produced by roller coasters, sexual stimulation, or exciting adventures is pleasant for most people, while the arousal due to a dental drill, extreme hunger, or school tests is unpleasant. We do not have an explanation yet of why some things are positively motivating and others are not, but it is likely that the answer is more complex than either drive-reduction or homeostatic theory would indicate.

Although we do not fully understand motivation, we do know a considerable amount about the sources and operation of specific motives. Let us now turn our attention to some of these motives.

BASIC PHYSIOLOGICAL MOTIVES

Some motives are directly linked to physiological needs or mechanisms. We cannot survive without food, water, oxygen, or sleep. When we are deprived of vital substances, we are usually motivated to obtain what is lacking. These are all positive motives—we need something and are reinforced when we obtain it. There are also negative motives, which cause us to avoid or escape from conditions that are threatening or uncomfortable. Pain serves as a signal that the body is in danger, and eliminating pain is a powerful motive. Similarly, extremes of temperature, some noxious odors and tastes, and very strong stimulation of any of the senses produce discomfort that motivates us to escape from its source. In addition to these motives that are directly tied to physiological needs, we have two extremely important and complex motives—sex and maternal—that involve physiological processes but are not strictly necessary for our individual survival. As we shall see, all of these physiological motives are affected by and interact with many other factors in the situation.

Need versus Motive

Before discussing how these basic motives operate, we should point out that not all physiological needs arouse corresponding motives. We need food and when we do not get it we feel hungry. But we also need specific substances in our food, and most of these are not linked to particular motives. Some, such as salt, can arouse a more or less specific desire for the missing element. Animals that have been deprived of salt or calcium, for example, show a tendency to prefer and seek out foods that are rich in those substances (Hughes and Wood-Gush, 1971). But this is an exception. A lack of magnesium, potassium, or thiamine produces no clear preference for foods containing these substances (Rozin, 1965; Adam, 1973). Similarly, protein deficiency prevents proper growth in children and can cause death, too little vitamin C causes scurvy, and too little iodine causes severe thyroid malfunction—but no one seems to feel a hunger for a particular protein group, vitamin C, or iodine.

On the other hand, animals that have been deprived of certain vital elements do tend to favor new diets, whatever they may be. In nature, this will sometimes cause them to switch from a poor diet to a better one, thus more or less incidentally replacing the needed substances (Rozin and Kalat, 1971). This is an impressive example of how an animal manages to obtain what it needs for survival despite the lack of motives that are linked directly to its needs. But if a

Almost any kind of gas, even poisonous, will satisfy the body's need for oxygen. People who work in deep mines or at high altitudes must guard against asphyxiation by harmful substances.

potassium-deprived animal is given a choice of a new diet rich in potassium and one that is not potassium-rich, it will show no preference for the former. Therefore, it clearly does not have a specific motive that can be satisfied by a specific substance. This indicates that the survival mechanism is quite chancy—it works only when a random change of diet happens to increase the supply of whatever is lacking.

Similarly, lack of air induces an almost overwhelming drive to obtain it. But virtually any gas that does not make us choke will satisfy this motivation—nitrous oxide or carbon monoxide will do fine. The body needs oxygen, of course, not just any kind of gas; but since there is no specific motive to find oxygen, people can asphyxiate without feeling any particular discomfort. This happens all too often when people warm up their cars in closed garages and are asphyxiated by carbon monoxide from the car's exhaust. It is also a common problem in deep mines and at high altitudes, where oxygen is scarce.

Just as the body does not always signal us that we need a particular substance, so it does not tell us that we are being exposed to a harmful stimulus. Ultraviolet rays and X rays are among the stimuli that can harm the body without arousing any motivation to escape. Only after the harm has been done (we are badly sunburned) do we become aware of it. Therefore, we must rely on warning systems external to ourselves. For example, workers in deep mines used to keep canaries as pets. The birds would collapse at the first whiff of poisonous gases, warning the miners to escape even though they were unable to sense the gas themselves. And people working near radiation wear a badge that warns them when they have received too much radiation.

Motives as Warnings

Motives that are linked to physiological needs are essentially warnings. Without these signals, the organism does not know what it needs or what to avoid. When the organism is in its typical environment it reacts more or less automatically. Poisonous substances usually taste bad, lack of oxygen is usually associated with lack of air, ultraviolet stimulation eventually causes pain (as with sunburn), and most vitamins and minerals will be obtained from the normal diet for the organism. But when the organism tries to live in a foreign or unusual environment these signals may prove inadequate. This is particularly true of humans because we have greatly altered our environment and are now living in situations for which our bodies were not designed. Under these circumstances, we need additional aids such as those described above. We have developed over thousands of generations to survive in certain environments, and our needs as well as our warning devices have evolved to meet the demands of these environments. The limitations of our biological heritage appear when we find ourselves in situations we have not faced before or which have not generally existed before on earth.

HOW MOTIVES OPERATE—THE EXAMPLE OF HUNGER

Hunger has been studied more extensively than any of the basic motives. Therefore, let us consider what we know about hunger as an example of the great complexity of the motivational process and the ways in which physiological, cognitive, and social factors are all involved.

Clearly, the longer the organism has gone without food, the stronger the hunger. As you can see in Fig. 9.1, this is a straightforward relationship—the body is deprived of something it needs, and the longer the deprivation the greater the need. But how is the body's need for food translated into the experience of hunger?

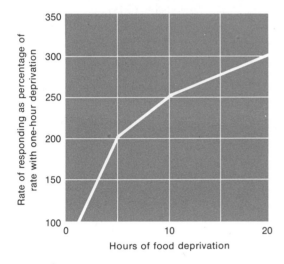

Fig. 9.1
Rate of responding and food deprivation

After twenty hours of deprivation, rats press the lever three times as rapidly as after one hour of deprivation. (From Clark, 1959)

Stomach Contractions

Most people would probably say that when their stomach is empty, they are hungry; when it is full, they are not. More specifically, it seems as if we experience "pangs" of hunger when our stomach undergoes contractions. With this in mind, Cannon (1934) conducted an experiment in which he had a student swallow a small balloon attached to a length of tubing. The balloon was then inflated so that it loosely filled the stomach. Contractions of the stomach compressed the balloon slightly and could therefore be easily recorded, as shown in Fig. 9.2. The subject was instructed to press a button when he felt particularly hungry. He usually pressed the button just after his stomach had contracted.

This seems at first glance to answer the question of what causes sensations of hunger, but it turns out to be far from the whole story. In the first place, many people say that they never experience stomach contractions, but do feel hungry. Their observations are supported by people whose stomachs have been removed. Obviously, these people do not experience stomach contractions, and yet they also report feeling hungry (Hoelzel, 1927).

Moreover, if stomach contractions produce hunger, the message must be transmitted from the stomach to the brain. However, a

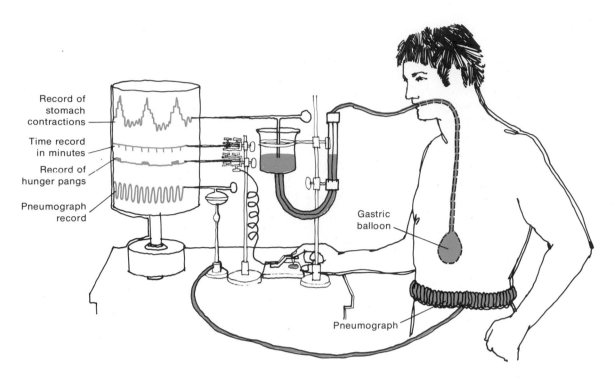

Record of
stomach
contractions

Time record
in minutes

Record of
hunger pangs

Pneumograph
record

Gastric
balloon

Pneumograph

Fig. 9.2
Cannon's experiment on hunger pangs and
stomach contraction

number of studies (Morgan and Morgan, 1940) have indicated that cutting the sensory nerves between the stomach and the brain does not eliminate hunger. Rats who had stomach contractions and whose stomach nerves were no longer connected to their brains still behaved as if they were hungry when they had been deprived of food. In short, these experiments indicate that stomach contractions alone could not be producing the sensation of hunger.

Cellular Depletion

One determinant of hunger may be the nutritional state of the body. When the blood and tissues are low in nutrients, the individual feels hungry (Mayer, 1955). This is the most basic source of hunger—the body really does need the food and it is somehow signaling its deprived state. But when people are fed high-calorie diets intravenously until the nutritional level of their blood is high, they still report feeling hungry (Jordan et al., 1974). Even though the body does not need food, the person experiences a motivation to eat. Such a diet can reduce the feelings of hunger considerably, suggesting that the tissues and blood must receive certain specific nutrients in order to eliminate the sensation of hunger. And in all cases of intravenous feeding, once the blood is rich in nutrients, the person is unable to eat much, even though he feels hungry. Nevertheless, the experience of hunger is at least partially independent of the level of nutrients in the blood.

Tasting and Swallowing

Other research has demonstrated that the reduction of hunger is controlled partly by the sensation of tasting and swallowing the food.

MOTIVATION AND PERFORMANCE

We generally assume that there is a simple relationship between motivation and performance: the stronger the motivation, the more intense and frequent will be the relevant behavior. An increase in hunger leads to more eating and searching for food, greater thirst to more drinking, and more intense pain to more vigorous efforts to escape. However, this does not mean that higher motivation will always lead to *better* performance. On the contrary, the quality of the performance will sometimes be improved and sometimes be hurt by increased motivation. As a general rule there seems to be an optimal level of motivation for every task—the level at which performance will be best. Motivation that is lower or higher will interfere with performance; and the more complex the task, the lower the optimal level. This is sometimes called the *Yerkes-Dodson law* after its discoverers (see figure).

The main reason for this complex effect of motivation on performance is that increased motivation increases the strength of all responses, not necessarily only the correct one. If there is only one possible response or if there are few competing responses, higher motivation should improve performance. If you are

running a race, it should help to have very high motivation. As you wait at the starting block, there is only one stimulus that matters (the sound of the gun) and only one possible response (running). Higher motivation should make you respond more quickly to the gun and then run faster. However, if motivation is too high, you may become so aroused that you jump the gun when you hear a car backfire or just see the starter about to fire. And during the race, you may be so motivated that you do not pace yourself or you may look behind you to see where the other runners are. Thus, with this and other simple behaviors (such as learning an easy list of words or answering simple questions), the optimal level of motivation will be quite high, but beyond that level performance will be less good.

With a complex task that involves difficult actions and many competing responses, the optimal level is lower. High motivation causes you to give incorrect responses or respond to irrelevant cues. If you are working on an intricate problem under moderate motivation, a phone ringing will probably be somewhat distracting. If your motivation is higher, you may leap out of your chair when the phone rings. Similarly, in taking a difficult test, too high a level of motivation will cause you to be distracted and will also make you give many incorrect answers. Being nervous about a test will thus improve performance on simple exams but interfere with performance on complex ones (Mandler and Sarason, 1952). High arousal also interferes with problem solving by increasing functional fixedness and preventing you from finding the unusual response to the problem (Glucksberg, 1962); while moderate levels of of arousal improve problem solving (Suedfeld, Glucksberg, and Vernon, 1967). So, when you are taking a test, worry about it a lot if it is simple but not if it is complex (which unfortunately, is just the opposite from the way most of us react).

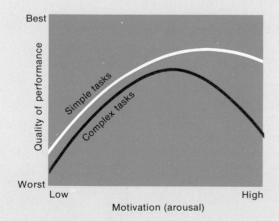

Best

Quality of performance

Simple tasks

Complex tasks

Worst

Low   High

Motivation (arousal)

Box 9.1

Miller and Kessen (1952) compared the effects of injecting food directly into the stomachs of rats with the effects of giving them the same amount of food through the mouth. When the mouth was bypassed, the rats' hunger apparently was reduced—but the reduction of hunger was much stronger when the rats were allowed to taste the food. Thus, the reduction of hunger is associated to some extent with the sensations of eating. On the other hand, animals allowed to eat food that passes from the mouth to the esophagus and then out of the body through a tube are never satisfied. They do not stop eating. Apparently some food in the stomach is necessary to turn off eating.

The Hypothalamus

There is considerable evidence that certain discrete areas of the hypothalamus play a role in eating. In particular, it has been suggested that the ventromedial hypothalamus is a *satiety center*. This conclusion was based on the observations that electrical stimulation localized to this area caused a hungry animal to stop eating (Hoebel and Teitelbaum, 1962), and that if the ventromedial hypothalamus was destroyed, animals would eat very large meals as if it were very difficult for them to become satiated (Brobeck, Tepperman, and Long, 1943). The result is that such animals become obese (see Fig. 9.3). Another part of the hypothalamus, called the ventrolateral hypothalamic area, has been called the *eating center*. This is because electrical stimulation there induces eating in a satiated animal and destruction of this area causes a reduction of eating that may last for several weeks. Animals suffering from damage in this area are therefore very thin. It has been proposed that these two centers antagonistically control eating, with the ventrolateral hypothalamus initiating a meal and the ventromedial hypothalamus stopping it. Support for this contention has been the observation that various internal stimuli associated with feeding reach these areas of the hypothalamus. For example, the hypothalamus receives information as to the taste of food, the amount and content of food in the stomach, the amount of sugar in the blood, and so on.

More recent research (Hoebel and Teitelbaum, 1966) suggests that these centers of the hypothalamus are more concerned with the maintenance of body weight than with eating per se. An already obese rat given a lesion (injury) of the ventromedial hypothalamus does not overeat. Likewise, a rat that is thin prior to a lesion of the ventrolateral hypothalamus does not undereat after the lesion. In both instances the food intake of the lesioned rats is relatively normal, suggesting that the overeating and undereating usually observed is an attempt by the brain to raise or lower the level of fat. There is evidence that obese animals with lesions of the ventromedial hypothalamus will try to maintain their new obese weight. If such rats are forced to become even fatter by overfeeding, or if they are starved so that their weights become normal again, they will quickly revert to their normal "obese" state when allowed to eat freely. Likewise, rats with ventrolateral hypothalamic lesions will maintain their newly acquired thin weights. These hypothalamic lesions therefore do not disrupt the weight regulatory system; rather, they simply change the weight level that the brain is attempting to maintain.

Fig. 9.3
Obesity in rat caused by destruction of ventromedial hypothalamus

Another area of recent research casts doubt on the long-standing idea that discrete centers within the hypothalamus are responsible for motivated behaviors. Technological advances in neuropharmacology have made it possible to destroy only neurons containing certain specific chemicals and to spare others when appropriate drugs are applied to the brain. Studies using these techniques have revealed that the symptoms commonly attributed to destruction of the ventrolateral hypothalamic area may be due to destruction of certain neurons passing through the lateral hypothalamus on their way to higher centers of the forebrain. Destruction of these axons at any point along their pathway including the ventrolateral hypothalamus will cause decreased food intake and loss of body weight. However, these recent findings should not obscure the fundamental observations that the brain has very powerful control mechanisms over food intake and body weight.

Cognitive and Social Factors

Stomach contractions, blood-sugar level, the sensation of eating, and hypothalamic activity all play a role in the arousal of hunger and the amount of eating. But there is still more to the story, particularly with people. Although we generally eat more when we feel hungrier, and this depends to some extent on how long it has been since we last ate, we are also sensitive to external factors that have nothing to do with physiological needs. Our awareness of the social situation and other cognitions also affect when and how much we eat.

Most of us tend to eat when it is "time" to eat. We are accustomed to having lunch around noon and dinner around six or seven. When noon rolls around, we usually have lunch whether or not we are particularly hungry. It is time to eat, so we eat. Moreover, we are greatly affected by the sight and smell of food. Everyone has probably had the experience of eating a big meal, feeling too full to finish what was on the plate, and yet "finding room" for some dessert that looked tempting. Regardless of whether the body needs food, our hunger can be aroused by appropriate stimuli and we sometimes eat even if we are not hungry at all.

Obesity—"fats" versus normals Some people are more sensitive than others to external stimuli. Research by Stanley Schachter and his associates suggests that some people get fat because they eat more in response to the social and cognitive situation than in response to the needs of their bodies. In our society, where there are constant stimuli associated with food, these people eat more than their body needs and become obese.

One difference between "fats" and normals appears in their response to the sight of food; another relates to the difficulty of obtaining or eating the food. In one study (Nisbett, 1968), obese and normal subjects were offered ham and roast beef sandwiches cut into thirds, but the number of thirds they were shown differed in two conditions. In one, they were given a plate with three thirds and told there were more sandwiches in a refrigerator and they could help themselves. In a second condition, they were given a plate heaped high with thirds of sandwiches, more than anyone could eat. In both conditions there

STANLEY SCHACHTER

INTERVIEW

JEAN NIDETCH

As her press release says, Jean Nidetch has "helped to change the shape of the world." She is the founder of the hugely successful Weight Watchers International corporation, the multimillion dollar company devoted to helping people lose weight. Jean herself trimmed down from 214 pounds to 142 pounds and decided to carry the word to others with a weight problem. This interview was conducted by phone, but even so, Jean's lively personality still comes through. We should note for those who do not already know it that the basic program of Weight Watchers includes attendance at weekly meetings where members are weighed, hear talks related to their problem, and tell about themselves, plus a carefully regulated, well-balanced diet that doesn't leave you hungry. The idea behind Weight Watchers is that you can lose weight not by starving or depriving yourself of tasty foods, but by learning how to eat properly.

Q: What are some of the reasons you feel that people overeat?

A: I think it is a hunger, but the "hunger" must be in quotes because it is not a hunger for food. You can satisfy hunger for food with asparagus or green pepper, but people who are overeaters seem to fall into one of two categories: sweets or starches. Very often people will say "I

The lady realized at that second that her weight could have prevented her from saving her child. And then she was ready to lose weight.

---

never eat dessert" and "I don't know why I'm overweight," and they weigh two hundred or three hundred pounds. Well, they don't go in for desserts, but their "hang-up," their "Frankenstein" as we call it, is starches. That could mean something like eating a whole loaf of bread during the night. A lady once said to me she never knew she consumed a whole loaf until, in the morning, she found the wrapper in the wastebasket!

Q: Do you mean you think her eating was unconscious?

A: Well, let's say, it's subtle. We have the tendency to justify what we do. If it's a dessert we can rationalize that we passed up dessert two days ago at somebody's party and therefore "we're entitled." Then we feel guilty, and we eat more to reduce the guilt. You will hear someone say in a restaurant, "Why did you let me eat that?" or "I didn't really need that." Well, I think they *did* need it in their own mind, for security.

Q: You use the words security and guilt. It sounds as if you're suggesting that people eat because

of certain problems they may have.

A: Well, people do seem to have a compelling need because they plot how to buy chocolate-covered cookies while they're dieting. People who live in the cold part of the country shop "in case there's a snowstorm and guests drop in," but, very often, the friends would be happy with just tea and an apple.

I think anyone in the world can change, can lose weight, but the decision must be a personal one. There is a great reluctance to change just because somebody else tells you. That's why a doctor who tells an overweight patient "you might die of a heart attack because you are overweight," doesn't usually get him to do anything. But have him walk on the street and catch a glimpse of himself in a store window, or have a lady go to a party where somebody makes a remark about how she's changed—that's "the moment of truth." A woman told me that she was sitting on the porch of her house somewhere in the Midwest and her little girl was coming across the street. She saw a car coming down the street toward the girl and the woman couldn't get out of the chair fast enough to help. That was for her The Moment. Fortunately, the child wasn't hurt, but what happened was that the lady realized, at that second, that her weight could have prevented her from saving her child. And then she was ready to lose weight.

Q: Weight Watchers sounds a lot like Alcoholics Anonymous—the person finally is forced to admit the problem and makes a decision to change.

A: Yes, we've been compared to AA and I feel it's a flattering comparison. What we are both doing is telling it like it is—they have a drinking problem, we have an eating problem. But the alcoholic has an advantage—you can hide the fact that you drink, but not that you're fat. We try to tell it straight and help reeducate people about their eating habits. But each person must decide to change.

Q: Do you think fat people have a poor impression of themselves?

A: I think there is a stigma attached to being fat, and they are treated differently. I have asked employers if they had two people, with the same background and everything else, but one was fat, which one would they hire and they say, of course, "I would hire the thin one." I asked one man why and he said "because if somebody didn't think enough of themselves to look their very best, then maybe they'd forget to give me a phone message." I wanted to be thin because I always felt that I was living in a different world as a fat kid. I didn't do the things normal children do—I wouldn't be caught dead in shorts. Summertime was disastrous because for a thin person summer means beach, bathing suits, fun. For a fat kid it is awful.

Q: Why is it that some people get fat and others don't?

A: Well, there are people who eat and don't gain weight. Some thin people eat half a sandwich and are full. Whatever that "thermostat" is that controls eating, it's different for them but it does control them. Overweight people clean the plate even if the food is no good—maybe because eating is their only joy.

Q: What are some of the techniques you suggest for losing weight?

A: Learn to eat slower. I watch people in restaurants, and fat people never put down the fork: they hold it, talk with it, almost like a "weapon." Thin people put it down, relax, sit back and enjoy the music. Also, telling someone else what you're doing is a great aid. That's why our groups work—everyone has the same problem and no one cares about your education or how much money you have in the bank.

Then, be patient. People who give up a piece of cake and then jump on a scale will be disappointed. Weigh yourself once a week. If you're eating out, make a selection before anyone else. Don't take a day off—your stomach doesn't know it's a birthday or Christmas. People say to me "I gained twenty pounds after I got married or went on vacation." Well, vacations and marriage aren't fattening—they are just times when we tend to justify improper eating.

Comment

Many of Jean Nidetch's general ideas about eating habits agree closely with those offered by Stanley Schachter and are supported by his research. For example, she acknowledges that people often eat not because they are hungry (for nutrition), but because of an appetite for a specific food or for some unspecified need other than hunger. This suggests that eating habits may be learned, and, as she mentions later, one of her techniques is to teach people new habits of eating. Certainly, we do learn to crave or like certain foods more than others and presumably each person learns different appetites with different strengths. But thus far this does not explain specifically why some people get fat and others do not, unless we want to say that some people never learn to control their eating.

Ms. Nidetch's conclusions about fat people also agree with some of the important points raised by Schachter. Fat people eat whatever is in front of them and are unaffected by the quality of the food (and, Schachter would add, are also unaffected by how recently they have eaten or how "hungry" they are). Obviously, if your food thermostat (to use Nidetch's term) does not control your eating, you will tend to get fat.

Ms. Nidetch mentions specific techniques for losing weight: eating slower, ordering first at a restaurant, talking with other people who are overweight. In common-sense terms, why might the specific techniques she mentions work?

was plenty of food, but in the first the subjects had to make some effort (going to the refrigerator) to get more. Normals ate the same amount, two sandwiches, whether or not they had to go to the refrigerator. In contrast, the obese subjects ate less than one and a half sandwiches when effort was involved, but more than two and a third when the plate was full.

In another study (Schachter and Friedman, 1974), subjects sat next to a bag containing either shelled or unshelled almonds. The condition of the almonds had no effect on normals—they ate the same quantity regardless of whether they had shells. But the obese subjects were almost totally affected by whether or not they would have to peel off the shells. When the nuts were already shelled, eighteen out of twenty subjects ate some; when the nuts were un-shelled and work was required, only one obese subject out of twenty ate any nuts.

An additional piece of evidence on the difference between normal and obese people comes from a study (Schachter, 1971) on eating habits in relation to structured and unstructured time. To the extent that obese people eat because it is time to eat (that is, noon for lunch), they should be more likely to miss lunch on days when time is less clearly structured, whereas normals, who eat because they are hungry, should be relatively unaffected by this. Sure enough, as shown in Fig. 9.4, normals and obese miss just about as many lunches on weekdays, but on weekends, with less structured time, obese miss many more lunches. This body of research demonstrates that although everyone's eating must be controlled to some extent by internal feelings, fat people are much more strongly affected by external factors than are normals.

Summary

Motives that are directly linked to physiological needs are necessary for the survival of the individual. When you need food, water, or air or when you are in pain or suffering from extremes of temperature, strong motives are aroused that must be satisfied. Yet, as we saw in the example of hunger, even these physiological motives are extremely complex and are affected by a wide variety of factors other than the actual physical need. As you might expect, motives that are less closely tied to physiological needs are even more strongly affected by social and cognitive considerations.

OTHER BASIC MOTIVES

As we stated earlier, a small number of motives appear to be shared by all people (and many animals) but are connected to specific physiological processes only partly or not at all. The three most important motives of this type are the maternal, sex, and curiosity drives.

Maternal Behavior in Animals

Many female animals seem to have an innate drive to care for their newborn offspring. Much of this behavior is purely instinctive—the cow licks the new calf clean, shows it how to nurse, and protects and takes care of it. A mother cat performs similar actions, and also

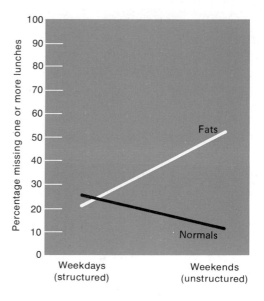

Fig. 9.4
Missing lunch and obesity

When time is structured, as on weekdays, fats and normals miss about the same number of lunches. When the day is less structured, many more fats miss lunch, presumably because they are less sensitive to the internal cues of hunger. (After Schachter, 1971)

carries her kittens around with her when she moves, retrieves them if they wander too far, and even makes sure that all of them get enough milk if they outnumber her nipples. These maternal motives are extremely powerful. There are countless descriptions of animal mothers risking their lives to protect their young from danger. Apparently even the strong urge for personal survival is sometimes weaker than the maternal drive to save the young.

The strength of maternal motivation has been confirmed in laboratory research. In a classic study by Warden (1931), rats in one box had to cross an electric grid to reach another box that contained various reinforcements—food, water, a sexually active animal of the opposite sex, or a newborn litter. Each of these reinforcements was paired with rats in appropriate motivational states. As shown in Fig. 9.5, female rats endured a greater shock to reach their offspring than they would to get food, water, or sex. We might note that for both males and females, thirst was stronger than hunger and sex was the weakest of all. This order may not hold for all species or all conditions, but the study does indicate the remarkable strength of the maternal motive.

Hormonal factors While much of this maternal behavior appears to be instinctive, it is triggered by specific physiological factors, particularly certain hormones secreted by females in large amounts just before and after they give birth. When one of these hormones, prolactin, is present, females engage in maternal behavior appropriate to their species—they build nests, lick their young, nurse them, and care for them. In fact, if prolactin is injected into a female who has not recently given birth or is a virgin, it still produces these maternal patterns of behavior; but injecting prolactin into males does not produce the maternal behavior. Although prolactin is present naturally in both sexes, the maternal response caused by it is present only in the female. Therefore, although the father may play a major role in

Fig. 9.5
Relative strengths of motives

Female rats endured more shock to reach their own young than to reach any other goal. The order of the other motives was the same for both sexes. The figures indicate the number of times an electrified grid was crossed during a twenty-minute test period. Once across the grid, the animal was given thirty seconds in the goal box and allowed to attend to the litter (maternal), lick a water bottle (thirst), have one nibble of powdered food (hunger), or engage in preparatory sex behavior (sex). (From Warden, 1931)

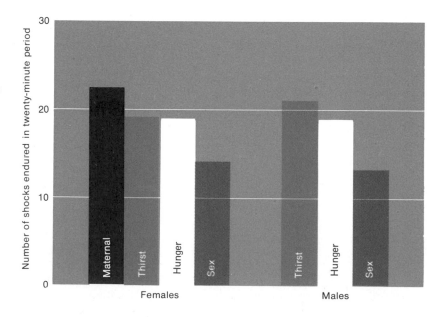

raising, feeding, and protecting the young, in most nonhuman species, maternal motives are much stronger in the mother than in the father.

Human Maternal Motivation

Although there has been little controlled research into human maternal behavior, it seems clear that most mothers are intensely motivated to care for their children. They spend vast amounts of time feeding, cleaning, and soothing their infants. They sacrifice time, money, and energy—and like other animals, most human mothers will risk their lives to save their children.

In humans, physiological and instinctive mechanisms are thought to be less important than in other animals. Accordingly, the group of motives termed "maternal" need not be limited to mothers. Appropriate hormones are present in new mothers, of course, and probably stimulate maternal feelings and behavior. But social factors also play an important role and these are not restricted to one sex or to actual mothers. Particularly with the recent relaxation of sex roles, both parents can share in raising the child and the father also may feel strong "maternal" motivation (see Chapter 13).

The Sex Drive

The sex drive is similar to maternal motivation in that neither is essential to individual survival. An animal can go without sexual activity throughout its entire life and suffer no observable ill effects. Obviously the species is not in the same situation—without sexual (or maternal) behavior, there will be no new animals to maintain the species. This dichotomy distinguishes the sex drive markedly from other basic drives, which are necessary for both the individual and the species.

Hormonal factors There are two types of sex hormones, *androgens* and *estrogens*. Although these are sometimes called "male" and "female" hormones respectively, both sexes have some of each type. The sexes differ primarily in the relative amounts of the two kinds of hormones. Adult male humans have five times as much androgen as females, while adult females have between five and ten times as much estrogen as males, the greatest concentration occurring at the time of ovulation (Turner, 1971).

These hormones have two important functions. They control the development of sexual characteristics, such as the genital organs, breasts, body hair, and body fat. They may also determine basic changes in the brain that make it in some sense either male or female. Giving testosterone (androgen) to infant female rats reduced normal female sexual behavior and increased male sexual behavior (mounting) when the animals were adults (Harris and Levine, 1962; Whalen and Nadler, 1963; Levine, 1966). In other words, the presence of androgens for a brief period soon after birth influences sexual behavior many months later. The specific mechanism underlying this result is not known, but it appears that normal male sexual development depends on the presence of androgens in infancy.

BOX 9.2

CONFLICTING MOTIVES— APPROACH-AVOIDANCE

Arousing a motive causes an animal to direct its actions toward a particular goal. A positive motivation such as hunger for a particular food, liking for someone, or sexual attraction will make someone seek the object on which the motive centers; negative motives such as fear or hatred will cause someone to avoid the object. However, both kinds of motives often focus on the same object or behavior. You may like someone but be afraid of him, enjoy smoking but worry about it causing cancer, or have a craving for chocolate but fear it will give you acne. The existence of both positive and negative motives produces what is called an *approach-avoidance conflict.* You want to come closer but you also want to avoid the object. The resolution of such a conflict depends on the relative strengths of the two motives. Obviously, if one is much stronger than the other you will be mainly influenced by the stronger one. If you are terrified of cancer and have only a mild appetite for smoking, you probably will not smoke; in contrast, if you crave a cigarette and have only a vague fear of cancer, you will smoke.

As long as one motive is much stronger than the other, the situation is

The sex hormones also affect the strength of the sex motive. When the hormone level is low, sexual drive is low; when the level is high, the drive is higher. This is most clear with female animals, although not so clear with human females. At the time of estrus (the mating period), hormonal levels are high and the animal is both more receptive and more attractive to the male. Removal of the ovaries and consequent elimination of sex hormones stops sexual behavior in female rodents, dogs, cats, and probably most other animals. Injecting estrogen can restore mating behavior, thus demonstrating the controlling and activating effects of the hormone. Similarly, castrated males engage in less sexual behavior than normal, but their sexual behavior increases when they are given testosterone (Whalen, 1964).

Independence from hormones It is extremely important to realize that the sex hormones are only one factor determining sexual motivation and behavior. In many species removing a female's ovaries stops sexual behavior. But in some species, a castrated male will continue

simple. But if both are about the same strength, what determines which motive will prevail? The figure illustrates an important characteristic of approach and avoidance motives, which is that they tend to have somewhat different gradients. Both motives are naturally strongest right next to the object, but the avoidance motive drops off more sharply. As one gets further and further away, it seems much less frightening, whereas the approach impulse usually declines less rapidly—even at some distance away, the object is appealing. The result of this is that an animal may move closer and closer to the object only to stop before reaching it because the avoidance motive has finally equalled the approach motive in strength. Rats that were both shocked and fed in a box at the end of an alley tended to run down the alley rapidly at first, but slowed down and usually stopped before reaching the box (Miller, 1959). The stronger the shock, the further from the box they stopped; the stronger their hunger, the closer they approached. Similarly, a squirrel might desire the nut in your outstretched hand but fear being too close to such a large creature. In such a conflict, the squirrel will approach only so near and then stop.

People often face approach-avoidance conflicts. When they do, we say they are *ambivalent* about something or someone. They like to drink, but worry about becoming dependent on it; they love their parents, but get angry at them; they like a friend very much, but feel jealous. Indeed, much of the conflict in our lives comes from motives that contradict each other. We have many motives that are relevant to any particular action or person; some are positive and some negative. These conflicts produce hesitancy, indecision, and, at the extreme, anxiety and serious mental problems. As we shall see in Chapter 16, much of psychotherapy is aimed at trying to uncover and resolve conflicts like these.

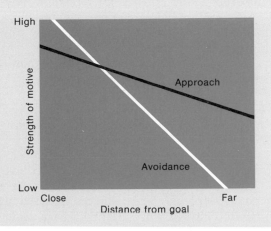

to engage in sexual behavior for a considerable length of time or even indefinitely. For example, male rhesus monkeys were still quite active sexually a year after being castrated (Phoenix, Slob, and Goy, 1973).

This lack of dependence on sex hormones is especially true of higher animals, and particularly of humans. Men with very high levels of sex hormones may still have low sex drives and vice versa. Castrated men have been reported to have high sexual motivation and to maintain the capacity for sexual intercourse for as long as twenty or thirty years. In women the lack of correlation between hormonal level and sex drive is even more marked. For example, female sexual desire and capacity seem to be largely unaffected by removal of the ovaries. Similarly, injecting male or female hormones into a person ordinarily has little effect on their sex drive (Kennedy, 1973).

Psychological factors Hormones, the recency of sexual activity, and other physiological factors play some role in human sexual motivation, but not the major role. Unlike almost all other mammals, women do not have periods in which they cannot have sex, and neither men nor women require the presence of a receptive partner to become sexually aroused. Indeed, human beings are much more influenced by psychological factors. We can be aroused by the thought of someone we consider sexually attractive, or by pictures, books, words, odors, and fantasies. Many kinds of stimulation that seem irrelevant to sexual arousal are in fact arousing for some people. A roller coaster ride, a certain kind of food, an automobile—almost anything is sexy for someone and can arouse sexual motivation. We shall discuss sexual behavior in detail in Chapter 13. For the moment, the important point is that in humans this basic motive is controlled by a combination of physiological and social factors just as is hunger.

Curiosity

If you put a cat in a new house, it will run around investigating it. A rat put into a new cage will sniff all the corners of the cage, walk back and forth, and look all around its new surroundings. A chimpanzee will work for hours to solve a complicated puzzle, and will perform a wide variety of behaviors in order to be allowed to see some new object. All of these behaviors are motivated by what we call curiosity. The curiosity motive is characterized by manipulation of new objects, by exploration, and by activity in general.

Curiosity is a surprisingly strong motive in the behavior of many animals. In one study (Butler and Harlow, 1954), monkeys were put in a cage that had two doors. When the monkey picked the right door, it opened and the monkey was able to look out. The other door stayed closed. Even though the only "reward" was a view out of the box, monkeys could learn to discriminate between the right and the wrong door. In addition, if they could see something interesting, such as a moving toy train, they responded more rapidly than if they could look only at an empty room.

It also appears that, just as with people, chimpanzees get tired of the formerly novel stimulus once curiosity is satisfied. When their curiosity is aroused they will learn to turn off lights, move sticks, and so on; but after a while, when the novelty has worn off, they perform the behavior less frequently. Nevertheless, new objects arouse the motive again, and behaviors associated with curiosity (such as exploration) increase (Welker, 1956).

LEARNED MOTIVES

Some motives are related to neither physiological needs nor innate mechanisms. Instead they are learned or acquired by the individual. We discussed in Chapter 3 how a stimulus that was initially neutral can acquire reinforcing properties and become a secondary reinforcer. You can teach a dog to salivate at the sound of a bell by giving it food each time the bell sounds; you can then teach it to salivate at the sight of a black square simply by sounding the bell, even when no food is presented. In other words, the dog is now motivated by the bell rather than by the food.

Fig. 9.6
The curious monkey

A monkey will do a latch puzzle such as this many times over.

In a classic study by Neal Miller (1948), rats learned to fear a previously neutral stimulus. They were put in a simple box with white and black compartments separated by a door. In the experiment, the rat was first given a strong electric shock in the white compartment and the door was opened by the experimenter. The rat soon learned to escape the shock by running through the door into the black compartment. Next the rat was put in the white compartment, no shock was given, and the door was opened only if the animal turned a wheel. The result was that the rats learned to turn the wheel in order to escape from the white compartment. When they could not escape, they crouched, defecated, and showed all the typical signs of fear. In other words, having been hurt in the white compartment they learned to be afraid of it, and this learned fear motivated them to learn a response that freed them.

Human behavior is determined even more by learning than is the behavior of other animals. This is particularly true of motives. Although dogs do acquire motives such as pleasing their masters, most of their behavior is controlled by such basic motives as hunger, thirst, and sex. Humans too are motivated by hunger, thirst, sex, and other basic drives, but many complex, learned motives are also factors in determining how they behave.

Specific Learned Motives

There are two different kinds of learned motives—specific and general. Specific learned motives involve specific objects. Through our experiences we develop a positive or negative attraction for a specific object and we become motivated to obtain or avoid that object. For example, we may learn to enjoy caviar and champagne, to root for the Lakers, to hate cities, to fear snakes, and so on. When the specific motivation involves food, we generally call it an *appetite*. Appetites are as varied as human beings; one person may acquire a taste for wine and will pay enormous prices or drive miles out of the way to get a specific wine. Another person may never develop a taste for it. There are many specific motives in addition to appetites. The desire for possessions—a particular car or home, an item of clothing, a special toy—is a powerful motive for many people. Positive and negative feelings about *people* are also strong motives and greatly affect our behavior toward others.

In combination, specific learned motives play a major role in determining an individual's behavior. Some of them, such as the desire for a particular person as a lover or a friend and an individual's relationship with his parents, have a substantial effect on behavior just by themselves. But more important, these appetites, likes and dislikes, and specific goals are involved in almost every aspect of the individual's life. Even when a person satisfies a basic motive such as hunger, the particular way in which it is satisfied is determined by that person's specific appetites. Naturally, an extremely hungry person will eat whatever is available. But people usually try to decide what kind of food they are hungry for. When this happens they are involved in specific learned motives, rather than just physiological hunger. Although these specific motives rarely have names and are generally not stressed very strongly by psychologists, perhaps more than any other factor they determine what an individual is like, what she wants, and how she behaves.

General Learned Motives

The other type of learned motive is directed at a general goal rather than a specific object. In our society, motives of this sort include desires for power, position, fame, love, and achievement. Sometimes it is difficult to distinguish between specific motives and general motives. For example, someone who seeks money for the position and power it may bring is demonstrating a general motive; someone who acquires money for its own sake (such as the fabled miser running his fingers through his gold) is demonstrating a specific motive. But since both people are seeking money, it may be difficult to tell the difference between their motives. General motives usually involve long-term goals toward which an individual might strive for a lifetime. They involve many aspects of behavior rather than being focused on certain objects.

The need for achievement The learned motive that has been investigated most thoroughly is the need for achievement. Researchers have demonstrated that some individuals possess stronger achievement motives than others (McClelland et al., 1953). These authors developed a reliable measure of the strength of a person's achievement motives—usually abbreviated to n-ach. They used a variety of tests, but relied heavily on the Thematic Apperception Test (TAT), a projective test that will be discussed in more detail in Chapter 14. The basic technique is to show an ambiguous picture and have subjects tell a story that describes what they think is going on. These stories are then scored in terms of the amount of concern for achievement they indicate. Using this test, McClelland and Atkinson demonstrated that the achievement motive had important and consistent effects on a wide range of behaviors such as performance on tests (see Fig. 9.7), choice of major in college, success in career, and choice of work partners.

The achievement motive is an excellent example of the complexity of learned needs. It is not a simple motive nor does it have simple effects. Indeed, there is strong evidence that n-ach is composed of two related but different motives: desire for success and fear of failure. Though both involve achievement, they have quite different implications in terms of response to outcomes and risks. People relatively high in fear of failure will avoid potential failure situations. They particularly avoid tasks of intermediate difficulty, where they may fail and others may not. In contrast, they worry little about very easy tasks, where they are bound to succeed, or about very difficult ones, where everyone will fail. Exactly the opposite is true of people with high motivation to succeed and relatively low fear of failure. For these people, neither the easy nor the difficult tasks have much appeal. They will succeed in the easy tasks and may fail in the hard ones— but so will almost everyone else, and so their success will mean little. They seek out intermediate tasks, where they have some chance of success and where any success will carry real meaning (Atkinson and Litwin, 1960). One study (Isaacson, 1964) showed that this held true for men who were choosing subjects in which to major. More of the

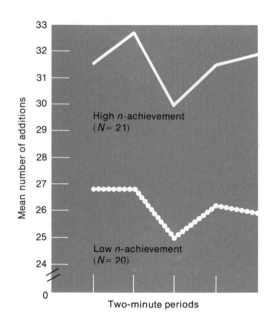

Fig. 9.7
Need achievement and problem solving

High n-ach subjects consistently solve more simple math problems than low n-ach subjects. (After Lowell, 1952)

high-success men chose intermediate-difficulty majors than did men with a high fear of failure.

Achievement motives and expectations also affect people's reactions to success and failure. People high in success motivation generally expect to succeed. Achieving success means relatively little to them and they tend to work less hard afterwards—but failure comes as a blow and makes them increase their efforts. In contrast, people with high fear of failure usually expect to fail. When they succeed instead, they are greatly encouraged and work harder. But failure reinforces their belief in their own fallibility and they work less hard in the future (Weiner, 1970). These patterns of behavior are obviously due to a complex interaction of motives themselves and people's understanding and evaluation of the situation. Whether a task is seen as hard or easy is exceedingly important, as is the reason people think they succeed or fail. As we shall see in the next chapter, more and more psychologists believe there is a strong cognitive element in both motives and emotions, and that the effect of a particular motive such as need for achievement depends in part on cognitive and social factors in the situation.

Other general motives Other general motives include the desires to achieve peace, justice, a role in society, and meaning in life; the expression of creative impulses; and many others. They are not directed toward specific objects, but they affect many decisions individuals make throughout their lives. On a day-to-day basis they may be relatively unimportant, but over the long run they govern the direction of people's lives. In a sense, they affect a person's style rather than any particular behavior. For example, in our society both high and low achievement-motivated people are likely to go to school and to work, but the former will generally work harder than the latter and take a greater interest in homework, grades, and success. The specific behaviors may not differ much, but the energy and time put into them will vary markedly. Thus, specific learned motives affect our daily behavior by causing us to perform particular acts and seek out particular objects. More general motives affect us primarily by changing our outlook, our style, and the specific decisions we make that affect the way we lead our lives.

Social motives: liking Our discussion of the hunger motive demonstrated how complicated even seemingly simple motives are in humans. Hunger may appear to be controlled mainly by physiological mechanisms, but, as we have seen, it involves many cognitive, social, and personality factors. This interaction of various factors is even more pronounced in learned motives, especially those that are primarily social in nature. Since liking for other people is such a basic motive in human interaction, it can serve as a further illustration of the complexity of human motivation. Although the topic of liking is generally discussed in the context of social psychology, let us consider it here as an example of a social motive with which everyone is familiar.

Animals other than humans also have likes and dislikes both within and outside their own species. Pet cats and dogs have favorite people; a horse will ride better with one jockey than with another; and animals in the zoo treat their feeders and trainers very differently

Box 9.3

A HIERARCHY OF NEEDS AND MOTIVES

Abraham Maslow (1954) advanced the idea that there is a hierarchy of needs and motives that ranges from simple, physiological needs to much more complex, psychological ones. Maslow believed that the goal of human life is for all people to express themselves fully, fulfilling their maximum potential. He called the ultimate achievement *self-actualization,* a term he applied to the process of fulfilling yourself, reaching your goals, using all your talents and skills, and in essence becoming the most productive, creative person that you can.

In order to self-actualize, we must first satisfy the lower needs. First to be satisfied are the *physiological needs*, including hunger, thirst, elimination of pain, and so on. Obviously, we must satisfy these in order to survive. Moreover, as long as they are not satisfied, we will concentrate so much on them that we will be unable to deal with higher motives.

Next in the hierarchy come *safety needs*, which include feeling secure from attacks, from pain, from invasions of privacy, and so on. If we are constantly afraid of being hurt or of someone bullying us, we will not satisfy these needs and thus cannot go on to seek satisfaction of other needs. As we shall see in Chapter 12 on child development, Erik Erikson also stressed the need for security as the most basic need in childhood. Both he and Maslow agree that a child who is not taken care of and given warmth and attention will not develop a sense of security about the world and may perhaps always face life with deep feelings of insecurity.

Love and belongingness needs are the third group in the hierarchy. These include friendship, acceptance, a sense of belonging, sexual satisfaction, and love. Although Maslow does not place as much importance on these needs as does Freud, they both agree that these are basic motives that must be fulfilled if the individual is to be healthy. Surely we can all understand that one must feel loved, have friends, and receive some sexual satisfaction in order to achieve any kind of happiness. Moreover, when these needs are frustrated, it is difficult to concentrate on other needs.

Once we have satisfied the three basic types of motives, we can progress to dealing with what Maslow calls *self-esteem needs*, which generally involve feeling good about ourselves. We need to have pride and confidence in ourselves, in our abilities and skills, and in our achievements and competence to deal with the world. These needs are satisfied in part by expressing our potential, by mastering various skills, by success, and by achievement. They are also dependent in part on the respect and acceptance we receive from others. They are thus closely related to love needs, but focus specifically on ourselves, on our own self-esteem.

from strangers. Frank Beach (1969) has demonstrated that dogs have clear preferences among themselves. He showed that male dogs have clear favorites among the females, and the females have equally strong preferences, encouraging some males and totally rejecting others. A male who was rejected by his favorite might not even approach a less desirable, but willing, female. And a female would spurn some males even when more favored males were not around. Whether this is simply a pattern of sexual attraction among dogs or something more general is unclear, but there is little question that dogs and other animals have likes and dislikes within their own

Self-actualization needs

Self-esteem needs

Belongingness and love needs

Safety needs

Physiological needs

And finally we reach the highest level of motives—*self-actualizing*. This level involves having an aim in life, goals toward which we strive, and the expression of our full potential. In addition, according to Maslow, the goals must be broad and generally humanistic in nature. Wanting to be creative, searching for beauty, striving for peace, fighting for justice are the kinds of goals that lead to self-actualization. The goals must be positive and must involve higher human ideals. Only people who have satisfied the four lower types of motives can achieve self-actualization; and few people ever do reach this stage.

It is possible to argue with some of the details of this theory. Some may consider love motives higher than self-esteem needs or may put sex lower in the scale than a need for security. And it seems likely that you do not have to satisfy a particular level of motive completely in order to achieve some satisfaction of higher needs. Someone who is occasionally hungry or is not totally secure might still be a great painter or fight for peace. But the basic idea seems quite convincing. Some needs are more urgent and necessary than others for our survival. If we do not satisfy these needs, we are distracted from almost everything else and cannot fulfill our potential. This viewpoint has become an important aspect of *humanistic psychology,* a general approach to psychology that emphasizes humaneness and positive factors in people.

species. However, social motivations are more prevalent and of greater importance among human beings. They are not limited to purely sexual behavior, but play a major role in all of our social interactions. Four major factors affect human liking—familiarity, similarity, complementarity, and reinforcement. We will consider each in turn.

Familiarity. People tend to like more and rate more positively anything that is *familiar*. For example, research by Zajonc (1968) has shown that the more often someone has seen a word, the more likely

ROBERT ZAJONC

he is to give it a positive meaning. Nor is this effect limited to words. Zajonc demonstrated that the more often a picture of a face was shown, the more the subjects thought they would like the person pictured. These results appear in Fig. 9.8. Other studies (Saegert, Swap, and Zajonc, 1973) actually had subjects sit across a table from each other different numbers of times. Although there was no talking and no obvious interaction of any kind, the more often they met, the more often subjects said they liked the other person. In other words, for reasons that are not yet clear, simply being familiar with another person produces a positive motivation toward that person.

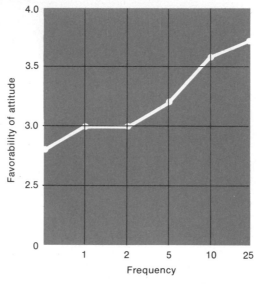

Fig. 9.8
Familiarity and liking
The more often subjects see a face, the more they say that they like the person pictured. (From Zajonc, 1968)

Similarity. Another factor affecting liking is *similarity*. We like people who are similar to us on almost any dimension—ethnic background, intelligence, athletic ability, interests, artistic talent, and personality, to name a few. There is no question that similarity plays a major and perhaps dominant role in friendships and may be even more important in marriages. Computer dating services, in which the participants list various facts about themselves and are then matched with others who have similar characteristics, are based on this fact.

The importance of similarity has been demonstrated in a large number of experiments. In one, Theodore Newcomb (1961) took over a dormitory at the University of Michigan and assigned students to rooms on the basis of questionnaires. In some rooms he put two students who were very similar, while in the others he put dissimilar students. At the end of the semester he asked each student how much he liked his roommate and the other people in the dormitory. He found that roommates who were previously selected as being similar ended up liking each other and being good friends, while those who

THEODORE M. NEWCOMB

were dissimilar tended to dislike each other and not to be friends. Similar effects have been found in short-term laboratory experiments (Byrne, 1961).

There are several specific reasons why similarity is so important but perhaps the most important one is that people who are similar are more likely to reinforce each other, to share pleasant experiences, to get along, and not to have conflicts.

Complementarity. Under most circumstances and on almost all dimensions, people like those who are similar to them and not opposite. The one exception occurs when one person's needs tend to be satisfied by and complement those of another. For example, a person who likes to talk a lot will get along very well with someone who loves to listen. Someone who needs to be dominant in a situation or relationship would clash with someone with similar feelings, but not with someone who either does not care about being dominant or—even better—likes to be submissive. The sadist and the masochist, the passive person and the active one, the sloppy person and the one who loves to clean up, all satisfy each other's needs and will often form strong relationships based on this *complementarity*. However, it is likely that they will be similar in most other characteristics, even though these particular ones are opposite. In general, when people have similar roles in the relationship, as is the case in most friendships, similarity will be dominant and complementarity will play a relatively small role. When two people have somewhat different roles, as happens in many professional relationships and some marriages, complementarity may become important.

Reinforcement. All the other reasons why we like other people can probably be accounted for in terms of rewardingness. Almost by definition, we like people who have characteristics that we consider positively rewarding. The specific characteristics that are judged most positively will vary from time to time, culture to culture, and individual to individual. But underlying most or all of these judgments is the principle of *reinforcement*.

A specific instance of the effect of reward is that we tend to like someone who likes us. In fact, having someone tell us (or someone else) that they like us may be the most universal and powerful reward that another human being can give us. There are, however, some twists to this effect. In the first place, hearing someone say she likes us is more reinforcing when we can believe her. Research by Jones (1964) has shown that the effect of hearing someone say something nice about us is considerably reduced when we think the person has something to gain by saying it. However, even people who are thought to be "ingratiating" (that is, saying nice things not because they believe them but to get something from the person they are flattering) tend to be liked more than people who do not say anything positive. In other words, it is nice to hear good things about ourselves, and we tend to like the people who say them regardless of whether we fully believe them or trust them.

The consistency of people's positive statements about us also affects how much we like them. Figure 9.9 describes a study by Aronson and Linder (1965) that revealed that while hearing positive statements makes you like a person more than hearing negative ones, hearing a person change from negative to positive statements increases liking even more. There are two explanations for this effect. First, the original negative statements caused the subjects some self-doubt and produced feelings of rejection that were quite negative. When the later statements became positive, they were not only rewarding in themselves but also reduced these negative feelings. This presumably made the positive statements even more reinforcing and thus increased the liking for the person making them. The other

Fig. 9.9
Liking in response to another's evaluation

Subjects met with someone a number of times, and after each meeting overheard the other person saying something about them. In one condition, the other person made positive statements throughout the study. In a second condition, the statements were negative throughout. In a third, the evaluation changed from negative to positive during the session. The results showed that you will probably like the most someone who begins with negative evaluations of you and becomes increasingly positive. (After Aronson and Linder, 1965)

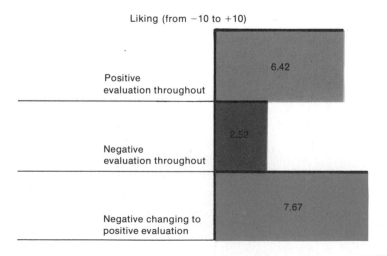

Liking (from −10 to +10)

Positive evaluation throughout — 6.42

Negative evaluation throughout — 2.52

Negative changing to positive evaluation — 7.67

explanation is closely related to the ingratiation effect and to the importance placed on sincerity. When the speaker immediately made positive statements, he may have appeared to be either a softy who likes everyone or the kind of person who always says nice things even if he doesn't believe them. In contrast, the person who started by making negative statements and then changed to positive probably appeared to be a tougher and more discerning judge. Obviously, he is not the kind of person who likes everyone or always says nice things. Thus, when he came around to liking the subject, his positive evaluation was probably seen as more sincere, carried more weight, and was accordingly more reinforcing. It is more rewarding to be praised by a careful, discriminating person, and therefore that person is liked more.

This is one example of how complicated interpersonal rewards can be. And despite the great number of studies on liking, it is obvious that we still do not have a complete understanding of the motive. We can list factors that generally increase liking, but we cannot specify whether a particular person will like another person. Clearly, we are a long way from knowing all the details that produce friendship and liking. ■

Summary

1. Motivation is defined as arousal associated with a specific goal. In the learning process, the motive determines the goal to be activated and the direction behavior associated with that goal will take.

2. Since motivation and reinforcement are closely related, theories of reinforcement help to explain motivation. Drive-reduction and incentive theories explain motives that involve reducing arousal. Homeostatic theory and the idea of adaptation level explain in part motives that involve either reducing or increasing arousal. According to homeostatic theory, adaptation level (an organism's ideal level of arousal) is maintained by the animal's motivation to reduce or increase arousal as necessary. But while reinforcement theories are useful in understanding motivation, they do not fully explain why some things are positively motivating and others are not.

3. Motives linked to physiological needs usually tell the body what it needs and what to avoid. But not all physiological needs are linked to *specific* motives. For example, any gas that does not make us choke, even though it may be lethal, can satisfy our need for air. In such cases our motives are inadequate signals.

4. Although the basic physiological motives are fairly simple, motives such as hunger, sex, and maternal behavior, as well as learned motives, involve a complex interplay of physiological, cognitive, and social factors. Some findings on the hunger motive, which has been studied extensively, are as follows: (a) Stomach contractions, blood-sugar level, the sensation of eating, and activity of the hypothalamus all play a role in the arousal of hunger and the amount of eating. (b) In humans particularly, awareness of the social situation and other cognitions also affect

eating behavior. (c) Research on fat people indicates that they respond more to cognitive and social factors than to internal stimuli.

5. Maternal motivation in nonhumans is largely instinctive and very powerful. Although there is little research on human maternal motivation, it is thought that instinctive mechanisms play a smaller role for humans than for nonhumans. Hormones influence maternal behavior in both human and nonhuman species, and social factors play an important role for humans.

6. The sex drive differs markedly from most other basic drives in that satisfaction of the motive is not necessary for the survival of specific individuals within a species. Hormonal factors influence the sex drive in several ways: (a) they control the development of sexual characteristics; (b) they appear to influence the development of male and female sexual behavior; and (c) they affect the strength of the sex drive, particularly in nonhuman species. Nevertheless, the strength of the sex drive in humans is influenced more strongly by numerous psychological, cognitive, and social factors than by hormones.

7. Curiosity is a surprisingly strong motive for both human and nonhuman animals, particularly when we consider that the motive is satisfied merely by the opportunity to see or explore some new object. Curiosity is characterized by manipulation of new objects, exploratory behavior, and activity in general.

8. Motives that are learned or acquired rather than related to innate mechanisms are particularly significant in human behavior. Specific learned motives involve specific objects as varied as an appetite for a particular food, the desire for possessions for their own sake, and feelings about people. General learned motives are focused on general, long-term goals rather than on specific objects. Both types of learned motives determine to a large extent what a person is like and how she behaves.

9. The need for achievement (n-ach) is a learned motive that is stronger in some people than in others. This extremely complex motive probably comprises two related motives: the desire for success and the fear of failure. The need for achievement consistently affects a wide variety of behaviors.

10. The desire to be liked by others is a basic social motive for nearly everyone. Four important factors affecting positive motivation toward others are familiarity, similarity, complementarity, and reinforcement, or rewardingness. Research on rewardingness indicates that hearing someone say he likes us is reinforcing, but is even more so when we can believe the person. Moreover, it is more rewarding to be praised by a discriminating person than by one who likes everyone.

RECOMMENDED READING

Berscheid, E., and E. H. Walster. *Interpersonal Attraction,* 2d ed. Reading, Mass.: Addison-Wesley, 1977. A short summary of the social-psychological approach to liking. Easy reading yet thorough.

Glickman, S. E., and P. M. Milner, Eds. *The Neurological Basis of Motivation.* New York: Van Nostrand Reinhold, 1969. Rather technical and detailed, but covers many of the important issues up to the time the book was published.

Maslow, A. H. *Motivation and Personality.* New York: Harper, 1954. The early book by Maslow that presents his most interesting ideas. Fine descriptions of people he considers to have achieved self-actualization.

Weiner, B. *Theories of Motivation.* Chicago: Markham, 1972. Compares several theories of motivation in relation to the need for achievement.

We should not pretend to understand the world only by the intellect; we apprehend it just as much by feeling.
Carl Jung, Psychological Types

The ruling passion, be it what it will
The ruling passion conquers reason still.
Pope, Essays

10 Emotions

Definition of emotions ■ Theories of emotion ■ The James-Lange theory ■ Activation theory ■ Physiological/cognitive interpretation ■ Expressing and identifying emotions ■ Emotion and behavior: aggression ■ The effects of emotions

When someone is described as "inhuman," what qualities does this person lack? Usually not brains, experience, or perceptual capacity. No, what it probably means is that the person shows no emotions. People constantly seek to satisfy their motives and maximize their satisfaction, but it is rare to find a person doing this unfeelingly. People care about what they are doing. They may feel concerned or delighted, angry or bored, but they feel something most of the time. These feelings may help them function more effectively, or they may be distracting or irrelevant to their immediate motives. But these feelings, which we usually call *emotions*, are the essence of humanness. Someone who seems not to experience them will strike us as less than human.

Although everyone "knows" what we mean by emotions, they are very difficult to define precisely. We all agree that hunger and thirst are not emotions, even though they produce strong internal feelings and are associated with physiological reactions. Similarly, someone who craves a hot fudge sundae is said to be feeling an appetite rather than an emotion, while the same person confronted with a bowl of fried ants might react with disgust and loathing, which are normally considered emotions. In particular, the distinction between emotions and motives is both arbitrary and ambiguous.

DEFINITION OF EMOTIONS

Although we cannot offer a perfect definition of emotions, we can give two elements that must be present before a feeling can be called an emotion. First, *emotions always involve either physiological arousal or depression.* Anger, fear, and ecstasy are associated with a heightening of the physiological activity of the body, while dejection and sorrow involve a slowing down of some bodily processes and speeding up of others. The arousal or depression can range from very slight to extreme, but if there is no noticeable change from the usual physiological state, we would not ordinarily call the feeling an emotion. Second, *emotions all seem to be either positive or negative feelings.* They involve likes and dislikes, happiness and sadness, attraction and repulsion. This is not always true of motives. When someone feels hungry, that does not necessarily imply that she is feeling either good or bad. Achievement motivation can sometimes be pleasant, sometimes unpleasant, and often neutral. In contrast, emotions are always evaluative. Someone who is sad is feeling bad; someone who is happy is feeling good.

There is never any ambiguity about whether an emotion is positive or negative—people can agree almost perfectly on which emotions are positive, which are negative, and even how positive or negative each of them is. You may have mixed feelings about an event—you feel happy that your competitor lost out, but guilty about feeling happy; you feel elated about receiving a promotion, but also nervous. Yet each separate emotion is clearly positive or negative. Mixed feelings, it seems, do not really mix. You simply become aware of two or more distinct, conflicting emotional responses to a single event.

Emotions are closely related to motives because the satisfaction or nonsatisfaction of a particular need often produces an emotional reaction. Although hunger is not an emotion, eating when one is hungry will probably arouse pleasure, which is an emotion. Similarly, sexual impulses are not themselves emotional states, but satisfying them will produce pleasure or ecstacy while not satisfying them may result in sorrow or dejection. This also holds for negative motives such as pain. The avoidance of pain is a motive; the emotional state that goes along with it would probably be called fear, panic, or terror, depending on how strong it was. There is not always a one-to-one relationship, but emotions often seem to be produced by the satisfying or not satisfying of particular motives.

Although we do not have any simple, one-line definition of emotions, these two essential factors do at least give a fairly clear idea of what we mean by emotions: they must involve physiological arousal or depression and they always have a strong evaluative component.

Because it is so difficult to produce a definition, most psychologists rely on a listing of emotions in order to be sure that everyone understands what we mean. Table 10.1 lists a large number of words that refer to people's feelings. Indicate in the space provided whether you consider each an emotion and then compare your ratings to the consensus answers given at the bottom of the table. As we have noted, people usually agree quite well as to what is and is not an emotion, and which emotions are stronger than others. Rage is more intense than anger, which is stronger than annoyance; terror and panic are stronger than fear, and so on. Although the table does not list all the emotions that people identify, it should be clear that people generally agree on what is an emotion even though there is no precise definition.

THEORIES OF EMOTION

Now that we are in some agreement as to what we mean by emotions, we can consider the major theories of emotions. These theories attempt to explain what causes emotions and also what determines *which* emotion we feel.

The James-Lange Theory

Psychologists William James and Carl Lange independently proposed an explanation of emotions that runs directly counter to most people's intuitions. In essence, they said that people feel emotions only because they are aware of their bodily reactions. The physiological response *precedes* and *causes* the emotional experience. This idea is diagrammed in Fig. 10.1.

For example, if you are walking down the street and are suddenly accosted by someone with a gun, you will first react with a variety of physical symptoms. Your stomach will tighten, your heart will beat faster, and so on. Then your awareness of these physiological responses will cause you to experience fear. Or imagine that you decided to run from the attacker; according to the James-Lange theory,

Table 10.1
WHICH OF THESE COMMON STATES ARE EMOTIONS?

	Yes	No		Yes	No
Rage			Sorrow		
Hunger			Sexual arousal		
Itching			Anger		
Disgust			Grief		
Fear			Terror		
Curiosity			Sleep		
Joy			Happiness		
Annoyance			Surprise		
Success			Thirst		
Pain			Amazement		

Indicate your own choices before reading the answers most people give. The states that are usually considered emotions are rage, disgust, fear, joy, annoyance, sorrow, anger, grief, terror, happiness, surprise, and amazement.

Fig. 10.1
The James-Lange theory of emotions

The physical response occurs first and the awareness of this response is the emotion. We say that our stomach is tight, our knees are weak, so we must be afraid.

Box 10.1

BRAIN FUNCTION AND EMOTIONS—THE LIMBIC SYSTEM

It is well established that there is a close relationship between brain functions and emotions. In particular, the *limbic system*, which consists of several brain structures including the hypothalamus, hippocampus, septum, and amygdala (see Chapter 8), is involved in controlling certain emotional reactions. Manipulation of any part of the limbic system in experimental animals leads to changes of emotional behavior, especially the arousal of fear, anger, aggression, and other humanlike emotions. Similarly, animals that have suffered specific lesions (injuries) of discrete areas of the limbic system suffer permanent changes in emotions. For example, lesions within the septum or within certain areas of the hypothalamus produce an animal that overreacts in an aggressive fashion to almost any stimulus input. These animals are often said to exhibit chronic rage. Lesions in certain areas of the amygdala, on the other hand, produce docility or tameness even in wild, ferocious animals. Some circus performers have used animals that were stated to be wild but that had actually suffered surgical destruction of parts of the amygdala.

The actual mechanism by which the limbic system controls emotion is unclear. It is known, however, that in addition to eliciting emotional behaviors, stimulation of particular sites within the limbic system can cause a variety of internal bodily responses. For example, limbic stimulation can cause epinephrine to be secreted from the adrenal glands, the stomach to "tighten," most glands to secrete hormones in greater or lesser amounts, and so on. In other words, the changes in physiological arousal known to be an important aspect of emotion are themselves under the control of the limbic system. Furthermore, sensory input from the internal organs feeds back into the limbic system as well as to other parts of the brain. So the limbic system not only controls one aspect of emotion but also is sensitive to emotionally related responses occurring within the body.

It is interesting that sexual behavior is also under the control of the limbic system. A lesion within certain parts of the amygdala can produce an animal that will try to copulate with almost anything. Similarly, lesions of other areas of the limbic system can produce an animal that will never mate again. Since reproduction and the emotions of love and pleasure are so intimately related, the importance of the limbic system is again emphasized.

MacLean (1960) has postulated that there are two functional subunits within the limbic system. One is concerned with the preservation of the individual and the other with the preservation of the species.

you will then experience fear because you are running—you will not be running because you are afraid.

Criticism of James-Lange theory Modern research in the physiology of the brain lends some support to the James-Lange idea that the physiological reaction causes the emotion (see Box 10.1). However, there is one obvious difficulty with the original statement of the theory. It would be absolutely essential for each emotional state to have a specific physiological reaction connected with it. In order for someone to know he was afraid because of his bodily state, he would have to be able to distinguish the bodily state that goes with fear from the one that goes with anger or surprise or sorrow or any other emotion. But it now seems clear that this is not plausible. Careful studies of physiological responses associated with various emotions in humans have found only small and inconsistent differences among

Stimulation of the first provides a number of different emotional states and responses consistent with this hypothesis. Animals might eat or drink if food or water is present, or might attack an animal standing nearby. Lesions of these areas of the brain produce deficits in these kinds of responses. Stimulation of that part of the limbic system concerned with preservation of the species, on the other hand, causes an increase in sexually related behaviors, maternal behaviors, and the secretions of hormones that control reproduction.

Thus, the limbic system does play a role in the arousal of many emotions. This suggests that the physiological reaction could precede our feeling an emotion, as the James-Lange theory states.

Neural control of aggression

It is possible to change an animal's emotional behavior by stimulating certain areas of the limbic system. Dr. José Delgado stopped this charging bull by transmitting a radio-controlled signal to an electrode he had implanted in the bull's brain.

them (Ax, 1953; Schachter, 1957). In fact, it is now generally accepted that whatever differences in physiological responses do exist are probably quite subtle and difficult for the individual to recognize. Thus, it seems implausible that individuals can distinguish one emotion from another merely by recognizing differences in their physiological state.

In addition, the James-Lange theory describes the sequence of events in the opposite order from what most of us intuitively think happens. We ordinarily think of emotions as having motivating properties—we run *because* we are afraid—but this theory says that we are afraid because we run, which sounds incorrect. The James-Lange theory has largely been superseded by later theories. Its major contribution is the emphasis it placed on people's awareness of their own physiological reactions, which, as we shall see, is one of the central ideas in more recent theories.

Box 10.2

PREFRONTAL LOBOTOMIES

Although the neural basis for emotions is generally stated to be the limbic system, higher animals such as some primates and humans may have other emotional centers. This was dramatically discovered in the 1930s by a researcher named Jacobsen (1935), who was teaching chimps to respond in a particular kind of apparatus. One chimp, Becky, became so emotional when she did not receive the desired reinforcement that Jacobsen withdrew her from the experiment and subjected her to a form of experimental surgery in which a small part of the frontal lobes was surgically disconnected from the rest of the brain. Amazingly, after the operation, Becky's emotional problems appeared gone. She now performed very well in the learning situation, did not become over-emotional, and had no apparent intellectual deficit as a result of the surgery.

Jacobsen presented these findings at a scientific meeting. A psychiatrist named Moniz noted the similarity between Becky's presurgical symptoms and those of some of his own patients. He therefore decided to try the operation upon some of his more emotional patients. He had a high degree of success in his first few patients and so reported in a scientific journal. One result was that thousands of humans suffering from emotional problems were subjected to the surgical procedure called the prefrontal lobotomy (see Chapter 16). Unfortunately, the results were not always as rosy as originally pictured. Many patients died during surgery and many others, although their emotional problems were cured, became little more than vegetables for the rest of their lives. They could initiate no behaviors and had to have other people clothe, feed, and care for them all of the time. Still others were not cured at all. The widespread problem associated with this form of surgery and the apparent abuse of the operation in some instances finally led Congress to outlaw the procedure in the 1950s. Interestingly, prefrontal lobotomies were not outlawed until another method of handling individuals with extreme emotional disorders had become available. Tranquilizers, the most commonly used treatment today, also became available in the mid-1950s.

Activation Theory

This theory, which was presented first by Walter Cannon (1927) and revised by Donald Lindsley (1951) and others, proposes that *arousal* is the essence of the emotional state. The physical reactions occur *at the same time* as the emotion, since the arousal *is* the emotion (see Fig. 10.2). Rather than distinguishing among the various types of emotions, this theory holds that emotion is more or less a unitary experience involving a heightened arousal of the whole organism. Since there are few if any differences among emotional states, there is no reason to talk about different emotions. It is the arousal that is crucial and nothing else.

Activation theory has its weaknesses also. There is no question that arousal is an important element in emotions. As we said earlier, we think of emotions as always involving physiological reactions and feelings—usually strong ones—as well. Emotions are not neutral; they must involve some kind of response. But the response does not always involve arousal. Sorrow, despondency, and depression are emotions, and they involve a depressed state rather than a strong arousal. Thus, this emphasis on heightened activity would seem to apply only to certain kinds of emotions and not to others. In addition, just as not all emotions seem to involve arousal, so not all arousal is emotion. Running a hundred yards causes the heart to speed up, but it does not produce an emotion. (Winning the race would, but not the running itself.) Failure to specify when arousal is an emotion is another weakness of activation theory.

Finally, a complete theory must account for the *variations* among emotions. Not all emotional experiences are the same. Even those emotions that seem to involve arousal—such as fear, anger, and surprise—differ greatly in how we experience them. Someone who is angry behaves and feels differently from someone who is afraid or surprised. It is all very well to focus on the importance of the aroused state, but it is essential to explain what produces the different kinds of emotional experience. Since activation theory does not do this, it is at best a limited explanation of emotions.

Physiological/Cognitive Interpretation

The best explanation of emotions available today is that they are produced by a combination of physiological reactions and the individual's interpretation of the situation. The person is aware that she is aroused (or depressed), but the emotion she experiences depends on *why* she thinks she is aroused and what it means (see Fig. 10.3). In

Fig. 10.2
Activation theory of emotions

The physical response and emotion appear simultaneously. The physical arousal *is*, in fact, the emotion.

Fig. 10.3
Physiological/cognitive theory of emotions

Physical response appears first; the person is aware of the response and of the situation, and interprets the arousal as fear.

order to decide this, she uses all the information at her disposal, including her knowledge of the current situation, what occurred previously, and her own mental and physical state. If she is facing a mugger, she feels physiological arousal and interprets it as fear, because that is the appropriate response to such an experience. Feeling a slowdown within herself and knowing that someone she loved has just died, she decides she is experiencing sorrow; while if no one has died but she has just lost her job, she might decide she is feeling disappointment or depression.

Like the James-Lange theory, this theory assumes that emotions require both arousal and awareness of that arousal. The vital addition is that the person *interprets* the causes, meaning, and significance of this arousal in terms of his understanding of the circumstances in which it occurs. Unlike the earlier theory, this physiological/ cognitive interpretation does not assume that each emotion has a specific physiological response. On the contrary, the nature of the physiological arousal is relatively unimportant. Since identical physical arousals can be interpreted in various ways, the full range of emotions can be produced.

Although this theory emphasizes the cognitive interpretation of what is happening, the physiological reaction is also necessary to produce an emotion. If you are not aroused, you will not feel an emotion even if the situation makes it appropriate. For example, you are expecting an exam and know that ordinarily you would be worried. If you do not feel tense physically, you will assume that, for some reason, you are not worried this time. Indeed, that is exactly how we define a lack of emotion—no physical reaction. Thus, this theory emphasizes that *both* a physiological response and an appropriate interpretation are essential if we are to feel emotions.

The Schachter-Singer experiment An experiment by Stanley Schachter and Jerome Singer (1962) explored just this point. In order to show that emotion was a joint effect of physiological arousal and cues from the situation, they *varied* each of these elements separately. Some subjects were injected with the hormone epinephrine, which produces increased heartbeat, tremor of the hands and legs, and generally heightened physiological activities. These symptoms correspond with the physical symptoms found in people who are experiencing strong emotions such as anger and fear. Thus, subjects who received the hormone had one of the two conditions that are supposedly necessary to produce emotions. Other subjects received injections of a placebo (a neutral drug that has no physical effect) and therefore did not experience the physiological symptoms.

Schachter realized that the subject must not know that his physiological arousal was caused by a drug. If he knows that the physiological responses are caused by the injection, he will not feel emotional. In other words, if he has an appropriate physiological explanation for his physical state, cues from the situation will be much less important. Therefore, only those subjects who are physiologically aroused and do not know that it was caused by the drug should respond to external cues with strong emotions.

Accordingly, some subjects who received the epinephrine were told that it would cause the very symptoms that it actually produced.

JEROME E. SINGER

These "epinephrine-informed" subjects were expected to feel little or no emotion because they knew what had caused their physiological arousal. Other subjects, "epinephrine-ignorant," were told nothing about the effect of the drug. Since these subjects did not have as good an explanation of their physiological arousal, they were expected to respond more to external cues and feel more emotional.

Each subject was tested in a social situation designed to provide cues appropriate to either anger or euphoric happiness. In both conditions, the subject sat in a room with another person (actually an assistant or confederate of the experimenter). In the euphoric situation, the confederate sat quietly for awhile and then began acting very happy. He began doodling, making paper airplanes, and playing basketball with crumpled paper and a wastebasket. He encouraged the subject to join him in these playful activities and generally acted light-hearted, silly, and happy. In the anger condition, the confederate began muttering annoyed comments, complained about the personal questionnaire they were both filling out, and ended up pounding his fist on the table and acting angry at the whole situation. In this way, the subjects were exposed to cues that would encourage them to label the situation either euphoric or angry.

To summarize, there were nonaroused subjects (those who received a placebo), aroused subjects who knew that arousal was caused by the drug, and aroused subjects who were ignorant of the drug's effects. These subjects were all exposed either to anger- or euphoria-producing cues. The results supported the physiological/cognitive theory of emotions. The drug-unaroused and the drug-aroused but informed subjects did not experience strong emotional arousal (see Fig. 10.4). In both the euphoria and anger conditions, they felt and acted as if they were quite unemotional, and they did not differ appreciably for the two conditions. The drug-aroused ignorant subjects were more emotional; they felt euphoric in the euphoric condition and angry in the anger condition.

In a related study (Schachter and Wheeler, 1962), some subjects were given a placebo and others were given chlorpromazine, a tranquilizer that suppresses physiological arousal. Those who received the tranquilizer laughed less at a funny movie while those who received the placebo reacted normally. These findings show that emotions depend on *both* physiological arousal and the social situation. They also indicate that the subject's interpretation of the whole situation is important, because if he attributes his physiological arousal to a nonemotional cause, he will not feel emotions.

Zillmann's experiments In both of these studies, the physiological state was produced artificially by means of a drug. Two experiments by Dolf Zillmann demonstrated similar effects with other kinds of arousals. In the first experiment (Zillmann, 1971), each subject watched either a violent, sexy, or neutral film. The neutral film produced little arousal, while the others aroused feelings connected with violence or sexuality. Then the subjects were given a chance to express aggression toward someone who had insulted them. Zillmann predicted that the angrier they felt, the more aggression they would express. Furthermore, if they interpreted the extent of their anger in terms of how aroused they were, they should feel angrier after either

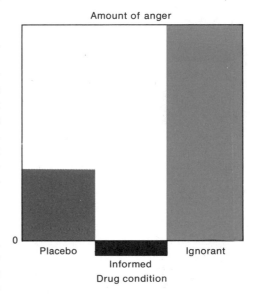

Fig. 10.4
Cognitive and physiological states and emotions

Subjects who received an arousing drug and were ignorant of its effects became angry when exposed to an angry confederate. Subjects who received a neutral drug or were informed of the effect of the active drug showed little anger. Similar results were obtained when the situation involved euphoria rather than anger. (After Schachter and Singer, 1962)

the violent or the erotic film. Since they were aroused and knew that they had been annoyed, they should interpret their feeling as anger regardless of what film they watched. Sure enough, both sexual and violent films produced more aggression than the neutral film. The second experiment (Zillmann, Katcher, and Milavsky, 1972) showed that subjects who were annoyed and who then simply peddled on an exercise bike also increased their aggressive behavior. Presumably, these subjects interpreted their purely physical arousal at least in part as increased anger.

Cognitive appraisal Schachter assumed that arousal precedes the individual's interpretation of the situation. In fact, Schachter produced the arousal chemically in most of his work, so that it was largely beyond cognitive control. Other investigators have approached the theory of emotions somewhat differently, emphasizing the effects of cognitive appraisal on the amount of arousal (Arnold, 1960; Lazarus, 1968). Richard Lazarus has suggested that how we interpret a situation will to some extent *determine* our physiological reactions to it. In a series of studies, Lazarus and his associates showed subjects films that most people find quite horrifying. One of the films is of subincision, an ancient ritual among some primitive tribes, in which adolescent boys have their penises cut deeply (understandably upsetting to the college-age males in the audience) and the other is a safety film that includes graphic scenes of terrible accidents. These films usually produce very strong physiological responses in viewers—but either before or during the film, experimenters gave some subjects special instructions designed to encourage them to view the scenes objectively or to deny their unpleasant aspects. Figure 10.5 shows the results of one experiment (Lazarus et

RICHARD S. LAZARUS

Fig. 10.5
Cognitive preparation and emotional reaction
Some subjects are instructed to deny the unpleasant aspects of the film (denial group), others to be objective and intellectual (intellectualization group), while others receive no special instructions (control). The first two groups have less strong physiological (skin-conductance) responses to vivid scenes of accidents. (From Lazarus et al., 1965)

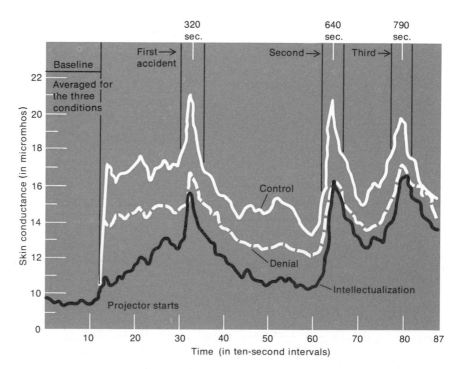

al., 1965). As you can see, cognitive preparation or guidance does decrease the physiological reactions substantially.

This line of research makes the valuable point that our physiological reactions must themselves be explained. Why do we become aroused when facing a mugger, expecting an exam, or talking to an opinionated person? Why do some physical processes slow down when someone we love dies or we get a rejection note from graduate school? Although some physical responses are innate—touching a hot stove produces an immediate withdrawal and also a danger reflex that involves a speedup of the heart and other processes—most human responses are not. They have been learned by the various mechanisms we have discussed in Chapters 3 and 4. Some reactions have been so well learned that they are automatic, but others occur only if we recognize that the appropriate stimulus is present. You will almost certainly become aroused automatically at the sight of a person charging at you with a knife, but you will probably not be automatically aroused by a dog running toward you, because you must first decide if the dog is friendly or dangerous. This means that some cognitive appraisal of the situation often takes place *before* there is a physical response. Therefore, cognitive interpretation enters into the emotional reaction in two ways—determining to some extent whether arousal is produced and how much, and then deciding the meaning of the arousal once it occurs.

Inappropriate emotions The physiological/cognitive theory of emotion helps to explain why people frequently experience inappropriate emotions. If you misinterpret a critical aspect of the situation, you will probably feel the "wrong" emotion. A big dog rushing at you may well arouse fear. If the dog jumps on you and gently licks your face, you may feel a little foolish, but at least you know what is going on. More subtle misinterpretations occur in our dealings with other people. We interpret a joke as an insult, or courtesy as friendliness, and in each case feel an emotion that does not fit the situation. A common confusion is between sexual arousal and love. We are with someone, find ourselves aroused, and may decide that this is caused by our affection for the other person—that is, we feel we are in love. If the physiological arousal is reduced by sexual activity, we may find that the feeling of love has disappeared. Since sexual attraction and love are so closely connected, this is an especially likely confusion and one that is difficult to avoid. Yet the implications of the two emotions are usually quite different and will have different effects on our behavior.

In addition to feeling the "wrong" emotion because of misinterpretations, we often feel an emotion that is too strong for the situation. We all know how it feels to overreact to a situation, becoming furious at a minor insult or suddenly depressed at a slight disappointment. One explanation is that our state of physiological arousal has been raised or lowered by other unrelated factors and we then interpret our emotional reaction in terms of this too-high or too-low state.

The studies described earlier illustrate just how this can operate. In Zillmann's studies, subjects who had been aroused—by either an erotic movie or rapid peddling on an exercise bike—became angrier when insulted than subjects who were not aroused. Schachter's subjects who were aroused with epinephrine became angrier or more euphoric than unaroused subjects, and those given chlorpromazine laughed less than those who did not get it. Similarly, if you are very tired from lack of sleep or if you have drunk a lot of alcohol (which lowers the level of arousal), you are more likely to become depressed and sad. And if you are hyped up on coffee, cigarettes, a stimulant, or tension, you may become far too angry when someone annoys you, or too euphoric and giddy over a minor success. You may wonder why you feel so elated or angry or depressed when the situation does not seem to warrant it; and the answer may be that you are feeling the appropriate emotion but its strength is artificially raised by your physical state.

Conclusions In light of these experiments, the physiological/cognitive interpretation theory of emotions seems reasonably satisfactory. It takes into account the importance of the bodily state but also explains how individuals experience such a wide variety of emotions. Since there are a great number of possible external situations, it is easy to see how the wide range of emotions can be aroused. Subtle distinctions among external cues will produce subtle differences in the emotional state.

Furthermore, this theory explains why different people experience different emotions in the same situation and why the same person experiences different emotions when in the same situation at different times. The strength of the emotion depends on the intensity of the physiological response. An external situation that might arouse anger at one time may produce annoyance at another, depending in part on your bodily state. If you are tired and less responsive, your body will not become as aroused and you will probably not experience as intense an emotion. Logically enough, the reverse holds for those emotions that involve depressed bodily activity. An experience that makes you feel depressed when you are tired and generally unresponsive might produce a milder emotional response if you were wide awake and generally aroused. Moreover, the theory allows for the fact that individuals interpret a social situation in different ways. Depending on how they interpret it, they will experience different emotions or perhaps no emotions at all.

EXPRESSING AND IDENTIFYING EMOTIONS

Although people all over the world probably experience very much the same kinds and the same range of emotions, they *express* them in many different ways. Naturally, the behavior that emotion produces will vary greatly from one situation to another. You do not always punch someone just because you are angry; you do not always cry when you are sad. This effect on behavior will vary from individual to individual and even for the same person at different times. And of course cultures differ considerably in the extent to which they allow or encourage different kinds of expression. These culturally shaped behaviors are not really expressions of emotion itself, but rather activities that are motivated or caused by emotions. But to what extent do people differ in how they show their emotions? Assuming most people do not conceal their emotions—they either try to express

"Afterwards, on my becoming very intimate with Fitz-Roy [the captain of the Beagle], I heard that I had run a very narrow risk of being rejected on account of the shape of my nose! He... was convinced that he could judge of a man's character by the outline of his features; and he doubted whether anyone with my nose could possess sufficient energy and determination for the voyage. But I think he was afterwards well satisfied that my nose had spoken falsely."
Charles Darwin

Figure 10.6

them or simply allow them to occur—how similar are individuals and cultures in the facial and bodily gestures they employ?

In 1872, Charles Darwin proposed that all people express emotions in the same way, and that, in particular, each emotion is represented by a particular facial expression. Darwin believed that people's personalities and feelings are reflected in their faces, but, as you can see in Fig. 10.6, he realized that it was not always easy to "read" a face accurately. Since then there has been a great deal of research dealing with two related questions—how accurate are perceptions of emotions from facial expressions, and how consistent are these expressions across cultures?

The Accuracy of the Perception of Emotion

Can you tell from someone's expression whether she is feeling anger or disgust, fear or surprise, love or sadness? Although we all tend to believe we are experts at this kind of judgment, most research indicates that we are not as accurate as we might hope. Research on this issue has generally involved photographing someone's face as he tries to portray various emotions, and then asking subjects to identify the emotion being expressed in each picture. Findings from such research have been quite mixed. Some studies indicated that the judgments were no better than chance (Guilford, 1929; Sherman, 1927) while others have shown quite a high degree of accuracy (Langfeld, 1918; Thompson and Meltzer, 1964).

One result has emerged quite consistently from this research. Although people may not clearly recognize a particular emotion, they

Fig. 10.7
The Schlosberg emotion circle

Emotions fall into approximately six groups, which can be placed along two dimensions: pleasantness-unpleasantness, and attention-rejection. The closer the emotions are on the circle, the more likely they are to be confused. Other emotions, such as jealously or rage, can be placed somewhere on this circle in terms of the two basic dimensions plus intensity. The photographs are placed according to how subjects ranked them on these dimensions. (From Schlosberg, 1952)

can identify *classes* of emotions. People usually group emotions into classes. In judging facial expressions, people often confuse emotions that fall in the same class, but seldom mix up emotions from different classes. Love may be confused with happiness but rarely with anger or contempt; anger may be confused with determination, but not with surprise. To test this observation, Schlosberg (1952) arranged six groups of emotions around a circle (see Fig. 10.7) so that groups closer

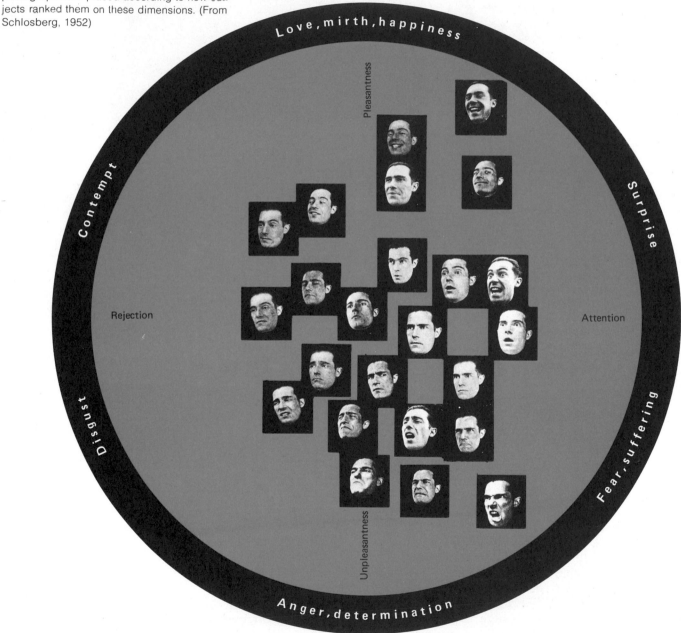

CONTROLLING YOUR EMOTIONS

The physiological/cognitive theory has important implications for the possible control of our emotions. Since emotion depends on cognitive interpretation as well as physiological arousal, we should have a fairly good understanding of the situation and therefore some control over our emotions. If we recognize the source of our arousal, realize how aroused we are, and know exactly what is going on, we should be unlikely to experience an inappropriate emotion. We will be more likely to respond correctly and efficiently.

Imagine that a friend disagrees with you on some minor point. You feel strongly aroused, know that your friend has annoyed you, and presume you are angry. But if you know that you are hyped up on five cups of coffee, you can explain the strong arousal in terms of the coffee and are less likely to act enraged. On the other hand, if you forget that you have drunk a lot of coffee, or if you have taken some other drug and are unaware that it produces arousal, you may become unreasonably angry.

Similarly, if you are less responsive than usual to the person you love, you might interpret this as a decrease in your feelings. But if you know that you are terribly tired or depressed for some reason, you can explain your lack of response in terms of fatigue or depression, and not feel that your love is waning. Conversely, the excuse, "Not tonight, I don't feel well," gives the partner a physical explanation for what might actually be a lack of sexual interest. The physical excuse is more acceptable and makes the partner feel less rejected.

Knowledge of your recent experiences is also vital. If you are with someone and you feel very angry, you might assume that the other person had annoyed or frustrated you. But recalling that you were just stuck in traffic for two hours will enable you to explain your anger in terms of this prior frustration, so that you will not take it out on the innocent bystander.

This does not mean that understanding the situation will necessarily enable you to control your emotions entirely, nor that this would be desirable. Emotions are aroused by complex factors and it is usually difficult for an individual to have much control over their strength or quality. What you can do is try to avoid inappropriate emotions that might lead to destructive or inefficient behavior, and yet to recognize that emotions are a basic part of human life that affects everyone's behavior.

Box 10.3

together were more similar and more likely to be confused. He found, and others supported this contention (Thompson and Meltzer, 1964; Frijda, 1968), that an emotion is more likely to be mistaken for one in a group that is only one scale point away than for one in a group that is further away. Contempt is less likely to be confused with anger than with disgust, and even less likely to be mistaken for fear or surprise.

However, there are some basic problems with this research. How can you decide what the "correct" answer is? An actor has been asked to portray an expression, but did he do it well? Did he do it the way other people would? Did he overdo the expression, producing an extreme portrayal that does not accurately represent the way the emotion is usually expressed? These questions are closely connected with the question of whether expressions of emotions are universal. If they are, it suggests that there are "right" ways of expressing an emotion.

Are Expressions Universal?

Recent research provides some indication that a particular facial expression is identified as the same emotion by people all over the world. Ekman, Sorenson, and Friesen (1969) showed college students in Argentina, Brazil, Chile, Japan, and the United States the same set of pictures and asked them to provide an emotional label. There was a high degree of consistency in the responses; regardless of their national origin, the subjects saw the face as portraying the same emotion. However, the difficulty with this study was that American films and television shows are popular in all of these countries and the students may simply have learned how Americans (or more precisely, American actors and actresses) express each emotion. Certainly there are Hollywood conventions for showing love, fear, and hate. The slightly open mouth and the wide-open, somewhat glazed eyes staring ahead, for example, are meant to represent adoring love. Although people may not look like that in real life, anyone familiar with the Hollywood representation would recognize it.

A second study eliminated this possibility (Ekman and Friesen, 1971). This time the subjects were natives of New Guinea who had seen no movies, had had no contact with Westerners, and spoke no English. Each subject was told a brief story that would usually elicit a particular emotion. For example, for sadness, "A man's child has died and he feels very sad." Then the subject was shown three photographs, only one of which was supposed to represent the right emotion, and the subject was asked to pick the correct photograph. Adults chose correctly over 80 percent of the time; and children, who were given only two photographs to choose from, selected the right one over 90 percent of the time.

This and other similar work suggests that people do express emotions in similar ways. There are obviously considerable variations even within a society and presumably the variations are greater across cultures. But there is enough consistency so that our perceptions of the emotion being expressed by someone from a totally foreign culture should have some general validity. We can probably tell at least what kind of emotion is being expressed, even if we cannot narrow it down to the specific emotion.

EMOTION AND BEHAVIOR: AGGRESSION

Most emotions can be expressed quite freely. If you are happy, you can smile; if you are sad, you can cry; if you are angry, you can sulk or slam a door. There may be some value or status connected with not showing emotions (being the strong, silent type has long been admired in our country), but generally the expression of most emotions and the corresponding behavior is allowed or even encouraged by society.

However, this is not true of certain emotions. In particular, most societies place considerable restrictions on expressing sexual and aggressive feelings. Just because you are angry, you cannot slap the stranger next to you, hurl a book at your professor, or throw the coffeepot at a waitress. We shall discuss sexual behavior in detail in Chapter 13. Since aggression is such an important problem for soci-

FREE EXPRESSION OF EMOTIONS

Although there are few laws against the expression of most emotions, our society, and especially the white, middle-class subculture, has tended to view open emotionality as weakness, particularly in men. This is evident in the heroes we admire in our literature and films. Our masculine heroes—typified by John Wayne and more recently Clint Eastwood and Charles Bronson—have traditionally been strong, silent men who may feel deeply but who rarely express these feelings openly. Women, on the other hand, have been encouraged to express emotions more freely. If a woman burst into tears in public it was perfectly normal and acceptable because she was a woman. Perhaps the greatest exceptions to the unwritten rule were the attitudes toward sexuality and aggression. In contrast with all other emotions, men have been allowed to express sexuality and anger much more freely than women. Clint Eastwood could sleep with a woman or get into a brawl with the bad guy because he had to have an outlet for these "masculine" feelings. On the other hand, a good woman was expected to keep such feelings (if she had them) under control.

As we shall discuss in Chapter 13 on sex and adult development, the patterns described above appear to be changing.

The feminist movement has had a significant influence on American women in freeing them from traditionally feminine attitudes and roles. Similarly, this movement has helped many men to recognize that they need not act "masculine" all the time. Indeed people now recognize that men and women have both "masculine" and "feminine" traits and that these qualities are common to all human beings. A result of this awareness is that many women are expressing their sexual and aggressive feelings more openly, and many men are learning to express sorrow and show fear.

The humanistic movement has also contributed to these changes. One of the goals of encounter groups and various humanistic therapies (see Chapter 16) is to get participants to express emotions openly in order to achieve greater self-awareness. Thus, in therapeutic settings it is fairly common to see men cry in front of others.

In spite of these changing patterns, we should realize that most men still find it difficult to let their feelings show and that many people in our society still consider emotionality a sign of weakness. Fundamental changes in attitudes always take a long time, but perhaps in the future ours will be a society in which showing feelings is accepted as the human thing to do.

ety, let us consider it now as an example of the complex relationship between emotions and behavior.

The Arousal of Aggressive Feelings: Frustration and Attack

Because aggressive feelings do not always lead to aggressive behavior, two separate questions arise in dealing with aggression. First we must see what *arouses* aggressive feelings, and then we shall turn to the factors that determine whether aggression will be *expressed.*

Frustration Probably the most important producer of aggressive feelings is *frustration*. Someone who is prevented from reaching a goal, or whose activity is blocked, tends to feel aggressive. Indeed, this so-called *frustration-aggression hypothesis*—first proposed by a distinguished group at Yale (Dollard, et al., 1939)—is one of the basic principles of behavior. The effect has been demonstrated repeatedly with animals, and also in a number of studies with humans. For example, Funkenstein, King, and Drolette (1954) asked subjects to speak as rapidly as possible but gave them acoustical feedback that interfered with their performance. In another situation, they asked subjects to remember digits that were read aloud, but made the task difficult for them by annoying them while they were trying to learn. These frustrations resulted in clear physiological reactions, particularly an increase in blood pressure. In addition, the subjects, who had been quite calm and relaxed before the experiment, reported that they were highly aroused, angry, and aggressive afterwards. We are all familiar with this response to frustration—a car in front of you does not move when the light turns green and you feel an immediate frustration and anger directed toward the person blocking the road.

Attack The other major causes of aggressive feelings are annoyance and attack. When someone bothers or assaults us, one common response is to become angry and aggressive toward that person. There are a great many studies in which someone insults or annoys a subject and measures of aggressive feelings are taken. All of these indicate that the person who has been annoyed becomes more aggressive, and her aggressive feelings tend to be directed sharply at the person who annoyed her. Although no goal has been blocked and no frustration has occurred, the aggressive feelings are aroused in response to the attack.

Aggressive Behavior: Instinctive or Learned?

Once someone feels aggressive, what determines whether or not he will express that impulse in actual behavior? One possible explanation is that it depends on *instinct.* Some ethologists (scientists who study animal behavior in natural environments) such as Konrad Lorenz (1966) believe that aggressiveness is an instinctive reaction in humans—that in certain situations we feel and act aggressively due to a built-in mechanism. This kind of instinctual notion is extremely difficult to test because it is virtually impossible to rule out all cultural influences. As a result, there is no convincing evidence in favor of the aggressive instinct in humans. Most psychologists believe that instincts generally play a relatively small role in human behavior, particularly in complex social interactions. Although there may be some instinctive aspects to aggressive behavior, the current consensus is that it is inaccurate to think that specific situations trigger an aggressive instinct or aggressive behavior.

In contrast, *learning* and *imitation* play a major role in determining when people will express aggressive impulses. A child is constantly disciplined for behaving aggressively, sometimes more severely than at other times. After a while, he learns to make distinctions among situations, among people, and among kinds of behaviors. Not only does he learn to control his aggression in general, but he develops rules that tell him when it is acceptable to express aggressive feelings. Aggression is more acceptable on the football field than in a department store; verbal aggression is generally more acceptable than physical; aggression against equals is more acceptable (but also more dangerous) than against inferiors. In addition, people unfortunately learn that it is more acceptable to be aggressive toward certain kinds of people than toward others. These prejudices and bigotries are present in almost all societies, which select certain of their members to be the recipients of aggressive feelings and behavior.

Aggression is learned by all the usual mechanisms that we discussed in Chapters 3 and 4. Rewards, punishments, association, and imitation are all extremely important. The classic study by Albert Bandura described in Chapter 3 demonstrated the power of imitation in controlling aggressive behavior. This power of imitation creates some unforeseen effects when parents physically punish children for behaving aggressively. Studies by Sears et al. (1953) demonstrated that spanking a child for fighting does cause him to be less aggressive at home. However, once he is away from the home, he is actually *more* aggressive than children who were punished less severely. The punishment evidently is associated only with the home, where the child is likely to get caught—but the imitation of the adult's aggressive behavior toward him is carried over to other situations. Apparently, the parent who says "Do what I say, not what I do" is bound to be disappointed.

Who Is Aggressed Against? Displacement

Even when people do express their aggressive feelings in action, they do not always direct them toward the person who aroused them in the first place. This may be because the person is too strong, unassailable, or for some reason unavailable, or because such direct aggression clearly would bring more trouble than satisfaction. You do not usually punch your boss if she annoys you, run over a policeman who has been directing traffic too slowly for your taste, go to Washington and kick a senator who has voted to increase your income taxes, or even yell at a friend who is annoying you. If you do not express these aggressive feelings, you will almost certainly find someone else to serve as the object of your aggression. This is called *displacement*. It follows the rule of stimulus generalization—the more similar the substitute object or person is to the original cause of the aggressive feelings, the more likely it is to elicit aggression and the stronger the aggression will be if it occurs. This has been demonstrated nicely with a variety of animals. In a study by Miller (1948), a rat learned to attack another rat when it was given an electric shock. If the other rat was not present, the trained rat would instead attack a toy rat that was put in the cage. This displacement also occurred for plastic dolls, other toys, and even rags (see Fig. 10.8). However, as the object became less and less similar to another rat, the likelihood and the amount of aggression decreased.

As with other kinds of stimulus generalization, the dimension along which the people are similar can be almost anything that seems important. Much of the aggression in society is probably due to displacement along very complex and subtle dimensions. For example, adolescents normally have some feelings of anger or frustration directed against their parents. As the source of power in the family, parents inevitably produce some of the child's frustrations and are blamed for others as well. This arouses anger that is sometimes expressed directly against the parents, but much of the time is not. Certainly school administrators, teachers, policemen, and members

Fig. 10.8
Aggression displacement

Witches were popular scapegoats in the six-teenth century.

Table 10.2
DEVIANCY AND AGGRESSION

Person doing the choosing	For shock	For reward
Deviants	2.18	3.73
Nondeviants	3.91	2.82

Figures are number of deviants chosen for each task. Deviants choose other deviants for reward and not for punishment; nondeviants select deviants for punishment and not for reward.

Based on Freedman and Doob, 1968.

of the government represent the same kind of authority as parents, and the rebelliousness and anger adolescents sometimes express against them is often due to displacement. Of course, there may also be legitimate reasons for being angry at these authority figures, but at times the anger takes its basic strength from the deep frustrations felt in childhood.

Displacement and prejudice Prejudice is also due in part to displaced aggression. People are frustrated and angered by those more powerful than themselves and by uncontrollable circumstances. But the farmer cannot attack the sky for not giving him rain, the factory worker who loses her job because of bad economic conditions cannot attack the boss, and someone who has to wait all day long for a plumber to repair the water heater cannot attack the plumber. Since they cannot express their aggression toward the source of their frustration, these frustrated people may express their aggression against people whom it is safe or acceptable to attack.

Almost every society and subgroup of a society picks certain kinds of people to serve as objects of aggression. These so-called scapegoats are usually relatively weak, easily identified, and in some way different from the rest of the group. Scapegoats naturally differ from society to society and from subgroup to subgroup within a society. Blacks, Mexicans, Poles, Catholics, Jews, Southerners, Easterners, the young, the old, women—and almost any other group in our society—are the object of prejudice in some subculture. Aggressive feelings aroused by all of the frustrations and annoyances of life are directed against these objects of prejudice.

This tendency to distrust and mistreat people who are different is a powerful phenomenon. A study by Freedman and Doob (1968) showed that it occurred even when subjects did not know *how* the other people were different but only that they were in some way different. In this study, subjects took a complex personality test; some were told that they had received typical scores, while others were told that they had received quite deviant scores. Nothing was said about the meaning of the test, but some people were clearly labeled deviant (different from the norm) while others were not. Then the group as a whole chose one of their members to play a special role. In some instances, this role was highly desirable because it would involve winning extra money. In other cases, it was undesirable because the person would receive strong electric shocks. As you can see in Table 10.2, nondeviants picked other nondeviants for the good role (winning money), and deviants for the bad role (getting shocks). Deviants picked deviants for the good role and nondeviants for the bad role. In other words, even though they knew nothing about the other person except whether she was deviant, people favored others who were like themselves and treated "different" people badly.

Catharsis

One of the most controversial questions about aggression is whether expressing or witnessing it reduces subsequent aggressive behavior. The idea is that expressing the aggression, "gets it out of your system," usually called *catharsis*, reduces the aggressive drive, and thus reduces aggressive behavior. However, there is considerable evidence that encouraging or allowing people to be aggressive simply teaches them that it is acceptable or even desirable to act that way. Therefore, attempts at catharsis, rather than decreasing aggression, may actually increase it. Although this controversy is not yet fully resolved, it does seem that the effect depends largely on the particular circumstances.

If a very angry individual is allowed to express aggression against the actual source of her anger, then she is less likely to be aggressive in the future. But if she is not particularly angry to begin with, or if she expresses aggression against someone other than the source, the reduction in her aggressive drive will be relatively unimportant compared to what she learns about aggression being acceptable. Catharsis will not occur.

In one study (Doob and Wood, 1972), a confederate of the experimenter angered some subjects and was neutral toward others. Some of these subjects then gave electric shocks to the confederate; others watched the experimenter shock the confederate; and others neither witnessed nor expressed any aggression. Afterwards, they were all allowed to give electric shocks to the confederate. The results are shown in Table 10.3. As you can see, when angry subjects either witnessed or expressed aggression against their tormentor, their subsequent aggression was reduced. However, when they were not angry to begin with, giving or witnessing shocks actually increased their aggressive behavior.

Table 10.3
CATHARSIS AND AGGRESSION

	After subject gave shocks	After experimenter gave shocks	No shocks given
Subject angry	6.80	7.60	10.67
Subject not angry	8.07	9.73	6.60

Figures represent the number of shocks. A subject who was initially angered by the confederate gave fewer shocks after either giving some shocks himself or witnessing the experimenter shock the confederate. A subject who was not annoyed actually gave more shocks after giving or witnessing shocks to the confederate.

Based on Doob and Wood, 1972.

In other words, the catharsis effect is quite limited. If the boss makes you angry, yelling at a secretary will probably *not* decrease your tendency to hurt the boss if you ever get a chance. In contrast, smashing the boss's desk or spilling a drink on him at the next office party will decrease the likelihood that you will hurt him again in the future (if you ever get a chance). But since the catharsis effect is limited, encouraging children or adults to express aggression in some relatively acceptable form, such as on the football field or in verbal competition, will not make them less aggressive people. On the contrary, it may actually increase their aggressiveness in other situations.

This is evident even when the individual merely witnesses aggression. Many studies (Bandura, 1965; Walters and Willows, 1968)

LEONARD BERKOWITZ

have demonstrated increases in aggression after subjects watched a violent film. In one such study (Berkowitz and Geen, 1966), some subjects saw a violent boxing film (*Champion*, starring Kirk Douglas), while others saw a mild, nonviolent film. All were then given the opportunity to express aggression. Those who had seen the boxing film were more aggressive. Apparently, simply watching violence has two effects—it tends to teach the person that violence is acceptable, and it also immediately arouses some sort of aggressive feeling in many individuals. (It also may work just by producing arousal in general. As we saw earlier, Zillmann (1971) produced aggressiveness with erotic movies and bicycling.) Whatever the reason, viewers are more aroused and more likely to express the aggression, and accordingly they are much more likely to perform aggressive acts.

The Effect of Television on Aggression

Because of this dual effect of witnessing aggression, it might seem that for most people the great amount of violence on television would have a negative effect. It teaches the child that violence is a common and apparently acceptable part of society, and it may also momentarily arouse aggressive feelings. According to this line of reasoning, children who watch a greal deal of television and learn about society from it are more likely to be aggressive than those who do not.

Although virtually all of the laboratory research suggests that viewing violence, whether on television or in the movies, increases aggressiveness, it is difficult to generalize from this work to the real world. Most children in our society do not need television dramas to teach them that violence is present in our world. Newspapers and magazines, news and sports on television, their parents' conversation, and what is going on around them every day teach children that there is a lot of aggression in our society. They already know this and therefore television violence in crime shows may not teach them anything new and may accordingly have little effect on their attitudes toward violence.

In addition, children seem to be able to make a distinction between television and the real world. Although parents are often shocked at the violence in children's cartoon shows, there is no evidence that it has any adverse effect on the children, who appear to understand perfectly well that these are cartoons, not people. It is worth remembering that there was strong and widespread opposition to the Vietnam war among college students, and yet they were the first generation of children raised with heavy exposure to television. In other words, even though watching a violent program in the laboratory momentarily increases aggressiveness, watching many such programs in one's home may have little or no effect.

In order to answer the question of the effects of television violence we need research in natural settings. Unfortunately, this is very difficult, time-consuming work and little of it has been done. One ambitious study by Seymour Feshbach and Robert Singer (1970) involved children at public and private schools. The children were put into two groups, one of which was required to watch at least four hours a week of violent shows on television, while the other group was not allowed to watch any violent programs. Measures of aggressiveness taken before, during, and after the study indicated that those who watched violent programs were actually *less* aggressive than the other group.

However, this study should be considered with caution. It is quite possible that those children who were not allowed to watch violent programs felt deprived and angry because they were prevented from seeing some of their favorite shows. This anger would increase their aggressiveness. In addition, several studies (Wells, 1972; Leyens et al., 1975; Parke et al., 1977) produced results inconsistent with those reported by Feshbach and Singer.

At the moment the issue is unresolved. It seems highly likely that television violence has different effects on different children. A child who is very aggressive to begin with might get ideas of how to express that aggressiveness. There are anecdotal stories of children who watch a program dealing with kidnapping and go out and kidnap someone, or who see a program on arson and then set a fire. In these instances, television is not increasing aggressiveness, rather, it is giving the child bad ideas that might otherwise not occur to him. Other children might be so excited by the violence they view that they become aggressive themselves. In contrast, others may find that watching violent programs relieves some of their own aggressive feelings. Thus, the violent programs might have harmful effects on

INTERVIEW

Crime:
The Commissioner
and the Convict

Robert J. diGrazia was the commissioner of police in Boston at the time of the interview. He is a great big man with a warm smile and friendly manner. Sitting behind a huge desk surrounded by radios and flashing lights—part of an impressive communications system—he talks sincerely about the problems faced by police in fighting crime. He is obviously upset by politicians who he thinks are using the problem of crime for their own ends, but he is also upset by what he considers the police's lack of attention to the real problems. He thinks the publicity given to crimes and the violence on television have very detrimental effects, and he also believes that the increasing amount of leisure time as well as weakened family structure contribute to crime. Perhaps most important, he thinks that severity of sentencing is unimportant but that what counts is the probability of being caught and sentenced. It is too low now; deterrence will work only if certainty is much higher.

Q: Let's start with the obvious question—why is there so much crime these days?

A: I think one of the big reasons is that no one's bothered with the root causes. It might be easy to illustrate it with "Find a Salk vaccine like we did for polio." What

ROBERT J. DIGRAZIA

Such a small percentage go to jail now . . . so crime does pay.

we do now is get the people after the fact, like with polio we used to put them in braces. Now we put them in jail. What we have to do is look for *before* the crime— the socioeconomic situation, the education, job opportunities, the way people are forced to live.

Also, you have to blame politicians who are enamored with safe streets and law and order and our lovely boob tube.

Q: What does law and order have to do with it?

A: Well, people are easily led or misled. If someone talks about something a lot, you're going to have people become involved in it. In San Francisco, my hometown, we'd go for months without a suicide, then we'd have one, and then we'd have several right away. The same way that if you have a TV movie about highjacking, the airlines would get hundreds of calls right after it. As for law and order, it was a great slogan, but it took attention away from the real issues such as the socioeconomic situation. Also, and I'm not saying we shouldn't discuss it, but if it sounds like everybody's being robbed and murdered, some people are going to think that's the way to go.

Q: And violence on TV?

A: Oh, it's unbelievable. In every single program you see it happen. It teaches people to do the same thing.

Q: What can society and the police in particular do about crime now, given the socioeconomic situation and the violence on television?

A: First, we should be selecting for the police *talent* instead of looking for somebody who's 6'4" and 225 pounds [describing himself]. It's what's in a person's mind and heart that matters, not whether they are black, white, yellow or brown, or male or female. You have to teach them they are dealing with human beings day in and day out. And as long as other people aren't going to take the initiative, we have to do as much as we can to displace crime. We're not going to eliminate it, but we can displace it.

Q: Do you think it's as simple as that, if it doesn't happen here, it's going to happen somewhere else?

A: Absolutely. You're going to have people prey on people closest to their residence because it's handy. Granted you might deter some because they have to travel farther, but let's face it, they're going to travel.

Q: So you think deterrence isn't going to work?

A: Well, reducing it somewhat. But it's a small amount. As we make it tough in one area, we see it breaking out in other areas.

Q: What about this recent trend that the answer—particularly with juveniles—is to put them in jail and leave them there longer. The argument against "revolving door justice."

A: It's not so much the length of time or that there be mandatory sentencing. What is really important is the *certainty* of the sentence. Such a small percentage go to jail now—maybe 5 percent of the 20 percent we convict—that they know that they won't go to jail. So crime does pay and you might as well go out and take your chances. Certainty would be a deterrent.

Q: Do you think there has been a general breakdown or decrease in morality and that it filters down to the kids?

A: Well, I wouldn't want to go back to the days when 85 percent of the people worked on farms or long, long hours in the cities. Back then they worked, ate, slept, and worked the next morning. I like my leisure and I'm not saying we should go back to the past, but it's just not as strict a society as it was.

Q: But there are other societies like Sweden that are very free and prosperous with low crime rates and where the public obeys the law.

A: I think the family unit is very crucial. I don't care if there are legal binds, but it is important for love and discipline to be demonstrated. If there is a strong family unit, it would help a lot.

CARL VELLECA

*I actually believe prisons
are for punishment*

Carl Velleca is an inmate in a Massachusetts prison. He is a remarkable man—quite obviously bright, witty, sharp, and natural. He astounded the community by running for public office, claiming that he had a right as much as anyone and that he knew more about crime and other problems than people who had not served time. Although he lost, he got a great deal of publicity and has become a spokesman for the rights of prisoners. He blames TV, decline in morality, and unequal justice for the increase in crime.

He feels that prisons should be tough, that the criminal owes a debt to society and that punishment will deter crime. But justice must be equal for all—if it isn't we lose respect for the law, we feel helpless, and our moral sense declines. He makes a distinction between professional criminals, who have chosen crime as a way of life to "earn a living," and people who commit wanton crimes for fun or excitement. The former can be rehabilitated perhaps by giving them self-respect, but they are less dangerous anyway. The "crazies" are another story, and he does not have a solution for them.

Q: I'd be interested in knowing your views on why there's so much crime these days.

A: When they talk about penology I think they are starting at square ten when they should be starting at square one. You have to go to the first part of the Bill of Rights where it says all men are equal. It just doesn't happen. The same day that Spiro Agnew pleaded guilty [and got a suspended sentence and a small fine], two kids from Roxbury got six months for breaking a window.

Q: Why does that cause crime?

A: These poor kids, they just know that the cards are stacked against them. They feel if they haven't got the brains, the only way they're going to get a broad or a nice car is steal. You have to put legislation in that if you violate the public trust, you go to jail. We had a judge here who was a tough judge. Then they found out he was on the take. He sent five hundred guys to jail, but all he got was reprimanded. So people don't bother trying to stop crime on the streets. Some guy's attacking a woman, like the Kitty Genovese incident [see page 567], but people just walk by because it's useless.

Q: You think that there's a decline, a moral decline?

A: Positively. Let's face it, TV is molding the shape of the country.

Q: Do you think the kids are influenced by what they see on TV?

A: They can't help but be. I'm strictly for the first amendment —no censorship—but boy they've got me changing a little bit. My friends in prison, they're no angels, but they have a certain amount of honor. Some kid came in and robbed a house and raped and killed the babysitter. That never happened like it's happening now.

Q: Why do you think we have these violent crimes more now?

A: I think the Vietnam war had a lot to do with it. The kill syndrome was there because their ideals have been shattered by My Lai and things like that. TV is bringing it out also.

Q: Let me ask you a different question. What is it like to be in prison?

A: Prison is a state of mind. To me it's a challenge. I actually believe prisons are for punishment.

Q: That's how it *should* be, prisons for punishment?

A: Positively. You commit a crime, you go to jail. The only thing they give you is that you can earn self-respect. Instead of these crazy sentences, if they commit a crime, they owe a debt to society. Let them pay it some other way. Let them clean the rivers. Two blocks from here, houses are falling down. Let the inmates do the work.

Q: Do you think this would stop people from committing crimes? Would it be a deterrent?

A: I think it would narrow the base. There will always be an element of criminals. But let's try to make it so they're not ones that indiscriminately kill people.

Q: What would you do with the others—the crazies?

A: You've got to put them away.

Q: Would you treat juveniles differently?

A: You have to treat them individually. I think they should be in age groups and try to give them self-respect. There's a program in Massachusetts working with the retarded. I've seen professional criminals working with the retarded and during the process they gained the insight, "What am I doing? Look how lucky I am. I'm healthy."

Q: Let me ask you this. Juvenile delinquents commit crimes and often they don't go to jail or stay in for a short time.

A: We've got to stop that. You can't say first thing—"You're free." It depends on the crime. I might give a kid two shots if he breaks a window twice—give him a break—but if he attacks a girl viciously that's got to be treated differently. And you can't make it easy. It's important that the first sentence is not easy. If you commit a crime, you have to be punished. Like when you're little and you do something wrong and your mother hits you. I think the old rock pile had merit. 'Cause as the kid was banging rocks, he could be saying, "Hey, I could be getting $4.50 an hour for this!" I think another thing that is missing is family honor. I could go into a gang war and kill seven guys and my mother would come and visit me. But if I ever took an old lady's handbag, my mother would absolutely shoot me. My family would disown me.

Comment

The commissioner and the convict both think that television has increased the amount of violence in our society. The commissioner makes the point that, at least, people who watch television may get bad ideas, such as the hijacking he mentions. How do Commissioner diGrazia's views and those of Carl Velleca fit in with the research on the effects of television on aggression?

Both men emphasize the importance of the family. We have discussed the role of physical punishment, and how children who are punished physically for fighting in the home may learn not to fight there but will learn to fight even more elsewhere because they imitate their parents. In what other way might the family and family life affect an individual's tendency to commit crime? Consider this question as you read Chapter 12, in which the role of discipline is discussed.

Another point of agreement between the two men is the importance of the certainty of punishment. They assert that the severity counts for less than the knowledge that you will be caught and punished. How does this fit in with what we know about schedules of reinforcement and especially the difference between partial and 100-percent reinforcement? Remember that each time you get away with a crime, you have been reinforced for that act.

some and relatively mild or even positive effects on others. It is fair to say that most psychologists believe that violence on television does increase aggressiveness and is therefore generally more harmful than helpful. But the evidence for this view is not yet conclusive.

THE EFFECTS OF EMOTIONS

Emotions help make us human. Both pleasant emotions, such as joy, and unpleasant ones, such as sorrow, bring richness and color to our lives. Because they are such a vital part of human life, it is doubtful that anyone would truly want to do away with emotional reactions. Nonetheless, emotions have strong motivating properties that often interfere with healthy, productive reactions to the world. When we say that someone is being emotional, we usually mean that his behavior is irrational and disorganized. But emotions also have positive, energizing effects. Let us look at these two opposite consequences of emotions.

It is both reasonable and functional to be afraid when you are in a dangerous situation. Your body becomes aroused for action, you focus clearly on the crucial elements of the situation, and your fear probably helps you to function efficiently. A certain level of fear will prevent you from being reckless and at the same time provide you with the energy and the motivation to behave appropriately. A pilot who suddenly discovers that one of her plane's engines is on fire *should* be afraid. Fear should stimulate her to fly the plane with every bit of skill she possesses in order to bring it home safely. If she were not afraid, she might take the situation less seriously, behave in a slower, less energized manner, and perhaps not give the problem all the attention it deserves.

On the other hand, becoming too terrified will interfere with her reactions. Instead of just energizing her system, terror may paralyze her—she may be unable to act, or may act too swiftly and precipitously, without considering all of the possibilities. In this situation, as in many others, a moderate level of arousal produces the best possible response. And as we saw with motivation in general, the optimal level of arousal is related to the complexity of the behavior—the more complex the behavior, the lower the level of arousal that will give the best performance.

The same is true of many other kinds of emotions. In one sense, we might think that never feeling anger would be ideal. But it is probably most efficient to become angry when the situation warrants it; for example, if someone has injured you or someone else. If you feel no emotion, you may not be motivated to do anything about the situation or to protect yourself in the future. Of course, a very high level of anger or rage might involve you in a fight or in some kind of violence that would be destructive and perhaps illegal. Once again, an intermediate level suited to the situation is most effective.

Such moderation seems less appropriate to more positive emotions such as joy and love. Of course, an overwhelming love for another person often does interfere with normal, rational, efficient behavior, and can even interfere with the relationship itself. Despite this, most people would not agree that a moderate level of love is the ideal state. Strong feelings of love may lead to inefficiency, but they lead to delight as well.   ■

Summary

1. Although emotions are difficult to define precisely, we can say that they contain the following two elements: (a) they always involve either physiological arousal or depression; and (b) unlike motives, they are always evaluative.

2. Theories that attempt to explain what causes emotions and what determines which emotions we feel include the James-Lange theory, activation theory, the physiological/cognitive interpretation, and cognitive appraisal.

3. The James-Lange theory proposed that the individual's physiological response precedes and causes the emotion. While research on the limbic system provides some support for this idea, recent studies have cast considerable doubt on it. At present its major contribution seems to be the emphasis given to people's awareness of their physiological reactions.

4. According to activation theory, emotion is synonymous with arousal; thus, there is no need to distinguish among various types of emotions. However, this idea fails to account for emotions that involve a depressed state (such as sadness) nor does it account for variations among emotions.

5. The physiological/cognitive interpretation assumes that emotions require both arousal (or slowdown) and awareness of that arousal, but adds the crucial idea that the emotion that is experienced depends on the person's cognitive interpretation of the situation. Experiments by Schachter-Singer and Zillmann support this view.

6. Research on the effects of cognitive appraisal on the amount of arousal has contributed the important understanding that cognitive interpretation determines to some extent whether arousal takes place and how much arousal, and then decides the meaning of the arousal once it occurs. Cognitive appraisal helps to explain why we sometimes feel the "wrong" emotion in a situation.

7. Physiological mechanisms, specifically the brain structures in the limbic system, play an important role in the arousal of many emotions, including fear, anger, aggression, and sexual pleasure. Although we do not know precisely how the limbic system controls emotions, we do know that stimulation of areas of the limbic system causes various bodily responses related to emotional behavior.

8. It seems clear that people in many different cultures experience very similar emotions. Research has concentrated on whether or not facial and bodily gestures associated with emotional expres-

sion are similar across cultures and whether people can identify a particular emotion from these expressions. Studies show that people are able to identify *classes* of emotions from facial expressions and that facial expressions for various types of emotions are universal.

9. Since aggressive feelings are experienced by everyone and expression of such feelings is a serious problem in our society, aggression has been the subject of much study. Aggressive feelings are produced by frustration, annoyance, and attack (being bothered or assaulted). Learning processes, including rewards, punishments, association, and imitation, play a major role in determining when people will act on their aggressive feelings; instinct (in humans) probably plays a relatively small role.

10. When aggressive feelings and behavior are directed at a substitute rather than at the actual cause of the feelings, we call the process *displacement*. Miller has demonstrated experimentally that the more similar the substitute person (or object) to the original cause of the aggressive feelings, the more likely that person is to elicit aggression and the stronger the aggression will be if it occurs.

11. Prejudice can be accounted for in part by displaced aggression. People who are frustrated and angered by those in a more powerful position may displace their aggressive feelings onto scapegoats who are weak or acceptable to attack.

12. Catharsis refers to the idea that expressing aggressive feelings reduces the aggressive drive and thus reduces aggressive behavior. However, this idea should be approached with caution, since there is evidence that in some circumstances attempts at catharsis actually increase aggression rather than decrease it. Moreover, there is no question that the catharsis effect is quite limited.

13. Most psychologists believe that watching violent programs on television increases aggressiveness and is generally more harmful than helpful. However, the research is not yet conclusive because few studies have been conducted in natural (nonlaboratory) settings and because social, personality, and situational factors may influence how a child reacts to a violent program. It seems likely that the effect depends in part on the child himself, with some children becoming aroused and others experiencing a catharsis of aggressive feelings.

RECOMMENDED READING

Ekman, P., W. V. Friesen, and P. Ellsworth. *Emotion in the Human Face.* New York: Pergamon Press, 1972. This book deals with the expression and recognition of emotion through the face. It describes fascinating attempts to determine whether all people express emotion in similar ways.

Lorenz, K. *On Aggression.* New York: Harcourt, 1966. The ethological approach. Not really a very good book, but the first few chapters are excellent and very good reading.

Schachter, S. *Emotion, Obesity and Crime.* New York: Academic, 1971. Describes research and theory relating the arousal of emotions to questions of why people get fat and why they commit crimes. Very well written.

Zuckerman, M., and C. D. Spielberger, Eds. *Emotions and Anxiety: New Concepts, Methods, and Applications.* Hillsdale, N.J.: Lawrence Erlbaum, 1976. A recent book that covers a lot of ground.

I believe it to be true that dreams are the true interpreters of our inclinations; but there is art required to sort and understand them.
Montaigne, *Essays*

Marijuana inflames the erotic impulses and leads to revolting sex crimes . . . one girl, known for her quietness and modesty, suddenly threw all caution to the wind. She began staying out late at nights.
Daily Mirror, UK, 1929

11 States of Consciousness

Sleep ▪ Dreams ▪ Hypnosis ▪ Meditation ▪ Mystical experiences ▪ Psychoactive drugs ▪

We were all in a house—my mother, some other people, and I—relatives maybe. It must have been Thanksgiving or some other holiday, because a nice dinner had been prepared and we were all sitting around on pillows eating and talking. My mother and I were arguing about religion. She kept telling me things would go better in my life if I would only follow the religious teachings I'd been brought up with. Then she told me I should have a hysterectomy. At this point in the conversation I began to realize that we were all in danger. FBI agents had surrounded the house and were going to set it on fire—like in the Patty Hearst case. I was the only one who recognized the danger, so I told everyone to go down to the basement. I knew that we would be safe there and I knew that somehow parrots—the tropical birds—would be involved in our rescue. Then, suddenly I was at a flea market alone looking for a long, gold chain to wear as a necklace. I found several that I liked, but when I looked at them more closely I realized they all had a cross hanging from the end. I didn't want to buy a chain with a cross hanging from it. (Personal Communication)

I opened my eyes to find the living room vibrating with brilliant colors . . . My limbs were trembling. I felt a tingling sensation in my fingers . . . I lost myself in the whirling colors funneling up like a huge mushroom spreading over me. I could now make out numbers, letters, and words in vivid colors.

[An apple is placed in his hand] I was astounded by the extraordinarily delicious taste . . . The process of chewing seemed to go on forever . . . Words were useless; speech a waste of time. I could not walk . . . I found myself creeping along the floor . . . [In the kitchen] I sniffed the cloves and their fragrance seemed to envelop my whole being. I became the odor as I inhaled and exhaled. (Aaronson and Osmond, 1970)

Obviously these are not descriptions of normal human behavior. People do not perceive objects in this way; their sense of time is not usually this variable; their motives are not this confused; their memories are not this distorted; and in general they do not behave like this. Yet these are real experiences of real people. The difference is that they are experiences of people not in the usual waking state but in other states of consciousness. The former is a dream, the latter a drug-induced state. In these altered states, as well as under hypnosis, in mystical states, and in meditation, we can have experiences and behave in ways that are vastly different from when we are awake. It is not accurate to consider wakefulness the only "normal" state—the other states are normal, we can all experience at least some of them, and the experiences in them can have a powerful effect on us. However, because these other states obey somewhat different rules from the waking state, it is important to consider them separately. In this chapter we shall discuss sleep and dreaming, hypnosis, meditation, mystical experiences, and the effects of psychoactive drugs.

SLEEP

Fatigue greatly affects perceptions and behavior, but it is still considered a form or degree of wakefulness. Sleep is a distinctly different state, even though the transition from being awake to being asleep may be almost imperceptible. Anyone who has ever tried to fall asleep and been unable to no matter how fatigued is well aware of this distinction. Indeed, there are clearly observable differences between sleep and wakefulness. During sleep there is a much greater relaxation of the muscles, less responsivity to stimulation, and a characteristic brain-wave pattern. And, as we shall see, there are also distinctions among stages of sleep.

Patterns of Sleep

Most animals sleep about the same amount and at the same time every day. Some sleep at night as we do, in part because they rely so heavily on their sense of sight for capturing game or finding food. But a whole world of animals sleeps during the day and is active at night. Some zoos have "night houses" in which you can observe this nocturnal counterpart to the daytime animal kingdom.

Although humans seem quite flexible about their sleeping schedules, everyone gets used to a particular pattern, and it can be extremely difficult to adjust to a new pattern. If you usually sleep from midnight to 8 A.M. and then stay awake all one night, you will probably be somewhat inefficient and generally disorganized next day—more so, perhaps, than you would expect just from lack of sleep. You may also find it hard to fall asleep the next night. This effect is familiar to people who fly across several time zones. The resulting "jet lag" interferes with behavior and thinking to such an extent that many corporations require their executives to rest for a day or two after a long trip before conducting any important business. This is one more phenomenon of modern life that evolution did not prepare us for. As we noted in Chapter 9, the limitations on our mechanisms of adaptation and on our built-in warning systems become most apparent when we face new environmental stresses that we ourselves have produced.

The difficulty of adapting to these kinds of time changes is magnified by "biological clocks" that seem to be present in most animals. The processes of the body have certain patterns, called *circadian* ("about a day") *rhythms* because they are more active at certain times of day and less at others. Although it is possible to change it over a period of several days, the rhythm does not respond quickly to abrupt changes in the individual's sleeping pattern. Thus when people who usually sleep at night start to work nights and sleep during the day, they will have difficulty because their bodies are still on the original rhythm. Their high internal activity level during the day will interfere with sleeping while the low level at night will reduce their energy.

Stages of Sleep

Most of us probably make a rough distinction between light sleep and deep sleep, but research has indicated that there are actually four

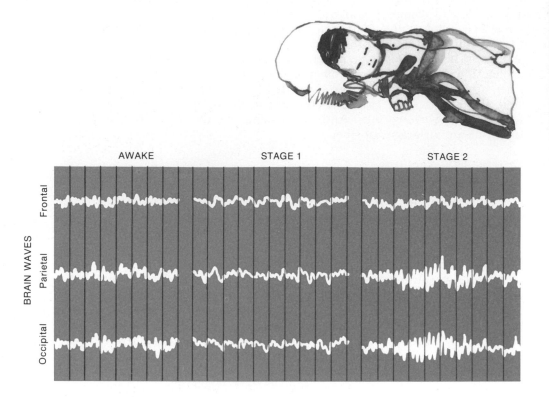

Fig. 11.1
Brain waves (EEGs) during wakefulness and levels of sleep

The closer together the waves, the more mental activity. Note that the dream state is more active than the other levels of sleep. (After Kleitman, 1960)

different stages of sleep. Mental activity can be measured by attaching electrodes to the head and recording electrical impulses in the brain. This record is called an *electroencephalogram* or *EEG*. By means of this technique, it has been shown that mental activity becomes less and less as we go from Stage 1 to Stage 4 sleep (Dement and Kleitman, 1957). As you can see in Fig. 11.1, the first two stages have small, rapid waves; these waves become slower from one stage to the next until in Stage 4 there are only large, slow *Delta waves*. Since it is the speed rather than the size of the waves that indicates activity, clearly there is less going on in Stage 4 than in Stage 1. Also, as one goes from Stage 1 to Stage 4, the body is less reactive to external noises (Williams, Tepas, and Morlock, 1962). A telephone ringing or someone entering the room will produce less of a reaction in Stage 4 than in any of the other stages. Measures of bodily activity also suggest that the organism is more slowed down in the deeper stages, less active physiologically. Blood pressure, heart rate, and respiration all decrease during sleep, and do so more in these deeper stages (Snyder et al., 1964). Finally, and most conclusively, the individual is harder to awaken from Stage 4 than from Stage 1. Thus, all of these measures indicate that there are stages of sleep that range from light to very deep.

STAGE 3   STAGE 4   REM SLEEP

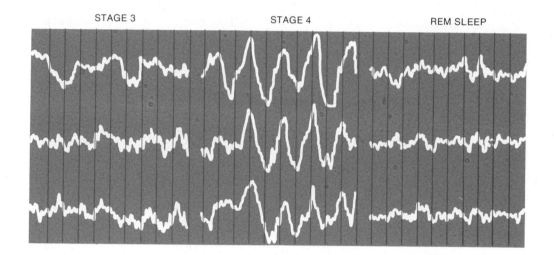

REM sleep That is not the whole story, however. The most important and fascinating discovery of this research is that during Stage 1 a unique phenomenon occurs. Aserinsky and Kleitman (1953) noticed that at certain times while the individual is in Stage 1, a series of dramatic changes occur. First, the subject's closed eyes begin to move very quickly, almost as if watching something. This so-called *rapid eye movement*, or REM, is so characteristic of this phenomenon that it has come to be called REM sleep.

Second, as you can see in Fig. 11.1, EEG's indicate that REM sleep is also characterized by high mental activity. Stage 1 is generally a fairly active time, but it becomes even more active when rapid eye movements are occurring. Third, the bodily functions also become more active. Temperature increases, and other measurements show that there is a considerable amount of arousal. Fourth, although this is a period of heightened activity in many ways, the muscles, paradoxically, become extremely relaxed. In fact, almost all muscle tone is lost, as if the muscles have been in some way detached from the activating mechanism in the brain. Yet occasionally a muscle will be activated despite this apparent uncoupling, and twitching will occur. Thus, REM sleep is a complex and contradictory combination of symptoms—heightened activity in terms of eye movements, brain waves, and other physiological indicators, but extreme muscle relaxation. In addition, despite the fact that individuals are in Stage 1 during REM sleep, it is extremely difficult to wake them up. These contradictory symptoms have caused some people to call REM sleep *paradoxical sleep* to reflect these seeming inconsistencies.

The Function of Sleep

It is clear that sleep is necessary for the normal functioning of any animal. A total lack of sleep produces not only fatigue but also much more extreme reactions such as depression, disorganized activity, hallucinations, and eventually even death. An animal that has not slept for a long time will lapse into sleep almost instantly if it is not deliberately kept awake. Keeping a person awake is a particularly vicious form of torture. It has frequently been employed in the so-called brainwashing of political prisoners, in which the goal is to weaken and disorient the individuals to the point that their most basic beliefs and values can be altered.

On the other hand, people seem to be able to recover from a lack of sleep very quickly. Peter Tripp, a New York City disc jockey, stayed awake for two hundred hours to get publicity for the Polio Fund (and perhaps for himself as well). Accounts of this ordeal describe how he became severely depressed and distracted, lost the ability to pay attention for more than a few seconds, could not work simple math problems, and developed extreme hallucinations. He saw the clock as an actor made up to be Dracula, imagined flames coming from his bureau, and thought a doctor was actually an undertaker. Yet he was able to perform the necessary functions of the show, organized records and commercials, and never did anything terribly inappropriate while he was on the air. But perhaps the most impressive aspect of the case was that after two hundred hours without sleep, one good thirteen-hour sleep removed virtually all of the bad effects and he appeared perfectly normal again. In other words, sleep deprivation can have dramatic negative effects, but these do not appear to last once the person gets some sleep. There may be some point beyond which the effects are not reversible, but we do not know what that is for humans.

It is not clear why sleep is necessary or why being deprived of it produces such strong reactions. There is little question that we need a certain amount of sleep to function normally, and that eventually a lack of sleep would be fatal. Sleep appears to refresh and revitalize the body; without it many of the vital mechanisms appear to run down or operate poorly. Yet we do not know how this revitalization is accomplished, nor why just resting does not have the same effect.

The Function of REM Sleep

Just as animals need sleep, there is some indication that they also need a certain amount of REM sleep. The need is not as obvious and the effects are less extreme, but research by Dement and others (Dement, 1960; Dement and Fisher, 1963) suggests that REM deprivation may also have negative effects.

One research technique is to deprive subjects of REM sleep but let them have other kinds of sleep by waking them up whenever rapid

WILLIAM C. DEMENT

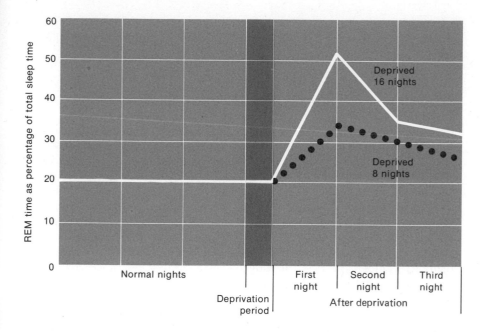

Fig. 11.2
REM sleep after deprivation

A subject is allowed to sleep but prevented from having REM sleep. When he is then allowed to sleep without any interference, the amount of REM sleep increases greatly from a normal baseline, in direct proportion to how long he was deprived. (After Dement, 1965)

eye movements begin. They may get the normal amount of sleep, but they will not get any REM sleep. They can then be compared to people who were awakened the same number of times but during a different phase of sleep. In this way all the subjects will get the same amount of sleep, but some will get little or no REM sleep while the others will get the normal amount.

The research shows that there is a clear tendency to make up for REM sleep that has been lost (Dement, 1960). As you can see in Fig. 11.2, someone who has had no REM sleep for eight days will have more than usual when given the chance. In fact, the additional REM sleep is almost exactly the amount that was lost during the deprivation period. It is almost as if the body needs a certain amount of REM sleep, and when it does not get it the need builds up. This same pattern occurs with other animals such as cats and dogs. Thus, the first finding is that animals get a regular amount of REM sleep each night and, if not, will have additional REM sleep to make up for what they missed.

The second finding is much less certain. A number of experimenters (Dement, 1965; Hoedemaker et al., 1963) have concluded from the previous result the animals need REM sleep and that if they do not get it they will suffer negative consequences. People who volunteered to go without REM sleep for long periods of time did appear to be more nervous and irritable than usual, and some of them actually got quite upset. In addition, cats who were deprived of REM sleep seemed to observers to be extremely nervous and jumpy (Jouvet, 1964). But these judgments were quite subjective; generally this research has not run adequate controls, and other studies have not confirmed these observations (Sampson, 1965). Thus there is still some question whether people or cats actually do suffer noticeable ill effects just because they are deprived of REM sleep. Humans and cats that are so deprived certainly function more or less normally and suffer no evident physical disability. In short, it is not clear that animals really need REM sleep in order to function normally.

DREAMS

People dream during REM sleep. A person awakened during REM sleep usually reports having just dreamed—the percentage of dream reports ranges from 75 percent (Kremen, 1961) to 93 percent (Stoyva, 1965). Someone awakened from non-REM sleep rarely says that he was just dreaming—percentages range from 0 percent (Dement, 1955) to 34 percent (Goodenough et al., 1959). When a person reports dreaming during non-REM sleep, the dreams tend to be less well remembered and less well organized (Monroe et al., 1965). Therefore, most researchers feel that full-fledged dreams occur only or mainly during REM sleep and that most of the time someone is in REM sleep, she is in fact dreaming. In other words, for an adult human being, REM sleep and dreaming are almost synonymous. This implies that REM sleep could be a different state of consciousness from either wakefulness or other kinds of sleep. The individual is not awake, but neither is her mind at rest. There is a strong contradiction between the active mind and the very relaxed muscles.

Who Dreams?

It is difficult to be certain whether everyone dreams. We do know that everyone has REM sleep. In fact, all people of the same age appear to have just about the same percentage of REM sleep. As you can see in Fig. 11.3, infants have a great deal of REM sleep, with the amount decreasing somewhat up to the age of four and then staying about the same. That pattern holds for the percentage of total sleep that is made up of REM sleep, but people tend to get less sleep as they get older. Therefore, the actual hours of REM sleep do decline somewhat with age. But at all ages and for all people, REM sleep does make up at least 20 percent of the total time spent sleeping, and that means at least an hour and a half to two hours of REM sleep each night.

Because everyone has REM sleep, most investigators have concluded that everyone must dream. Since REM sleep is so closely associated with dreaming, it does seem as if even people who cannot recall dreams probably do have them. But the only clear indication of whether or not a dream has occurred is the person's own memory of it. If he does not remember, all we can say with certainty is that he did or did not experience REM sleep.

There is no question that some people normally recall a great many dreams in vivid detail while others recall few or none. This also occurs if people are awakened from REM sleep. Once again, some people will consistently report dreams while others will not. But the nonreporters have the same amount of REM sleep as the reporters (Antrobus, Dement, and Fisher, 1964). Therefore, our best guess at the moment is that everyone does dream, but some people, for one reason or another, do not remember their dreams.

Certainly dreams are difficult to remember. Sometimes you wake up and vividly recall exactly what you were dreaming, but most

"Falling" dreams are very common. They may represent fear of falling, but also may involve concerns about loss of control, sexuality, excitement, and probably other areas as well.

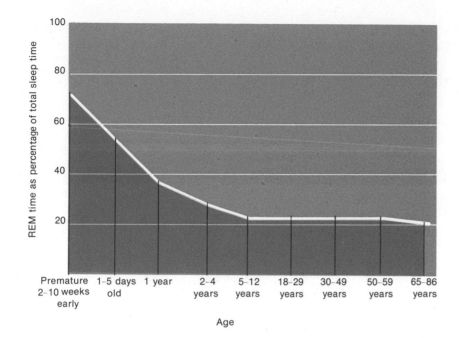

Fig. 11.3
REM and age

Newborns and infants have much more REM sleep than older children, but there is little change after about the age of five. (After Kales, 1968)

of the time a dream seems vague once you have awakened. In fact, unless you tell someone what you have dreamed, write it down, or at least rehearse it immediately, even those portions that you remember on awakening will soon disappear. Most of us have had the experience of waking up after a dream and remembering it perfectly, but being unable to recall even the simplest details a few hours later.

This aspect of dreams is closely related to the problem of memory consolidation that we discussed in Chapter 4. In a sense, dreams are experiences or bits of information given under conditions that tend to make them difficult to remember. The individual is in a relatively nonattentive, nonaware state. The dreams themselves are usually disorganized or confusing, and the material often seems illogical. Furthermore, the dreamer makes no effort to learn or rehearse the material as it appears. As we would expect from research on memory, information presented under these circumstances can be remembered immediately afterwards, but, unless something is done to consolidate it, it will soon be lost. Rather than going into long-term memory where it would be retained, most of it simply disappears from the memory store. On the other hand, if the person consolidates the information by saying it out loud, writing it down, or rehearsing it to himself, it is much more likely that he will remember. If you tell someone a dream immediately after awakening, you can then recall the dream yourself even much later. Thus, the difficulty of remembering dreams should not be considered mysterious or strange. Any information presented under these circumstances would be hard to recall, and dreams are no exception.

Freud's Theory of Dreams

Sigmund Freud called dreams "the royal road to the unconscious." He believed (1953; original 1900) that dreams are manifestations of hid-

BOX 11.1

THE CONTENT OF DREAMS

Although dreams can be very strange, eerie, and seemingly unique, there is actually a considerable amount of consistency in what people dream about. As you can see in the table, 83 percent of the college students interviewed reported dreaming at least once in the last few months about falling, 77 percent dreamed about being attacked or pursued, and 71 percent dreamed about trying repeatedly to do something. While it is hardly surprising that they also dreamed often about school, sex, and even food, dreams dealing with severe fright, losing a loved one, snakes, and fire are not so obviously related to their daily lives. Presumably, many of these dreams had symbolic significance. For example, falling, trying repeatedly, and arriving late all may involve fear of failure or loss of control, but they may also have sexual significance for the individual.

THE TWENTY MOST COMMON DREAMS OF COLLEGE STUDENTS AND THE PERCENTAGE HAVING EACH TYPE OF DREAM

Type of dream	Percentage of students
Falling	83
Being attacked or pursued	77
Trying repeatedly to do something	71
School, teachers, studying	71
Sexual experiences	66
Arriving too late	64
Eating	62
Being frozen with fright	58
A loved person is dead	57
Being locked up	56
Finding money	56
Swimming	52
Snakes	49
Being inappropriately dressed	46
Being smothered	44
Being nude in public	43
Fire	41
Failing an examination	39
Seeing self as dead	33
Killing someone	26

Source: Griffith, Miyagi, and Tago, 1958

den conflicts, desires, and unconscious impulses. As we shall see in more detail in Chapter 14, one of the central points of Freud's theory of psychoanalysis is that everyone has unconscious impulses, fears, and desires that have important effects on their lives. Freud felt that these impulses were always trying to come to the surface, to be expressed in some way. One such way is in dreams. When individuals are asleep, their ordinary controls and defenses are weaker and the impulses are therefore more easily expressed.

Manifest and latent content There are two additional aspects to this theory of dreams. First, the unconscious impulses are not expressed directly; they appear in disguised form. According to Freud, the content of the dream is based on the activities of the day and current concern of the dreamer. This is the so-called *manifest content*. If the person has just taken a plane ride, she may dream about flying; if she is studying for a test, she might dream about the test. But this manifest content of the dream conceals the so-called *latent content*, which is much more important. The unconscious impulses and conflicts are represented in the dream in disguised and distorted ways. Various disguises are used, such as *symbolization* (something stands for something else), *condensation* (two or more things are combined into one and time is condensed), and *displacement* (the focus of the conflict is shifted to someone or something else). For example, suppose you are very angry at your teacher and a friend. You may have a dream in which you swing a baseball bat at an oddly shaped football that has long hair and a piece of chalk stuck to it. A possible interpretation is that the bat stands for a weapon (symbolization), the football represents both your teacher and friend (symbolization and condensation), and your anger has been displaced to sports. Thus the true meaning of the dream appears in the manifest content but in a distorted and ambiguous form. It is not always easy to discover the latent content of a dream. Part of psychoanalysis consists of analyzing dreams to discover their hidden meanings.

It is not an accident that the latent content appears in disguised form. These unconscious impulses and conflicts are upsetting and disturbing (you do not want to be angry at your friend), and so people manage not to think about them or to be aware of them during the day. But when sleep relaxes the defenses, the person's impulses and conflicts are expressed. However, they are expressed in a disguised form because otherwise they would be too upsetting. Expressing them reduces somewhat the stress they produce, but they have to be expressed in a way that does not make the person feel too uncomfortable.

Wish fulfillment This leads to the second aspect of Freud's theory, which is that all dreams represent wish fulfillment. He felt that every dream expresses an unconscious desire or wish of the dreamer. Even when the manifest content and latent content seem to be very upsetting and forbidden, Freud felt that they represented a wish on the part of the individual. For example, it is quite common to dream of one's parents dying. These tend to be unpleasant, even nightmarish dreams. Yet Freud would say that most people do have an unconscious wish for their parents to die and the dream is simply representing it; or perhaps the dream represents a wish for the parents to suffer, not necessarily die.

Purpose of dreams Freud felt that the purpose of the dream was to keep the person asleep by reducing the stress caused by unconscious conflicts. If these impulses and conflicts are not expressed at all, the stress builds up and might awaken the person. During the day, one's defenses are generally strong enough to keep these impulses under control (although, as we shall see, they do have important influences on behavior). At night, however, when the individual's defenses are weaker, these impulses are expressed more readily and might be so upsetting that they would wake him up. When the impulses are expressed in dreams, the stress is reduced somewhat and the individual can continue sleeping. And as we noted, the fact that they are disguised prevents the impulses from becoming too upsetting. Thus, a "successful" dream consists of a disguised expression of an unconscious conflict, which reduces the strength of that conflict and thereby allows the individual to stay asleep.

Freud's theory of dreams has transformed our thinking about this subject. Practically everyone now takes it for granted that dreams often have meaning and that their significance is sometimes disguised. The symbolic meaning of objects that appear in dreams is not only part of cocktail conversation, but is to some extent accepted by most psychologists. After all, we use symbols while we are awake, so why should we doubt that they occur in dreams? No one would have

Figure 11.4

any difficulty understanding the sexual symbolism shown in Fig. 11.4. In the appropriate context climbing a staircase could symbolize success, falling could mean failure, flying excitement, a long stick a penis, and so on. There are no consistent rules for what something symbolizes—objects and actions mean different things to different people and in different contexts. But the notion that dreams sometimes represent something other than their manifest content is now generally accepted.

Criticisms of Freud's view There are two points, however, on which many people disagree with Freud or at least take milder stands. Freud said that *all* dreams represent unconsciously motivated wish fulfillment. It seems more likely that this holds only for *some* dreams. Other dreams may represent conscious desires, conscious or unconscious fears, and sometimes more or less random mental activity. Just as the waking mind contains all sorts of thoughts and ideas ranging from well-organized plans and desires to haphazard, fleeting notions and momentary thoughts of individuals and objects, so does the mind when it is asleep. If someone is worried about taking an exam, a dream in which she fails the exam represents her fear rather than a wish to fail. Most people have really frightening nightmares occasionally. Feldman and Hersen (1967) report that 86 percent of college students had at least one nightmare in the last year. It is difficult to consider these as wish fulfillment rather than fears, but the fears may be very deep and perhaps unconscious.

There are also sometimes obvious conscious relationships between dreams and waking life. If someone is hungry he tends to dream about food. There is nothing hidden in the dream, nothing disguised; the person wishes to eat, so he dreams about food. Naturally, such a dream can also include disguised, unconscious conflicts, but at least some of the time it will be only an expression of a conscious desire.

In many other cases, the content of a single dream may include random associations to events of the day; conscious concerns, ideas, projects, and even distant memories that have been aroused by association with current activities. Sometimes dreams feature people we have not seen for many years, and we may wake up amazed that we even remembered them. This is a fascinating aspect of dreams, and one that is not fully explained. But even this need not be interpreted in terms of an unconscious wish or conflict. It may be that something during the day triggered the memory even though we were not aware of it at the time. Or it may be that when we are asleep, our associations are looser and freer and so more distant memories are stirred up.

Thus, the most likely explanation of the meaning of dreams is a variation of Freud's original analysis. We would accept Freud's proposition that dreams have meaning, that they involve disguised and distorted content, and that this content is often of unconscious origin. But we would add that not all dreams are disguised or unconsciously determined or represent wish fulfillment; sometimes they are manifestations of conscious fears and desires or even just random associations.

AGGRESSION IN DREAMS

As we have mentioned before, sex and aggression are the two motives most carefully controlled by our society. Most other motives can be expressed in action more or less whenever we want, but, according to society's rules, these two must be expressed only in certain circumstances and with certain people. We may not always follow these rules exactly, and of course each of us and each group in society has somewhat different rules. Nevertheless, even the person who is "freest" from societal constraints does not express either sexual or aggressive feelings whenever and wherever they occur. Therefore, it is not surprising that sex and aggression show up a great deal in dreams, where the rules and constraints are weaker or are entirely absent. Obviously, it is more acceptable to express sexual or aggressive feelings in dreams, because the dream is fantasy. Moreover, we generally assume that dreams are not under the control of the person having them, and thus no blame is attached to them (although if you dream about having sex with someone other than your usual partner, the partner might be jealous even though it was just fantasy because we also assume that dreams to some extent indicate our desires).

As we saw in the table in Box 11.1, sexual experiences, nudity, and various symbols that might represent sex occur often in dreams. The table shows that aggression is also very common. People dream often about murder, physical attacks, destroying property, and many other kinds of overt aggression. They also dream about aggression being directed at themselves. Freud would argue that these dreams express aggressive impulses that we do not or cannot express as behavior. Even the aggression directed at the self is an expression of feelings of guilt. Whether all dreams of aggression are due to specific feelings of aggression toward the objects or people in the dreams is questionable. But it is clear that we all have angers, frustrations, and irritations that we experience during the day and do not act on. When we are asleep, these feelings sometimes emerge in the form of dreams. Dreaming that you killed your mother does not mean literally that you would like to kill her, but it may mean that you are angry at her. In the same way, dreaming that your mother kills you does not ordinarily mean that you wish she would or that you are afraid she will. Rather it may mean that you realize she is angry at you, or that you feel guilty about not visiting or calling her and you think you should be punished, or it can mean that you are angry at her and the dream reverses the direction of the aggression. The point is that dreams of aggression often are expressions of negative feelings that we all feel but cannot express openly.

Box 11.2

Jung's Contribution to Dream Theory

Carl Jung, an important disciple of Freud's, offered a somewhat different view of dreams (see Chapter 14 for further discussion of Jung's ideas). Although Jung (1944) agreed that dreams have meaning and symbolism, he went further than Freud in his interpretations. He felt that dreams sometimes expressed unconscious memories and beliefs that were somehow common to all humanity. Each individual has access to a pool of these memories—what Jung called the *collective* or *universal unconscious*—but they generally do not appear when we are awake. They appear in our dreams and give us insights and knowledge that we cannot get in any other way.

This is a rather mysterious notion, with mystical overtones. However, put in a slightly different way it seems to fit more easily into scientific psychology. Jung felt that people have strengths and ways of thought that are rarely accessible to their conscious, waking mind. These creative, free forms of expression and thinking come out in dreams and, if remembered, can be helpful when the person is awake. In some sense, dreams become predictions of the future—not because the person is really seeing into the future, but because the dreams reveal possible actions by the person that she might not have thought of otherwise. In other words, it is not magic but insight into ourselves that dreams provide. As such, the theory is not entirely different from Freud's. The major difference is that Jung sees the function of dreams as more creative and positive—not just as a release of tension and protection of sleep but as productive mental activity.

HYPNOSIS

If a willing person relaxes, concentrates on some object such as a blinking light or a star fixed on the wall, tries to make his mind a blank or at least not think intentionally about other matters, and finally puts himself in another person's hands, sometimes he will become hypnotized. He is not asleep when this happens, but neither is he in a normal waking state. In fact, *hypnosis* has some of the characteristics of both wakefulness and sleep and in that sense is almost a combination of the two.

In many respects the hypnotized subject behaves quite normally. He responds to stimulation, and can work effectively on tasks, solve problems, and interact with other people. He is obviously much more alert and capable of reacting to the situation than is a sleeping person. Although you would be unlikely to confuse a sleepwalker with someone who is awake, it is much more difficult to recognize that someone is hypnotized.

On the other hand, there are certain characteristics of hypnosis that distinguish it quite clearly from both wakefulness and sleep. Although not all hypnotized subjects will have all of these symptoms, anyone who is deeply hypnotized will have many of them. Thus it is fair to say that a state of hypnosis tends to produce the following symptoms.

Heightened suggestibility. The most important characteristic, without which hypnosis would not really exist, is a heightened suggestibility. There is some question whether a hypnotized subject is generally more suggestible, but there is no question that she is more likely to accept and follow the suggestions of the hypnotist. In fact, all of the other important characteristics of hypnosis seem to follow from this

The hypnosis of consenting witnesses is increasingly being used as a police investigating tool. Police report that witnesses can frequently remember details that they have forgotten, repressed, or never consciously knew in the first place. However, there is no reliable scientific evidence to support this.

increase in suggestibility, combined with a tendency for the individual to place unusual reliance on the hypnotist.

Acceptance of distortion. Perceptual and time distortions suggested by the hypnotist are accepted unquestioningly. If the hypnotized subject is told that a white wall is painted red, that there is a dog on his lap, that someone who is actually in the room is invisible, that twenty minutes took only five seconds, or practically any other kind of distortion, he will tend not to question it. And he can focus his attention on one stimulus to the extent of hearing only one voice in a crowd or entirely ignoring a flashing light.

Acting out of suggestions. The hypnotized subject will perform acts, follow a sequence of behavior, and play a role suggested by the hypnotist. He will lift his arms, pretend he is a duck, act as if he were a policeman, and do whatever the hypnotist orders. One particularly fascinating demonstration of this is so-called *age regression*, in which the subject is told he is only a few years old and asked to act out his life at that time. Under hypnosis, some subjects can relive an earlier period of their lives with considerable accuracy and detail. Hypnosis can release some of the inhibitions that most of us feel and enable subjects to act out roles with more feeling and enthusiasm than they ordinarily would be able to display. However, there is no evidence that hypnosis improves ordinary memory (Cooper and London, 1973).

Distortion in the individual's bodily state. This can be produced by suggestion. The hypnotized subject can be told that her arm is rigid, and in fact she will be unable to move it. Subjects can be told that they do not feel sensation or pain in a particular part of the body and their sensitivity will decrease sharply (Hilgard et al., 1974). A standard test of hypnosis is to tell the subject to link her fingers together and then suggest that she is unable to separate them. Under deep hypnosis, subjects will be unable to pull their hands apart. Some subjects can make their bodies so rigid that someone can actually sit on them if they are placed with their head on one chair and their feet on another. Once again, although this seems to be a mysterious effect of hypnosis, many people have performed even more amazing feats of strength in emergencies. And, as we mentioned in Chapter 6, yogis and others sometimes attain remarkable control over their bodily processes without the aid of hypnosis.

Post-hypnotic amnesia (loss of memory). If it is suggested, most well-hypnotized subjects will forget what has occurred under hypnosis. They can also be given a *post-hypnotic suggestion*, a command to be carried out at a certain time. Then, even after they have been awakened, they will obey the command when the appropriate circumstances present themselves. Apparently these post-hypnotic suggestions can be extremely powerful even though the individual is unaware of them. An example of this is given in Box 11.3. Note that

Box 11.3

AN EXAMPLE OF POST-HYPNOTIC SUGGESTION

"During profound hypnosis the subject was instructed to feel that smoking was a bad habit, that he both loved and hated it, that he wanted to get over the habit but that he felt it was too strong a habit to break, that he would be very reluctant to smoke and would give anything not to smoke, but that he would find himself compelled to smoke; and that after he was awakened he would experience all of these feelings.

"After he was awakened the subject was drawn into a casual conversation with the hypnotist who, lighting one himself, offered him a cigarette. The subject waved it aside with the explanation that he had his own and that he preferred Camels, and promptly began to reach for his own pack. Instead of looking in his customary pocket, however, he seemed to forget where he carried his cigarettes and searched fruitlessly through all of his other pockets with a gradually increasing concern. Finally, after having sought them repeatedly in all other pockets, he located his cigarettes in their usual place. He took them out, engaged in a brief conversation as he dallied with the pack, and then began a search for matches which he failed to find. During his search for matches he replaced the cigarettes in his pocket and began using both hands, finally locating the matches too in their usual pocket. Having done this, he now began using both hands to search for his cigarettes. He finally located them but then found that he had once more misplaced his matches. This time however he kept his cigarettes in hand while attempting to relocate the matches. He then placed a cigarette in his mouth and struck a match. As he struck it, however, he began a conversation which so engrossed him that he forgot the match and allowed it to burn his finger tips whereupon, with a grimace of pain, he tossed it in the ash tray. Immediately he took another match, but again introduced a diverting topic by asking the audience in a humorous fashion if they knew the 'Scotch' way of lighting a cigarette. As interest was shown, he carefully split the match through the middle. One half of the match he replaced in his pocket in a time-consuming manner and tried to light his cigarette with the other half. When it gave too feeble a flame he discarded it and had to search for the second half. After striking this another interesting topic of conversation developed and again he burned his fingers before he made use of it. He apologized for his failure to demonstrate the 'Scotch' light successfully and repeated the performance, this time holding the flame in such a way as to ignite only a small corner of the cigarette from which he succeeded in getting only one satisfactory puff. . . ." (Erickson, 1939, pp. 342–344)

the man who was told not to smoke does everything possible to obey his instructions despite the fact that he wants to smoke and does not know that he has been told not to.

Is Hypnosis a Real Phenomenon?

From this list of reactions it might seem obvious that hypnosis is a very different state from normal wakefulness. However, some scientists remain skeptical about hypnosis. They argue that the supposedly hypnotized subject may be only in a highly suggestible state. Subjects do whatever the hypnotist asks because they have agreed to put themselves into her hands and to obey her. They are not asleep, they are not in an altered state of consciousness, they are simply trying their best to follow orders.

These skeptics (particularly Barber, 1969) say that in a normal wakeful state some people are indeed highly suggestible. If the situation is set up correctly, many people will perform acts and have sensory distortions without being hypnotized. Barber and Glass (1962) simply suggested a list of effects to a group of unhypnotized subjects. Even without a hypnotic trance, some of the subjects felt their arms grow heavy and then light, locked their hands and could not separate them, and had hallucinations of being thirsty and of their body being rigid. And Orne (1962) demonstrated that subjects who were told to pretend that they were hypnotized performed antisocial and dangerous acts just as readily as did hypnotized subjects. Other research has shown that the degree of suggestibility under hypnosis is highly related to how suggestible the person is when he is not hypnotized. This raises the question of whether hypnosis is really a different state of consciousness or simply a situation that demonstrates how highly suggestible some people are.

It is good to be skeptical about a subject that is still frequently associated with magic. Nonetheless, most current evidence favors the idea that hypnosis is a separate state or at least a powerful phenomenon separate from normal experience. The main argument for this position is that some of the effects produced by hypnosis either do not occur during wakefulness or can be produced only in extreme situations and with selected individuals. For example, the sensory hallucinations that occur quite readily under hypnosis are extremely difficult to produce in a normal, wide-awake person. Skeptics suggest that the hypnotized subject may be pretending that the white wall is really red or that the person is invisible. But under intense questioning, the hypnotized subjects usually insist that this is not the case. Similarly, the various bodily distortions such as stiff arms, locked fingers, and bodily rigidity can occasionally be duplicated by a waking person and could conceivably be faked, but it seems much more likely that hypnosis produces a real effect.

Research on the effect of hypnosis on pain provides strong evidence for this viewpoint. In a number of studies subjects were hypnotized and told that they would not feel pain; other subjects were given a placebo (a harmless drug) and told that it would eliminate pain. And a third group received neither hypnosis nor a placebo. All subjects were urged to withstand as much pain as they possibly could. Then they were exposed to a painful stimulus. In one experiment (McGlashin, Evans, and Orne, 1969) a tourniquet was applied to the right arm to stop the flow of blood. This ordinarily produces a great

THEODORE X. BARBER

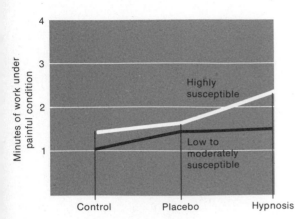

Fig. 11.5
Hypnosis and pain

A placebo increased ability to stand pain, but for good hypnotic subjects hypnosis produces a much greater effect. (After McGlashin, Evans, and Orne, 1969)

ERNEST R. HILGARD

deal of pain that continues to increase as the tourniquet is left on. As you can see in Fig. 11.5, the placebo did increase the amount of pain that was withstood compared to the control group, but for subjects known to be easily hypnotized, hypnosis produced an even stronger effect. In other words, even the urging of the experimenter plus the placebo instruction did not enable the subject to endure as much pain as did a strong hypnotic suggestion. A case study on one student showed that hypnosis actually reduced the physiological reaction to pain (Zimbardo, Rapaport, and Baron, 1969). Other studies have produced corresponding results, suggesting that hypnosis has a real effect on response to pain that cannot be duplicated simply by strong suggestion in the waking state.

Thus, our best current evidence indicates hypnosis is a state of consciousness somewhat different from either normal wakefulness or sleeping. It is characterized primarily by a heightened suggestibility, but it does not seem to be simply a highly suggestible normal state. On the contrary, deep hypnosis produces effects that are difficult or impossible to produce in a normally wakeful person.

Is Cooperation Necessary?

There are three questions most people ask when they think about hypnosis. Who can be hypnotized? Can people be hypnotized against their will? Can people be made to do something antisocial, dangerous, or immoral under hypnosis that they would not do if awake? The answer to the first question is that many people cannot be hypnotized even when they cooperate. Only about 60 percent can be hypnotized at all. Fewer than 25 percent can achieve deep hypnosis and experience post-hypnotic amnesia. And only 5 or 10 percent of the population go "deep" enough to have visual hallucinations (Hilgard, 1965). These figures are quite consistent across different populations. However, despite considerable research, no clear picture of the hypnotic subject has emerged. Hilgard, a leader in this field, suggests that good hypnotic subjects tend to be open to new experiences, interested in mental rather than physical activities, and not especially troubled or neurotic. Moreover, the good subject is not particularly weak or dependent (Hilgard, 1965). But these generalizations are highly speculative. At the moment, we are not able to identify with any certainty who will and who will not be a good subject. The only reliable method of finding out is to try to hypnotize the person and see what happens.

The answer to the question of whether people can be hypnotized against their will is almost certainly no. Indeed, the essential element in hypnosis appears to be a willingness to give up some control to the other person. Anyone who resists even slightly will probably not be hypnotized. It is conceivable that someone who is greatly fatigued or under the influence of a drug might be put under hypnosis against his will, but even this seems unlikely.

The answer to the third question is more complicated. Although there is little good, controlled research on the subject, the evidence from anecdotal descriptions and experienced hypnotists suggests that people cannot be made to commit crimes or immoral acts under hypnosis if they would not do them when they were awake. If someone is deeply hypnotized and told to go out and shoot the first person he sees, he will not obey. If a modest person is hypnotized in front of an audience and told to strip, the order will be disobeyed. A direct command to commit this kind of an act will not be effective as long as the person would refuse to do it when awake.

On the other hand, hypnotized subjects can sometimes be "tricked" into committing such acts. The hypnotist can change and distort the whole situation so that the act no longer seems criminal or immoral. For example, the subject can be told that she is carrying not a gun but a cigarette lighter, which she should point at the first person she sees and press the trigger. Under these circumstances, if she accepts this distortion of reality, the subject might shoot the gun. Or the person on stage can be told that he is alone in the shower, where taking off his clothes would be neither immodest nor indecent. Thus, although a direct request to commit antisocial acts might be refused, perhaps a skillful hypnotist can distort the situation and cause the individual to commit such acts.

Rowland (1939) asked hypnotized subjects to reach into a rattlesnake cage and pick up the "rope." Although it was a real snake, most subjects obeyed. Lyon (1954) told hypnotized subjects to pour "acid" on their hands and few did it, but when he then said that the acid was harmless, they all acquiesced. When Watkins (1947) told a soldier that the person in front of him was an enemy who was about to attack, the soldier lunged so fiercely with a bayonet that he had to be restrained. (In all cases, of course, the situation was arranged so that no harm could befall the subject or anyone else.)

Despite these demonstrations, considerable doubt remains as to the effect of hypnosis in these situations. In a symposium on this subject, Kline (1972) and Watkins (1972) both proposed that hypnosis could produce antisocial or harmful acts, but they agreed that the evidence was not yet sufficient to reach a firm conclusion. Orne (1972) took the position that the evidence is almost impossible to evaluate because it is difficult to separate the effects of hypnosis from those of any close relationship. Surely, someone would also perform many acts for someone they loved or trusted very much, and perhaps that is all hypnosis does. The subject may simply assume that the experimenter or hypnotist (or loved one) will not allow anything bad to happen, and therefore feels free to obey any command.

This research implies that hypnosis should be used with great care and people should not allow themselves to be hypnotized unless they fully trust the person doing the hypnosis. Although there is little evidence that anyone has used hypnosis for evil or unpleasant purposes, the potential for such use does exist.

MARTIN T. ORNE

Uses of Hypnosis

Hypnosis has found several uses in medicine and psychotherapy. It can be used to relax a patient so that certain kinds of medical procedures can be performed without anesthetics (Schafer, 1975). When no particular pain is involved but it is important that the individual be quiet and relaxed, hypnosis can also sometimes be successful. In addition, it can reduce the anxiety connected with operations and other medical problems, thus relieving some of the psychological suffering. Finally, hypnosis can sometimes reduce the pain sufficiently so that no anesthetic is necessary. This is particularly true in dentistry, where it is usually advisable for the patient to be awake but where pain can be quite severe. The patient can be placed under hypnosis and told that she will not feel the pain in her mouth, and then the dentist can proceed. This avoids the problems connected with anesthesia and is highly effective for hypnotizable patients.

Hypnosis is used in psychotherapy to relax the patient and sometimes to reduce resistance to therapy or to facilitate memory. It has also been used extensively in specialized therapies such as those that help a person stop smoking or eat less. The person is hypnotized, told that he will no longer like the taste of cigarettes or feel like eating much, and given a post-hypnotic suggestion to this effect (Stanton, 1975). As you can see in Box 11.3, these suggestions are often quite effective in producing temporary abstinence. Hypnosis is also used to fight specific fears, such as the fear of flying. Once again, the patient is hypnotized and told that she will no longer be afraid of airplanes. There have been few careful studies of these procedures, however, so it is difficult to evaluate their effectiveness.

MEDITATION

Hypnosis is produced by concentrating on an object or spot of light, trying to make your mind blank, and entrusting yourself to another person. A state of meditation is reached in a similar way, but without the necessity of another individual. Instead, the person who wants to meditate focuses on a word, object, or aspect of his own body, and by concentrating manages to achieve a state of consciousness that seems to be different from normal wakefulness.

There are various specific procedures by which people reach this meditative state. Zen Buddhism tells beginners to sit motionless and concentrate on their breathing, counting each breath and thinking of nothing else. They might then pay attention not so much to the number of breaths as to the process of breathing itself. This repetitive, continuous activity is like counting sheep when trying to sleep. It also resembles the procedure of counting backwards from one hundred by threes, mentioned in Chapter 4 as a way to keep someone from rehearsing information or thinking about anything other than the task at hand. Intense concentration on counting or a specific repetitive act tends to occupy the mind fully. Paying attention to one's own breathing probably also serves to turn the individual's perceptions inward and thus further facilitate the process of meditation. And as the individual becomes more advanced, he may concentrate on a *koan*, a riddle or paradox, that he has been given by his teacher. *Koans* such as "What is the sound of one hand clapping?" or "Show me your face before your mother and father met" may baffle a logical Western mind, but they are not designed to produce logical answers. Rather, their function is to help the individual detach himself from the rational, logical way of thinking. Yoga or transcendental meditation usually involves repeating a *mantra* (mystical phrase or invocation) to oneself over and over again. The mantra is usually a brief phrase, easily said and spoken softly, that the teacher gives to the pupil; it is supposed to be entirely private. Some schools of Yoga

use chanting out loud for the same purposes, a phrase being said over and over again, often for several hours. They also use visual images or *mandalas*, which can range from a simple circle to a complex figure (as shown in Fig. 11.6), and which the individual gazes at, trying to exclude all other thoughts and perceptions.

Meditation clearly produces substantial physiological effects. There is considerable evidence that brain activity during meditation involves an increase in alpha waves (Wallace and Benson, 1972; Kasamatsu and Hirai, 1966). In addition, skin conductance increases, and, as shown in Fig. 11.7, oxygen consumption drops sharply after as little as ten minutes of meditation (Benson et al., 1975; Wallace and

Figure 11.6

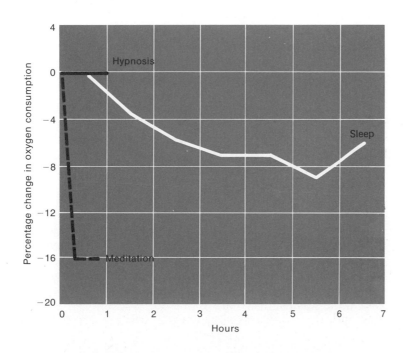

Fig. 11.7
Effects of meditation, hypnosis, and sleep on oxygen consumption

Meditation has a much faster and greater effect than sleep, while hypnosis has no effect at all. (From Wallace and Benson, 1972)

Benson, 1972). As you can see from the figure, this pattern is quite different from those of both hypnosis and sleep. Thus, while meditation may have some similarities to other states of consciousness, it is obviously different in important ways.

Moreover, people who have experienced meditation describe their subjective feelings as quite different from those of other states. In a controlled study, inexperienced subjects were asked to attempt a simple meditation exercise (Deikman, 1963). They stared at a blue vase and attempted to exclude or at least ignore all other thoughts and perceptions. They repeated this exercise on twelve different days. All subjects reported some reactions. Perceptual effects included an increase in the vividness and luminosity of the vase, and conflicting perceptions so that at one moment the vase seemed to "fill the field" while at the next moment (or even simultaneously) it took up only a small part of the visual field. The subjects said that time seemed to be shortened—their period of meditation seemed to last much less long than it actually did. External stimuli were excluded from their consciousness, almost as if a barrier had been erected. This barrier became increasingly strong with experience, so that by the twelfth session they were successfully screening out almost all external stimulation, even when the experimenter deliberately played music and introduced other distractions. Finally, there was a sense of personal involvement with or attachment to the vase—a feeling of being close to it emotionally.

Other reports, particularly by those who are much more experienced in meditation, are more dramatic. Meditation usually causes the person to feel relaxed, peaceful, and calm. However, on occasion it can have the opposite effect, making the person more aware of his own tension and anxiety. This seems especially true of inexperienced meditators. Meditation also seems to produce some perceptual and temporal distortions, and there is experimental evidence that deep meditation does cause strong resistance to distraction by external stimuli (Orme-Johnson, 1973).

Experienced yogis and other masters of meditation can produce dramatic effects that are easy to observe. Just as with hypnosis, meditation can lead to great resistance to or endurance of pain. One study (Anand, Chhina, and Singh, 1961) describes two yogis who had developed raised pain thresholds to the extent that they could keep their hands in cold water (4 degrees centigrade) for over forty-five minutes. During this period, both men continued to have elevated alpha waves, which ordinarily suggest great relaxation and total absence of pain. Apparently they managed to block the pain sensation from reaching their brains, rather than just being better able to endure the pain.

It is clear that we are far from understanding fully the processes by which meditation works, or the extent to which it can affect people's thoughts and behavior. At the least, it now appears that many people who practice meditation find it helpful to them in terms of relaxation, calmness, and perhaps some expansion of their ability to think about and deal with various aspects of their lives. But there is no evidence for the moment that it can serve as a form of psychotherapy (Smith, 1975).

MYSTICAL EXPERIENCES

In addition to the fairly well-established states we have discussed, there appear to exist experiences that are generally termed *mystical* or *peak*. These are not generally brought about by a specific action on the part of the individual; they cannot be produced at will, but occur more or less unexpectedly and suddenly. Moreover, those who experience them report that they are profoundly moving. While psychologists have not studied mystical and peak experiences systematically, it seems worth discussing them briefly because they are remarkably common and apparently do have important effects on people's lives.

Mystical experiences have been mentioned for thousands of years and are often associated with important religious figures. Jesus, the Buddha, and Muhammed are all described as having such experiences. St. Paul was knocked off his horse by a flash of light and underwent a spiritual transformation. Thomas Aquinas, G. K. Chesterton, the *shamans* (priests) of Indian tribes, and Balinese dancers all have described having some form of mystical experience. But such experiences are far more widespread than this. A survey of a cross section of Americans in 1973 found that 50 percent of the respondents said they had had a "religio-mystical experience," 45 percent said that they had at one time felt as though "they had become one with God or the universe," and 40 percent said they had at least once "had the feeling of being very close to a powerful spiritual force that seemed to lift you out of yourself." While the survey may not have been perfectly worded to assess true mystical experiences, it is clear that a great many people have had powerful experiences that they think of as mystical (Greely and McCready, 1975).

In *The Varieties of Religious Experience*, William James discussed mystical experiences, or what he called *ecstasy*. He noted that they appear to be brief, to defy specific description, to cause the person to feel in the grasp of a superior power, and to give the individual an overwhelming sense of understanding. Certainly, in almost all cases the experience is positive—the person feels happy, ecstatic, warm, joyful, and alive. In the 1973 survey, most of those who reported having the experience were religious in the sense of belonging to an organized religion and even attending services of some sort; and they tended to believe in life after death. Of course, it is difficult to know whether this religious feeling contributed to or was caused by the mystical experience. But it is clear that these people did feel something that affected them deeply and that seems to involve a different state of consciousness.

At the moment, we do not have any reliable information about such events. Freud thought they were similar to severe mental disturbance, a form of schizophrenia (see Chapter 15) involving strong hallucinations and an escape from reality. Others, such as Maslow, consider them basically healthy. Whatever their cause, it appears that a great many people experience them at one time or another and perhaps in the future we will begin to understand them more fully. All we can say now is that mystical experiences seem to be still another variation of that complex human condition called consciousness.

PSYCHOACTIVE DRUGS

Drug use in the United States in a year:

- 231 million prescriptions for psychoactive drugs
- 10 billion doses of barbiturates
- 3 billion doses of amphetamines
- 10 billion doses of tranquilizers
- 9 billion dollars spent on legally purchased drugs
- 18 gallons of beer, 10 quarts of hard liquor per person
- 19 billion dollars spent on alcohol
- 4,000 cigarettes per person over eighteen
- 9 billion dollars spent on cigarettes
- 45 gallons of coffee per person

As you can see from the list above, Americans use huge amounts of psychoactive drugs—those that alter mood, emotions, perceptions, or thought processes. Psychoactive drugs fall into three major categories: depressants, stimulants, and hallucinogens (see Fig. 11.8). Whereas depressants and stimulants alter mainly mood or level of activity (depressants lowering and stimulants raising activity), hallucinogens, including marijuana as a somewhat special type, appear to change the actual mode, style, and content of mental and perceptual experience and are therefore of greater interest to psychologists. For this reason, we shall describe the effects of the first two groups briefly and then discuss the hallucinogens in more detail.

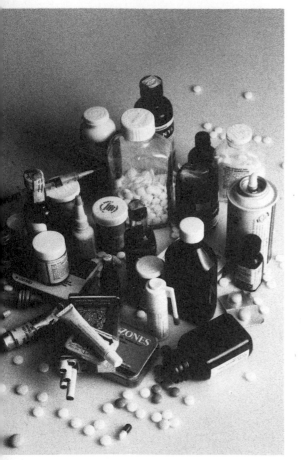

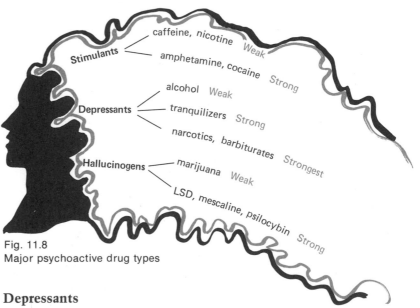

Fig. 11.8
Major psychoactive drug types

Depressants

A large group of drugs that includes alcohol, the barbiturates, the narcotics, and the minor tranquilizers all reduce the activity of the central nervous system. These drugs slow down reactions, reduce the strength of responses, and produce drowsiness, sleep, or even death depending on dosage.

Two depressants have become serious social problems: alcohol and heroin. Alcohol is the most widely used psychoactive drug in our society and many people (alcoholics) are addicted to it to the point where they suffer actual physical reactions such as sweating and tremors (withdrawal symptoms) if they are deprived of the drug. There is no foolproof cure for alcoholism. Psychotherapy and some forms of aversive conditioning (see Chapter 16) sometimes help. In addition, alcoholics anonymous, an organization composed of ex-alcoholics, provides a form of therapy based on group support plus a type of group therapy and confessions. Moreover, when the alcoholic feels in need of support, he or she can call the group and a member will always be available to talk or provide companionship. AA appears to be quite successful, especially if the alcoholic is highly motivated in the first place to give up alcohol.

© Jules Feiffer, courtesy Field Newspaper Syndicate

As everyone knows, heroin addiction is the cause of great misery, serious crime, and many deaths from overdoses in the United States. Addiction to heroin is both physical and psychological. Like other narcotics, heroin is very useful in relieving pain and at certain dosages produces a feeling of wellbeing, freedom from worry, exhilaration, and even extreme physical pleasure. After continued use, however, all of the narcotics and barbiturates become addictive—people require the drug and experience withdrawal symptoms if they do not get it. The addiction to heroin is both physical and psychological, and therefore successful treatment probably must include both physical and psychological approaches. One method of treatment consists of maintaining the addict on heroin or on a substitute such as methadone; while this does not cure the addiction, it eliminates the need to obtain the drug illegally and allows a gradual, controlled reduction in dosage. Some but not all studies of methadone maintenance have indicated substantial success in terms of reduced drug usage, fewer crimes committed by those treated, and better work records (Brecher, 1972; Freedman and Senay, 1973). An entirely different treatment is total abstinence combined with an alcoholics anonymous kind of program (Synanon), and still another is abstinence plus psychotherapy. No method is completely successful—heroin addiction is obviously very difficult to overcome.

Stimulants

This class of drugs includes caffeine, nicotine, amphetamines, and cocaine. Stimulants produce reactions opposite to those of the depressants, increasing central nervous system activity, speeding up reactions, and producing a feeling of lightheadedness, alertness, or even euphoria.

Stimulants have the positive effect of improving performance on many tasks and keeping someone awake when that is required. On the other hand, continued use of stimulants leads to a cycle of arousal followed by depression when the drug wears off. This produces increased dependence on the drug to avoid the depression, making larger and larger doses necessary. Minor side effects include restlessness, anxiety, and irritability. In the extreme, extended use of some stimulants can produce a state of severe mental confusion and a disorder similar to psychosis (see Chapter 15).

Hallucinogens

There are many drugs that alter the perceptions, thoughts, and feelings of people who use them. Various plants such as the tropical morning glory, the psilocybin mushroom, and hemp (cannabis) contain hallucinogenic substances; others, such as LSD-25, have been produced synthetically.

Effects of hallucinogens Although the effects of each drug are somewhat different and the dosage required varies enormously, they all can produce perceptual and temporal distortions, a sense of being detached from the body, and a variety of mysterious or mystical experiences. Subjects who have taken LSD, one of the strongest hallucinogens, have reported that walls seem to be breathing, floors move and flow, they see multicolored moving designs even with their eyes closed, objects flow around the edges, and they "see" music. In addition, subjects report that their self left their body, they were floating in space, they had peculiar sensations on their skin, they became another object or person, their body grew in size all on its own, and parts of them were paralyzed. Users also experience mystical sensations—feeling contact with unknown forces in the universe, seeing mystery in certain familiar objects, having levels of thought that are difficult to express in words, and experiencing a sense of joy.

However, despite the claims of enthusiasts, there is no evidence that hallucinogens expand the powers of the mind. People do not solve problems or produce great creations while under the influence of these drugs unless they are also able to do so in a normal state (Zegans, Pollard, and Brown, 1967).

Dangers of hallucinogens There is still great controversy over the dangers of hallucinogens. Among the more familiar chemicals, LSD is usually considered more powerful and potentially more dangerous than mescaline or psilocybin. Since all the drugs are illegal, they are usually obtained "on the street" or from unreliable suppliers of one sort or another. This means that users cannot be sure of what they are getting.

Apart from the legal problems, there may be physical and mental damage from hallucinogens. A number of researchers suggested that very large doses of LSD cause chromosomal damage that could produce birth defects. However, a thorough review of the research has concluded that there is no evidence linking LSD with birth defects (Egozcue and Irwin, 1970), and a recent textbook on drugs (Julien, 1975) largely discounts this danger of LSD.

On the other hand, there is no question that users sometimes have extremely negative reactions. These "bad trips" include feelings

Unpleasant and/or frightening hallucinations are among the risks associated with hallucinogenic drugs.

of horror, anxiety, confusion, and separation from everyone and everything in the world, a fear that someone was spying into their minds, general suspiciousness, and a doubt that they would ever return to normal. Bad trips seem to occur more often to people who are already somewhat disturbed or unstable (Ungerleider et al., 1968). They also may depend on the environment in which the drug is taken. A protective, stable, reassuring situation appears to reduce greatly the chance of a negative experience. When a negative reaction occurs it is usually brief—a few hours at most—but it can sometimes last for several days and may recur in "flashes" months or even years after the drug is taken.

On a short-term basis, hallucinogenic drugs can sometimes lead to dangerous or antisocial behavior because of the unrealistic mental states that they produce. There have been instances of people trying to fly out of windows, or walking aimlessly across a busy highway. In relatively rare instances, the feelings of being threatened or attacked that these drugs sometimes produce can lead someone to become violent, in an apparent attempt at self-protection from the imagined attacker.

Whether hallucinogens have any lasting negative effects is uncertain. There have been reports of serious mental disturbance caused or brought on by LSD and other drugs (Acord and Barker, 1973), but these are individual cases with no controls. If someone is disturbed to begin with, any strong or upsetting experience may precipitate a psychotic episode, and there is little question that hallucinogenic drugs can produce strong experiences. At the moment, therefore, it seems as if the greatest psychological danger of hallucinogenic drugs is the possibility of precipitating serious mental disturbance in someone who is already quite upset.

There is as yet no evidence about the long-term effects of regular use of any hallucinogens. Whether any of them change mental functioning, reduce the ability to concentrate, or have any other cumulative effect is unknown. The drugs are not habit-forming or addictive nor does tolerance develop, so in this respect they are not as dangerous as narcotics and barbiturates.

Marijuana

Marijuana is usually considered to be in a somewhat separate class from the other hallucinogens. The resin of the hemp plant *cannabis sativa* contains the hallucinogenic ingredient THC (tetrahydrocannabinol), which is the active ingredient in both marijuana and hashish. Marijuana is a mixture of dried stems, leaves, and flowers, while hashish is a stronger concentration of THC obtained from the flowers alone.

Although use of marijuana is generally not legal in the United States, a great many people in all sectors of society have tried it and large numbers continue to use it. A 1976 United States government study showed that a third of high-school students use it regularly and research indicates that more than 50 percent of college students have used it. However, the figures on regular usage vary considerably.

Reactions to marijuana are much more consistent and predictable than are reactions to LSD or mescaline. Generally, marijuana produces feelings of well-being, satisfaction, calmness, unexplained hilarity, and sometimes intense appetite for a specific food such as chocolate ice cream or pizza. Marijuana can also produce minor distortions of sensation; increased sensitivity to sound, light, and taste; changes in the perception of time; and, in extreme instances, illusions and hallucinations.

With very large doses, some tolerance may develop, but this does not occur at the doses normally taken in this country (Perez-Reyes, Timmons, and Wall, 1974; Renault, 1974). On the contrary, marijuana actually seems to produce stronger effects in experienced users than in people who are using it for the first time.

There are some reports that continued use of very large quantities of marijuana can produce negative effects, including feelings of persecution and anxiety, sleep disturbance, and impaired judgment. Moreover, marijuana can interfere with cognitive and physical functioning. It lowers performance on a wide range of intellectual tasks (Clark and Nakashima, 1968; Melges, Tinklenberg, and Hollister, 1971) and appears to make driving a car more difficult (Binder, 1971), though the effect is much less severe than that caused by drinking (Crancer et al., 1969). However, there is no convincing evidence that marijuana has lasting adverse effects on physical and mental functioning, nor that it is likely to lead to antisocial behavior.

Some researchers have suggested that marijuana can cause serious mental illness. Two retrospective studies of users and nonusers (Kolansky and Moore, 1972; Chopra, 1973) reported that those who had mental difficulties were more likely to have used marijuana than those who did not, and both concluded that the marijuana was at least in part the cause of the condition. These findings are considered far from conclusive because there are few controls in the research and the authors appeared to draw unfounded conclusions (Rosenthal, 1972; Zinberg, 1972). At the moment there is too little research available to settle this question decisively. Large and continuous doses of marijuana may precipitate mental conditions in people who are already disturbed, but in normal doses it appears to have little or no lasting effects.

Perhaps the major reason that American society has traditionally opposed marijuana use is that the drug is thought to reduce motivation to work hard. This drug's calming, tranquilizing effects may reduce the drive to be a hard-working, productive member of an industrialized society, at least while the user is under the influence of the drug. But in average doses that influence wears off in an hour or two. In fact, one controlled study showed that in college, light marijuana smokers had better grades than nonusers, and the few heavy users had grades only slightly below the abstainers (Good, 1971).

Thus, although there is some inconsistency in the findings, the current evidence seems to indicate that marijuana is not a particularly dangerous drug. Nevertheless, more research is required before we can accurately assess the very long-term effects of continued marijuana use. ■

Summary

1. While motivation, perception, and learning are major determinants of behavior, alterations in the state of consciousness can also have profound effects on behavior.

2. Sleeping patterns in humans seem flexible, but once a pattern is established it can be difficult to adjust to a new pattern. This difficulty is magnified by patterns of body processes called circadian rhythms.

3. There are four stages of sleep, which range from light to very deep. REM sleep, which occurs during the first stage, is characterized by high mental activity and, paradoxically, extreme muscle relaxation.

4. Sleep is necessary for the normal functioning of any animal. Sleep deprivation can produce extreme reactions, but people seem to be able to recover quickly once they get some sleep.

5. Dreams occur during REM sleep. Psychologists currently believe that everyone dreams but that some people do not remember their dreams.

6. There are three important aspects to Freud's theory of dreams: (a) Dreams are manifestations of hidden conflicts, desires, and unconscious impulses. (b) Dreams consist of manifest content and hidden, but more important, latent content. (c) Dreams are wish fulfillments. Dreams can have content of unconscious origin and represent wishes, as Freud asserted, but sometimes they are manifestations of conscious fears and desires or even just random associations.

7. Jung's view of dreams included the idea of the collective unconscious, a pool of unconscious memories and beliefs that are common to all humanity. Jung perceived the function of dreams as productive mental activity, while Freud believed they serve to release tension and allow us to remain asleep.

8. Hypnosis has some of the characteristics of both sleep and wakefulness. The following symptoms can be produced under hypnosis: heightened suggestibility; acceptance of distortion; selective attention; acting out of suggestions; distortion in the individual's bodily state; and post-hypnotic amnesia. It is almost certain that only cooperative subjects can be hypnotized and the available evidence suggests that people cannot be made to commit acts under hypnosis that they would not commit while awake.

9. Meditation produces substantial physiological and psychological effects. It appears that many people who practice meditation find it helpful in generating relaxation, calmness, and perhaps some expansion of their ability to think about and deal with various aspects of their lives.

10. Mystical or peak experiences occur more or less unexpectedly and suddenly. In almost all cases the person feels happy, ecstatic, warm, joyful, and alive.

11. Major categories of psychoactive drugs include depressants (alcohol, barbiturates, narcotics, and minor tranquilizers), stimulants (caffeine, amphetamines, and cocaine), and hallucinogens (such as LSD, mescaline, psilocybin, and marijuana).

12. As their name suggests, depressants produce depressive effects on the central nervous system. Stimulants produce physiological arousal and make a person feel more alert and active.

13. Hallucinogens produce distortions in perception and thinking. These distortions may be pleasurable but they may also be upsetting and frightening. Dangers include legal problems, overdose, negative psychological effects, and antisocial behavior.

14. The effects of marijuana are usually feelings of well-being and calm, sometimes hilarity, increased appetite, some perceptual distortions, and in extreme cases, hallucinations. Current research suggests that marijuana is not particularly dangerous.

RECOMMENDED READING

The titles of these books are self-explanatory. Each covers a different altered state in a fairly straightforward, interesting manner. The book on meditation is less scientific than the others and is, instead, an argument by a proponent of the value of meditation.

Dement, W.C. *Some Must Watch While Some Must Sleep*. Stanford, Calif.: Stanford Alumni Association, 1972.

Forem, J. *Transcendental Meditation: Maharishi Mahesh Yogi and the Science of Creative Intelligence*. New York: Dutton, 1973.

Hilgard, E. R. *The Experience of Hypnosis*. New York: Harcourt Brace Jovanovich, 1968.

Julien, R. M. *A Primer of Drug Action*. San Francisco: Freeman, 1975.

Ray, O. S. *Drugs, Society and Human Behavior*. St. Louis: C. V. Mosby, 1972.

Tart, C. T., Ed. *Altered States of Consciousness*. New York: Wiley, 1969.

Teyler, T. J., Ed. *Altered States of Awareness: Readings from Scientific American*. San Francisco: Freeman, 1971.

The childhood shows the man as morning shows the day.
Milton, Paradise Regained

A kiss from my mother made me a painter.
Benjamin West

12 Developmental Psychology

Physical growth and skills ■ *Perceptual development* ■
Piaget's stages of cognitive development ■ *Erikson's
stages of social development and personality* ■
Identification ■ *Moral development* ■ *Further
development*

t is almost impossible not to be amazed and fascinated by an infant's development into a full-fledged adult human being. We all know, of course, that this happens with remarkable consistency, but this transformation is a remarkable and incredibly complex achievement. The newborn human has almost all the usual features but few of the behaviors of mature adults. The infant nurses, cries, wets, thrashes about, responds to stimulation, and sleeps a lot. This diffuse being develops into an adult with an entirely different repertoire of responses, memories, beliefs, and values that enable it to function in our complex society and that also give it unique individuality. Some of this development is determined largely by a built-in maturation process, some of it depends on what the child experiences, and a great deal is due to an interaction of intrinsic characteristics and experience. We do not yet know all of the details about how this transformation occurs, but in this chapter we shall discuss what we do know—what factors affect development, what sequence it takes, what physical and psychological elements can interfere with it, and what specific incidents and experiences are especially important.

The study of child development is important and fascinating because it provides a background to our understanding of adult behavior. Only by knowing how the infant matures can we fully appreciate the behavior of adults. Moreover, any prospective parent, teacher, aunt, or uncle should know as much as possible about the factors that affect a child's development, for one day they themselves may be critical elements in the process.

In addition, child development relates to one of the most important themes of this book—that a human being is a product of innate characteristics plus experience. The innate characteristics provide a structure, in a sense the bones that experience fleshes out. Innate qualities set limits on perceptual, physical, and mental capacities, and the individual develops within these limits. Moreover, there is a dynamic interaction of innate characteristics and experience that is revealed dramatically when we trace the development of an individual from infancy to adulthood. By focusing on different aspects of development, we can also see how greatly the relative importance of the two elements varies, depending on the particular characteristics and the person's age. Innate characteristics appear to play a large role in determining physical and perceptual activity. They are less vital to cognitive functioning, and still less important in personality and social development. And as the child grows older, experience naturally becomes relatively more and more important.

This chapter is to some extent a review of the previous chapters and a preview of those to come. We shall consider first the child's physical growth and the development of physical skills. Then we shall discuss the development of perception and cognitive functions, referring to the chapters on these topics and on language. Finally, we will examine how the child develops morality and personality.

PHYSICAL GROWTH AND SKILLS

Prenatal Development

Every normal human embryo follows the same general course of development from the time the egg is fertilized until birth nine months later. The remarkable photographs shown in the color-plate section illustrate some of the stages of this development. At thirty days the embryo is smaller than a pea, has only a few rudimentary organs, and bears little resemblance to a human being. A few days later, hands and feet have begun to develop; by forty-four days, even though the embryo is only an inch long, it looks like a tiny human. After five months, the fetus is completely formed, and the next four months are devoted to growth and strengthening. This sequence is summarized in Fig. 12.1.

The normal progression from a fertilized egg to a human fetus is determined by genetic factors. But the process is dependent on a benign environment, and any serious interference with the health of the mother or embryo will threaten the normal development. Diseases, drugs, chemicals, lack of sufficient nutrition, and the emotional health of the mother can seriously affect the unborn child at particular stages of embryonic growth. For example, German measles (rubella) in a pregnant woman can produce abnormalities in her child—but only if she contracts the disease during the first three months of pregnancy. At that time, the embryo's nervous system is being formed and it is highly vulnerable. The disease interferes with normal development and often causes blindness, deafness, or brain damage. Yet after the first three months, German measles is almost always harmless.

Similarly, certain drugs can produce catastrophic effects if taken during certain prenatal periods, but will have no effect at other times. Hundreds of thousands of people took a tranquilizer called Thalidomide during the 1960s, believing it to have no serious side effects. It was later discovered that when Thalidomide was taken during the early stages of pregnancy, it inhibited the growth of the embryo's extremities. As a result, hundreds of babies were born with missing hands, arms, ears, or legs. This was perhaps the most publicized case of a drug that can interfere with normal growth, but not the only one. Mothers who are addicted to drugs often transfer their addiction to their children, thus producing one of the saddest phenomena of modern society—a newborn infant that is already addicted to heroin and shows withdrawal symptoms if he does not get the drug. Because of these examples and others, most obstetricians now urge pregnant women to take as few drugs as possible, preferably none at all. This insurance is necessary because we are not fully aware of all the side effects of even very common drugs.

In addition to diseases and drugs that interfere with embryonic development, there is some suggestion that severe emotional upset in the mother during the early stages of pregnancy can produce abnormalities such as a cleft palate. We do not know for certain that this happens and are not clear how it would occur. We do know that severe emotional stress produces a hormonal imbalance in the mother. This imbalance may be transmitted to the embryo and interfere with its normal growth.

Infancy

At birth the human infant already looks entirely human. The almost magical influence of genes has transformed sperm and egg into a complete, though tiny, human being. Different genes would have produced a different kind of animal with just as much certainty. Of

The embryo—conception to eight weeks

a) Grows from single cell to about one inch long.

b) At eight weeks basic structure has begun to emerge—face, mouth, nose and eyes appear; head is half of body; arms, legs, fingers, and toes appear; internal organs are present with heart beating, liver and kidney functioning; glands are secreting.

c) Neural system including brain begins working, producing some reflexes.

The fetus—eight weeks until birth (about forty weeks)

a) Third and fourth month, muscles develop—can open and close fist, suck thumb, move around; very rapid growth during fourth month.

b) Fifth month—internal organs in place; skin developed; hair and nails appear.

c) Sixth month—eyelids open; can cry; weighs about twenty-four ounces

d) Seventh month—brain develops rapidly; almost all functions in operation though some are weak; at this stage a premature baby can survive.

e) Eighth and ninth month—further development; much activity; rapid gain in body weight.

Fig. 12.1
Prenatal development

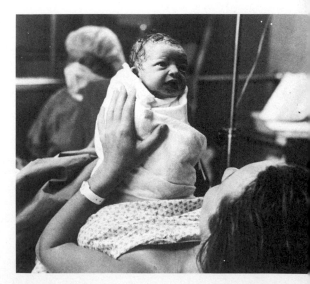

course, the particular genes governing this human being have also determined many qualities that distinguish it from other humans. Even at birth, the infant will differ from others in terms of size, weight, color of skin and hair, and various other traits. As the infant develops, more genetically determined characteristics will appear regardless of external influences. Eye color, curliness of hair, ultimate size, strength, and physiological sexual characteristics are all governed in part by genetic factors. But, as in the prenatal period, severe traumas or insufficient nourishment can interfere with normal development.

Innate responses Newborn babies have a small repertoire of innate responses. They will cry when they are hungry or uncomfortable and thrash about when they are upset or are disturbed by some external stimulus. They also show specific reactions to certain kinds of stimulation. Some of these are listed in Table 12.1. All of these responses are present at birth. Infants may have to try them a few times before they do them right, but little or no learning is necessary.

Emerging behaviors Though an infant is born with few innate responses, it develops a large number of physical skills in its first months and years. Figure 12.2 shows when some of an infant's earliest accomplishments tend to appear. All babies learn these skills in the order shown, but as you can see there is considerable variation in the age at which they are learned. Thus, parents who worry because their child is a "late" stander or a "late" walker should understand that there is a great deal of variation in the development of these

Table 12.1
SOME REFLEX BEHAVIORS IN INFANTS

Reflex	Behavior
Moro reflex (startle)	Sudden stimulus such as loud noise causes full extension of legs, arms, and fingers, with back arched and head thrown back. Disappears in third or fourth month.
Rooting reflex (searching and sucking)	Stroking cheek causes turn in direction of stroke; mouth opens and sucks. Obviously enables infant to find nipple and nurse.
Babinski reflex	Stroking sole of foot causes toes to fan and foot arch up. At about six months replaced by adult reflex with foot arching downward and toes curling.
Darwinian reflex (grasping)	When palm is stroked, infant makes a fist and grasps whatever is in the palm. The grip is remarkably strong, perhaps a holdover from a time when newborns had to hold onto their parent's fur or body.
Swimming reflex	Put in water face down, baby will make swimming movements.
Walking reflex	If held under arms with bare feet touching the floor or other surface, infant makes movements similar to walking. The reflex disappears at about eight weeks. This and the swimming reflex are very early preparations for behavior that appears much later; yet both the swimming and walking reflex disappear before the more advanced behavior develops.

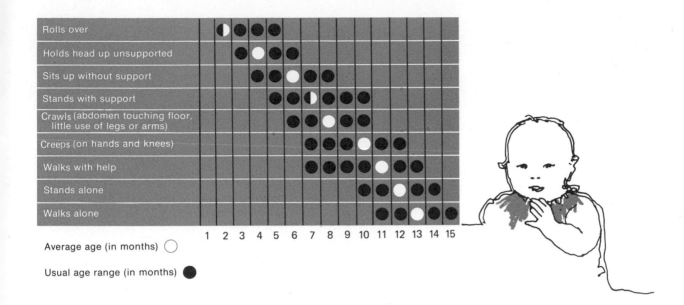

	1	2	3	4	5	6	7	8	9	10	11	12	13	14	15
Rolls over		◐	●	●	●										
Holds head up unsupported			●	○	●	●									
Sits up without support				●	●	○	●	●							
Stands with support					●	●	◐	●	●	●					
Crawls (abdomen touching floor, little use of legs or arms)						●	●	○	●	●					
Creeps (on hands and knees)						●	●	●	○	●	●				
Walks with help						●	●	●	●	●	○	●	●		
Stands alone										●	●	○	●		
Walks alone											●	●	○	●	●

Average age (in months) ○

Usual age range (in months) ●

---

skills. No baby can walk until she has developed the necessary physical strength and coordination. Some babies simply reach this point of development sooner than others.

Speeding Up or Delaying Development

As we have said, the sequence of physical development we have described is universal. Children will rarely stand until they have learned to crawl, and cannot walk until they have learned to stand. The same will be true of other learned physical abilities such as grasping objects, turning somersaults, or anything else. Basic skills will come before more complex ones. But can we accelerate the speed with which a child develops any particular skill? Many anxious, devoted, and ambitious parents believe that they can speed their child's physical development with instruction and encouragement. But the fact is that no amount of encouragement, practice, or careful training has an appreciable long-term effect on these basic childhood skills. It is possible to speed up or delay slightly the age at which a particular ability appears, but the effect is very small and soon disappears—if it appears early, other children soon catch up; if it appears late, the child quickly catches up to the rest of her age group. The relative lack of variability in physical development and its independence from environmental factors have been demonstrated in many studies with a wide variety of animals. In one experiment (Cruze, 1935) baby chicks were kept in the dark from birth so that they could not practice pecking. Normal newborn chicks can peck at grain but miss about 25 percent of the time. By the time they are five days old, they almost never miss. When the chicks that had been kept in the dark without practice were taken out after five days, they behaved just as normal chicks do—their pecking was almost perfect. Thus, lack of practice had no effect on the chicks' basic skills. They did need some experience in performing the action, but they did not need to learn it.

Fig. 12.2
Development of motor skills

Average age at which skill appears is shown by white circle (or white portion for half-years). The normal range is considerable, as indicated by the dark circles. In addition, children in different cultures may develop certain skills generally earlier or later than in other cultures.

Box 12.1

MULTIPLE BIRTHS

Twins and other multiple births are a fascinating phenomenon. Other species typically give birth to more than one offspring at a time, but humans and most large mammals do not. Thus, most people do not have a sibling of exactly the same age and most parents do not raise two children of the same age at the same time. The consequences of having twins or being a twin are largely unknown, but novelists and psychologists have been concerned with it for a long time. Throughout this book, we discuss research using twins—generally to answer broader questions, but always relying on the fact that identical twins share the same genes while both identical and fraternal twins share the same environment.

The incidence of twins varies greatly among different ethnic groups. White Americans have twins in about one out of seventy births; in England the rate is similar—about one in eighty. But in Nigeria it is one in twenty-two while in Japan twins account for only one of one hundred and sixty births (Gedda, 1961). This suggests that twinning is genetically determined, though there is not enough systematic research yet to prove it. We do know that fertility drugs of various kinds greatly increase the chance of having twins, and can lead to other multiple births—triplets, quadruplets, quintuplets, and even more. Children of multiple births tend to be smaller at birth and have a smaller chance of survival, and this is especially true with triplets and higher numbers. Although many more quadruplets, quints, and sextuplets have been reported in recent years (probably due to fertility drugs), very few have survived (or, at least, in few cases have all the children lived). However, there is no evidence that twins who do live are abnormal in any way.

Many other skills depend on a combination of maturation, experience, and learning. They will not appear until the animal is ready, and readiness seems to be determined by an interaction of maturation and experience. Once the animal is ready, the skills improve with practice. For example, the chicks in Cruze's study also tried to swallow the grain they pecked. Swallowing is a task that requires some practice. Normal chicks improve very rapidly in their ability to swallow the grain. At twenty-four hours they swallow less than 20 percent of the grain they peck but by day five they swallow more than 60 percent. In contrast, the chicks kept in the dark for five days were way behind the others. At five days, they could swallow only about 20 percent of the grain they pecked. But once they had a chance to practice, they caught up very quickly. By the eighth day all the chicks were equal in both pecking and swallowing. In other words, even with skills that require some practice, animals that have been held back learn rapidly and soon catch up with their peers.

The same is true of human infants. It is possible to teach a child to walk or to climb a little earlier than he normally would, but children who have not received special training and even those who have been deliberately held back soon catch up. For example, some Hopi Indian babies are bound tightly to a carrying board and therefore get little opportunity to move freely during their early months. Despite their immobility and inability to practice any physical skills, Hopi infants crawl, stand up, and walk about as soon as other infants. And those Hopis who are not bound walk at about the same time as those who are bound (Dennis, 1940). Similar results were found with infants in Russia who were swaddled (wrapped tightly in cloth) when compared to others who were not swaddled. The freer children walked a little sooner, but the others soon caught up.

Controlled experiments, in which some children are encouraged to perform physical activity while others are not, produce comparable results. Figure 12.3 shows what happened when one group of two- and

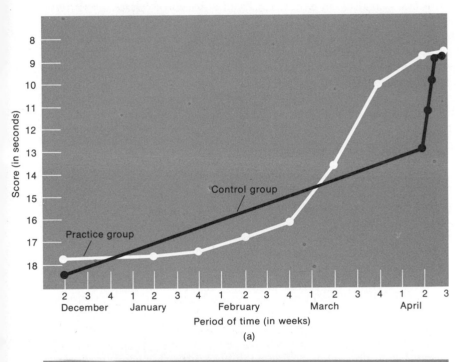

(a)

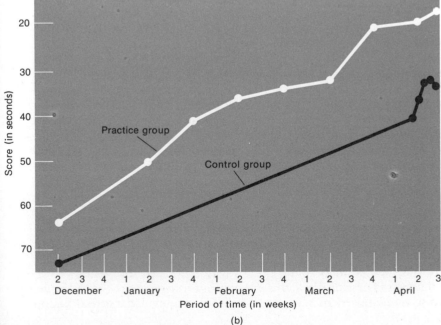

(b)

Fig. 12.3
Mean learning curves for two groups in (a) climbing and (b) cutting. The practice group trained for twelve weeks, starting in January. The control group trained only between the second and third weeks of April. (From J. Hilgard, 1932)

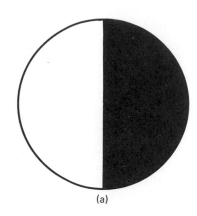

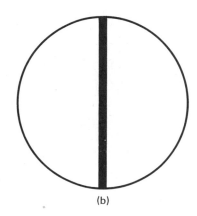

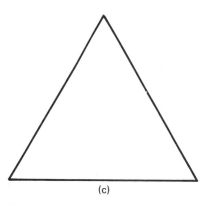

Fig. 12.4
Perceptual preferences of infants

Shown (a), almost all infants spend most of their time looking at the dividing line between the white and black parts of the figure. Shown (b), they look at the black vertical bar (Haith, 1966). In (c), infants focus either on one of the angles or on the sides (Salapatek and Kessen, 1966, 1973).

three-year-olds was given twelve weeks of practice in climbing stairs and cutting with a scissors while a control group was given no practice during that period (J. Hilgard, 1932). The children who got the training quickly became quite proficient at climbing and cutting. However, only one week was necessary for the control group to achieve the same climbing ability because the children were three months older and could benefit much more from the practice. In contrast, even after the week of practice, the control group was clearly inferior in cutting, probably because greater specific skill is required in that task. In general, a fixed amount of practice will have greater effects when children are more mature. It is possible to rush nature somewhat. In one study (Zelazo et al., 1972) infants were encouraged to walk by means of special exercises that were given them as early as one week of age, and these children did walk sooner than others. However, such efforts to speed up development are largely wasted. Whether or not they are encouraged, children are ordinarily ready to walk at twelve months and will walk just about then.

PERCEPTUAL DEVELOPMENT

The development of perceptual ability follows much the same course as the development of mechanical skills. As we mentioned in Chapter 2, the range of perception is determined almost entirely by innate factors. The human eye is sensitive to light of certain frequencies, and no amount of training will increase this range. Similarly, all humans appear to have certain built-in perceptual processes such as size constancy for short distances. As far as we can tell, every human infant who has even minimal exposures to visual stimuli develops some degree of size constancy very early in life.

A series of ingenious studies investigated the perceptual abilities of extremely young infants. The problems with this kind of research are obvious. When studying adult perception, the experimenter asks subjects to tell what they see or to respond in some simple way. But how does one find out what an infant is seeing? A number of psychologists decided to watch the infant's eyes in order to see what it looks at. The infant is shown a series of stimuli. The experimenter observes what he looks at in each presentation and also whether he seems to respond to a particular stimulus. For example, two- and three-day-old babies were shown stimuli similar to those in Fig. 12.4. The babies did not simply move their eyes around aimlessly. They focused consistently on certain aspects of the visual display. This research also indicates that infants prefer (in the sense of looking at more) black-and-white figures to colored ones. This indicates that even very young infants already have perceptual preferences and the ability to make some discriminations.

These demonstrations of perceptual skills in babies show the importance of innate factors in perception. Other research has shown that depriving animals of the chance to practice their perceptual skills has almost no effect on their development, as long as no physical damage is produced by the unusual circumstances. For example, chimpanzees raised in total darkness do not develop normal vision because their retinas deteriorate without exposure to light. But when rhesus monkeys were raised in diffuse, unpatterned light their retinas stayed healthy. When they were put in a normal situation, their vision was quite poor at first, but they caught up quickly and their perception of color, brightness, and size was soon normal (Wilson and Riesen, 1965). Just as with mechanical skills, being deprived of practice for many months does not necessarily permanently damage perceptual abilities that are innate. On the other hand, some experience with any skill is necessary for it to emerge, and different types of experience may produce somewhat different skills (Lerner, 1976). Moreover, in the Wilson and Riesen study, the deprived animals were below normal in discrimination of forms, depth perception, and other specific visual abilities.

Thus, as we mentioned in Chapter 2, certain aspects of perception are greatly affected by experience. Though basic processes and rules seem to be innate, the extent to which they develop depends on learning. The clearest example of this is depth perception. Depth perception at close range seems to be largely innate, but the development of depth perception at greater distances depends on experience. People who have no experience in seeing objects at great distances may not develop depth perception beyond twenty or thirty feet (see Chapter 2). As with so many other facets of human behavior, innate factors determine the basic process, but experience determines the degree and direction of development.

Critical Periods and Imprinting

We have seen that physical growth, mechanical skills, and perception develop largely independently of external factors. This is also true of a number of simple but crucial behaviors that appear in infancy. Newborn animals do not have to learn those behaviors that are necessary for their survival. Occasionally a kitten, calf, or human infant may have trouble finding and nursing at the nipple, but most of them nurse immediately and with little difficulty. Mothers report that human babies get better at nursing with experience, but they can do it reasonably well right from the start.

Though these behaviors occur without any specific training, they depend on one extremely important factor: the animal must be given a chance to perform the act during a certain period in its early life. Only if the behavior occurs during this *critical period* will the animal develop normally.

One illustration of the critical period occurs in newborn ducks. Konrad Lorenz (1952) showed that a newborn duckling will follow whatever moving object it sees first. Naturally the typical duckling sees its mother first, and follows her. This is obviously highly adaptive because she will lead her ducklings to safety and food. Millions of ducklings all over the world begin their lives by following their mothers. Largely by accident, however, Lorenz found that young ducklings cannot distinguish between their mother and other moving objects—even Lorenz himself. Figure 12.5 shows Lorenz doing a mild imitation of a duck walk and being followed by a line of ducklings. He was the first object they saw and so they followed him. This "following behavior," or *imprinting* as it is often called, is dependent on a

Figure 12.5

Fig. 12.6
Age and imprinting

The number of imprinting responses is closely related to the age at which the duckling is first exposed to the duck or object to be followed. If the first exposure is later than a day and a half (thirty-six hours), little or no imprinting occurs. (After Hess, 1959)

JEAN PIAGET

critical period. For the behavior to appear, the ducklings must be exposed to a moving object sometime in the first day of their lives. If they are not given an object to follow then, imprinting will rarely take place and the ducklings will respond with fear to strange objects. In fact, the critical period is a matter of a few hours. As shown in Fig. 12.6, imprinting is most likely between nine and twenty hours after birth and virtually disappears by thirty hours (Hess, 1958). Another example of critical periods is that kittens must be handled during the first few weeks of their lives or they will remain forever afraid of people and cannot be made pets.

However, critical periods may themselves be affected by experience. Moltz and Stettner (1961) showed that they could alter the critical periods of ducklings by raising them in rooms with no clear objects or structures and therefore depriving them of structured perceptual environments. Once again, it is apparent that development involves interaction of innate characteristics and experience.

PIAGET'S STAGES OF COGNITIVE DEVELOPMENT

The ability to form associations and concepts and to solve problems—in other words, to think—emerges in a fixed sequence. As with physical skills, although there are considerable differences in the *age* at which various cognitive abilities appear, every child goes through the same stages in the same *order*. These stages of cognitive development have been investigated most thoroughly by the Swiss psychologist Jean Piaget, who based most of his ideas on careful observations of a few children.

These intimate observations and subsequent controlled research led Piaget to propose (1952) that every child goes through four stages of development. These are shown in Table 12.2, which also indicates the approximate age at which the stage appears. Other authors such as Langer (1969) divide the process into as many as ten substages, but the basic sequence is similar. Let us consider each stage in turn.

"KEEP AN EYE ON THE KIDS FOR AWHILE, WILL YOU, JEAN?"

© 1974 by the American Psychological Association. Reprinted by permission of the APA and Richard D. Konicek, University of Massachusetts at Amherst.

Table 12.2
PIAGET'S STAGES OF COGNITIVE DEVELOPMENT

Stage	Age (approximate)*	Characteristics
Sensorimotor	Birth to 18 months	Develops motor skills; some sense of cause-effect relationships; little or no internal representation of external world; gradual development of object constancy.
Preoperational	18 months to 7 years	Development of symbolic thought; language development; little or no grasp of certain basic concepts such as conservation.
Concrete operation	7 to 11 years	Development of conservation and other basic concepts; rudimentary logic; little or no abstract thinking.
Formal operations	11+ years	Abstract thought; logical reasoning.

*Note that the ages are only approximate. The sequence appears to be invariant, but there is considerable variation in when a particular child attains each level of cognitive development.

The Sensorimotor Stage

For the first eighteen months to two years, children function in the *sensorimotor stage* of development. Their dealings with the world consist mainly of sensation and physical interaction. During this period, children become aware of elements of the world around them and begin to understand some of them. Their most basic discovery is that there is a separate world "out there." By manipulating objects and learning to control their own bodies, children make this essential discovery—there is a "me" and everything else is not part of me.

Object constancy A second crucial discovery, which occurs only toward the end of this period, is the realization that objects exist in their own right and continue to exist even if they cannot be perceived directly. In the first weeks of life, infants are barely able to focus on an object. By three or four months they easily focus on and follow a moving object. During this stage, motion seems to be an important factor in defining an object. If an object moves, infants are much more likely to identify it as a distinct entity than if it stands still (Nelson, 1971; Bower, 1971). Moreover, infants will follow the moving object with their eyes until it disappears from view or stops moving. However, until about sixteen weeks, infants behave as if the object ceases to exist when it disappears. They show no tendency to search for it when they can no longer see it. And if they are following a moving object that suddenly stops, their eyes do not continue along the line of motion as would an adult's.

By sixteen weeks, this has begun to change. Infants will track a moving object, will anticipate movement, and will continue tracking for a moment after the object stops (Bower and Paterson, 1973). And if an apple is partially covered by a cloth, infants will recognize that it is still an apple and will reach for it. Yet they still seem to have little sense of the permanence of objects. They will not find an apple that is totally covered by a cloth even if they have watched the cloth being

Fig. 12.7
Object constancy in infants

At sixteen weeks a child will not find the apple even though she has seen it covered and can see the bulge it makes.

put over it and can see the bulge it produces (see Fig. 12.7). Even at four or five months, most infants still act as if an object that is totally out of sight no longer exists (Bower, 1974).

By seven or eight months, objects have a greater degree of permanence—when they disappear children look for them. They will find the apple under the cloth even if it is fully covered. Yet it is only in the middle of their second year (fifteen to twenty months) that children will look for an object that disappeared some time ago. Only then do they seem to understand fully that objects have a reality totally beyond them, that they continue to exist whether or not they can be seen.

During this same period children learn to understand and deal with space, time, and causality. By the age of two, children can locate themselves in space and relate other objects to their position. They understand that there is a past that extends beyond the last few minutes. They not only perceive cause and effect, but can also reconstruct a cause-effect relationship even when only the effects are visible. For example, if they see a rubber ball come in through a door and bounce on the floor, two-year-olds will know that someone threw it even if they cannot see anyone. By the end of the sensorimotor period children have learned to deal with their environment in small ways, such as turning a bottle around in order to find the nipple, searching for a hidden piece of candy, and recognizing familiar objects.

Preoperational Stage

From about ages two to seven children enter a new stage of cognitive functioning, called the *preoperational stage*. Probably the most important development during this period is the acquisition of language. All normal children who are exposed to language develop the ability to understand and communicate with great facility. We have discussed this process in Chapter 5, but it is well to remember that language has profound effects on how children think and behave.

During this period children also begin to form concepts, to classify the world into categories, and to use objects symbolically rather than only literally. For example, children during this period often transform ordinary objects into toys. A kitchen pot becomes a ship, a book becomes a car and is moved around with appropriate engine noises, and a crude piece of wood can be a doll, dressed up and given tea. However, children are still highly egocentric, seeing everything from their own point of view. Children in this stage cannot understand that someone standing in a different spot actually sees the world differently, and less concrete differences in opinions, values, and needs are even more difficult for them to imagine.

Conservation At around the age of four children begin to understand such concepts as numbers, the relationship between objects, and classes and types of objects. One of Piaget's most interesting discoveries was that only in the preoperational stage does the concept of conservation *begin* to appear, and it is not mastered until the next stage of development. *Conservation* is the principle that a given quantity, weight, or volume of a substance remains the same regardless of its shape or configuration. Until this period children do not realize that four buttons are still four buttons however they are arranged, that altering the shape of a stick of toffee does not affect the amount of toffee, and that pouring water from a tall, thin glass into a short, wide one does not alter the volume of water (see Fig. 12.8).

The concept of conservation is so natural to adults and so much a part of our lives that it is sometimes difficult to accept that young children cannot understand it. More research has been done on this particular phenomenon than on any other aspect of cognitive development, and there is little doubt that until they are about four, children cannot grasp the principle of conservation. Asked to choose between four Tootsie Rolls spaced closely and four spread out, most children under four will choose the latter—presumably because they think they are getting more candy. Only at a certain stage of development that appears somewhere between age four and seven do children fully grasp the conservation of number, mass, and volume (Inhelder and Sinclair, 1969).

The effect of training on conservation The concept of conservation emerges from an interaction of experience and the state of development of the child's brain and training has little effect until children

Fig. 12.8
Lack of conservation

Although the young girl has seen the same amount of juice poured into the two jars, she chooses the taller one because she thinks it contains more.

are ready for it. Smedslund (1961) gave young children some idea of conservation a few years before they were supposed to be ready to grasp it. After his training, the children acted as if they understood that four Tootsie Rolls were only four Tootsie Rolls, no matter how far apart they were placed, and that water poured from a tall, thin glass into a wider glass remained the same amount of water. Yet when the experimenter used new stimuli or shook the children's faith in what they had learned, the supposedly trained children fell back on their own intuitive, nonconservation ideas. A control group of older children, who had acquired the notion of conservation naturally, retained the concept and looked for other explanations. It appears that the children who had received the training had merely memorized the idea but had not fully understood or accepted it. Other research by Inhelder and Sinclair (1969) showed that only children who were about ready to learn conservation on their own anyway benefitted from special training. On the other hand, some investigators have had considerable success in teaching conservation to young children (Siegler and Liebert, 1972). Whether or not conservation can be learned through early training, the mixed results all indicate how difficult it is for children to acquire conservation earlier than they are ready for it. At best, intensive training seems to speed up the process slightly.

As this research on conservation shows, young children may simply not understand concepts that are second nature to adults. Many misunderstandings and frustrations that occur between children and adults may be caused by the inability of most adults to understand or accept this fact. Children are not simply smaller and weaker versions of adults. As this work on conservation dramatically illustrates, the child's view and understanding of the world is in some respects markedly different from an adult's—so different that under some circumstances the child cannot grasp what the adult is driving at. Imagine the frustration of a parent whose child demands his orange juice in a tall, thin glass rather than a short, wide glass when it is perfectly clear to the parent that the same amount of juice is involved. Since a child of two is not able to understand this principle of conservation, it is up to the adult to make allowances. This work by Piaget on stages of development is perhaps the most convincing proof that children differ from adults in some ways, and no amount of explaining and teaching can alter this difference because the level of understanding depends on the developmental stage of the child.

Concrete Operations

The stage of *concrete operations* occurs between the ages of seven and eleven. According to Piaget, during this period children begin to understand the relationships among numbers and also arithmetic. They finally grasp conservation and learn to form concepts, to classify objects into hierarchies, and to produce an ordered series in terms of size or number. For example, if they know that Robert is the same size as Paul and Paul is the same size as Juan, they will understand that Robert is also the same size as Juan. Once again, these ideas seem so simple to us that we may find it difficult to accept that a bright child will not immediately grasp them. Nevertheless, until this stage of development occurs at approximately the age of seven, children are not able to do these kinds of mental operations.

Formal Operations

Between the ages of eleven and fifteen, the last stage of cognitive development emerges. The period of *formal operations* marks the development of abstract thinking, higher-level conceptualization, and the systematic forming and testing of hypotheses.

An important characteristic of this stage of cognitive functioning is that the individual is capable of formal, logical reasoning. While not all adolescents and adults use logic regularly or accurately, they can construct a line of argument, try to work out a problem deductively rather than try solutions randomly, and bring to bear rules and principles that they have learned. Whether it be math or social situations, someone in the stage of formal operations can approach the problem systematically, constructing and testing hypotheses in order to explain what is going on. In addition, at this stage individuals become capable of dealing with entirely hypothetical situations. If you ask a child of six how she would move a mountain of whipped cream through the city, she would probably object because there is no mountain of whipped cream and no one would want to move it if there were. An adolescent might think it was a silly question, but could accept it as a fanciful problem and try to work out a solution.

During the stage of formal operations, individuals first begin to shift some of their cognitive focus from the present, and to consider the past and the future as part of their world. Previous events are considered, discussed, and interpreted. The effect of current actions on the future plays an ever-increasing part in decisions, and long-term planning occurs. This perception of time as continuous, and of both history and the future impinging on our lives, emerges only at this stage. It is one of the basic qualities of human thought. Only humans know their history and imagine their future—and it is only at this highest stage of cognitive functioning that this perspective emerges.

In a sense, cognitive development is complete at this stage—no longer is the child "different" from adults. Naturally, additional experience and knowledge will add to the individual's cognitive abilities, but, according to Piaget, all of the basic kinds of thinking and mental processes such as those discussed in Chapters 3, 4, and 6, are now developed.

Piaget's work on cognitive development has been enormously influential, for he provided an outline of the sequence in which cognitive skills develop. Although everyone knew that children act smarter as they get older, the specific differences in thought processes had not been described in any detail before. Piaget's other major contribution was to point out that this development occurs in a fixed sequence that is universal. And this sequence depends on the interaction of experience with built-in mechanisms that take time to develop. The increasing cognitive skills of children are based on the maturation of these innate mechanisms. Training and experience have powerful effects on a child's life, but they cannot accelerate the appearance of these basic cognitive skills. They will emerge only when the mechanism is ready.

ERIKSON'S STAGES OF SOCIAL DEVELOPMENT AND PERSONALITY

ERIK H. ERIKSON

While children are developing the basic physical, perceptual, and cognitive skills, they are also beginning to form relationships with other people. Children's early interactions with other people form the basis for their later social behavior, their feelings about themselves and others, their values and morality, and their personal style. Those personal characteristics that make children unique individuals, that make up what is usually called their *personality* (their characteristic ways of dealing with the world and others), begin to develop very early in life and depend in large part on their first relationships with other people.

Like cognitive development, personality goes through a series of stages that are essentially the same for all people. We shall discuss Freud's theory of personality in Chapter 13. But Erik Erikson (1963), who was strongly influenced by Freud, has presented a framework that is particularly useful in considering the development of personality in childhood. Erikson describes eight stages of personality development. He sees each stage as centering on a problem that must be solved by the child and his parents in order for development to proceed along healthy lines. If it is solved, the child moves ahead with strength and freedom to the next stage and next problem. If it is not adequately solved, the child is burdened with an unresolved problem that may limit his freedom and strength for the rest of his life.

Erikson's specific conflicts are less important than the general principle on which his theory is based. Some psychologists argue that other conflicts occur at various stages and that the conflicts Erikson lists could conceivably occur at other times, either earlier or later. These details are not crucial. But the vision of children facing the world, trying to solve certain problems, with their personalities depending on the solutions, is extremely important. The eight stages are outlined in Table 12.3, but we shall discuss only the first four in detail because they are the ones that deal with childhood.

Table 12.3
ERIKSON'S STAGES OF PERSONALITY DEVELOPMENT

Age (approximate)	Crisis or conflict	Ideal outcome
1. Birth to first year	Trust vs. mistrust	Basic trust
2. Second year	Autonomy vs. shame	Self-control and confidence
3. Third thru fifth year	Initiative and doubt vs. Guilt	Independence and purpose
4. Sixth through puberty	Industry vs. inferiority	Competence
5. Puberty and adolescence	Identity vs. role confusion	Sense of identity, ability to give to others
6. Early adulthood	Intimacy vs. isolation	Sharing, warmth, love
7. Young and middle adulthood	Creative production vs. self-centeredness	Productivity, nurturance
8. Later adulthood	Integrity vs. despair	Satisfaction with one's life, wisdom

Based on Erikson, 1963.

First Year—Basic Trust versus Mistrust

During their first year of life babies form their initial impressions of what the world is like. According to Erikson, infants will learn to either trust or mistrust the world during this stage. At birth infants do not distinguish between people and things. They seem unaware that their own body is distinct from that of the rest of the world. This soon changes, and they begin to respond to people differently from other objects. Research shows that by the age of four months most infants will smile at any human face (Gewirtz, 1965) and will return a smile that is offered to them. Although smiling can be encouraged by reinforcement (Brackbill, 1958), the response seems to emerge largely independently of particular treatment or environment (Gewirtz, 1965). One of the pleasures of dealing with infants is their readiness to smile back. Unless they are particularly unhappy, babies will usually grace you with a smile if you appear in their line of vision.

Stranger anxiety Around four months, this behavior changes somewhat. As infants learn to distinguish among different human beings, they will respond more to familiar faces and less to others. And around eight or nine months most infants develop what has been called *fear of strangers* or *stranger anxiety*. At this stage, instead of smiling, infants respond with fear or hesitation when they see an unfamiliar face. Stranger anxiety usually appears first at six to eight months, increases for a few months, and then declines (Greenberg, Hillman, and Grice, 1973). The anxiety is not indiscriminate; infants are more frightened by strange adults than by strange children. In addition, research by Rheingold and Eckerman (1973) and others indicates that some children never experience stranger anxiety and even those who do may show it under some circumstances and not others.

Exactly why stranger anxiety develops and whether it would occur even in a totally benign environment are unknown. It may be an innate tendency, serving to protect infants from hostile strangers at a period when they are no longer immobile and may be less well protected by their parents. In any case, this is a stage most infants pass through, after which they are once again fairly open to strangers. Once this stage is passed, infants begin to interact with other people in more complicated and differentiated ways.

Development of relationships When children begin to react to and recognize other people, they also begin to form relationships with them. These initial relationships, particularly the primary one with the mother (or mothering adult of either sex), play a major role in the development of trust.

If children's needs are satisfied, if they are fed when hungry, kept warm and comfortable, nurtured, attended to, and made to feel that life is orderly and predictable, then they will develop what Erikson called *basic trust*. According to this concept, children form a lasting, profound acceptance of the world and confidence in it. Later events may shake this confidence, of course, but at the most basic level children learn that the world is not a dangerous place. But if they are not fed when they are hungry, if they are not kept warm, if life is unpredictible and unordered, children learn to mistrust it at this basic level and perhaps may never develop full confidence in the world outside.

In a sense, this concept resembles the idea of a hierarchy of needs (described in Chapter 9). When simple needs are satisfied, individuals can go on to higher and more complex needs. If the simple needs are not satisfied, individuals must constantly worry about them and are not free to develop further. Naturally there is a range of satisfaction—few infants have all of their needs totally satisfied. But according to Erikson and other theorists, the greater the satisfaction of these needs, the more trusting and healthy the individual will become.

Attachment Erikson's description of this first basic conflict between trust and mistrust is reinforced by research on the phenomenon of attachment. John Bowlby (1969) calls a strong, healthy relationship between the child and the parent *attachment*, which is a combination of positive feelings, dependence, trust, desire to be physically close, and a tendency to be less frightened when the parent is nearby. These feelings will naturally cause children to stay close to their parent, and if the distance between them becomes too great, both parents and children will make an effort to reduce it—children because they are afraid, parents because the child seems unhappy. Indeed, Bowlby considers attachment a mechanism whose main function is to keep infants close to their parent, since this is the period during which children begin to move around freely and they might well need the extra protection this would provide. Attachment tends to appear between five or six months at the earliest and a year at the latest, with most children developing it at about seven or eight months.

The most important aspect of Bowlby's theory is his belief that attachment is developed because of innate or intrinsic tendencies in infants. Because children need the protection of an adult, nature has provided them with various behavioral patterns designed to elicit attachment from the adult. Grasping, sucking, cuddling, and so on are necessary for infants to survive but also tend to keep them close to the mother, and in turn cause mothers to give infants a lot of attention. A more subtle example is the infant's smile. Almost all adult's like to see children smile and find it very rewarding. By smiling, infants reinforce those adult behaviors that satisfy their needs. And at the same time, the smile produces feelings of attachment to the infant by the adult.

Thus, Bowlby argues that attachment does not depend on only a simple reinforcement of the infant's basic physiological needs. Food and warmth are important but are insufficient by themselves to activate the feelings of attachment that are crucial to an infant's survival. It takes continual interaction with the parent to produce attachment. The more attention infants are given, the stronger attachment they develop. And infants have intrinsic behaviors that elicit this attention.

Of course, the satisfaction of basic needs forms a key element in the relationship between parent and child. For example, hungry children are usually fed by the mother or in the mother's presence, even if the mother is not breast-feeding. Thus, children learn to associate the satisfaction of hunger with the mother and also any frustration or lack of satisfaction. However, Bowlby, Erikson, and others emphasize that the relationship with the mother depends on much more than just feeding.

Harlow's artificial mothers. This view of attachment is supported by Harry Harlow's ingenious research on the nature of the infant-mother relationship in monkeys. Baby monkeys were reared apart from their mothers but were provided with artificial mothers of various kinds. Some of the artificial mothers consisted of soft terrycloth bodies with a head while the others were made of wire with no cover. In one experiment, the monkeys were fed from a bottle attached to the wire mother and received no nourishment from the soft, terrycloth mother. Nevertheless, the monkeys spent much more time clinging to the soft mother and also reacted to it as a source of security in exploring the world (see Figs. 12.9 and 12.10). They would keep one foot on the terrycloth mother while investigating the cage and if frightened would return and cling to the terrycloth. This indicates that the warmth and softness were more important in terms of establishing a relationship than was the nourishment (Harlow and Harlow, 1966; Harlow and Zimmerman, 1958).

However, even a cuddly artificial mother that produced nourishment was not sufficient for the monkey to develop a healthy personality. When the terrycloth and wire mothers were the only contacts the monkeys had during the first six months of their lives, the babies did not become normal adults. They were unable to interact socially with other monkeys, and had great difficulty mating. When they did mate, the females made inadequate mothers. In contrast, when they were exposed to other young monkeys at an early age they grew up normally. Evidently some social contact with other animals of the same species is absolutely essential for normal social development.

Attention and care in human attachment. Mary Ainsworth has provided some direct evidence for the importance of attention and care in the development of attachment in human infants (1969, 1970). This research indicates that if the mother has a positive attitude toward breast-feeding, attachment is likely to develop, but just the act of breast-feeding is not sufficient. And Schaffer and Emerson (1964) also showed that it is attention and feelings associated with it that produce attachment. Thus, although the reinforcement derived from satisfying hunger and relieving discomfort must play some role

Fig. 12.9
Harlow's wire and cloth mothers

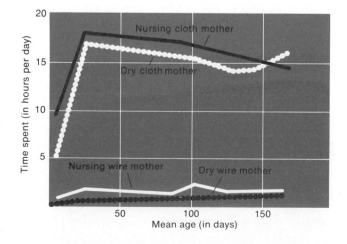

Fig. 12.10
Warmth versus nourishment

The infants prefer the cloth monkey regardless of whether or not it gives milk. (From Harlow and Zimmerman, 1959)

in the development of attachment, other, subtler factors also appear to be important. A strong, secure first relationship depends on adequate attention and a positive attitude on the part of the parent.

To sum up, the first year of life centers around the child's first relationship. If children are nurtured well—which means given tender, loving care—they form an attachment to their parent and a basic trust in the world. Otherwise, they become insecure and untrusting.

The Second Year—Autonomy versus Shame and Doubt

Erikson proposes that the second stage of development centers on the problem of independence. Healthy children have formed a strong attachment and now must begin to act on their own. The two lines of development are consistent. The stronger the attachment, the more secure and trustful the child, and the easier it will be for her to achieve some independence. The conflict occurs because the child must face the first demands of society.

This stage of development focuses on two crucial episodes that usually occur during the second year of life. Children must be weaned from the breast or bottle to more solid food, and later must be toilet trained. No matter what else they are required to do, in order to survive and to take their place in society, they must eat solid food and learn to control their bowels and bladder.

Weaning As far as we can tell, it matters little whether the baby is breast-fed or bottle-fed. But how the feeding is done and how the eventual weaning is accomplished are extremely important. The child's relationship with the mothering adult is the child's first introduction to the social world and much, therefore, depends on it. The act of feeding the baby, holding the baby, and providing nourishment can produce either warmth, security, and satisfaction or tension and anxiety. Similarly, the tenderness and understanding with which weaning is accomplished are crucial. Children must not feel rejected, but more independent. They should feel that they have accomplished something, not that their mother no longer wants to feed them.

Toilet training The socialization process is complex and infants must learn to control many different aspects of their behavior in order to fit into society. They have virtually no control over their needs or the expression of their feelings, and none is expected of them. But society requires adults and even fairly young children to control many of these behaviors most of the time. The expression of feeling and the satisfaction of needs are expected to occur only in appropriate circumstances.

Some needs, such as hunger and thirst, are expressed relatively openly in society. In contrast, other impulses, such as aggressive or sexual ones (discussed in detail in Chapters 10 and 13 respectively), are much more severely restricted. Most societies, and certainly Western, industrialized societies, demand that the individual express aggressive and sexual feelings only under limited circumstances. Eventually children will have to learn to control all of their needs and impulses, but naturally those that require stricter control will involve more difficulties and complications.

One of the first such impulses is the elimination of bodily wastes. Children must learn to control this natural function, committing it not whenever they feel the urge, but only when in the appropriate place. Thus, toilet training is a crisis in socialization and is also the first test of the child's ability to control herself and to fit into society. Just as feeding was the first test of how the world would treat the child, toilet training is the child's first test of herself. It is an episode in which she either learns confidence in herself and a feeling of mastery or develops doubt over her ability.

There is a dramatic contrast between success, which brings praise, and failure, which leads to embarrassment and criticism. You may remember how terrible it was to wet your pants in public as a small child, or even to have to go to the bathroom when one was not immediately available. Even as adults, we tend to get quite upset in this situation because of the possible consequences. Thus the negative aspects of failure are fairly easy to appreciate.

But there is also a strongly positive side to toilet training. You may have witnessed a child's great satisfaction when he manages to get to a toilet in time. Children often are delighted by their stools and admire them in the toilet. Adults may find it hard to understand the source of this delight, but children are only responding naturally to a productive accomplishment. In other words, toilet training can be a difficult experience, and often is, but it can also be greatly rewarding and give children a sense of confidence in their own strength, control, and productivity.

The outcome of toilet training depends to a great extent on when it is attempted and the patience of the parents. Attempts made too early are doomed to failure and frustration. As with so many other behaviors that we have mentioned, a certain degree of physical development is necessary for toilet training. The sphincter muscles and the child's awareness of how to control them are not sufficiently developed until around the middle of the second year. Although there is a wide range of ages at which toilet training is begun, it cannot be successful much before eighteen months—earlier attempts will subject the child to constant failures and the parents to frustration and disappointment, which will be communicated to the child. As a result, the child will probably develop a sense of inadequacy and lack of confidence. But if he is asked to control himself only when he can do so, he is more likely to succeed and to develop confidence.

Third to Fifth Year—Initiative versus Guilt

During these three years, children are capable of increasingly independent action and are constantly trying out new activities. This exposes them to danger and also tends to bring them into conflict with various rules of society. The parents and the rest of society face the dilemma of protecting and controlling children without discouraging this growing independence. The outcome of this conflict depends largely on how the children are disciplined.

Discipline The socialization process continues through much of childhood, and is accomplished in part by discipline (punishment) and rewards in one form or another. Since many of society's "rules" are quite arbitrary or at least beyond the understanding of young children, the parents must teach children what is and is not acceptable without expecting them to comprehend fully why that is so. To accomplish this, parents must rely on discipline when children do something wrong and reward when they do something right. However, the nature of the discipline and rewards is very important.

Some parents use objects and privileges for rewards and the denial of these plus physical punishment for discipline. Other parents use love, affection, and praise and the withholding of these. In the first case, children are being asked to behave in order to get rewards and avoid punishment; in the second case, they are being asked to behave in order to please their parents. There is a crucial and far-reaching difference.

While both techniques can produce obedience for the moment, there is good reason to believe that discipline based on love is much more effective in the long run. The main difference is that object reward and punishment do not seem to affect the children's internal evaluation of their behavior as much. Children who make their beds in order to earn a nickel or do not steal from the cookie jar because they are afraid of being hit tend to obey the rules only when the rewards and punishments are likely to occur. If they think they will not be caught and therefore not punished, there is little reason for them not to steal. Continual pairing of rewards with some behaviors and punishments with others may produce some tendency to evaluate those behaviors positively or negatively, but the link will be relatively weak.

In contrast, children who make their beds in order to get praise and do not steal because their parents will be disappointed in them tend to internalize these values. Accordingly, even when there is no chance of getting caught, they will be unlikely to steal because they have decided on their own that stealing is bad. Naturally not all discipline based on love is perfect, nor is discipline based on giving or withholding objects totally ineffective, but in general the former tends to produce a clearer moral sense and therefore to produce more lasting effects. As we noted in Chapter 10, physical punishment for aggression actually makes the child more aggressive outside the home. And extensive studies of juvenile delinquency (Glueck and Glueck, 1950, 1964) showed that aggression was much more common among children whose discipline had been based on objects and physical punishment than among those who were disciplined by the giving and withdrawing of love.

It is impossible to specify an ideal type and amount of discipline. Withdrawal of love appears to be very effective in teaching children to obey rules even when the authority is not around to enforce them. However, it seems likely that any kind of reasonable discipline (as opposed to severe beatings or other directly harmful means) can produce good socialization if done with love and understanding. In addition, consistency in discipline is very important. Children should not be punished one day for crossing the street alone and praised as independent for the same action the next day. Children like to know where they stand and they cannot form clear rules for their own behavior unless the parents are consistent in disciplining them.

Moreover, the goal of discipline is not to produce children who always obey rules but have no initiative. Such children may be easy to deal with, but they have not been adequately encouraged to express their own feelings and impulses. They may be so burdened with rules—and with feelings of guilt when they transgress these rules—that they are almost incapable of the independent behavior that is

STYLES OF DISCIPLINE

In addition to the particular kind of discipline that parents use, there are important differences in the amount and style of the discipline. Diana Baumrind has distinguished among three types of households and shown that they have quite different effects on children (Baumrind and Black, 1967). *Authoritarian* parents exert a lot of control, expect strict conformity and unquestioning obedience, and tend to be detached and cold. *Permissive* parents make few demands on their children, explain the rules they do have, and are generally warm and noncontrolling. The third type of parent, which Baumrind calls *authoritative*, exerts firm control but does it in a warm manner, explaining the reason for each rule and requiring obedience only because the child understands the purpose of the rule. On entering school, children from authoritarian homes are withdrawn, distrustful, and the most discontent; while children from authoritative homes are the most self-reliant, self-controlled, and confident.

Baumrind has suggested (1971) that there is an additional type of pattern, which she calls *harmonious*, in which parents exert almost no direct control. Instead, the children seem to know what their parents want and they do it without discipline or reward.

These are, of course, idealized descriptions. Most parents fall in between the various patterns, having some characteristics of each. For example, a parent may be strict on some issues but permissive on others, authoritative and rational at times but arbitrary and authoritarian at others, and exhibit some of the characteristics of the harmonious parent at still other times. However, Baumrind's research indicates that the type of discipline may be less important than the mood in which it is used; and that permissiveness is not necessarily best for the health and confidence of the child.

Box 12.2

necessary for an adult. The problem is to produce reasonable adherence to the family's and society's rules together with freedom of action and expression for the child.

Six to Eleven—Industry versus Inferiority

Once children enter school, their problems tend to focus on achievement rather than just expression. Again they want to accomplish things, to act on their own, but now they find that in addition to following some rules they must compete with other children and with abstract standards. When they succeed, they are encouraged to go further and feel good about themselves; when they fail, they are discouraged and may develop a sense of inferiority. Yet all children experience some failures and some successes. The crucial factor is how failure and success are handled by parents and teachers. Once again, the outcome depends largely on a balance of discipline, praise, and criticism. If children are praised for their accomplishments and their failures are sympathetically understood, they will tend to become strong and independent. If their successes are ignored or played down and their failures punished or criticized, they will become discouraged and insecure. As with discipline, it is important for praise and criticism to be given with love and consistency. It is a mistake to praise everything or to ignore all failures. Parents must be realistic, and accept how children actually are doing so that the children can accept themselves.

Box 12.3

GUILT AND HAPPINESS

Withdrawal of love is an effective type of discipline. Its immediate effect is to make children worry about losing that love and to feel guilty if they transgress. This guilt provides a strong, built-in control mechanism. However, there is some evidence that children who feel guilty (and therefore are well behaved) may become unhappy adults. In a study of adult happiness, Shaver and Freedman (1976) asked people whether they were happy and, among many other questions, whether they felt guilty as children. Very few childhood experiences appeared to be related to adult happiness, but guilt was. In general, those people who remember feeling guilty much of the time as children were less happy than the others. This finding is only suggestive, based as it is on a large-scale questionnaire and memories of childhood. Nevertheless, it does raise the possibility that techniques that are effective in controlling children's behavior may sometimes have harmful effects on the children in future years.

How Children Describe Parental Treatment

The three problems that Erikson emphasizes during the first ten or twelve years of a child's life involve trust versus mistrust, autonomy versus doubt, and severity of control and discipline. It is interesting that children focus on exactly these three problems when they consider their parents' treatment of them. Asked to describe how they are treated, children from early grade school to the beginning of high school divide parental treatment into three major categories: Acceptance-rejection, autonomy-control, and firm-lax discipline (Armentrout and Burger, 1972; Renson, Schaefer, and Levy, 1968). This holds for many different populations of children and remains largely constant across different ages. While this is hardly surprising, it provides some independent verification of Erikson's focus on these particular issues in childhood.

Children Affect Parents Too

Although we have been emphasizing the importance of how parents treat children, it is important to realize that to some extent this is a mutual relationship. Children are not entirely passive objects. They too act and react, and their behavior is one factor in how the relationship develops. In particular, children can elicit many affectionate responses from their parents or very few. Children who tend to smile a lot will in turn receive more smiles; children who cry a lot may get more attention than those that suffer quietly. Since children do seem to differ in these respects, probably in part for genetic or innate reasons, different children receive different treatment from parents partly as a result of how the children behave (Bell, 1968, 1974).

In other words, if a child turns out "badly" (upset, disturbed, criminal) it may not be entirely the parents' fault. Parents who seem unloving may be dealing with a child who is hard to love. But if we accept this proposition, we should also not give the parents all the credit when the child turns out well. There is an interaction of qualities of the child (for which the parents are responsible genetically but not otherwise) and experience, so both parents and child are partly responsible for whatever course a child's development follows.

We have discussed in detail the first four stages of Erikson's scheme, which bring the child to puberty. The rest of the stages focus on specific events and difficulties, but the basic problems are quite similar to those encountered earlier in life. We shall deal with some of the later stages in the next chapter, which explores sex roles and adult development. However, from these first crucial periods you can see that the development of children involves a constant interaction with their parents and the world, and the outcome of this interaction determines the kind of adults that emerge.

IDENTIFICATION

A phenomenon that has powerful effects on child development and magnifies the importance of children's early relationships is a strong tendency for children to imitate the behavior, mannerisms, and beliefs of one adult and to accept whatever this adult says. This mixture of affection, love, respect, and close copying has been called *identification*. Children model themselves after some figure in their environment. Early in life this person is usually the mother, but it can be some other mothering adult or the father if he plays a more prominent role. Whoever it is, the continuing presence of one (or at least a small number) of adult individuals in the child's life seems to be extremely important in normal development. Children use this model in order to shape their own behavior and personality and to achieve some sense of what they themselves are like and also of what is expected of them in the world. For these reasons, the lack of such an adult seems to leave children confused, uncertain of their own personality, low in self-awareness and self-esteem, and without a clear sense of morals or values.

There is evidence that children deprived of a consistent adult early in life suffer in this way. Infant monkeys that were separated from their mothers and from other adults became depressed and anxious (Kaufman and Rosenblum, 1967). Similarly, human children who are separated from their parents and put in hospitals or nurseries for extended periods of time become agitated and depressed. When English children during World War II were moved out of London to protect them from bombing and put in centers that did not have one permanent adult, many of them suffered severely. They "would lie or sit with wide open, expressionless eyes, frozen, immobile face and far-away expression as if in a daze. . . ." (Spitz and Wolf, 1946, p. 314). Children can apparently adapt reasonably well to brief separations, but extended periods without their mother or some permanent substitute often cause serious problems.

This does not mean that the traditional family situation is the only way in which an acceptable adult model can be provided. On the collective farm (kibbutz) in Israel, children are raised collectively. Almost from birth, infants on a kibbutz live in a communal nursery rather than with their parents. During the first year, the mother has most of the responsibility for care and feeding, but after that, responsibility shifts to the nursery and the mother tends to see her child only on weekends and in the evenings. Children are raised by specially trained people at the community nursery. These substitute mothers spend a great deal of time with the children and have no other responsibility on the farms. This has the obvious advantages of guaranteeing efficiency and expert care, relieving the mother of child-rearing responsibilities and freeing her to take an active part in farming duties. However, it does raise the question of whether "collective motherhood" of this kind will produce healthy children. Although the situation is unlike that in wartime England or of families with absent parents, the mothering adult, no matter how well trained and dedicated, does share her time among a large number of children and probably does not give any one child the amount of love he ordinarily would get from his own mother. However, the real mother does see the child daily—perhaps as much as most working mothers do in this country.

A number of studies of kibbutz children have yielded somewhat inconsistent results. Some research (for example, Rabin, 1965) seems to suggest that kibbutz children were slightly behind in mental development compared to comparable children raised in noncollective communities. Most other studies (for example, Kohen-Raz, 1968) found no differences between kibbutz and other Israeli children. Such comparisons are difficult because life on a kibbutz differs in many ways from life in other communities. One study tried to avoid this problem by comparing children on a kibbutz with those from a mosharim, a very similar kind of community, the major difference being that the mosharim does not raise children in the communal way. The results were that kibbutz children had higher self-esteem, more social interest, and higher identification with their parents.

This research, though inconclusive, indicates that raising children collectively with a trained, dedicated, and affectionate substitute mother does not necessarily produce obvious deficiencies and may even have some advantages. In short, arguments in our country that community child care centers have harmful effects on children should probably be largely discounted in the light of studies of the Israeli experience.

Sexual Identification

One effect of children's identification with a particular adult is the emergence of their sexual identity. Young children learn to behave "appropriately" for their sex through a process of reinforcement and identification with the same-sexed parent. This sexual identification has an enormous effect on most children, which endures throughout their lives. The process by which it occurs is the same that we described earlier, in that children adopt the behavior and values of the parent, but identification is concentrated on the parent of the same sex. Since this is a particular form of identification that is being increasingly questioned in our society, we shall discuss it in detail in Chapter 13 when we consider the whole question of sexual identification and sexual behavior.

MORAL DEVELOPMENT

Another important aspect of development is the formation of morality. In addition to learning the rules of society, all people develop their own personal sense of right and wrong that has profound effects on how they behave. The development of this moral sense is closely related to both cognitive and social development. How is morality acquired?

Learning

At the simplest level, the learning approach explains a considerable amount of moral development. There is little question that children acquire certain laws and rules through a process of learning and imitation. Children can be taught to resist or give in to selfish impulses if provided with a model who behaves in appropriate ways (Rosenkoetter, 1973). Similarly, aggression can be encouraged or discouraged by models (Bandura, Ross, and Ross, 1961; Baron, 1971). As Bandura and Walters point out (1963), self-control and obedience to rules are certainly developed in part through learning.

In addition, it is obvious that the particular rules required by the society in which children are raised must to some extent be learned. Societies throughout the world agree on very few standards of behavior. Murder within the group, parent-child incest, and perhaps stealing from friends are universally condemned by organized societies. But there are probably no other specific behaviors that all cultures agree are good or bad. Fighting, violence, and torture are frowned upon in some cultures and accepted or even encouraged in others. Stealing is wrong in most industrialized western cultures, but some subcultures within those societies might not agree, and whole other cultures seem to accept stealing as part of life that is not to be condemned (Benedict, 1934). Therefore, children must learn the specific rules of their subgroup by observing how others behave and by being deliberately taught what is considered right and wrong. Thus, in terms of the development of self-control, the general tendency to obey rules, and the knowledge of those rules, learning must play a role in moral development.

Identification

Identification also has an important influence on moral development because it leads children to accept the morality of the adult. It is not just a question of learning what that morality is—children may be exposed to many different views of morality. But once identification has occurred, children tend to pattern themselves after the person with whom the identification has taken place. Indeed, there is some suggestion that children who have no consistent adult figure, or who are treated so badly that identification does not occur, develop a weak and distorted sense of morality (Sears, Maccoby, and Levin, 1957). People with such weak morality are often called psychopaths. They do not obey any set of rules, and feel no guilt regardless of their actions. Although there are undoubtedly other reasons for the development of a psychopathic personality, the lack of identification, resulting in the absence of a moral sense, appears to be one of the most important. (See Chapter 15 for a further discussion.)

Stages of Moral Development

Both learning and identification provide partial explanations for moral development, but there also seems to be a large cognitive

LAWRENCE KOHLBERG

element. Piaget (1932) suggested and Kohlberg (1969) has elaborated the notion that there are stages of moral development that correspond roughly with the stages of cognitive development described earlier. The basic idea is that a certain level of development is necessary in order for children to reach a particular moral level, and that therefore all children will pass through the same series of moral stages.

Lawrence Kohlberg has described six stages that are presented in Table 12.4. As you can see, the earliest stages define morality mainly in terms of punishment and reward for the individual. Children obey the rules to avoid punishment (Stage 1) or to maximize rewards (Stage 2). They have no real sense of right and wrong, nor are they even concerned with how others feel about the action except insofar as they will provide reward or punishment.

The next two stages involve a more thorough understanding of conventional morality, and children now take into account what others would feel about their actions. Kohlberg calls the third stage "good boy or nice girl" morality. Children want approval, want to be considered good people. Intentions become important for the first time. If you "mean well" it counts for a lot. In the fourth stage, the concept of law is introduced. Children recognize and obey authority. If they transgress, they begin to experience guilt, which means some sense of right and wrong has emerged. The children themselves are beginning to feel that some actions are good and others bad regardless of their benefits to them. Children in this stage will not steal from a store for a variety of reasons. They may still be afraid of punishment, and they also recognize that it is considered wrong to steal, and that they would not be behaving correctly. Yet they still have no appreciation of why something is right or wrong and cannot question conventional rules, although they are beginning to share the norms of their society.

Table 12.4
KOHLBERG'S STAGES OF MORAL DEVELOPMENT

Stage	Description
Preconventional level	
1. Punishment is dominant	Obey rules to avoid physical pain
2. Hedonism—rewards and punishment	Obey primarily to obtain rewards and avoid punishment.
Conventional level	
3. Want to be liked	Try to be "good boy or girl," so that others will approve; conform to others.
4. Respond to authority	Obey authority's rules to gain acceptance and avoid censure; maintain social order; do one's duty.
Postconventional	
5. Legality and standards	Obey rules of society; want to appear moral to an impartial observer; uphold standards and laws.
6. Individual principles	Obey own ethical principles based on sense of justice, human rights and respect for the individual; be highly flexible.

Based on Kohlberg, 1969.

In the final two stages, individuals make their own decisions about right and wrong according to principles and values that they accept. Morality is somewhat relative—a given act must be considered in the broader context and in relation to general principles. One does not steal because it would upset the legal order and would be unfair to the other person (Stage 5). But at the ultimate stage, higher principles such as the value of human life are also considered and stealing would be allowed in order to save a life, feed a child, or produce more good than harm (Stage 6).

Although there are probably some minor variations, these basic stages have been found in a wide variety of cultures including the United States, Great Britain, China, Mexico, and Turkey. Moreover, the sequence is not dependent on religious differences, appearing in roughly the same order for Catholics, Protestants, Jews, Buddhists, Moslems, and atheists (Kohlberg, 1970).

It seems clear that these stages are produced by corresponding changes in the level of cognitive functioning. When children are confronted with a moral argument more advanced than theirs, they tend to be convinced by the higher-level child (Glassco, Milgram, and Youniss, 1970). Indeed, there is substantial evidence that all children, regardless of their age, prefer the highest-level moral argument that they are capable of understanding (Rest, Turiel, and Kohlberg, 1969; Rest, 1973). This does not mean that all people with sufficient intelligence have high moral values. Rather, these studies show only that how we deal with moral issues depends to some extent on our cognitive development. We may still act in immoral ways, but the way we think about moral issues will be at a higher level. In other words, even at the highest moral level, people are capable of dropping bombs on children, stealing from the helpless, and discriminating against certain groups, but these actions will be justified in complex moral terms with reference to higher principles rather than in terms of simple reward and punishment.

FURTHER DEVELOPMENT

We have traced development through childhood, showing how physical, perceptual, cognitive, social, personality, and moral changes occur as a joint result of genetic factors and experience. Naturally, development does not stop at the end of childhood. These early experiences form the basis for future growth and to some extent determine the direction in which the individual will develop. But people change throughout their lives, facing new situations, learning new patterns and dropping old ones, and acquiring new attitudes, values, skills, and ways of dealing with the world. Moreover, there are still some important episodes in the individual's life that have not yet occurred. As we shall discuss in the next chapter, the onset of puberty turns children into sexually mature adults and introduces a new and vitally important element into life. And, of course, education, careers, romantic relationships, marriage, children, and the anticipation of death all have profound effects on people's lives. The next chapter focuses on sex roles, sexual development, and these other aspects of adult life. ∎

Summary

1. The process of human development depends on both innate factors and experience. Early physical and perceptual development are largely determined by innate factors. The development of cognitive abilities, personality, social behavior, and morality are strongly influenced by experience, with innate characteristics playing a smaller role.

2. The normal development of the human from fertilized egg to infant can be threatened by a variety of physical influences such as disease, drugs, lack of sufficient nutrition, and the physical health of the mother. It has also been suggested that severe emotional stress in the mother produces a hormonal imbalance that can interfere with the normal growth of the embryo.

3. The development of mechanical skills and perceptual abilities in an infant follows an unvarying sequence that is dependent almost entirely on maturational readiness. While it is possible to teach children to climb or walk a little earlier than usual, other children catch up quickly when they are physically ready. Animals deprived of the chance to practice their perceptual skills catch up quickly when returned to a normal situation.

4. Lorenz's work with newborn ducklings provided the basis for the idea that there may be *critical periods* in development during which a particular behavior must occur if the animal is to develop normally. Other research suggests that critical periods may themselves be affected by experience.

5. Jean Piaget's observational research on children led him to propose that cognitive development occurs in a series of four stages: (a) sensorimotor, which includes the discovery that there is a separate world apart from the child, the development of object constancy, and the beginning of some understanding of space, time, and causality; (b) preoperational, which includes language acquisition, concept formation, and the beginning of understanding of conservation; (c) concrete operations, which includes understanding conservation and numerical relationships and learning to classify objects into hierarchies; and (d) formal operations, which includes the development of abstract thought, the systematic forming and testing of hypotheses, and logical reasoning.

6. Erikson viewed personality development as occurring in stages. Each stage centers around a problem that must be resolved in order for healthy development to take place.

7. The childhood stages of personality development, according to Erikson, are as follows: (a) Trust versus mistrust (first year)—How children are cared for and whether or not their needs are met will influence whether they look on the world with trust or mistrust. (b) Autonomy versus shame and doubt (second year)—The problems of weaning and toilet training will influence whether children gain confidence in their own control and productivity or whether they develop a sense of inadequacy. (c) Initiative versus guilt (third to fifth year)—Children's need for independence conflicts with their need to adhere to parental and societal rules. If a happy balance is achieved, children will develop a sense of independence and initiative. (d) Industry versus inferiority (six to eleven)—The successes and failures of the school years and how they are handled will affect whether chil-

dren become industrious or feel a sense of inferiority about their abilities.

8. Identification, the process in which children model their behavior after that of an adult they love and admire, is crucial to healthy adjustment. Children who are deprived of an adult model with whom to identify may become uncertain of their own personality, low in self-esteem, and lacking in a clear sense of morals or values. The adult model need not be the actual mother, and research suggests that children raised by a loving substitute mother figure will not suffer in adjustment.

9. The development of morality can be explained in part by the normal learning processes. Children are taught by their parents (or parental figures) to obey societal and family rules, and they also learn by observing how others behave and by imitating that behavior. Identification also plays a crucial role, with children patterning their behavior after that of the adult with whom they have identified. As suggested above, if for some reason identification does not occur, children may develop a weak sense or no sense of morality.

10. Moral development can also be explained in terms of developmental stages. Elaborating on Piaget's ideas, Kohlberg proposed that the development of morality occurs in stages that are dependent on the level of cognitive functioning. He identified six stages of moral development—from the lowest level, in which children obey rules to avoid punishment or receive reward; to the highest level, in which individuals make moral decisions according to principles and values that they have internalized. The stages described by Kohlberg have been found across a broad spectrum of cultures and religious groups.

RECOMMENDED READING

Erikson, E. H. *Childhood and Society.* New York: Norton, 1950. Erikson's view of child development. This is a warm, thoughtful book by an outstanding theorist and therapist.

Flavell, J. H. *The Developmental Psychology of Jean Piaget.* New York: Van Nostrand, 1963. Easier to read than Piaget himself, this book covers most of Piaget's theories with evaluation and comment.

Flavell, J. H. *Cognitive Development.* Englewood Cliffs, N.J.: Prentice-Hall, 1977. A thorough general introduction to this complex topic.

Lerner, R. M. *Concepts and Theories of Human Development.* Reading, Mass.: Addison-Wesley, 1976. A somewhat difficult text that describes development as an interactive process between biological characteristics of the individual and experience. A nice middle ground between those who stress one or the other.

Nash, J. *Developmental Psychology: A Psychobiological Approach.* Englewood Cliffs, N.J.: Prentice-Hall, 1970. A rather difficult textbook that presents the developmental field more from the point of view of physiology than most books. For those who are especially interested in this approach.

Piaget, J. *The Origins of Intelligence in Children.* New York: International Universities Press, 1952. The most comprehensible book by one of the greats. It concentrates on cognitive development, and provides a good introduction to Piaget's theory.

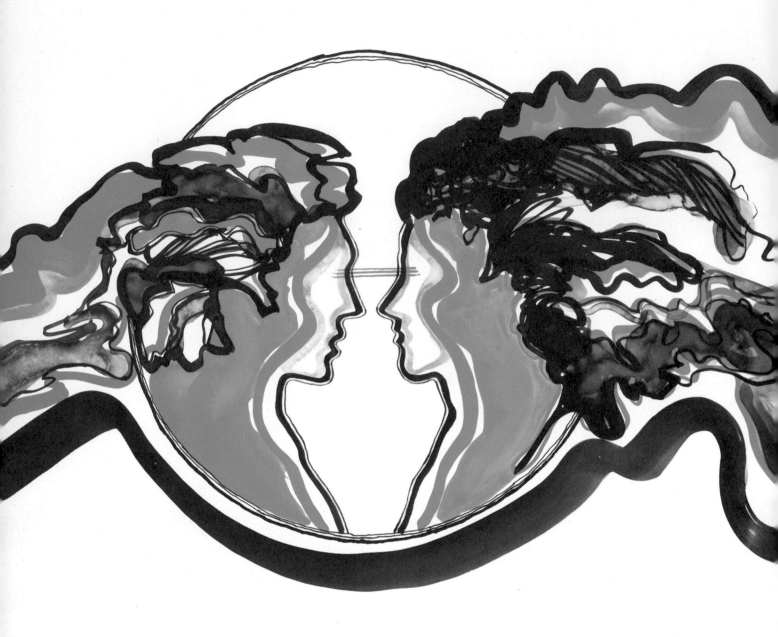

After sixteen years—that was seven years ago—I took a trip to Hawaii and the Caribbean for two weeks. Went with a lover. The kids saw it—they're all married now. (Laughs.) One of my daughters said, "Act your age." I said, "Honey, if I were acting my age, I wouldn't be walking. My bones would ache. You don't want to hear about my arthritis. Aren't you glad I'm happy?"
Studs Terkel, Working

13 Sex and Adult Development

Adolescence and sexual behavior ▪ *Current sexual attitudes and behavior* ▪ *Sexual deviance* ▪ *Sex roles* ▪ *Adult development* ▪ *Adolescence and the search for identity* ▪ *Occupation and career* ▪ *Marriage and family* ▪ *Middle age* ▪ *The later years*

Albert Einstein did poorly in school until he became interested in mathematics and physics during adolescence. Grandma Moses started painting in her late 70s. Jimmy Carter went from being a nuclear engineer to peanut farmer and then to president of the United States. Most of us are familiar with similar though perhaps less dramatic illustrations of how development continues after early childhood. We all know children who are noisy brats at eight but quiet, serious people at eighteen; and others who are withdrawn and insecure at ten but sociable and popular in college. And we can observe in our own lives substantial changes that took place after childhood. Until recently, psychologists tended to concentrate on development during childhood; indeed, this field used to be called child psychology. But more and more psychologists are broadening their view to include development throughout life, for of course we do continue to change and develop as long as we live. Although the early years may be especially important in that they lay the groundwork for future development, neither personality nor particular behavior patterns are fixed forever. The problems and experiences of adolescence and adulthood have great effect on our lives and play important roles in determining the kind of people we become.

After childhood, two new concerns appear that we must deal with more or less throughout our lives. The first is sexuality, which includes sex roles, actual sexual relations, relationships with sex partners, marriage, and family. The second can be defined broadly as a concern with the kind of life we want to lead, which includes career, lifestyle, and long-term goals. As we get older, we must face the problem of aging and the prospect of dying. And running through all of these specific problems is the important, but somewhat vague, search for happiness and satisfaction. Let us consider each of these in turn.

ADOLESCENCE AND SEXUAL BEHAVIOR

Although we sometimes think that sexuality begins at puberty, sexual behavior of a sort starts early in childhood. Stimulation of many parts of the body and particularly the genitals is pleasurable at all stages of life, including infancy. Baby boys get erections and babies of both sexes act as if they like genital stimulation. Moreover, children are fascinated by the sexual organs, play doctor with each other, and so on. Thus, interest in sex does not appear out of the blue at puberty. On the contrary, there is some experience with sex in childhood that provides a history out of which adult sexuality emerges.

However, sex clearly takes on much greater importance in people's lives with the onset of puberty. *Puberty* is the period during which we physically change from children into adults. The changes are dramatic. Almost all people experience a sudden spurt in growth, gaining as much as four or five inches and fifteen or twenty pounds in one year. The reproductive organs also develop rapidly during this period, and the so-called secondary sexual characteristics appear, including larger breasts for girls, facial hair and lower voices for boys, pubic hair for both sexes, and a general change in body shape. Puberty is defined as the achievement of physical sexual maturity and is marked by the beginning of menstruation in women and approximately by the appearance of sperm in the urine of men.

One important aspect of this developmental process is that puberty occurs over a wide range of ages. Girls reach puberty anywhere from ages ten to seventeen, boys from ages twelve to eighteen, and a few people may reach it even earlier or later than this. In addition, girls tend to achieve puberty on average about two years earlier than boys. This means that in any group of people between the ages of eleven and fifteen there will be a great deal of variation in the stage of development, and that, in general, girls will be ahead of boys. A seventh- or eighth-grade class will have a mixture of small boys who have not yet begun their growth spurt; tall, awkward boys right in the middle of their sudden growth; girls who are undeveloped sexually; and other girls who are both taller and more mature sexually. Moreover, because girls tend to reach puberty earlier, most of them will have reached puberty while most of the boys will not have. In fact, as shown in Fig. 13.1, due to the difference in age at which the growth spurt occurs, there is a period during which girls are on average actually taller than boys.

These sudden changes are often bewildering and produce a variety of conflicts. Some members of both sexes go through a period of awkwardness. Their coordination is sometimes poor because they are not used to their own size, they sometimes grow much taller before they gain enough weight to go along with their height, and so on. But these difficulties are much less serious than the problems adolescents encounter with their sexual maturity. Girls who mature early are often embarrassed because their breasts are so much larger than other girls', because they are menstruating before anyone else in the class, because they are attracting the attention of older boys, and because they do not know how to handle their new maturity. And late maturers of both sexes have the opposite problems—they are embarrassed because they are not yet women or men while others are sexually mature, and feel rejected because they do not get the attention their more mature classmates are attracting. While most adolescents are proud and happy at the appearance of sexual characteristics, this is typically mixed with feelings of uncertainty, embarrassment, and nervousness. Clearly, this period of transition from childhood is an exceptionally hard time for many people.

Pleasure versus Guilt

In the previous chapter we discussed the conflicts that occur at various stages of development during childhood. During adolescence, one of the major conflicts is between the enjoyment and other reinforcements that can come from sex and the guilt that is often associated with it; between acceptance and rejection of one's own body and desires. This is further complicated by the fact that adult sexual behavior depends on another person. Not only must you accept yourself, but you must find someone else to accept you. And, of course, sexual behavior is strongly controlled by the social values current in society and by the individual's own morality, which may or may not be the same as society's. Accordingly, young adults face enormous cross pressures.

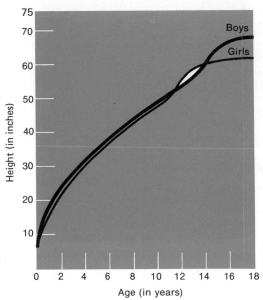

Fig. 13.1
Growth curves for boys and girls

Because girls' growth spurts tend to occur earlier, there is a brief period (shown in white) when girls are on average taller than boys. (After Tanner, Whitehouse, and Takaishi, 1966)

CURRENT SEXUAL ATTITUDES AND BEHAVIOR

Sexual behavior is greatly influenced by the prevailing values and customs of society, and these differ widely from place to place and from time to time. Most primitive, nonindustrial societies that have been studied have much freer attitudes toward sex than the more industrialized societies. Most nonindustrialized societies allow premarital sexual intercourse, and many of these encourage it. Adolescents are expected to engage in sex in most of these cultures, although certain restrictions are placed on them, such as not having sex with relatives. Sometimes, boys are allowed great freedom while girls are more restricted. But in virtually all of these societies, sex is an accepted fact of life in adolescence and even in childhood.

This relatively free attitude toward sex contrasts sharply with attitudes that prevailed in the United States for most of the twentieth century. During this period, it was acknowledged that adolescents had sexual impulses, but they were expected to control them. Certainly girls were not supposed to engage in sexual intercourse before they were married. And though boys were allowed somewhat more freedom, even they were somewhat restricted.

There has obviously been considerable change in these attitudes. Although sexual mores vary greatly among different communities and different families, the overall feeling about sex has become much freer. In most communities premarital sex by both men and women is expected if not always fully accepted. Perhaps more important, it is now understood that both sexes have sexual feelings and impulses, and that it is all right to enjoy sexuality. Indeed, one of the effects of the feminist movement is that women feel they have a right to enjoy sex as much as men. Sex is no longer a duty that a wife performs more or less under protest; it is now an act that she is supposed to take

How do you think the judges at this 1920 bathing beauty contest would react if they could see what is worn on our beaches today?

pleasure from—and if she doesn't, something is wrong either with her or with her husband. In other words, we have now gotten around to the attitude of most so-called primitive societies—that sex is an important and good thing in life, and that people should enjoy it.

It is extremely difficult to obtain reliable data on sexual behavior. Many people consider this aspect of their lives so private and personal that they will not discuss it, at least not with someone who is doing a survey. Others are willing or even enthusiastic about discussing it, but their answers are often dishonest. Some are embarrassed to give accurate replies, and therefore understate the level and type of their activity; while others use a survey to exaggerate their sexual prowess and freedom. And even if everyone who replied did answer truthfully (as many probably do), it is likely they are less restricted than those who do not answer at all, which again biases the results. Thus, surveys of sexual behavior must be viewed with skepticism and caution.

The earliest major work on sexual behavior was conducted by Alfred Kinsey in the late 1930s and 1940s (1948, 1953). More recently there have been many different surveys conducted both by mail (for example, Athanasiou, Shaver, and Tavris, 1970) and in person (for example, Hunt, 1974). Without going into great detail, let us cite a few of the most important findings on which these two recent large-scale studies agree. First, it appears to be fairly unusual now for someone to remain a virgin until marriage. Results varied, but only about 20 percent of the women and probably fewer than 10 percent of the men refrained from premarital intercourse. The figure for women is a dramatic change from Kinsey's survey, which found that more than half of the women were virgins at marriage.

In addition, there is considerable freedom in types of sexual activity. More than 70 percent of the respondents had at least tried oral-genital foreplay, and variations in positions for intercourse are quite common. More than 35 percent of males and perhaps 15 percent of females report having at least one homosexual experience during or after adolescence, and the figures would be much higher for homosexual experiences in childhood. It is interesting to note that these results are similar to Kinsey's despite gay liberation and the seemingly more liberal attitudes toward homosexuality that are prevalent today. In addition, although homosexuals are much more visible now than in the past, these recent studies indicate no change since Kinsey's survey in the number of people who consider themselves exclusively or primarily homosexual—it is still about 4 percent of the adult population.

A great deal of publicity, much of it rather lurid and sensational, has been given to "swinging"—exchanging sexual partners. There are magazines devoted entirely to it, many newspaper and magazine articles, and probably lots of thinking about it by many people. However, even the relatively liberal sample of respondents who return sex questionnaires have little experience with swinging, as shown in Table 13.1, and most of them participated only once. (It is fascinating to note that this somewhat radical expression of liberated sexuality is still generally called "wife-swapping," as if it were only the husband who participates or makes the decision.) More people had engaged in sex with more than one person at the same time (group sex), but

...u w....d like to meet some more. NYR, Box 12320.

EUROPEAN LADY, middle-aged, attractive, healthy, likes sports, music, happy life. Seeks cultured, secure gentleman of good character, 45-60. NYR, Box 12343.

ST. LOUIS AREA SINGLE MALES, British Universities graduates or onetime students, interested forming social club, write NYR, Box 12289.

TELEDATE. METROPOLITAN NEW YORKERS meet via closed-circuit TV. Only service in color, on 7 foot Video-Beam screen. Straight and gay clientele. Discreet, professional. Success assured. (212) 582-6201.

BAY AREA LADIES, running out of good books to read lately? Some warm, bright, funny woman will never lack for above if she can help a Berkeley male librarian, 49, NY Jewish intellectual type, too long in the stacks recently, to circulate again. NYR, Box 12374.

ATTRACTIVE, BRIGHT, PROFESSIONAL HAMPTON WOMAN, independent and human interested in meeting unattached man, 50+, confident, aware, interesting and good to be with. Please write about yourself—give name, phone number. NYR, Box 12380.

DC AREA MAN, 41, desires satisfying intellectual and sexual relationship with mature woman, 35-45, who shares enjoyment of great music, photography, literature. Box 1651, Springfield, Virginia 22151.

THE MAN FOR WHOM I AM SEARCHING won't be easy to find: Someone in his fifties or sixties who has the capacity to care, to understand and to be committed. I would enjoy meeting such a man and we could see if I am a woman who pleases him. NYR, Box 12306.

GAYS/BISEXUALS, receive free literature from the nation's largest gay social organiza-'on. Discretion assured. Call toll free (800) C-''----'- (21' ''4-3491, NYC,

Table 13.1
EVER ENGAGED IN "SWINGING SEX"

	Males	Females
Had engaged in mate swapping	5%	5%
Had engaged in group sex	15%	9%
Might engage in mate swapping	41%	22%
Might engage in group sex	50%	20%

For this sample, a relatively small percentage had engaged in swapping or group sex, and most of those only once, but a much higher percentage say they *might*.

Source: Athanasiou, Shaver, and Tavris, 1970.

Table 13.2
ATTITUDES TOWARD EXTRAMARITAL SEX

	Male	Female
Adds dimension to marriage	6%	3%
Permissible if both agree	23%	19%
All right but don't talk about it	5%	4%
All right in principle, but can be disastrous	22%	17%
All right for men only	2%	0%
Allowable only under very special circumstances	24%	30%
Always wrong	18%	27%

Source: Athanasiou, Shaver, and Tavris, 1970.

again, generally only once. Many people say that they have thought about it, but obviously thinking about an activity is an entirely different matter from engaging in it.

Attitudes toward sex have clearly changed even more than practices. As late as 1959 almost 80 percent of those polled thought that premarital sex was wrong in principle, while the figure dropped to only 9 percent in 1970. However, most surveys still report that people tend to link love, or at least romance, and sex quite closely. Casual sex continues to be frowned upon by many people. Moreover, extramarital sex is considered a clearly desirable addition to marriage by only a small percentage of people (see Table 13.2). Many people think it may be permissible or even desirable under some circumstances, but few believe that it will help a marriage.

Thus, there is no question that sexual behavior and values are freer now than they were twenty or thirty years ago. People engage in sex earlier, experiment more, have more partners, and are more accepting of what other people do even if they do not do it themselves. However, there continues to be a strong tendency to relate sex and love. For most people sex has not become a casual activity to engage

Box 13.1

SEX THERAPY

In response to the greater freedom regarding sex and to the continuing sexual difficulties that many people experience, there now exist therapies specifically devoted to sexual problems. A husband-and-wife team, William Masters and Virginia Johnson (1966), conducted research on sexual behavior by observing couples during the sexual act. This was an important change from previous work, which relied entirely on interviews and self-reports. Rather than having to rely solely on information that people provided about their sex lives, Masters and Johnson were able to observe directly and obtain information that might otherwise have been unavailable. Some people feel that this research invaded personal privacy, dealt in matters that should not be studied, and perhaps yielded invalid results because sex is usually a private matter, not performed in front of an audience. Nevertheless, it seems clear that Masters and Johnson did open up this vital area for more scientific study.

Perhaps most important is that Masters and Johnson developed a technique for treating certain kinds of sexual problems. They discovered that many people have difficulty accepting their sexual impulses, are embarrassed by them, are afraid to express or talk about them, and that they therefore have difficulty enjoying sex. Moreover, many people are inexperienced sexually and therefore do not know how to give or receive pleasure. Sex therapy encourages communication between the sexual partners (it is always done with couples) and at the same time, in a sense, teaches people to accept the pleasure that can be obtained from their bodies. The specific procedures differ considerably from one therapist to another and for different sexual problems. However, Masters and Johnson use two specific techniques that they claim are highly successful. First, couples are told not to engage in sexual intercourse or other forms of direct sex, but rather to start fresh, as if they had never engaged in any sexual behavior. They are told to start by caressing each other's bodies very gently, avoiding the genitals. This allows them to avoid the pressures of sex performance and still experience the pleasure that can be derived from their bodies. From there, they proceed very gradually, over a period of many days, to more and more intimate caresses until they engage in intercourse. Meanwhile, they meet

in simply for pleasure. The nature of the relationship with one's partner continues to be of great importance.

We might also point out that the increased freedom of expression has not necessarily reduced guilt, fear, and other problems associated with sex. Indeed, many therapists report that the increased freedom combined with women's liberation have made male impotence much more common than before. Moreover, young people now feel pressure to engage in sexual activity in order to be accepted. Thus, although we live in a relatively liberated time, sex remains a complex and troublesome area for many people.

SEXUAL DEVIANCE

Many states have laws declaring certain kinds of sexual activity illegal. In these states, it is a crime to engage in oral-genital or anal-genital sex, and homosexual acts are outlawed even between consenting adults (in 1976 the United States Supreme Court upheld these laws). Given the high percentage of people who engage in these

with the therapists, together and individually, to discuss their sexual feelings and problems. The second part of the treatment is that the partners are urged, in fact forced, to discuss their feelings and needs with each other. Most people have difficulty telling their partner exactly what they like and do not like, and this lack of communication naturally interferes with the full enjoyment of sex. In addition, some people have fears and conflicts that can interfere if kept hidden, but that the other person can take into account if they are known. Thus, encouraging the partners to talk openly about sex can make it easier for both of them to give pleasure to each other and enjoy sex together.

There are few rigorous studies of the effectiveness of these sex therapies. Masters and Johnson claim almost total success with all patients, and other therapists also feel that therapy is effective. As with therapy that deals with other psychological problems, however, it is not yet certain how effective this treatment is and what specific sexual problems it can solve.

VIRGINIA JOHNSON AND WILLIAM MASTERS

"forbidden" acts at one time or another in their lives, it seems absurd to consider them crimes. When over 50 percent of the population engages in oral sex, for example, it would be difficult to argue that it is not a normal part of the sexual repertoire. Nevertheless, there is a strong tradition in biology, ethology, psychiatry, and other fields to declare certain kinds of sexual acts natural and to exclude others. For example, Desmond Morris (1967) blithely asserts that the face-to-face position in sexual intercourse is the only natural one. He recognizes that people do use other positions, but contends that they are some-how deviant or biologically strange. Yet cultures differ sharply in what they consider the "normal" position. The face-to-face position was first introduced to Africa by the white missionaries, and, in fact, is still called the "missionary position" in their honor. The natives found it strange and unnatural compared to their usual means, which ranged from a rear-entry position to a somewhat unusual one in which the man knelt and pulled the woman to him on her back. The face-to-face position is probably the most common throughout the world, but is no more natural than any other.

Most psychiatrists and psychologists would not make any judgments about what is natural or unnatural. They do, however, consider certain sexual behavior unhealthy. When individuals engage in sexual behavior that limits their freedom, prevents them from having rewarding sexual experiences, or is harmful to others, there would probably be fairly general agreement that this was unhealthy. Someone who enjoyed sex in front of mirrors, or when the partner wore black boots, or standing up in a canoe, would not necessarily be unhealthy, unless this person could enjoy sex only under these very special circumstances. Similarly, oral-genital sex is by now widely accepted as normal adult behavior; but someone who engaged only in oral-genital sex and did not enjoy genital to genital contact would be severely limited. Nevertheless, the trend certainly seems to be toward considering even these sexual predilections as within the realm of normal behavior as long as individuals seem relatively happy with them.

In contrast, sexual behavior that harms others is certainly considered unhealthy and abnormal. Rape and child molesting are clear examples of deviant sexual behavior. Also considered deviant, though presumably less harmful, are people who derive sexual pleasure entirely or largely from exhibiting themselves (exhibitionism) or watching others engage in sex (voyeurism). Thus, although the current trend is to accept a wide variety of sexual behavior as normal, this does not extend to behavior that is dangerous or harmful to others.

Is Homosexuality Deviant?

A great many people have had at least some homosexual experiences. Most men (over 60 percent) and a large percentage of women (at least 30 percent) report that they had some sexual interactions with members of the same sex during childhood. This appears to be a usual part of growing up. Isolated homosexual experiences are also quite common for adults. There are, however, some people (about 4 percent of the population) who are primarily or exclusively homosexual. These people are attracted to and are sexually satisfied only by members of their own sex. The term *homosexual* can refer to either a man or a woman, but female homosexuals are often called lesbians.

Until recently, homosexuality was considered a mental illness by the American Psychiatric Association. In 1973, in part under pressure by the Gay Liberation movement (the word *gay* being a common term for homosexual) and in part in response to changing values, the association took the position that homosexuality was not an illness in the usual sense. Nevertheless, there remains a strong sentiment among psychiatrists, psychologists, and certainly the general public that homosexuality is unnatural and unhealthy.

One justification for this view is that homosexuality does not fulfill the biological purpose of reproducing the species. Clearly, heterosexual intercourse must take place in order for the species to survive, and to the extent that one believes the basic purpose of the sexual impulse to be reproductive, homosexuality would be unnatural. But it is obvious that sexual behavior among humans plays a much wider role than reproduction. The widespread use of birth-control techniques and the sharp drop in the number of pregnancies demonstrate that people have sex whether or not they want to have children. In addition, from a biological point of view, sex serves many purposes other than reproduction. It is a strong bond tying people together; it underlies love and friendship; and it is a strong motive for many other behaviors. Although the ultimate survival of the species depends on the reproductive function of sexuality, many other crucial aspects of human behavior are affected by the sexual urge.

In the abstract, homosexuality is not necessarily harmful to the person engaging in it or to others. When those involved are consenting adults, no obvious damage is done to the individuals. If they are exclusively homosexual, they cannot have children and raise a family, which does limit them in one important aspect of life. But some people, homosexual or otherwise, choose not to have families and this is not necessarily unhealthy. Therefore, except insofar as society discriminates against homosexuals and makes their lives difficult, there seems to be nothing inherent in homosexuality that would of itself produce unhappiness, frustration, or a lack of productivity. Accordingly, whether homosexuality is unhealthy must depend largely on whether it is limiting and restrictive for a particular individual. And this probably depends to a great extent on the underlying reason for that person's homosexuality.

Two participants at the New England Gay Conference

Causes of Homosexuality

We are far from understanding fully why some people are homosexuals. Although it has been suggested that there are genetic or innate causes, no one has found reliable physiological or physical differences between homosexuals and heterosexuals. Although some male homosexuals do appear quite feminine and some female homosexuals quite masculine, this is by no means a universal characteristic of homosexuals—many times quite the opposite. In other words, there are no consistent physical differences and no evidence of any biological or physiological cause. It is conceivable that a boy who looks very feminine will be more likely to be approached by homosexuals, may have a less masculine image of himself, and may for these reasons have a greater tendency to become homosexual than someone who looks more masculine. But this would then be due primarily to the social and cultural stereotype of a homosexual's appearance rather than to any innate causative factor.

Although little is known about the origins of homosexuality, it seems likely that it is caused by a variety of psychological and social factors. It is possible that some people become homosexual because, largely by accident, they have had bad sexual experiences with the opposite sex and relatively good ones with the same sex. Many people's first sexual experiences are homosexual, and if these experiences are satisfying the person may continue to desire sexual contact with others of the same sex. This would be especially true if subsequent experiences with the opposite sex were difficult or unavailable (for example, if the person goes to schools or camps of one sex, is in military service, and so on).

Another possible cause of homosexuality is that the person develops a personal identity appropriate to the opposite sex. A boy who is raised without a father or other male adult may identify with his mother and think of himself as female rather than male. Similarly, a girl might be rewarded for behaving like a boy and thus develop a masculine image of herself (Money, Hampson, and Hampson, 1957). In either case, the individual will have a confused or reversed sexual identity.

In some cases, homosexuality may be due to considerably more complex factors such as deep psychological problems, traumatic sexual experiences, or other experiences that cause people to have strong conflicts regarding sex. They may feel guilty about sexual feelings for the opposite sex or may be taught that members of that sex are dangerous or evil (all women are out to seduce them, all men are ogres, women should be pure, and so on) and will turn away from heterosexual activities. Some children will develop an aversion for members of the opposite sex, especially as sexual partners, and associate them not with pleasure and love but with pain and guilt. Accordingly, if they develop any sexual feelings and behavior at all, it will often be homosexual in nature.

The various causes of homosexuality have different implications for the treatment of homosexuals. In the past most psychiatrists and psychotherapists automatically assumed that homosexuality was a condition that therapy should attempt to remove. It now seems as if it should be treated only if it makes the individual unhappy. The point is that homosexuality is not necessarily bad or unhealthy per se, but only to the extent that it limits or interferes with the individual's life.

SEX ROLES

A person's sex probably has as profound effects on his or her life as any other single characteristic. As far as we know, throughout history and in every society and culture, males and females have been treated differently. They are given different duties, privileges, rights, and responsibilities. These sexual stereotypes have serious consequences for both sexes. In almost all areas of life, certain behaviors and activities are considered more appropriate for one sex than for the other, and this puts considerable pressure on the individual to conform to

TRANSSEXUALISM

For reasons that we are far from under-standing, some people develop a strong image of themselves that is appropriate to the opposite sex. A man who considers himself a woman or a woman who con-siders herself a man are sometimes called *transsexuals*. They are not to be confused with people who behave in some ways that are considered inappropriate for their sex. A somewhat feminine man or mas-culine woman is not generally a transsex-ual, nor are most homosexuals. These people may have weak sexual identifica-tion, they may simply refuse to accept society's idea of how their sex should be-have, they may be sexually attracted to the same rather than the opposite sex—but they are not transsexuals. The trans-sexual really feels that he or she has been born into the wrong body.

Until recently, transsexuals had no choice except to live with their problem. Probably many became transvestites, wearing the clothes and adopting the manners of the opposite sex; some were homosexuals; some tried to live as a member of the sex they were born into; and almost certainly most were exceed-ingly unhappy. Modern medicine has made it possible for at least some trans-sexuals (now estimated at about 3,000) to change their appearance and their bodies so that in large measure they can actually change their sex. Hormone treatments can cause male breasts to enlarge, the figure to become more rounded, and re-duce beard growth. For women, hormones affect skin texture, increase the growth of the beard, firm the muscles, and deepen the voice. The transformation is often quite striking—a handsome man becomes an attractive woman or the other way around.

Changing the sexual organs is, of course, much more difficult than altering other aspects of appearance. For a male, the drastic surgery involves castration, removal of part of the penis, and the fash-ioning of a vagina and labia. For a woman, the uterus and ovaries are removed, the

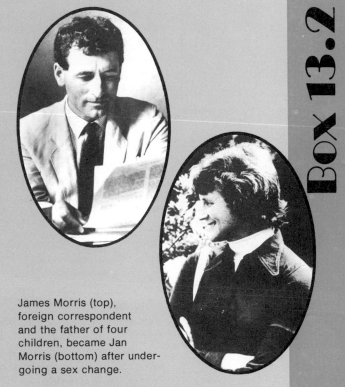

James Morris (top), foreign correspondent and the father of four children, became Jan Morris (bottom) after under-going a sex change.

breasts may be reduced in size, and some-times a penis-like organ is constructed. While the surgeon cannot actually dupli-cate the real organs and various limita-tions remain on sexual activity and en-joyment, the operation is still remarkable. In the female-to-male operation, in fact, the person may even be able to achieve sexual climax because tissue from the clitoris is left intact.

There is considerable controversy over the desirability of these sex-change procedures. Some psychologists and psychiatrists feel that the person needs therapy, not surgery, in order to make a good adjustment to life. With sex roles being less and less strictly defined, it would seem that even someone with a strong transsexual identification could live a reasonable life without changing sex. On the other hand, those who favor these sex-change procedures feel that they are the only way the individual will ever be happy. As transsexuality becomes more common, perhaps we will find out if this is the answer to cross-sexual iden-tification.

BOX 13.2

How to Tell a Businessman from a Businesswoman

A businessman is aggressive; a businesswoman is pushy.

A businessman is good on details; she's picky.

He loses his temper because he's so involved in his job; she's witchy.

When he's depressed (or hungover), everyone tiptoes past his office.

She's moody so it must be her time of the month.

He follows through; she doesn't know when to quit.

He's confident; she's conceited.

He stands firm; she's impossible to deal with.

He is firm; she's hard.

His judgments are her prejudices.

He is a man of the world; she's been around.

He drinks because of excessive job pressure; she's a lush.

He isn't afraid to say what he thinks; she's mouthy.

He exercises authority; she's power mad.

He's close-mouthed; she's secretive.

He's a stern taskmaster; she's hard to work for.

this stereotype. For example, in the United States certain jobs are considered masculine and others feminine. Engineering, medicine and some other sciences, business, truck driving, and accounting have long been thought of as mainly jobs for men; nursing, teaching, biological science, and being a librarian, dancer, or, of course, housewife are considered appropriate for women. This stereotyping has two effects. First, it tends to make people feel that they should go only into fields that are considered "right" for their sex. Thus, women feel pressure not to become engineers or physicists while men feel that they should not become librarians or dancers (Bacon and Lerner, 1975). Moreover, women tend to underrate their own intelligence and to choose "women's" fields because they think they are less qualified than men (Farley, 1974). And when women do succeed, both men and women tend to assume it was because the women tried especially hard (Feldman-Summers and Kiesler, 1974) or were lucky (Deaux and Emswiller, 1974). Finally, people are often excluded from fields because of their sex. At least until recently, it was much harder for a woman to get into medical or engineering school than for a man, and it was harder to get good jobs once she was graduated. These patterns are changing under pressure from the feminist movement and the Human Rights Council, but there is considerable evidence that bias against women continues in many fields (and perhaps also against men in a few fields, but this is less widespread).

Moreover, when a woman does get a job in a "man's field" she often is treated differently and less well than a man in the same field. There are many stories of women executives being asked to take the minutes in a meeting or to get the coffee because these are women's jobs. And if a woman is assertive and successful in business, she is often considered "bitchy" while a man with similar characteristics would be thought of as forceful and dynamic.

Sex typing poses problems for men as well. They are supposed to be aggressive, strong, dynamic, successful, and scientific. A man who is not interested in being successful financially or would like to be a dancer encounters considerable pressure. More generally, a man who is inclined to be unassertive and gentle finds that these characteristics are considered inappropriate for him even though they are fine for a woman. This puts considerable pressure on men to uphold the male role, to struggle for success, to make a lot of money, and to be dominant and assertive. While many men fit into this role easily, others do not. Those who do not, often feel as if they are failures or not "real men" simply because they are not living up to a stereotype. Thus the feminine stereotype tends to limit a woman's freedom of choice and to exclude her from various jobs, while the masculine stereotype exerts pressure on men to fulfill the dominant role and may stifle their creativity and individuality. Clearly, both stereotypes limit people's freedom and produce prejudice against deviants of both sexes. These sexual distinctions have been around for so long that they seem to be a fact of life. Yet at times through history isolated individuals have questioned them, and recently, under the influence of the feminist movement and other pressures from society, our views of sex roles have begun to change radically. More and more research has shown that sex differences that were taken for granted actually do not exist. Even more basically, the very idea of different roles for the two sexes is now seriously questioned by many people.

Sex Differences

An individual's sex is determined genetically, with females having two X chromosomes and males having an X and a Y. This genetic difference is reflected in physical differences—some important, some minor. Obviously the sexual organs are different, as are some secondary sexual characteristics such as the size of the breasts, shape of the body, and the amount of facial and body hair. Men tend to be taller, heavier, and stronger than women. More profound is the fact that only women become pregnant, bear children, and have the ability to nurse them. In addition, women have menstrual cycles that are accompanied by changes in the hormonal balance of their systems, and women always have a higher level of female sex hormone than do men (though both sexes have both male and female sex hormones). There are a number of other physical differences, but they are generally of less importance than those listed above.

The obvious physical differences between the sexes have caused people to assume that there are also many differences in personality, intellectual functioning, ability, and social behavior. Some such differences do seem to exist, but many fewer than has generally been supposed. In a massive work, Eleanor Maccoby and Carol Jacklin (1974) reviewed all of the research on sex differences and concluded that only a few were firmly established. Before reading further, look at the list in Fig. 13.2 and indicate which differences you think exist and which do not.

As indicated in the figure, boys are not more active at birth than girls, men are not smarter or more logical than women, women are not more suggestible than men, and so on. Most of the "differences" that pictured women as weaker, less competent, less independent, and less active in terms of personality or intellect have turned out not to exist. There are, however, some differences that do seem to be quite consistent.

Aggressiveness At all ages, males appear to be more aggressive than females. This begins as early as two or three years of age (Pedersen and Bell, 1970; McIntyre, 1972), continues through early childhood (Omark, Omark, and Edelman, 1973), and persists in adolescence and adulthood (Titley and Viney, 1969; Shuck et al., 1971). In addition,

ELEANOR MACCOBY

CAROL JACKLIN

Fig. 13.2
Sex differences

Indicate which differences you think exist. Results of the research findings are given elsewhere on this page. How well did you agree?

		Yes	No
a)	Boys are more sensitive to visual stimuli than girls are.	☐	☐
b)	Girls are more sensitive to auditory stimuli than boys are.	☐	☐
c)	Girls have better memories for verbal material.	☐	☐
d)	Boys imitate less than girls do.	☐	☐
e)	Men have higher IQs.	☐	☐
f)	Women are better at verbal tasks.	☐	☐
g)	Men are better at quantitative tasks.	☐	☐
h)	Men are more creative and original.	☐	☐
i)	Men have greater spatial ability.	☐	☐
j)	Men are more logical and analytical.	☐	☐
k)	Young boys are more curious and explore more than young girls do.	☐	☐
l)	Women are more submissive than men are.	☐	☐
m)	Men are more aggressive than women are.	☐	☐
n)	Women show more dependency than men do.	☐	☐
o)	Women are more sociable than men are.	☐	☐
p)	Infant boys are more active than infant girls are.	☐	☐
q)	Girls are more timid than boys are.	☐	☐

Answers to Fig. 13.2
The following receive substantial support; the rest do not: c, f, g, i, k, m.

boys are more likely to imitate aggressive adults than are girls (Bandura, Grusec, and Menlove, 1966). As we shall discuss below, there is little indication that boys are reinforced more for aggressive behavior or punished less. The evidence suggests that parents punish aggression in either sex and encourage it in neither. Since the sex difference in aggressiveness appears so early, and since it also is present in primates and many other animals, it may be that it is hereditary. Perhaps males are born with a genetically determined predisposition toward aggression.

Verbal ability Females tend to be superior in terms of verbal ability at all ages. As early as seventeen months, girls are better at language than boys (Clarke-Stewart, 1973). Girls out-perform boys on a variety of verbal tests during childhood (McCarthy and Kirk, 1963), and are better readers (Cotler and Palmer, 1971). During adolescence they continue to be superior to boys and the difference may even increase (Backman, 1972; Svensson, 1971).

Quantitative and spatial ability In contrast, boys tend to be superior to girls in quantitative and spatial abilities. Neither difference appears in early childhood, but around puberty and especially in adolescence a clear difference emerges. In particular, boys are better at the rod and frame test, which requires the subject to recognize a vertical

BOX 13.3

METHODOLOGICAL ERRORS PRODUCE SEX DIFFERENCES

Psychologists have often reported substantial sex differences that disappeared when better controlled studies were conducted. For example, many studies found that women were more conformist than men and were less good at problem solving. However, recent research has suggested that these earlier findings were due to specific aspects of the experimental situation rather than to actual differences between the sexes. Both kinds of studies tended to use material that was more familiar to men than to women. Conformity studies often involved mathematics or perceptual judgments, while the problem-solving research almost always used examples taken from areas of primarily masculine concern, such as automobiles, mechanics, and mathematics. Since most women are less familiar with and therefore feel less comfortable with these kinds of problems than do men, they are less certain of themselves and are less adept at dealing with the material. Their lack of confidence increases their conformity, while their lack of familiarity naturally makes problem solving more difficult. When feminine materials are substituted the differences reverse or disappear (Sistrunk and McDavid, 1971). As you can see from the table, the total degree of conformity was actually slightly less for women than for men.

AMOUNT OF CONFORMITY BY MALES AND FEMALES FOR ITEMS CONSIDERED MASCULINE, FEMININE, AND NEUTRAL

| | Type of item | | | |
	Masculine	Feminine	Neutral	Total
Males	34.15	43.05	39.65	38.95
Females	42.75	34.55	39.10	38.80

Source: Adapted from Sistrunk and McDavid, 1971.

line despite a tilted background (Witkin, Goodenough, and Karp, 1967; Saarni, 1973) and to pick out designs from complex patterns (Nash, 1973). There is some suggestion that these differences on spatial tests are due to the fact that these tests are seen as more masculine than feminine and that the materials tend to be male oriented. Boys also perform better on a wide variety of quantitative tasks (Droege, 1967), including the quantitative part of the Scholastic Aptitude Test (Bieri, Bradburn, and Galinsky, 1958). However, remember that these differences in quantitative and spatial skills appear mainly during adolescence and may well be due to different training or encouragement rather than any innate differences.

In general, it is important to note than even on those variables that show differences between the sexes, there is a great deal of overlap. Many girls are more aggressive than many boys; many boys are better at verbal tasks and poorer at quantitative and spatial tasks than girls; and so on. Thus the overall differences do not imply that any individual boy or girl is automatically better or worse than the other sex at a particular skill. To put it another way, the similarities, even on these variables, are much greater than the differences.

The Origin of Sex Roles

Although there are few consistent differences between the sexes in terms of personality or ability, society has developed very clear sex roles that are remarkably similar at different times in history and in quite diverse cultures. Why did these sex roles develop?

One explanation is that the physical differences between men and women required considerable differentiation in their roles. This was certainly true in primitive societies, where the fact that women could bear and nurse children must have had the most profound consequences. In the absence of birth control, women of childbearing years are pregnant much of the time. When they are not, they usually have just given birth and are in the process of nursing their young. This constant cycle of pregnancy, nursing, and pregnancy must have been almost universal—at least until the age of modern medicine— and is common even today in much of the nonindustrialized world. Although healthy women can be quite active while pregnant, they are somewhat limited during the later stages. And, of course, nursing mothers necessarily must stay close to their children. Consequently, tasks that required either a great deal of exertion or traveling far from the home were largely performed by men. Therefore, it is not surprising that hunting, soldiering, herding, and any other activity that required being away from the home for extended periods would be done by men and not by women.

This early differentiation of roles was probably the beginning of a sexual differentiation that then extended into virtually all aspects of life. Courage, strength, initiative, and independence were crucial for the men and must have been greatly encouraged. In contrast, the women's roles required diligence, warmth, domestic skills, and perhaps most important a willingness to give up adventure, excitement, and initiative. Thus, it is easy to speculate that this early distinction in work roles became extended to more general personality traits that were deemed appropriate to each sex.

The world has changed enormously, however, and in our own society, at least, most or all of this biological justification no longer

INTERVIEW

BETTY FRIEDAN

The women's movement is like no other revolution before. There's no escaping it. Virtually every man comes home to a woman every night.

Although no important movement was ever caused by one book, it is fair to say that the publication of Betty Friedan's The Feminine Mystique *marked the beginning of the feminist movement in our time. Her book challenged women to examine their condition in American society, and women responded in great numbers. As the movement grew, Ms. Friedan recognized the need for a cohesive organization to which women could turn for support. She founded the National Organization for Women (NOW) and was elected its first president. A passionate spokesperson for women's rights (and, indeed, for men's liberation as well), Ms. Friedan frequently is asked to lecture on college campuses. Her recent book,* It Changed My Life, *describes what has happened to the women's movement and to her own life since the publication of* The Feminine Mystique *nearly fifteen years ago.*

Q: Let's start by talking about why the women's movement was so enormously successful.

A: It did not happen because I or anyone else somehow bewitched the otherwise happy housewife. It came as a result of an evolutionary development. You know, Freud once said that anatomy is destiny. And the identity of woman from time immemorial has been defined almost entirely in terms of her childbearing role. Female fulfillment was different from human fulfillment. It was defined in terms of her relations to man, as wife, mother, sex object, taking care of children, and involved the great glorification of the housewife. This feminine mystique was so enshrined that a woman who was dissatisfied thought something was wrong with *her.*

Q: If she wasn't entirely happy, it was her problem.

A: Yes. If waxing the floor was less than a peak experience, it was her problem. I called it the "problem that has no name" because women were feeling this malaise, trying to live this role, while the world was going on without them. But more and more women were having children younger and having fewer children, and work didn't depend any more on brute muscular strength but more and more on capacities that women share. So equality was possible. And women had control of their childbearing.

Q: Contraception was very important.

A: Yes. And then finally, this next great leap of women was informed and infused by the black movement just as the original women's suffrage movement was in the nineteenth century by the abolition of slavery. A whole generation of women took part as students, or otherwise supported or watched the blacks say, "Freedom now with dignity." And women said, "Me too."

Q: Yes, I'm sure that's true. But what is fascinating is that it seems as if the women's movement, which in some ways was given its start or at least stimulated by the black movement, has been so much more successful, has had its effect so much more quickly.

A: Well, I talk about that in my new book, *It Changed My Life.* The women's movement is like no other revolution before. There's no escaping it. Virtually every man comes home to a woman at night. Children are born of women. If something fundamental is going to happen to women, it will affect all of society. Suddenly half the population began to examine their own condition in concrete daily terms—in the home, office, everywhere. And so much of the pathology in our society stems in part from the obsolete, unequal sex roles as they have been enshrined in the family and every other institution. Pathology built up by excessive dependence of the woman, by the denial of her energies and abilities. Because she was frustrated and angry, she took it out on herself, her children, and her

men. And now it is out there in the open. In psychological terms, several whole generations at once went through a mass identity crisis. Of course, there are certain situations that are more likely to make feminists. There were many more divorces, and the divorced woman, being brought up to think all she needed was to get a man to take care of her, is now faced with taking care of herself. And then there were all the women who went to college, participated in the student movement, and then found themselves at home with their kids. Or a woman did get a job but wasn't promoted in the office, was paid half what a man was, and then had to rush home to do the housework.

Q: And if she happened to be successful in the office, then she'd come home and be a housewife again.

A: Right, right. And you see, the denial of our personhood was so general. We were bombarded with it by the media, churches, political parties, and the conditions of employment. So once we recognized this, we needed a movement to change things, to break down the barriers. But the women were ready for it.

Q: One interesting question is where were the men during all of this? How did they react?

A: Well, some men were threatened.

Q: Sure.

A: But mostly, they were going along. They were even pushing the women in many instances. I noticed it almost from the beginning. Men would come in and say "I bought your book for my wife."

Q: Why did they react that way?

A: I have several reasons. One is that this was not a revolution of an oppressed class, women, trying to overthrow men. Men are here to stay also. Women may have been defined too much in terms of love and sex alone, but you're not going to tell women to give up their need for love. They may have been defined too much in terms of motherhood, but the generative impulse is not going away. Women do have husbands and they do have children.

Q: If women don't have them, no one else is going to!

A: Right, so we're stuck with that. And second, the sexual, social bonds are there so that men are immediately affected by what goes on and they are affected for the good. It is better for a man if his wife is bringing home a good paycheck; better for him if he comes home at night and his wife isn't climbing the walls.

Q: How did all of this affect men's sex roles?

A: Well the masculine sex role rebellion was going on at the same time. Men were saying: "I don't have to have a crewcut, I don't have to have big muscles, I don't have to be dominant and superior to prove that I'm a man. I can be tender, sensitive, gentle. I can admit sometimes that I'm afraid." You know in 1972, just a few years ago, Muskie was ruined as a presidential possibility because he cried in New Hampshire, provoked by that awful letter. And now Ford cried, Reagan cried, everybody cries and it's OK.

Q: Do you think we're moving toward a situation of no sex roles?

A: Something like that, though what we're really getting is an opening of options and possibilities. Some will do the traditional thing, some won't. But

we will still be left with the fact that we come in two basic packages—male and female. There are differences.

Q: But they do seem to be minor ones.

A: If you think of the total life span, they are less important than they used to be. Muscular strength, childbearing are less important than they were.

Q: Do you think there are any basic psychological differences?

A: Well, every cell of the male and female has forty-eight chromosomes, and all except one are alike. That's probably about the size of the difference—one out of forty-eight. That could be very important, we don't know, but there are always the forty-seven identical chromosomes.

Comment

Betty Friedan's view of sex roles coincides closely with those presented in this text. Physical strength and childbearing capacity were very important earlier in our history, and sex roles based largely on physical differences were established and then reinforced by many forces in society. But with changing needs and with better contraception, strength and childbearing became less important and women began to realize that they were being excluded from much of life. The movement was so successful because reality had already changed and society's values had not yet changed to come more in line with reality. Moreover, the need of women to fulfill their potential (one of the important needs in Maslow's hierarchy––Chapter 9) had been frustrated and was striving for actualization.

As Ms. Friedan notes, the change in sex roles affected both men and women. Many men were faced with women who no longer fit into traditional roles and this upset some men but pleased others. At the same time, men began to be freed from their traditional roles and today more men feel free to express their feelings more readily without fear of being considered unmasculine. As we noted earlier, there do seem to be some differences between males and females that may be innate. But these differences are relatively minor (perhaps one chromosome out of forty-eight, as Friedan suggests) and, in any case, there is a good deal of overlap. Whether sex roles will disappear entirely is uncertain and perhaps unlikely, but as Betty Friedan says, there is now much greater freedom to choose whatever role and behavior suits a person best.

has any force. With birth control and changing patterns of family size, women tend to have many fewer pregnancies than they did before. In addition, children are generally breast fed for a shorter time if at all, with much more dependence on bottle feeding. Women no longer need to be physically restricted by pregnancy or by the necessity of caring for children. In addition, there is now much less dependence on physical strength than there was in primitive times, so that this factor also is less important than it used to be. Thus there are no longer solid biological reasons for sex-role distinctions. Yet despite this fact, there is little doubt that such distinctions still exist. Therefore, it is important to understand how these sex roles become defined.

Social factors So much has been written about sex roles that the basic processes are probably quite familiar to everyone. Because virtually all parents share society's image of the distinction between men and women, boys and girls tend to be treated differently almost from birth. Although infant boys and girls do not differ appreciably in how they act, parents tend to impose on infants and older children their own expectations for how the sexes should behave.

However, it is both important and fascinating that the differences in how boys and girls are treated are much subtler and more specific than one might have imagined. There is no consistent evidence that parents spend more time with children of one sex than with the other, nor that mothers and fathers individually favor a child of either sex in terms of attention (Beckwith, 1972; Pedersen and Robson, 1969). In addition, the research shows no differences in the amount of warmth or affection given to the sexes (Kagan, 1971) nor in the degree to which the two sexes are restricted in their activities (Sears, Maccoby, and Levin, 1957; Baumrind and Black, 1967). Moreover, there are no differences in parental reactions to aggressiveness, sexuality, or dependency on the part of children. While this research is by no means conclusive, it suggests that parents treat children of either sex quite similarly in many crucial respects.

On the other hand, certain specific differences in treatment do emerge. There is little question that parents are more "physical" with boys than with girls. They respond more to physical, motor behavior of boys (Lewis, 1972), handle boys more roughly (Moss, 1967; Yarrow, Rubenstein, and Pedersen, 1971), and are much more likely to play physically with boys, bouncing them around and so on (Tasch, 1952). Perhaps consistent with this, boys receive more physical punishment than girls (Minton, Kagan, and Levine, 1971; Newson and Newson, 1968). In general, it appears that girls are seen as more fragile than boys and they are treated accordingly. The greater aggressiveness that boys display may be a reaction to the greater physical aggressiveness they receive. Children are highly imitative, and boys may imitate their parents by being physical and aggressive themselves.

The one area in which parental treatment seems to differ most involves behavior that is considered appropriate for one sex or the other. This includes specific behaviors—such as choice of toys, dress, games, and careers—and also a vague conceptualization of femininity and masculinity. Moreover, the concern about appropriateness seems to concentrate primarily on the boy rather than the girl. For example, if a girl chooses a toy or activity that is generally considered mas-

Louisa May Alcott describing the
twins Daisy and Demi:

"

**"At three, Daisy demanded a 'needler'
and actually made a bag with four
stitches in it; she likewise set up
housekeeping . . . while Demi learned
his letters . . . the boy early developed a
mechanical genius. . . . Of course,
Demi tyrannized over Daisy, and
gallantly defended her from every other
aggressor; while Daisy made a galley
slave of herself, and adored her brother.
. . ."**

Daisy was a

**"rosy, chubby, sunshine little soul . . .
who seemed made to be kissed and
cuddled, adorned and adored."**

Demi was

**"of an inquiring turn, wanting to know
everything" and committed "pranks
with which dear, dirty, naughty little
rascals distract their parents' souls."**

"   *Little Women*

Figure 13.3

culine, parents do not mind very much; but they get quite upset if
boys choose feminine toys or games (Lansky, 1967). When the parents
choose, they are very careful to pick sex-appropriate choices for boys,
but are less concerned for girls (Fling and Manosevitz, 1972). In
general, parents and especially fathers may become very disturbed if a
boy seems to have feminine characteristics and tastes. Maccoby and
Jacklin quote from Goodenough (1957, p. 310), who reports a father's
response to the question as to whether he would be disturbed if his
son showed femininity. The father replied: "Yes, I would be, very,
very much. I can't *bear* female characteristics in a man. I abhor
them." It is easy to imagine how such a father would teach his child
to behave.

In addition to the kinds of treatment just discussed, there are, of
course, countless other ways in which children are taught to fit the
role appropriate to their sex. Boys are taught to play with guns, trains,
trucks, erector sets, and chemistry sets, and are encouraged to take
part in athletics. Girls are given dolls, cooking sets, and books, and
are encouraged to dance and play the violin. Traditionally children's
fiction has encouraged this distinction, describing boys involved in
masculine activities and girls in feminine ones. The quote from *Little
Women* given in Fig. 13.3 is a typical example. This is a fine novel
with considerable sensitivity and characterization. In addition, the
heroine is a strong-willed, independent, and intelligent woman who
in many respects would be considered "liberated" by modern
standards and certainly was by the standards of the day. Yet the book
includes descriptions in which sex roles are very clearly defined.

Naturally, this sex-role socialization is not entirely perfect. Girls
are sometimes reinforced for masculine behavior and boys for
feminine. Some parents make these distinctions much less than
others, and even those parents who do treat boys and girls differently

are not perfectly consistent. Both sexes are often punished for being aggressive and rewarded for being obedient. But even when parents are relatively even in their treatment of the two sexes, society bombards the children with masculine and feminine images. Advertisements, stories, television, even nursery rhymes all tell the boy to act masculine and the girl to act feminine.

In addition to these direct reinforcements, sex roles are produced by the powerful mechanism of identification. We have discussed this in some detail in the chapter on development and will return to it again in discussing personality. Stated briefly, children tend to model themselves closely after a parental figure and there is enormous pressure within the family for the boy to identify with the father and the girl with the mother. Accordingly, children tend to imitate the same-sex parent, to accept his or her values or behaviors, and in general to accept that parent as a model of correct behavior. As we have mentioned before, imitation is a very strong and efficient mechanism of learning that does not require any direct reinforcement. Therefore, once a child has identified with the same-sex parent there will be a strong tendency to behave the same way as that parent even in the absence of any differences in reinforcement for the two sexes.

Thus, differential reinforcement, identification, and constant exposure to society's image of appropriate behavior for the two sexes shape the child's sexual identification. Under most circumstances this produces a substantial difference in self-image and in behavior patterns for boys and girls. By the time they are adults, they have in turn accepted society's distinctions, and their attitudes, values, and behavior to some extent conform to them. Various studies show that older children show clearer sex differentiation than younger ones. For example, in choosing between masculine and feminine toys the preference for same-sex toys increased sharply from age five to age eight (DeLucia, 1963). This indicates that the learning of sex roles is a continuous process.

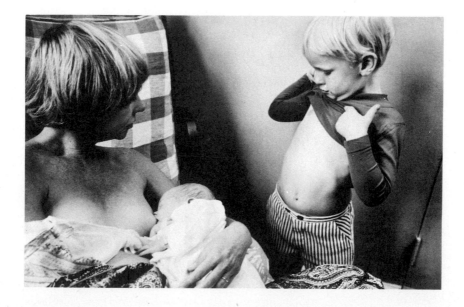

Changes in Sex Roles

In recent years, there have been changes in society that have weakened the traditional sex-role distinctions. The vast increase in the number of people attending college has been one such factor. As we will discuss in Chapter 18, college tends to be a broadening experience in which strongly held values and attitudes often change. Getting away from home, from the relatively homogeneous environment in which you grew up, and being exposed to new ideas and the relative equality of men and women on the college campus has probably played a major role in breaking down traditional sex roles. In addition, the greatly increased emphasis on intellectual achievement has weakened the biological and physical reasons for making such distinctions. For these and various other reasons, people have begun to challenge the traditional roles and are often able to escape from them. Women are now able to accept and cause others to accept their desire for a career, independence, and strength. They can now show interest in mechanical engineering, physics, medicine, or being a jockey. They can be as aggressive and tough in business as can men without necessarily being disliked any more than a man would with similar characteristics. Similarly, men can be interested in clothes designing or cooking, can be submissive and quiet and not care too much about a career, and still be accepted by society. And both can decide not to get married, not to have children right away (there is still pressure to have children at some time), and to take equal responsibility for raising the children. Clearly, roles are being reevaluated and it does seem as if this will result in a substantial decrease in the strength of sex roles and an increase in freedom of choice for both sexes.

"*I want you to know, gentlemen, that at this moment I feel I have realized my full potential as a woman.*"

Drawing by Frascino; © 1973 The New Yorker Magazine, Inc.

ADULT DEVELOPMENT

Adolescence and the Search for Identity

In describing stages of development, Erik Erikson describes adolescence as a time in which the individual faces a crisis of identity. The adolescent asks the questions: Who am I? What do I want to do? What can I achieve? Where am I going? At this stage of life, most people can no longer depend on their parents entirely for guidance—instead they must make some important decisions on their own and develop a sense of themselves as individuals. Naturally, this process of search for identity has been going on before and will continue throughout life, but it seems to be most crucial during adolescence.

We have already discussed one aspect of this identity crisis—sex roles and sexuality. Certainly this is one central issue facing the adolescent. But there are many more. All people must decide on a set of values and beliefs that to some extent will guide them and affect their behavior. Adolescents typically begin to question the values of their parents and of society in general. Whereas earlier they might have accepted them simply because parents or other authorities held them, now they must decide which values they really hold. Naturally, we are all affected by what we learn from our parents and peers, but during adolescence everything is to some extent in question, including some values we have held for many years. This is the time that people "rebel" against their parents, sometimes to the point of automatically disagreeing with everything their parents say in order to establish their own independence.

Along with this rebellion against parents and authorities comes an increased reliance on peers. It is very important to be accepted by the group, which often means doing what everyone else is doing and avoiding being different. Thus it is a time of fads. One year everyone wears jeans, has long hair, and listens to rock music; the next year more formal clothes, short hair, and country and western music may be "in." Adolescents are trying out various styles and roles, while at the same time keeping contact with their peers. As a group they may be liberals at one time, conservatives at another; aiming toward college or deciding to move to a farming commune; thinking about being doctors or wanting to get into the movies. Through it all they are trying to find an identity that feels comfortable and right to them, and that also fits into the world around them.

Although there is no question that adolescents often face an identity crisis, it would be a mistake to think that the crisis is over at the end of adolescence or that our identity then becomes firmly fixed. On the contrary, we must deal with the question of who we are throughout our lives. It is sometimes suggested that our major life crises occur during adolescence, where sexual identity is most important; around twenty, when we make a career choice; at forty, when we must decide to accept our current life or change it; and finally at sixty, when we face old age and the prospect of dying. At each point (and some may face other crises at other times) the crisis involves our whole image of ourselves and our decisions are based on and also affect those images.

Occupation and Career

One of the most difficult and far-reaching decisions adults must face is the choice of an occupation. Although there are no legal ties to a particular career (as there are to a marriage partner), it is often more difficult to change careers than to form new attachments. Of course, many people do change careers both early and late in life. Nevertheless, the choice of a career often determines the direction of a person's life.

This choice is especially difficult in times of high unemployment, because there is the additional concern about getting a job once you have completed your training. In recent years, the number of jobs in teaching, architecture, and many other professions had declined. In fact, horrifying statistics are available (see Fig. 13.4) that compare the number of people looking for jobs with the number of jobs offered. Thus, more and more people are being forced to take the job situation into account when considering what career to pursue.

A general question for everyone is what career will be most suitable for them in terms of their talents and interests. Some people may freely choose not to pursue a professional career, or for that matter any career at all. And although some fields have relatively few jobs available, it may be worthwhile to compete for those jobs if this is the field you are most suited for. In other words, the choice of career should be based on many considerations, among them one's own interests as well as opportunity and economic expectations.

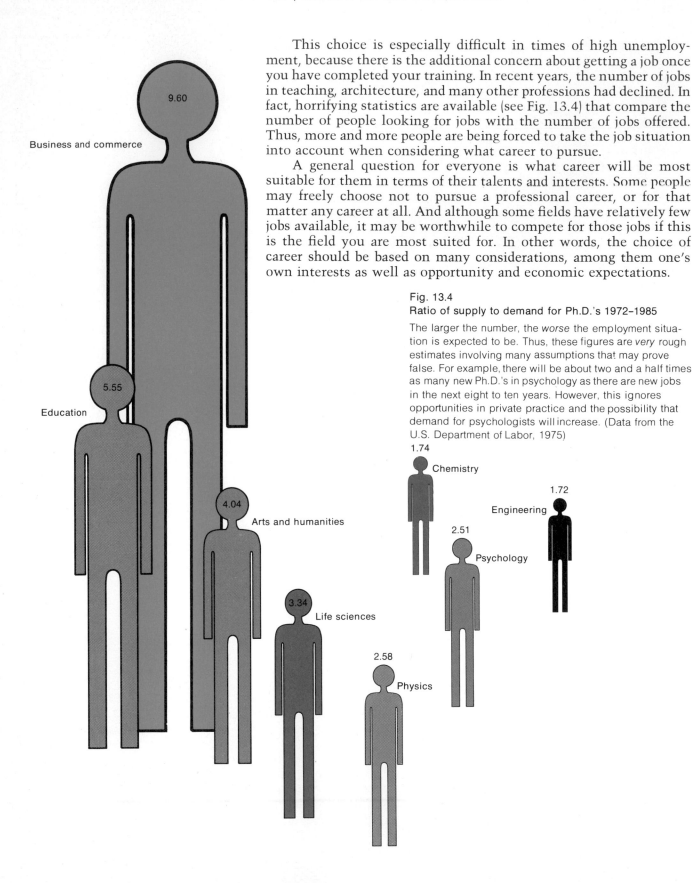

Fig. 13.4
Ratio of supply to demand for Ph.D.'s 1972–1985

The larger the number, the *worse* the employment situation is expected to be. Thus, these figures are *very* rough estimates involving many assumptions that may prove false. For example, there will be about two and a half times as many new Ph.D.'s in psychology as there are new jobs in the next eight to ten years. However, this ignores opportunities in private practice and the possibility that demand for psychologists will increase. (Data from the U.S. Department of Labor, 1975)

Business and commerce 9.60

Education 5.55

Arts and humanities 4.04

Life sciences 3.34

Physics 2.58

Chemistry 1.74

Psychology 2.51

Engineering 1.72

Of course, it is not easy to decide what kind of work will interest and suit you. Talking to people in the field and trying to gain some experience before finally committing yourself can be some help to you in making the decision. In addition, several tests, such as the Cuder Preference Test and Strong Vocational Guidance Test, are available that try to provide insight into your suitability for various careers. These vocational interest tests ask a series of questions (see Fig. 13.5) to assess the kinds of activities that interest you, and then compare your answers with those that have been given by people in the field and with descriptions of the field to see how well they match. The results should be considered only as indicators, but they can often help you clarify your goals.

Marriage and Family

As adolescents grow into young adults, they become increasingly concerned with forming long-term relationships, and in particular with the possibility of marriage and a family. All cultures throughout recorded history have been built around the institution of marriage, which is a more or less permanent, legal pairing of a man and a woman. The characteristics of marriage differ somewhat among societies. A few allow polygamy (a man having more than one wife), a very few allow polyandy (a woman having more than one husband), but most define marriage as an exclusive relationship between one man and one woman. In all societies, marriage means that the man and woman take on certain responsibilities toward each other, and to some extent will share each other's lives "for better or worse," as the traditional Christian marriage ceremony states.

Clearly, marriage plays a central role in the social structure. It is an important factor in social relationships, social status, and lifestyle. It provides an institution for bringing children into the world and raising them. It serves to give each person's life a kind of stability, based on reciprocal responsibility.

In recent years there has been considerable questioning of the central and universal role of marriage. Some people are asking whether marriage is necessary for everyone or for them in particular: they note that love, which in our society has always been presumed to be the basis of marriage, often seems to be lacking in the relationship; and they wonder whether other kinds of relationships and institutions might not be preferable. Much of this questioning has arisen because so many marriages in our country end in divorce. As you can see in Fig. 13.6, the divorce rate has risen dramatically during this century. Whereas our grandparents generally assumed they would marry for life and tended to stay married even if they were not fully satisfied, more than a quarter of the marriages today lead to

In each pair, select the activity you would prefer.		
1. a)	Working on mathematical problems.	1. ___
b)	Arranging the furniture in a room.	
2. a)	Arguing a case before a jury.	2. ___
b)	Delivering a baby.	
3. a)	Talking with people about their problems.	3. ___
b)	Teaching a class in psychology.	
4. a)	Designing a building.	4. ___
b)	Solving mathematical problems.	
5. a)	Studying a chest x-ray.	5. ___
b)	Painting a picture.	
6. a)	Scrubbing test tubes.	6. ___
b)	Arranging the furniture in a room.	
7. a)	Grading exam questions.	7. ___
b)	Doing chemical analyses.	

Fig. 13.5
Vocational guidance test items

These are similar to the items used on some of the vocational guidance tests. The individual's responses are compared with responses of people who are actually in the various fields, and the assumption is that the more similar the responses, the more the person taking the test would like that particular field. This kind of test indicates what occupation the person would like—not necessarily what he or she would be skilled at or successful in. The latter is measured by aptitude tests such as the medical or law school boards.

Fig. 13.6
Divorce rates

The percentages are based on the total number of marriages and divorces each year. This does not give a precise measure of how many of the marriages end in divorce, but it does indicate that, for example, for each one hundred marriages in 1974 there were forty-four divorces.

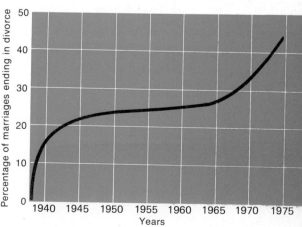

BOX 13.4

WORKING WOMEN

The number of women who hold paid jobs has increased steadily since the turn of the century. As you can see in Fig. (a), the increase was especially sharp between 1930 and 1940 and from 1960 to the present. Today almost 50 percent of the women in the United States hold jobs, a total of almost forty million women. Moreover, working women come from all economic levels and marital situations (see Fig. (b)). It is no longer taken for granted that a woman will marry, have children, and stay at home. Although clearly many women are still principally homemakers, the number is much less than it used to be.

As we mentioned earlier, there are more and more opportunitites for women to enter fields that used to be almost entirely limited to men. Medical schools now admit over 30 percent women whereas just a few years ago they admitted fewer than 10 percent. Similar changes have occurred in law schools and in graduate schools in most fields, and are beginning to take place in business and engineering. Moreover, women are getting jobs on assembly lines, driving trucks, as police officers, and in all sorts of supposedly masculine fields. Thus there is little question that a qualified woman who really wants to get into a particular occupation has a better chance than she used to. Almost no field is entirely closed.

However, the picture is far less rosy than that description might imply. Although the fields are now technically open, there still appears to be strong opposition to letting women into some fields and women themselves often restrict their own choices. It took great effort to get women admitted to West Point because for some reason it was argued that only men could fight or lead other soldiers. Once they were admitted, women actually dropped out less fre-

(a)

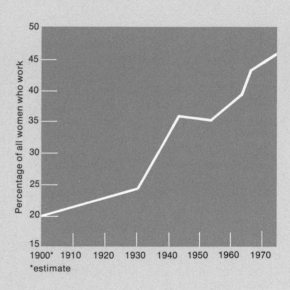

divorce, with the rate being more than 50 percent in some areas. In addition, social values have changed so that it is no longer considered so awful to be divorced, and many more people consider it an alternative if they are dissatisfied.

Both increased divorce rates and altered views of marriage are probably also caused by our changing ideas about sex and the woman's role in society. Now that women are seeking jobs and careers alongside men, these women no longer consider marriage the ultimate goal. Today's women also tend to be more experienced sexually,

quently than men. Similarly, most police departments resist hiring women officers except for special assignments, presumably because strength and aggressiveness are considered necessary for the job. And once more, women officers appear to be doing just fine. The same story could be told about dozens of fields—resistance followed by grudging acceptance. Yet the resistance continues. Figure (c) indicates that most women still work in traditionally "feminine" occupations. This

may be changing gradually as more women enter the work force, but it is important to realize that even with almost 50 percent of women working, there is a long way to go before women have the same freedom as men in selecting and pursuing a career.

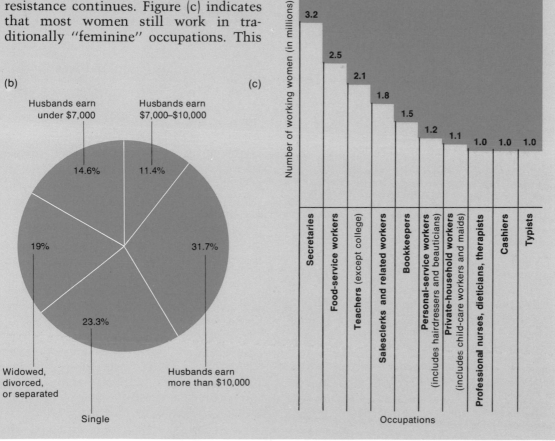

(b)

Husbands earn under $7,000 — 14.6%

Husbands earn $7,000–$10,000 — 11.4%

19%

31.7%

23.3%

Widowed, divorced, or separated

Single

Husbands earn more than $10,000

(c)

Number of working women (in millions)

3.2 — Secretaries
2.5 — Food-service workers
2.1 — Teachers (except college)
1.8 — Salesclerks and related workers
1.5 — Bookkeepers
1.2 — Personal-service workers (includes hairdressers and beauticians)
1.1 — Private-household workers (includes child-care workers and maids)
1.0 — Professional nurses, dieticians, therapists
1.0 — Cashiers
1.0 — Typists

Occupations

and with the more relaxed sexual attitudes neither women nor men need seek marriage as the only outlet for their sexual needs.

Despite these changing views and the high rate of divorce, and despite the various alternatives to traditional marriage that have been proposed (see Box 13.5), most men and women in our society do marry and raise a family. They marry later; couples often postpone having children for many years (this, of course, is made easier by reliable birth-control methods); and they have fewer children than they used to (the average per couple is now about two children

BOX 13.5

ALTERNATIVES TO TRADITIONAL MARRIAGE

Cohabitation

The simplest and by far the most common alternative to marriage is cohabiting, or living together without a legal marriage. A great many people of all ages* live together as couples and have relationships that are probably quite similar to a formal marriage. They share financial responsibilities, divide the work in their home, see friends as a couple, and so on. Many of them also consider each other exclusive sexual partners so that they are as faithful (or unfaithful) as marriage partners. Moreover, many of these relationships last many years. It is difficult to get accurate figures on the duration of these kinds of relationships, but given the high divorce rate, they are probably almost as stable as marriages. Some people who live together even have children and raise them in much the same way as married couples. Society still does not generally accept cohabitation to the extent that it does formal marriage, however, and this is especially true when the couple have children. Therefore, most couples tend to get married if they have children or avoid having children if they do not wish to marry.

In addition, there are a variety of legal problems connected with cohabitation. The partners are not legally responsible for each other, cannot as easily inherit money from each other (though obviously this is not an important consideration for young people), cannot obtain social security benefits as spouses, and so on. If disaster strikes and permission is necessary for medical care, for example, a cohabiting partner cannot legally give such permission. And finally, for many people, even those who have no moral objections to cohabiting, there is a desire for marriage because it represents a formal and symbolic commitment to each other. Therefore, despite the enormous increase in the number of people who spend at least some of their lives living together without marriage, a formal, legal marriage continues to be the ultimate choice of a vast majority of Americans.

Limited, Trial, or Term Marriages

Some couples have experimented with marriages that do not involve the usual lifelong commitment. They agree to be married for a limited period of time, or to try it out for a few years and then choose whether to continue the arrangement. This is done either with or without a legal ceremony, but the idea is that both people are committing themselves fully for the agreed-upon period. The rationale behind trial marriage is that no one knows how a marriage will work until it begins. Even living together is not a complete test of what a marriage will be, because the formal marriage often alters the relationship. Some people are frightened or worried by the total commitment of marriage; others thrive under this kind of commitment. The trial marriage formally recognizes this uncertainty, and theoretically allows the partners to avoid the feeling of being trapped and also the guilt if they want to get divorced. Whether this arrangement works is unclear. It is probable that at the end of the two-year or five-year term, anyone who wants to end the arrangement is under almost as much pressure and feels almost as much guilt as a person in a formal marriage. But the idea is appealing and some people are trying it.

Marriage Contracts

Closely related to trial marriage is the idea of a marriage contract that spells out

---

* Recently many older people have begun living together instead of marrying because by remaining single both can retain their full social security benefits.

in detail exactly what each partner wants and expects from the relationship. The marriage itself is legal, but the contract would simply be an informal agreement that would specify the couple's own rules rather than the unwritten rules of traditional marriage. The marriage partners may or may not share financial responsibilities, may or may not expect sexual fidelity, may or may not want children. They may also specify in advance the division of labor in the household, the amount of freedom each wants, and so on. Probably very few couples actually draw up such a contract, but the idea of it may have affected the way many couples enter marriage. More and more people do specify what they expect and question some of the traditional roles. Even if they do not write down these arrangements, they enter the marriage with a clearer view of what each of them wants.

Open Marriage

The term "open marriage" refers to a legal marriage in which the two partners agree that they will be free to do what they want in terms of their social and sexual lives. In particular, each is free to have extramarital sexual relationships and neither is supposed to be jealous or upset by the other's activities along these lines. Whether they discuss these other relationships with each other depends on their agreement, but they are not restricted in any other way. As we have mentioned, some married couples do have extramarital affairs; so the open marriage is meant to be a way of allowing what happens anyway. The idea is appealing to many people who find it difficult to accept total monogamy. Currently, we have no evidence one way or the other on how successful such arrangements are. Sexual jealousy is a very strong emotion and probably cannot be eliminated simply by an agreement. Moreover, sexual relationships outside the marriage are always po-

tentially threatening to the primary relationship and may weaken or destroy it. Yet this is a more open and honest kind of relationship than one in which the partners secretly have affairs. The open marriage has received a good deal of publicity but not very much acceptance. Married people may be somewhat more accepting of extramarital affairs than they used to be, but there are few marriages that involve a total acceptance of sexual relationships outside the marriage.

Group and Communal Marriages

Perhaps the most extreme alternative is a marriage (not recognized by law) of more than two people. The idea is that a number of couples will live together, sharing responsibilities and sexual relations. This is supposed to solve the problem of sexual exclusivity—people are free to have sex with other partners as well as their spouse—without producing jealousy since the sexual relations are with someone else in the marriage. It is also supposed to provide more variety, excitement, and sharing of experiences (not just sexually) because each member of the marriage brings special attributes, interests, and talents that can be shared by all. As with open marriage, the idea is appealing in theory; but there is little evidence that it has caught on and considerable anecdotal evidence that it rarely works. Perhaps the reason is that it is hard enough to live in harmony with one other person, and the group may intensify the normal problems and personality clashes. Although communal living and communal marriages were somewhat popular for a brief period in the sixties, they seem to be out of favor now.

Table 13.3
CHANGES IN EXPECTED BIRTHS

Year	Total expected	% expecting to have		
		no children	1 or 2	3 or more
1960	3.1	23.4	35.1	38.4
1965	3.1	23.3	38.2	35.4
1970	2.6	22.7	54.9	18.8
1975	2.3	25.1	59.9	12.7

The number of children expected by childless wives has decreased since 1960. The decrease is *not* due to a change in those planning to have no children. Rather it is caused by many fewer planning to have more than 2 children.

Source: Current population reports, 1975.

compared to more than three only twenty years ago, as shown in Table 13.3). In short, people are questioning whether marriage will make them happy and fulfilled, and seem to experiment sexually much more before getting married, but legal marriage remains the ultimate choice of the vast majority of our population. And even those who get divorced are very likely to remarry, apparently preferring to try again rather than remain single. It is interesting to note that studies of satisfaction with life (Campbell, Converse, and Rodgers, 1976; Shaver and Freedman, 1976) indicate that married people tend to be happier than those who are single (see Box 13.6) perhaps suggesting that with all its faults, marriage does satisfy most people's needs better than the alternatives.

Middle Age

To most young people, "middle age" probably sounds terrible, but actually these are the years that a large percentage of the population considers their happiest. Between the ages of thirty and sixty careers and family become established, creativity of various kinds is at its height, and in many ways people find their place in life. Of course, this is a long period and there is considerable question as to what ages should be included in "middle age." Some people consider middle age to be from forty to sixty, others from thirty to fifty, and still others thirty-five to sixty-five. It does not really matter what age range is chosen because different people face the problems and enjoy the satisfactions of middle age at different times. The important point is that once the problems of early adulthood have been more or less settled, one's life usually becomes more settled and structured. Instead of making monumental decisions such as whom to marry, whether to have children, and what job to pursue, we are dealing with ongoing concerns produced by these choices. Thus, middle age is a time of consolidation and productivity, and to some extent of acceptance.

In recent years, however, more and more people are experiencing crucial changes during and after middle age. To begin with, the high divorce rate in the United States causes a series of upheavals in many people's lives. From a marriage with children, home, and social life

MARRIAGE AND HAPPINESS

Although married people say they are happier than single people, as shown in the figure, the effect of being single seems to differ considerably for men and women. As they get older, women who have never married report being more and more unhappy, with single women over forty being the least happy. In contrast, men appear to get used to being single. As they get older they report being slightly less happy up to forty, but after that they say they are actually happier than before and happier than men their age who are married. There is not yet enough evidence to say what effect second marriages have on happiness. The indication at the moment is that a second or even third marriage provides no less happiness than a first marriage, especially for men.

All of these findings should be considered in light of changing views on marriage, divorce, and women's role in society. It may be that the apparent burden of being a single woman over forty will be relieved by new ideas of equality between the sexes and the acceptance of the single life. Nevertheless, the current findings are virtually identical to those that have been obtained in the past. Perhaps the effect of marriage, sex, and age on happiness will change slowly if at all.

Source: Shaver and Freedman, 1976.

BOX 13.6

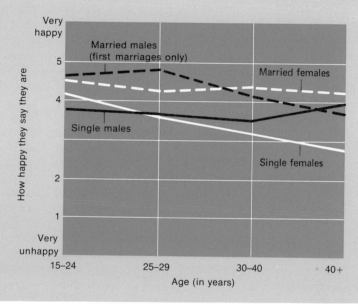

they return to life as a single person and then often back to family life if they remarry. The divorce is often complex and painful, particularly when children are involved. Both the man and the woman must adjust to being single, meeting new people, and engaging in a totally different social life while at the same time maintaining responsibility for the children. Remarriage may involve children from a previous marriage and children from the new marriage. And, of course, both the single life and a new marriage typically produce enormous changes in the individual's social life, bringing new friends, new patterns of socializing, perhaps a totally new economic and social

Divorce Announcement

John E. and Louise E. Tumultuously announce a few cosmic happenings.

John and the children have moved to New York City.

Louise has moved to San Diego. We are dissolving our marriage.

circle. While adjusting to being single again or to a new marriage may be difficult, it can also open up new possibilities and provide new experiences. Indeed, a unique phenomenon in the United States today is the large number of middle-aged people who are single or newly married.

As important as divorce and remarriage are, perhaps an even more dramatic change that can occur during middle age is starting a new career. Many people—particularly men—during their middle years begin to evaluate whether they are successful in their careers. Have they made enough money, achieved a high enough position, fulfilled their potential, or contributed enough to society or to their friends and family? Not everyone can be equally successful in these respects, and some people must face the fact that they have not achieved as much as they would have liked. Others who are successful must deal with the question of whether that success was what they really wanted and whether it has brought them the happiness and satisfaction they expected. Sometimes a man realizes at the age of forty or so that he is not fully satisfied with what he is doing. Having realized this, most people nevertheless remain in their job and wait for retirement, or perhaps try to alter the job sufficiently to make it more interesting. But others look around for something new. Although as we have said, it is very difficult to change careers, some people do. Architects decide to go to law school, lawyers become artists, business executives try farming, and so on. These changes are obviously not easy, but with sufficient desire, work, energy, ability, and probably luck they are possible.

Furthermore, a great many women are now seeking careers after their children are grown. These women are returning to school, receiving advanced training, or entering the work force. For such women, middle age, rather than being a time of settling down, may be a period of growth and change. It may also be a period of considerable strain because in seeking a career they may be disrupting established patterns in their marriage; and of course they are competing with younger women for jobs.

Finally, middle age is also the time when we must face the fact that we will not live forever. People become more and more concerned about their health and security. We worry about losing our attractiveness, our sex appeal. In women these concerns may arise as early as age thirty-five, but they probably become focused at menopause, when the ovaries cease to produce egg cells, menstruation stops, and the woman can no longer have children. There is also a decrease in the production of estrogen, which can cause "hot flashes," a loss of muscle tone, and a decline in physical appearance. These changes are frequently accompanied by changes in mood or by depressions. It seems likely that these depressions are caused primarily by the physical changes, but perhaps they also can be accounted for in part by the feeling of postmenopausal women that they are no longer attractive and desirable as sexual partners. Moreover, it is around this time that the children have grown up and left the home. A woman who has spent her younger years devoting herself exclusively to raising her family may now begin to feel useless. How will she fill the remaining twenty or even thirty years of her life?

While middle-aged men do not experience the profound biological changes that women undergo, they often do experience fears of

FACTORS IN HAPPINESS

Although no one knows how to guarantee happiness, it appears that certain factors in one's life contribute more to happiness than others. A survey on happiness (Shaver and Freedman, 1976) asked people to indicate how happy they were in various aspects of their lives and then related this to their overall happiness. As shown in the table, social factors ranked very high. Sex and being in love were important for all groups; friends and social life were critical for single people, while mar-

riage and partner's happiness were at the top for married people. Career and recognition were also high on the list, as was personal growth. Material considerations—finances and where one lived—and even health counted for less, as did religion, attractiveness, and being a parent. On the other hand (not shown in the table), having guiding values (as opposed to religion per se) was also an important contributor to happiness. Thus we do not know how to achieve happiness, but we have some ideas about what areas of our lives are most likely to provide it.

BOX 13.7

THE SIXTEEN PILLARS OF HAPPINESS: THE IMPORTANCE OF EACH OF THE FOLLOWING ITEMS TO GENERAL HAPPINESS, RANKED IN ORDER

	Single men	Single women	Married men	Married women
Friends and social life	1	1	8	7.5
Job or primary activity	2	3	4	7.5
Being in love	3	2	2	1
Recognition, success	4	4	7	5.5
Sex life	5	6	6	4
Personal growth	6	5	1	5.5
Financial situation	7	9	10	13
House or apartment	8	10.5	11	14
Body and attractiveness	9.5	8	16	16
Health and physical condition	9.5	7	13	9
City you live in	11	13	14	11
Religion	12	10.5	12	12
Exercise, recreation	13	12	15	15
Being a parent	—	—	9	10
Marriage	—	—	3	2
Partner's happiness	—	—	5	3

Source: Shaver and Freedman, 1976.

losing their sexual attractiveness and prowess. It is not uncommon for a man facing this prospect to divorce his wife of many years and marry a much younger woman—perhaps in an attempt to show that he is still young and potent.

Thus, toward the end of middle age, everyone finally realizes the obvious fact that they are no longer young. In addition to physical changes, people begin to approach the age of retirement, must make plans for their later years, and so on. Psychologists have devoted regrettably little time to these problems, but in recent years the field of adult development has begun to attract much more attention. As we live longer and longer, and a larger percentage of the population is in middle or late life, it becomes increasingly important to understand the developmental process during these periods.

The Later Years

Until fairly recently in human history, very few people lived long enough to enter what we now call the later years. Average life expectancy as recently as 1880 was only thirty-three years for white males in New York City and was as low as twenty years for black males in the South. Overall, life expectancy in the nineteenth century was no more than forty for any group anywhere. Now, however, the average life expectancy for all groups in the United States is greater than sixty years, with white females having the highest and black males still the lowest (see Fig. 13.7 for more detailed figures). Moreover, at least 50 percent of all those born now will live beyond sixty-five, with the figure rising to over 80 percent for white females. Thus, by far the majority of our population will live past sixty-five and have to deal with the problems of old age.

Fig. 13.7
Changes in life expectancy in the United States during this century

Life expectancy increased sharply but has now largely leveled off. Differences between males and females and between whites and nonwhites remain. The latter is probably due mainly or entirely to a difference in economic level. (Data from the U.S. Office of Vital Statistics)

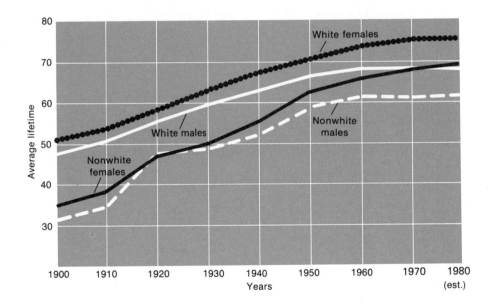

Some of the problems that we usually attribute to old age are more imagined than real. There is no evidence, for example, that mental ability declines very much as we get older. Some older people think a little more slowly and have somewhat weaker short-term memories, and therefore are less agile with mental arithmetic and other such tricks (Schaie and Strother, 1968). But by and large, the important mental functions decline very little if at all even when people are very old (Schaie, Labouvie, and Buech, 1973). We all know of many people in their late seventies and older who are still extremely sharpwitted. Indeed, some of the world's most important figures have been active at seventy, eighty, and even ninety (see Fig. 13.8). Thus one major concern of older people—that their minds will

PABLO CASALS
Cellist who gave concerts and conducted until his late 80s.

JUDITH LOWRY
Became an actress in her later years, and gained a following in her 80s for her role as spunky Mother Dexter in the television series *Phyllis*.

GEORGIA O'KEEFE
American artist known for paintings of the Southwest desert; still active at 89 (1976 date), has lately taken up pottery.

ANNA MARY ROBERTSON (Grandma Moses)
Started painting in late 70s; painted until late 90s.

EDVARD MUNCH
Played a pivotal role in the development of Expressionism; recovered from a "nervous breakdown" in 1908 and painted into his 80s.

HENRI MATISSE
Painted, sculpted, and designed until the age of 85.

QUEEN VICTORIA
Queen of England for sixty-four years until her death at 82.

HANS HOFMANN
"Philosopher-king of abstract expressionism"; first famous as a teacher; not until 1958, when he was nearly 80, did he turn to painting full time.

ANDRE MALRAUX
French philosopher, writer, critic, hero of the French Resistance; volunteered at age 70 to drive a tank in the war of independence in Bangladesh.

MARTHA GRAHAM
America's most influential modern dancer; now 84, she has choreographed and danced for over 50 years.

ARTUR RUBINSTEIN
Still giving piano concerts in late 80s.

BUCKMINSTER FULLER
Philosopher, author, and architect, continues to pursue a vigorous and active career at the age of 83.

Fig. 13.8
Famous people active in old age

not function well—is generally unfounded unless they have a physical illness that directly affects the brain.

The same is true of sexual ability. Both men and women experience sexual desire and are able to take part in sex for as long as they live, barring specific physical disabilities. In fact, men in their seventies and eighties can still sometimes sire children. Older people usually are less strong and vigorous than younger people, of course, and their sexual activities will consequently decrease also. But this does not mean that sexual activity stops any more than it means that all athletics cease. Often a decrease in sexuality is due not to physical factors, but to a feeling that it is unseemly or inappropriate for a man or woman of seventy-five to still be interested in sex. Masters and Johnson (1966), the pioneering researchers on sex, make the strong point that if older people are still capable of sexual activity there is no reason to think it is unnatural.

While intelligence and sexuality do not decline as much as people might imagine, there is no question that most older people do face some real problems. Typically, they have been forced to retire from their profession. This presents a number of difficulties. In the first place, they may suffer an immediate loss or decline of income. A great many older people find that they have much less money to spend than they did before, and that inflation makes the income they do have go less far than it used to. This is a serious problem for these individuals and for society. To be old may be difficult; to be old and poor is a lot worse. For this reason labor unions and the government have put more and more emphasis on retirement and pension plans. Indeed, in many labor-management disputes the key issue is pensions rather than current wages.

The problem of losing income is serious, but for many people an even more serious problem with retiring is the loss of something to do. As long as a person works, he or she can feel valuable and valued. The danger of retiring is that the individual may suddenly feel useless. When this occurs, it often produces depression and can lead to a decline in the person's health and vitality. It seems very important for all people, young and old, to have something to do, whether it be work, a hobby, traveling, or taking care of grandchildren. The older person who keeps busy and active seems to live longer and remain happier.

Fortunately most people do not suffer this decline following retirement. The notion that as soon as people retire they immediately lose their health and die is simply not supported by the evidence. A study of retirement by Streib and Schneider (1971) found that fewer than a quarter of retired people felt useless and lost their health as a result. As you might expect, those who retired voluntarily felt better

This couple, still practicing dentistry in their nineties, is living evidence that people who stay busy and active live longer and remain healthier and happier.

than those who were forced to retire, but even among the latter group a majority coped quite well.

The final problem in all senses of the word is facing the prospect of death. While we all know that we will die, it is difficult for many people to accept this fact. Naturally, older people must face death directly. They see their friends and relatives dying, and they know that they, too, will eventually die. For many years, death was a forbidden topic in American society. Long after sex was discussed with considerable freedom, death continued to be taboo. In recent years, this has changed somewhat. In 1977, for the first time, the *Annual Review of Psychology* included an article on psychological perspectives on death (Kastenbaum and Costa, 1977). More and more psychologists, sociologists, and therapists (Kübler-Ross, 1969, for example), and many popular and scholarly books are focusing on how to prepare for death. Both the individual who dies and his or her friends and relatives often have enormous problems before and immediately after the death. While there are no easy solutions to these problems, it appears that facing the prospect directly, talking about it, and making plans can be of considerable help. This work also raises a number of serious questions such as whether to tell someone that he is dying. Friends often keep this information from the person, thus treating him to some extent like a child and also subjecting themselves to the additional burden of maintaining the secret. Since the person who is dying tends to know it anyway, he, too, sometimes tries to pretend that he is not and everyone suffers more than is necessary. On the other hand, perhaps under some circumstances, for particular individuals, it is kinder not to tell. Further work on the problems of dealing with death may give additional information on this and other crucial questions. At the moment, we do know that this is a terribly difficult subject but that, in general, facing death directly is better than pretending it will not happen. ∎

Summary

1. Although the study of human development has tended to concentrate on the childhood years, psychologists are becoming increasingly interested in the concerns of adolescence and adulthood, particularly sexuality, careers, long-term goals, and aging.

2. Puberty, the achievement of sexual maturity, is marked by the onset of menstruation in women, sperm in the urine of men, and the development of the sexual organs and secondary sexual characteristics. The maturing young person often has feelings of pride mingled with uncertainty over the changes. A primary conflict during adolescence concerns the appropriate expression of sexual feelings.

3. Data on sexual attitudes have been collected primarily by survey research, pioneered by Alfred Kinsey. Information from surveys should be viewed cautiously because the intimate nature of the subject results in some dishonest responses. It is apparent that American sexual attitudes and expression are considerably freer than in the past; however, people still tend to relate sex and love and freer attitudes have not eliminated guilt, fear, and other problems.

4. Whether a particular sexual behavior is deviant (abnormal) is often determined by law. A psychological definition of deviance would include behavior that limits the individual's freedom, prevents rewarding sexual experiences, or is harmful to others. Homosexuality is still considered by many people to be deviant, but whether or not it is in fact unhealthy depends on the underlying reasons for the homosexuality and whether it makes the person unhappy or is harmful to others. A variety of factors probably influence the development of homosexuality, among them early homosexual experiences that were happy, identification with the role of the opposite sex, or psychological conflicts about sex.

5. Sex roles involve behaviors and activities that are considered appropriate for members of each sex. Historically, sex roles probably originated from the physical differences between the sexes, which determined the activities men and women performed and fostered the qualities required for these activities. Other factors influencing sex roles are differential reinforcement of boys and girls, identification, and exposure to societal expectations. Recently, various factors have weakened sex-role distinctions and the result may be an increase in freedom of choice for both sexes.

6. Research on sex differences indicates that of the many differences that were thought to exist between the sexes, only a few actually do exist and there is considerable overlap on these. Differences appear in aggression (males are higher), verbal ability (females are higher), and quantitative and spatial abilities (males are higher).

7. Adolescence marks the beginning of adult development. As well as maturing sexually, the individual usually undergoes an *identity crisis*; that is, a search for a sense of oneself as an individual. The identity crisis is characterized by a breaking away from parental authority, an increasing reliance on peers, and attempts to find an answer to the question, Who am I?

8. Adult development includes the following stages: early adulthood, when we search for a marital partner and choose a career; middle age, when we evaluate our lives and decide to accept or change things; and the older years, when we face old age and the prospect of dying.

9. Choice of a career is a far-reaching decision. Some important considerations are one's interests, one's economic expectations, and opportunities in the desired field. Vocational interest tests are useful in indicating a person's suitability for various careers.

10. In spite of high divorce rates, altered views of marriage, and alternatives to traditional marriage, the institution of marriage is still the choice of most people. A recent survey indicated that married people tend to be happier than single people.

11. With major decisions about marriage, career, and childrearing largely in the past, many people feel settled and content in middle age. Others, however, experience many upheavals. Divorce, changing one's career or lifestyle, and worries about health, aging, loss of attractiveness, and income are all potential crises.

12. The idea that people in their later years will have decreased mental ability is largely unfounded. Except for short-term memory, the important mental functions decline very little in old age. Similarly, the idea that old age rules out sexual activity seems to be based on societal expectations rather than on fact. The real problems of old age involve loss of income, a feeling of uselessness after retirement, and the necessity to face death.

RECOMMENDED READING

Conger, J. *Adolescence and Youth: Psychological Development in a Changing World.* New York: Harper & Row, 1973. One of the best short books on adolescence.

Friedan, B. *The Feminine Mystique,* 2d ed. New York: Norton, 1974.

Maccoby, E., and C. N. Jacklin. *The Psychology of Sex Differences.* Stanford, Calif.: Stanford University Press, 1974. A complete summary of research on sex differences. Encyclopedic, difficult, certainly a high-level book, but it is all here for those who are interested.

Masters, W. H., and V. E. Johnson. *Human Sexual Response.* Boston: Little, Brown, 1966. The first book by this team. Describes how they study sexual behavior in the laboratory and some of their findings. An important book.

A wonderful fact to reflect upon, that every human creature is constituted to be that profound secret and mystery to every other.
Charles Dickens, A Tale of Two Cities

To love oneself is the beginning of a lifelong romance.
Oscar Wilde, An Ideal Husband

14 Personality

Theories of personality ■ *Constitutional or physiological theories* ■ *Psychoanalytic theories* ■ *Personality development—Freudian theory* ■ *Criticisms of psychoanalytic theory* ■ *Neo-Freudian theories* ■ *Social learning theory* ■ *Humanistic psychology and self-actualization* ■ *Comparison of the personality theories* ■ *Personality assessment* ■ *Some specific personality traits*

rite down ten statements that describe yourself or someone you know very well. Some of these statements probably refer to sex, occupation or college major, physical characteristics, and perhaps abilities. These are very important qualities, but we do not ordinarily think of them as the person's personality. Personality is something more—it involves how the person differs from other people, how she or he acts under various circumstances, and how he or she responds to other people; in other words, the unique style that is theirs.

For example, suppose you say that someone is named Nancy Arrowsmith, is a lawyer, twenty-six, single, and works in a large firm. Then you add that she is a white American, short, beautiful, and intelligent. We already know quite a bit about her, but we do not yet know anything about her personality—we do not know "what she is like." Only when you say that she is witty, independent, ambitious, aggressive, warm, extroverted, and sincere do we begin to get a sense of her as a person. These characteristics involve what we usually call personality because they describe how she behaves and feels.

It is not easy to give a formal definition of personality because the concept is actually somewhat vague. However, a few classic definitions might give a clearer idea of how the term is used. Gordon Allport described personality as "the dynamic organization within the individual of those psychophysical systems that determine his characteristic behavior and thought" (1961, p. 28). A typical textbook definition defines personality as "the most characteristic integration of an individual's structures, modes of behavior, interests, attitudes, capacities, abilities and aptitudes." (Munn, 1966, p. 637) And Raymond Cattell offers a somewhat different notion: "Personality is that which permits a prediction of what a person will do in a given situation" (1950, pp. 2-3).

Although each of these definitions gives a general idea of what we mean by personality, none of them is entirely adequate. It is important to realize that the essential element of personality is that it includes those factors (whatever they are) that distinguish one individual's behavior and thought from another's and that are consistent from one time to another. We shall see that there is some controversy about just how consistently people do behave, but there is no doubt that some consistency exists. At the least, a person will be likely to behave the same way in two identical situations. This consistency, the tendency to behave in characteristic ways, is the basis of personality.

The second crucial point is that people differ in the way they behave. If everyone acted the same way in all situations, there would be no study of personality. Whereas most fields of psychology concentrate on similarities among people, personality assumes and studies differences—it focuses on what makes people unique. Indeed, personality shows up *only* in situations in which people behave differently. Blinking at a bright light, jumping at a sudden noise, or eating when you are very hungry tells us little or nothing about your personality because everyone responds the same way. Only when there is some freedom of action, when responses are not automatic, does personality become evident.

In studying personality, psychologists have dealt with several different problems. First, they have attempted to describe the major aspects of personality and how they develop; second, they have devised tests to assess personality; and third, they have investigated certain personality characteristics that seem to have major effects on our behavior. We shall consider each of these in turn.

THEORIES OF PERSONALITY

There are more than enough theories of personality to fill a book by that name (Hall and Lindzey, 1970), but they can be divided into several general classes. Some theories explain personality largely in terms of innate or physiological factors; others explain it in terms of dynamic interactions between the individual's innate needs and her experiences; others use principles derived from research on learning; and still others conceive of personality as existing within the person, waiting to emerge. As we discuss these different theories, it is well to keep in mind that they are not necessarily contradictory. Rather, they tend to concentrate on different aspects of the process and to answer somewhat different questions. The various theories often contribute compatible ideas that together increase our understanding of this extremely complicated phenomenon.

CONSTITUTIONAL OR PHYSIOLOGICAL THEORIES

These theories suggest that personality is determined in large part by the biological constitution of the individual. Just as there are innate differences in perceptual and cognitive abilities, so there are innately determined differences in personality. In particular, these theories have concentrated on the relationship between personality and physique, or presumed neurological differences in the brain.

Sheldon's Body Types

The idea that people of differing physiques have different personalities goes as far back as the ancient Greeks and is a widely accepted popular belief. The stereotype of the slow-moving but jolly fat person and the quiet, introspective thin person are part of popular culture. William Sheldon (1954) attempted to demonstrate these relationships systematically.

First, Sheldon identified three basic types of physical structure: *endomorphic*, characterized by a soft, rounded, unmuscled body; *mesomorphic*, characterized by a tough, muscled, angular structure; and *ectomorphic*, characterized by a thin, lightly muscled, slim build. Extreme examples are shown in Fig. 14.1. While few people are perfect examples of any of these types, everyone can be classified according to how closely his body resembles each type. (You might try rating yourself and other people you know.)

Next Sheldon attempted to show that endomorphs tended to be even tempered, tolerant, and slow reacting; that mesomorphs were aggressive, adventurous, and callous; and that ectomorphs were restrained, inhibited, self-conscious, and overreactive. Although there is probably some tendency for the body types to go along with these personalities, most psychologists now feel that the relationships are

Body Type

ENDOMORPH—
Soft, rounded,
unmuscled

MESOMORPH—
Hard, angular,
muscular

ECTOMORPH—
Thin, sharp-featured,
little muscle

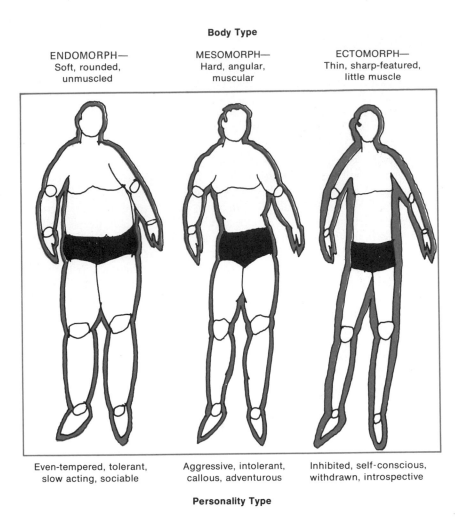

Even-tempered, tolerant,
slow acting, sociable

Aggressive, intolerant,
callous, adventurous

Inhibited, self-conscious,
withdrawn, introspective

Personality Type

Fig. 14.1
Sheldon's theory of body and personality types

weak. The particular physique does not seem to produce a specific personality often enough for this theory to be generally accepted.

On the other hand, there is little question that physique plays some role in shaping personality, not because it determines personality directly, but because it affects how one is treated by the world. For example, strong, muscular people may be encouraged to be athletes, and taught to be aggressive and assertive and to take risks. Thin, weak people may learn early in life not to get involved in fights, to be quiet in order to protect themselves, and to depend on intellectual power for success. The physique does not produce the personality, but society treats us differently depending on our builds and therefore teaches us to act differently. Thus, the importance of Sheldon's work is that it stresses the contribution of biological and genetic factors, which have often been ignored by American psychologists.

Eysenck's Three-Factor Theory

Hans Eysenck (1967) began his work by obtaining personality measures on a great many people. He then claimed to have demonstrated by means of statistical analysis that all human personality could be described in terms of three basic characteristics: *introversion-extroversion* (antisociability, inhibition, and intenseness versus sociability and easygoing openness), *neuroticism* (anxiety and nervousness versus calm and self-assurance), and *psychoticism* (severe disturbance versus general health).

The next step is the important one for our purposes. Eysenck asserted that these psychological factors are associated with and caused by neurological differences. He said that introverts have a weak inhibitory potential in the brain while extroverts have a strong one. This would cause introverts to respond strongly to external stimuli and to condition easily, while extroverts would respond weakly and condition slowly. Because introverts respond strongly to pain and other stimulation, they become anxious, worried, nervous, and generally neurotic. In contrast, the extroverts, who respond weakly to external stimulation, learn less control, are less anxious, and more willing to face social stimulation.

This is a fascinating and provocative idea. As we shall discuss in Chapter 16 on therapy, there is good reason to believe that responsivity in the brain is associated with mental disorders such as depression; and drugs that affect this responsivity can reduce depression. Therefore, differences among people in responsivity at the neurological level might cause differences in personality. However, the research on this theory has produced inconsistent results. Eysenck and his associates generally report supportive results (Eysenck, 1959), but others do not (Spence and Spence, 1964). Eysenck predicts that extroverts will be more likely to be criminals because they do not learn to control their behavior, but another study (Iwawaki and Cowen, 1964) found that criminals did not differ in extroversion from female high-school students, and that juvenile delinquents were very low in extroversion.

Thus, the theory has not been well supported by the data. Nevertheless, there is good reason to believe that neurological differences can affect personality. You will recall from Chapter 9 that the work on hunger indicated the importance of hypothalamic functions, and also that Schachter found substantial differences between "fats" and normals in their reaction to external stimuli. Therefore, although the particular neurological factors stressed by Eysenck may not be the critical ones and may be less consistent than he claims, this would seem to be a fertile field for research. Recent progress in our understanding of brain functions may enable us to find more consistent relationships between physiological differences and personality.

PSYCHOANALYTIC THEORIES

A large group of personality theories stress the interaction between the individual's innate needs and characteristics and the environment. These theories take constitutional factors into account, but generally assume people are similar on these and that they therefore do not play an important role in producing differences in personality. The major emphasis is on what people experience in life and how these experiences relate to their basic, innate qualities. Freud's psychoanalytic theory is the central formulation, but many other theories have developed and altered some of the original concepts.

Freud's theory of psychoanalysis starts with the assumption that we all have powerful innate needs and impulses that are shaped by and conflict with the needs of society. Although innate needs such as hunger and sex must be satisfied to some extent, no society or even family can exist if people express their impulses with total freedom. Unless some control is imposed, we have too many aggressive, sexual, destructive, and selfish motives for us to live together harmoniously. Infants can flail about, scream, and strike out blindly when they are uncomfortable or hungry. Adults who behaved this way would cause havoc. Similarly, children tend to express their sexual and pleasure-seeking impulses immediately and directly. Although modern sexual values sometimes urge us all to do this ("If it feels good, do it," "Do it till you're satisfied"), society could not survive for long if everyone actually acted this way. You cannot take anything you want, nor can you express your sexuality or your aggressive feelings with total freedom. Thus infants must be taught (socialized) to control some of their impulses and to express them only under certain limited conditions.

Everyone must experience this training in order to become an adult who can live with other people. However, this training produces conflicts between the innate impulses and the rules of society. According to Freud, this conflict and the way it is resolved produces personality. Or, to put it slightly differently, personality is in fact our characteristic way of dealing with these conflicts. With this idea in mind, let us discuss some of the major elements of the theory.

The Unconscious

Perhaps the most influential aspect of psychoanalytic theory is the concept of the *unconscious*. Freud asserts that we have motives, feelings, memories, and thoughts that we are not aware of—that are, in his terms, unconscious. This does not mean that the unconscious is an entity that actually exists somewhere in the brain, but rather that we are aware (conscious) of some mental functioning and unaware (unconscious) of other functioning.

The point of this idea is that unconscious motives are assumed to affect our behavior. This is not an easy notion for most people to accept. It seems as if when we think of something we are aware that we are thinking of it, and that when we feel motivated we are aware that we are feeling it. In all of our actions, it seems as if we know what we are doing and why.

However, Freud has pointed out many convincing examples of unconscious motivation affecting behavior. We often make slips of the tongue, saying the opposite of what we mean or making other mistakes in our speech. Freud suggests that many of these errors (sometimes called Freudian slips) are expressions of our unconscious feelings. For example, you might say to your rival for someone's affections, "I'm very sorry to meet you," when what you meant to say

Sigmund Freud and his daughter Anna Freud

was the socially acceptable (but untrue), "I'm very happy to meet you." Similarly, we often forget a piece of information or someone's name because the information is upsetting, because we are angry at the person, or for some other reason. Although errors of this sort can happen by accident (the mind does not always work perfectly), it does seem as if a disproportionate number are connected with disturbing events or occur when we are nervous and upset. In addition, Freud points out that dreams (see Chapter 11) and various kinds of mental disorders are caused by unconscious thoughts and feelings. Thus, although many psychologists dislike the term "unconscious" and prefer to state the phenomenon in other terms, most people do accept the idea that some of our behavior is affected by mental processes of which we are unaware.

The Id, Ego, and Superego

The second major aspect of psychoanalytic theory is the separation of mental processes into three parts: the id, the ego, and the superego. According to Freud, each of us has three separate but closely related psychological processes that together determine our behavior. Although Freud often wrote of them as though they were separate parts of the brain, they are not in fact specific organs. Rather, they are separate *functions* of the brain that constitute our personalities.

The id The basic source of energy and motivation is called the *id*. It is composed of our primitive, innate physiological needs collected together. The most important of these make up two groups: *libido*, which consists of the positive, sexual, loving impulses; and *thanatos*, which includes destructive, aggressive impulses. These innate motivational forces provide the energy behind all of our behavior.

The id follows what Freud called the *pleasure principle*, which means that it is concerned solely with seeking maximum satisfaction of needs and desires. It is totally uncontrolled, caring about and being

Fig. 14.2
The id, the ego, and the superego

affected by only primitive satisfactions. Newborn babies, for example, are essentially only id because all they care about is satisfying their needs and being comfortable. However, soon babies must learn to take some part in satisfying their own needs—the parent will not always do it for them. Since the id is incapable of performing this function (it is pure impulse and cannot form plans or deal with the world), another function begins to emerge. This is the start of the ego.

The ego The *ego* is the individual's personal identity, her aware, conscious, deliberately functioning mind. The ego contains all of our perceptual and cognitive functions such as language, thinking, and reasoning. It is the part of the mind that deals with the external world and seeks to satisfy the individual's needs. It follows the *reality* *principle*, which means that by and large it is rational and logical, and is able to delay gratification in order to achieve greater satisfaction later. In a sense, the ego is the "I" that we think of as ourselves.

Part of the function of the ego is to control the impulses of the id but also to maximize their satisfaction. In general, the ego is devoted to preserving the individual, doing what is best for her survival and growth.

The superego The *superego* is the conscience of the individual. It contains the rules, values, and morals that tell us what is right and what is wrong. These rules help us decide what course of action to take in a given circumstance, but they also sometimes conflict with our impulse to seek satisfaction. The superego is thus our own version of society's limitation on our freedom.

The superego also contains our vision of perfection, our *ego ideal*. This is the image of ourself that we would like to achieve. Whenever our behavior approaches this ideal self, we feel good; when it deviates, we feel guilty. Thus, the superego controls and directs our behavior by providing built-in reinforcements.

Dynamics These three parts of our minds cooperate but are also in constant conflict. The id consists of impulses we want to satisfy, the superego says that only certain ones are allowed, and the ego tries its best to satisfy the impulses within the limitations of the superego and the outside world. Personality is the particular compromise we work out within ourselves. For example, we all have sexual impulses from the id. Society puts restrictions on these—we cannot caress anyone who happens to attract us or leap on any sexy person who walks by. The superego also places restrictions on our sexual behavior because we feel that certain things are wrong even if we could get away with them. Operating within these limitations, the ego (our conscious, active mind) does what it can to find sexual satisfaction, seeking acceptable people and places, planning seductions, finding romantic locations, and generally planning our sex life. It is a tricky and difficult interaction, and in this area, at least, most people have difficulty avoiding frustration on the one hand and guilt on the other. But how we handle this, how we react to sexual feelings and situations, is an important aspect of our personality. The same applies to all other basic impulses, such as anger, aggressiveness, hunger, fear, and so on, though the conflicts are generally less difficult than with sexual urges.

Anxiety and Defense Mechanisms

One of the central ideas of Freudian theory is the concept of *anxiety*, which is a particular kind of discomfort, nervousness, and psychological pain caused by conflicts between the id and superego. Anxiety is distinguished from ordinary fear or nervousness because it does not have a real object or reason. We are afraid of a poisonous snake that is right in front of us, nervous about an important exam, or worried about being liked by our friends. In each case, we know why we are uncomfortable, and the discomfort has a reasonable cause. But anxiety arises from conflicts within us and does not have a real object or a logical cause. In fact, there is nothing to be afraid of, we are not going to be hurt, and no one is going to bother us.

Fear and anxiety may focus on the same object or situation. It is sensible to be afraid of a rattlesnake in front of you or of meeting one while hiking along a country trail; to worry about all snakes or about meeting one while walking on the main street of a big city is not. The former is fear; the latter is anxiety. Sometimes the distinction is not entirely clear and is one of degree, but the more unrealistic the concern, the more it is anxiety rather than fear.

Because anxiety is unrealistic, it is much harder to deal with than ordinary fear. We cannot take logical steps to reduce anxiety the way we can with fear. If you are frightened by a snake, you can run away, kill the snake, or decide that it is not dangerous. But if you are anxious about all snakes and constantly worried that one is going to appear in front of you, it is more difficult if not impossible to take any logical actions to reduce that anxiety. Instead, we use various techniques, called *defense* mechanisms, that are specifically designed to reduce or avoid anxiety. Defense mechanisms operate by either distorting the source of the conflict or obscuring the conflict entirely, but in either case they reduce anxiety by making the conflict less conscious, by making us less aware of it. The major defense mechanisms are denial, repression, projection, displacement, reaction formation, and rationalization and intellectualization (see Fig. 14.3). Although they all serve the same purpose, they work in quite different ways and tend to have different effects.

Denial The simplest, most primitive way of dealing with anxiety, denial consists of pretending that the source of anxiety does not exist. For example, someone who is anxious about snakes may simply deny that there are any snakes in Kansas. If you were anxious about getting cancer, you might deny any symptoms that appeared. Instead of going to a doctor when you felt a pain, you would ignore the pain and pretend it wasn't there. This makes you less anxious because you do not have to worry about the pain being caused by cancer; but it is obviously foolish and dangerous because the pain might, in fact, be a symptom of some illness. Thus the anxiety about cancer causes you to behave irrationally and actually makes it more likely that you will become seriously ill.

Fig. 14.3
Defense mechanisms

Denial	Pretend it doesn't exist; ignore it.
Repression	Push into unconscious; forget it.
Reaction formation	Think or behave the opposite of what you want or fear.
Projection	Imagine the other person feels what you feel; reverse the direction.
Displacement	Change object from one with high conflict to one with less.
Rationalization	Make up "logical" reasons for actions or feelings.
Intellectualization	Avoid emotional involvement by discussion, debate, "objective" consideration.

Repression Repression is the same process as denial, but focuses on feelings and emotions. If you are very angry at your father but are made anxious by this feeling, you might make it unconscious, pretend you do not feel it. If you are sexually attracted to your brother or sister (an unacceptable feeling), you may repress this impulse to avoid the anxiety that it would arouse. Repression reduces anxiety by making you less aware of the impulse, and therefore less aware of any conflict it might create. On the other hand, as with denial, you are not dealing with the conflicts and eventually they will have important, negative effects. They will be expressed in dreams, or in slips of the tongue, and may produce mental disturbance if they are severe enough.

Projection This defense mechanism consists of assuming that someone else has your own feelings. If your anger at your mother produces too much anxiety, you may project that feeling and decide that she is angry at you. We do this often in our daily lives when we decide that someone we do not like does not like us; or that someone we have been mistreating is mistreating us. The advantage of projection is that the other person takes on your guilt, and you can still treat her badly because now she deserves it. Projection seems to be a major element in prejudice, in which one group decides that the other group is acting badly and therefore deserves to be mistreated.

Displacement We have already talked about displacement in the section on aggression in Chapter 9. As we noted, displacement occurs whenever we direct our feelings or actions not toward the primary object but toward some substitute. If you are angry at a friend but do not want to or cannot attack him, you may attack someone else. This helps you avoid the anxiety of dealing with the unacceptable impulse of anger toward someone you care for, but still allows you to express your anger.

Reaction formation We sometimes cover up an anxiety-arousing feeling by expressing its exact opposite. To use a simple case, if you do not like a friend's date, you may make a special effort to be nice to him. Parents who are angry at their children often lean over backwards to be loving because they cannot admit their feelings of anger. However, the true feelings usually show through. In being nice to the date, you may make such a show of it that it becomes obvious that you are being insincere. The angry parent who tries to be loving may show her anger by smothering the child with love or forcing the child to eat too many sweets and therefore get fat.

Rationalization and intellectualization These two defense mechanisms are familiar to most of us. Rationalization consists of making up complex, seemingly rational arguments to explain an anxiety-arousing or conflict-producing event. We might say "I don't mind not getting into medical school because there is too much emphasis on money in the medical profession and I really wanted to work in community health programs"; or, "It is just as well that she was busy Saturday night because I hate this whole business of having to have a date on the weekend." Also, the boy who hits his younger sister because he is jealous of her might say that he did it to teach her not to cross the street alone. In all cases, the individual has provided a logical reason to explain away a result that was unpleasant or unacceptable.

Intellectualization carries this process one step further. It consists of dealing with anxiety by treating the whole situation in objective, rational, unemotional terms—talking endlessly about the implications of the event, why it might have happened, what Kant would have said about it, and so on. The anxiety aroused by tests, anger, love affairs, or almost anything else can be reduced by putting everything into intellectual terms and ignoring the emotions that ordinarily go with the situation.

The defense mechanisms are important because in a sense they are part of our personality. The particular mechanisms people favor make them different from people who use other defenses. To return to our example of dealing with sexuality and guilt, people who repress sexual feelings in order to avoid anxiety will obviously have different personality characteristics from people who project the feelings and assume that everyone else also has strong sexual impulses. People who use intellectualization in this context will tend to be unemotional and not get involved in love relationships, while reaction formation might cause people to avoid any expressions of sexuality by acting cold and impersonal. The point is that how we deal with conflicts and in particular the defense mechanisms we employ are integral parts of our personality and are one of the elements that make us the kind of person we are.

Personality Development—Freudian Theory

Since personality is thought to emerge from the interaction of innate needs and experience, it is obviously closely connected with the process of socialization. As children learn the rules of society and begin to control their impulses, their personalities develop. Although this interaction of internal needs and external restrictions continues throughout life, it is especially evident during the early years; therefore, Freud placed great emphasis on the first few years of life in shaping personality. Later theorists in this tradition agree that the early years are especially important, but subsequent experiences are also assumed to play a substantial role in personality development. For example, psychiatrist Harry Stack Sullivan (1953) does not minimize the importance of the early years, but feels that the juvenile and adolescent periods have profound effects on the individual's ability to make friends and form love attachments.

Infantile sexuality The most controversial aspect of Freud's theory, the one that caused him to be practically ostracized from the medical community, is his emphasis on early childhood sexuality. According to Freud, the libidinal, sexual impulses are present at birth and are expressed even by infants. The notion of a sexy six-year-old or, God forbid, a sexy six-month-old came as a thunderbolt to the staid Viennese medical community. Even now, with our greater acceptance of sexuality, the idea of young children having sexual impulses is difficult for most people to accept. It is important to keep in mind, however, that Freud was not talking about a two-year-old literally engaging in adult sexual behavior. When Freud discussed sexual impulses in childhood, he meant pleasurable feelings derived from various parts of the body. Even in childhood it feels good to have parts of the body stimulated. It is only in puberty that these pleasurable impulses become more and more centered around the genitals and become what we usually think of as sexual. Before that, however, these impulses have a profound influence on the child's behavior and how they are expressed plays a very important role in the development of personality.

Stated in these terms, it should be easy for anyone who has observed children to accept the fact that they do derive pleasure from their bodies. Many animals enjoy being touched, stroked, and petted. Similarly, young children enjoy being touched and fondled. Infants like to suck on nipples even when they are not getting milk. The sensation of having something in their mouths is pleasurable. What is upsetting for many adults is that even infants like to have their genitals touched. Since they are not yet supposed to have sexual urges, and since adults are not allowed by our society to touch their own or other people's genitals in public, the sight of a child "playing with himself" is disturbing. Yet it is no different from the same child sucking on a nipple or an old towel—it is a primitive expression of pleasure taken from one's own body. Children seek pleasure of this sort from various sources and from different parts of their bodies, and the interaction between these strivings and the rules of society play a major role in their personality development.

Psychosexual stages and personality Freud felt that children went through periods during which pleasurable sensations and concerns centered around a particular zone of the body—oral, anal, and then phallic. During each period, the conflicts among the various parts of the personality and society focus on that area of the body and on events connected with it, such as weaning and toilet training. How these conflicts are resolved is thought to be an important factor in personality development.

Freud argued that people who did not resolve these conflicts would become *fixated* or stuck at that stage of development, and would always have problems that related to the original conflict. Fixation at the oral stage, in which independence from the mother and nipple is crucial, causes an *oral personality* who is always troubled by dependency. Such a person would tend to be overly dependent on others or to be fearful of being at all dependent. Fixation at the anal stage, in which toilet training and control are critical, causes an *anal personality*—one that is overly concerned with control, possessions, and cleanliness.

Perhaps the most famous Freudian notion is the *Oedipus complex*, which is supposed to occur during the phallic stage, between the ages of four and six. The name comes from the Greek myth in which Oedipus, a king of Thebes, kills his father and marries his mother (without knowing their relationships to him until afterwards). According to Freud a boy in the phallic stage is tempted to do just that. He is in some sense sexually attracted to his mother and hostile to his father. While he still loves his father, he is also afraid of him because they are rivals and because the boy has these forbidden impulses toward his mother. The healthy resolution to this extremely difficult

Fig. 14.4
The Oedipus complex

The boy loves his mother and fears his father, who is a rival and also stronger. To resolve the conflict and reduce the fear, the boy identifies with his father. This allows him to share the mother's love, no longer fear his father, and also get some satisfaction from his father's relationship with his mother.

Drawing by Chas. Addams; © 1972 The New Yorker Magazine, Inc.

"Why can't you be more like Oedipus?"

situation is for the boy to identify with his father, take on his characteristics and values, and try to be like him. In this way, he receives some vicarious satisfaction of his sexual impulses toward his mother and need no longer be afraid of his father. This resolution enables the boy to have sexual feelings toward women without guilt or fear, because he is doing what his father does; it also allows him to deal with authority and to accept the moral values of his father's world. Unresolved, this conflict makes it difficult to experience sexual feelings without guilt and causes the boy to be afraid of and angry toward all authority figures. More generally, the resolution of this conflict enables the boy to develop feelings of love and friendship as he becomes an adult. (Freud described a similar situation for girls, the Electra complex, but it seems considerably less plausible.)

It seems likely that the process of resolution continues through much of our lives. Certainly most adolescents also feel both positive and negative feelings toward their parents, and resolving these feelings is one of the major aspects of growing up. Indeed, even adults feel these same conflicting feelings toward their parents, and in many cases they are not fully resolved.

Criticisms of Psychoanalytic Theory

We should note that there is a considerable amount of controversy surrounding details of Freud's psychoanalytic theory. Although there is fairly general agreement on some of the ideas (the importance of childhood experience, sexual feeling in infants and children, interaction between the child and the parents, identification with the parents' moral values and behavior), there is disagreement over specific points and much of the emphasis. For example, conflicts, are not necessarily as sexual as Freud suggests. Difficulties in toilet training are obviously upsetting, but the idea that someone who experiences them is thereafter fixated at the anal period and will always be overly concerned with retention and control is harder to accept. Similarly, the specific aspects of the Oedipus complex are doubtful. Not all children are sexually drawn to the parent of the opposite sex, nor do all of them fear the parent of the same sex. But the idea that children both love and compete with their parents seems sound. Children often say, "I hate you," or even, "I'll kill you." They do not mean either literally, but they do feel anger and fear toward their parents who are so much stronger than they and who deny them so many pleasures. Thus, all children must at some point resolve these contradictory feelings toward their parents, and one way to do this is to identify with one or both of them and to adopt their values. This reduces the conflict between the children and parents, and allows the children to love the parents without feeling so angry. In other words, many of Freud's general descriptions are accepted as perceptive views of what goes on in childhood, while the specific descriptions and emphases are questioned.

We should also mention that Freud based most of his work on mentally disturbed patients, and therefore his theories may be more applicable to disturbed than to relatively healthy people. And, as we noted earlier, most of psychoanalytic theory is presented in terms of the male child. Despite the fact that most of Freud's patients were women, he seemed more interested in or at least more perceptive about men. Therefore, many of the details of the theory are probably more accurate for men than for women.

Neo-Freudian Theories

Freud's psychoanalytic theory had enormous influence on how people think about personality. However, it must be realized that he was one person, seeing other people from his own viewpoint. This does not mean his ideas are incorrect, but it suggests that they are somewhat limited. His followers often disagreed with him on important points and both expanded and changed the theory.

Carl Jung Freud's most famous follower was Carl Jung, who broke away from the master and formed his own school, called *analytic psychology*. Although he accepted much of Freud's theory, Jung also believed that all people to some extent looked to the future, and tried to develop their own potential and to achieve unity among the parts of their personality. Thus, there was a more dynamic, striving, creative force than Freud recognized.

Another important idea of Jung's was that people had two kinds of unconscious. In addition to their own personal unconscious, they had a reservoir of all of the memories, traditions, and experiences of the human species, called the *collective unconscious*. This is a somewhat mystical notion, but could be related somewhat to the idea that human biological inheritance plays a role in personality.

Alfred Adler Adler was another disciple who split from Freud to set up his own school, in this case *individual psychology*. The central

CARL G. JUNG

theme of Adler's psychology is that everyone is striving for superiority. Everyone has feelings of inferiority and tries to overcome them. Adler thought that this feeling of inferiority came about because all people have some physical deficiency, some organ or part of the body that is inferior, and they spend their lives trying to overcome this deficit. An alternative is that all people feel inferior as children because adults, and in particular parents, are bigger, stronger and smarter; and the children spend their lives trying to become as strong as their parents. In either case, Adler's view is that we are dominated by aggressive feelings in the fight for superiority. This striving is controlled mainly by the ego and is entirely conscious. Unconscious forces play a relatively small role, if any—instead people are master of their own fate, and every action reflects their individual styles and personalities.

Ego psychology The major trend in neo-Freudian psychoanalytic thinking over the past twenty-five years has been toward more and more emphasis on *ego functioning*, the conscious processes that involve thinking, planning, perceiving, and problem solving. While not denying the role of unconscious phenomena, theorists such as Anna Freud (Freud's daughter) and David Rapaport have given more attention to how the ego deals with the conflicts it faces, rather than to the conflicts themselves. They argue that everyone faces the same conflicts and has the same motives, but people handle them differently. Some deny that they have sexual feelings, some express them and suffer guilt, others express them under certain limited circumstances or toward certain kinds of people and not others. In other words, as we mentioned in discussing defense mechanisms, how you deal with your motives and conflicts is an integral part of your personality and one major source of your individuality. Freud also stressed the defense mechanisms, but tended to think of them as something to get rid of; the ego psychologists accept them as a normal part of personality.

SOCIAL LEARNING THEORY

A very important development in personality theory has been the growing influence of the *social learning theory* of personality. This approach differs considerably from the constitutional or physiological in that it explains personality almost entirely in terms of experience rather than innate or biological factors. According to social learning theory, personality is learned just as is anything else. The particular learning principles that are stressed vary depending on whose learning theory is being considered, but the basic idea is that we develop our personality by the same mechanisms and principles by which we learn to play tennis, eat with a fork, speak a language, or anything else.

In 1950, John Dollard and Neal Miller presented an extended analysis of personality in terms of reinforcement theory (Dollard and Miller, 1950). B. F. Skinner has worked along somewhat similar lines, but has stressed operant conditioning (1971). And Albert Bandura has developed social learning theory, which combines all of the principles of learning in an attempt to explain and control human behavior (Bandura, 1977). Since there is ample evidence that classical condi-

ALBERT BANDURA

tioning, operant conditioning, contiguity, and imitation all produce learning, it seems most reasonable to employ all of them in trying to explain something as complex as human personality.

Using the full range of learning mechanisms, we can explain the emergence of personality in terms of a series of relatively small and discrete bits of learning. To begin with, infants develop positive reactions to their mother because she is associated with the reduction of hunger, the pleasant experience of being held, and other positive situations. Children are taught by positive reinforcement and punishment to behave in certain ways and express certain emotions. They imitate those around them and thereby acquire their modes of behavior, their styles, and their values. Also, as we mentioned in Chapter 9, children learn motives—to achieve, to be successful, to be artistic, to be liked, and so on. Although we are all exposed to similar experiences, our environments and specific experiences differ enough so that each of us learns a somewhat different set of behaviors, motives, values, and information. Moreover, we develop different ways of expressing our motives because we imitate different people and are reinforced for slightly different actions. Since each of us is exposed to a unique set of experiences, models, and reinforcements, we become unique. And according to this explanation, our personality is simply the sum total of all these bits of learning expressed in behavior.

The learning approach to personality can explain why we are all different and also why people in similar cultures and from similar backgrounds tend to have much in common. Clearly, the more similar your background, the more similar your experiences will tend to be and therefore the more similar your personalities should be. Yet people from very similar backgrounds, even identical twins who grow up together, can have different personalities because no two people ever have identical experiences throughout their lives.

Factors in the Learning of Personality

Although personality is assumed to be learned according to the same principles as anything else, certain factors seem to be particularly important with respect to personality. For example, imitation plays a major role in the development of personality and it is clear that children do not imitate everyone equally. On the contrary, as noted in Chapter 3, children are more likely to imitate people who are prominent and powerful than those who are unimportant or weak (Bandura, Ross, and Ross, 1963), and also to imitate people whom they see being reinforced. It follows from this that children are more likely to imitate parents than any other adult. The mother and father (or other parent figures) play a dominant role in their lives, are constantly present, and, from the children's point of view at least, are very powerful. They control most reinforcements, and it probably seems that they receive lots of reinforcements themselves. Thus, children would be expected to learn more of their behaviors and values from their parents than from any other people, especially during the early years when they are exposed to relatively few outside forces. Once we enter school, the influence of our parents is reduced somewhat because there are other important adults and also other children to imitate and learn from. And, of course, as we get older and our circle of acquaintances grows, the relative influence of our parents steadily diminishes.

Learning theories of personality do not place the same emphasis on the early years as do psychoanalytic theories. In fact, most learning theorists do not think that the early years play a predominant role in shaping personality. On the other hand, they acknowledge that our experiences early in life can have profound and lasting effects, often relatively more important than later learning. One explanation of this in learning terms is that learning during the first few years involves little or no language. We learn by imitation and reinforcement, but we cannot label what we have learned. When any learning occurs without verbal labels and associations, it is harder to talk about, harder to remember clearly, and presumably harder to deal with on an intellectual level. If children learn conflicting values or behaviors (for example, it is pleasurable to touch your body but you may be punished for it) and cannot put this into words, the conflict may be harder to verbalize later and therefore harder to resolve.

The learning approach to personality explains conflicts in simple terms that we have already discussed (see Chapter 9 on motivation). When we are rewarded for some action but also punished, we develop conflicting tendencies and are in what we have called an approach-avoidance conflict. As we get closer to the goal or to performing the behavior, the avoidance gets stronger and stronger and the conflict increases. You have probably seen a child reach out for a cookie or something else she is not supposed to touch. She puts her hand out, slows down as the hand gets closer, and finally stops just before touching. If she manages to touch it, the approach tendency was stronger; if she stops, the avoidance was stronger. We all face these kinds of conflicts constantly, in simple situations such as wanting an ice cream sundae but wanting also to diet, and in complex, highly emotional situations involving jobs, friendships, and so on. Dollard and Miller would say that under these conflict-producing situations we experience anxiety—indeed, that anxiety is the emotion that is aroused when we are in an approach-avoidance conflict. Thus, whereas Freud explains anxiety in terms of unconscious conflicts, learning theory sees it as a result of approach-avoidance conflicts of any kind.

Implications of Social Learning Theory

Learning theorists tend to assume that personality is more changeable than do most other theorists. Whereas the other theories take the position that personality is a fairly basic characteristic that changes only very slowly if at all during life, the learning approach views personality as just another bit of learning that can be unlearned or reshaped. Personality is seen as a set of learned responses to particular situations. Naturally, by the process of stimulus generalization, what is learned in one situation will generalize to others. If you learn to be aggressive in the home, you will probably be aggressive in many other situations that are similar to situations in the home. But much of the learning will be quite specific to a situation, and you will learn different behaviors in other situations. Thus, you may learn to be aggressive in the home but not at all aggressive in school. Therefore, learning theorists see personality as less general than do most other theories—particular characteristics apply to particular situations, not to all situations. (See Box 14.1 for a more detailed discussion of these differing views of personality.)

As we said above, the implication of this notion is that personality can be changed with relative ease. If personality is a unitary trait that operates in all situations, it is obviously extremely powerful and broad. To change it, you would have to teach people to change their behavior in a great many situations, and that is difficult. But if personality consists of responses that are relatively specific to particular situations, changing the response would involve a relatively minor change in behavior. Therefore, learning theorists generally assume that personality can be altered by teaching individuals to change their behavior in particular situations. As we shall see in Chapter 16, this view has profound implications for therapy.

Social learning theory makes the extremely important point that personality is determined in large part by our experiences, and that the effect of these experiences can be understood in terms of basic principles of learning. While this has not yet given us specific knowledge of how a particular personality develops or how a given experience will affect personality, it has taken some of the mystery out of the process of personality development. Probably without meaning to, psychoanalytic theories often make it seem as if the development of personality follows different rules and principles than those that govern the rest of psychology, and that what we know about perception, learning, and motivation does not really apply to personality. The learning approach has countered this notion, and shown that personality, like every other psychological phenomenon, must obey the basic rules of psychology.

HUMANISTIC PSYCHOLOGY AND SELF-ACTUALIZATION

Carl Rogers, Fritz Perls, Erich Fromm, and Abraham Maslow have contributed to an approach to personality that is quite different from the others we have been discussing. Although there are substantial differences among their individual approaches, they may all be considered *humanistic*. Instead of dealing mainly with explanations of *how* personality develops, humanistic psychologists concentrate on how personality *should* develop; and instead of emphasizing similarities among people, they focus on the uniqueness of each individual. According to the humanistic view, all people have certain unique talents, abilities, feelings, and potentials to express. To the extent that individuals manage to express them they are *self-actualized*, and in this sense their lives are successful and full.

The proponents of the humanistic school differ somewhat in their explanations of where these inner potentialities come from, but they all agree that they exist. The crucial assumption is that somewhere in each of us is our "true" personality, trying to express itself against the pressures in the world. Thus, instead of discussing the formation of personality in childhood, the humanists deal with how personality emerges if given a chance and how certain factors can interfere with this emergence. As Abraham Maslow states, "Full healthy and normal and desirable development consists in actualizing

Box 14.1

DOES PERSONALITY EXIST?

This may seem like a strange question since we are devoting a whole chapter to discussing personality, but a number of prominent psychologists have recently asked whether personality really exists. They are not denying entirely the existence of personality in the sense that people have inclinations to behave, think, act, and interact in certain ways and with certain styles. Rather, they are questioning whether global personalities exist that determine a person's actions across a wide variety of situations and over a long period of time. They readily agree that some people are more competitive at school, more aggressive in sports, or more interested in painting than others, but they question whether there is such an animal as an "aggressive" or "competitive" or "artistic" person. They argue that people differ in different situations and that a person's behavior is not so consistent in different situations as to support the idea of a basic, general personality within the individual.

Walter Mischel of Stanford University is the most outspoken exponent of the idea that personality may not be a useful concept (1973). He bases his argument primarily on the lack of evidence in favor of personality. He points out that despite years of research in this area, few if any studies demonstrate consistent behavior across a number of different situations. That is, there is no evidence from the research literature that people who are aggressive in one situation are consistently aggressive in others, that people who are submissive in one situation are consistently submissive in others, or that honesty, charity, liberalism, or any other personality characteristic shows up consistently in different situations. On the contrary, he asserts, there are studies that show that people who are honest in one situation will be dishonest in another — they will cheat in school but not in a game; they will steal but will not cheat; and so on. Thus, says Mischel, it is difficult to argue that there is such an entity as an "honest person." In other words, honesty does not exist as a unitary general characteristic of people.

Instead Mischel argues that behavior patterns are determined by the situation. While people do differ across situations, they are extremely consistent from one situation to another similar situation. Someone who does not cheat in school on one occasion will not cheat on another; and the more similar a situation is to that of the classroom, the less likely it is that he will cheat. This kind of consistency is not, of course, what we normally mean by personality. Personality implies consistency across different situations, not just similar ones. Thus, this position essentially removes the idea of global personality traits and substitutes for it behavior that is specific to situations.

this nature, and fulfilling these potentialities, and in developing its maturity along the lines that this hidden, covert, dimly seen, essential nature dictates, growing from within rather than being shaped from without." (Maslow, 1954, pp. 340–341)

The idea that all people are unique and have within themselves their full potential is an appealing one. The direct implication is that the role of society is to encourage and support individual growth, giving maximum freedom to express one's inner tendencies. Unlike Freud, who emphasized the necessity of socialization and control, humanistic psychologists feel that an authoritarian parent or a strict environment will interfere with the person's development. Even loving parents can do harm if they make decisions for their children or try to encourage them along preconceived lines of development. The mother who gives her son piano lessons because she wants him to be

However, Mischel has not suggested throwing out the concept of personality. Rather he thinks we should concentrate on other aspects of a person that tend to produce consistency in behavior. He has determined that five kinds of characteristics are particularly useful in predicting what an individual will do in a particular situation:

1. Competencies—what the person is good at, what skills, abilities, knowledge she has.
2. Categories and personal constructs—how the person organizes and views the world. We have already seen that perception is a basic factor in human behavior, and clearly differences in the perception and understanding of the world will have great importance.
3. Expectancies—what the individual expects to happen to him in particular situations as a result of his behavior. If you typically expect movies to be terrible, you will probably avoid them; if you usually expect people of the opposite sex to like you, you will behave differently on a date than if you have the opposite expectation.
4. Values—the person's tastes, incentives, likes, and dislikes. If you like horror movies, you are more likely to attend them than a romance; if you like clothes you are more likely to read fashion magazines and go shop-

ping than if you don't care about clothes.
5. The person's rules of behavior—this is similar to ethics but also includes personal rules that may be quite specific, such as a policy not to argue with your parents no matter what. You may become furious at them, but this rule (if you manage to follow it) will prevent you from arguing.

While these are very interesting suggestions, it is too early to know whether studying these variables will be more productive than studying traits. For the moment, we do know that consistency is greater across similar situations than across different situations. The only question is whether enough consistency exists across different situations to indicate that people do have global personality characteristics. In any case, it is important to keep in mind that what is commonly thought of as a personality trait may be an oversimplification or may not be the basic, underlying characteristic. Thus, we should not be surprised to find that people behave seemingly inconsistently when in fact their behavior may be consistent with some characteristic of which we are not aware. In studying and describing personality we must take into account the great complexity and diversity of personality types. People are not simple creatures, and their personality structures in particular are complex.

a great musician may think she is doing the best for her child, but may not be if the child's natural inclinations are not musical. The enlightened father who wants his daughter to be a doctor may be working against this particular girl's innate talent for physics or dancing. In other words, the ideal environment is one that allows and encourages children to express their own feelings and to develop unique interests and abilities.

A closely related aspect of humanistic theory is Maslow's hierarchy of needs and motives, which was discussed in Chapter 9. Although it is possible to argue with his particular sequence of needs or even that some are higher than others, his point is well taken that some needs are more basic and urgent than others in the sense that individuals must satisfy them first. Someone who is hungry cannot easily concentrate on being creative; a person who lacks love and

security will find it difficult to pursue justice; and so on. However, it is probably inaccurate to say that the basic needs must be *fully* satisfied before others can be expressed (a somewhat hungry or sexually unfulfilled person can still create works of art or fight for justice), but it does seem likely that to the extent that basic needs are frustrated they interfere with higher motives.

This is quite a different position from that taken by Freud, who felt that certain needs, such as sexual and aggressive impulses, when not expressed could be thc basis for creative energy. Since he saw these id impulses as the prime source of human energy, artistic creativity and any other higher motivation were simply different forms of expressing these basic needs. In contrast, Maslow sees self-actualization as the primary source of energy, and believes frustration of a need is unhealthy.

The major contribution of the humanistic approach is to focus attention on allowing the individual's inner nature to express itself. It is not necessary to accept the view that our inner nature is formed at birth—our potential can be seen as a product of innate factors plus experience. But humanistic psychologists make the valid point that society often frustrates our needs and creative impulses. A girl may have decided by the age of six to be a lawyer. Her decision was based on identification with a parent plus events involving conditioning, and her own innate intelligence and other abilities. However, this desire may be continually frustrated by a society that says that most women do not become lawyers, that puts various obstacles in her path, and that may try to convince her to become a housewife or nurse instead. Similarly, a boy may learn early in life to be easygoing, not to have strong achievement motivation, and not to strive hard for financial success. Perhaps he would like to be an artist or just take any job that does not require too much hard work. As an adolescent, he finds enormous pressures from his family, friends, and school to be "successful," to achieve good grades, to get a "good" job. His artistic nature is frustrated rather than encouraged. Whether these interests and inclinations are present at birth or develop in childhood, there is little question that during adolescence many people find that their environment does not encourage them to express their own, personal feelings. Yet most people would be happier, more productive, and more fulfilled if they were not only allowed but encouraged to "do what they want" rather than what society decrees is right for them.

COMPARISON OF THE PERSONALITY THEORIES

Although the four major approaches to personality that we have described may sound at times very different, they are actually more complementary than contradictory. The social learning approach concentrates almost entirely on the *process* by which personality develops. Unlike constitutional or psychoanalytic theory, it does not attempt to describe specific incidents, innate characteristics, or conflicts that affect personality. Rather it is a general statement of how any incident will affect the individual's personality. According to this approach, the same mechanisms that affect any kind of learning will affect personality. Personality is learned from all the individual's experiences with the world. It is the sum total of all the positive and negative reinforcements, the associations, the various kinds of conditioning, and imitation. People learn to be a particular kind of personality in much the same way they learn to speak French, although presumably the number and complexity of the incidents is greater.

A possible conflict between this approach and either the constitutional or psychoanalytic approaches is in terms of the role played by instinctive impulses. The constitutional theory, of course, deals almost exclusively with these innate factors, and psychoanalytic theory places considerable stress on them. Since learning theory is largely an environmental approach, it may appear to conflict with the others. However, all learning theories do accept the fact that an individual is born with various needs and capacities. Indeed, classical conditioning depends on the existence of unconditioned stimuli and responses; and operant conditioning depends on the existence of basic drives, the satisfaction of which is reinforcing. Thus both these forms of learning assume the existence of innate needs upon which the conditioning depends. The difference between the learning approach and the others is the extent to which these innate needs are emphasized. Learning theory views individuals as born with some needs but otherwise being shaped almost entirely by their environment. At the other extreme, constitutional theory sees individuals shaped largely by innate characteristics, with experience playing a relatively minor role. And psychoanalytic theory emphasizes a dynamic interaction between children's innate needs and their experiences. Humanistic psychology does not disagree with the others, but stresses individual uniqueness, and seems to imply people are born with certain talents and impulses. In this sense, psychoanalytic theory and learning theory are much closer to each other than they are to the constitutional or humanistic approaches. Although Freud does stress instinctive impulses, the basic assumption of both psychoanalytic and learning theories is that how people are treated during their early years (and later) will shape their personalities, and thus both place a great deal of emphasis on experience.

In general, these theoretical approaches taken together seem to provide quite a good description of personality development. Innate differences probably play a larger role in personality than psychoanalytic and learning theories suggest, but not the primary role indicated by the constitutional theories of either Sheldon or Eysenck. Innate characteristics, both those on which people differ and those that they share, surely interact with our experiences and, according to the principles of learning, shape our personality. The kinds of situations and considerations suggested by Freud and other psychoanalytic theorists are helpful in understanding just what goes on in childhood and how experiences affect personality, even if some or all of the specific ideas are questionable. And humanistic psychology emphasizes that society often interferes with rather than encourages the expression of individuality. So while we still do not know many of the details of personality development, these theories provide a framework within which we can consider specific factors to see how they determine personality.

PERSONALITY ASSESSMENT

The theories we have described attempt to describe the principles, critical incidents, and dynamics of personality development, but tell us little about specific personality types. Sheldon and Eysenck suggest that there are only three basic kinds of people, and Freud describes three types of personalities depending upon where a person is fixated. However, these are obviously limited descriptions considering the enormous range of human beings. In a major attempt to provide a more complete categorization of personalities, Raymond Cattell (1973) identified the sixteen basic factors listed in Fig. 14.5. The list allows for much greater diversity than just three factors, but even so it seems incomplete. Surely warmth and sense of humor, to name just two, are also important aspects of personality. Moreover, other investigators using techniques similar to Cattell's have found somewhat different sets of factors. Clearly, it is very difficult to compile a complete list of basic traits that everyone can agree on and that enables us to describe all people's personalities completely.

For this reason, a great deal of effort has been devoted to devising tests that will allow us to assess certain specific aspects of personality. None of these tests is expected to give a complete description of anyone's personality, but each test is supposed to measure a certain trait or set of traits. While it is not fully successful, personality testing in one form or another pervades our society. It goes on all the time informally whenever we meet someone (does he look honest? is she a warm person?), and is done formally as part of the entrance requirements to some professional schools, in connection with hiring by many corporations, and by the government for all sorts of purposes. We have already discussed in Chapter 7 some of the difficulties in measuring intelligence; testing personality is even more complex and difficult.

Problems in Measuring Personality

To begin with, all of the problems encountered in testing intelligence are also encountered in the testing of personality. Bias can be introduced by the choice of materials, by communication difficulties between tester and test-taker, and by the way in which the test is administered. If the person being tested does not understand the test or responds negatively to the testing situation, the results will give an inaccurate picture of his personality. Just as in intelligence testing, the test must be appropriate for the person taking it, and must be given in a standardized, bias-free manner. However, this is just the beginning. Much more serious difficulties involve finding a test that really measures the personality trait you are interested in (determining validity) and making sure that the person taking the test responds honestly.

How would you go about making up a test that measured whether someone was warm or honest or self-assured? These are complex concepts and we are not completely certain how they affect behavior or what questions or responses will assess these qualities adequately. Indeed, that is why we want a personality test—because it is difficult to tell what the person is like without such a test. But if we do not know what responses to look at, how can we know what

1. Reserved_____Outgoing
2. Less intelligent_____More intelligent
3. Affected by feelings___Emotionally stable
4. Submissive_____Dominant
5. Serious_____Happy-go-lucky
6. Expedient_____Conscientious
7. Timid_____Venturesome
8. Tough-minded_____Sensitive
9. Trusting_____Suspicious
10. Practical_____Imaginative
11. Forthright_____Shrewd
12. Self-assured_____Apprehensive
13. Conservative_____Experimenting
14. Group-dependent_____Self-sufficient
15. Uncontrolled_____Controlled
16. Relaxed_____Tense

Fig. 14.5
Cattell's sixteen basic traits

Each trait is scored on a continuum labeled at either end.

kind of a test to use? As we shall see, there are various possible solutions to this problem, but none that is entirely satisfactory.

The other difficulty is that even if we know what questions to ask, the person taking the test may deliberately or accidentally try to disguise his true personality. On an intelligence test almost everyone tries to score as high as possible. Only under extraordinary circumstances would someone deliberately give the wrong answer on an IQ test if he knew the right one (for example, he wanted to fail the test so he wouldn't be drafted). But the situation is entirely different on personality tests. People want to appear in a favorable light, they want to give a good impression of themselves, and if there is some characteristic they do not like about themselves, they may try to conceal it. Or even if they happen to like that characteristic, they may conceal it if they think other people will not like it. Thus, people will not readily admit that they are dishonest, weak, submissive, overly aggressive, or anything else negative about themselves. Moreover, people are not entirely open in answering questions about their personality and therefore their responses are not always accurate reflections of their true feelings or inclinations. This means that even if a valid test could be designed, there is the additional difficulty of making sure that the answers are accurate.

Types of Personality Tests

All personality tests attempt to deal with the various problems we have just described. Each type has certain advantages and certain disadvantages, coping relatively well with one problem and less well with another. The major distinction among types of tests is between those that ask questions about personality directly and those that try to get this information indirectly.

Direct tests One way of finding out whether someone is anxious, honest, sexually inhibited, or anything else is simply to ask. Thus, many tests of personality ask, "Are you aggressive?" or, "Do you get into many fights?" or, "Do you have a police record?" and similar direct questions pertaining to whatever characteristic is being measured. The assumption is that someone who is aggressive will tell you, or at least that he will respond honestly about how many fights he has had and whether he has a record. Using this self-rating and these other indications, the test should give a picture of how aggressive the person is.

A slightly less direct type of test asks straightforward questions, but the relationship between the questions and personality traits is less clear to the person taking the test. For example, a widely used test of personality is the Minnesota Multiphasic Personality Inventory (MMPI), which includes hundreds of items such as those shown in Fig. 14.6. Although the questions are direct, it is difficult to know just what they are supposed to be measuring. Thus the person may be less likely to conceal the correct answer. This test and ones like it attempt to give a general picture of someone's personality, particularly an overall assessment of adjustment and neuroticism. However, there is little evidence that these tests provide much more than a very general picture—they are not useful for measuring specific personality characteristics.

I wake up fresh and rested most mornings.

There seems to be a lump in my throat much of the time.

I do not always tell the truth.

I believe I am being plotted against.

Criticism or scolding hurts me terribly.

Even when I am with people I feel lonely much of the time.

My sex life is satisfactory.

Fig. 14.6
MMPI items

Direct tests have the great advantage that you know what you are asking and the person taking the test knows what is being asked. If you are interested in aggressiveness, you ask about fighting or general aggressiveness; if you want to know whether someone is sexually active, you ask about sexual activity. The questions are straightforward and to the point. When the person taking the test is cooperative, when she wants to tell you what she is like, these tests are efficient, highly reliable means of finding out. Also, when the qualities being measured are those we are usually willing to talk about openly, these tests do not suffer much from people concealing their true natures. As we shall discuss later, direct tests have proven useful as measures of anxiety and are widely used by social psychologists to assess feelings at a given moment, political attitudes, and other characteristics that tend not to be hidden.

The major difficulty with direct tests is that people are not always willing or able to give honest answers to direct questions. For example, in the anxiety test there are a number of questions dealing with physical symptoms. Some of these are probably answered honestly most of the time. People are willing to say they sweat a lot even if this is not an entirely admirable characteristic. But people may be less willing to admit that they have diarrhea often, or that they have the shakes. Other tests that ask questions about sex ("Are you often impotent?" "Do you have an orgasm every time you make love?") are even more likely to elicit inaccurate responses. And asking someone if he is honest is obviously not very useful, because if he isn't, he will lie. Some people have no problem answering the most personal questions, but other people will be very concerned about appearing in a good light even if the answers are supposed to be totally confidential. Since it is difficult to be certain that people are responding honestly, these tests are of questionable value.

Moreover, people sometimes cannot give you an accurate answer even if they want to. We do not really know our own personalities fully. We may have unrealistic images of ourselves, think we are better or worse or different from what we really are. Can you say with full confidence how humorous, sincere, warm, or aggressive you are? You may think you are very warm and loving, but other people may have a different view of you. Thus, asking someone what she is like will give you her own image of herself, and that is not necessarily an accurate one. This serious problem led psychologists to construct personality tests that attempt to measure personality indirectly.

Projective tests The main form of indirect test is a *projective test*, in which you are asked to respond to an ambiguous stimulus (often a picture) and your responses are presumed to reveal something about you. The name *projective* comes from the assumption that you project your own feelings on to the stimulus. If you feel angry, the anger will show up in your answer; if you are concerned about sex, that will be reflected in what you describe, and so on. Since no direct questions are asked, the assumption is that there will be less distortion of your true personality than in direct tests.

The idea behind projective tests is that we all perceive the world differently and that to some extent our perceptions are determined by our own characteristics. But the more ambiguous the stimulus, the greater role our own qualities play. For example, if you were asked to

Figure 14.7

Figure 14.8

describe the drawing in Fig. 14.7, you and virtually everyone else would say it was a boy holding a dog or something quite close to that. The picture is highly realistic and you merely describe it. But Fig. 14.8 is much more ambiguous and will elicit hundreds of different responses since no one can tell for certain exactly what is being represented. Presumably, you could tell little about people's personalities from their responses to the first figure since everyone would give the same answer. But you could tell more from the second figure because the responses would differ according to individual perceptions and personalities.

One of the most widely used projective tests is the *Rorschach Inkblot Test*, which was first published in 1921 (see Fig. 14.9 for an example). A thorough review of the research on this test indicated that it has low reliability and validity (Cronbach, 1970). Despite this finding, psychologists who use the Rorschach claim that it is very useful for them but that it requires a great deal of skill and practice to use it correctly. They argue, perhaps with some justification, that most tests of reliability and validity are based on scoring by inadequately trained administrators. Thus, some very experienced and highly skilled psychologists may be able to employ the Rorschach as a good measure of personality.

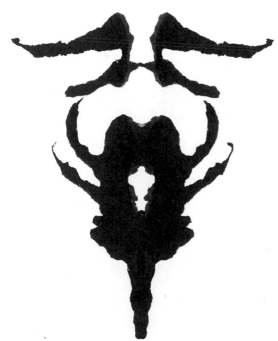

Fig. 14.9
The Rorschach Inkblot Test

The design shown is similar to those used on the test. Individuals are asked what they see in the picture.

14.10

The Thematic Apperception Test

This picture is similar to those used in the TAT. The instructions are to say what is happening in the picture. The assumption is that people will project their own needs, conflicts, and concerns on to the ambiguous picture.

The other major projective test is the *Thematic Apperception Test* (TAT), an example of which is shown in Fig. 14.10. The stimuli for this test are less ambiguous than those for the Rorschach, but still leave lots of room for each individual to see different things. The story that is told about the picture is assumed to reflect the concerns and feelings of the person telling it. As we shall discuss later, the TAT has proven to be reasonably reliable and to provide useful measures of certain personality traits.

The Status of Personality Testing

There is little doubt that at times far too much reliance has been placed on personality tests. There are those who think these tests give such accurate results that we can use them to decide who is going to commit a crime, who is a security risk, who is unstable and so on; and that we can then make crucial decisions about the person's life solely on the basis of the test results. These are incorrect and dangerous assumptions. Personality tests vary considerably in their reliability and validity, but even the best of them are far from perfect. Personality tests can give useful hints and suggestions about an individual's personality. If someone scores high on need achievement, he may indeed have very high achievement motivation; if he scores neurotic, perhaps this should be taken into account. But it is a serious mistake to base important decisions about a person's life entirely on a test of this sort. Skilled testers consider the test one piece of evidence to be used along with interviews, knowledge of the person's life, and current behavior. Used in this way, a psychological test of personality can be a valuable tool in many different situations; but no test should be expected to stand entirely on its own as a definitive measure of personality.

"*Rorschach! What's to become of you?*"

Copyright © 1976 by permission of *Saturday Review* and Sidney Harris.

JURY SELECTION

A fascinating application of psychology to the legal system involves the selection of juries. As you know, in any criminal trial each side is allowed to challenge juries whom they feel will be unfair or prejudiced. Some of the challenges are based on "cause," which means that there is clear reason to believe that the individual is biased on one side or the other. An extreme example would be someone who was related to or knew the defendant personally. Similarly, if the defendant is charged with robbing a bank, employees or stockholders of the bank would probably be excused automatically. In addition, anyone who already knows too much about the case, who holds opinions clearly favorable to one side or the other (hates banks), or for any reason has already made up his mind, will not be used. But the interesting situation arises when there is no obvious cause but the lawyer thinks that the individual would not be good for the case. Each side is allowed a number of so-called peremptory challenges—they can excuse some people without giving a cause. And it is on these decisions that the lawyer typically uses intuition and hunches. Indeed, it is often said that the most important skill a trial lawyer can have is selecting a good jury.

Recently, a number of social scientists (Schulman et al., 1973) have used techniques drawn from psychology and sociology to provide more rigorous evidence on which to select jurors. Rather than relying on intuition, Richard Christie and the others gather information on a sample of people living in the area where the trial is being held. The survey finds out attitudes toward the trial and relates them to various demographic characteristics of the people such as age, sex, race, religion, and so on. It may reveal, for example, that for this particular trial, older, white, nonreligious women are the most favorable to the defendant, while younger, religious people of both sexes and races are less favorable. Using a large number of such variables, Christie and his colleagues can guess as to how favorable any particular juror is likely to be. They do not actually interview the people who are called as jurors, but base their estimates on a broad sample of people who are similar to the actual jurors.

Armed with the information, the lawyer can decide whether a prospective juror will be favorable, unfavorable, or neutral to his or her side. Sometimes this estimate is just what the lawyer would have guessed independently (for example, young, college-educated, upper middle class people will be more lenient than older, less well-educated people in a trial involving bank robbery). But often the research produces unexpected results and allows the lawyer to pick a better jury than might otherwise have been possible.

This may turn out to be a powerful technique that will have considerable effect on trials. For the moment, it has been used primarily on the side of radical or highly liberal defendants, generally against the government. However, it should be realized that anyone can use this method, and eventually the side having the most financial resources will be able to do the most complete survey. If both sides do these surveys, the effect will largely be cancelled, except that, perhaps, it will serve to exclude extremely biased individuals who might otherwise serve on the jury. On the other hand, since these surveys are expensive and time consuming, there is the possibility that the rich defendant and the government will be able to conduct them while poorer defendants will not. If this occurs, the result will be to bias the case against those who cannot perform such a survey. Perhaps the answer would be for any such survey to be available to both sides, thus assuring that they derive equal benefit from it and both get a fairer jury.

This is one example of how a powerful psychological technique that is originally devised to benefit one group can sometimes backfire and actually hurt the group it was supposed to help. More generally, it makes the point that any scientific advance can be used in many different ways, not necessarily the ones that the inventors or discoverers had in mind.

BOX 14.2

1. America is getting so far from the true American way of life that force may be necessary to restore it.
2. Obedience and respect for authority are the most important virtues children should learn.
3. What this country needs most, more than laws and political programs, is a few courageous, tireless, devoted leaders in whom the people can put their faith.
4. An insult to our honor should never go unpunished.
5. There is hardly anything lower than a person who does not feel a great love, gratitude, and respect for his parents.
6. The businessman and the manufacturer are much more important to society than the artist and the professor.

Fig. 14.11
The authoritarian scale

Answer the questions on a scale from −3 (disagree strongly) to +3 (agree strongly). The explanation and scoring are given elsewhere on this page.

Explanation and scoring for Fig. 14.11: The higher your score (that is, the more strongly you agree with each of these items), the higher you score on authoritarianism. Other versions of this test reverse or reword some of the questions so that agreement does not always indicate the same thing. This controls the tendency some people have to agree with or disagree with questions regardless of their content.

SOME SPECIFIC PERSONALITY TRAITS

While some theorists proposed explanations of personality, and others attempted to describe personality, some investigators have concentrated on specific personality characteristics that seem to play an important role in human behavior. In particular, there has been a great deal of research on four such characteristics—authoritarianism, machiavellianism, the need for achievement, and the tendency to experience anxiety.

Authoritarianism

In part as a response to fascism in World War II, a group of investigators headed by Else Frenkel-Brunswik studied a trait that they called *authoritarianism* (Adorno et al., 1950). They believed this characteristic was a combination of conventional ways of thinking, rigidity, an attitude that authorities should be strictly obeyed, a tendency to be very aggressive toward those who deviate from conventional norms, a preoccupation with toughness and power (what we might now call the "macho" or male stereotype of strength), and an overall cynicism about human nature. Researchers expected authoritarian people to be politically conservative, to vote for "law and order," to favor elitist as opposed to popular justice, and to oppose freedom of sexual expression and modes of dress, racial integration, and so on.

The authoritarian personality is identified by a test that consists of a wide variety of items designed to measure the various characteristics just listed. Some of the items are shown in Fig. 14.11. You might give your answers and then score yourself to see where you fall on the scale.

Research on the authoritarian personality has produced mixed results. As expected, high authoritarians do tend to be politically conservative, preferring Nixon to Kennedy in 1960 (Leventhal, Jacobs, and Kudirka, 1964) and to McGovern in 1972 (Shikiar, 1975). However, they have not always proved to be more conformist (Gorfein, 1961), were not chosen as military leaders by their peers (Hollander, 1954), and were not more willing to report "hippie" than "straight" shoplifters (Steffensmeier, 1975). Thus, even though the description of the authoritarian personality sounds as if it captures the essence of a type of person we all know, the evidence has not demonstrated that it is a particularly useful way of describing personality.

Machiavellianism

A particularly fascinating personality characteristic involves the ability and tendency to manipulate other people. Richard Christie has called this trait *machiavellianism*, after the sixteenth-century author of *The Prince*, which dealt with how to use guile, deceit, and opportunism in interpersonal relations. Christie and Geis (1970) constructed a test to measure this characteristic. Before reading further, you might look at the items in Fig. 14.12 and score yourself according to the key given there. The major qualities of a high machiavellian (high mach) are a relative lack of affect in interpersonal relations (they don't care much about other people), a lack of concern with conventional morality, and weak or nonexistent commitment to any ideology. Clearly, caring about other people, morality, or ideals will cause us to treat people fairly and honestly, while a lack of these feelings allows us to treat people any way necessary to get what we want. As you can see from the items on the scale, the high-mach person believes that you should tell people what they want to hear (not be honest), that there's a sucker born every minute, that most people are not especially good or kind, and that you shouldn't trust anyone. This is a highly cynical view, but apparently it is held by many people who are good at getting what they want, at least in some situations.

Christie and his associates demonstrated that high-mach people are especially effective in winning games or bargaining encounters. The high mach is untrusting and untrustworthy, and often takes advantage of others who are more trusting. Moreover, high machs tend to be more persuasive—they usually win other people over to their side of an issue, while being unconvinced themselves. In interpersonal relationships, we would expect that high machs (who tend to be less involved) would usually have a dominant position because they are typically the cool person who has to be won over.

1. The best way to handle people is to tell them what they want to hear.
2. One should take action only when it is morally right.
3. Most people are basically good and kind.
4. Most people who get ahead in the world lead clean, moral lives.
5. Barnum was wrong when he said that there's a sucker born every minute.
6. It is hard to get ahead without cutting corners here and there.

Fig. 14.12
The machiavellian scale

Answer the questions on a scale from −3 (disagree strongly) to +3 (agree strongly). The explanation and scoring are given elsewhere on this page.

Explanation and scoring for Fig. 14.12: Agreement with questions 1 and 6 and disagreement with questions 2–5 indicate high machiavellianism. If you reverse the scores for 2–5 (that is, change a +3 to a −3), the higher your score, the higher you rate on this trait.

Need for Achievement

We have already discussed the achievement motive in some detail in Chapter 9. It is measured on certain TAT pictures by counting the references to achievement and success that appear in the stories. There is little question that some people are more concerned with success and achievement than others. These concerns can change over the course of an individual's life and even from one month to another, but some recent work has shown that they tend to remain fairly constant over many years.

Although achievement motivation is an important characteristic of an individual's personality and can have important effects on behavior, these effects are generally quite complicated. For example, high need achievement would ordinarily be expected to lead to harder work and therefore to better performance in school. While some studies do find this relationship (Littig and Yeracaris, 1963; Shimoyama, 1974), others do not (Bendig, 1959; Brown, 1974). The explanation may be that harder work is not always productive—trying hard may help but trying too hard may lead to anxiety and interfere with performance (Rand, 1973). On the other hand, higher need achievement has been shown to relate consistently to higher occupational goals and to affect the difficulty of the major that a student chooses (Isaacson, 1964).

As discussed in Chapter 9, achievement motivation is considerably more complicated than simply high or low. People vary in wanting success and also in fearing failure, and these two tendencies produce complex effects on behavior. However, it is clear that need achievement is an important element in our personalities and that it has strong effects on how we act.

Anxiety

Some people appear to experience a great deal of *anxiety*; that is, they worry about things; are fearful, apprehensive, and nervous; and ex-

1. I am often sick to my stomach.
2. My sleep is restless and disturbed.
3. When embarrassed I break out in a heavy sweat which is very annoying.
4. Life is often a strain for me.
5. I feel anxious about something or someone almost all the time.
6. I blush about as often as others.

Fig. 14.13
The anxiety scale

Answer the questions true or false. The explanation and scoring are given elsewhere on this page.

perience various physical symptoms that indicate this anxiety. Freud thought that anxiety was the result of unconscious conflicts and fears; therefore, it is not surprising that it has been extensively studied. This characteristic of high anxiety is also closely related to the factor Eysenck called neuroticism, which involved the contrast between being calm and assured or nervous and worried. Research on anxiety seems to indicate that it has consistent effects on people's behavior.

In 1953, Janet Taylor constructed a simple test of anxiety that was based mainly on physical symptoms (see Fig. 14.13). It was called the Taylor Manifest Anxiety Scale (or TMAS) because it referred to anxiety that was evident (or manifest) in the person's behavior and responses. A great deal of research has indicated that high-anxiety people do behave differently from low-anxiety people in a wide variety of situations. For example, anxiety is related to mental disturbance, as shown by the fact that university students rate lower than psychiatric patients (Taylor, 1953). In addition, high-anxiety people perform better on easy tasks and less well on complex ones (Spence et al., 1956). Some people experience anxiety particularly in connection with taking tests. As we would expect from the Yerkes-Dodson law (see Chapter 9), this so-called *test anxiety* can sometimes improve performance on simple tests, but typically interferes with performance on more complex ones (Mandler and Sarason, 1952). It may be helpful to remember that it can actually hurt your score to be too anxious before an exam. If you do feel exceedingly anxious, relaxing and easing your tension will probably cause you to do better. But if your performance involves relatively simple tasks, such as a sprint in track, high anxiety will probably be beneficial.

Explanation and scoring for Fig. 14.13: The more questions you answer true, the higher your score on manifest anxiety. This scale is based largely on physical symptoms that tend to indicate anxiety, and the more you have these symptoms, the greater your general anxiety level.

These are just a few of the particular personality characteristics that have been studied. Research has also been done on the need for affiliation, aggressiveness, honesty, and many other important traits. In addition, as we discussed in Chapter 13, there has been a great deal of interest in "masculinity" and "femininity" and in whether there are personality differences between the sexes.

A particularly important area of research that is closely related to personality is work on mental disorders. In a sense, this research also involves personality, but the emphasis is on maladjustment and problems rather than on the usual or normal development. However, the theories and research that deal with personality provide the background for understanding so-called psychopathology, and that is what we shall consider in the next chapter. ∎

Summary

1. Personality refers to individual behavior and thought patterns that are consistent from one time to another. In studying personality, psychologists concentrate on differences among people, on what makes them unique.

2. There are many theories of personality, but they fall into four general classes: constitutional (physiological), psychoanalytic, social learning, and humanistic.

3. Constitutional theories propose that personality is determined by innate factors, and focus on the relationship between personality and the physiological makeup of the individual. Sheldon suggested that body type (endomorphic, mesomorphic, or ectomorphic) determines personality traits; and Eysenck explained personality in terms of neurological differences.

4. Psychoanalytic theory emphasizes the dynamic interaction between innate qualities and life experiences in determining personality. Freud proposed that many unconscious motives, feelings, and thoughts affect our behavior and that personality consists of three separate brain functions that are sometimes in conflict. The *id* consists of primitive impulses that demand immediate satisfaction; the *ego*, the rational, conscious mind, tries to satisfy the impulses of the id in socially acceptable ways; and the *superego*, the conscience and vision of our ideal self (ego ideal), includes the individual's moral code.

5. According to psychoanalytic theory, conflicts between the id and the superego produce *anxiety*, a kind of psychological pain that has no real object or external cause. In order to reduce anxiety we use defense mechanisms such as denial, repression, projection, displacement, reaction formation, rationalization, and intellectualization.

6. Freud asserted that personality development occurs in psychosexual stages. At each stage (oral, anal, or phallic), sexual impulses from the id focus on certain zones of the body, and the child's desire to express these impulses comes into conflict with the rules of society. If the conflict is not resolved, the individual becomes fixated at the stage in which the conflict occurs.

7. Neo-Freudian theorists such as Carl Jung and Alfred Adler expanded and also challenged Freud's ideas. Jung introduced the idea of a collective unconscious shared by all of humanity, and Adler stressed the role of conscious aggressive feelings in shaping personality. Modern *ego psychologists* stress conscious processes and investigate how the ego deals with the conflicts we all face.

8. Social learning theorists believe that personality is formed through the normal learning processes of association, reinforcement, and imitation. They think that early experiences influence personality, but they do not accept the Freudian notion that early experiences are predominant. Moreover, whereas Freud believed that anxiety is caused by unconscious conflicts, learning theorists believe it is aroused by approach-avoidance conflicts.

9. The emphasis of humanistic psychologists (including such people as Carl Rogers and Fritz Perls) is on *self-actualization,* the development and expression of a person's unique talents, abilities, and potentials. This theory implies that personality is innate and waiting to emerge. Thus, what is important is not to control unconscious impulses, as Freud asserted, but to provide an environment that encourages the expression of one's potential.

10. The problems encountered in accurately measuring personality are similar to those encountered in measuring intelligence. Communication difficulties, bias introduced by choice of materials, and questions of reliability and validity may influence the results. In addition, great care must be taken in determining what questions to ask, since people may answer dishonestly if they feel their answers will cast them in an unfavorable light.

11. The major types of personality tests are direct tests and projective tests. A useful direct test is the MMPI, which attempts to conceal the relationship between the questions asked and the personality traits they are designed to measure. The projective test requires the subject to respond to an ambiguous stimulus. Projective tests are based on the idea that our personality characteristics to some degree determine our perceptions, and therefore our responses will reveal something about our personality. The Rorschach Inkblot Test and the Thematic Apperception Test (TAT) are the best-known projective tests.

12. Certain personality traits have been singled out for extensive study because of their important effects on human behavior. These include authoritarianism, machiavellianism, the need for achievement, and anxiety.

RECOMMENDED READING

Freud, A. *The Ego and the Mechanisms of Defense.* New York: International Universities Press, 1946. Anna Freud presents the beginning of ego psychology. The defense mechanisms are seen as part of the personality rather than simply a means of avoiding anxiety.

Freud, S. *New Introductory Lectures on Psychoanalysis.* New York: Norton, 1933. The simplest presentation of Freud's theories on just about everything.

Hall, C. S., and G. Lindzey, Eds. *Theories of Personality*, 2d ed. New York: Wiley, 1970. Still the best description of all the theories of personality.

Mischel, W. *Personality and Assessment.* New York: Wiley, 1968. An advanced book that forcefully criticizes the assumption that people have personality traits.

Mischel, W. *Introduction to Personality.* New York: Holt, 1971. One of the best textbooks in this field. Presents a broad range of theory and research, with more than the usual emphasis on the role of learning and with Mischel's skepticism about personality traits.

Mullahy, P. *Oedipus: Myth and Complex.* New York: Hermitage Press, 1948. Probably the clearest presentation of Freud's theories. A well-written, relatively brief book that covers most of the major points.

Everyone is a moon, and has a dark side which he never shows to anybody.
Mark Twain, Pudd'nhead Wilson

As I was walking on the stair
I met a man who wasn't there.
He wasn't there again today.
I wish, I wish he'd stay away.
Hughes Mearns, The Psychoed

15 Psychopathology

Mental health—a definition ■ *Types of psychopathology* ■
Neuroses ■ *Personality disorders* ■ *Psychoses* ■
Causes of psychopathology ■ *Prevalence of*
psychopathology

e all occasionally say that someone is acting "crazy" or "insane." A friend doesn't like our favorite movie, and we tell him he's nuts. Someone goes swimming in the winter and we say she's crazy. We call people lunatics when they act odd, eccentric, or just disagree with us; and other people call us the same things. And we all do act strange at times. We get peculiar ideas about something, develop odd tastes, and behave irrationally and illogically. We worry much more than seems necessary about an exam; we are terribly sensitive about our looks; we are afraid to fly or go to a party or call someone up for a date. We may imagine that someone hates us, when they actually feel neutral or even like us. We have all kinds of fears and concerns that are out of proportion to the situation. All of this is natural and normal; it is merely an expression of natural concerns. Indeed, we are exhibiting our own individuality by taking some problems or concerns more seriously than others might, and behaving differently from others. However, some patterns of thought and behavior are so disruptive and harmful that we do consider them abnormal, and we consider someone who exhibits these patterns to be suffering from a mental disorder.

In this chapter we shall first try to define mental health and its opposite, psychopathology (mental disturbance or disorder). Then we shall discuss the major types of psychopathology—neuroses, personality disorders, and psychoses. Next we consider various theories of the causes of psychopathology, and finally we deal with the prevalence of psychopathology.

MENTAL HEALTH—A DEFINITION

In order to decide that some behavior is unhealthy it is obviously necessary to have a clear concept of health. Mental health is such a complex idea and involves so many philosophical and psychological considerations that we cannot define it in simple terms. Instead, we rely on several criteria, although no one of these is entirely satisfactory by itself. Nevertheless, together they provide a useful and applicable definition.

Is the Behavior Good for the Person?

The first criterion of mental health is whether the individual's thinking and behavior are good for him and others. By "good" we mean that the person is free to satisfy his needs, seek reinforcement, avoid unpleasant situations, and deal with the world effectively. In Maslow's terms, healthy individuals are free to self-actualize, to satisfy basic needs and proceed to seek satisfaction of the higher needs. Within the limits of the environment and rules of the society, they are able to fulfill their potentialities.

From a slightly different point of view, positive feelings are healthy and desirable, while negative feelings are not. This is particularly true of feelings about the self. Thus, self-confidence, self-respect, and self-acceptance are healthy, while self-hatred and excessive shyness are not. Openness, sociability, affection, warmth, and love are expressions of health, while isolation, anxiety, fear, distrust, and hatred are usually unhealthy.

This is not to say that truly healthy people never experience negative feelings. Clearly, someone who does not mourn the loss of a loved one or feel anger at injustice is less sensitive and healthy than someone who experiences these feelings. But by and large, within the limitations of the environment, healthy people are free to act and their behaviors and thoughts lead toward positive feelings, while unhealthy people are restricted, closed in, and tend to experience negative feelings regardless of the situation.

In trying to define healthy behavior it is essential to keep in mind that the degree and duration of the behavior and feelings are critical. It may be very healthy to spend some time alone. Some people need to be by themselves for long periods in order to think clearly, to write or paint, to solve problems, or to get in touch with their feelings. But never seeing other people would be unhealthy. Similarly, it is perfectly normal to experience self-doubt. The point is that most emotions and feelings are within the realm of normalcy, as are most behaviors. When the emotions or behaviors become extreme, when they take over your life, or when they last too long, they start to damage you and then we think of them as a mental disturbance.

Is the Person in Touch with Reality?

The second criterion is whether the individual is in touch with reality. By this we mean that she is aware of what is going on around her, knows where she is, sees objects and activities realistically, and does not perceive anything that is not there. There is, of course, a fine line between having different or original perceptions and not perceiving reality. Artists, creative thinkers, and social critics often interpret scenes or activities much differently from most people. And composers may actually "hear" their music as they are writing it even though no one is playing it.

Differences in perception or understanding do not mean that someone has broken with reality. Nevertheless, some people, under some circumstances, do lose touch with the external world and do perceive stimuli that are not there. When this happens to any considerable extent, it naturally tends to interfere with the individual's ability to cope with the world. If you think you are being followed by giant green lizards, you will have difficulty acting freely. If you think you are Napoleon and give everyone orders, you probably will not get along well with other people. Except under very special circumstances, people who do not perceive what is going on accurately will not be able to function well and will not be able to pursue their own needs effectively. Thus, in terms of our first criterion, a break with reality would almost always be unhealthy.

Is the Behavior Markedly Different from the Norm?

Third, a behavior or pattern of thought that differs greatly from the norms of society may indicate disturbance. This does not mean that we should use a purely statistical criterion—average is not necessarily good; deviation is often healthy. Indeed, much of society's vitality comes from people who break with the usual rules, who have original ideas and act differently from most of those around them. Neverthe-

Expression of individuality or mental disturbance?

less, someone who behaves very differently from other people may be disturbed. Someone who runs naked down the main street in town may be perfectly healthy—it may be a publicity stunt or just exuberance. But if he does it often, we begin to wonder. The deviation is not proof of disturbance, but it is sometimes an indication of it.

Difficulty of Applying These Criteria

Although these three criteria are plausible indicators of mental health, in practice they are difficult to apply because behaviors must be considered in terms of particular individuals and their circumstances. For example, as we have noted, people who avoid contact with other people would ordinarily be unhealthy. Since other people are a major source of satisfaction for a wide variety of needs, avoiding people is automatically restricting. On the other hand, under some circumstances this behavior may be highly adaptive. In Nazi concentration camps, some prisoners managed to survive by creating an internal world of their own and screening out contact with other individuals. And some of those who hid from the Nazis for years in total isolation managed to survive, while those who were unable to stand the isolation did not. Similarly, members of various religious orders maintain seclusion from the world, and we do not consider them unhealthy. Thus, even this extreme behavior cannot be declared categorically unhealthy.

In addition, the criteria for healthy behavior differ in different societies. The extreme aggressiveness in some American Indian societies and the equally extreme passivity in others have been described in detail by Ruth Benedict (1934) and other anthropologists. An average person taken from either of those societies would be considered deviant in most other cultures. And some cultures that are surrounded by antagonistic neighbors may teach all of their members to be afraid of strangers, to be constantly alert to danger, and so on.

Finally, some cultures show great respect for someone who hears voices, goes into catatonic trances, and suffers severe breaks with reality. Whereas such people would be considered "crazy" in our society, they become important members of those communities. Thus, a determination of mental health must be made to some extent in the context of the mores and values of the particular culture.

However, this cultural and situational perspective should not obscure the fact that under most circumstances certain behaviors are healthier than others. Even if the situation requires isolation or encourages a fear of strangers, these behaviors are not healthy in a broader sense. Individuals who behave in this manner are more restricted, less free to pursue their needs, than people who do not. The behavior may be temporarily adaptive in a particular context, but all that means is that it is a reasonable response to an unhealthy environment. In other words, although any given behavior must be evaluated in context, we can apply a general rule that the greater the freedom of action and the more realistic the perceptions, the healthier the human being.

Health as a Continuum

It is essential to keep in mind that there is no sharp division between the healthy and unhealthy person (see Fig. 15.1). All people have many of the concerns and exhibit many of the behaviors of mentally disturbed persons. In any society, practically everyone will share certain fears, conflicts, troubles, and frustrations. Some of these fears will be realistic, some less so, but even the unrealistic fears will be felt by most people. Furthermore, those aspects of life that tend to

Fig. 15.1
Health as a continuum

Everyone has some mental and behavioral difficulties. There is no clear dividing line between someone who is "healthy" and someone who is not. There may, however, be a clearer distinction between severe disturbance (psychosis) and less serious problems.

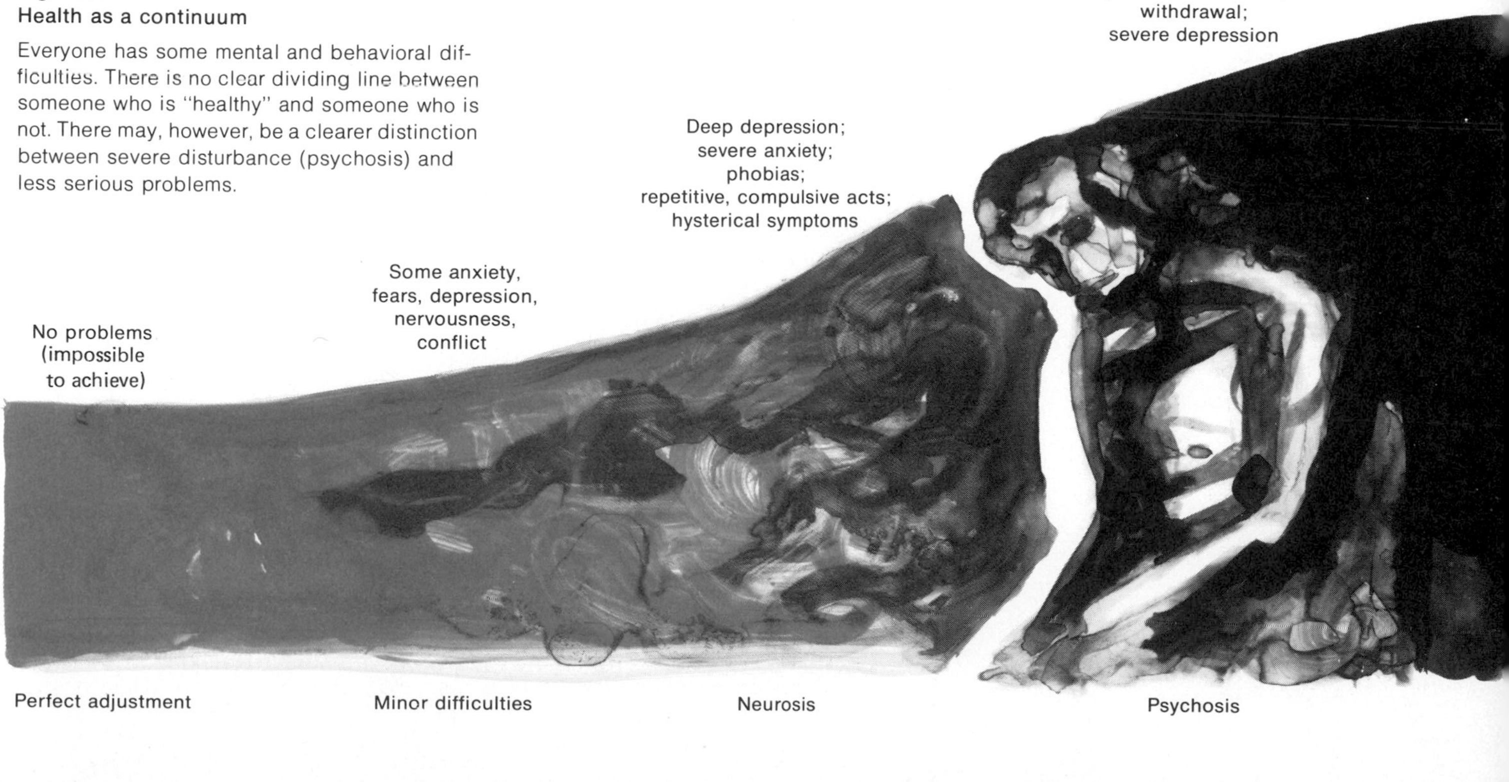

Hallucinations; paranoid fantasies; withdrawal; severe depression

Deep depression; severe anxiety; phobias; repetitive, compulsive acts; hysterical symptoms

Some anxiety, fears, depression, nervousness, conflict

No problems (impossible to achieve)

Perfect adjustment   Minor difficulties   Neurosis   Psychosis

arouse conflict in everyone are the same ones that, when taken to extremes, produce mental disturbances. The difference is one of degree and duration. The conditions we shall describe below involve more severe and more lasting restrictions and breaks with realty than most people experience and are therefore considered disorders.

TYPES OF PSYCHOPATHOLOGY

Fig. 15.2
Mental disorders

The major classes of psychopathology are neuroses, personality disorders, and psychoses. Within each class, there are several types that we shall consider in detail. Keep in mind that an individual may not fit perfectly into any category or may have aspects of more than one condition. The categories, which are shown in Fig. 15.2, are useful primarily as convenient groupings of common symptoms rather than as precise descriptions of specific disorders.

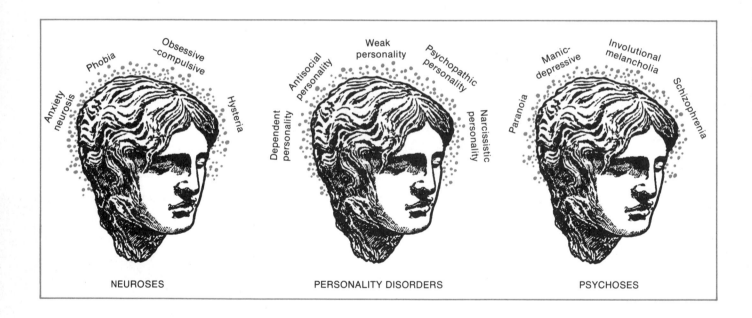

NEUROSES   PERSONALITY DISORDERS   PSYCHOSES

NEUROSES

The most common type of mental disturbance is called *neurosis,* from the Greek root meaning nerves. This is an appropriate term because the major characteristic of neurosis is nervousness, or, as it is usually called, anxiety. Neurotics are in touch with reality and can generally function reasonably well in society. But they have developed fears or behavior patterns that interfere substantially with their freedom of action. Different names are given to the neurosis depending on the particular pattern of symptoms. The types of neuroses are listed in Table 15.1, and we shall discuss each in turn.

Table 15.1
TYPES OF NEUROSES

Classification	Symptoms
Anxiety neurosis	Feels anxious and nervous much of the time. May be associated with specific situations (e.g., parties, work) or "free-floating" (not associated with any particular object or situation).
Phobia	Excessive fear of a particular object or situation. Whenever near object, is overcome with great anxiety.
Obsessive-compulsive	Repetitive actions or thoughts. Is "forced" to repeat certain behaviors over and over. Constantly thinks and worries about specific things.
Hysteria	Development of specific physical symptoms with no organic cause. Typical symptoms include blindness, paralysis, and fainting.

Anxiety Neurosis

The major symptom of an *anxiety neurosis* is a very high level of anxiety. This feeling of nervousness and fear may be entirely unfocused—the person feels it almost all the time rather than in connection with particular objects or situations—in which case it is usually called *free floating anxiety*. In severe cases an anxiety neurotic may experience acute anxiety attacks that are accompanied by physical symptoms such as shortness of breath, dizziness, pounding of the heart, nausea, or even fainting. But even under less stressful circumstances, the neurotic suffers from strong anxiety that is extremely unpleasant and makes it difficult to act freely and spontaneously.

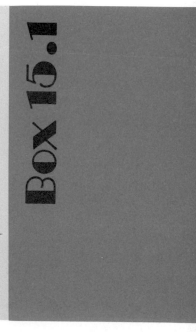

NERVOUS BREAKDOWNS

If we were to judge from movies, novels, and everyday conversation, we would conclude that by far the most common form of psychopathology is the nervous breakdown. However, this term does not refer to any particular condition and has no technical or scientific meaning. Rather, people use the term "nervous breakdown" very loosely to describe a condition in which someone is so upset that he or she can no longer continue functioning normally at home, at work, or in interpersonal relationships. A woman who must take a leave of absence from work because she is too nervous to concentrate on what she is doing or a man who cannot deal with his children and wife and must get away for a while are said to have suffered nervous breakdowns.

What are called nervous breakdowns range greatly in severity. More serious ones probably are symptoms of anxiety neuroses, depression, and at the extreme, various forms of schizophrenia. But mild nervous breakdowns may be simply temporary reactions to severe stress. Life has become very difficult, problems have mounted up, and the person needs some time to rest. This period of rest would generally be fairly brief, and then, refreshed, the person can return to normal living. It is almost as if we need a vacation from regular life occasionally; and, in fact, the normal vacations people take may serve the purpose of preventing stress from building up too much.

The difference between normal, everyday concern and neurotic anxiety is partly a matter of severity, but also involves the ability to deal with these feelings. We all feel anxious under some circumstances, but can usually cope with these feelings and try to reduce them. Most people are anxious when taking exams, for example—this is a reasonable reaction and reasonable steps can be taken to reduce it. But neurotics cannot deal with their anxiety. Taking the ordinary steps to reduce the fear—studying very hard or talking to other students—has little effect. The neurotic might study for twenty hours a day for four days hoping that this will reduce his anxiety, but all it does is make him so tired or so anxious that he cannot take the exam at all. Thus, people with anxiety neuroses typically do less well in almost all aspects of their lives because they are constantly burdened with the pressures of their neurosis.

ANXIETY ATTACK

Sue, a recently married, twenty-year-old college student, had been experiencing anxiety attacks for approximately a year when the therapist first saw her. Without warning her heart would begin to pound, her breathing would become difficult, her hands would sweat profusely, her stomach muscles would tighten, and she would feel flushed and feverish. Although she had frequently experienced these sensations, she could not stop herself from feeling that she was about to die. At the same time she knew—somewhere in the back of her mind—that if she only closed her eyes and rested, she'd feel normal again within an hour.

Sue's first anxiety attack had occurred as she was leaving a crowded football stadium. The only previous event that appeared connected with these feelings was a panicky reaction the night before to a TV story about a nightclub fire which trapped and killed thirty people. Her second anxiety attack occurred during an argument with her husband about whether to wear slacks or a dress to a family party. Sue didn't remember the details surrounding the third attack or the fourth or all the others which she had experienced since. The attacks were coming almost every day now—whenever any one disagreed with her, when she encountered strangers, when she drove in congested traffic, when she shopped in crowded stores. They happened at parties and in classes, restaurants, theaters, houses, and even her own apartment. Lately, Sue had been trying to avoid the places where the attacks occurred most often. Consequently, she was spending a great deal of time in her apartment, venturing out into the world primarily to seek help. The many physicians whom she consulted found nothing medically wrong with her and eventually she was referred to a psychiatric clinic. (Davidoff, 1976, p. 401)

Table 15.2
TYPES OF PHOBIAS

Classification	Symptom
Claustrophobia	Fear of enclosed places
Agoraphobia	Fear of open places
Acrophobia	Fear of high places
Nyctophobia	Fear of the dark
Xenophobia	Fear of strangers

Phobia

A *phobia* is similar to anxiety neurosis except that instead of individuals feeling general anxiety, they become abnormally afraid of a particular situation or object. The fear usually has some basis in reality, but it is magnified far out of proportion. It is so strong that the phobic cannot stand being near the object of her fear. There are a wide variety of phobias, some of which are listed in Table 15.2. Fear of snakes, spiders, closed spaces, and heights are some of the most common. In all cases it seems as if the object of fear is either symbolic of an inner conflict or resulted from a particularly terrifying experience for the individual.

Drawing by Perry Barlow; © 1940 The New Yorker Magazine, Inc.

"See me again in a week, Mrs. Martin, and remember claustrophobia never killed anyone."

Most of us have some fears that are not entirely realistic. Some people love to fly in planes, while others are always worried while they are in the air. Some people like dogs, others are afraid of them; some people like snakes, others are revolted by them; and so on. These fears, even when they are unrealistic, should not be considered phobias unless they are so extreme that the individual is literally overwhelmed by them in the presence of the object. Someone who is nervous on a plane does not have a phobia; someone who cannot bring himself to board a plane does. As with all the other neuroses, it is the extremity and the lack of control over the symptom that make it neurotic.

Obsessive-Compulsive Neurosis

Obsessive-compulsive neurotics feel anxiety connected with particular situations or events, and in order to reduce that anxiety develops behavior that involves the constant repetition of certain acts or thoughts. These repetitive acts distract them or allow them to avoid the situation. For example, a common compulsive habit is continuously washing the hands. In Shakespeare's *Macbeth*, after the king has been murdered, Lady Macbeth tries to wash away the imaginary spot on her hands and the guilt it symbolizes. Some neurotics wash their hands to cleanse them from the guilt associated with thoughts about or actual masturbation. As long as they are in the act of washing their hands, the guilt they may feel is temporarily relieved because they are symbolically cleansing themselves. In addition, while they are washing they are temporarily distracted from their conflict and that also reduces anxiety. Someone who is abnormally anxious in social situations may go through a very complicated ritual whenever she enters a room or meets a new person. She may have to touch everything three times, straighten all the pictures on the walls, or shake hands in a special way. This distracts her from the actual social situation, and at the same time helps to temporarily relieve her anxiety.

In a minor way practically everyone has some compulsive habits. Some people cannot study unless the radio is on, others must line up their papers and pencils very neatly before they can get to work, others are compulsively neat. This kind of behavior affects all of us, but neurotics cannot stop themselves from doing it. If they do not perform the required acts, they are overwhelmed with anxiety and can barely function at all. Thus, once again, neurotics simply carry to an extreme the kinds of behavior that occur in relatively healthy individuals.

Obsessive thinking—constantly dwelling on some problem or action—is also a characteristic of this neurosis. Whereas normal people might sometimes worry about whether they locked the door when they left the house, neurotics may worry about it to such an extent that they can think of nothing else. Most premed students worry about getting good marks and getting into medical school. This is natural. But some think about this constantly and it interferes with almost every aspect of their lives. This is obsessive thinking.

OBSESSIVE–COMPULSIVE SYMPTOMS

A girl who began masturbating at the age of thirteen told her mother about the practice. Her mother warned her that masturbation would make her insane and that she would never be clean again. The girl developed migraine headaches and was afraid to go to sleep at night. She felt dirty all the time and began to wash her hands and genitals hundreds of times a day. (Reported in Rosen, Fox, and Gregory, 1972, pp. 159–160)

A boy whose mother was extremely overprotective and whose father mistreated him became very attached to his grandfather. He began to worry constantly that his grandfather would die. He pictured the house catching on fire, being struck by lightning, or falling apart in a strong wind. When these thoughts occurred, he performed magical, ritualistic acts such as touching something to ward off the danger. If he stepped on a crack while having a frightening thought, he felt compelled to step on the crack again to cancel the thought. Eventually he performed more and more compulsive acts, such as spending an hour or more touching objects in the room. He developed special techniques for cancelling the thoughts and removing the danger. For example, in his room he would point to the southwest (a lucky direction for him) four times (a lucky number), but then might have to repeat this $4 \times 4 \times 4 \times 4$ (256) times to be certain. (Reported in White, 1964, p. 264)

Hysterical or Conversion Neurosis

The most dramatic form of neurosis, called *hysterical or conversion neurosis*, involves the development of an actual physical disability for no physical reason. Hysterical neurotics actually become blind, lame, paralyzed, and so on, despite the lack of a physical cause. This is not a question of faking a symptom to avoid an unpleasant situation, as a child might pretend to be sick to avoid school (although it is similar in that the neurotic develops the symptoms in order to avoid an anxiety-producing situation). Healthy people know that they are faking, do not actually get sick, and can stop acting whenever they want. The neurotic who has become blind cannot see even if she wants to and no amount of effort on her part will enable her to see.

Cases of this sort are common among soldiers and other people who face extreme danger. In one classic and relatively simple case described by Robert White (1956), a flyer suddenly began losing consciousness whenever the plane went above eight thousand feet. When questioned about it he declared that he was unaware of what was happening, and that he was unafraid and very much wanted to continue flying but consistently blacked out at altitude. Since this made it impossible for him to fly and therefore to face the extreme dangers that he had been subjected to for many months, the symptom protected him from a situation that had produced more fear and anxiety than he could handle. As long as the hysterical symptom persists, the individual is safe from the particular situation he fears and therefore from the anxiety it would arouse. Thus, despite the enormous restrictions on the individual's freedom of action that are produced by these conversion symptoms, they continue because they reduce what might otherwise be unbearable anxiety.

HYSTERICAL—CONVERSION NEUROSIS

Curt Z., a 35-year-old married father of three, had enjoyed perfect health until two months before he applied for treatment. At that time he experienced a choking sensation, accompanied by tightness in his neck and a bandlike constricting sensation in his abdomen. He was also unable to move his legs for about fifteen minutes. Following this episode he became dizzy and fainted, and when he recovered, discovered that he could not speak. A physician was summoned, and he gave him an injection to put him to sleep. The following morning he could speak again, but only in a hoarse and barely audible voice which he retained for almost a month, until his normal speaking voice spontaneously returned. After that he again lost his voice for periods ranging from less than a day to close to a week on numerous occasions. During the month before seeking treatment Curt had one to eight attacks daily, lasting between five minutes and one hour. These attacks were marked by a choking sensation in the throat, tightness in the neck, occasional side-to-side jerking motions of the head, hives on his arm and face, profuse sweating, and nausea. After the onset of his illness he severely limited his work around the butcher shop, leaving the bulk of the work to his father and mother. His appetite was undisturbed, but his sleep was disrupted with frequent awakening. For the first few weeks of his illness, Curt remained in his room, only leaving it to eat or go to the doctor's office. After that he began to leave his room and attempted to move around the house, but usually when he did so he had a recurrence of symptoms. He became very gruff with the children, slept late, and went to bed early in a state of exhaustion. Whenever he fainted he became worried that he might have seen or done something he shouldn't have while unconscious. (Zax and Stricker, 1963, pp. 163–164)

PERSONALITY DISORDERS

Whereas neuroses are characterized by the presence of anxiety, personality disorders have no specific symptoms of this type. Instead, they consist of the development of a set of behaviors or personal characteristics that are harmful to either the individual or to other people in society. It could be said that people with personality disorders simply have bad personalities—they are too aggressive or too dependent, cannot form friendships, are immature, are reckless beyond usual bounds, enjoy only weird sexual activity, or have any other highly deviant characteristic. As long as the behavior is unimportant (she eats only Italian food, he can enjoy sex only with the light off), we would probably not classify the condition as a disorder. But when the characteristic is central enough to influence a wide range of behaviors, or tends to involve very important kinds of behavior, the condition becomes a personality disorder.

Many people who do not have specific symptoms but find that they are not enjoying life or are much less successful than they should be probably suffer from personality disorders. In fact, this has become quite a common condition of people seeking therapy of various kinds. For one reason or another, such people have developed patterns that are not adaptive in their society and that continually interfere with their lives and with those around them.

Psychopathic Personality

A particular personality disorder of special concern to society is the *psychopathic personality*, which is characterized by an inability to

PSYCHOPATHIC
PERSONALITY

Donald S., 30 years old, has just completed a three-year prison term for fraud, bigamy, false pretenses, and escaping lawful custody. . . . With less than a month left to serve on an earlier 18-month term for fraud, he faked illness and escaped from the prison hospital. During the ten months of freedom that followed he engaged in a variety of illegal enterprises. . . . By passing himself off as the "field executive" of an international philanthropic foundation, he was able to enlist the aid of several religious organizations in a fund-raising campaign. The campaign moved slowly at first, and in an attempt to speed things up, he arranged an interview with the local TV station. His performance during the interview was so impressive that funds started to pour in. However, unfortunately for Donald, the interview was also carried on a national news network. He was recognized and quickly arrested. During the ensuing trial it became evident that he experienced no sense of wrongdoing for his activities. He maintained, for example, that his passionate plea for funds "primed the pump"—that is, induced people to give to other charities as well as to the one he professed to represent. . . .

By all accounts Donald was considered a willful and difficult child. When his desire for candy or toys was frustrated he would begin with a show of affection, and if this failed he would throw a temper tantrum; the latter was seldom necessary because his angelic appearance and artful ways usually got him what he wanted. Similar tactics were used to avoid punishment for his numerous misdeeds. At first he would attempt to cover up with an elaborate facade of lies, often shifting the blame to his brothers. If this did not

work, he would give a convincing display of remorse and contrition. When punishment was unavoidable he would become sullenly defiant, regarding it as an unjustifiable tax on his pleasures. . . .

His sexual experiences were frequent, casual, and callous. When he was 22 he married a 41-year-old woman whom he had met in a bar. Several other marriages followed, all bigamous. In each case the pattern was the same: he would marry someone on impulse, let her support him for several months, and then leave. One marriage was particularly interesting. After being charged with fraud Donald was sent to a psychiatric institution for a period of observation. While there he came to the attention of a female member of the professional staff. His charm, physical attractiveness, and convincing promises to reform led her to intervene on his behalf. He was given a suspended sentence and they were married a week later. At first things went reasonably well, but when she refused to pay some of his gambling debts he forged her name to a check and left. He was soon caught and given an 18-month prison term. As mentioned earlier, he escaped with less than a month left to serve.

It is interesting to note that Donald sees nothing particularly wrong with his behavior, nor does he express remorse or guilt for using others and causing them grief. Although his behavior is self-defeating in the long run, he considers it to be practical and possessed of good sense. Periodic punishments do nothing to decrease his egotism and confidence in his own abilities, nor do they offset the often considerable short-term gains of which he is capable. (Hare, 1970, pp. 1–4)

control impulses and a lack of guilt connected with one's actions. As we said in Chapter 10, one major effect of socialization is to teach children that certain impulses and behaviors can be expressed only under certain circumstances, and that others, such as a desire to kill someone, should not be expressed at all. The superego, conscience, or moral sense is the result of this aspect of the socialization process. It monitors our impulses, generally preventing unacceptable behavior, and producing guilt when such behavior occurs. Virtually everyone develops this kind of control mechanism to one degree or another. Accordingly, most people do delay some gratifications, suppress certain impulses, are not violent or sexually aggressive whenever they feel like it, and usually obey the laws and rules of their society. Probably everyone transgresses these rules at one time or another, but normal people tend to experience guilt when they do.

Psychopaths lack this control mechanism (Cleckley, 1950). They do not experience anxiety, they do not have a moral sense, and they do not experience guilt. As might be expected, they do not delay gratification, they seek to satisfy their needs whenever they can, they do not follow the rules of normal society, and they also seem to show little deep emotion about anything or anyone. Psychopaths commit amoral, criminal, antisocial acts with no qualms about their morality and often with little long-range purpose. They commit them on the spur of the moment, simply because they feel like it.

Psychopaths are not out of touch with reality. On the contrary, they often can be very charming, friendly, and able to function well in society. Unlike neurotics, who are restricted by their condition, psychopaths are perhaps freer than most people because they are not burdened with the sense of morality or guilt. Accordingly, people tend to like psychopaths at first meeting, not realizing that their friendly behavior is entirely superficial and that they are capable of an almost unlimited range of antisocial acts. Generally, psychopaths go through life getting involved in a series of impulsive, antisocial acts that may or may not get them in serious trouble. But aside from these incidents, they function well and in fact may be successful in our competitive society if they have developed at least a minimal ability to delay gratification and plan ahead.

Most delinquents and criminals are not psychopaths. They usually have developed a sense of morality, even though it may be somewhat different from that of the rest of society, and they do distinguish between acceptable and unacceptable acts. They may be willing to steal or even to kill, but would not steal from friends, would not be disloyal, would not hurt a woman, or whatever. In other words, they may be willing to break certain laws of society and commit acts that most other people would not, but they do have a code of ethics that may be just as strong as someone else's. In addition, most criminals are capable of forming deep personal relationships, experiencing strong emotions, and so on. In contrast, psychopaths do not experience love or affection. Some criminals are psychopaths, but they are the exception.

As we discussed in Chapter 12, the development of morality seems to depend on internalizing the values of one's parents or some other adult. In order for this to happen the child must be exposed to one consistent adult during the early years of his life. When there is no such person (as occurred in child-care centers during World War II, and still occurs in many institutions for orphans and in homes where

Marlon Brando as Don Corleone in the movie *The Godfather*. Although they are the perpetrators of widespread crime, including murder, professional criminals may have a strict code of ethics and their own highly developed sense of morality.

Box 15.2

THE INSANITY PLEA

Canadian and American law requires that in order for people to be held responsible for a crime they must have some knowledge that what they did was wrong and some conscious intent to commit the act. Although this criterion may sound reasonable in principle, it is exceedingly difficult to apply in practice. It becomes especially complicated when apparently sane defendants claim that they were insane at the time the act was committed and were therefore not responsible for their actions. Insanity is a recognized defense almost everywhere, but lawyers, psychologists, and psychiatrists have a great deal of difficulty deciding what they mean by legal "insanity."

The earliest ruling on insanity is the McNaughton rule set forth in 1843. The rule states that at the time of the act the person must know the "difference between right and wrong" and must specifically know that what he was doing was wrong. In extreme cases, this rule works fine. A schizophrenic may believe that the man walking toward him is Jack the Ripper and is about to kill him; therefore he shoots the man in self-defense. Although it turns out that the dead man was only asking for directions, most courts would not want to hold the killer responsible in a criminal sense. He did not know that what he was doing was wrong because of a severe break with reality. Similarly, if a woman believes that she is God and everything belongs to her, and if she then strolls into a store and walks off with a television set, she does not know that she has committed an unlawful act. Again, according to the McNaughton rule, she would be innocent by virtue of insanity. So far so good.

However, most psychologists see the law as too narrow. It does protect extreme cases, but it does not protect other people who commit crimes under the influence of severe mental disorders even though they may in some sense know the difference between right and wrong. There are cases of people who believe that they have been ordered by God to kill someone, or who suffer from uncontrollable fits of rage and cannot control violent acts during these fits. They may know that what they are doing is wrong in the eyes of the law, but they do not stop themselves either because they think they have sufficient reason (an order from God is hard to refuse) or because they cannot control their actions. From a psychological point of

no adult takes an interest in or expresses love to a child), the conscience does not develop and the individual fails to be socialized in this very critical way. It seems likely that this is at least one possible cause of a psychopathic personality. Another possibility is that highly inconsistent discipline and attention, even from the same person, prevents the child from forming normal values (Buss, 1966).

There is also some evidence that psychopaths have less reactive autonomic nervous systems than most people. When psychopaths are given electric shocks, their heart rate, galvanic skin response (sweating), and respiration rate change much less than normal (Lykken, 1957; Hare, 1970). However, while these differences may be due to actual neurological differences, they may be caused simply by the fact that psychopaths are less anxious about everything, including injury to their own bodies.

Narcissism

One of the most common personality disorders and a leading topic of research among psychoanalysts is *narcissism*, named after the figure

view these people are severely disturbed and are not really responsible for their actions.

In some jurisdictions the law allows insanity as a defense if the act was committed because of an "irresistible impulse." The person knew the act was wrong, but was under the control of irresistible inner forces. The difficulty with this view is that almost anyone could claim that he committed an act because he could not resist the temptation. If you see a beautiful piece of jewelry, want it very much, and scoop it up, should you be excused? Most people would say no; yet you could claim that you did have an impulse you did not or could not control.

The key issue is between "did not" and "could not." Unfortunately, neither the law nor psychology provides a way of making that distinction. Again, the extreme cases can be decided fairly easily. For example, *kleptomania* is a condition in which people constantly take things on impulses they apparently cannot control. When someone steals all sorts of things including objects he does not need, when he or she (it is more common among women) does not sell the objects and does not even use them, and when the stealing is totally unplanned, we are probably will-ing to believe that the person is suffering from kleptomania and is not just a thief. So we would not hold this person responsible for the crime. But except in extreme cases, how do the courts decide? Many people engage in spontaneous shoplifting. They see something they want and they take it without paying. They know it is wrong, and they are not mentally disturbed according to most accepted criteria. So in these cases we would not accept an insanity plea even though the act was impulsive.

Because the determination is so difficult, most legal jurisdictions have stayed with the original rule. Even though it is very strict, it seems to be the only one that can be used with reasonable confidence. This means that many greatly disturbed people are convicted of crimes and punished as criminals rather than provided with therapeutic treatment.

A viable solution is to change the focus from the determination of guilt to the question of treatment. If the person has committed the act, find her guilty. Then decide whether she should be sentenced to prison or receive treatment. Some states actually have two separate trials—one to determine guilt, the other to decide if the person is legally insane.

in Greek mythology who pined away for love of his own reflection in a pool. The gods turned Narcissis into a flower that usually grows near water, but modern people with this condition do not have this particular solution available. Psychoanalyst Otto Kernberg (1974) describes the narcissist as someone who is totally self-absorbed and can think about and care for only himself or herself. Such a person is superficially smooth and effective in social interactions, but underneath this apparently successful adaptation is beset by very serious problems.

Narcissists think they are the center of the universe, are egotistical, and are incredibly ambitious. They have grandiose fantasies involving wealth, brilliance, beauty, and power. No fantasy is too extreme for their ambition. Yet they also suffer from basic insecurity and feelings of inferiority and need constant admiration from others to sustain them. Everyone must love them or they feel totally rejected. Even great success does not satisfy them—all achievements become empty. Thus, whatever they accomplish they feel bored, dissatisfied, and unfulfilled. It is as if they are constantly hungry and no food could ever alleviate this craving.

In addition, narcissists rarely if ever really care for other people. They use people and discard them ruthlessly when they no longer satisfy their needs. Moreover, they are terribly envious of anyone else's success and therefore find it almost impossible to form a relationship with anyone who is at all accomplished or successful. Thus, narcissists' lives are empty—success means nothing, they are bored with life, and they cannot achieve any lasting, meaningful relationships.

This is, of course, an extreme description. As with all conditions we have been considering, most people have some of these characteristics. We have grandiose fantasies, our achievements are often less satisfying than we expected, we are envious of others, we are self-centered, and have difficulties forming good relationships. But narcissists carry all of this further and it dominates their lives.

In recent years the incidence of narrcissistic disturbance in our society has been rising. It has been suggested that part of the fault may lie with the consciousness movement, which places too heavy emphasis on the self—self-expression, self-understanding, and self-concern. This may make people overly concerned with themselves to the exclusion of caring for others. Another explanation is that people are turning inward because of the growing feeling today that individuals can no longer have significant impact on social or political change. Whatever the causes, it is clear that the disturbance is widespread. Many people seem to have everything one might desire—wealth, position, success, admiration, love—and yet are dissatisfied with the achievements and cannot return the love.

Drawing by Chas. Addams; © 1974 The New Yorker Magazine, Inc.

"Is there someone else, Narcissus?"

PSYCHOSES

The most severe forms of mental disturbance are called *psychoses*. Although there is not always a clear dividing line between the behavior of neurotics and psychotics, many people believe that the conditions are entirely different, with psychoses, particularly schizophrenia, involving specific physiological causes, which is not true of neuroses. But one critical difference definitely exists—psychoses always involve some break with reality. Neurotics may suffer extreme symptoms of various kinds, but they are generally in touch with reality. Their vision of the world may be bleaker than that of healthy people, but they see the same world. This is not true of psychotics. To some extent, in some way, their reality is markedly different from that of healthy people. Psychotics may hear voices, see visions, think they are being followed, or think they are God or Napoleon. They may also feel very sad and forlorn even though nothing especially bad has occurred. And they believe in their reality, not other people's. Almost all psychotics have some idea what is going on around them. And fortunately we no longer accept old notions of lunatics who must be chained up to prevent them from hurting other people. We also know that most psychotics are capable of functioning reasonably well in many situations. Nevertheless, a psychosis does involve some substantial break with reality. The type of break and symptoms vary among the three major types of psychosis—manic-depression, paranoia, and schizophrenia.

Manic-Depressive Psychosis

People in this condition are either terribly and inappropiately depressed, wildly and inappropriately elated, or swinging from one state to the other. In the depressed state, they are extremely passive, often do not eat, may cry a lot, and have little interest in life or even in staying alive. Statements such as, "I have nothing to live for," "the world is a horrible place for me," and so on, characterize their mood. Although this kind of depression is almost always precipitated by a crisis such as the death of a loved one or loss of a job, depressives react more intensely and for much longer than healthy people would. We all feel a sense of loss at times, but manic depressives never seem to get over the loss. In addition, the depression is far more severe than what most people experience, is not relieved by more favorable life experiences, and in general has little to do with reality.

Although depressive patients are unlikely to harm others, suicide is a distinct possibility during the depressed states. In addition, depressives have so little interest in life that they often fail to take care of themselves. Therefore, although they are usually in relatively good touch with day-to-day reality and are quite capable of functioning, depressives are often hospitalized for their own protection.

A special kind of depressive reaction, called *involutional melancholia*, tends to occur fairly late in life, often around the menopause for women. It has many of the same symptoms as a depressive psychosis, but is usually less serious and involves less of a break with reality. There is some indication that it is brought on by hormonal changes in the body, by specific events such as the menopause, or just by a general feeling of getting old. As with manic-depressive psychosis, loss of interest in life and thoughts of suicide are major symptoms.

Although severely depressed people have many different symptoms, Arnold Beck (1967) has described certain characteristics they all seem to have in common. He says that they all have negative views of themselves, have negative expectations about the future, and tend to interpret all experiences negatively.

Negative view of self Depressed people think they are worthless and underrate all of their abilities and traits. No matter how successful,

Virginia Woolf suffered from severe manic depression for most of her life, finally committing suicide. Yet between bouts with her illness, she wrote some of the outstanding novels of our century.

famous, and skillful they are, depressed individuals cannot accept their own achievements and constantly find fault with them. They believe that no one could love or value them because they are not worthy. Furthermore, if they realize that they are depressed, they even blame themselves for this.

Negative expectations Depressives have a pessimistic view of the future. Nothing is going to go right for them. Anything that could possibly go wrong will. If they get in a car to drive downtown, they assume they will get struck in traffic or have an accident. If they love someone, they assume the love will not be reciprocated, or the loved one will die. And these gloomy expectations are often visualized in great detail so that the person suffers even if nothing bad actually happens.

Negative interpretations of experience Everything that happens is interpreted in the worst possible way. Minor difficulties, such as getting delayed in traffic, are seen as a serious frustration; losing a few dollars is felt as a major loss. Getting a B+ on a paper is a failure because it was not an A; an A is interpreted as a mistake or undeserved. The successful artist thinks she is a failure because another artist is more successful. In all cases, whether the outcome is good or bad, the depressive finds some way to make it seem worse.

The manic phase of this condition is considerably rarer. People who are enormously depressed or feel they are about to be overwhelmed by such depression, may sometimes resist this feeling by

MANIC SPEECH

A woman of forty-two, married, mother of two, became upset about a property transaction in which she feared she and her husband were going to be cheated. She lost her appetite, could not do household chores, had difficulty sleeping, and started to drink. She feared she was going to die and spent almost all of one night praying while completely undressed. When she was finally admitted to a hospital, she was noisy, restless, and seemingly out of contact. Her speech was very rapid. For example, when asked about her trouble, she replied:

Would you like to be tied up here? I had an Easter suit to wear. I would like to have a higher priced one. Will you please leave my husband in here and get me out of here— please, deliver me anywhere—I won't give another word because I want to get out of here. Before twelve o'clock we will be millionaires. You are trying to get my confession and put me in a garbage can and put the

cover on—go to hell and stay there. I will cut you all to pieces. I will put a bullet right in you. I won't listen to you because you know more than I do—get out of here, go to hell. I'd rather die than be the way I am.

And on another occasion, after she had left the hospital and returned.

. . . I feel good, how do you feel? I said when I solved the crime I'd come back and see you, didn't you, it's God's will. I don't know what it is but I can tell why you are writing. I still have blood and new—true, true-who-who.

Note that despite the excited, frantic tone of the speech, there is indication of deep concern, guilt, and depression. The patient feels she has something to confess, that she is being punished, and that she would rather be dead than where she is. (Based on Zax and Stricker, 1963, pp. 33–35)

acting in the opposite manner. They pretend to be happy about everything, talk a great deal, are extremely active, and say that everything is as good as it possibly could be. Moreover, the manic state is typically quite fragile and brief. While in the manic phase, individuals ignore reality in much the same way as depressives. Unhappy events and negative experiences do not noticeably alter the mood. They might, for example, giggle at the death of a loved one rather than showing sorrow. However, the mood is easily shattered, with the person plunging precipitously into a depressed state.

Paranoia

This is a relatively rare condition in which individuals seem to be in perfect contact with reality in all respects except one—they have a persistent delusion of some sort. These delusions generally follow certain patterns. They may be delusions of grandeur: the paranoid is the emperor, the king of the world, Jesus Christ, Superman, or the world's greatest scientist. Paranoids may also have so-called *ideas of reference*; that is, they believe everyone is talking about them and thinking about them. Whenever they walk down the street people are whispering behind their back, laughing, and pointing at them. Finally, and most important, paranoids tend to have feelings of persecution. People are out to get them; there is a worldwide plot to kill them; the FBI, the CIA, or just the neighbors are conspiring against them. Their mail is being opened, their phones tapped, people trip them intentionally on the street, and so on. Paranoids may have one or all of these delusions, but typically they all go together. Clearly paranoids think they are extremely important, the center of activities. The most fascinating aspect of paranoia is how complex and internally consistent the delusions can be. There is some tendency for paranoids to be extremely intelligent, and their fantasies are often brilliantly worked out and defended against all of the seemingly contradictory evidence from reality.

As with almost every other disturbance, normal people often have paranoid feelings. When the neighbor makes a lot of noise, we may think he is doing it deliberately to annoy us; when a newspaper isn't delivered, the newsboy is out to get us; when our phone doesn't work, it is being tapped. Usually we know that we are imagining these things or that some of them may be true but there is no general plot to "get" us. Paranoids, on the other hand, really believe in these plots. They interpret all the typical annoyances of daily life in terms of a vast conspiracy. And since people are often nasty, since phones sometimes are tapped, since mail occasionally is opened, the paranoid fantasy is constantly reinforced. (Even paranoids have enemies.) The plausible argument that there is no reason for such plots against them is unconvincing to paranoids because they see themselves as exceedingly important people. Therefore, it is usually extremely difficult to shake their delusional symptoms, which often persist indefinitely. Since paranoids are otherwise in close touch with reality they may function quite well in most phases of life. The difficulty is that they must always be on guard against their persecutors, and sometimes can be extremely dangerous when they decide to fight back. Although there are few full-fledged paranoids of this type, many people do have strong paranoid feelings that they carry with them throughout life.

Schizophrenia

The most serious type of mental illness, which shows the most dramatic breaks with reality and most frequently necessitates hospitalization, is *schizophrenia*. Although the term means "split mind," schizophrenics do not in fact have two distinct personalities. The image of someone being rational, kind, and gentle one moment, and a raving, homicidal maniac the next does not apply to schizophrenics. Unfortunately, however, this image has often caused society to be unduly afraid of people with this disorder. With rare exceptions, schizophrenics are not wild, uncontrolled, or dangerous. There are occasional acute periods during which patients may be agitated and even violent, but these occur in a relatively small percentage of the cases and then only for a short time. Thus, although schizophrenics are severely disturbed and usually do need intensive care, they are not usually a threat to other people.

Symptoms of schizophrenia Schizophrenia is always characterized by one or more of the symptoms listed in Fig. 15.3. Probably the one condition that is constant in all kinds of schizophrenia is that to some extent the thought and perceptions of schizophrenics are different from what is going on in the real world, and the schizophrenics do not

Fig. 15.3
Major symptoms of schizophrenia

INAPPROPRIATE AFFECT
Laughs or cries suddenly without reason
Laughs at sad story
Shows little emotion; blank expression

STRANGE THOUGHT PATTERNS
Weird speech
Unusual associations
Illogical connections

WITHDRAWAL
No rapport with other people
No interaction at all

BIZARRE BEHAVIOR
Strange gestures
Public sexual acts—masturbation, nudity
Jumps around, dances

FANTASY NOT DISTINGUISHED
FROM REALITY
Hallucinations—visual, auditory
Delusions of grandeur, persecution
Irrational beliefs—Martians, strange religions

MULTIPLE PERSONALITIES

Schizophrenia means "split personality," but a schizophrenic actually has only one personality. There are, however, cases of one individual displaying two or more fully formed, complete personalities, with each of them being unaware of and out of contact with the others. The fictional Dr. Jekyll and Mr. Hyde is an example of such a multiple personality. The mild-mannered, kindly scientist Dr. Jekyll at times became the evil, violent Mr. Hyde, and when one side of the personality was in command, the other side was totally absent.

This is a rare condition, with few well-documented cases. *The Three Faces of Eve* (Thigpen and Cleckley, 1957) is a widely read, popular book that describes Eve White, a woman of twenty-five, who sometimes took on an entirely different personality who called herself Eve Black. The two personalities were almost perfect opposites. Eve White was quiet, competent, and industrious. She wore conservative clothes, had a soft voice, and was generally a serious, thoughtful person. Eve Black was flamboyant and irresponsible. She wore provocative clothes, had a coarse voice, and was generally light-hearted, thoughtless, mischievous, and sexually active. Moreover, Eve Black was allergic to nylon while Eve White was not. About eight months after Eve White began psychoanalysis, a third personality called Jane emerged who combined elements of both Eve White and Eve Black. In time, Eve also assumed numerous other personalities, among them the Spoon Lady who collected spoons and the Blue Lady who wore only blue.

Eve's psychiatrist concluded that Eve's multiple personalities had their origins in a highly traumatic childhood experience—when Eve was five she was forced to kiss the corpse of her dead grandmother. After many years of therapy, Eve was able at last to achieve a fully integrated personality whom she decided to call Evelyn.

Other multiple personalities that have been described in detail are Sybil, whose sixteen different personalities were formed as a defense against unspeakable abuse during her childhood by a schizophrenic mother (Schreiber, 1973); and Jonah (Ludwig et al., 1972), who at various times exhibited four quite different personalities ranging from the shy, conventional Jonah to the belligerent, tough Usoffa Abdullah.

As with all kinds of psychopathology, multiple personalities should be considered the extreme instances of a much more common phenomenon. All of us have different sides to our character. The same person can be gentle and loving at one time in one situation and tough and aggressive at another. We all have both conventional and unconventional impulses that often conflict with each other. Yet most people are aware of these diverse aspects of their own personality and do not see themselves as more than one distinct personality. The difference is one of degree, which is probably why stories of true multiple personalities are so fascinating to many people. The true multiple personality carries several steps further what most of us recognize as a part of our own character.

Chris Sizemore, shown here with her painting entitled *Three Faces in One*, which symbolized her multiple personalities, was the true-life subject of *The Three Faces of Eve.*

BOX 15.3

Examples of schizophrenic condensation, fusion, and abnormal cognition appear in this drawing done by a schizophrenic. Because they are all strong, an ancient warrior, a horse, a mythical bird, mountains, and people are partially identified and fused. The patient wants to convey an ideal of grandeur and strength.

recognize this difference. The specific, observable symptoms of schizophrenia can probably all be traced to this basic cause. Schizophrenics are responding to internal, unrealistic stimuli and therefore their behavior often looks bizarre. This relationship between the internal world of schizophrenics and their overt behavior is often indicated by their responses to hallucinations and delusions. Schizophrenics will respond to voices and visions that no one else perceives. They may also have paranoid feelings of persecution or of being controlled by external forces.

The other most common symptom of schizophrenia is *inappropriate affect*—the expression of emotion inappropriate to the situation. Schizophrenics may be dull and apathetic most of the time, laugh suddenly as at a private joke, cry with no apparent cause, and so on. In general, this inappropriate behavior, particularly the sudden laughing or crying, is in response to an internal world known only to the schizophrenic.

Schizophrenics also often have strange and illogical thought patterns. They may be talking about one subject and jump to a seemingly unrelated one, then go back, and then switch to another all without pausing. They form unusual verbal associations, make up their own words, and generally do not follow logical or consistent trains of thought.

Although schizophrenics often retain their full intelligence and can think rationally and solve problems when they are in touch with reality, even when they are functioning well they will typically think and express themselves in strange ways. For example, when asked to explain the meaning of the saying, "When it rains it pours," a schizophrenic replies with the somewhat sensible, but typically

EXAMPLES OF SCHIZOPHRENIC SPEECH AND WRITING

Q: Why are you in the hospital?
A: I'm a cut doctor, donated by double sacrifice. I get two days for every one. That's known as double sacrifice; in other words, standard cut donator. . . .
Q: Well, what do you do here?
A: I do what is known as the double criminal treatment. Something that he badly wanted, he gets that, and seven days' criminal protection. That's all he gets, and the rest I do for my friend.
Q: Who is the other person that gets all this?
A: That's the way the asylum cut is donated.
Q: But who is the other person?
A: He's a criminal. He gets so much. He gets twenty years' criminal treatment, would make forty years; and he gets seven days criminal protection and that makes fourteen days. That's all he gets.
Q: And what are you?
A: What is known as cut donator Christ. None of them couldn't be able to have anything; so it has

to be true works or prove true to have anything, too. . . . A double sacrifice is what is known as where murder turns, turns the friend into a cut donator and that's what makes a daughter-son. (Cameron, 1947, pp. 446–467)

An essay entitled "Mother of Man"

This creation in which we live began with a Dominant Nature as an Identification Body of a completed evolutionary Strong Material creation in a Major Body Resistance Force. And is fulfilling the Nature Identification in a life Weaker Material Identification creation in which Two Major Bodies have already fulfilled radio body balances, and embodying a Third Material Identification Embodiment of both. (White, 1964, p. 514)

schizophrenic, response: "Nothing more nor less than very wet weather."

Finally, schizophrenics tend to withdraw from social interaction, and to be uncertain where they are and what time it is. In extreme cases they withdraw entirely, no longer talking or reacting, and in a final stage not even moving. Rather than face reality, which they find unbearable, they construct, and then withdraw to, their own inner world.

PARANOID SCHIZOPHRENIA

Mel, a forty-five-year-old bachelor, lived alone in a rented room. He spent his welfare check as soon as it arrived—mostly on books and drawing supplies. He had no umbrella and no winter coat. He often went days without eating anything but chocolate bars. Mel's pleasures were simple: He enjoyed lighting matches; he liked to sketch; he was fond of browsing in bookstores; most of all he loved sitting in coffee houses talking to college students.

Mel described himself as a free-lance inventor, mathematician, scientist, and philosopher. He claimed to have known Einstein and Schweitzer. He insisted that Henry Kissinger sometimes called him for advice. The list of foreign and American presidents who'd consulted him was impressively long; he'd also spoken before the United Nations; and from time to time he'd advised Standard Oil, General Electric, and many other similar corporations. Mel's accomplishments were not confined to advice. He had also invented the color television and the electric can opener; most importantly, he was on the brink of discovering the cure for cancer.

Despite appearances to the contrary, Mel asserted that his inventions had made him rich, a millionaire many times over. But success had brought some heavy burdens with it. As Mel saw it, the heaviest one was envy. Out of envy several state senators were having him tailed and were trying to put him away in a mental hospital. (Davidoff, 1976, p. 411)

Types of schizophrenia Although all schizophrenics have some of the symptoms described above, there are enough differences among them that a number of distinguishable varieties of the condition have been recognized. The American Psychiatric Association lists nine types of schizophrenic reactions, but most therapists deal primarily with the five major varieties listed in Table 15.3. The distinctions among the various types are often arbitrary and difficult to make. A patient may have a combination of symptoms, may resemble one type at one time and another at another, and may also be diagnosed differently by different doctors. Given these differences in classification, it is well to consider the types of schizophrenia not so much as distinct conditions, but rather as general descriptions of the range of symptoms that occur in schizophrenia.

An important point should be made about schizophrenia. There is sometimes a tendency to think that people with these conditions are crazy but happy because many of them laugh a lot and seem to be unconcerned with what is going on in the world. Personal accounts by schizophrenics and observations of their behavior, however, as well as knowledge of what is causing the condition, provide evidence that this is extremely unlikely. In her book *I Never Promised You a Rose Garden*, Hannah Green makes it clear just how miserable schizophrenics are, and this is confirmed by almost every other description by cured or semicured psychotics. The giggling and "happi-

Table 15.3
TYPES OF SCHIZOPHRENIA

Classification*	Symptoms
Infantile autism	Begins at a very early age, perhaps at birth. Extreme withdrawal and lack of reactivity to any kind of stimulation, especially social. Does not form social relationships, learns little if anything, may not speak at all. Rarely responds to treatment—the most hopeless condition. This may be a special disturbance that does not really belong with the other types.
Simple schizophrenia	Also usually begins at an early age, but less severe than infantile autism. May show up in childhood or early adolescence. Individual displays a lack of interest in activities, makes few or no friends, and gradually withdraws from life. Emotional reactions tend to be restricted, activity level is low, ability to deal with the world is poor. Usually the condition is progressive, with all symptoms becoming more and more severe. The condition rarely involves hallucinations or other kinds of extreme behavior. Rather, the person seems to "run down," almost like a watch that has been wound up and is running slower and slower. Responds poorly to treatment.
Hebephrenia	When most people think of schizophrenia, they think of this condition. It involves most of the extreme symptoms including hallucinations, delusions, and strange behavior and thought patterns. Usually the most excited of the conditions, with sometimes violent activity, uncontrolled behavior, and odd movements and gestures. Responds relatively well to treatment, particularly drug therapy.
Paranoid schizophrenia	Somewhat similar to paranoia except that the person does not usually have as complete a paranoid system and also often has hallucinations and inappropriate affect. May be hostile and violent, since thinks other people are enemies. Also responds relatively well to treatment.
Catatonia	This condition is characterized by extreme withdrawal, little or no emotional response, and sometimes total immobility and lack of speech. This lack of activity may be interrupted by brief periods of great excitement.

* These categories are largely for convenience. With the possible exception of infantile autism and simple schizophrenia, the other conditions are generally not distinct. People will usually have symptoms from various categories, and it is difficult if not impossible to classify most schizophrenics into a particular category with any precision.

SCHIZOPHRENIC– HEBEPHRENIC TYPE

Kenneth, an eighteen-year-old boy, had always had difficulty interacting with other people, got into fights, was withdrawn, left school, and could not hold even menial jobs. Became very religious when he burned a small painting of Christ and heard a voice saying, "Whosoever shall burn me will be thrice saved." He began to draw crosses on walls and mirrors, attended church five times every Sunday, and prayed aloud in his back yard while also shouting that the world was coming to an end. In the hospital he felt that the whole world had become a dream, that God was within him, and that he was born two thousand years ago. Kenneth believed that he would soon control everything, including electricity, that people would run from him, and that he heard angels calling him Jesus. Yet he felt that shadows in the halls were snakes trying to kill him. Throughout his affect was flat except for occasional laughter at inappropriate times. (Zax and Stricker, 1963, pp. 65–66)

ness" are a fragile defense against overwhelming anxiety and misery. Even *hebephrenics*, the most cheerful and least inhibited of the schizophrenics, typically lapse into long periods of depression and crying. The fantasy worlds do sometimes provide some comfort and protection, but often they do just the opposite, containing as they do threatening voices and delusions of persecution. Thus, it is a mistake to consider schizophrenics happy lunatics. On the contrary, they seem to be burdened with such great cares and fears that they are unable to remain in the real world. Their retreat is only to relative safety, not to happiness and tranquility.

AUTISM: THE CASE OF PETER

Peter nursed eagerly, sat and walked at the expected ages. Yet some of his behavior made us vaguely uneasy. He never put anything in his mouth. Not his fingers nor his toys—nothing. . . .

More troubling was the fact that Peter didn't look at us, or smile, and wouldn't play the games that seemed as much a part of babyhood as diapers. While he didn't cry, he rarely laughed, and when he did, it was at things that didn't seem funny to us. He didn't cuddle, but sat upright in my lap, even when I rocked him. But children differ and we were content to let Peter be himself. We thought it hilarious when my brother, visiting us when Peter was 8 months old, observed that "that kid has no social instincts, whatsoever." Although Peter was a first child, he was not isolated. I frequently put him in his playpen in front of the house, where the school children stopped to play with him as they passed. He ignored them too. . . .

Peter's babbling had not turned into speech by the time he was three. His play was solitary and repetitious. He tore paper into long thin strips, bushel baskets of it every day. He spun the lids from my canning jars and became upset if we tried to divert him. Only rarely could I catch his eye, and then saw his focus change from me to the reflection in my glasses. It was like trying to pick up mercury with chopsticks.

His adventures into our suburban neighborhood had been unhappy. He had disregarded the universal rule that sand is to be kept in sandboxes, and the children themselves had punished him. He walked around a sad and solitary figure, always carrying a toy aeroplane, a toy he never played with. (Eberhardy, 1967, pp. 257-258)

CAUSES OF PSYCHOPATHOLOGY

There is still a great deal of controversy about what causes the various conditions we have described. The central questions are as follows:
1. Do genetic and physiological factors play a role? Most experts agree that they play no role in the neuroses, but there is disagreement about the psychoses, particularly schizophrenia.
2. Assuming that experience plays some role, to what extent are events early in life crucial? Psychoanalysts tend to stress very early experiences, especially relationships within the family, while behaviorally oriented psychologists place much more emphasis on experiences throughout the individual's life.

Organic Causes

It is clear that some mental disturbance is produced by actual physical damage or deterioration. This is most obvious in psychotic behavior produced by specific damage due to disease, chemicals such as alcohol, trauma, or deterioration produced by aging, and probably in infantile autism, which appears almost at birth. In these cases, the initial and underlying cause of the mental disturbance is the physical condition. The more difficult question is whether less obvious organic factors cause or play a role in other mental disorders. Research has focused on genetic and specific physiological factors.

Genetic factors Heredity plays a substantial role in susceptibility to a wide variety of physical illnesses, including tuberculosis, heart disease, and possibly cancer. It is not surprising, therefore, that researchers have asked whether there is a hereditary factor in mental disorders. At the moment there is little reason to believe that heredity plays a role in the neuroses, but there is substantial evidence for a genetically determined predisposition toward schizophrenia.

As with most investigations of genetic factors (see the discussion of the hereditability of intelligence in Chapter 7), research consists largely of studying family members who share similar genes, and seeing how often they share the same mental conditions. If people who have more similar genes are more likely to share symptoms, this strongly suggests that heredity plays some role. However, it is necessary to eliminate the possibility that people with similar genes have been exposed to similar environmental factors because they are in the same family. Therefore, researchers have developed the ingenious technique of comparing identical twins with fraternal twins. The genes of fraternal twins are no more similar than those of any siblings (brothers and sisters), while identical twins have identical genes. Thus, to the extent that heredity is important, there should be about the same amount of agreement in symptoms among fraternal twins and siblings, while the agreement should be much higher between identical twins.

Many studies have compared the degree of agreement between the following groups: a child and his parents, siblings, fraternal twins, and identical twins. If, for example, one fraternal twin had schizophrenia, in how many cases would the other fraternal twin also have it? As shown in Fig. 15.4, which summarizes the results of this work, the closer the genetic structure of the other person, the more likely the individual was to have the same condition. Only about one person in a hundred has schizophrenia at any one time, but if one parent has it, the chances are about ten out of a hundred that the child will. If one sibling has it, the chance of another sibling having it goes up to 14 percent. The rate is about the same for fraternal twins, but the agreement between identical twins is very high—ranging from 25 percent to over 80 percent, with an average of about 45 percent. Since twins of both types share very similar experiences—they are the same age, both twins, members of the same family, and so on—the greater agreement among identical twins is most likely due to the greater similarity of their genetic makeup.

However, this evidence is not entirely conclusive. The possibility exists that the greater agreement is due to the fact that identical twins are treated more similarly than are fraternal twins. After all, they look almost exactly alike, are less likely to be able to establish separate personalities, and therefore almost certainly share more similar experiences than do fraternal twins. They may also be more closely tied emotionally, so that if one of them becomes disturbed it

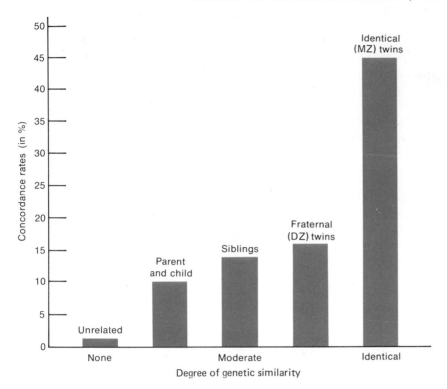

Fig. 15.4
Degree of genetic similarity

The greater the genetic similarity, the higher the likelihood that if one person is schizophrenic the other will be also. Members of the same family have higher concordance than unrelated persons, and identical twins, with identical genes, have much higher concordance than siblings or fraternal twins.

would be more likely to upset the other. Thus, the findings strongly suggest a genetic role in schizophrenia but cannot be considered definite proof.

Additional evidence for the role of heredity comes from studies of children raised by foster parents. When the natural parents are schizophrenic, the likelihood of their children also being schizophrenic is greatly increased (Wender, Rosenthal, and Kety, 1968; Heston, 1970). Since all of the children were removed from their parents' home very early in life, this result cannot be due to how the natural parents treat the child. The conclusion is that it is due to genetic factors.

The evidence overall strongly suggests that heredity plays some role in schizophrenia. Some early research (for example, Kallman, 1946) almost certainly overstated the role of genetic factors and misled some people into concluding that heredity was the major or perhaps the only cause of schizophrenia. More careful research, such as the massive study by Kringlen (1969), seems closer to the truth. He found a substantial (38 percent) agreement between identical twins, but clearly the remaining 62 percent leaves lots of room for other causes. It now appears that genetic factors do not by themselves produce schizophrenia or other mental disorders but do make the individual more or less susceptible to various conditions.

Specific physiological causes There has been a continuing search for specific organic causes of schizophrenia. Sarnoff Mednick (1970) has suggested that it is due in part to temporary deprivation of oxygen during pregnancy, which causes brain damage, possibly centered around the hippocampus (see Chapter 8). This damage in turn produces the symptoms we call schizophrenia, or at least makes the individual more susceptible to the development of these symptoms.

Mednick's theory has not received wide acceptance because the evidence is still unconvincing to most psychologists. Criticism has also been leveled at the idea that hippocampal damage would produce the symptoms of schizophrenia (Kessler and Neale, 1974). Nevertheless, the idea that brain damage is involved in schizophrenia remains plausible.

Another suggestion has been that schizophrenics might have some specific deviations from normal bodily chemistry that would account for the condition. For a short time there was great excitement about a substance called *tarexin*, which was taken from the blood of schizophrenics and which some researchers (Heath et al., 1957) claimed produced schizophrenic symptoms in normals. However, other experimenters could not replicate those results (for example, Siegel at al., 1959) and the idea has generally been dropped. More recently, Wise and Stein reported (1977) that schizophrenics' lack of a biochemical agent may cause damage in the "pleasure" centers of the brain. In addition, some of the psychedelic drugs, such as LSD and mescalin, can temporarily cause schizophrenic-like symptoms. Although these conditions are clearly different from schizophrenia, the fact that they can be produced by a chemical suggested that schizophrenia might have chemical causes.

Unfortunately, this research too has thus far failed to produce any answers. Most of the initial findings either do not hold up when the experiment is repeated or seem to lead nowhere. Although there are many promising findings, at the present time there is no definitive evidence that the body chemistry of schizophrenics differs in any way from that of healthy persons. There is, however, substantial reason to believe that psychotic depression is due to organic factors. In particular, it seems likely that at least some depressives suffer from unnaturally low reactivity in the brain. As we shall see in Chapter 16, chemicals that increase neural reactivity are often successful treatment for depression.

In addition, there is strong evidence that physical factors are a partial cause of some mental disturbances. We have already mentioned that involutional melancholia tends to occur around the menopause in women and somewhat later in men. The psychological feeling of getting old and particularly of no longer being able to bear children is undoubtedly an important factor in this condition. However, the hormonal changes that occur during menopause almost certainly contribute. Similarly, many women suffer a so-called *postpartum depression* after giving birth to a child. Here again, the psychological pressures of motherhood following the long period of pregnancy are the major cause of the depression, but the physical changes in the body also play a role. At the moment we do not know of any close links between physical factors and most of the neuroses. Nevertheless, it seems likely that various organic conditions will be found to be precipitating or aggravating causes in a number of mental disorders.

The Role of Experience

There is broad agreement that experience plays an important role in the development of all of the mental disorders. Even in conditions that clearly are due largely to specific organic damage, such as brain injury or senility, psychological factors are quite important. Seemingly identical injuries may produce severe disturbance in one person and not in another. Individual experiences and personality seem to affect susceptibility to mental disorders even when the precipitating cause is obvious physical damage. And clearly, experience will have relatively more importance when there is no physical damage. Thus neuroses, personality disorders, and psychoses are generally assumed to be caused at least in part by individual experiences.

As we saw in discussing theories of personality (Chapter 13), both the psychoanalytic and social learning approaches stress the importance of experience. These theories are also useful in helping us understand how mental disorders develop. Let us consider each of these approaches in turn.

Psychoanalytic theory of mental disorder Psychoanalytic (Freudian and neo-Freudian) theories explain all of the mental disturbances in basically the same way. Some unacceptable wish, conflict, impulse, memory, or desire is repressed and made unconscious because the individual cannot tolerate it consciously. This unconscious content constantly strives for expression while the ego continually fights against it. All mental disturbance is essentially the result of this battle, with the specific symptom being the manifestation of the defensive mechanisms. For example, as we described earlier, the obsessive-compulsive neurotic who is concerned about masturbation may wash his hands constantly in order to relieve the guilt associated with the unacceptable desire and also to keep himself occupied so that he will be distracted from the source of his anxiety. The bombadeer who was terrified of being killed repressed that fear but fainted whenever he was above eight thousand feet, thus guaranteeing that he would not be able to fly. Each symptom is used to keep the unconscious impulse repressed and thereby ward off anxiety.

According to this theory, the severity of the condition is determined by the type of unconscious conflict, and by the stage of psychosexual development at which it appears. The emphasis is on conflicts that develop early in life. The earlier in life the problem occurs, the more serious will be the mental disturbance. As we described earlier (Chapters 12 and 14), children face a series of crucial conflicts, each of which must be adequately resolved in order for them to progress in a healthy manner. As they resolve each conflict, children grow in strength, their egos become better developed, the relationship between their conscious and unconscious desires becomes more resolved, and they are better able to face and deal with later problems. If the earliest conflict is not solved well, naturally it will be the most difficult to cope with later and the amount of damage will be the greatest. The later in life the conflict appears, the better able people will be to cope, and the less damage it will do.

Thus, conflicts that revolve around the initial problem described by Erikson of trust versus mistrust will lead to the most serious conditions. If a child is not fed and comforted at birth, she may never develop an integrated personality. Most psychoanalysts would trace very severe psychosis to this early stage. In Erikson's terms, the child has never developed basic trust in the world. Accordingly, at some stage in life, when other problems appear as precipitating causes, this child may retreat entirely into a schizophrenic fantasy life. The specific nature of the unconscious conflicts may vary, but they will always concern in part the need for being taken care of and the fear that this need will not be met.

When the conflicts appear at later stages, during the anal or Oedipal period, the disturbances may be somewhat less severe, but they can still be very serious. On the theory that someone who did not resolve the very earliest conflict probably could not resolve later ones, most schizophrenics are thought to have serious conflicts stemming from all of the crucial stages of development.

Neuroses and personality disorders are generally thought to stem from the same childhood conflicts as psychoses, but the individual was better able to resolve them. Therefore the anxiety connected with a particular conflict is less, the adjustment mechanisms are better integrated, and when symptoms appear they are accordingly less severe. Although neurotics have difficulty dealing with the world, unlike the psychotics, they have not broken with reality. The following example illustrates how a particular conflict might lead to a neurotic condition.

A woman who has an unresolved conflict about her sexual feelings may experience anxiety whenever she is with men. She is afraid that she will show her own "forbidden" sexual feelings. (Bear in mind that according to Freudian theory, all or most of the conflict is unconscious—in fact the woman would deny vigorously that she felt any sexual feelings at all under these circumstances.) The result of this unconscious conflict is that she feels enormous anxiety whenever she is with men. This could produce an anxiety neurosis, in which she experiences anxiety in these situations. Or it could lead to an obsessive-compulsive neurosis in which, perhaps, she touches everything in a room twenty times, turns around five times, washes her hands three times before shaking hands with a man, and so on. This would distract her from her conflict and also, no doubt, make her less attractive, thereby reducing the chance that she will be approached sexually. Or she could develop a hysterical symptom such as blindness that would make it much harder for her to meet men and also less attractive when she did meet them. And a final possibility would be the development of a phobia, perhaps a great fear of social gatherings, which would prevent any social interactions with men.

All of these results would be due to the unconscious conflict and all (except the anxiety neurosis) would serve to reduce the anxiety. According to Freud, the particular symptom chosen is not purely random, but has significance in terms of the particular conflict and the individual's history. But the process is about the same for all conditions.

Because the emphasis in psychoanalytic theory is on conflicts that develop early in life, research on schizophrenia has focused largely on the relationship between the mother and child. Researchers hypothesized that the mothers of schizophrenics would be cold, ungiving people who never gave the baby the warmth and attention it needed. These so-called *schizophrenogenic* mothers would produce children who were themselves so cold and withdrawn that they become mentally disturbed. However, research results have been inconclusive; in many cases, it is difficult to establish that mothers of schizophrenic children differed substantially from mothers of children who developed normally. When differences are found, they are not consistent. Clausen and Kohn (1960) found mothers of schizophrenics to be cold, anxious, overcontrolling, and restrictive. Wolman (1965) found them to be tyrannical but self-sacrificing, and to demand unceasing love. Klebanoff (1959) found that parents of schizophrenic, brain-injured, and retarded children were more possessive and overcontrolling than mothers of normal children. Lidz, Fleck, and Cornelison (1965) found that parents of schizophrenics fought between themselves. Kokonis (1973) reported that parents of schizophrenics had weak sex-role identification. In other words, there are many differences but not always what the theory predicts.

It should be noted that research on the early relationship between mother and child is fraught with difficulties. Most of it is retrospective; people are trying to remember how a mother acted ten, fifteen, or twenty years ago and such memories are vague and often distorted. In addition, there is always the possibility that even if the mother was cold and withdrawn, she may have behaved this way because her child did not respond to her normally. As noted in Chapter 12, children also affect parents. In other words, it could be that the child was withdrawn and the mother gave less love because the child was less rewarding to her.

Research has shown a greater than normal incidence of schizophrenia among lower-class children (Hollingshead and Redlich, 1958). This suggests that economic pressure within the family may interfere with the child's development. And there also is evidence (Hilgard and Newman, 1961) that schizophrenics are more likely than normals to have lost one of their parents early in life. Thus, the research presents a somewhat mixed pattern. Most of it is consistent with the psychoanalytic idea that disruption of the home or mistreatment early in life are the causes of schizophrenia. However, the findings are far from definitive and we must await additional research to provide support for this explanation.

Social learning and behavior therapy Another approach is to consider psychopathology a problem in learning. According to social learning theorists such as Albert Bandura (1969) and behavior therapists such as Joseph Wolpe (1969), people acquire psychopathology through interaction with the environment just as they acquire a vocabulary, knowledge of physics, or achievement motivation. Whereas some people learn to deal well with the world, other people develop unhealthy or maladaptive ways of behaving that are destructive, that cause conflicts with others, and that make it difficult or impossible for them to cope with problems. These maladaptive behaviors are what we mean by psychopathology. (See Box 3.7 for a discussion of learned helplessness, a learning explanation of depression.)

Thus, the development of psychopathology must follow all the basic learning principles we described in Chapters 3 and 4. Operant

JOSEPH WOLPE

BOX 15.4

PSYCHOSOMATIC CONDITIONS

Just as physical conditions can produce mental disorders, so is the reverse true. We have already seen that people can deliberately control their own brain waves, can cause their hearts to speed up or slow down, that under hypnosis and meditation individuals can achieve physical control over their body (which is rare if not impossible in normal states), and that there is some evidence to indicate conditioning of internal processes such as insulin shock and blood pressure. It should therefore not be surprising that disturbed mental conditions sometimes produce physical illnesses.

Sometimes this relationship is straightforward. For example, someone who is always nervous or excited may have an enlarged adrenal gland. The reason for this is simply that the adrenal gland is more active, and becomes larger. This is not necessarily an unhealthy condition, but it does show one direct effect of mental state on the body. A subtler effect is the formation of stomach and duodenal ulcers. Psychoanalyst Franz Alexander (1950) proposed that ulcers were caused by specific psychological conflicts. People who were constantly torn between being aggressive and passive were supposed to be particularly subject to ulcers. Hard-driving business executives are often required to be extremely assertive and aggressive at work, but many of them also have the natural desire to let other people make their decisions and take care of them. This conflict, according to Alexander, causes a constant flow of excess gastric juices that eventually may produce an ulcer. This speculation was based on observation of patients but received remarkable support from experimental research on monkeys (Brady et al., 1958). In a series of studies, pairs of animals were subjected to electric shocks at unpredictable intervals. One of the animals (the so-called executive monkey) was given the responsibility of turning off the shock. By pressing a lever at least once every twenty seconds, he could avoid or terminate the shock. In other words, both monkeys received the identical amount of shock, but one of them had the job of operating the lever. Only the executive monkey developed ulcers. The situation is not exactly analogous to Alexander's notion of the passive-aggressive personality, but it does appear that having both the worry and responsibility produced the

JOSEPH V. BRADY

and classical conditioning, association, and imitation all play a role. Rules of timing, size of reward, schedules of reinforcement, discrimination, and stimulus generalization apply to neurotic behaviors just as they apply to any other behavior. Someone with hysterical blindness has learned this behavior because it was reinforced at some time; obsessive symptoms are learned because they enable the person to escape unpleasant situations; and so on.

Proponents of this approach are applying well-established principles of learning to the explanation and treatment of psychopathology.

ulcers. The psychological state of having to be alert and operate the lever led to the physical damage.

A similar, more recent experiment, on the other hand, had the opposite result (Weiss, 1972). In this study the "executive" monkey was given a warning signal and by turning a wheel could avoid the shock entirely. Under these circumstances, the executive fared better than its helpless partner.

It seems likely that both decision making and lack of control are stressful. In the earlier studies, there was no clear warning, so the executive had the responsibility of constantly deciding whether to press the lever without getting a clear reward. This is like many real situations in which you have to make difficult decisions and will not know for some time, if ever, whether you were right. But if your decision immediately turns out to be correct, as in the Weiss study, it is better to have power to control our own fate (see Box 3.7).

At the present time research on psychosomatic medicine is in an early state. Although a few links between mental and physical conditions have been established, there are vast areas yet to explore. It is likely that psychological factors play a role in the development of asthma and hypertension, but the connection has not been demonstrated conclusively. Some researchers have suggested that practically all of our physical conditions are brought on or at least aggravated by our mental state. This may be too extreme a position; nevertheless, mental tension and disturbance probably have profound effects on the physical state of our bodies.

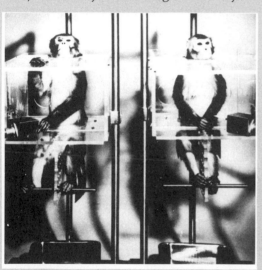

The executive monkey

JAY WEISS

If someone pronounced a particular word strangely or had bad form in tennis, everyone would assume that this was due to poor learning and would try to teach the person the correct way of doing things. Although psychopathological behaviors are much more complex, they should, according to this view, be dealt with in the same way. Since we have a large body of information about learning, we should use it to enable people to learn the right way of behaving; that is, learn to get rid of their psychopathology and to develop healthier ways of behaving.

This view of the causes of mental disturbances is not necessarily inconsistent with the psychoanalytic approach. As we discussed in Chapter 14, both theories place considerable emphasis on the individual's interaction with the world, and consider mental disturbance the result of unhealthy or stressful experience. But the psychoanalytic explanation focuses on specific events and conflicts in the individual's life, mostly those occurring in the very early years, while social learning theory deals with more general processes. In a sense, social learning theory provides a rigorous, experimentally verified framework for the more specific statements of psychoanalytic theory.

There is one crucial disagreement between the two approaches. The psychoanalytic approach always assumes that a symptom is the result of an underlying conflict, and that removing a symptom without dealing with the conflict will result in some other symptom appearing—so-called *symptom substitution*. Most social learning theorists do not believe this—they maintain that a symptom is the result of learning, so that once it is removed no underlying problem remains.

Despite their differences, the psychoanalytic and social learning theories both stress the role of experience in mental disorders. Organic factors clearly cause some conditions and make individuals more susceptible to others, such as schizophrenia. But interactions with the world are at the heart of neuroses and are also critical in most psychoses.

PREVALENCE OF PSYCHOPATHOLOGY

Neurosis, personality disorders, and psychosis are extremely common. Except for tooth decay and the common cold, they are probably more prevalent than any physical illness. Although it is difficult to get accurate figures, it has been estimated that probably one person in ten will suffer from a psychosis at one time or another. Careful studies in New York City and New Haven, Connecticut (Hollingshead and Redlich, 1958; Myers and Bean, 1968) support this rough estimate. Of course, at any one time only 1 percent of the population or fewer are actually psychotic, but that still means that almost half the people occupying hospital beds are psychotic or suffering from some other mental condition. Neurosis is even more prevalent. It is almost impossible to get accurate estimates, because neurotics are rarely hospitalized and because the determination of whether or not someone is neurotic is often very difficult. Also, many people who are disturbed will nevertheless not think of themselves as neurotic and will not seek professional help. Various studies have produced estimates of the number of neurotics ranging from 5 percent of the adult population to as high as 37 percent. The most careful observations (Srole et al., 1962, 1974; Leighton et al., 1963; and so on) indicate that between 20 and 30 percent of the population have symptoms serious enough to interfere with and restrict their daily lives.

These rates of mental illness are approximately the same for big cities and small towns and even for small, nonindustrialized tribes in

Australia and Africa (Dohrenwend and Dohrenwend, 1974). While living in New York City, Chicago, or any other major urban center may put certain additional pressure on the individual, it does not appear that it increases the incidence of mental disturbance. As we shall discuss in Chapter 19 on environmental psychology, crowding is not a factor in mental illness. Nor does it appear that simply living in a city increases the chance of being neurotic or psychotic. There are, however, systematic differences between socioeconomic classes in terms of psychosis, with lower-class people having a much higher rate. This may be due not so much to actual incidence as to the ability of more affluent families either to take care of psychotic members themselves (for example, hiring a nurse) or to place them under private care where the case is less likely to be recorded. There do not seem to be comparable class differences in rates of neurosis, although there is some suggestion that the type of neurosis suffered varies by class.

Clearly, mental disturbance is remarkably widespread. It seems as if barely a majority of the population manages to get through life without suffering from either neurosis or psychosis. The typical reaction to this fact is horrified disbelief. What is wrong with our society that so many people are mentally disturbed? But it is well to have some perspective on this problem.

The psychological and social development of the individual from birth to adulthood is exceedingly complicated and treacherous. If we think of all the experiences, problems, conflicts, and cross-pressures that children are subjected to, it seems a miracle that anyone can get through them and manage to adapt to society. Children must learn a vast number of things about the world, how to take care of themselves, who everyone is, what various things are, and, of course, language. They must also learn very subtle, complicated, and often contradictory pieces of information having to do with acceptable behavior, morality, and the expectations of parents and society. With all of this, they must somehow manage to achieve a compromise between their own needs and desires and the limitations placed on them by other people. It is an incredibly complex task and it should be no surprise that many people have difficulty making a satisfactory adjustment.

This is not to say that such a high rate of mental illness is inevitable but only that it is understandable given these enormous pressures. It is to be hoped that in the future, psychologists will better understand the processes involved in the development of personality and will be able to reduce somewhat the incidence of mental disturbance. It is also hoped that the methods of treating these disturbances will improve to the point where the disturbances can be more readily and quickly cured. For the moment, however, we must accept this high rate of mental disturbance and do what we can to understand and treat the condition. ▪

Summary

1. Although mental health is a complex and somewhat subjective concept, there are certain criteria that help us distinguish between healthy and unhealthy behavior. Thinking or behavior that encourages self-actualization and that is in touch with real-

ity is usually considered healthy, while thinking or behavior that prevents the expression of one's potential or that indicates a break with reality is usually considered unhealthy. Behavior that consistently deviates greatly from the norm is often an indication of some disturbance, though of course it may be perfectly normal.

2. The term psychopathology refers to mental disturbance or disorder. The three major classes of disorders are: neuroses, personality disorders, and psychoses.

3. A neurosis is characterized by the presence of anxiety and the inability of the individual to take positive action to reduce the anxiety. Instead, neurotics develop behavior patterns to avoid the problem. Neurosis is less severe than psychosis in that people are not out of touch with reality and can function fairly well, but to a greater or lesser extent the anxiety prevents freedom of action. The most prevalent types of neurosis are anxiety neurosis, phobias, obsessive-compulsive neurosis, and hysterical or conversion neurosis.

4. Personality disorders consist of behaviors or personal characteristics that are harmful to the individual or to other people. Narcissism is a particularly common personality disorder in which the person is egotistical and has fantasies of wealth and power, but also suffers from feelings of insecurity and inferiority. In addition, narcissists are unable to care deeply about others. A psychopathic personality is characterized by the lack of a moral sense and the inability to delay gratification, experience guilt, or care about others.

5. Psychosis is the most severe form of psychopathology and involves some type of break with reality. The three major types of psychosis are manic-depression, paranoia, and schizophrenia.

6. Manic-depression incorporates two related states. In the manic state, which is brief and easily shattered, the person is wildly elated; in the depressive state, the person experiences severe negative feelings about self, other people, and events. Manic-depressives break with reality in that nothing that happens—either good or bad—has much effect on their mood.

7. Paranoics have a persistent delusion (false mental conception), such as the belief that one is Jesus Christ. They also have irrational feelings of persecution. Many people have paranoid feelings at one time or another, but in the true paranoic, the delusional symptoms persist.

8. Schizophrenia is the most serious type of mental disorder and the one that most often requires hospitalization. Schizophrenics experience fantasies and hallucinations, exhibit illogical thought patterns and inappropriate affect (expressing emotions that are not appropriate to the situation), and may withdraw entirely into an inner world.

9. Research on the organic causes of schizophrenia has focused on the roles of heredity and body chemistry. In studying the influence of heredity on schizophrenia, researchers have developed the technique of comparing identical twins with fraternal twins. Findings strongly suggest that there is a genetic role in schizo-

phrenia but that hereditary factors do not by themselves produce schizophrenia. Research connecting brain damage to schizophrenia has not been widely accepted, but the connection remains plausible. Similarly, there has been little evidence that the body chemistry of schizophrenics is different from that of healthy persons.

10. Psychoanalytic theories view mental disturbance as the result of a struggle between unconscious desires or impulses and the rational mind (ego), which tries to prevent their being expressed. Since resolution of conflicts at the earliest psychosexual stages is essential to healthy development, conflicts unresolved early in life will produce the most serious disorders (psychoses). Neuroses and personality disorders result from the same conflicts as psychoses, but the individual was better able to resolve them.

11. Social learning theorists and behavior therapists believe psychopathology is acquired by the ordinary learning processes—classical and operant conditioning, reinforcement, imitation, and the like. The disorder is in essence maladaptive behavior that has been learned. While they have different emphases and disagree on the question of symptom substitution, both psychoanalytic and learning theories stress the role of experience in mental disorders.

12. Mental disturbance is a serious and widespread problem. It is estimated that one person in ten will suffer from a psychosis at one time or another and that between 20 and 30 percent of the population have symptoms that interfere with their daily lives.

RECOMMENDED READING

Beck, A. T. *Depression: Clinical, Experimental and Theoretical Aspects.* New York: Hoeber Medical Division, Harper & Row, 1967. An influential book about depression. Not easy reading. An advanced text, but about as good coverage of the topic as can be found.

Coleman, J. *Abnormal Psychology and Modern Life,* 5th ed. Glenview, Ill.: Scott, Foresman, 1976. One of the most widely used textbooks in the field. No particular approach or theory is stressed—a quite balanced presentation.

Davison, C. C., and J. M. Neale. *Abnormal Psychology.* New York: Wiley, 1974. The behaviorist view of the problem.

Freud, S. *New Introductory Lectures on Psychoanalysis.* New York: Norton, 1933. Not new, of course, but the best review of his theory, including the development of psychopathology.

Szasz, T. S. *The Myth of Mental Illness: Foundations of a Theory of Personal Conduct.* New York: Harper & Row, 1961. As the title says, this book presents the view that it is a mistake to talk in terms of mental illness, that the analogy to medical disease is misleading and inaccurate.

Fortunately, analysis is not the only way to resolve inner conflicts. Life itself still remains a very effective therapist.
Karen Horney

If anything affects your eye, you hasten to have it removed; if anything affects your mind, you postpone the cure for a year.
Horace, Epistles

16 Treatment of Psychopathology

Who does therapy? ■ *Types of treatment* ■ *Organic techniques* ■ *Psychological techniques* ■ *Psychoanalytic psychotherapy* ■ *Behavior therapy* ■ *Behavior therapy and psychoanalysis compared* ■ *Humanistic therapies* ■ *Other psychological techniques* ■ *Evaluation*

For centuries, the mentally ill were treated with the cruel hostility of ignorance. The painting below by the sixteenth-century artist Hieronymus Bosch satirized the ignorance of the day, when patients were deluded into thinking their madness was caused by ''stones of folly,'' which must be plucked from their head. The doctor's funnel symbolizes fraud, while the jug represents the devil. In the drawing below, an insane patient is kept in ''the crib'' at a New York institution in 1882.

Attitudes toward psychopathology have changed dramatically during the last two centuries. Until quite recently, minor disturbances were either ignored or considered merely a problem of willpower, while severe disturbances were thought to be due to spirits that were inhabiting the person. People who heard voices or went into trances might be highly respected or even worshipped if the public decided that they were inhabited by good spirits; but most of the time the spirits were assumed to be evil and the people were loathed and feared. Treatment was often inhumane. Psychotics were usually forced to live apart from the rest of society, either driven from the community or, in later times, put in insane asylums that were often worse than prisons. Because their condition was caused by an evil demon, a common form of treatment was torture, which was intended to drive out the demon.

Humane treatment also involved elaborate techniques to cast out the evil. Medicine men performed dances, prescribed herbs, and engaged in complex rituals to rid people of evil forces. Similarly, Western religions developed complicated procedures—*exorcisms*—for casting out devils (as popularized in various movies including *The Exorcist*).

More sophisticated methods that were supposed to involve scientific principles began to emerge in the eighteenth century. Occasional use was made of magnets applied to the body to draw out the evil or alter the internal forces. And Anton Mesmer, who discovered hypnosis, attempted to accomplish the same end with the use of animal magnetism—a force held to reside in some individuals—which he focused by the use of a wand or a large vat filled with magnetized water. By this time, there was a gradual move away from the notion of evil spirits, but the emphasis was still on unexplained, uncontrolled forces within the body that had to be eliminated. It was only in the nineteenth century that people began to understand that psychosis and other severe mental disturbance might have psychological or physical causes.

Charcot, Breuer, and Freud began to treat mental disorders in a new way. Since almost all of these early pioneers came from a medical tradition (Freud was a physiologist), they tended to view mental disturbance in much the same way as they would a physical illness.

The patient was "sick," and needed to be treated. Although now we recognize that there are a number of problems with the concept of "mental illness" (see Box 16.1), at that time it was both revolutionary and hopeful. It meant that a mental disorder was not caused by evil spirits, that people should not be stigmatized because of it, and most important, that there was a chance the condition could be cured. Thus this new view led to a dramatic shift toward humane and systematic treatment.

However, even now many people feel that psychopathology is not so much a condition as a weakness. According to this view, people with enough willpower should be able to solve their own problems and deal with their own conflicts without outside help. People who are extremely anxious or phobic are just scared; all they need to do is to get hold of themselves, show some determination, and they will overcome their difficulties.

While no one would tell a crippled polio victim that he will be able to walk if he puts his mind to it, or a child with poor eyesight that she will be able to see if she only concentrates harder, mental

THE CONCEPT OF MENTAL ILLNESS

The discovery that mental disorders were a form of illness was a great improvement over the earlier notions that involved devils or inherent evil. This meant that the condition had a specific cause and might respond to treatment. The search for a cure made sense. However, there is now some question whether the concept of mental illness is appropriate.

The major argument against it, given by Thomas Szasz in *The Myth of Mental Illness* (1971), is that the medical analogy does not fit. Except for those conditions that are caused by specific organic or genetic factors, there is no underlying cause. The symptom itself *is* the problem. Pneumonia is caused by a virus; a skin rash is caused by a fungus. Kill or weaken the virus or the fungus and the symptoms will disappear. And if you cover over the rash or remove it without treating the fungus, the rash will probably reappear. But in mental disorders, the symptom is mainly a problem in living, a maladaptive behavior that must be unlearned or replaced. The person is not sick in the medical sense of the word any more than someone who fails a math exam because he has learned the wrong answers. In both

instances, appropriate learning will eliminate the problem. Many behavior therapists agree with this point of view, and the term "disorder" or "disturbance" is generally replacing "illness."

On the other hand, as you would expect, psychoanalytically inclined therapists would dispute this position. They feel that there is an underlying cause, and that treatment should focus on removing it. This makes the concept of mental illness more appropriate and even useful in that it implies that the patient is sick, cannot function normally, and needs help.

Whichever position is favored, there is more and more concern for the rights of those with mental or behavioral disorders. Most states still allow people to be put in mental hospitals even against their will at the request of one or more physicians, even if the physicians are not specialists in psychiatry. And once in the hospital, the burden of proof may be on the patient to prove that she is sane enough to be released. New laws are gradually being introduced that make it much harder to put someone in a hospital against her will and much easier for her to get out.

Box 16.1

disturbances have been given much less understanding. This has certainly been true in the United States, where tradition holds that people should be strong, independent, and able to take care of themselves. While we are expected to turn to physicians for medical care and teachers for instruction, for some reason mental conditions are considered a person's own fault.

Fortunately, more and more people are coming to accept the fact that psychopathology is quite common, is no more the person's fault than any other difficulty, is not a sign of inherent weakness or lack of willpower, and very often requires expert care. During the last twenty or thirty years most colleges have provided therapy as part of their medical program, and an extremely high percentage of students have taken advantage of this. Since so many college students have at one time or another received some therapy, they are naturally much more accepting of this approach. This does not mean that any conflict or unhappiness should cause someone to go to a therapist, but when the conflict becomes severe enough to interfere with individuals' lives, they should feel free to seek professional help.

In this chapter we shall discuss current treatment of psychopathology—who does it and the particular methods they use. The techniques include physical-organic procedures such as electric shock and drugs, and psychological approaches such as traditional psychoanalytic therapy and behavior therapy. Finally, we consider the question of the effectiveness of these treatments.

WHO DOES THERAPY?

There are now several disciplines that deal with psychopathology. As you can see in Table 16.1, psychiatrists, psychoanalysts, clinical psychologists, and psychiatric social workers all receive systematic training in treating these conditions. The table outlines some of the differences in the educational experience of these specialists, but there is a great deal of overlap in both training and the treatment they offer (see Box 16.2). In fact, differences in treatment offered by the various specialists are often due more to their theoretical orientation, personal experience, and even personality than to their specific training.

Table 16.1
WHO TREATS PSYCHOPATHOLOGY?

Discipline	Training	Methods favored
Psychiatrist	Medical degree plus psychiatric internship and residency	Traditional psychotherapy, organic treatment, eclectic
Psychoanalyst	Same as psychiatrist plus psychoanalytic institute	All of above but especially psychoanalysis
Clinical psychologist	Ph.D. in psychology with clinical internship	All psychological methods, behavior therapy
Psychiatric social worker	Master of Social Work	Psychological methods, group therapy, work with family

CLINICAL PSYCHOLOGISTS, PSYCHIATRISTS, AND PSYCHOANALYSTS

Many people have difficulty distinguishing among psychologists—especially clinical psychologists—psychiatrists, and psychoanalysts. Members of all of these disciplines treat mental disturbance and often use similar techniques. The one clear distinction involves training and the educational degree that is held. A clinical psychologist attends graduate school in psychology, takes part in a clinical internship that consists of practical training in a treatment center (such as a mental hospital or clinic), and receives a doctoral degree in psychology. A psychiatrist attends medical school, does a psychiatric residency (again in a clinical setting), and receives an M.D. (doctor of medicine). A psychoanalyst in almost all cases also goes through medical school and a psychiatric residency and then attends an institute for psychoanalysis where intensive training in practical techniques of therapy is given. (A few nonmedical people are allowed to attend the psychoanalytic institutes, but they are the rare exception.) Thus, psychiatrists and psychoanalysts are physicians; clinical psychologists are not. Accordingly, the former can prescribe drugs and medical treatments and the latter cannot. However, many clinical psychologists work with physicians and can therefore arrange to have drugs prescribed when necessary.

All three disciplines use a variety of therapy techniques, but there tend to be some differences among the specialties. Psychoanalysts use traditional Freudian methods; psychiatrists often make greater use of drugs than the others do; and clinical psychologists often favor behavior therapy and other techniques that have grown out of psychological research. However, it is important to realize that there is considerable variation among the specialties, and that a member of any one may use most of the techniques available. Thus, some psychiatrists use behavior therapy, while some psychologists use traditional psychotherapy, and so on. Moreover, most people who provide treatment for mental disturbance employ a variety of methods rather than relying on only one.

Many other people receive some less formal training in dealing with disorders of thought and behavior. Clergymen, teachers, lawyers, and the police often take courses in this field. Thus, more and more people are available to give some form of treatment and some understanding to those suffering from mental disorders.

TYPES OF TREATMENT

A great many different techniques and approaches are used in the treatment of mental disorders. However, one basic distinction that should be pointed out is between approaches that involve organic, physical treatment and those that do not. Often physical and psychological methods are used together, but the emphasis of the two approaches is clearly quite different. Therefore, we shall first discuss electric shock, drugs, and other physical therapies and then turn to a consideration of such psychologically oriented methods as psychoanalytic therapy, behavior therapy, and various humanistic therapies.

ORGANIC TECHNIQUES

The assumption underlying all organic techniques is that the condition is due at least in part to physical causes. If there is something wrong with the person's brain function, if there is chemical imbalance or any other physiological cause, organic treatment may be effective. This kind of therapy is especially appropriate with conditions that appear to have organic causes, such as schizophrenia, but it can also be useful with conditions that are largely psychological in nature. Although organic techniques do not deal with psychological conflicts or learning problems, they can alleviate symptoms and make it easier to treat the patient psychologically if that seems necessary. In addition, with the exception of psychosurgery, organic treatment is relatively cheap and efficient and is therefore widely used. New organic treatments are constantly being tried. At the moment, the most successful are electroshock treatment of depression and drug therapy for a variety of conditions.

Electroshock therapy

Passing a powerful electric current through a person's head appears to be a useful treatment of severe depression. In this procedure, usually called *electroconvulsive shock* (ECS), electrodes are fastened to a patient's head and a current ranging from 7 to 130 volts is applied for one-tenth to one-half a second. This produces a convulsion consisting of a sudden flexing of the body. All the muscles contract at once, the arms and legs are thrown outward, and the whole body becomes rigid. This is followed by a so-called *clonic phase*, in which there are minor convulsions and jerking contractions of the arms and legs. The full convulsion lasts for one-half to a full minute. After the convulsion, the patient remains unconscious for some time—between ten and thirty minutes—and upon awakening is drowsy, confused, and often has a headache and other pains.

Electroshock treatment sounds primitive and barbaric. The idea of passing an electric shock through someone's head sounds too similar to execution to be easily accepted as a therapeutic treatment. Nevertheless, there is substantial reason to believe that electroshock therapy produces consistently positive effects in cases of severe depression (Noyes and Kolb, 1963; Wortis, 1960). Both psychotic depression and involutional melancholia seem to respond well to this treatment. Exactly why it has this effect is unclear, but it is difficult to argue with its success.

On the other hand, there is considerable question about the long-term effects of extended courses of electroshock therapy. Most psychiatrists and psychologists believe that eventually it causes memory loss, an inability to concentrate, and perhaps an actual reduction in intellectual ability. Even one shock produces an almost total loss of memory for recent events. Typically patients cannot remember what happened during the hour or two before they received the treatment and some patients also lose memories that go back as far as several days. On the other hand, there is little evidence of any long-term memory loss, or of any negative physical side effects. Depressives who receive five or perhaps ten treatments are often greatly helped by them. But schizophrenics who have received hundreds are not only not helped but probably suffer substantial damage (Leukel, 1957). Partly because of the likelihood of negative effects and partly because of the availability of new drugs, less reliance is being put on shock therapy than in the past.

Psychosurgery

The most radical form of physical treatment involves actual surgery on the brain. It was believed that if you cut some of the pathways between the prefrontal lobe and the hypothalamus you would thereby reduce the flow of emotions and disturbing thoughts. This procedure, called *prefrontal lobotomy*, or leucotomy, was introduced in 1937 by Moniz and improved by Freeman and Watts in 1942 (see Box 10.2).

Prefrontal lobotomy did seem to reduce anxiety and make patients calmer. Unfortunately this was accompanied by a loss of personality—after the operation, patients were typically cheerful, inane, complacently stupid, unconcerned about the world, and unable to feel strong emotions or attachments. Their intellectual ability was also somewhat reduced, but this effect was overshadowed by the personality change. In other words, although the operation sometimes reduced the most severe anxiety connected with a mental disturbance, the cost was enormous in that individuals were no longer the same people as before. The surgery is a success but the person disappears.

Today lobotomies are no longer performed. However, a great deal of research is being done on other kinds of psychosurgery and it may be that sometime in the future we will know enough about the relationship between brain structure and mental activity to devise surgical procedures that can effectively treat mental disturbances without producing negative consequences.

Chemical Therapy

By far the most important advance in organic treatment involves the use of drugs. As we discussed in Chapter 11, there are all sorts of chemicals that have dramatic effects on people's moods, calming them if they are nervous and making them more excited and energetic if they are depressed. A few of these are extremely useful in the treatment of psychopathology. Generally they fall into two classes—tranquilizers and antidepressants.

Major tranquilizers Although rauwolfia (a medicinal extract from a family of somewhat poisonous trees and shrubs) was known to the Indians for centuries, its major derivative reserpine has been used in the systematic treatment of mental disturbance only since about 1954. At about the same time an even more important drug, chlorpromazine, was synthesized. These so-called major tranquilizers have two effects that are of profound importance in the treatment of psychotics—they calm people and also directly reduce some psychotic symptoms.

As their name implies, the tranquilizers lower people's level of excitement and activity. People who take them are not totally calm or without anxiety, but uncontrolled behaviors such as shouting, screaming, aggressiveness, and temper tantrums are greatly reduced.

Because they are much less likely to harm themselves or others, patients can be given much more freedom. Old-fashioned methods of restraint such as padded cells and straitjackets are rarely if ever needed. In addition, since they are calmer, the patients are more accessible to the various methods of psychotherapy, which we shall discuss later.

The other effect of these drugs, particularly chlorpromazine, is to *reduce psychotic symptoms directly*. Schizophrenics who take these drugs tend to hallucinate less, have fewer delusions and more appropriate affect, and generally appear less disturbed. It is unclear whether the drug eliminates the symptoms permanently or only suppresses them temporarily, but there is little question that chlorpromazine makes it possible for patients to be released from mental hospitals. Considerable research has demonstrated that the use of tranquilizers plus psychotherapy is more effective than psychotherapy alone (May, 1971); and there is some indication that the drug is effective by itself.

The tranquilizers have revolutionized the treatment of schizophrenics, particularly in large mental hospitals. As was mentioned above, the hospitals use fewer restraints, allowing patients to use the grounds or even to hold jobs on the outside, and many more patients are released. Since 1954, when chlorpromazine and other drugs were first widely used, the number of patients in mental hospitals has declined sharply (see Fig. 16.1). This does not mean that the tranquilizers alone have solved the problem of schizophrenia, but they have had a dramatic positive effect.

In addition to the major tranquilizers, which relieve psychotic symptoms, the minor tranquilizers such as meprobromate (Miltown or Equanil), Librium, and Valium are commonly used in the treatment of neurosis and mild anxiety. These drugs do not solve the person's problems or remove the sources of anxiety, but they often reduce the unpleasant symptoms. This obviously makes the individual less uncomfortable and more responsive to other forms of therapy.

Fig. 16.1

Patients in public mental hospitals

The number rose steadily until the introduction of drug therapy in 1955. Since then the numbers have declined sharply despite an increase in the total population of the country. (Data from National Institute of Mental Health)

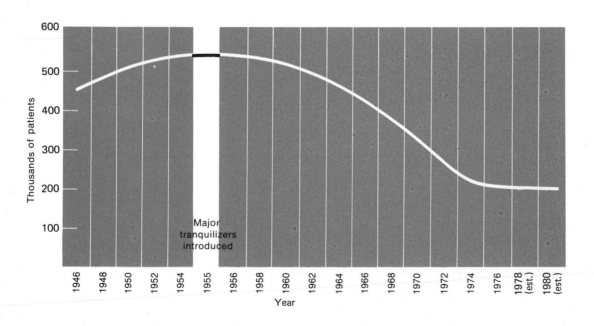

Antidepressants Depressed people need to have their mood elevated. As we explained earlier, they are sad and inactive, feel they are worthless, and are sometimes suicidal. Stimulants such as the amphetamines produce a general arousal, but they do not alter the depressed mood and thus are useless in the treatment of depression. However, a number of drugs do have a specific antidepressant effect. Imipramine (usually marketed as Tofranil), amitriptyline (Elavil), and related drugs have been shown to have some success in relieving depression (English, 1961). In addition, the natural element lithium reduces manic symptoms and relieves depression. Although more research is needed on its effectiveness, it is certainly the most promising development in recent years. A great many people appear to have been helped greatly by it (Davis, 1976; Fiéve, Platman, and Plutchik, 1968). Unfortunately, some of these drugs appear to have severe side effects. Iproniazid, which was quite effective, turned out to be so toxic that it is no longer used; and the other drugs, including lithium, must also be employed with great care. Moreover, although there have been promising reports, the beneficial effects of the drugs are not yet firmly established. Despite these problems, the antidepressant drugs do appear to provide a promising alternative to electroshock therapy for severe depressives, and drug therapy in these cases will probably become more and more common as research and development continue.

How Do the Organic Treatments Work?

An extremely important question concerning all of the organic treatments is how they work. ECS is literally and figuratively a shock to the system, and one notion of how it works is that it somehow interrupts depressed people's obsession with their problems. Unlike most people, depressives never seem to recover from severe blows such as a loved one dying or the loss of a job. They seem fixated on the loss and remain in a state of mourning. Perhaps the shock allows them to "start over" and at least temporarily not think about the specific loss. Clearly, this is not a satisfactory explanation, but we do not know the specific mechanism involved.

The antidepressants seem to operate by affecting the synthesis or breakdown of chemicals involved in synaptic transmission in the brain. The low level of reactivity shown by depressives may be due to an abnormally low level of these chemicals, thus causing less responsiveness at the neural level. The drugs increase the level of the critical chemicals and thereby increase neural responsiveness. Conversely, lithium seems to reduce the level of these chemicals and thus reduces the overresponsiveness that is characteristic of manics. These explanations are still somewhat speculative, but they provide a consistent, logical explanation of how the drugs work and also of why the person is depressed in the first place.

PSYCHOLOGICAL TECHNIQUES

The organic treatments, especially the major tranquilizers, have revolutionized the treatment of schizophrenia and have had considerable impact on other conditions. Despite their effectiveness, however,

"Now to start with, let's make a list of all the famous and important men who were short."

many therapists feel that they do not fully solve people's problems. In most cases, some sort of psychological treatment is necessary to accomplish that. Therefore, even people who receive drugs or other physical therapy are generally advised to get some psychological treatment as well. The disturbance is assumed to be due at least in part to the individual's experiences, whether they involve unresolved conflicts or maladaptive learning, and treatment must be directed at this psychological cause. The major psychological approaches are psychoanalytic psychotherapy with its many variations; behavior therapy; and humanistic therapies; but we shall also discuss several other techniques.

Psychoanalytic Psychotherapy

Since Freud began publishing his major works on psychoanalysis, there have been many changes in psychoanalytic treatment. New types of therapy both related to and different from traditional psychoanalysis have focused on different aspects of the process, different problems, and different techniques. However, Freudian and Neo-Freudian ideas have had enormous influence on virtually all kinds of therapy. Thus, despite the increasing interest in the use of behavior therapy and other new techniques, psychoanalytic therapy is still extremely influential and widely used.

We have already discussed the major points of psychoanalytic theory in Chapters 12, 14, and 15. Those aspects that are most relevant to techniques of psychotherapy are that (1) the early years of life are especially important in shaping personality, centering around oral, anal, and sexual conflicts; (2) in order to avoid overwhelming anxiety, individuals sometimes use defense mechanisms to force into the unconscious conflicts they are unable to handle in a realistic way; and (3) mental disturbances are caused by these unconscious conflicts, with the individual's symptoms being a direct result of the defense mechanisms. From this description of the cause of mental disorders, Freud concluded that psychotherapy would be successful if it accomplished two goals: (1) it brought the unconscious conflict and its surrounding events into the conscious mind, and (2) it enabled the individual to "work through" this conflict and resolve it. Table 16.2 summarizes the major aspects of psychoanalytic therapy.

Table 16.2
KEY ASPECTS OF PSYCHOANALYTIC THERAPY

Type of therapy	Method
Free association	Patients say whatever occurs to them with no censorship.
Interpretations	Therapist offers suggestions or possible explanations of patients' problems. Also suggests meaning of symbols, dreams, and specific acts of resistance.
Resistance	Patients are assumed to resist telling some thoughts and dealing with some conflicts, and to fight therapy to some extent.
Transference	Patients develop emotional involvement with therapist, with both positive and negative feelings. This relationship represents many different relationships that were important in the patients' lives.
Insight and working through	Patients achieve insight into their problems and work them through (resolve them) in the therapeutic relationship.

Free association The first problem is to discover the specific unconscious conflicts that are causing the condition, and to trace them back to their origin. When he first began treating neurotics, Freud experimented with hypnosis and was amazed to find that some hypnotized patients were able to recall memories, dreams, and early events in their lives that they could not remember in a waking state. Although hypnosis was efficient and seemed to speed the memory process, Freud soon abandoned it because it seemed to interfere with other parts of the treatment and often produced unreliable memories. Instead, psychoanalysis relies on free association to reveal unconscious conflicts.

Free association consists of having patients say anything that comes to mind. Some form of free association is a basic element in all psychoanalytically oriented therapies. Patients are told to let their minds wander freely, to censor nothing, and to say anything and everything that they think of. Nothing is too small, too trivial, too silly, or too awful to be told to the therapist. Although no one can associate entirely freely, the idea is that the train of associations will be revealing, as will be specific information that is expressed. When patients tell everything, small clues are unearthed that might otherwise be concealed. Something that the patient might dismiss as unimportant, or conceal as too awful or damaging, may come out during this process.

One special source of information is the patient's dreams. As we mentioned earlier (Chapter 11), Freud thought that all dreams were expressions of unconscious wishes. The material in the dream is often symbolic or distorted, but it may reveal a great deal about the patient's problem. Therefore, patients are encouraged to remember their dreams and to discuss them in the therapy sessions.

Interpretations To help patients recall memories and understand their conflicts, the therapist makes *interpretations*. That is, he sometimes suggests the meaning or significance of a particular piece of information. At the simplest level, he may point out that a patient never mentions her younger brother. At a more complex level, he might suggest that her conflict involved jealousy of her brother and feelings of rejection by her mother. Interpretation may also deal with the possible meaning of a dream, the symbolic significance of a symptom, or any other aspect of the patient's condition. It is assumed that the therapist can sometimes suggest meanings that might not occur to a patient. The experienced therapist should be quite cautious in making interpretations, and present them only as suggestions rather than as the truth. Sometimes the interpretations will turn out to be correct, sometimes they will not.

Resistance to therapy Psychoanalysts assume that to some extent patients resist or fight the therapy. Modern psychoanalysis, influenced by innovators such as Anna Freud and David Rapaport, places a great deal of emphasis on these defensive mechanisms. Rather than concentrating on the unconscious conflicts themselves, these therapists stress the role of the defense mechanism and resistance to therapy. In interpreting and analyzing various forms of resistance, therapists help the patients understand the dynamics by which their symptoms have appeared, and eventually to uncover the hidden conflicts.

Resistance to therapy can take many forms. If a patient always arrives late or arrives late for sessions in which he is about to discuss particularly disturbing material, for example, the therapist will probably point out that he may be trying to avoid (or resist) the therapy. In addition, patients can avoid discussing disturbing material by talking constantly about recent movies they have seen, by concentrating on trivial incidents in their lives, by making up stories, or most dramatically by not talking at all. In all cases, the therapist will eventually point out to the patient that he is resisting the therapy and help him try to understand the source of that resistance. The most subtle form of resistance is to censor what is supposed to be free association. The patient talks freely about all sorts of subjects but carefully avoids certain topics that are particularly crucial. By noting where the resistance occurs, the therapist begins to understand what material is involved in the unconscious conflict and can make the patient aware of it also.

Transference One of the key assumptions of psychoanalytic therapy is that the relationship between the patient and the therapist assumes great importance. A therapy session is, of course, a social situation in which the patient tells the analyst all about herself. The therapist in turn reveals little about himself, and instead tries to be entirely accepting and sympathetic without being personal. Under these circumstances, the patient usually forms a strong emotional attachment to the therapist. This emotional response, called *transference*, can be both positive and negative, just as in other strong relationships. When transference takes place the therapist comes to symbolize a variety of crucial relationships in the patient's life. The patient will respond to the therapist as she has to the other people to whom she is strongly attached. She may be jealous of the therapist's other patients, be hurt when the therapist takes a vacation, get angry when the therapist ends the hour, and so on. By analyzing and interpreting these responses and the emotional attachment, the therapist gains clues to the patient's problem and also helps the patient work out the conflicts.

In a sense, the transference becomes a model of the patient's relationship with other people. In dealing with her feelings toward the therapist, the patient lives through her other relationships. It is almost as if she is role-playing her earlier experiences with her mother and father and with other crucial people in her life. The assumption is that if she can work out her feelings toward the therapist and deal with him on a rational basis, she should eventually be able to resolve conflicts that are based on difficult relationships with other people.

Working through The least clear aspect of psychoanalytic treatment is the process called *working through* the problems. Freud discovered quite early that simply making the unconscious conflicts conscious did not ordinarily cure the patient. Once they were understood, these conflicts still had to be resolved. But just how to resolve them is not entirely clear. We have already discussed one important mechanism, that of transference. When patients understand their problems, they can work them out in terms of their relationship with the therapist. In addition, by talking about them, understanding their source, reliving the early experiences, and confronting similar conflicts in other day-to-day relationships, patients gradually resolve the underlying conflict.

For example, as we noted in Chapter 12, one common conflict involves anger at and fear of one's father, which develops during the Oedipal period. A man with this kind of conflict may have great difficulty expressing aggression and forming relationships with men, and may have ambivalent attitudes toward sex—both desiring it and feeling guilty about it. Once the source of this conflict is understood, the patient can begin to deal with his pent-up aggressive feelings. He may express some of them toward the therapist, and discover that he will not be rejected or criticized just because he is sometimes angry. Similarly, when he expresses sexual feelings, either toward the therapist or toward a woman, he may be reassured when the therapist does not become angry at him and condemn him. Once again, this is working through the Oedipal conflict in which the boy is competing with the father for his mother's love. He is afraid to express his love toward his mother or his anger toward his father because his father may punish him. When the therapist does not punish or disapprove of the patient, this fear is lessened. And in expressing these same feelings toward people in the real world, the patient discovers that they too will be accepting of moderate levels of aggression and sexuality. Thus, he not only understands the source of his conflict but is able to reduce it by expressing the forbidden impulses and not being punished. This description is, of course, an oversimplification of the actual process, and as we said above, the specific mechanisms are not fully understood. It may be that working through actually consists of unlearning the maladaptive behavior or learning new, more adaptive alternatives, as we shall discuss later.

Duration of the treatment Patients typically have from one to five therapy sessions a week (a session now usually lasts forty-five minutes, down from the famous fifty-minute hour). The length of treatment varies greatly. Psychoanalytic psychotherapy often deals with quite specific problems, such as anxiety about work or impotence, and in these cases the treatment might last only a few months or half a year. When the treatment is for no specific problem but rather a general difficulty in life, it takes much longer, often many years. In recent years, there has been more and more emphasis on relatively short-term treatment of specific problems, particularly by analytically oriented psychiatrists, psychologists, and social workers. However, unlike with some other therapies, no attempt is generally made to fix the length of treatment ahead of time.

Behavior Therapy

Behavior therapy takes a quite different approach from psychoanalytic therapy. This form of therapy applies established techniques of learning to modify the patient's behavior.

All of the psychologically oriented therapies are based largely on the assumption that the disorder is the result of experience—it is learned. The proponents of behavior therapy such as Joseph Wolpe, Arnold Lazarus, and Albert Bandura argue that since the maladaptive behavior has been learned, treatment should consist of systematically unlearning the undesirable behavior and substituting new behaviors. In order to do this, behavior therapists use techniques of learning taken directly from the extensive research in this area (see Chapters 3 and 4). In other words, instead of relying on the traditional methods of therapy that grew up primarily by a process of trial and error, behavior therapists use methods of teaching that are rigorously based on theory and research.

As we mentioned in the previous chapter, behavior therapists do not believe that the symptom is due to any underlying conflicts. Rather, the symptom is the condition, and therefore *it is the symptom that they treat.* For example, a patient who is afraid of snakes is not assumed to have any underlying reason for this fear other than a learned aversion to snakes. Accordingly, the behavior therapist attempts to teach the person not to be afraid of snakes. There is little or no concern about any other conflicts in the person's life. Treatment consists of extinguishing this fear and substituting positive behavior. A number of specific techniques are used to accomplish this.

Systematic desensitization A procedure called *systematic desensitization* is based on the principle that it is impossible to be relaxed and anxious at the same time. The patient constructs a hierarchy of situations or objects of which she is afraid (see Table 16.3). For example, someone who is frightened of snakes might describe situations ranging from hearing the word snake, seeing a picture of a snake, seeing an actual snake at a distance, being closer and closer to the snake, and finally actually touching the snake. The closer the

Table 16.3
KEY ASPECTS OF BEHAVIOR THERAPY (SYSTEMATIC DESENSITIZATION)

Step	Description
Specify the problem	Patient states the specific problem as clearly and completely as possible.
Construct hierarchy	Patient lists a series of events or situations that range from most frightening to only mildly frightening.
Learn desensitization	Therapist instructs patient in how to relax completely.
Systematic desensitization	Patient begins at least frightening point on the hierarchy and tries to relax while imagining (or engaging in) that situation. Once this is accomplished, patient moves to next step, until whole hierarchy is completed.

person is to the top of this hierarchy, the more anxiety would ordinarily be aroused.

In desensitization, the patient first learns to become completely relaxed. This requires several sessions, and hypnosis or drugs may be used as aids. The patient relaxes her muscles as completely as possible, and gradually is able to feel totally calm and peaceful. After she is able to accomplish this easily, she tries to imagine the mildest situation in her fear hierarchy. Whenever she begins to feel anxious again, she forgets the frightening situation and concentrates on relaxing. Eventually, she may be able to imagine the frightening situation and remain entirely relaxed. Once she has accomplished this (which may take a few minutes or several sessions), she moves on to the next level of the hierarchy, proceeding by slow steps to more and more frightening situations. By a process of generalization, simply imagining these situations while being relaxed often enables the patient to face the real situation without being afraid.

A similar but more direct technique is to place the patient in the actual situations. Once again, the patient tries to relax and is then put in the least frightening situation in the hierarchy. For example, she might be shown a picture of a snake while she is in a relaxed state. In

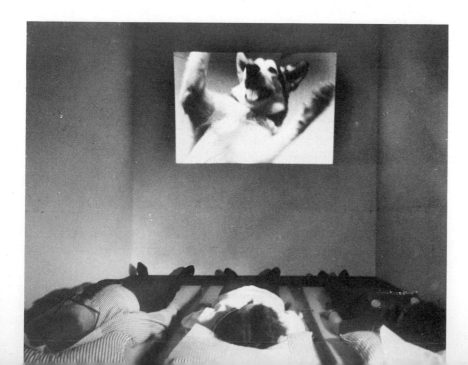

Fig. 16.2
Systematic desensitization

The use of film can be an effective desensitization technique. The patients here are undergoing treatment for their fear of dogs.

subsequent sessions, she moves up the hierarchy until she may actually be able to touch a snake without being afraid. Bandura (1969), Wolpe (1973), Lazarus (1971) and others have reported great success in eliminating phobias by these procedures.

Modeling Another technique employed by behavior therapists is *modeling* or *imitation*. A patient with a particular fear is told to identify with someone who is actually present or who is shown in a movie. The other person is shown in situations that ordinarily would arouse anxiety in the patient. By watching this model, and seeing that she is not suffering or afraid, the patient learns not to be afraid himself.

Aversive techniques Behavior therapists also sometimes use negative reinforcement, punishment, or aversive learning techniques. For example, patients who have a particular behavior that they would like to be rid of are punished whenever they perform it. This procedure is essentially the opposite of the desensitization technique. An alcoholic might set up a hierarchy ranging from actually drinking to approaching a bottle and finally just thinking about alcohol. In the conditioning procedure, he might pick up a glass of alcohol (or just imagine doing it) and receive a strong electric shock or hear a painfully loud noise (see Fig. 16.3). After a while, he will associate this aversive stimulus with drinking. Next, this will be paired with even entering a bar or buying a bottle of alcohol, and finally even thinking about alcohol will be punished. Eventually, the patient will learn to avoid alcohol because it will have unpleasant associations. In a sense, the behavior therapist is producing a phobia, just as with desensitization he is removing one.

Positive reinforcement Positive reinforcement can be used in much the same way to teach particular behaviors. Whenever the patient performs the desired act she is rewarded with verbal approval, candy, money, or whatever is most appropriate. This technique has been used especially in the treatment of severely disturbed children whom it is difficult to reach any other way. Just as Skinner could shape the behavior of pigeons, these reinforcement techniques can be used to shape the behavior of humans. A severely disturbed child who is being taught to speak might first be reinforced for any noises he made, then for speech-like noises, then for words, and finally for sentences. As Sherman (1963) and others have shown, this shaping procedure is sometimes effective with very disturbed patients.

Behavior Therapy and Psychoanalysis Compared

Both behavior therapy and psychoanalytic psychotherapy are based on the assumption that the condition being treated is caused by the individual's experience. Individuals are not born with problems but develop them through interactions with their environment; in short, they learn them. Thus, although psychoanalysts would not use this terminology, both therapies are designed to enable individuals to unlearn or replace with new learning the source of their difficulty. However, the two approaches differ in a number of important respects.

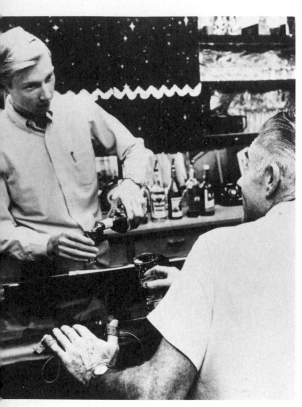

Fig. 16.3
Aversive learning and alcoholism

Table 16.4

ASSUMPTIONS AND PRACTICE OF BEHAVIORAL
AND PSYCHOANALYTIC THERAPY

Behavior therapy	Psychoanalytic therapy
Symptom is the condition; no underlying cause	Symptom is result of underlying conflict
Treat symptom, do not look for cause	Look for cause
No symptom substitution expected	Symptom substitution expected
All experiences given equal weight	Early life weighted heavily
Uses techniques derived from learning research	Uses free association, interpretation, and insight
Relationship with therapist incidental, although good relationship helpful	Relationship with therapist critical; patient works through conflicts by transference to therapist
Relatively short-term—rarely as much as a year	Wide range, but often long duration—many years of therapy

As we discussed in the preceding chapter, the major differences involve the existence of underlying conflicts and symptom substitution, the importance of early experiences, and the role of the relationship between therapist and patient (see Table 16.4).

Underlying conflict versus symptoms Psychoanalytic theory assumes that the symptom is a result of an unconscious conflict. According to psychoanalytic theory, the phobic is afraid of snakes *because* they represent unacceptable or frightening sexual impulses; the obsessive-compulsive taps three times because that distracts him from his unconscious wish to curl up and be dependent and the tapping may also symbolize his mother's comforting heartbeat or the rocking of his crib. Therefore, removing the symptom without treating the conflict would lead to *symptom substitution,* with new symptoms replacing those that disappeared. In contrast, behavior therapy denies that there is any underlying conflict. The symptom is the problem, and it is simply due to maladaptive learning. The phobic is afraid of snakes because she was very frightened by one once; the obsessive-compulsive taps three times because he found at some time in his life that it removed his anxiety about something and he was therefore reinforced for tapping. Some behavior therapists do not accept any symbolic explanations; others might agree that the snake at one time stood for sex, but would argue that the connection is no longer important. All that matters is the symptom itself, and the symptom was learned because of specific circumstances and patterns of reinforcement in the individual's life. If you remove the symptom, you have solved the problem. No substitute symptom will appear.

This is perhaps the most important difference between the two approaches because it leads to quite different courses of treatment. As we have mentioned, behavior therapy focuses on the symptom throughout the treatment, using whatever techniques are available to relieve and then remove entirely the particular maladaptive behavior. Psychoanalytic therapists argue that other symptoms will then appear—that removing a symptom without treating the cause can produce great anxiety and even precipitate more severe breakdowns. There is far too little evidence to provide a definitive choice between these alternatives, but at the moment there is little question that behavior therapy does relieve some symptoms without having any negative effects; and there is no convincing evidence that symptom substitution occurs with any regularity (Yates, 1970).

The importance of early experiences Both approaches emphasize the effects of experience, but while psychoanalytic theory assumes that what happens to someone during the first few years of life is especially critical and will tend to have much more influence on the person than later events, behavior theory makes no such distinction. Although this is a difference in degree, it has considerable impact on how therapy is done. The psychoanalyst assumes that life within the family during a child's early years is almost always involved in mental disorders. Therefore, the therapy tends to focus on and relate to

Box 16.3

REINFORCEMENT AND TOKEN ECONOMIES

Some of the most dramatic successes of behavioral techniques have come from the treatment of severely disturbed psychotic patients and autistic children who are totally out of touch with reality. These people are almost impossible to reach through usual methods of psychotherapy because they do not respond to anything that anyone does. If a child never speaks, free-association techniques are obviously not going to work. But these people can feel pain and appreciate food and other rewards. Thus, techniques involving rewards and punishments have a chance of working.

Lovaas (Lovaas and Koegal, 1972) has shown that even autistic children who never respond to people can be taught and eventually perhaps reached by behavioral techniques. He used electric shocks and other methods that may sound primitive or cruel, but he argues that these children are doomed to a terrible life unless they can be reached in some way. With these techniques, Lovaas and others have treated autistic children who have never been able to take care of themselves. In some cases, the children learned to eat at a table, go to the bathroom, change their clothes, and even participate in the family to some extent. Although these methods have not produced cures (most autistic children probably have some form of severe brain damage), behavior therapy seems to have had some success where no other method has had much success at all.

Severely disturbed adults in mental hospitals are also difficult to treat, but they are more accessible than autistic children. One method, the so-called *token economy*, consists of rewarding people for certain acts and punishing them or more often withholding rewards for other acts (Ayllon and Azrin, 1968). For example, patients on a ward would be given actual tokens when they made their beds, cleaned up, went to meals on time, and participated in social events. These tokens could then be exchanged for special foods, weekends at home, or any other desirable privilege. Token economies of this sort have been quite effective in hospitals, prisons, and even homes (Maley, Feldman, and Ruskin, 1973). Reward and punishment operates everywhere. The achievement of the token economies is to make the operation systematic and explicit. The patient knows exactly what will happen as a result of a particular act. As we discussed in Chapter 12 on child development, consistent discipline (and the token economy is a form of discipline) is especially effective in producing social, moral behavior.

these early incidents. In contrast, behavior therapy may not consider early events at all.

The role of the therapist-patient relationship As we described earlier, psychoanalytic theory considers the emotional feelings of the patient for the therapist to be of great importance. Transference (positive or negative emotional response) is a key element in the therapy because it is part of the process by which patients discover and work out their problems. In behavior therapy transference is not an issue. Patients may indeed develop strong feelings for the therapist, and positive feelings generally make the therapy proceed more smoothly, but emotional attachment is not essential for the treatment to work. Just as a good teacher can help students learn math whether or not there is a strong attachment between them, so a good behavior therapist can enable the client to unlearn maladaptive behavior regardless of the patient's feelings for the therapist.

THE ETHICS OF BEHAVIOR CONTROL

Behavior control or modification has received much bad press. "Behavior mod," as it is often called, has been made to sound like an all-powerful, futuristic method of forcing people to behave in certain ways. And it has been attacked for interfering with the basic freedom of the individual. Although it is conceivable that the methods could be used unethically, behavior control is really a new term for the systematic use of methods and procedures that have been around for a long time and are used everywhere from prisons to families.

The essence of behavior control is to use reinforcements to get people to behave. Parents do this all the time with their children and with each other. They smile, and give a cookie, a kiss, or a pat when the other person does what they want; they frown, take away a privilege, or give a slap when the behavior displeases them. Rewards and punishments are also given in all institutions no matter how enlightened or free. Those in charge always prefer some behavior to others, and they always reward some actions and punish others (if only by withholding rewards). Certainly, mental hospitals and prisons do this quite deliberately. Thus, the idea of using rewards and punishments to control behavior is nothing new.

What is new is that some attempts are now being made to use reinforcements systematically. In a prison, instead of leaving the rewards and punishments up to the whim of a particular person in authority, the whole institution has specific rules with specific reinforcements given for specific acts. Presumably this makes the system more effective, but it does not change it substantially. Prisoners are no less free than before, but they are more likely to get the specified reinforcement for a particular action on their part.

However, when a system of this kind becomes highly routine and effective it does involve some threat. Although the inmates can now count on more consistent responses from the authorities, they also know that their behavior is being watched more closely. Moreover, they probably *feel* more control is being exerted because the reinforcements are more explicit. Most people are afraid of thought or behavior control, and any system that suggests either of these is highly suspect. The burden is on those using behavior control techniques to convince people that the system actually removes some of the worst aspects of life in an institution, such as being subject to arbitrary responses on the part of the authorities. Thus, although behavior control is not a mysterious form of control and may generally have excellent goals, it should be used with caution.

Box 16·4

There are other differences between the psychoanalytic and behavioral approaches to therapy, but these are the most important. It should also be noted that behavior therapy is done mainly by psychologists and perhaps some social workers; while psychoanalytic therapy is done by psychiatrists, social workers, psychologists, and, of course, psychoanalysts. However, behavior therapy appears to be gaining rapidly in popularity and acceptance. In addition, it is widely incorporated into treatment programs in mental hospitals in the form of token economies or similar systems. Thus, even though it is often not the only form of therapy given, behavior therapy is now becoming increasingly important in the treatment of hospitalized patients.

Humanistic Therapies

A variety of therapeutic techniques are based to some extent on humanistic approaches to psychology. As we mentioned in previous

Box 16.5

OTHER KINDS OF TREATMENT AND THERAPY

Primal Therapy

This form of therapy is based on the premise that people's problems are caused by very basic needs being frustrated. The need for nurturance, love, warmth, or freedom is not satisfied or is denied by the individual. This produces a primal pain that can be dealt with only if it is brought to the surface. This is accomplished by weakening the individual's defenses by isolation and lack of sleep and then encouraging the expression of this pain. When the process is successful, the person is supposed to experience a *primal,* and utter a *primal scream* that expresses the pain and suffering that has been bottled up until then. The emphasis obviously is on emotions and expression, with the basic assumption being that getting them out into the open will solve the person's problems.

Reality Therapy

In direct contrast to primal therapy, reality therapy emphasizes understanding and logic. The therapist helps the individual to understand the implications of his or her actions and beliefs, to plan for the future, and to follow the course of action most likely to satisfy the person's expressed goals.

Gestalt Therapy

One version of humanistic therapy, Gestalt is usually conducted in groups with the therapist dealing with one individual at a time. Many of the assumptions are derived from psychoanalytic theory, but there is additional emphasis on acting out fantasies and becoming aware of one's feelings at the moment, and particularly on the humanistic goals of self-actualization and concern for others.

Transactional Analysis

Another type of humanistic therapy, transactional analysis is similar to Gestalt therapy but places greater emphasis on honesty. In TA the individual is perceived as having three ego states: (1) the Parent, who acts, thinks, and feels like the individual's parents; (2) the Adult, who deals with current reality, gathering facts and being objective; and (3) the Child, who feels or behaves like the individual as a child. The Parent and Child states have both positive and negative aspects, and the goal in dealing with others is to express the positive aspects of the appropriate ego state. Communications between people are called *transactions.* Some people play psychological games with each other and the transactions in these games are not open and honest. The goal of transactional analysis is to learn to give up negative behaviors, express posi-

chapters, psychologists such as Maslow, Perls, and Rogers have a somewhat different view of personality and mental disturbance than Freud and his followers. These humanistic theories differ considerably among themselves, but they all contain the idea that individuals have much of their potential within them and that it is society's responsibility to encourage its development while interfering as little as possible with its expression. In terms of therapy, this seems to imply that people also have within them the ability to solve their problems and to grow and that therapists must be especially careful not to impose their standards or values on clients. This point of view has been incorporated into a number of specific therapeutic systems (some of which are described in Box 16.5).

Probably the most important and influential type of humanistic therapy was developed mainly by Carl Rogers (1951, 1970) and is called *nondirective, client-centered* therapy, or, more recently, *person-centered* therapy. As in psychoanalytic therapy, the patient

tive feelings, stop playing psychological games, and become more authentic.

EST

This is quite different from the other treatments because it is not meant to be therapy in the usual sense of the word. EST stands for Erhard Seminar Training, a sixty-hour course designed to change a person's life in positive ways. The course is conducted in very large groups, usually of well over a hundred people, and is run according to a rigid script, with the participants required to follow strict rules such as no smoking or drinking, using the bathroom only at specified times, and so on. The group listens to speeches from the leader, sits for a long time in one place, does various exercises such as imagining certain situations and encounters, and also may engage in discussions with the leaders. The emphasis is on accepting oneself completely, feeling the power to do almost anything, and being close to and open to all people. There is a strong mystical and fascist flavor to EST, as well as a messianic zeal that is not generally present in the other therapies. In many ways, it is more similar to scientology and other such quasi-religious movements than to psychological therapy. We include it mainly because it has received a lot of attention in recent years, but it should probably not be considered a legitimate therapy.

Two other types of therapy are shown in the above photos. At left, Ida Rolf probes deeply into a patient's muscles, which she claims have been damaged and thrown out of alignment by physical reactions to past emotional experiences. This painful massage, called "Rolfing," is necessary to relax the muscles and release damaging emotional memories. At right, Moshe Feldenkrais demonstrates from his repertoire of body exercises that he feels can help practitioners alter their patterns of thinking and feeling. Ultimately, Feldenkrais claims, these exercises can be used to relieve the symptoms of diseases of the nervous system and reverse the symptoms of aging.

CARL R. ROGERS

(client) talks about his problems and the therapist listens. But more emphasis is placed on allowing the patient to discover his own problem, and interpretations are minimized. Thus the therapist is unlikely to say that it seems as if the patient is angry at his father or has sexual conflicts unless the patient has already made this quite explicit. On the other hand, especially in his recent work, Rogers does stress the personal reactions of the therapist and feels that the therapist can tell the client these reactions, not as interpretations of the client's problems but rather as the therapist's personal views and feelings. The therapist would not say that the patient had a sexual problem (an interpretation), but she might say that the client's sex life seemed limited or strange or whatever she happened to feel. It is felt that this feedback enables a client to understand how other people react to him and that for this reason the therapist's comments are very important. In other words, unlike in psychoanalysis, where the therapist tries to be impersonal, in person-centered therapy the therapist acts like a real person, with her reactions and feelings expressed.

In addition, the client's problems are not considered primarily in terms of early experiences. While not denying that what happened

A "SILENT YOUNG MAN" — AN EXAMPLE OF PERSON-CENTERED THERAPY

Therapist Carl Rogers selected this interview as an example of his method. The client was twenty-eight years old, had been hospitalized for nineteen months when the therapy began, and was diagnosed as a schizophrenic.

C: I just ain't no good to nobody, never was, and never will be.

T: Feeling that now, hm? That you're just no good to yourself, no good to anybody. Never will be any good to anybody. Just that you're completely worthless, huh?—Those really are lousy feelings. Just feel that you're no good at all, hm?

C: Yeah. [Muttering in low, discouraged voice] That's what this guy I went to town with just the other day told me.

T: This guy that you went to town with really told you that you were no good? Is that what you're saying? Did I get this right?

C: M-hm.

T: I guess the meaning of that if I get it right is that here's somebody that—meant something to you and what does he think of you? Why, he's told you that he thinks you're no good at all. And that just really knocks the props out from under you. [Jim weeps quietly.] It just brings the tears.
(Silence of 20 seconds)

C: [Rather defiantly] I don't care though.

T: You tell yourself you don't care at all, but somehow I guess some part of you cares because some part of you weeps over it. . . .

C: I'm gonna take off.

T: Huh?

C: I'm gonna take off.

T: You're going to take off? Really run away from here? Is that what you mean? Must be some—what's the—what's the background of that? Can you tell me? Or I guess what I mean more accurately is I know you don't like the place but it must be that something special came up or something?

C: I just want to run away and die.

T: M-hm, m-hm, m-hm. It isn't even that you want to get away from here to something? You just want to leave here and go away and die in a corner, him?
(Silence of 30 seconds)

T: I guess as I let that soak in I really do sense how, how deep that feeling sounds, that you—I guess the image that comes to my mind is sort of a—a wounded animal that wants to crawl away and die. It sounds as though that's kind of the way you feel that you just want to get away from here and, and vanish. Perish. Not exist.
(Silence of 1 minute)

C: [almost inaudibly] All day yesterday and all morning I wished I were dead. I even prayed last night that I could die.

T: I think I caught all of that, that—for a couple of days now you've just wished you could be dead and you've even prayed for that—I guess that—One way this strikes me is that to live is such an awful thing to you, you just wish you could die, and not live.
(Silence of 1 minute, 12 seconds)

T: So that you've been just wishing and wishing that you were not living. You wish that life would pass away from you.
(Silence of 30 seconds)

C: I wish it more'n anything else I've ever wished around here.

T: M-hm, m-hm, m-hm. I guess you've wished for lots of things but boy! It seems as though this wish to not live is deeper and stronger than anything you ever wished before.
(Silence of 1 minute, 36 seconds)

T: Can't help but wonder whether it's still true that some things this friend said to you—are those still part of the thing that makes you feel so awful?

C: In general, yes.

T: M-hm.
(Silence of 47 seconds)

T: The way I'm understanding that is that in a general way the fact that he felt you were no good has just set off a whole flood of feeling in you that makes you really wish, wish you weren't alive. Is that—somewhere near it?

C: I ain't no good to nobody, or I ain't no good for nothin', so what's the use of living?

T: M-hm. You feel, I'm not any good to another living person, so—why should I go on living?"
(Silence of 21 seconds). . . .

C: I might go today. Where, I don't know, but I don't care.

T: Just feel that your mind is made up and that you're going to leave. You're not going to anywhere. You're just—just going to leave, hm?
(Silence of 53 seconds)

C: [muttering in discouraged tone] That's why I want to go, 'cause I don't care what happens.

T: Huh?

C: That's why I want to go, 'cause I don't care what happens.

T: M-hm, m-hm. That's why you want to go, because you really don't care about yourself.

You just don't care what happens. And I guess I'd just like to say—I care about you. And I care what happens.
(Silence of 30 seconds) [Jim bursts into tears and unintelligible sobs.]

T: [tenderly] Somehow that just—makes all the feelings pour out.
(Silence of 35 seconds)

T: And you just weep and weep and weep. And feel so badly. (Jim continues to sob, then blows nose and breathes in great gasps.)

T: I do get some sense of how awful you feel inside —You just sob and sob. (Jim puts his head on desk, bursting out in great gulping, gasping sobs.)

T: I guess all the pent-up feelings you've been feeling the last few days just—just come rolling out.
(Silence of 32 seconds, while sobbing continues)

T: There's some Kleenex there, if you'd like it—Hmmm. [sympathetically] You just feel kind of torn to pieces inside.
(Silence of 1 minute, 56 seconds)

C: I wish I could die. [sobbing]

T: You just wish you could die, don't you? M-hm. You just feel so awful, you wish you could perish.
(Therapist laid his hand on Jim's arm during this period. Jim showed no definite response. However, the storm subsided somewhat. Very heavy breathing.) (Silence of 1 minute, 10 seconds)

Comments: Note that the therapist responds largely by restating what he believes the client is feeling, and that he does this even when no words have been uttered. Another important aspect of this therapy is that the therapist expresses his own feelings, as when he says that he does care what happens to the client. Rogers comments that that response was a "spontaneous feeling which welled up in me, and which I expressed. It was certainly not planned and I had no idea it would bring such an explosive response." Rogers also remarks that following these sessions there was no sudden, dramatic improvement in the client, but that there was steady improvement that eventually led to the client's leaving the hospital. Eight years later, the client was, in Rogers' words, "a solid, employed citizen, living a rather limited social life, but content." (Rogers, 1967, pp. 141-144)

early in life can be important, person-centered therapy focuses more on the present than does traditional psychotherapy.

One technique that is used by therapists is to mirror or repeat clients' statements in order to clarify them. The idea is that the therapist can select statements that seem especially important, and by repeating them focus the client's attention on them. Also, hearing something from someone else's lips sometimes sharpens the thought or feeling. However, it should not be thought that these kinds of repetitions are done regularly or that it is an easy matter to select which statements to repeat. Just as a psychoanalyst must be very careful what interpretations to make and when, so the person-centered therapist must use all her skill in choosing which statements to focus on. A good example of this method is given in the case.

This kind of treatment seems to be particularly appropriate for people who are not seriously disturbed and for children, who naturally have difficulty in the more complex process of psychoanalytic therapy. It is a very optimistic and humanistic approach in that it does not assume an underlying conflict or early disturbance; rather, it views patients as temporarily having difficulty focusing their resources on their own problems. Once they clarify their own feelings and learn to accept them, they will be able to deal with whatever problems they are encountering.

Other Psychological Techniques

Play therapy This technique is designed primarily for use with disturbed children. Because they would have difficulty talking in therapy and describing their feelings and experiences, they are instead given games to play. Some of these games involve doll houses with dolls that represent the various members of the family. Others are just any game the therapist thinks the child might enjoy. During the game, the therapist observes and occasionally interprets the child's behavior. Playing the game usually relaxes the child, who then sometimes makes revealing statements, talks about his feelings, and sometimes acts them out during the course of the play. In other words, instead of using words and verbalizations as the substance of the therapy, play therapy relies on games to elicit the same kind of information. In *Dibs in Search of Self*, Virginia Axline (1947) provides a moving description of play therapy.

Group therapy There are a variety of therapeutic techniques involving groups. The essential idea is that discussing one's problems with other people under the direction of a therapist can produce many of the same positive effects as individual therapy. It is sometimes used for efficiency—there are too few therapists to go around and obviously they can see more patients if they see them in a group. However, it is also used for quite different purposes than individual therapy. In cases where someone has difficulty accepting herself, thinks that her problems are unique or worse than anyone else's, it is sometimes very useful to be in group therapy. The patient usually discovers that other people have the same types of problems, that she is no worse off than anyone else. This leads to self-acceptance and has the additional benefit of increasing the patient's sympathy for and understanding of others.

An important assumption behind much of group therapy is that many problems involve relationships with other people. Perhaps the patient cannot get along with people, is afraid of them, is overly competitive, and so on. Since our personalities are shaped largely through interactions with others, it is not surprising that many of our difficulties revolve around social situations. The group session is a social situation, of course, and requires that patients interact with other people. Thus the group elicits many of the social difficulties and also provides an appropriate place to deal with them. Just as individual psychotherapy may allow people to work through their relationships with key people in their lives, the group allows them to work through a wide range of social relationships.

Encounter groups In recent years as part of the humanist movement, there has been great interest in what used to be known as a "T" group (training group, or sensitivity group) but is now generally called an *encounter group.* Encounter groups have as few as five or six and as

PLAY THERAPY—
DIBS IN SEARCH OF SELF

Virginia Axline, a noted therapist, has described a course of play therapy with a boy she calls Dibs. *Dibs in Search of Self* is a moving, thoughtful book that gives insight into the process of treatment, the difficulty of dealing with a child's problems, and the thoughts that run through the therapist's mind as she tries to help the boy.

Dibs is a very disturbed child who does poorly in school, cannot get along with anyone, and is very withdrawn. He acts mentally retarded but shows moments of high intelligence. By the end of the treatment he is getting along with everyone, doing well in school, and testing at the top end of the IQ distribution. Here are a few excerpts.

(Dibs speaks first)
"There are so many things in the world. There are all kinds of people. I see some cars and trucks. And these people. There are all kinds of people. Sometimes I am afraid of people."

"Sometimes you are afraid of people?" I said, hoping he would be encouraged to go on.

"But sometimes I'm not afraid of people," he added. "I'm not afraid of you. . . ."

"You don't feel afraid when you're with me?" I commented.

(A moment later) "I am a boy," he said slowly. "I have a father, a mother, a sister. Grandmother has always loved me. But not Papa. Papa has not always loved me."

"You feel sure of Grandmother's love, but not so sure Papa has always loved you?" I remarked.

Dibs twisted his hands together. "Papa likes me some better now," he said.

"You feel Papa likes you better now?" I felt this was a very delicate situation; any prodding would cause Dibs to scurry away into the underbrush of his impassive silent defense.

"Some little better," Dibs said. He twisted his hands together as though he felt agitated. "I have a microscope," he said . . . Dibs was off again into the safe world of his intellectualism.

Dibs locks mother and father dolls into a playhouse and pretends it is on fire. "They want to get out but the house is burning. . . . They scream for help. I weep. I weep."

"Do you weep because the mother and father are locked in the house and can't get out and the house is burning?"

"Oh, no!" Dibs replied. "I weep because I feel again the hurt of doors closed and locked against me," he sobbed.

"You are feeling again the way you used to feel when you were alone?" I said.

(At the end of the hour) It had been a rough hour for Dibs. His feelings had torn through him without mercy. The locked doors of Dibs' young life had brought him intense suffering. Not the locked door of his room at home, but all the doors of acceptance that had been closed and locked against him, depriving him of love, respect and understanding he needed so desperately. . . . When he left the playroom he seemed to leave behind him the sorrowful feelings he had uprooted there. . . . (Axline, 1947, pp. 150–155)

many as thirty, forty, or even one hundred and fifty members. They meet for as little as one hour and as many as forty hours, and interact under the guidance of one or more group leaders.

The small and large groups function somewhat differently. In the smaller groups, there is intensive interaction among all the members, with the one essential rule being that they are supposed to be free and open with one another (similar to more traditional group therapy). Everything should be expressed, including embarrassing, unpleasant, and intimate reactions. The premise is that most of us have learned to be too defensive, that people should be honest with each other, and that releasing our feelings is helpful in many ways. It makes interpersonal relationships stronger and better because they are no longer based even in part on dishonesty. Moreover, this open expression allows individuals to convey various aspects of their personality that may have been discouraged by society; it allows them to get more in touch with their true nature and potential.

The larger groups start with the same basic assumptions, but generally do not operate in quite the same way. Instead, various individuals are selected as examples and, as Perls puts it, are "put on the hot seat." By observing the interaction among them, the leader, and a small number of group members, the whole group shares their experience.

This goal of total openness is very appealing to many people. The group provides a place where they can release feelings without being condemned for them. If they are angry at someone in the group, they are not only allowed but encouraged to tell the person they are angry. If they are sexually attracted to someone, they can say that also. The rigid, formalized interactions that make up most of our daily lives are thrown aside, and instead the participants are openly emotional, sexual, aggressive, and so on. This is such an unusual experience that encounter groups produce strong reactions in the participants. People cry, throw tantrums, become extremely upset and emotional, laugh, and often feel euphoric. The group sessions are designed to elicit strong emotions, and particularly in the long, so-called *marathon groups,* they are usually successful.

Although this experience is exciting and moving for some people, there is considerable question as to what effect it has on their lives. The goal is to make them more open, sincere, and in touch with their feelings and those of others, but at the present time there is little evidence that encounter groups generally achieve this goal. In one study of encounter groups (Lieberman, Yalom, and Miles, 1973), most participants felt that the group had produced a positive effect, but the study relied entirely on self-reports. In addition, even with the relatively short-term encounter group in this study, a few students seemed to be adversely affected.

Of course, there are so many different kinds of groups that it is unfair to judge them all together. Practically every conceivable variation has been employed. Some of the more extreme are nude encounter groups that are openly sexual and violence-oriented groups in which participants are deliberately beaten in order to elicit an emotional response. And the leaders of the groups range from highly trained, serious therapists to people who are engaged in therapy for questionable reasons. Thus, the variation in response of people to the groups must be due at least in part to the difference between the groups themselves. Because there is so little research, all we can say now is that legitimate, well-run encounter groups seem to be powerful experiences, which most people respond to favorably but which may produce negative reactions in a small percentage of participants.

EVALUATION OF THERAPIES

Research Problems

Assessing the effect of psychotherapies is one of the most difficult tasks facing research psychologists. It is obviously extremely important to know whether a therapy works, and which therapies work best. However, despite the considerable amount of research on this problem, we do not have conclusive answers yet because almost all of the studies are flawed in some way. Most of the difficulties in doing precise research on this issue involve measuring success and equating both patients and therapists.

First, since it is difficult even to define mental health, it is obviously even more difficult to agree on measuring it. Presumably the best procedure would be to observe someone for an extended period of time in his real-life setting, devise careful measures to assess his productivity and health, and then see how well he is doing. Obviously this is virtually impossible in terms of time and money, not to mention the difficulty of finding a situation in which such observation would be possible. Thus, studies of the effectiveness of therapies usually depend largely on the reports of the patients themselves or of the therapists. Unfortunately a patient's self-report is of questionable value, because people who invest a great deal of time and money in some form of treatment are likely to say that they were helped even if they were not. Some studies have used physiological measures and questionnaires, but these too are to some extent under the control of the patient and their interpretation is not always straightforward. Therefore, most of this research is at best suggestive and definitive conclusions await much more extensive and elaborate research, which should be one of the major goals of psychotherapists.

Second, patients who go to behavior therapists may be different from those who go to psychoanalysts, and those who go to psychoanalysts are probably different from those who go to humanistic therapists. Obviously, if one group of patients is more disturbed or more difficult to treat for any reason, comparison of success rates would be meaningless. In addition, it is essential to equate the therapists in terms of experience and quality. It is rare for a given person to be equally well trained in several therapeutic techniques. Even if she is experienced in several methods, she will probably be more enthusiastic and more confident about one method than another. Thus it would be unfair to compare the amount of success she had using one method with that using another because presumably she will be better at one than at the other. A more sensible approach is to compare the success rates of different therapists, each doing the kind of treatment she favors. But this raises the problem of equating them in terms of experience, ability, and interest in the research. If one therapist is more skilled, enthusiastic, committed to his procedures, or even more concerned about the research than another, a comparison of their success rates would tell you more about the therapist than about the type of therapy. It is possible to approximate solutions to all of the methodological difficulties, but none of the research today has done so satisfactorily.

The Effect of Psychological Therapies

The field of psychotherapy was shocked by an article published by Eysenck in 1953. He attempted to compare the success of psychoanalytic therapy with the success of what he called *eclectic therapy*, in which a variety of approaches was used. Comparing the success rates of the two different approaches with a control group who were not treated, Eysenck reported that all three groups showed about the same improvement—roughly two-thirds of those receiving psychoanalytic treatment, eclectic treatment, and no treatment at all showed considerable improvement. Since the psychotherapy was no better than no treatment, these were extremely surprising and discouraging results.

This study had the positive effect of stimulating people to devise new methods of treating mental disturbance. However, it also has been used as evidence against all kinds of psychotherapy, which is unfortunate because the study is deeply flawed and almost impossible to interpret.

Spontaneous recovery The most serious difficulty with Eysenck's article concerns the figure of two-thirds as the improvement rate for untreated controls—what is usually called the rate of *spontaneous recovery*. This is a critical figure, because all therapy must be compared to what happens when nothing is done. It seems clear now that the figure is based on incorrect and perhaps even biased judgments. Kiesler (1966) and Bergin (1971) have shown that Eysenck made many errors in computation and judgment to produce the figure.

HALFWAY HOUSES

Since the introduction of the major tranquilizers, few mental patients spend much of their lives in hospitals. The drugs remove or at least reduce most of the disruptive symptoms and allow the patient to be released from the hospital. However, most patients are not ready immediately to return to society without some treatment or support. They need to reorient themselves, to learn again how to get along with other people, to cope with what others might think about their hospitalization, and in general to adjust to the fact that they are no longer in the protected environment of a hospital. All of a sudden they have many more responsibilities and are more or less on their own. This is a heavy burden to bear and people who have just gotten out of a hospital often are not ready for it.

One attempt to make the transition from hospital to society easier is the *halfway house.* There is considerable variation in the services provided by halfway houses. Some provide the ex-patients with extensive services, including therapy, vocational training, job placement, and so on. Some are residential so that the ex-patients can live for a while in a protected environment and also hold a job in the outside world. And some are mainly places for ex-patients to go to be together; that is, they serve as a social center where ex-patients will be accepted and understood.

It is too early to assess the effectiveness of this program. However, there is little question that at the least the halfway houses provide a source of comfort and security to people who would otherwise have to face the world without support. It may be that the optimal way to treat most psychotics is not in a hospital at all, but in an outpatient clinic combined with some type of halfway house. This would minimize the abrupt transition from hospital to society that now exists.

Box 16.6

Bergin reviewed all the studies he could find (see Table 16.5), and reports a median spontaneous recovery rate of only 30 percent. The very highest is 52 percent and that includes patients classified as slightly improved. Thus, on the basis of the best data currently available, it is obvious that a large majority of people with mental disorders do not recover spontaneously. Indeed, even the figure of 30 percent may be misleading, since many of the people considered controls may have received some treatment or at least guidance without the knowledge of the person doing the research.

Reasons for Optimism—Other Studies

With this baseline figure of about 30 percent, we can be much more optimistic about the effects of therapy. Almost all studies of this problem show an improvement rate greater than 30 percent and many produce rates of improvement well above 75 percent. For example, a long-term follow-up study conducted by a psychoanalyst (Schjelderup, 1955) reported that twenty-two out of twenty-eight neurotics were greatly improved as much as twenty-four years after they had received the treatment. In this case, the evaluation was done entirely by the psychoanalyst himself and must be considered in that light.

A similar study by a behavior therapist (Wolpe, 1960) found an impressive 90-percent improvement rate more than a year after the therapy had ended. Once again the evaluation was done primarily by the therapist, and only those patients who had attended at least

Table 16.5
SPONTANEOUS RECOVERY FROM NEUROSIS—NO TREATMENT

Study	Percentage improved
Friess and Nelson (1942)	29
Friess and Nelson (1942)	35
Shore and Massimo (1966)	30
Orgel (1958)	0
Materson (1967)	38
Vorster (1966)	34
Hastings (1958)	46
Graham (1960)	37
O'Connor (1964)	0
Cappon (1964)	0
Endicott and Endicott (1963)	52
Koegler and Brill (1967)	0
Paul (1967)	18
Kringlen (1965)	25

Source: Bergin, 1971.

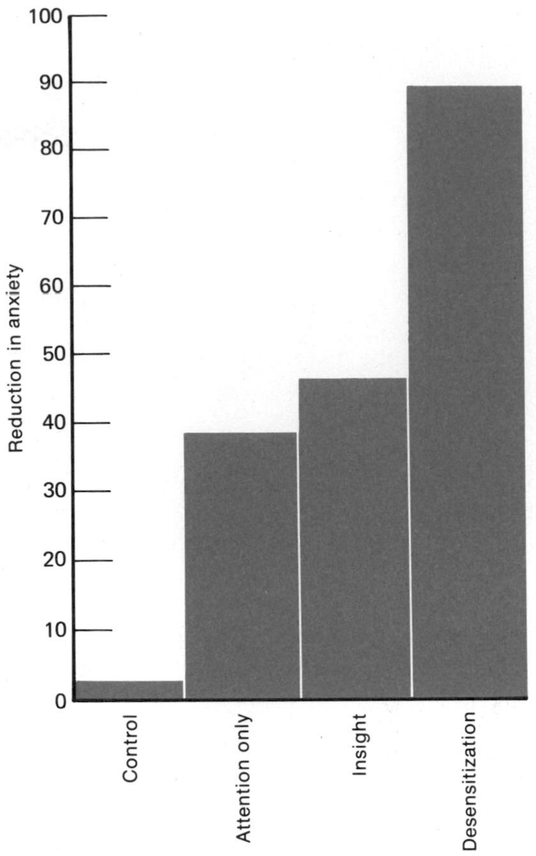

Fig. 16.4
Effects of various therapeutic techniques

All methods produced more anxiety reduction than the no-treatment control, but desensitization was clearly the most effective. (After Paul, 1966)

fifteen sessions were included, so that the most difficult cases were possibly not included. Nevertheless, as with the psychoanalytic study, the findings are certainly encouraging.

A study by Paul (1966) compared different treatment techniques. Students who were anxious about giving public speeches were randomly assigned to four conditions: (1) control, which received no treatment; (2) a group that received attention from the therapist but no systematic therapy, and a drug that was supposed to reduce their anxiety but which was actually just a placebo; (3) a psychotherapy group, which stressed insight and interpretations; and (4) a systematic desensitization behavior therapy group. Afterward, the effects of the procedure were measured by observers' ratings, subjects' self-reports, and physiological indicators of anxiety. Some of the findings are summarized in Fig. 16.4. You can see that all "treatment" conditions were more effective than the no treatment control. In addition, the insight group was more effective than the attention group, but the behavior therapy group was the most effective of all. The comparison between the two real therapy conditions may be questionable for the

Table 16.6
RATES OF IMPROVEMENT WITH PSYCHOTHERAPY

Source	Type of therapy	Percentage cured or improved
Jones (1936)	Psychoanalytic	68
Knight (1941)	Psychoanalytic	76
Wolpe (1958)	Behavior	90
Lazarus (quoted in Paul, 1969)	Behavior	86
Neustatter (1935)	Eclectic	50
Miles, Barabee, and Finesinger (1951)	Eclectic	58

reasons mentioned earlier in our discussion of research problem in this area. Nevertheless, the most important result of this study is that systematic treatment, whether it be insight oriented or behavior oriented, was quite effective in reducing the students' anxiety. Naturally, the condition was not particularly serious to begin with, but it is reassuring that treatment was successful.

Two thorough reviews of most of the research on psychotherapy (Bergin, 1971; Howard and Orlinsky, 1972) concluded that those who received psychotherapy do show appreciable improvement (see Table 16.6). The authors avoid providing an estimate of the actual percentage of patients who improved; there are so many problems with the studies and so many unresolved factors that any such figure might be misleading. Nevertheless, there is substantial reason to believe that psychotherapy is a powerful experience that can probably be even further improved by an openness to new therapeutic techniques and more systematic research on what factors in the treatment are most crucial. ■

Summary

1. Attitudes toward psychopathology have advanced considerably from the belief that mental disturbances were caused by evil spirits. Nineteenth-century psychoanalytic theory introduced the more scientific idea that disturbed people were afflicted with an illness that could be treated like a physical illness. And in recent years behavior therapists have preferred the term "disorder," since they consider the disturbance a problem in learning.

2. Organic treatments for mental disorders are based on the assumption that the condition is due in part to physical causes. Of the organic treatments, tranquilizing drugs are being used most widely. They have been very helpful in alleviating the anxiety and symptoms of psychotics, and making these patients more accessible to psychological treatments. Antidepressant drugs, especially lithium, seem to be effective treatments for depression.

3. Psychoanalysis is based on the Freudian idea that mental disturbances are caused by unconscious conflicts. Free association and analysis of the patient's dreams are used to bring the conflict into

the open. Through transference the patient forms a strong emotional attachment to the therapist, who comes to symbolize important relationships in the patient's life. An understanding of transference enables the therapist to help the patient work through the conflict. Working through involves learning to express emotions hitherto suppressed, mentally reliving early experiences, and learning to face similar conflicts in present relationships.

4. In behavior therapy, techniques based on extensive research in learning are used to help the patient unlearn undesirable behavior and substitute healthy behavior. In contrast to psychoanalysis, behavior therapy denies the existence of an underlying conflict. The symptom is the problem and is due to maladaptive learning. Thus, treatment is focused on the symptom itself. The primary techniques for teaching the new behavior are systematic desensitization, modeling, aversive techniques, and positive reinforcement.

5. Humanistic therapies emphasize that each of us has the capacity for solving our own problems. The focus is on treating present problems, although past experiences are not ignored. In person-centered therapy, developed by Carl Rogers, therapists offer few interpretations, express personal reactions to patients, and provide feedback by carefully selecting revealing statements that patients have made and repeating them back. This mirroring process is intended to help patients become more aware of their feelings and thoughts.

6. Play therapy is designed to be used with disturbed children who are not likely to be able to verbalize their feelings and experiences. As play proceeds the child may act out feelings or make statements that offer clues to the nature of the conflict.

7. The idea behind group therapy is that many mental disorders revolve around interactions with other people. The group setting fosters an atmosphere in which the patients can work through many kinds of interpersonal problems.

8. Encounter groups encourage open, honest expression of feelings as a means of strengthening relationships and helping individuals get in touch with their true nature.

9. Evaluation of the effectiveness of psychological therapies is hampered by numerous research problems. Since the evaluation process often relies on self-reports by the patient or therapist, the results must be interpreted cautiously. In addition, it is difficult to equate patients in terms of how disturbed they are, and therapists in terms of their experience and ability.

10. Eysenck's studies of the success of psychoanalytic therapy, which found a 67-percent rate of spontaneous recovery, were seriously flawed by errors in computation, judgment, and interpretation. More careful studies found a spontaneous recovery rate of 30 percent, which indicates that a majority of patients with mental disorders do not recover spontaneously. Several other studies have shown that patients who undergo treatment

are helped to various degrees, and it seems likely that new therapeutic techniques and more systematic research will increase the rate of recovery.

RECOMMENDED READING

Axline, V. M. *Dibs in Search of Self.* New York: Ballantine, 1964. A lovely, moving account of therapy with a young boy. Gives a clear picture of how play therapy combined with a Rogerian method operates.

Green, H. *I Never Promised You a Rose Garden.* New York: New American Library, 1971. A woman's brilliant and touching description of psychosis and treatment. One of the finest novels on this subject.

Kesey, K. *One Flew Over the Cuckoo's Nest.* New York: Viking, 1962. A novel about mental hospitals. Moving and dramatic.

Lieberman, M. A., I. D. Yalom, and M. B. Miles. *Encounter Groups: First Facts.* New York: Basic Books, 1973. There is not much good research on encounter groups, but this book presents whatever is available.

O'Leary, K., and G. Wilson. *Behavior Therapy.* Englewood Cliffs, N.J.: Prentice-Hall, 1975. A clear presentation of how behavior therapy deals with various conditions.

Rogers, C. R. *Client-Centered Therapy.* Boston: Houghton Mifflin, 1951. Although somewhat out of date since Roger's ideas have changed, this book still presents one approach to psychotherapy better than any other.

Wolpe, J. *The Practice of Behavior Therapy.* New York: Pergamon Press, 1969. One of the most vocal and influential behavior therapists describes his work and theory.

No man is an islande entire unto himself.
John Donne

You don't live in a world all alone. Your brothers are here too.
Albert Schweitzer on receiving the Nobel Prize

17 Social Psychology

Social concerns ▪ *Social perception and attribution theory* ▪ *Affiliation* ▪ *Social facilitation* ▪ *Competition versus cooperation* ▪ *Groups*

magine yourself sitting alone in your room reading, watching television, or just daydreaming. Try to picture exactly how you are feeling and what you might be doing. Now imagine that someone else is in the room with you, or even watching you from across the street. Whether or not you know the other person, whether or not you interact in any way, the whole situation has changed. The presence of another person will have profound effects on how you feel and act. You will no longer feel free to perform certain acts, and you will be more self-conscious, more concerned about how you look, and probably less relaxed. And if you begin interacting with the other person in any way, the changes are even greater. This is a simple illustration of the fact that other people are the most important stimulus in almost any situation. We are social animals. Except for a few basic physiological needs, our motives are directly or indirectly related to and indeed defined by other people. The field of social psychology attempts to describe and explain how we are affected by social considerations.

Almost all of the phenomena we have been discussing in this book depend to some extent on contact with others. Perception is shaped by our interactions with people; most of what we learn is through social contact; our way of thinking, motives, emotions, language, and personality depend largely on social interactions. In this chapter and the next we shall discuss some of the most important motives and concerns that are primarily social in nature, and shall consider specific effects of social situations. We shall start with some general social considerations, then discuss why and when people want to be together, some of the simple effects of being with others, and how being in a group affects our behavior. In the next chapter we shall deal with the broad question of social influence, how groups and individuals affect our attitudes and behavior.

SOCIAL CONCERNS

Almost all of the motives we have mentioned thus far involve other people to some extent. Even the innate motives such as hunger and curiosity are affected by the social situation, and obviously sex, the need for achievement, and so on depend greatly on other people. However, these motives can exist and even be satisfied apart from other human beings. We have sexual feelings in part for physical reasons, we have them when we are alone, and we can partially satisfy them by ourselves. The need for achievement is learned through social interactions, but once learned can be felt even on a deserted island and can be satisfied by accomplishing something on our own. In contrast, certain motives and concerns are purely social. They cannot exist or be satisfied without other people. Moreover, these motives tend to be aroused whenever we are with other people and therefore play a major role in all of our social interactions. The most important of these motives are the desire to be liked and accepted, the fear of being deviant, and the need for social comparison. As we shall see, all of these are closely related because they center on other people's reactions to us, but each has a slightly different emphasis and different effects.

Need for Acceptance and Liking

We mentioned in Chapter 9 that one of our most powerful motives is the desire to be liked by other people. This is probably learned through a process of reinforcement that begins in infancy and continues throughout life. Most of our basic needs are satisfied either directly by other people or in their presence. Babies get food from their parent. When they are uncomfortable, they are comforted by their parent. If the mothering adult is not present, their needs will not be satisfied and they will be more likely to be uncomfortable. Thus, the parent is associated with positive reinforcements and the absence of the parent often with punishment, such as the discomfort of a wet diaper or hunger pangs. Next, discrimination begins and babies learn that when the parent is happy or feeling kind, more reinforcements appear than when the parent is angry. And soon babies learn that it is very important to make the parent like them, to make the parent smile. A mother or father's smile becomes a reinforcement in itself—a secondary reinforcer of great strength. As we go through life, this generalizes to all other people. When they like us, we expect rewards from them; when they dislike us, we expect no reward, or punishment. Moreover, simply having them like us is a secondary reinforcement even without any other reward, while having them dislike or reject us is unpleasant. People may differ in how strongly they feel this need to be liked, but for almost all of us it is one of the dominant factors in our lives.

Clearly we want the people we know and care about to like us. We also want people whose behavior can affect us to like us—fellow workers, our boss, teachers, uncles, aunts, the tough guy down the block, the popular girl in school, the leader of the team, and so on. But what is remarkable is how strong this motive is when it involves people we do not know at all and who can never have any effect on our lives. If you drive through a town, stop to get gas, and have a brief interaction with the gas-station attendant, you want even him to like you. If he sneers at you, it is unpleasant; if he smiles, it is pleasant. Yet it does not really matter in any rational sense—you have no expectation of future contact, and the gas will go into the car however he feels about you. The simple fact is that you are pleased if you make a good impression and displeased if you make a bad impression. This will matter less than it would with someone who has more impact on your life, of course, but it does matter. We have learned this motive very early in life, we are continuously reinforced, and we generalize the motive to all people. Thus, in any social situation, one of our overriding motives is to make other people like and react positively to us, and to some extent we are always concerned about the possibility that they will not.

Fear of Being Deviant

Closely related to this first concern is a fear of being different or *deviant*. People feel that if they are too different they will be treated badly, rejected, and not liked; therefore there is a tendency to avoid being or appearing deviant. People presumably learn this concern through experiences in which they are in fact rejected because they are deviant or in which they witness someone else being rejected for

Although we consider this painting by Manet, entitled "Luncheon on the Grass," a classic example of impressionistic art, Manet's own contemporaries branded him as an unbalanced, uncultured deviant because of what they considered a radical departure from traditional artistic modes and subject matter.

this reason. They may also be told by parents or others that it is dangerous to be too different. Thus, again by the usual processes of learning, they learn to avoid being deviant.

There is considerable evidence that deviants are actually treated badly in many circumstances. We have already described experimental studies in which people who were labeled as deviant, with no other details about how they differed, were denied good jobs and given bad ones (Freedman and Doob, 1968). The same treatment is given to members of a group who hold positions different from the majority (Schachter, 1959). And, of course, we are all familiar with the sad fact that prejudice consists largely of mistreating people who are different. Therefore, the fear of being deviant is generally highly adaptive—deviants are treated worse, so avoiding being a deviant is likely to lead to better treatment.

One of the striking aspects of our treatment of deviants is that the direction of deviancy does not matter as much as one might think (Freedman and Doob, 1968). That is, being different in a positive direction leads to almost as much bad treatment as being deviant in a negative direction. Very smart people are subjected to the same kind of rejection as are very dumb people; very rich, very poor—all suffer somewhat from being different. Naturally, having the positive attribute has other compensations—it is better to be rich than poor—but you will still face potential rejection if you deviate too much from the norm. Thus, even on clearly positive traits, many people try to avoid being too different. A college student may conceal that she is well educated or very smart if she is with a group of noncollege people; a rich person will conceal his wealth when he is with less well-to-do people, and so on. By hiding their deviant characteristic, people are more likely to fit in and to be accepted. Once again this varies considerably from person to person, but most people are strongly motivated to avoid being deviant and are often concerned about this possibility.

Social Comparison

We all have a strong tendency to evaluate ourselves on a wide variety of qualities. Are we smart, beautiful, intelligent, sexy, and successful? Also, we want to know if we are responding appropriately in a given situation—are we right to be feeling sad, happy, or disgusted? This need to know where we stand has a strong cognitive component—we want to understand the situation and ourselves—and is associated with the first two concerns about being liked and not being deviant.

On some characteristics, an objective measure exists. If you want to know how tall you are, you can use a ruler; if you want to know how well you did on a test or how fast you can run, you can get a grade or be timed on a stopwatch. But on even these characteristics—and certainly on those where there is no objective measure, such as beauty, emotions, or success—the only way you can really find out where you stand is by comparing yourself to other people.

Leon Festinger (1954) proposed in his theory of social comparison that in the absence of objective criteria for evaluating performance, people will seek out others with whom to compare themselves. Moreover, according to Festinger, we tend to seek out other people who are already fairly similar to us because the information we get will be more useful. If you want to know how good you are at tennis, you want to compare yourself with someone who is roughly comparable. If you are just starting, you don't want to play Jimmy Connors—it will not tell you anything when he beats you. Instead, you want to play someone else who is either also starting or who has been playing only a short time. If you win, you are doing pretty well; if you lose, your progress has been slow. Research has supported this idea that in comparing talents, skills, feelings, or anything else, you seek out those who are in the same situation as you and are roughly comparable to you on other characteristics (Samuel, 1973; Zanna, Goethals, and Hill, 1975).

There are many other motives that involve social interactions, but these three are the ones that seem to be entirely social in nature. They arise from social situations, can be satisfied only within social situations, and almost always affect our feelings and actions when we are with other people. As we shall see during this and the next chapter, these concerns of wanting to be liked, fearing deviancy, and seeking social comparison affect a wide variety of social behaviors. In a sense, they are the three major themes that run through all of social life.

With these considerations in mind (and without forgetting that many other motives such as sex, need for achievement, and aggressiveness play critical roles), let us turn to some basic social phenomena. We shall start with social perception, and then discuss affiliation, the effects of the presence of another person, the effects of being in a group, and finally how groups as a whole function.

SOCIAL PERCEPTION AND ATTRIBUTION THEORY

How we perceive the world greatly affects our attitudes and behavior. We discussed this in Chapter 2, where we saw that people differ in their perceptions of depth, susceptibility to visual illusions, and so on. Clearly, these differences in perception will produce differences in behavior. If you lack depth perception at distances over thirty feet and perceive a huge lion as only six inches tall, you are less likely to run away than if you see it accurately. The effect of perception on behavior is especially powerful in social situations, where so many stimuli and judgments are ambiguous and where, as a result, there are much greater differences in our perceptions.

As we mentioned earlier, our expectations tend to affect our perceptions because, whenever there is any ambiguity, we see what we expect to see. If we expect our team to play fairly and the other team to cheat, we will probably perceive the game that way even if, objectively, the two teams are playing the same way. If we think someone is an unpleasant, aggressive person, we tend to interpret all of her behavior in those terms. On any given occasion she might be perfectly pleasant and friendly, but we still may perceive her actions as aggressive because we expect them to be. This complex relationship between expectations, perceptions, and behavior plays an important role in all social interactions.

Stereotypes and Prejudice

The effect of expectations and perceptions is especially evident in prejudice. We all learn certain *stereotypes* about groups of people through our interactions with members of those groups and from information provided by friends, parents, and society. Thus we might learn that Germans are industrious, Scandinavians are blond, Chinese are mathematical wizards, and Italians are passionate. We also learn negative stereotypes about all sorts of national or racial groups. These stereotypes, whether positive or negative, tend to affect our perceptions of individual members of each group. If we think that Germans are industrious, we will probably perceive a particular German as industrious even if he is not an especially hard worker. And if we think Jews are pushy or blacks athletic, we will perceive members of these groups as conforming to our stereotype. Naturally, we all differ in how strongly we hold these stereotypes and how much we are affected by them, but our expectations about a group tend to affect our perceptions.

Clearly, this is one of the causes of prejudice. If we have a negative stereotype about a group, this causes us to have more negative perceptions of a member of that group than we would if we did not have the stereotype. Any ambiguous actions by individuals who belong to the group may be interpreted negatively rather than positively. Since prejudice is, in part, a result of stereotyping, one way to reduce prejudice is to eliminate stereotypes. This is not easy and may not get rid of prejudice completely, but it is one positive approach. In addition, being aware that we have stereotypes and making an effort not to let them affect our perceptions are also positive steps in reducing prejudice. We may honestly believe that all Germans are industrious (perhaps they are more industrious than other people),

This is a posed photo showing how the Italians might behave if they conformed to a common stereotype. Preconceptions such as "all Italians are passionate" are one of the primary causes of prejudice.

but we can still treat each particular German the same way we treat any other person.

Liking and Social Perception

Our perception of other people affects how much we like them, and this operates in the other direction also. As we discussed in Chapter 9, we tend to like people who are similar to us. But it is also true that once we decide we like someone, we tend to *perceive* them as more similar to us. This is particularly true of married couples and other people who spend a lot of time together. Fill out the personality scales in Fig. 17.1 for yourself and for your best friend or someone you are close to. Then have the other person do the same, and compare your ratings. You will probably find that you rated the other person as more similar to you than he or she actually rated himself or herself. Husbands and wives almost always think that their spouse is considerably more similar to them than they are, and are surprised to find that they disagree on many things and do not have personalities that are quite as close as they thought.

Fig. 17.1
Personality descriptions of self and friend

Using the scales below, first put a check where you think you fall; then put an X where you think a close friend falls.

Dishonest	Honest
Happy	Sad
Dominant	Submissive
Pessimistic	Optimistic
Humorous	Not humorous
Weak	Strong
Active	Passive
Liberal	Conservative
Nervous	Calm
Warm	Cold

As might be expected, the opposite is true with people we do not like. We assume that their attitudes and values are further away from ours than they actually are. And these two tendencies have the joint effect of dividing the world more sharply than it should be. We all tend to perceive people in two groups—those we like, who are similar to us, and those we dislike, who are dissimilar. Actually, there is a lot more overlap than we usually think, but our perceptions sharpen the distinctions.

Attribution Theory—The Perception of Causality

One aspect of perception that is particularly important in social situations concerns the perception of *causality*. Whenever anything happens in the world, we look for what caused it. When the event involves inanimate objects or natural phenomena the cause is usually obvious and straightforward—the car stopped because I stepped on the brake, or it rained because of a weather front. Even if we do not understand the scientific principles involved, we have a clear perception of what caused what. But with human behavior, and particularly in social situations, perception of causality is much more difficult.

A critical reason for this difficulty is that human behavior is motivated. As we discussed in detail in Chapter 9, people generally act because they *want* to do something—they are internally motivated, not forced to act (like the car) by external forces. And our perception of people's motives and intentions is a crucial factor in our reactions to social phenomena.

Attribution theory, an important development in social psychology, deals with how we decide what motivated a particular act or behavior; in other words, how we *attribute* causation (Heider, 1958; Jones and Harris, 1967; Kelley, 1967). Whenever we observe a person's behavior, we decide whether the person acted for internal or external causes, whether she wanted to act that way or was forced to, and what specific internal or external causes are involved. For example, if a person you do not know well says she likes you, you will probably try to attribute her statement to some cause. Perhaps she said it for external reasons such as simply to be courteous, or perhaps she said it because she wants something from you. If she is applying for a job and you are doing the hiring, she might say something nice just to get the job. Or maybe she really does like you.

If you decide she really does like you, then you tend to think about why she likes you. To what should you *attribute* her liking? Is it your looks, your charm, your sense of humor, or something else? Perhaps, sadly, you decide that she is undiscriminating and likes everyone. Each of these decisions has an effect on your response to the situation and your actions toward the other person. As we discussed in Chapter 9, we almost always like someone who says they like us. But the more we think they are saying it because they really feel it, the more we like them. To the extent that we attribute their behavior to outside forces or to a lack of discrimination, we will be less impressed and will like them less (Jones, 1964).

Rules affecting attribution In any social situation, our attribution of causality tends to follow certain rules. Kelley (1967) proposed that *consistency* and *distinctiveness* of the behavior are two crucial factors. If someone behaves consistently from one situation to another—if, for example, someone is always aggressive or likes all science-fiction movies—we tend to attribute his response to internal causes. We assume that he is an aggressive person or is a science-fiction fan. In contrast, if he likes a particular science-fiction movie but dislikes others, we would assume that the movie itself was causing his response—that is, that his reaction was determined by external causes. In addition, the more distinctive the behavior, the more likely we are to attribute it to external causes. If someone hates all science-fiction movies but likes this one, we would naturally think that this was an especially good movie (external cause). Similarly, if a man is unfriendly to most people but is extremely friendly to you, it would seem that your characteristics are causing this unusual behavior (external cause) rather than some characteristic of the man. Various studies have supported these predictions in a variety of situations (MacArthur, 1972; Karaz and Perlman, 1975).

We also attribute internal motivation more to powerful people than to people who seem weak. Presumably we assume that people with strong positions or high status are freer to do what they want and are therefore less influenced by external pressures (Thibaut and Riecken, 1955). In addition, the less external pressure we see and the less people have to gain from their actions, the more we attribute them to internal motives. In the extreme case—if there is a gun to someone's head, for instance—we assume that whatever the person does is for external reasons. When soldiers are captured by the enemy and then make speeches against their own country, the speeches carry very little weight because we know that the captives are under great external pressures and that they probably do not mean what they are saying.

We also form perceptions of the causes behind our own actions and feelings. If you feel depressed one morning, you may decide that it is because you had a fight with a friend the night before; but you can also attribute it to the fact that you did not get enough sleep. If you are very nervous and irritable, you look around for a reason. One possibility might be that you are nervous about an exam; an entirely different one would be that you drank four cups of coffee at breakfast. Clearly, the implications of each explanation are quite different.

We saw this attribution process at work in Schachter and Singer's experiments on emotions (Chapter 10). When subjects were aroused by an injection of epinephrine and then exposed to someone who acted angry, the subjects became angry. The physiological arousal plus the cognitive-social stimulation produced an emotional state. However, the subjects' knowledge of the effects of the injection was crucial. When they knew that the epinephrine produced the arousal, they attributed their arousal to the drug rather than to their own emotions and became less angry. When they did not attribute arousal to the drug, they perceived the situation differently and became angrier.

Similarly, attributions play an important role in social relationships. Suppose you find that you are excited whenever you are with a particular person of the opposite sex, that you want to be with that person, and that life seems better and more interesting when you are. Under these circumstances many people begin to wonder whether they are "in love." Often the crucial question is whether the excitement is due entirely to sexual attraction and arousal, or to deep feelings of attachment, caring, and so on. The distinction is difficult to make and attributing the feeling simply to sex obviously leads to totally different consequences than attributing it to love. One point is that incorrect attributions can lead to serious mistakes: I am depressed rather than just tired; I am nervous rather than just on a coffee jag; I am in love rather than just sexually aroused. Knowing the cause of our own emotions and feelings can help us understand ourselves better and avoid misinterpreting situations and reacting inappropriately to them.

Actor versus observer The attributions we make about our own behavior are quite different from those we make about other people's behavior. In particular, when we are the person performing the behavior (the actor) we usually exaggerate the importance of external factors, whereas when someone else is acting and we are the observer, we stress the importance of internal factors (Jones and Nisbett, 1971). In one study (Nisbett et al., 1973), male students were asked to explain why they had chosen their girlfriend and also why their best friend had chosen his girlfriend. In talking about their own feelings, the students listed all sorts of characteristics of their girlfriend (factors external to them), but they attributed their friend's feelings mostly to his own characteristics (internal factors).

We also assume that other people will behave more consistently from one situation to another than we do ourselves. We reason that because their behavior is chiefly motivated internally, it follows that they will be consistent, whereas we are more influenced by changing factors in the situation and therefore will not behave as consistently. This might explain in part why most people believe in consistent personality traits even though they themselves often behave inconsistently (see Chapter 14 for a discussion of this issue).

The difference between attributions of the actor and observer implies that we place blame differently. If we commit a wrongful act, we tend to blame external pressures (I cheated because the temptation was too great, because everyone else cheats, because she showed me her paper, and so on) whereas if someone else commits the same act we tend to blame his personality (he cheated because he is dishonest, wants to get into medical school and has no principles, and so on). One way to overcome this tendency is to put ourselves into the shoes of the other person and imagine how he must be feeling; in this way we can minimize this difference and begin to appreciate that other people also are exposed to strong external pressures (Regan and Totten, 1975).

AFFILIATION

Human beings are gregarious animals. We almost all live with and interact constantly with other people. Because this tendency to associate with others, to *affiliate*, is such a universal characteristic of our species, it provides a good example of how social behavior is controlled by a combination of innate factors, learning, and specific social motives.

EDWARD JONES

Instinct and Innate Characteristics

An instinctive drive to affiliate may have been built into our genetic structure by the Darwinian process of natural selection (see Chapter 8). According to this basic biological principle, a wide variety of characteristics will appear in any species by the chance operation of various factors that produce alterations in the genes. Those characteristics that have high survival value will tend to be retained and passed on to other generations, and eventually will become part of the basic heredity of all members of the species. Those characteristics that have low survival value will tend to disappear. In these terms, it is clear that a tendency to affiliate would have high survival value and should be retained. This was certainly true thousands of years ago, when survival was a great deal harder than it is now. Those early people who happened to have a genetically determined inclination to band together would be able to protect each other from wild animals, build shelters, hunt game, and care for their young much better than those people who preferred solitary lives. The gregarious people would tend to live longer, have larger families, and therefore pass on their heredity to more people. It is plausible that over many hundreds of generations, a genetic tendency to affiliate would become more and more a part of our hereditary base. Thus, people who are born now may have a genetically determined instinct to affiliate.

As with explanations of other behaviors in terms of instinct, this is almost impossible to test. People do affiliate, they do this more or less from birth, and almost no one is entirely solitary. All of this fits the notion that affiliation is instinctive, but there is no hard evidence one way or the other. Accordingly, all we can say is that virtually all human beings do seem to be gregarious and there may be some instinctive component to this behavior.

Whether or not affiliation is instinctive, it certainly is determined to some extent by other innate characteristics of human beings. More than any other animal, human infants are dependent on their parent for survival. Newborn deer can walk immediately. Within a few months they can run fast enough to keep up with the herd. Infant dogs, cats, lions, and almost any other mammals are almost self-sufficient within a few months, and by the end of the year can defend themselves against most predators. Chimpanzees and gorillas mature somewhat more slowly, but are very powerful within a few years and reach adulthood by four or five. In contrast, human infants are totally helpless at birth and continue to be extremely dependent for some time. They do not even walk until about a year, and certainly could not find food or defend themselves for many years after that. Conceivably, a mature child of six could survive in an entirely benign environment, where edible foods were within easy reach and where there were no predators. But by and large humans are dependent on others for their existence at least until the age of eight, and where predators exist for many years after that. Thus, simply because of this very slow rate of maturation, humans must affiliate with others for many years in order to survive.

This means that both adult and infant humans are necessarily gregarious for a long time. Infants need at least one adult to feed and protect them, and under most circumstances that adult needs at least

BOX 17.1

BIRTH ORDER AND AFFILIATION

Schachter discovered almost by accident that people who are born first in their family differ considerably in terms of affiliation from those who are born later. When first-borns were made afraid, they showed a much stronger preference for being with other people than when they were not afraid. But later-borns did not differ in their preference whether they were afraid or not afraid. Moreover, this is not due to the size of the family. A first-born in a family with only one child has the same reaction as a first-born in a large family; and a third-born of three children reacts the same as a third-born of seven children (see Figure). In other words, the cause has to do with order of birth, not family size.

This difference between first-borns and later-borns influences the kinds of jobs they take and their responses to stress. First-borns are much less likely than later-borns to be fighter pilots or skydivers (lonely professions). In addition, when they have psychological problems first-borns tend to seek psychotherapy (relying on someone else), while later-borns are much more likely than first-borns to be alcoholics (a solitary solution).

The reason for this difference is far from certain. One plausible explanation has to do with how parents treat their first-born children. Usually, parents are very nervous about their first child, rush to its aid whenever it seems unhappy, spend a lot of time with it, and particularly try to console it when it is afraid. The second child also gets a lot of care, but by this time the parents have learned that children are less fragile than they thought. The parents have gained some confidence, are less worried, and know more about what is a serious problem. When the first-born falls, the parents rush over; when the second-born falls, the parents probably look over and see that it is still alive and not seriously injured. By the time the third child arrives, the parents

are much less likely to spend a lot of time with it. Thus, the children are given different amounts of attention, especially when they are afraid or nervous. Children learn to depend more or less on other people as a result of the amount of attention they are given. Therefore, first-borns learn to depend on others a great deal; second-borns less so; and so on. And later in life, the first-borns continue to seek out others when they are afraid more than do later-borns.

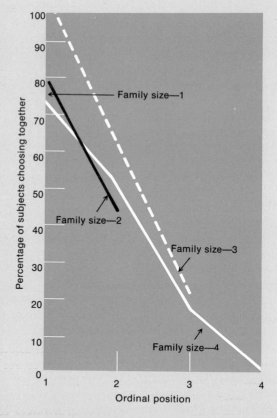

When they are afraid, people born earlier in a family affiliate more than those born later. Note that the size of the family has no effect. (From Schachter, 1959)

one other to provide for other family needs. In other words, whether or not there is an instinctive tendency to affiliate, because of the innate helplessness of infants, human beings must stay together in order for their infants to survive.

Satisfaction of Needs and Learning

However, there is more to affiliation than what we have discussed, because even after people reach adulthood and are no longer dependent on others for survival they almost always continue to affiliate. There are very few hermits, and they are almost always considered extremely strange. There are various reasons for this continued affiliation. In the first place, adult humans do need others for the satisfaction of various needs. In addition to sexual needs, people have all sorts of learned motives, such as the need for achievement, the need for respect and esteem, the need to be praised, and so on, that can be satisfied only by other human beings. In addition, because most reinforcement has been associated with the presence of other people, we have learned that other people are generally positive. Just as with other learned behaviors, we learn to affiliate because we are often rewarded when we do. As we discussed in Chapter 3, affiliation is a learned drive—being with people is a secondary reinforcement. Therefore even after our innate needs have been satisfied, we continue to affiliate because we have learned to do so and because various acquired motives are satisfied only when we are with other people.

Social Motives

Up to now we have been talking in quite general terms. People affiliate for instinctive or innate reasons, because they have learned to affiliate, and to satisfy a wide variety of needs. We also affiliate because the presence of other people serves certain specific purposes that are largely social and cannot be met in any other way. A series of studies by Stanley Schachter (1959) and others has focused on two major factors in affiliation—the reduction of fear and the need for social comparison.

Fear reduction In laboratory experiments, Schachter told subjects that they were going to receive electric shocks, and described these shocks as either severe ("These shocks will hurt, they will be painful . . . but, of course, they will do no permanent damage") or mild ("What you will feel will not in any way be painful . . . it will resemble more a tickle or a tingle than anything unpleasant"). Then these subjects—who were presumably either quite frightened or only slightly frightened—were given a choice of waiting with other people or being alone while the apparatus was made ready. The strong-shock, high-fear subjects showed a much stronger tendency to affiliate than the mild-shock, low-fear subjects. Apparently being able to talk about the situation or just having other people around is reassuring. Indeed, Wrightsman (1960) showed that frightened subjects who waited with other people did become somewhat less frightened. If you think about the survival value of affiliation, this effect makes good sense. It is exactly when you are frightened that being with others should be

PHILIP ZIMBARDO

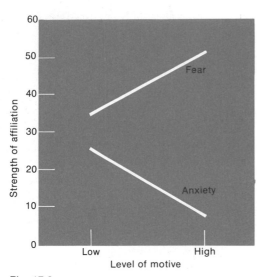

Fig. 17.2
Motivation and affiliation

Fear increases affiliation but anxiety reduces it.
(After Sarnoff and Zimbardo, 1961)

most helpful since they are supposed to provide protection and support.

A later study by Irving Sarnoff and Philip Zimbardo (1961; replicated by Teichman, 1973) made the important point that increased affiliation occurs when people are frightened but not when they are anxious or nervous. In this experiment, high and low fear was aroused the same way as in the original study; but other subjects were made to feel either high or low anxiety by having them anticipate experiences that were potentially embarrassing (such as sucking on a metal breast shield—high anxiety—or a lollipop—low anxiety). Then all were given a choice of waiting alone or with other people. As shown in Fig. 17.2, high fear increased affiliation but high anxiety reduced it. Being with others reduces fear, but it increases anxiety because we are worried about being embarrassed and will be even more embarrassed when other people are around. As we would expect in terms of the basic social concerns of being accepted and not appearing deviant, anytime we are nervous about seeming strange or looking foolish, we will tend to avoid social contact rather than seek it out.

These findings imply that frightening situations such as air raids, waiting to take an exam, or preparing to be operated on will cause people to affiliate. In fact, there is ample anecdotal evidence that people are highly gregarious during periods of stress such as war, natural disasters, or personal hardship. On the other hand, anxiety-arousing situations such as waiting to go on an important date (for people concerned about social competence) or waiting to hear about getting into medical school should cause people to avoid affiliation.

Social comparison Another factor that leads to affiliation is the need for social comparison. As we mentioned earlier, we all have strong tendencies to compare ourselves to others in order to find out how we are doing relative to them, and also to discover if we are responding appropriately to any situation. These concerns are especially strong when we are confronted with an unfamiliar or strange situation, where we are not certain just what and how much we should be feeling. Being frightened by an impending electric shock is just such a situation, and indeed Schachter has shown that one of the reasons high fear leads to affiliation is that people want to compare themselves to others. As predicted by Festinger's theory of social comparison (1954), this desire to affiliate is quite specific—people want to be with others who are similar to them, not with people who are different. When they are expecting a shock, people want to be with others who are also expecting a shock. As Schachter (1959) says, "Misery doesn't just love company, it loves miserable company."

Other research has shown that whenever people are unsure of their own reactions they want to affiliate with others in order to find out if they are reacting properly. The more information we have about our own reactions and those of others—the more certain we are—the less we need to compare ourselves and the less we affiliate (Gerard and Rabbie, 1961). Unfamiliar feelings, such as severe hunger experienced by usually well-fed college students (Schachter, 1959), also increases affiliation, again because we want to compare our feelings to those of others.

Thus, affiliation is determined by a variety of factors. It may have an instinctive basis. It certainly is caused by innate characteristics that make us dependent on others for survival and for the satisfaction

OBJECTIVE SELF-AWARENESS

The presence of another person affects us mainly by causing us to be concerned about how we are being evaluated and how we are appearing. Throughout our lives, the extent of this concern varies greatly depending on many characteristics of the situation. When other people are present we are more concerned; when the other people are important to us, our concern increases still more; and if we are specifically told that we are being evaluated, our concern becomes greater still. It is also possible to have these concerns even when we are alone. Sometimes, we picture ourselves as others see us; we ask, "How do I appear to others?" or we "step outside ourselves" and take a relatively objective view of our behavior. Whenever we do this, our concern about being evaluated (even if it is by ourselves) increases.

Shelley Duval and Robert Wicklund (1972) have called this tendency to look at ourselves as others would *objective self-awareness*. They have shown that when this kind of awareness is aroused, people behave quite differently from when it is not aroused. The major effect seems to be that people tend to act more in line with what they think are the correct social norms, to try to behave properly, and to perform well. Just as is the case with social facilitation, when our objective self-awareness is aroused, we perform simple tasks better and complex tasks less well (Liebling and Shaver, 1973). We are also less aggressive if that is the correct behavior (Scheier, Fenigstein, and Buss, 1974), or more aggressive if that seems appropriate (Carver, 1974). In other words, whatever the norms are, we are more affected by them when we are more self-aware.

Perhaps the most fascinating aspect of this work is the techniques by which

ROBERT WICKLUND

objective self-awareness is produced. Having a television camera running, being observed through a two-way mirror, or just having other people in the room all work. But the most powerful and ingenious method is to have the person sitting in front of a mirror. When you see yourself in a mirror, you immediately become more aware of yourself as a person, you begin to look at yourself from the outside, and you become more objectively self-aware. (This is not due to suspicion about the mirror being a two-way mirror; suspicion is removed by having mirrors sitting on a table or by making it obvious through other means that no one is looking through the mirror.) Try it for yourself. Sit in front of a mirror while you perform some task. It does make you conscious of yourself in a way that you rarely are when you cannot see your own face. And this self-consciousness causes you to be more aware of how you are behaving and to be more concerned about behaving properly. Thus, just as the presence of others arouses these concerns, we can arouse them in ourselves by looking in a mirror or even just thinking about ourselves and our behavior.

BOX 17.2

of needs. Affiliation is reinforced throughout life and therefore becomes a learned motive. And specific factors such as the reduction of fear and the need for social comparison also increase the desire to be with other people.

SOCIAL FACILITATION

There is a world of difference between being alone and having even one other person present. As early as 1920, Floyd Allport, one of the first systematic social psychologists, discovered that the presence of other people often improves our performance on a variety of tasks. He called this the *social facilitation effect* because performance was facilitated (improved) by being in a social situation. This effect has been demonstrated not only with humans, but also with ants, cockroaches, birds, and other species. For example, an ant by itself dug fifty grams of sand in ten minutes, while a pair of ants together dug one hundred grams of sand in the same time each, even though they were not helping each other in any way (Chen, 1937).

These findings seemed so consistent that at one time they suggested the existence of some sort of "group mind." The presence of other people somehow enhanced performance by raising the individual's consciousness, or brain power. Although there was no clear explanation for the effect, it was widely believed that being with other people would always improve performance.

However, a more careful analysis of the results plus some recent research indicates that this is not the case. Although the presence of others often improves performance, it sometimes has the opposite effect. We now know that whether a performance gets better or worse in the presence of others seems to depend largely on the type of task.

Zajonc (1965) has proposed an explanation for these diverse results. Whenever members of the same species are present, individuals become more aroused. They are motivated to do well, more concerned about their performance, and generally have higher drive. As we discussed in Chapter 9, the effect of increasing drive depends on the particular task. In general, high drive improves performance on simple, well-learned tasks and interferes with performance on complex or new tasks. It does seem as if those tasks on which performance improved (such as canceling vowels and simple arithmetic) are relatively simple, while the others (such as logical deduction and harder arithmetic) are more difficult.

This dual effect of the presence of others has been neatly demonstrated in a series of studies involving both humans and cockroaches (Zajonc et al., 1969; Hunt and Hillery, 1973). People learned simple or complex mazes alone or with others watching, and cockroaches also learned simple or complex mazes (different ones from those the people worked on) either alone or with another cockroach present. The results, shown in Fig. 17.3, are that humans and cockroaches do better on a simple maze when there is company, and worse on the complex maze. Apparently, having another member of the same species present increases arousal and therefore affects performance.

Social Evaluation

The particular type of arousal may vary somewhat, and it is almost certainly different for cockroaches and people. There is, however, some evidence that for people the specific motive that is aroused in the presence of other people is related to our basic concerns about being liked and not appearing deviant. Whenever someone else is present, we tend to worry about how they are perceiving us, and

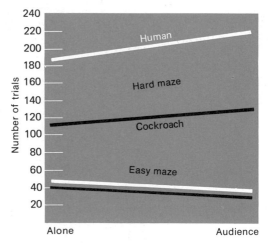

Fig. 17.3
Audience, task difficulty, and performance by humans and cockroaches

Both humans and cockroaches learn an easy maze faster but a hard maze more slowly with an audience. (Naturally, different mazes were used for humans and cockroaches.) (After Zajonc et al., 1969 (cockroach data); Hunt and Hillary, 1972 (human data))

whether we are acceptable. This is sometimes called *social evaluation*. Think back to the situation described earlier in which you first imagine you are alone and then realize that someone is watching you. At least part of the change in your behavior occurs because you do not want to appear foolish or to perform any act that is not socially acceptable (a typical example is picking your nose, but you can probably think of others). You want to be accepted and this motive is aroused whenever other people are present.

Several experiments have provided some support for the idea that concern about evaluation is the motive that is involved in the social facilitation effect. In one study (Cottrell et al., 1968) the social facilitation effect occurred only when the other people present were actually watching the subject. When they were blindfolded, performance by the subject did not differ from when he was alone. This is a rather weird situation (the subject probably wondered what was going on), but it does demonstrate that more than just the presence of another person is necessary to produce the effect. Henchy and Glass (1968) and Paulus and Murdock (1971) further showed that only when the subject expects to be evaluated by the other people is there any effect. All of these experiments suggest that concern about evaluation is at least one source of arousal.

COMPETITION VERSUS COOPERATION

One of our basic choices in social interactions is whether to compete or cooperate with other people. Some kinds of situations are set up so that we are forced to compete. In poker, tennis, getting into graduate school, and political elections one person is going to win and another is going to lose. These are called *zero-sum games*. But in other situations the gains and losses do not have to add to zero—you can both win. These are called *non-zero-sum games*, and are typical of most social interactions. Business dealings, relations among countries, informal social relations—most of our social interactions need not involve a loss to one person so that the other can win. In all of these instances, people can cooperate in order to maximize the gains to both sides, or they can compete.

Unfortunately, there seems to be a general tendency for people to compete even when they could do much better by cooperating. Apparently, the desire to do "better" than someone else is often more important than doing as well as you can yourself. This was demonstrated in a classic study by Morton Deutsch and Robert Krauss in 1960 using a game involving the Acme and Bolt trucking companies. This simple game is played on the board illustrated in Fig. 17.4. The object is for each player to get his or her truck from its starting point to its destination as quickly as possible. The problem is that the shortest route for both sides is along a one-lane road that they must use in opposite directions. Obviously, the solution is to take turns using the road so that both sides can complete the course quickly, because the alternative route is long and slow. So, the question is whether the subjects will cooperate and do well or compete and do poorly.

Sad to say, much of the time both subjects insisted on using the one-lane road first. This meant that the two trucks met head-on and sat

MORTON DEUTSCH

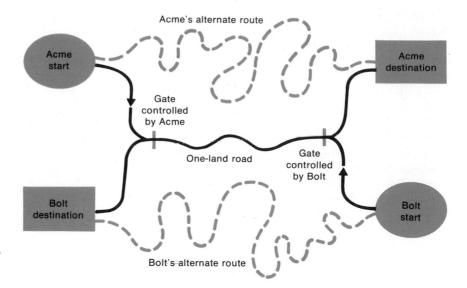

Fig. 17.4
Trucking game

The players try to reach their destination quickly, but the best route requires sharing the use of a one-lane road. People often refuse to cooperate, especially when gates are provided as threats. (From Deutsch and Krauss, 1960)

there for a while, the subjects laughed nervously but did not retreat, and eventually they both lost. When they were provided with barriers with which they could prevent the other side from using the road, the results were particularly bad—each side erected its barrier, used the long road, and both did terribly. Similar results have been found with other games and in many different societies. For reasons that we do not fully understand, it seems to be more important to win than to do well.

Moreover, the stakes that are involved do not change the result. Offering participants substantial amounts of money, as high as nine dollars, does not consistently increase cooperation (Gallo and Sheposh, 1971; Oskamp and Kleinke, 1970). And providing threats of various kinds generally makes things worse. Whenever one or both sides are given a threat, they tend to use it and that increases competitiveness. As we have seen in international affairs during this century, raising the stakes and the power of weapons does not necessarily lead to more cooperation. The one factor that does increase cooperation is greater communication between the participants. If they are allowed, or better still forced, to talk to each other, they are more likely to help each other. Communication does not guarantee cooperation, but it improves the chances.

Friendships and romantic relationships often involve the same kind of processes. Two friends or lovers may compete and play all sorts of games with each other to see who is stronger, who is dominant, or who can get the most while giving the least. Similarly, parents and children may compete to see whose will is more powerful. Children sometimes deliberately do something to annoy the parent, even if the action is not especially rewarding for the child. At the same time, parents may place restrictions on the child mainly to "show who's boss" even if the rule makes little sense and is almost certain to cause conflict. Even in close, loving relationships there seems to be a tendency to compete rather than cooperate fully. Perhaps this is because many people have very strong needs to be dominant; that is, they must show that they are stronger than the other person.

Although it is somewhat chancy to generalize from laboratory experiments such as these to complex world situations, this research may also be applicable to international politics. Countries do seem to compete even when their own self-interests should make them cooperate, and high stakes or greater threats do not improve the situation. On the other hand, increased communication such as provided by the "hot line" between Washington and Moscow, summit meetings, and the UN probably increase the chances of cooperation. Perhaps the ideal situation is one we see often in bargaining between customers and sales-people at used-car lots and country fairs. The salesperson continually pretends he is selling the item at a great loss to himself, that the customer is getting an incredible bargain while he, the seller, is immediately going into bankruptcy. When the sale is completed the customer feels she has "won" the bargaining, the sales-person also feels (probably correctly) that he has "won," and both are happy. In a sense they have competed to their mutual advantage. Such tactics might well be used in international bargaining.

GROUPS

Up to now we have been talking primarily about social situations that involve interactions between only two people. Society is made up of many groups, however, ranging from large ones such as the Democratic or Republican parties to small ones such as a group of five friends, a bridge club, or a family. We all are members of many different groups, and this membership greatly affects our behavior. Let us discuss one key characteristic of groups—leadership—and then consider two specific ways in which groups influence our actions—conformity and risk taking.

Leadership

An almost universal characteristic of groups is that they have leaders. Groups of chickens, lions, cattle, jackdaws, baboons, and practically every other animal have one member or pair of members who are more or less in charge. This individual makes decisions, and chooses where to hunt, which direction to travel, when to stop, and so on. Most human groups also have one person who plays a dominant role in the group's affairs. Although in most cases the human leader cannot make decisions all by herself, the leader has more influence than any other member and often has the deciding voice in what the group will do. Even in informal groups of friends, there is often one person who acts as leader; and, of course, most formal groups have a recognized leader.

We still know very little about the personal characteristics that produce leadership. Some people seem to be "born" leaders—whatever group they are in, they emerge as its leader. This ability or quality is sometimes called *charisma*, but no one has been able to say

INTERVIEW

Abe Burrows is one of Broadway's outstanding figures. As a playwright, director, and performer, he knows show business very well. Some of his best-known productions are Guys and Dolls, Can Can, Silk Stockings, Cactus Flower, *and* How to Succeed in Business Without Really Trying, *for which he won the Pulitzer Prize in 1961. His recent revival of* Guys and Dolls *using an all-black cast was a tremendous hit. When we talked to him he was involved in preparing several new projects. Burrows is a man of enormous energy, always on the go, a professional.*

Q: In working with actors you're faced with the challenge of getting them to do what you think is right for the play, yet generally you can't order them to do anything. How do you get them to follow your lead?

A: First of all, you have to learn that what is generally called "temperament" is really insecurity. There is no person who goes out on the stage without being nervous. Stage fright is very common and some people have violent stage fright. Al Jolson did, believe it or not. Helen Hayes cheerfully admits to it and so do many others. Actors are up there exposing themselves. An actor on stage sometimes feels naked but the play clothes him in some security. What goes on between the actor and the director is a semi-parental situation. The actor is like the director's offspring. The director in the role of a status symbol must realize that the

ABE BURROWS

. . . You have to remember that you're the figure of authority without being authoritarian.

actor is nervous and decide how to handle it. First it is best if he can avoid showing that he is nervous himself—which he is—you can't fake your own security. But he should really try to be definite and positive. The director should do his homework and come to rehearsal prepared. He should know what he wants from his actors. After that you have to treat each person differently and see how it works out.

Q: You are saying that you have to deal with people in a way that works for you personally. You can't make up rules ahead of time.

A: Yes, but you have to remember that you're the figure of authority without being authoritarian and dictatorial—try to get authority and equality.

Q: What do you do if an actor or actress says I won't do that, you're wrong about that?

A: You have to be prepared to lose. You can't make an actor do something that he really doesn't want to do—the actor is out there, you aren't. So you've got to figure a way, sometimes it's a compromise, or maybe find out why he won't, maybe show him why it would be good if he could do it, maybe let him try it once. I've sometimes said, we'll run it through once and see how you feel, and it frequently comes out well. Other times the actor's version is better than my version and I have learned to accept that gracefully and gratefully.

I know certain directors who think of actors as the enemy, just as some parents think of their children as the enemy. But it really is a collaboration. Sure you defer to the one with experience, but you still have to work it out together. When I did my first show, with George Kaufman, I said to my wife, "I'm going to do everything he tells me to do." She said "Everything?" And I said, 'Yeah, everything." And I really learned. When I felt a little strength on my part, then I made suggestions and argued, but at the beginning I accepted his authority.

Q: As a director, in a sense you have to be the eyes of the audience for the actor. How do you do this?

A: Well, I have a funny idea about audiences, which is that they coalesce into one. Shows in Washington, D.C. are a good example. People go there from all over the country, every branch of government, every kind of work. They sit in the balcony or orchestra. And somehow or other I am thrilled by the fact that they listen and two minutes into a good comedy they are all laughing at the same time. They all applaud the same things and there is a magic that happens—they become one.

Q: Do audiences differ in terms of who is in them, such as whether the members are all similar as opposed to all different?

A: A good audience is a mixed audience. I have seen nights where it is a benefit, all ladies from the same club, and if one of them doesn't like it, they all don't. But give me a heterogeneous audience, they may start with different reactions, but the laughter starts and they all share it. And people from thousands of miles away, different races or anything, they all usually end up reacting the same way.

Q: Then how do you picture how an audience will react?

A: I go by my own reaction. I have to. I'm the audience; and if I like it, they will; if I don't like it, they won't. I've had people say to me, "Abe, I like your show, but will the guy in Kansas like it?" I say right away, "*You* didn't really like it. If you have to question what somebody else would think about it, you didn't give yourself to it." Incidentally, if the audience begins to disagree with me, I'd better find myself another business.

Q: But don't people in the theater sometimes say that's a "New York" show and won't do well on the road?

A: I've heard people say it, but I don't believe it. *Guys and Dolls* was supposed to be a New York show but it played all over the country and is still playing.

Comment

Leadership is one of the most important and least understood phenomena of group dynamics. A theater director, such as Abe Burrows, is the leader of the show. He has a certain degree of legitimacy because he has a title and presumably has demonstrated in the past that he deserves it. On the other hand, the cast has not selected him—he has been picked by someone else, the producer. Thus the director must prove himself. Burrows talks about how he cannot order an actor to do something and must compromise. Also that, as in a family, the director provides security to the actor as well as guidance. This fits in well with the research we've discussed on leadership because an appointed leader usually cannot command in the same way as someone who is elected. Leaders must get the cooperation of the members by proving their ability and also by providing something the members need—in this case security.

Burrows' view of an audience is an interesting example of how members of a group can sometimes lose their individual identities. The audience responds together—perhaps not unanimously as he implies—but people are caught up in each other's responses. Do you think this reaction is similar to conformity, or is it more closely related to contagion produced by being in a mob or crowd?

A final point raised in the interview is that actors are very nervous about appearing in front of the audience. Although they are professionals and have a script, there is always the fear of exposure. As we mention in this chapter, one of the most important motives aroused in social situations is the fear of rejection or appearing deviant. The actor is in front of everyone and has no protection. Thus it is understandable that he or she is often especially concerned about being accepted and liked (and not making a fool of himself).

Leadership is one of the most outstanding characteristics of a successful politician.

exactly what produces it. We can list some people who have it—famous people such as Napoleon, Julius Caesar, John Kennedy, Elizabeth I—and you all probably know others who are natural leaders. However, no single personality trait or ability accounts for this tendency to assume leadership. It is probably a complex combination of traits, with many different combinations having the same effect.

Although we do not know the personal qualities that produce leadership, we do know other characteristics that tend to make someone a leader. In the first place, people of higher status or who bring special powers to the group are often chosen as leaders. One study (Strodbeck, James, and Hawkins, 1958) showed that high-status people (professionals, officials, and so on) were much more likely to be elected members of juries than were people of lower status. There is considerable anecdotal evidence that taller soldiers are usually selected as squad leaders, stronger men as captains of football teams, and more courageous boys as leaders of teenage gangs. Similarly, smarter, more attractive, more competent women (or men) are more likely to become leaders of their group. In addition, in many groups, people who talk a lot are likely to be perceived as the leader even if there is no formal vote. In one experiment (Bavelas et al., 1965), quiet members of a group were encouraged to talk by being reinforced whenever they said anything, and simply talking more made these people go way up in the group's estimation of their leadership abilities. This and other studies (Regula and Julian, 1973; Sorrentino and Boutillier, 1975) also showed that it is quantity of talking that counts. The quality of the remarks does make the people seem more competent, more influential, and better contributors, but only quantity relates to leadership. Indeed, someone who talks a lot may be disliked considerably, yet he is still perceived as having strong leadership abilities (Stang, 1973).

Obviously, just talking does not guarantee that you will become a leader. But it seems clear that a high level of participation, sociability, and assertiveness tends to be necessary for leadership. The strong, silent type may sometimes become a leader, but it is more often the strong, talkative person.

One consequence of the importance of communication in determining leadership is that any restriction on people's ability to communicate freely greatly decreases their influence and the possibility that they will be leaders. The critical importance of communication channels is a basic tenet of revolutionaries. In any coup d'etat, control of the nation's communications is essential. In *Seven Days in May* (a fictionalized account of a plot to overthrow the American government), the basic plan of the plotters was to isolate the president and take command of the emergency communication network. In actual revolutions, the palace or central house of government is usually surrounded as soon as possible, and the radio station begins broadcasting that the government has been overthrown. Control of the communications networks not only has tactical advantages in terms of deploying troops and issuing orders, but also tends to convince the undecided portions of the population that the person doing the broadcasting is in fact in command.

This effect has been demonstrated in studies involving small groups (Leavitt, 1951). Five people are given a task to perform, but

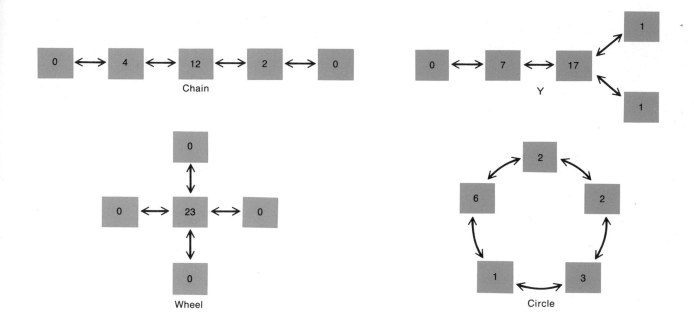

they are put in separate rooms and their communication is carefully limited. Sometimes everyone is allowed to talk to everyone else. In other groups, each person is allowed to talk to only two others (the circle formation), in some one person can talk to everyone while everyone can talk only to that person (the wheel formation), and so on. As you can see in Fig. 17.5, members of these groups differ considerably in the freedom with which they can communicate. When the members are asked to name the leader, their choices are strongly related to the communications setup. As shown in the figure, the more centrally located the person, the more likely it is that he will be named leader.

Legitimacy of leadership Some leaders are elected while others are appointed or hold their position for other reasons, such as heredity (royal families of most countries). Whenever leaders have not been chosen by the members of the group, there is a question of whether they are legitimate—do they deserve to have their power. And there is evidence, as you would imagine, that appointed leaders tend to have less influence and power than those who are elected (Raven and French, 1958). This means that people who are not elected to an office of leadership must try to establish that they have a right to that position.

This was potentially a very serious problem for Gerald Ford, who was the first United States president not elected in a national election. Other vice-presidents have succeeded to office, but in all cases they were elected to the vice-presidency. Although Ford was appointed through the legal process, he was not the choice of the people and to some extent that was a problem throughout his term.

A final note about leaders is that they must not be too different from the rest of the group. Ideally, good leaders will have more

Fig. 17.5
Communication networks and leadership

Only people connected by a line can communicate directly to each other. The more people someone can communicate with, the more often he or she is chosen as leader of the group, as shown by the numbers in the squares. (After Leavitt, 1951)

advanced and progressive views than the rest of the group, will be innovative, and will involve the group in new kinds of activities. However, there is ample evidence that leaders who try to be too innovative or who are too different soon lose their positions. We can watch effective politicians deal with this problem by taking many popular positions to solidify their power, and then (and only then) introducing some new ideas. As we shall see, the reason for this avoidance of deviancy is that probably the most important characteristic of groups is strong pressure for everyone to be the same.

Conformity

All groups exert powerful pressure on their members to agree with the rest of the group; that is, to *conform*. Every member of a gang wears the same outfit, every member of a group of friends is supposed to share the same tastes in clothes, movies, music, and everything else. Naturally, this is rarely the case—people do differ considerably even if they belong to the same group. But there is always some pressure to conform to the group norm.

The enormous power of social pressure of this type has been demonstrated in a famous experiment by Solomon Asch (1951), con-

BOX 17.3

CROWDS AS ATTENTION-GETTERS

Up to a point, larger groups produce more conformity. Larger groups also have the effect of attracting more attention. A march by twenty people is obviously less important than a march by twenty thousand. When three people picket a building it is less impressive and probably has less effect than when a hundred picket. A simple demonstration of this effect of numbers is provided by a study (Milgram, Bickman, and Berkowitz, 1969) in which people on a crowded street in New York City suddenly stopped and stared up at a sixth-floor window. One, two, three, five, ten, or fifteen people composed the group that did the staring; and another experimenter counted the percentage of passersby who stopped and the percentage who looked up at the same window. As you can see in the figure, the larger the group of starers, the more effect their staring had. Whereas only 4 percent stopped next to a solitary starer, 40 percent stopped for a group of fifteen. This is probably not so much a matter of conformity as it is the attention-getting power of the larger group, but it does have

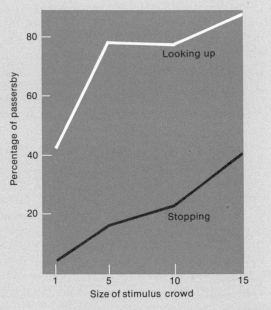

the same effect—it causes more people to copy the behavior. It might be noted that even in this situation, increasing the size of the group beyond a certain point does not increase its effectiveness substantially. A group of five causes about as high a percentage to look up as does a group of fifteen, although the larger group does cause more people to stop.

ducted as follows. A group of six or seven "subjects" sit around a table and make a series of perceptual judgments. For example, they are shown the stimuli in Fig. 17.6 and asked which of the lines on the second card is most similar in length to line x. The group members give their judgments out loud, one at a time, in the order that they are sitting around the table. All of the judgments are fairly easy, and sure enough on this trial everyone says line b. The procedure continues in this way for a series of trials, with the groups giving unanimous decisions on every one. The task is trivial, the experiment rather boring and commonplace.

However, on the eleventh trial something entirely different happens. The first subject looks carefully at the stimuli and then in the same tone as before carefully gives the wrong answer. He says, for example, line a in the figure rather than line b. The next subject gives the same wrong answer, as do the third, fourth, and fifth. Finally it is the sixth subject's turn to respond and he finds himself in a perfect conformity situation. The first five "subjects" are of course confeder-

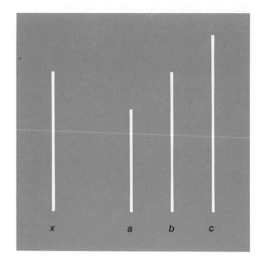

Fig. 17.6
Stimuli in Asch experiment

(a)

(b)

(c)

(d)

(e)

Fig. 17.7
The Asch experiment

In Asch's conformity study, some subjects are able to maintain independent judgment throughout. Most, however, are unable to do so and yield to group pressure on at least one trial. (a) The experimenter gives instructions. (b) The critical subject, number 6, listens to the instructions. (c) He makes his first judgment disagreeing with the consensus. (d) He leans forward as the next set of lines appears. (e) He feels conflict as he listens to new, incorrect peer judgments.

Drawing by Lorenz; © 1976 The New Yorker Magazine, Inc.

ates who have been instructed how to respond on each trial. The one real subject does not know this and is faced with the dilemma of giving what is clearly the correct choice and disagreeing with the whole group or giving the same response they did even though he knows it is wrong. Note that there is no ambiguity, little or no possibility that the other subjects are more expert or have knowledge that is not available to the real subject; the stimuli are right in front of them and the judgment is simple and straightforward.

The results are dramatic. Over a great many experiments, many different kinds of stimuli, and a wide variety of subjects, conformity occurred on approximately 35 percent of the trials. Some subjects never conformed; some conformed on all trials; but overall, subjects gave the incorrect (but conforming) response about one time in three.

It is important not to underestimate the strength of the pressures in this situation. Being faced with a seemingly incorrect but unanimous opinion by a group of people who seem more or less comparable to oneself is usually quite upsetting, particularly when the judgment involves the evidence of one's own senses. Normally we trust our perceptual judgments, and it is therefore difficult to accept disagreements. Confidence in one's own judgment is probably as great here as in any other kind of situation, but conformity occurs because it is so difficult to disagree with the whole group. We are all familiar with such situations. They may involve a movie that we like and everyone else dislikes, a political opinion, religious beliefs, or anything else. And when values and attitudes are involved rather than the less ambiguous stimuli used in the Asch study, even more conformity occurs. This does not mean that people necessarily change their opinions when faced with a majority. Rather the major effect is an overt conformity (appearing to agree) to the group even if the internal attitude is not affected at all.

The amount of conformity that occurs is affected by many factors. Up to a point, the larger the group, the more expert the members, the higher their status, the more the individual is likely to conform. By the same token, the greater the anonymity of the subject and the greater his confidence in his own judgments, the less conformity will occur. In other words, factors that increase the importance of trustworthiness of the group will increase pressure toward conformity, while factors that increase the subject's confidence or decrease his fear of rejection will decrease conformity.

Unanimity The most important factor in producing conformity is the unanimity (complete agreement) of the rest of the group. If even one person defects from a group as large as fifteen, the amount of conformity is sharply reduced (Asch, 1951; Morris and Miller, 1975). This occurs regardless of whether the one dissenter gives the correct response. As shown in Table 17.1, Allen and Levine (1969) have demonstrated that a subject who gives the correct response reduces conformity just about as much as someone who dissents but gives a response that is even more incorrect than that of the majority. If a subject is asked the color of a wall that is obviously green, and everyone else says it is red, the subject will probably say it is red. But if one other person says the wall is green, or even that it is yellow, conformity almost disappears. In other words, the effect of breaking the unanimity is not due primarily to a reduction in confidence in the majority's opinion. If that were the case, the dissenter who gives an

Table 17.1
AMOUNT OF CONFORMITY WITH UNANIMOUS MAJORITIES
AND WITH ONE DISSENT

	Type of Judgment		
	Perception	Information	Opinion
Unanimous	.97	.78	.89
One dissent—correct	.40	.43	.59
One dissent—more incorrect than majority	.47	.42	.72

Based on Allen and Levine, 1969.

even more incorrect response would have little effect. Rather, breaking the unanimity appears to make deviancy more acceptable and less threatening, and therefore easier. Further, any mistreatment by the majority or embarrassment will be reduced accordingly.

This dramatic effect of breaking unanimity provides a strong argument for freedom of speech. It suggests that even one deviant voice can have the effect of encouraging others who also disagree with the majority but are afraid to express themselves. It may also explain why totalitarian governments and orthodox religions do not tolerate even minor dissent. They are apparently aware that even one small dissent, which is meaningless in itself, can encourage others and eventually have a very great impact.

Risk Taking in Groups

It is widely believed that groups tend to be more conservative than individuals. Bureaucratic decisions arrived at by group consensus are usually thought to be more moderate, less innovative, and less risky than decisions made by a single executive. Although there may be some truth to this belief because of the necessity of reaching a compromise solution that is acceptable to everyone in the group, there is also strong evidence against it. In fact, many studies have demonstrated that groups produce a so-called *risky shift;* that is, being in a group causes individuals to favor riskier decisions than they would make by themselves.

People are often faced with a choice between a course of action that has a good chance of working but a fairly small payoff and one that has a small chance of working but a big payoff. Should you dig a wildcat oilwell with a small chance of making a fortune, or develop an already established area with a good chance of striking oil but making much less money? Should the college senior selecting a graduate school pick a school with very high standards where her chances of getting a degree are relatively small, or one with relatively low standards where almost everyone finishes? In each case, there is a choice between a relatively safe alternative and a riskier one.

A series of studies (Dion, Baron, and Miller, 1970; Stoner, 1961; Wallach and Kogan, 1965b) has compared individuals to groups in terms of the riskiness of their decisions. Throughout this work it appears that for most kinds of material and many different kinds of subjects, being in a group produces riskier choices than individuals would make by themselves. But sometimes groups make people more conservative. Why do these shifts—either risky or conservative—occur?

Although a number of explanations have been offered, it now seems likely that the effect is due to two factors: cultural values, and the number of arguments produced for each side of the decision. Depending on the situation, a given culture or subculture will tend to place a higher value on risky behavior or on conservative behavior. We respect and admire people who make decisions that are in line with these values. When someone is in a group, these cultural norms are made more salient or important. The individual by herself might not think about them very much and would be relatively uninfluenced by them. In the group, she is more aware of them and accordingly her judgment is more influenced. Therefore, to the extent that the cultural norm favors riskiness, decisions made in groups will be riskier; when the norms favor conservatism, groups will produce conservative shifts.

A somewhat different explanation of the group effect on choices is that it is due mainly to the second factor we mentioned, the type of arguments that are produced in the group discussion (Vinokur, Trope, and Burnstein, 1975; Ebbesen and Bowers, 1974). When the group gives more risky arguments, there is a risky shift; when it gives more conservative arguments, there is a shift toward caution. The important point is that for some reason being in a group causes individuals to construct new arguments that they might not have thought of by themselves. And these new arguments tend to be riskier for most choices than those individuals make up when they are alone.

These two explanations—cultural values and type of arguments—are not entirely contradictory. It would seem that the arguments are the process by which the shift occurs; but the existence of cultural values probably accounts for the production of different types of arguments when people are in groups. In other words, being in the group reminds people of the cultural value and they then produce arguments in line with the cultural value. The importance of the new research on the type of arguments is that it explains the risky shift in terms of social influence—group members are persuaded by the arguments they hear, rather than just by already existing social values.

Groups as Mobs

As early as 1896, LeBon noted that large groups of people sometimes took on a quality and behaved in ways that were quite different from the normal behavior of individuals. Members of a mob will perform acts that they would never consider doing if they were alone. This is most striking and frightening when the acts involved are immoral or violent—lynchings, the killing a few years ago of a referee at a soccer match in South America, racial riots, the burning of huge areas of cities, and so on. Interviews with participants reveal that they are often law-abiding, quiet people who are actually shocked at what they have done. Nevertheless, caught up in the mob and influenced by the strong pressures and dynamics of the situation, they commit acts that run strongly counter to their own personality and even their own self-interest.

Some instances of mob behavior are simply due to panic. The individuals find themselves in threatening situations and are unable to deal with them rationally. One or more people become frantic, and this breakdown spreads through the group until it produces a panic. A tragic example of this phenomenon is the behavior of people in a building that catches fire. Although there is ample time for everyone to escape through the available exits, in desperation people stampede to the doors, blocking them, and then no one is able to escape. All too often, firefighters find thirty people pressed against a door, jamming it closed, even though it would have taken only a few minutes for everyone to get out if they had taken turns.

A demonstration of panicky behavior is provided in a study by Mintz (1951). Each subject is given one end of a string, while the other is attached to a small wooden spool. All of the spools are placed in one bottle that has a neck just wide enough for one spool to pass through at a time. When the bottle begins to fill with water, the subjects try to get their spools out safely. Unless they cooperate fully, the spools will jam in the neck of the bottle. This is, in fact, what happens. Even though there is no actual danger or any particular incentive for getting out first, traffic jams develop. A later study by Harold Kelley and his associates (1965) showed that threatening subjects with electric shock if they did not escape produced more disorganization and more traffic jams. Since even these relatively mild situations can cause a breakdown in organization, it is not surprising that real life threats can often lead to disorganized and panicky behavior.

Deindividuation

But panic is not the only explanation for mob behavior. When people are in a group, they sometimes tend to submerge their own personalities in the group and as a result feel less responsible for their own behavior. This is called *deindividuation*. When this happens, people are less concerned about behaving correctly, following their own moral codes, and worrying about the consequences of their actions. The individuals' own values become less important, and they are therefore more likely to commit actions simply because the rest of the group is doing them. The result can be that groups engage in antisocial, illegal, and destructive behavior that would not occur if the people were by themselves. The extreme case of this is a large group that becomes a mob and commits acts of lynching, arson, rioting, and so on. Few if any individuals would commit these acts alone, but in the mob everyone participates.

Note that there are two important forces producing this mob behavior. On the one hand, there is this phenomenon of deindividuation, a loss of a sense of personal responsibility. On the other there is the strong pressure toward conformity to the group, which carries people along once the action has started. Thus, most riots and other kinds of mob behavior are probably started by a few individuals who are strongly motivated or weakly principled. Once the action has started, the dual influences of conformity and deindividuation enable it to spread through the mob.

One implication of deindividuation is that anything that makes individuals less identifiable or more anonymous—in any way reduces their sense of individuality—is likely to reduce the ordinary restraints on behavior, and in the extreme, may produce antisocial behavior. As we shall discuss in Chapter 19, this may be a major factor in urban life, where the huge population causes most people to feel largely

Supported by a policeman, a radio and television shop owner and his staff attempt to keep the crowds out of the store after the owner offered second-hand television sets for one-fourth of a cent each.

Fig. 17.8
Anonymity and aggression

Anonymity has been shown to reduce the individual's inhibitions against aggressing. The photo above is of the subjects in Zimbardo's (1959) experiment. The photo on the facing page shows a gathering of the Ku Klux Klan.

anonymous most of the time. Even in small groups, reducing individuality tends to produce more antisocial behavior. In one experiment (Singer, Brush, and Lubin, 1965), some subjects dressed in normal clothes and were called by their names while others wore identical, bulky lab coats and were never addressed by name. In discussions that required the use of obscene language, subjects in the low-identifiable conditions were much freer than the others. There were fewer pauses, livelier discussions, and a greater willingness to use obscenity when the subjects were relatively anonymous. Of course, this is not so much antisocial behavior as a reduction in embarrassment and restraint. A study by Philip Zimbardo (1959) also had some of the subjects wearing lab coats and hoods as shown in Fig. 17.8. He found that those wearing the hoods gave more electric shocks to a female subject than did those who were dressed normally. Apparently, minimizing the chance of being identified reduces various restrictions on behavior ranging from fears of embarrassment to moral values against violence. ■

Summary

1. The field of social psychology attempts to describe and explain those motives and behaviors that are related to and defined by our interactions with other people.

2. Motives that are purely social in nature include the desire to be liked and accepted, the fear of being deviant, and the need for social comparison.

3. The need to be liked and the related fear of being deviant are probably learned through experiences early in life and are constantly reinforced as we grow up. Our desire to be liked is remarkably strong and tends to make us avoid appearing too different from others, since people who are deviant (even in positive ways) tend not to be accepted.

4. According to Festinger's theory of social comparison, when there are no objective criteria against which to measure performance, people will compare themselves with others who are similar to them.

5. Our perceptions and expectations strongly affect our social interactions. Incorrect or unreasoned perceptions are responsible for the tendency to form *stereotypes* (standardized images of others based on incomplete information), and stereotyping in turn encourages the formation of prejudices. Our perceptions affect whether or not we will like another person, and once we decide we like someone, we tend to perceive her attitudes as more similar to our own.

6. *Attribution theory* attempts to explain how we decide the causes for a particular act or behavior. When we are observing another person's behavior, our decision about the causes is strongly influenced by the consistency and distinctiveness of the behavior and by how powerful the person is who is performing it. We also attribute causes to our own behavior, and we tend to believe we are motivated by external factors and that others are motivated internally.

7. Affiliation, the tendency to associate with others, is a universal human characteristic. We affiliate for innate and perhaps instinc-

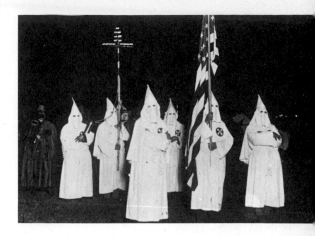

tive reasons, because we have learned to do so, and because being with others satisfies a wide variety of needs. Specific factors including the reduction of fear (but not of anxiety) and the need for social comparison increase our desire to affiliate.

8. The presence of other people may either help or hinder performance on a task. A logical explanation proposed by Zajonc is that the presence of others increases arousal, which is beneficial to performing some tasks and not others. The specific motive aroused when we are performing a task with other people present is probably concern about their opinion of us.

9. Studies have demonstrated that even in social situations where cooperation will result in gains for all concerned, people still tend to compete with each other. One factor that does increase the chances of cooperation is communication among participants.

10. In most cases persons who become leaders of groups probably possess different combinations of complex personality traits such as personal magnetism (charisma), intelligence, competence, physical attractiveness or strength, and verbal assertiveness. There is evidence that leaders who are not perceived as legitimate tend to have less influence than those who are perceived as having earned or deserving their position.

11. The most important factor in producing conformity is *unanimity*, the complete agreement of the rest of the group; conversely, when unanimity is broken by even one dissenter, conformity is sharply reduced. Once the dissenter has broken with the group, disagreement is perceived as less deviant and more acceptable.

12. Contrary to what one might expect, being in a group causes individuals to make more innovative, riskier decisions than they might make on their own. This is probably because the members of the group offer more arguments in favor of riskier decisions. In addition, our society generally places a higher value on innovative behavior than on conservative behavior and the individuals in a group try to conform to this cultural value. When society would prefer a conservative decision on a particular issue, the group then makes conservative decisions.

13. Antisocial behavior in mobs may be produced by panic, or by *deindividuation* (submerging one's personality in the group) and conformity. Deindividuation may be an important factor in antisocial behavior in general, because it makes the individual more anonymous and thereby loosens normal restraints on behavior.

RECOMMENDED READING

Aronson, E. *The Social Animal*, 2d ed. San Francisco: Freeman, 1976. A brief, very well written, interesting presentation of some aspects of the field of social psychology.

Freedman, J. L., J. M. Carlsmith, and D. O. Sears. *Social Psychology*, 3d ed. Englewood Cliffs, N.J.: Prentice-Hall, 1978. An easy-to-read text that is comprehensive without being encyclopedic.

Goffman, E. *Stigma*. Englewood Cliffs, N.J.: Prentice-Hall, 1963. A sociologist's view of how people deal with deviancy.

It were not best that we should all think alike; it is difference of opinion that makes horse races.
Mark Twain, Pudd'nhead Wilson

There is a mistaken zeal in politics . . . By persuading others, we convince ourselves.
Junius, Letters

18 Social Influence

Increasing compliance and obedience ■ *Altruism, equity, and social justice* ■ *Bystander intervention* ■ *Attitudes* ■ *Learning theory approach* ■ *Cognitive consistency theory* ■ *Changing attitudes*

f someone asked you to deliver painful electric shocks to a stranger who had never done anything to you, you would be outraged that anyone could even suggest such a thing. If you were offered money for giving the shocks, you would refuse even more vehemently—imagine being "bribed" to harm someone. Yet under some circumstances many people will give strong, possibly lethal shocks to a total stranger who has a heart condition and who screams with pain at each shock that is given.

An advertisement in a New Haven newspaper offered to pay three dollars an hour for participation in a psychological study being conducted by Stanley Milgram (1963). The volunteers arrived in pairs, were told that it was a learning study, and that one would be the teacher and the other the learner. The teacher's job was to read a list of words to the learner, test him on the words, and, whenever he missed one, give an electric shock. The teacher sat in front of an impressive shock machine (shown in Fig. 18.1) that had levers with labels identifying shock levels from 15 volts ("slight shock") to 450 volts ("danger—severe shock"). Before beginning, the teacher was given a sample shock that was quite painful and told that it was only 45 volts. The learner was put in another room and strapped into a

Fig. 18.1
The Milgram shock box

(a) The shock box. (b) Electrodes are attached to the learner's arm. (c) and (d) A "teacher" refuses to continue delivering shocks as requested by the experimenter.

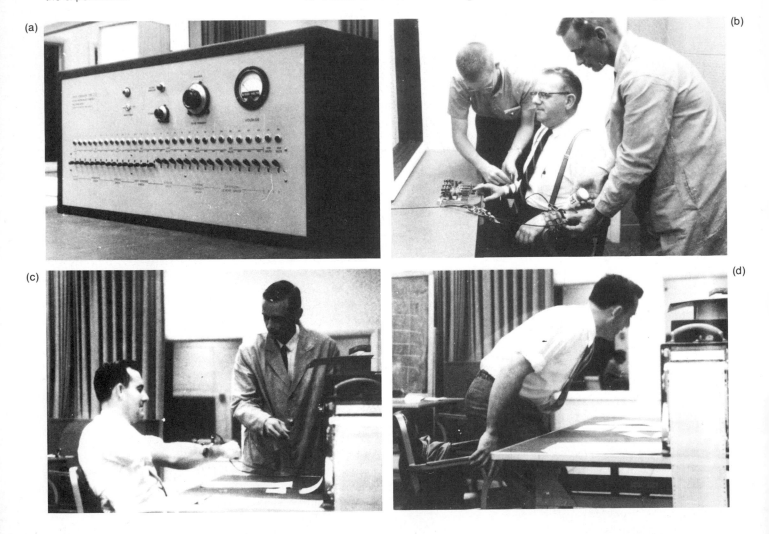

chair, and electrodes were attached to his arm so that he could not remove them. At this point he mentioned that he had a mild heart condition and was assured that the shocks would not harm him.

So the teacher knew the learner had a heart condition, that the shocks were quite painful even at low levels, and that the learner could not escape. At this point, communicating by intercom, the teacher read a list of words; the learner got some right, but then began to make errors. On each error, the teacher was supposed to press one of the levers, starting at the lowest level and moving up one level for each error. Pretty soon, the learner began to yell whenever a shock was given, then to complain, to beg to be released, to say that his heart was bothering him, and finally to pound violently on the wall and stop answering entirely. Through all of this the experimenter continually urged the teacher to keep going, saying that the experiment demanded it and that he, the experimenter, took all the responsibility.

Under these conditions more than half of the subjects delivered shocks all the way up to the maximum level of 450 volts. Even though the learner begged for mercy, screamed in pain, and eventually stopped replying, the subjects continued to deliver shocks as requested by the experimenter. They were paid only a few dollars for this, had no obligations to the experimenter, and were ordinary, decent human beings. Yet if the shocks had been real and the learner really had had a heart condition, they might very well have committed murder. And perhaps you would have done the same.

STANLEY MILGRAM

Actually, of course, the learner was a confederate of the experimenter. He was not really strapped in, received no shocks, and followed a careful script throughout, with most of his responses tape recorded ahead of time and simply played back. But the subjects did not know this—most of them fully believed that they were giving shocks that were exceedingly painful and possibly dangerous. How can we explain this?

Before attempting to answer that question let us note that many psychologists have expressed concern about the ethics of this particular study. There seems to be a general feeling in the field that the subjects in this experiment were exposed to a potentially harmful experience, which is never justified. Milgram has replied that he took many precautions and spent a great deal of time after the study talking to the subjects and reassuring them. However, the critics feel that these precautions were insufficient, and that no research should be conducted that involves the possibility of substantial harm to the participants. This is a continuing issue among psychologists and there is no easy answer. But most of us feel that we should be exceedingly cautious about what we expose subjects to and that we should protect them at all costs. Therefore, it is unlikely that this particular experiment will be repeated.

Now, to return to the question of how to interpret the findings. Milgram has suggested that this study shows that people will blindly obey authority and will perform any act, no matter how awful, if they are ordered to do it and if someone else accepts responsibility for the results. He says that this is why people stood by or even helped while millions of Jews were exterminated by the Nazis, and this could be extended to similar atrocities against Armenians, blacks, and many other groups.

This is much too strong a conclusion to be drawn from this demonstration. It does not show that people will perform unspeakable acts when ordered. What it does show is the great strength of *social pressure*.

The subjects gave the shocks because they were in a social situation that put great pressure on them to obey instructions. Consider the situation. They have agreed to be in an experiment, they have undertaken some obligation to do what the experimenter wants, they trust the experimenter, and he says that he takes all responsibility. He is right next to them, telling the subject to press the lever, and it is very hard to refuse. Although the subject worries about the health and well-being of the learner, he tends to assume that the experimenter would not let anything really bad happen and it is much easier to do what is asked than to ruin the experiment.

The same thing happens when the behavior affects only the individual himself. We are all familiar with being in a doctor's waiting room and being told by the nurse to go into a small room, undress, and wait for the doctor. We know that the doctor is busy, that we may have to wait for half an hour or more; nevertheless we docilely take our clothes off and sit in our underwear (or in a hospital gown if we are lucky), not even taking along the year-old magazine we were reading in the waiting room. Why do we do this? Because the situation is set up for us to obey, we are in the hands of the doctor and staff, and so we do what they tell us.

If a situation is constructed to put pressure on the person, to make it difficult to refuse, many people will succumb to that pressure. That does not mean that people are weak or always obedient—it means that with sufficient control over the social situation, you can exert tremendous social pressure that most people will be unable to withstand.

Throughout our lives we are affected by our social environment. Our perceptions, emotions, habits, beliefs, feelings, and behavior are shaped by the people around us. In addition, and this is unique to social life, other people *deliberately* try to influence our thoughts and behavior. They attempt to make us believe something or act in a particular way even if this runs counter to our long-standing feelings and habits. And, as we saw in our example, social influence is enormously powerful. This chapter deals with how our behavior and attitudes are influenced by social factors, and how we can resist that influence. We shall start with a number of factors that affect behavior directly, and then turn to a consideration of attitudes—how they are formed and changed, and how they influence our actions.

INCREASING COMPLIANCE AND OBEDIENCE

When people do what they are asked to do, we say they are being *compliant* or *obedient*. The terms can be used almost interchangably, but we generally use the term obedience in referring to the behavior of children or animals, while the term compliance is usually applied to adults. Many variables affect the degree of compliance; some are direct and some quite subtle and indirect.

Drawing by O'Brian; © 1964 The New Yorker Magazine, Inc.

As we would expect from research on learning and reinforcement, it is relatively easy to increase obedience through the use of rewards and punishments. If you want a dog to come when you call, giving it a dog biscuit every time it obeys will certainly help. If you want a child to make her bed, eat her spinach, or stop fighting, rewarding the appropriate behavior will increase obedience. And punishing inappropriate behavior will also make the child more obedient. Similarly, providing a model for the child to imitate will increase compliance if the model performs the desired behavior. In other words, all the basic principles of learning apply to compliance as they do to so many other kinds of behavior.

In the real world, however, there are usually severe limitations on the applicability of these simple learning principles. We are often not in a position to provide rewards or punishments large enough to elicit the desired behavior. For practical, ethical, or legal reasons we cannot threaten people with severe punishments or with big rewards. If you want a child to stop fighting when he is away from home, you cannot follow him around constantly, rewarding him for being a good boy and punishing him for being bad. If you want someone to give to charity, obviously you cannot threaten to burn down her house if she refuses. Although this is exactly the kind of inducement that is supposedly used by gangsters in the protection racket, the Girl Scouts or cancer fund would not find this an appropriate appeal. Thus, in a great many situations, we would like someone to comply with a request but are in no position to provide strong reinforcement. What other procedures increase compliance?

Group Pressure

We have already seen that group pressure is extremely powerful. People will tend to go along with whatever a group wants in terms of actions and beliefs. If you are a member of a social group of any kind, there is great pressure on you to conform to the demands of that group. If everyone else wants to go to a movie, you will probably go along even if you hate movies. If everyone in a group gives to charity, you will also. And so on. Note that this conformity occurs even without any direct pressure or threats. There is always the implied threat of rejection by the group, and that is generally sufficient to produce conformity.

Situational Pressure

Milgram's shock study is a dramatic example of the strength of situational pressure. Whenever a situation is constructed so that individuals feel they have no choice about their behavior, they will tend to be extremely compliant. This lack of choice is generally in the eyes of the participant rather than in reality. That is, it is your *perception* of choice that is important. You may in fact be perfectly free to refuse without suffering any consequences, but if you perceive no choice, you will obey. In Milgram's study, the subjects could have refused to give the shocks. Clearly, nothing would have happened to them except that the experimenter would have been disappointed. The small amount of money involved was unimportant, and in any case, they were paid in advance. Yet, because they felt they had little choice, a great many complied with the experimenter's demands.

Tina has never had a Teddy Bear.

A mother's love. A doll to cuddle. Tina knows nothing of these things. But she does know fear, rejection, and hunger.

For just $15 a month, you can help save a child like Tina.

Through our "adoption" program you can help provide a child with a better diet, clothes, medical attention, school. And even a toy or two.

But don't wait. There are so many. And somewhere, right now, a child is dying from starvation and neglect.

Write to: Mrs. Jeanne Clarke Wood, Children, Incorporated, P.O. Box 5381, Dept.   Richmond, Va. 23220 USA

☐ I wish to "adopt" a boy ☐, girl ☐, in
  ☐ Asia, ☐ Latin America, ☐ Middle East,
  ☐ Africa, ☐ USA, ☐ Greatest Need.
☐ I will pay $15 a month ($180 a year).
  Enclosed is my gift for a full year ☐, the
  first month ☐. Please send me the child's
  name, story, address and picture.
☐ I can't "adopt," but will help $ _____.
☐ Please send me further information.
☐ If for a group, please specify.

_____
Church, Class, Club, School, Business, etc.

_____
NAME

_____
ADDRESS

_____
CITY   STATE   ZIP
U.S. gifts are fully tax deductible.
Annual financial statements are available on request.

CHILDREN, INC.

What type of inducements are being used in this advertisement for Children, Inc.?

We face this kind of situation quite often in our lives and we generally are extremely compliant. Even though no reinforcements are offered, even though no group pressure is applied, we obey orders whenever they are given in such a way and in the kind of situation that seems to provide no choice. This does not mean that people are especially compliant. In fact, we break all kinds of rules, fight authority in many ways, and are not particularly obedient in our daily lives. But whenever the perception of choice is removed, compliance is greatly increased.

The Foot-in-the-Door Technique

To induce people to comply with a request, it is often effective to start with a much smaller request. Once people have agreed to a minor favor, they are much more likely to agree to the larger one also. Freedman and Fraser (1966) asked housewives to sign a petition requesting senators to work for legislation to encourage safe driving. Several weeks later, these same housewives plus others who had never been contacted were asked to post in their yard a large, unattractive sign that said, "Drive Carefully." Whereas only 17 percent of those who had not been contacted before agreed to post the sign, over 55 percent of the women who had signed the petition also agreed to put up the sign. Although the explanation for this effect is not entirely clear, it seems likely that it involves a sense of participation and a change in the individuals' perceptions of themselves (Pliner et al., 1974; Snyder and Cunningham, 1975). People who would ordinarily hesitate to get involved have difficulty refusing the very minor request, and once having agreed to a political act are more willing to commit another one.

On the other hand, recent work (Cialdini et al., 1975) shows that compliance can also be increased by starting with a large request and following it with a much smaller one. If someone asks to borrow a hundred dollars, you will probably refuse; but if she then asks to borrow a quarter, you may be more likely to lend her the money than if she had not started with the big request first. In labor negotiations, both union and management start by demanding the world. The union wants a 30-percent raise, ten days more vacation, seven-hour days, two-hour lunch breaks, retirement after ten years at full pay. Management offers a 1-percent raise, longer work days, higher productivity, half-hour lunch breaks, and retirement at sixty at quarter pay. Eventually they compromise. The idea is that in contrast to the initial demands, the final settlement seems reasonable for both sides.

Thus, you can increase compliance to a large request by starting with a small one, and you can increase compliance to a small request by starting with a very large one. In the first case, the effect seems to be due to a change in the person's self-image; in the second case, it is a perceptual or contrast effect that makes the small request seem even smaller by comparison with the large one.

Guilt

Compliance is also increased by feelings of guilt. Whenever we break a rule or do something that we consider morally wrong, we experience a sensation of guilt. This is especially true when our actions hurt

PATRICIA PLINER

someone, even if the harm was accidental. If you unintentionally brush against a lamp and break it, you usually feel guilty despite the fact that you obviously did not mean to cause the damage. If you are driving carefully and hit someone who runs in front of the car, you feel guilty even though it was not really your fault. A number of studies have demonstrated that when we feel guilty we are much more likely to be compliant than when we do not feel guilty. Telling a lie, delivering electric shocks, breaking an expensive machine, scattering valuable notes—all increase compliance to subsequent requests.

Merrill Carlsmith and Alan Gross (1969) experimented using a procedure similar to that employed by Milgram. Subjects delivered either electric shocks or just buzzes to a confederate who played the part of a learner. Afterwards, the subjects were asked by the confederate as a favor to make a series of phone calls in connection with a campaign to save the California redwood trees. In the buzzer (low-guilt) condition, 25 percent of the subjects complied, whereas in the shock (high-guilt) condition 75 percent complied. The arousal of guilt tripled the percentage of those who helped the confederate. Similar strong effects have been found in the other studies (Freedman, Wallington, and Bless, 1967; and so on). Sue Wallington (1973) showed that guilty subjects voluntarily punish themselves. And other experiments by Judy Regan (1971) and Carlsmith, Ellsworth, and Whiteside (1969) suggest that allowing the guilty person to confess or even just to talk about what had happened reduces the effect (see Fig. 18.2). Transgression produces guilt that can be relieved by self-punishment, confession, or helping someone.

ALTRUISM, EQUITY, AND SOCIAL JUSTICE

Up to now we have been talking primarily about somewhat negative motivations for compliance. However, people do have positive feelings for others and often will gladly help people who are in need. This kind of cooperative, helping behavior when nothing is expected in return is sometimes called *altruism*—doing good is its own reward. Although altruism may be elicited by guilt (the rich man who has exploited people and then gives to charity), it can also be caused by feelings of sympathy for others and by what has been called *social justice* (Homans, 1961) or *equity* (Walster, Berscheid, and Walster, 1975). These terms refer to the feeling that all people should get what they deserve according to their needs and efforts—a sense that the world should be fair. When this principle is violated, most people have a tendency to try to restore equity. For example, if one person receives more than he deserves, he will tend to share it with others; if someone else receives less than she deserves, there will be a tendency to give her enough to make things equal. This does not mean that everyone is always fair with everyone else, and obviously some people are greedy. But in addition to these selfish feelings, most people do have a sense of justice and will feel some pressure to produce equity when they can.

Subjects who win more than they deserve in a game tend to give some of their winnings to the person who lost (Berscheid and Walster,

Fig. 18.2
Guilt, confession, and compliance

Feeling guilty increases compliance, but confessing reduces compliance somewhat, presumably because guilt is reduced. (After Carlsmith et al., 1968)

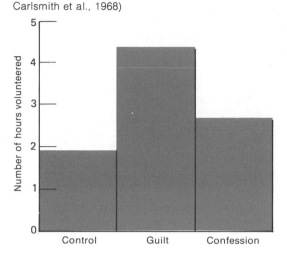

ELLEN BERSCHEID

Table 18.1
GUILT, SYMPATHY, RESTITUTION,
AND HELPING

Condition	Percentage helping
Control	16
Sympathy—witnessed accident but did not cause it	64
Restitution—caused accident and can help victim	39
Guilt—caused accident but can help only someone else	42

1967). Witnessing a misfortune befall someone also arouses these kinds of feelings. Subjects who have seen someone have an accident are more likely to help that person in the future and are also more likely to help an entirely different person than if they had not witnessed the accident in the first place. Presumably, generalized feelings of social responsibility and justice are aroused, which carry over to other situations. In a nice study along these lines (Konečni, 1972), subjects watched a pedestrian get bumped into and drop her groceries (sympathy condition), others bumped into the pedestrian themselves (guilt condition), while still others neither observed nor were involved in the mishap. Then all subjects were given an opportunity to help that person or an unrelated person pick up a bunch of cards that had fallen on the ground. As you can see in Table 18.1, either witnessing or causing the accident greatly increased the amount of help that was given, even when the person needing the assistance was not the one who had previously suffered. Why sympathy alone produced even more helping is unclear. Perhaps the guilt and restitution groups want to get away from the scene because it reminds them of their guilty act.

A study by Melvin Lerner (1974) demonstrated that feelings of equity are present in young children as well as adults. Kindergarten-age children played a game and were given rewards to distribute among themselves. At this age, the children distributed the same number of rewards to everyone regardless of how much they had contributed—what Lerner called *parity*. A few years later, however, children have a more complex sense of fairness and reward each other in part according to how much they have participated. Those who did more expected to receive more and, in fact, were given more.

Elaine and Bill Walster and Ellen Berscheid wrote an extensive article (1975) in which they describe a wide variety of implications of *equity theory*. They suggest that the sense of justice can enter into almost all social relationships and interactions. It can produce altruistic behavior when we see someone in distress. It can affect the distribution of rewards or any other resource so that people receive what they deserve. Equity can also play a role in friendships, romantic relationships, and even teacher-student interactions. To the extent that each person has a sense of equity, he or she will want to get as much from the relationship as is put in and will also want the other person to get as much, and only as much, as the other contributes. Both teachers and students, for example, tend to feel that hard work should be rewarded; and both feel that something is wrong when this does not happen. Thus a teacher who knows that a student worked hard is probably inclined to give a higher grade, even if the paper is not better than one from a student who worked less hard. One difficulty with this is that often the student knows he worked hard, but the teacher does not because all the teacher sees is the finished paper, not the work that went into it. Thus, the student may feel unjustly treated while the teacher is unaware of the lack of equity. Similarly, many students are not inclined to work hard in a course when the teacher does not seem to be making much effort. Teachers who come to class poorly prepared or give the students little attention should not be surprised when students maintain equity by also paying little attention and not doing the work.

Thus far there has been little research on these broader implications of equity theory. We do not know how strong these feelings of justice are in most people, nor when they are more important than other strong feelings such as the competitive impulses we discussed in the previous chapter and our selfish tendencies to get as much as we can from a situation or relationship. However, it is perhaps reassuring that most people do seem to be motivated at least at times by feelings of justice and equity.

BYSTANDER INTERVENTION

Under what conditions will people spontaneously help a stranger who is in distress? Bibb Latané and John Darley (1970) have called this *bystander intervention* and have attempted to discover what factors determine whether help will be given. Their research has focused on the effect of being alone versus with other people. Interest in the problem stems in part from a series of dramatic incidents in which bystanders did not help.

Kitty Genovese, a young woman, was brutally attacked at three o'clock one morning. She screamed for help loud enough and long enough for at least thirty-eight people to hear her. Many of them came to their windows to see what was happening, yet no one called the police or came to her assistance.

Eleanor Bradley tripped and broke her leg on a crowded street. In great pain, she lay on the sidewalk calling for help. Hundreds of people passed by, but she lay there for forty minutes before help came.

We know that there are many other incidents in which people *do* offer assistance, in which they show great bravery and compassion. What determines whether people will respond to others in distress?

Darley and Latané's most fascinating finding is that the presence of other people often reduces the amount of help that is offered. In one study (Latané and Darley, 1968), subjects were either alone or with other subjects when smoke began to pour into the room. A subject who was alone was much more likely to report the smoke to the experimenter than subjects who were with others. Subjects in another experiment (Latané and Rodin, 1969) heard a carefully rehearsed act from an adjoining room. First they heard a chair fall, then a woman screamed and yelled "Oh my God, my foot. I . . . I . . . can't move . . . it. Oh . . . my ankle. I . . . can't get this . . . thing . . . off me." She sounded in great pain and was obviously pinned under some object. Of subjects who were alone, 70 percent tried to help the victim in some way; with two subjects together, only 40 percent helped; and when a confederate of the experimenter simply sat there and did nothing, only 7 percent of the subjects helped.

The explanation seems to be that when the situation is ambiguous subjects interpret it in part in terms of what others are doing. If other people are present and do not help, the subject assumes that no help is necessary or that for some reason it would be inappropriate to help. Ambiguity is a critical variable. For example, in the New York subway, a person who fell down and clearly needed help was given help almost every time (Piliavin, Piliavin, and Rodin, 1975). In another study (Clark and Word, 1974) help was almost always given

Strangers rush to help an earthquake victim in Guatemala. Are these people different from those who walked by Eleanor Bradley as she lay on the sidewalk calling for help, or is it the situation?

in unambiguous situations (from 91 percent to 100 percent of the time), but in highly ambiguous situations, people who were alone were more likely to help than people in a group. Thus, being with other people does not always reduce bystander intervention—it does only when the situation is so ambiguous that everyone interprets the situations by watching what others do.

Although this does not fully explain why people failed to help Kitty Genovese and Eleanor Bradley, it may be that in fact most people were unsure just what the situation was. A less optimistic explanation is that many people are afraid to get involved or simply in too great a hurry to offer help. However, before accepting this negative view of human nature, we must remember that people often do offer help (as in the subway study) and that work on equity and social justice shows that we do care about others and do offer assistance under many circumstances.

To sum up, removing the perception of choice, applying group pressure, and arousing feelings of guilt, social justice, or obligation all increase compliance and helping. In addition, getting someone to agree first to a small request makes it more likely that he will agree to a larger request, and starting with a large request will increase compliance with a small one. These are all ways of affecting behavior directly. But although they have dramatic effects, they work only as

Box 18.1

BRAINWASHING

During the trial of newspaper heiress Patricia Hearst there was a great deal of talk about brainwashing. The defense claimed that after she was kidnapped she had been brainwashed into changing her attitudes and joining her captors in illegal acts. However, it is not at all clear just what those defense attorneys and other people mean by this term, nor how it differs from ordinary persuasion and influence of the type we have been discussing. Obviously, people can be convinced by strong arguments. If a student changes her political or religious views after four years in college, we would hardly say she was brainwashed, even though she might have been exposed to a great deal of persuasive pressure. How is brainwashing different from ordinary persuasion?

The term seems to imply the use of coercive persuasive techniques. The person may be a captive who cannot escape the persuasive arguments. Perhaps the messages are misleading, unusually constant, or given when the person is exhausted either physically or mentally.

There may be some use of physical force, torture, or some other dramatic and illegitimate method. The notion is that attitudes are changed against the will of the person, without giving him a "fair" chance to resist. In addition, some people who talk about brainwashing seem to believe that it involves extremely powerful methods that are almost irresistible. However, there is no evidence to suggest the existence of any such methods. People may be somewhat more easily persuaded when they are held captive or are weak physically, but there are no magic tricks to change attitudes and, in fact, the attempts at brainwashing that we know about were not especially successful.

Whether there was a systematic attempt at brainwashing in Patty Hearst's case is uncertain, but we do know that during the Korean conflict of the 1950s, the North Koreans and Chinese Communists undertook large-scale programs to change the opinions of American prisoners of war. The particular techniques used by the Chinese are remarkably similar to some of the procedures we have discussed in terms of compliance. As

long as the person is in the actual situation. In contrast, behavior can also be affected by changes in attitudes; and once an attitude has changed, it will usually continue to affect behavior for a long time. The effects are often small, but they will persist if the attitude has really been altered. Therefore, a great deal of attention has been devoted to the study of attitudes—how they develop and how they can be changed.

ATTITUDES

Our behavior is greatly influenced by our knowledge. We do not try to drive to England, because we know that the ocean will get in the way. We do not try to drive at all if we know that our car is out of gas, or that there is a tornado blowing outside. Someone goes to a particular church in town because he is Catholic and he knows it is a Catholic church; someone else goes to a movie theater because he knows what movie is playing and believes that it is a good movie. All of these relationships are obvious—we have certain information and we act in accord with it.

We are also influenced by *attitudes*, which are combinations of cognitions (facts) and feelings (emotions, likes, and dislikes). We

Schein (1956) reports, the two major techniques were to make prisoners feel guilty and to employ a version of the foot-in-the-door procedure. Individuals were encouraged to confess their misdeeds, to admit that they had committed all sorts of wrongs from childhood to the present. Everyone has done some things he considers wrong, and admitting these sins in public is likely to arouse feelings of guilt. The foot-in-the-door technique consisted of getting prisoners to do something inconsequential, such as leading a discussion of the Communist system or admitting that capitalism was not perfect. From there, the demands were increased gradually until the prisoner was asked to condemn everything about the capitalist system or other aspects of his country and accept Communism fully. These specific procedures were often combined with methods that created extreme discomfort, lack of sleep, loss of privacy, humiliation, and so on to weaken the prisoner's resistance in general.

However, the success of these techniques has usually been greatly overstated. Although thousands of American prisoners were subjected to brainwashing attempts in Korea, only a handful chose to stay in North Korea after the war and most of those subsequently changed their minds and asked to return. (In fact, in 1976 the one American who stayed in China returned to the United States for a visit, stating that he wanted to see his relatives and the country in the Bicentennial year.) Apparently, even weak, lonely, and uneducated soldiers were able to resist this extremely intensive attack on their attitudes. As we have said, longstanding attitudes are exceedingly resistant to change as long as the attitudes are firmly held in the first place. People do, of course, change their minds about issues, but generally that happens when the attitudes are not strongly held to begin with or when they are exposed to very convincing arguments that they have never heard before. Brainwashing sounds frightening and powerful, and no doubt is. But there is little reason to believe that anyone has devised a procedure that actually results in changing firmly held attitudes with any consistency.

know that a church is Catholic—this is a fact; we like or believe in Catholicism—this is an attitude, because it involves *affect* or emotion. An attitude can center on anything. We have attitudes about people, objects, actions, ideas, concepts, and ideals. Attitudes can involve general categories such as dogs, presidents, love, or studying; or specific objects such as a favorite cat, Jimmy Carter, the girl next door, abortion, or spinach. Anything about which we have information and feelings can be the focus of an attitude.

The information about the central topic makes up the cognitive component of the attitude. For example, the knowledge that Elton John is a singer, English, short, and writes his own music constitutes part of the contents of an attitude about him. The emotional component consists of feelings toward Elton John such as excitement, attraction, and liking. And the attitude produces a behavioral tendency that includes an inclination to buy Elton John's records, go to his performances, and watch him on television.

Unlike facts, which are relatively easy to change given new information, attitudes are resistant to change. There are wide variations in the strength of this resistance depending on the degree of commitment, how long it has been held, and the strength of the emotional feelings. But in general people do not give up an attitude without some kind of struggle because it requires overcoming the emotional component.

THEORETICAL APPROACHES TO ATTITUDES

Learning Theory Approach

There are two major theoretical orientations to the study of attitudes—learning theory and cognitive consistency. Carl Hovland, Irving Janis, and others (Hovland, Janis, and Kelley, 1953) have used principles derived from research on learning in order to understand attitude formation and attitude change. Their view is that attitudes are learned according to the same laws as anything else. The processes of classical and operant conditioning, association, and imitation produce attitudes exactly as they produce any other kind of learning.

According to learning theory, a negative attitude toward heroin might be learned by the following steps: (1) You first hear the word when a parent mentions how terrible heroin is, thus producing a negative association to heroin. (2) You gather bits of information about it, such as that it comes as a powder, it is often diluted and injected, it is expensive, there are many heroin addicts, and so on. Many of these elements will have little or no evaluative component, but will add to the total attitude. (3) Then you might meet someone who takes heroin and tells you how wonderful it is. This is your first positive association. (4) You have a series of contacts with people who have had experience with heroin and tell you how terrible it is. Or, perhaps, they are unpleasant and you associate them with heroin. (5) You also hear that it is illegal, clearly a negative association. (6) You may be reprimanded or even punished for talking about heroin or suggesting that you might try it—negative reinforcement. (7) Your parents, teachers, and friends may say generally bad things about heroin, and you imitate their positions. Overall, although you may be exposed to some conflicting positions, your attitude will be negative because there have been many more negative reinforcements, models, and cognitive elements. If your experiences were different, it would also be possible to build up a positive attitude. Presumably, the attitude then consists of all the pieces of information plus the evaluative component, which has been learned partly through the individual element and partly directly.

Cognitive Consistency Theory

Although no one disagrees with the idea that attitudes are in part learned, the other major theory stresses the interrelationship between cognitive and emotional elements. *Cognitive consistency theory* starts with the assumption that people tend to seek consistency (agreement or balance) among their cognitions, feelings, and behavior. Whenever inconsistency exists or a new piece of information is introduced, individuals will do what they can to minimize conflict among the various elements. Thus, new information or experiences are not just added to the list—to some extent they are interpreted and altered to fit the existing attitude. The key question, however, is what determines whether things are consistent.

Balance model The simplest answer is provided by Fritz Heider's (1958) *balance model*. This deals primarily with attitudes toward other people, although it could be applied to almost any attitude. The essence of this model is that if you like someone, your other likes and dislikes should be similar; while if you dislike someone, your attitudes should be dissimilar. This is diagramed in Fig. 18.3, which shows a voter's feeling toward a local member of congress, and both people's attitudes toward pollution. There are eight possible arrangements of the three plus or minus signs. According to the theory, those on the left are balanced (consistent) and will tend to remain as they are, while those on the right are unbalanced (inconsistent) and will tend to change toward one of the balanced structures. For example, if the voter likes the member of congress, the member of congress likes pollution, and the voter hates pollution, an imbalance is created and there will be pressure on the voter to change by deciding either that she does not like the member of congress or that she likes pollution. A third possibility is for the voter to distort the congress member's position and convince herself that the congress member also does not like pollution. Any of these changes will produce a balanced, more consistent arrangement. The important point is that imbalance tends to lead to attitude change—about either the person or the object involved. Heider's position is that this change would be due not to learning principles but to the drive toward cognitive consistency.

One implication of this model is that positive and negative statements do not always produce the intended effect. If someone you dislike says something positive about someone you like, you may actually dislike the person more than before. The reasoning in terms of consistency is that if this stinker likes Fred, Fred must not be very nice. Similarly, if someone you dislike attacks Fred, you will like Fred even more than before (my enemies' enemies are my friends). It is also

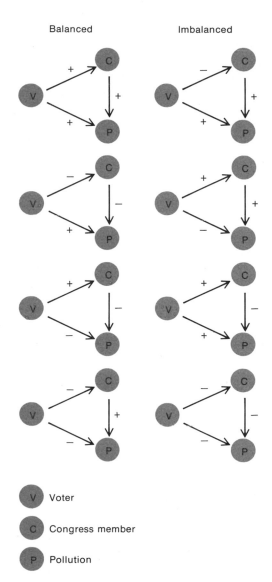

Fig. 18.3
Balance model of liking

Imbalanced situations have an odd number of negative signs and tend to change to balanced configurations. For example, at the upper right, a voter who likes pollution but dislikes the congress member who also likes pollution will tend to either like the congress member more or dislike pollution.

	Yes	No
1. I love Harry. Harry doesn't love me.	☐	☐
2. I want to be rich. I am poor.	☐	☐
3. I love Barbara. I deliberately hurt Barbara.	☐	☐
4. I like Republican politics. I voted for a Democrat.	☐	☐
5. I am hungry. I am sitting in class not eating.	☐	☐
6. I bought a Chevy. I preferred a Ford.	☐	☐

Fig. 18.4
Are these pairs of cognitions dissonant? The answers are elsewhere on this page.

Answers to Fig. 18.4

1. No. Love is often not returned.
2. No. Unfortunately, not everyone gets everything they want.
3. Yes. It follows from loving someone that you would not deliberately hurt that person.
4. Yes. If you favor Republicanism, you should not vote for a Democrat.
5. No. Generally you do not eat in class even if you are hungry.
6. Yes. You should buy the one you prefer.

Remember that each pair is evaluated by itself. Other cognitions might eliminate the dissonance; for example, in #6, "but the Chevy was cheaper."

true that you will judge people in part by their likes and dislikes. If an unknown person attacks something you already dislike or praises something you like, you will be inclined to like her. Politicians appear to be well aware of the powerful effect of attacking unpopular causes and supporting popular ones. This is particularly effective when the politician is relatively unknown to begin with. An unknown conservative attacks welfare cheats, whom the public generally dislike. The neutral source attacks a very negative group and becomes more positive. This is known as the "I'm against sin" ploy. Similarly, unknown politicians take stands in favor of popular causes, such as safe streets, strong America, or lower taxes. The neutral source supports a popular cause making the politician very popular. This is the "I'm in favor of motherhood, America, and apple pie" gambit. Although no single tactic of this sort will actually make a neutral politician popular, it is an extremely effective technique that causes almost all politicians to search as hard as possible for unpopular causes to attack and popular ones to support—not so much to affect the popularity of the causes, but to increase their own popularity.

The theory of cognitive dissonance By far the most influential consistency theory is Leon Festinger's *theory of cognitive dissonance* (1957). According to this theory, inconsistency, which is termed *dissonance*, exists whenever a person holds two cognitions and the opposite of one follows psychologically from the other (see Fig. 18.4). If you have the cognitions that you hate any kind of drugs and that you smoke marijuana, dissonance would be aroused because if you hate drugs it follows that you should not be using one. And if you hate organic chemistry but are studying it very hard, that too should arouse dissonance.

According to this theory, the inconsistency between the two cognitions is defined entirely psychologically. Dissonance exists only when the individual *thinks* that the cognitions are inconsistent. Even if they are logically inconsistent, dissonance will not be aroused if for some reason the individual does not recognize or accept this inconsistency. If he does not know the rules of logic or has an unusual system of logic or is simply unaware of the logical inconsistency, dissonance will not be aroused.

The amount of dissonance in any situation is determined by the number of dissonant elements (those that disagree) relative to the number of consonant ones (those that agree), and the importance of these elements. The total amount of dissonance depends on the whole cognitive system. Studying organic chemistry is inconsistent with your knowledge that you dislike the subject. Having the cognition that you want to go to the movies would increase the amount of dissonance because it is also inconsistent with studying. On the other hand, adding the cognition that you want to go to medical school and need the course would reduce the amount of dissonance because that is consistent with studying organic chemistry. In addition, some elements have greater implications and are more important than others. Giving up your whole social life is probably more important than missing a movie. Therefore, if the only cognition you had relative to studying was missing the movie, there would be less dissonance than if your whole social life were at stake.

Dissonance reduction. The central idea of the theory of cognitive dissonance is that dissonance is like a drive or a motive. Arousing dissonance is unpleasant, and once it exists the individual tries to reduce it by adding consonant elements or eliminating dissonant ones. And often this results in changing attitudes and judgments. For example, Aronson and Mill (1959) invited a number of college women to join a discussion group on the psychology of sex. The women were told that the group had been meeting for some time and that they would be replacing someone who had dropped out. Before joining, however, they were told that they would have to pass a brief screening test to demonstrate that they could talk freely about sex.

The key element of the experiment consisted of variations in the severity of this "initiation test." The "severe initiation" consisted of reading aloud twelve obscene words and two lurid, explicit descriptions of sexual activity. The "mild initiation" involved reading aloud words that were sexually related but not obscene. A third group did not undergo any initiation. Everyone who took a test was told that she had passed.

Then all subjects listened to, without participating in, one session of the group that she was going to join. This was a tape-recorded meeting that was deliberately made extremely dull. The participants interrupted themselves, did not finish sentences, said almost nothing of any interest, and in general were uninformed and boring. After enduring this discussion, each subject rated the group on a variety of scales, including interest level, intelligence, and so on. Those who had undergone the severe initiation rated the group higher than those who had endured only the mild initiation, who in turn rated it higher than the no-initiation group. As we would expect from dissonance theory, the more effort that is expended to join the group, the more dissonance there would be if the group were less good than expected and the more likely the person is to increase the evaluation of the group so as to reduce this dissonance. A later study by Gerard and Mathewson (1966) demonstrated the same effect when subjects endured seemingly irrelevant electric shocks in order to join the group. This eliminated the possibility that the severe initiation in the first study made the group *seem* more interesting because the initiation itself was sexier and more provocative.

A practical application of this dissonance phenomenon involves the so-called introductory low price offer that is common in merchandising. As an encouragement to customers, a new mouthwash or some other product is sometimes introduced at a very low price for a few weeks and then raised to its normal price. Dissonance theory suggests that this might not be a good practice. The reasoning is that customers who pay the full price from the beginning will become more committed to the product than those who buy it at a discount price. In terms of dissonance, the less one pays, the less one is likely to convince oneself that the product is valuable. Just as a severe initiation makes the group seem better, so a high price makes the product more attractive. An experiment conducted in a chain of discount stores, the results of which are shown in Fig. 18.5, supports this theory.

Contributions of cognitive consistency theories Probably the most important contribution of cognitive consistency theories is to em-

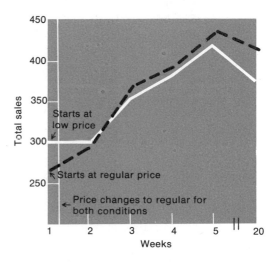

Fig. 18.5
Effect on sales of introductory low-price offer

The curves show the sales of a thirty-nine-cent bottle of mouthwash that was introduced at either twenty-five cents or the normal price. Naturally, more mouthwash was sold at twenty-five cents than thirty-nine, but when the regular price was instituted there was a clear reversal. Those stores that had used the introductory low price ended up selling less mouthwash than those that had introduced it at the full price, and this effect was still strong after twenty weeks. (From Doob et al., 1969)

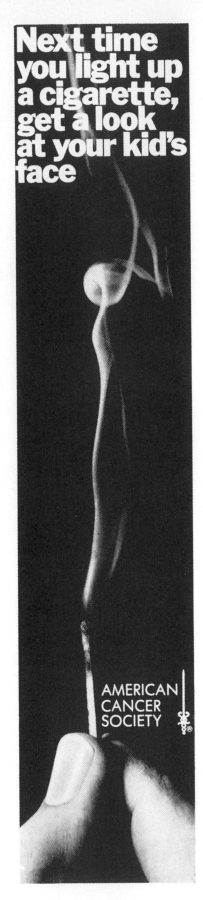

Next time you light up a cigarette, get a look at your kid's face

AMERICAN CANCER SOCIETY

phasize the interrelationships among the various cognitive elements in an attitude, and to stress that people are not passive receptacles for new information. When people hold an attitude and are exposed to a new experience that is related to it, they do not react in exactly the same way as they would if they did not already have the attitude.

A positive statement about heroin will have different effects on attitudes toward heroin depending on the person's initial position. If this is the first information she has, the learning theory explanation is perfectly appropriate. She will simply form a mild positive attitude toward heroin. However, once she has some information and some evaluation, that same piece of positive information will be processed at least in part in terms of what already exists. If it is consistent with the initial position it will be integrated and will support it. But if the initial position is negative, the new information is inconsistent and will not carry as much weight. Rather, the individual will do what she can to minimize its effect, to distort or reorganize the information so that it will be consistent with her attitude.

This is a major explanation of why people are so resistant to attempts to change their attitudes. New information that ordinarily would be sufficient to produce a positive attitude toward heroin will not be accepted passively. Instead there will be pressure to maintain the original attitude by making the new information consistent with it. In fact, research indicates that once an attitude has been formed, subsequent information has much less effect than information received earlier (Luchins, 1957). This is sometimes called the *primacy* (first) effect because first impressions of people or first opinions tend to dominate over later impressions or information. We hang on to our attitudes by weighting new information that disagrees with us less heavily than information that agrees, and by distorting information if necessary.

CHANGING ATTITUDES

Because attitudes are assumed to affect behavior, a great deal of time, effort, and money are spent trying to change people's attitudes. We are exposed to almost incessant television and radio commercials, advertisements in newspapers, magazines, and on billboards, leaflets, speeches, and informal discussions all designed to alter our attitudes. Having a more favorable attitude toward Crest, Chevrolet, or Winston cigarettes may not ensure that we will buy those products, but it makes it more likely. Therefore, billions of dollars are spent on advertising; and many billions of hours are devoted to trying to change attitudes in one way or another.

The typical attitude-change situation involves someone (the communicator) who delivers a message (the communication) that is directed at someone else (the audience). Whether the attitude changes depends on many factors, but all of them involve whether we trust the message and whether it is strong enough to change our minds.

Do ads such as this affect your attitude toward smoking?

Factors Affecting Attitude Change

Prestige of the communicator A major element that affects our trust in the persuasive message is the prestige of the person giving it. *Prestige* is a general term that includes expertise, respect, integrity, and similar characteristics that make you accept someone's statements more readily. As you might expect, the higher the prestige of the source, the more likely it is that a message will produce attitude change. Carl Hovland and Robert Weiss (1951) showed that a message from noted physicist J. Robert Oppenheimer and other high-prestige sources had more effect than the same messages from untrustworthy sources such as the Russian newspaper *Pravda* or unknown people. Similarly, T. S. Eliot's judgments of poetry had more influence than similar judgments from Agnes Stearns, a student at Mississippi State Teacher's College (Aronson, Turner, and Carlsmith, 1963).

This is an obvious but powerful effect. Of course we will trust and be swayed more by Eliot's opinions than by an unknown student's. But the effect is quite complex. Our trust in a message also depends on whether we think the other person has anything personally to gain from convincing us. If we attribute selfish motives to the other person, we are less influenced. We saw in discussing liking and attribution theory that someone who says he likes us is less impressive when he is trying to sell us something because we attribute his statement not to his true opinion but to baser motives. Similarly, if someone is trying to influence our opinions, we are less affected if a change in our opinion will help the other person. When during an oil crisis oil companies argue for higher prices for gas, we are not impressed because we know they will benefit; but if a consumer advocate group takes the same position, we are more likely to be influenced. Another study (Walster, Aronson, and Abrahams, 1966) showed that criminals arguing for curbing police power had little influence, but when they argued for more police power, they were more influential than when police took that position. Thus, trust depends not only on the prestige of the person, but also on whether he has anything to gain from the issue. Even someone you ordinarily would not trust can be influential if he seems to be arguing against his own self-interest.

How high would you rate the prestige of each of these men as communicators? Do you think Walter Cronkite or John Dean would be more effective in persuading you to change your attitude?

INTERVIEW

Jerry Della Femina is chairman of the board of Della Femina, Travisano and Partners, a well-known New York advertising firm. He is a very warm, appealing man who looks a little like television's Kojak, but has none of Kojak's aggressiveness, as least as far as I could tell. It is not surprising that most of Della Femina's ads are humorous, since he is almost always smiling, telling a joke, or laughing at someone else's. His opinions on advertising are evidently respected, since he is frequently quoted in news magazines and occasionally appears on television. He seems to enjoy his work, thinks he is making advertising more humane, and admits that he loves publicity.

Q: Let's say you are going to advertise a product, to convince people to buy it. What kinds of things do you think about—how do you approach it?

A: The first thing any advertising writer does is come to grips with the fact that he is a salesman and we assume the role of the person who is going to make the purchase. We take into consideration his fears, strengths, and his economic situation. For example, transport yourself into a nice restaurant where you're about to order a bottle of wine. First you have to call over this character who looks intimidating; you look down the wine list and can't pronounce any of the names no matter how much French you had in school and the person you're with

JERRY DELLA FEMINA

The job is to get yourself liked. Make contact, be human. My way of doing this most of the time is through humor.

---

is going to be embarrassed by this, and anyway, you don't know what wine to order even if you could pronounce it. So when you are selling wine, you come up with a hero—the hero wine that solves all these problems. Our wine is a liebfraumilch, but we don't call it that because it's hard

to pronounce—we call it Blue Nun. The people we are selling to don't have to be sophisticated or very bright—they just have to have about $3.89. And they would much rather say Blue Nun than liebfraumilch.

Then we realize that our man is afraid to order because he doesn't know which wine goes with what food.

Q: He is afraid that he will do something awful and the wine steward is going to sneer at him.

A: Right. So we save him again. Our wine goes with meat, goes with fish, goes with vegetables, goes with anything. And our advertising messages repeat that over and over.

Q: At other times it won't be embarrassment but some other problem. You try to analyze the motive and then solve the problem?

A: Right. We're in the business of pushing buttons. Everyone has buttons that someone can push. When I went out to buy a car for my daughter I read all the ads. The guy who got me was the one who said "safe car for your family." The ad says it has a steel cage, it's got this and that, it's safe. I bought it.

Q: All right, let's say you found the motive. Now, of course, there is the question of putting it across. What are the kinds of techniques that work?

A: The things that work best *for* me are the things that work best *on* me. What works best for me doesn't insult my intelligence. The job is to get yourself liked. Make contact, be human. My way of doing this most of the time is through humor. People would rather be with somebody who makes them laugh or makes them think or excites them. [Della Femina's agency is famous for witty, clever ads. For a cat food called Meow Mix, writer Neil Drossman created the slogan "the cat food cats ask for by name." In the commercial, brand-conscious cats are "interviewed" and all of them say "meow" except the last, who barks.]

Q: Some people in advertising seem to use ads that are deliberately annoying or grating. The idea is that if it grates enough, you will remember it. Do you believe that?

A: I believe you'll remember it. I think if it's a short-run sale, it can be grating and get away with it. I don't think it's a way to make friends over a long run.

Q: One of the considerations in advertising is that you have to get the person's attention. How do you do that?

A: It's not difficult to get their attention. People are willing to listen, so that's not the problem.

Q: Let me ask one more question. You find the person's motives, get their attention, and project a pleasant image, but there are products for which you want to say something. You want to say that it is better than another product, that it provides particular advantages, and so on. And you have to convince the listener. How do you do it?

A: I think the most important point is that they like you and trust you and the trust comes from technique. People trust people who make them laugh, and laugh on their grounds—not silly. Also, they are going to trust us for certain aspects of our technique. For example, when you're talking about a major purchase like an automobile, I believe in a lot of copy. A lot of copy says to the consumer, "Hey, there's a lot to be said. This person realizes that this is a tremendous purchase for me. This is serious. And he is being serious with me. He may have some fun with me at the beginning, but he knows this is important." And so I trust him because he understands and he wouldn't lie to me.

Comment

Perhaps more than anything else, Jerry Della Femina stresses the relationship between the advertiser and the target. If we like the ad and therefore like him, we will be influenced. This belief fits in nicely with Carl Hovland's idea that trust is a crucial element in attitude change. We must trust the source of the message if we are to be influenced; and presumably if we like the person, we are likely to trust him. Della Femina uses humor to produce this liking and trust. Other advertisers approach the problem by using movie stars, athletes, learned-looking announcers, white-haired "doctors," walls lined with books, or by saying "laboratory studies show," "national survey finds." All are designed to make you trust the message, and most want you to like the person presenting it. Can you think of any products you buy because you trust the ads?

Della Femina also tries to find the right approach for each product—the button for each person. What he means is that the message must tell you that you will get exactly what you want from the product—confidence (Blue Nun wine), safety (the car), or whatever is important to you. And at least in these cases this button is not the main function of the product, which is to be drunk and enjoyed or to take you to and from work. Presumably, Della Femina thinks it is harder to convince you that his wine tastes better or his car drives better than it is to convince you that the product will satisfy some other, less central, need. There is no research on this point, but it is worth considering whether attitude change in general is more effective when the message concentrates on incidental issues. Do political campaigns work best when the real issues (economics, foreign policy, education, and so on) are stressed or when they deal mainly with side issues such as the candidates' personal lives, their personality and looks, their military records twenty years ago, how much they paid in taxes, and so on. As we mentioned earlier, in politics, attacks on the individual (often purely personal attacks) are more effective than discussions of real issues.

During our interview Della Femina said that he does not believe that pairing an attractive man or woman with a car or other product is especially successful. Yet many advertisements use just this technique. Presumably this type of advertising is based on principles of association and reinforcement. It is rewarding to look at the person and therefore you will be more likely to look at or buy the object. What other mechanism might be involved—a more cognitive one? Also, to the extent that it works, why should an unpleasant or jarring commercial lead you to remember a product more? Think back to the chapter on human learning and memory and the interview with Harry Lorayne in which he discusses the "slap in the face" method of memorizing material.

Discrepancy of the communication Let us say that a friend of yours hates the field of psychology. You think it's a terrific field and you want to change her attitude. A major decision you must make in trying to convince her is how much *discrepancy*—that is, variation or disagreement—there should be between her opinion and your communication. Should you tell her that psychology is the most wonderful field in the world (large discrepancy between her opinion and the communication), that psychology is pretty good (moderate discrepancy), or that psychology is OK (slight discrepancy)? The answer is that under most circumstances, moderate discrepancy will produce the most change.

In general, the relationship between discrepancy and attitude change is curvilinear, as shown in Fig. 18.6. The reason is that at slight discrepancy there is relatively little pressure to change because the inconsistency between the initial and proposed attitude is small. And even if change occurs, it will be slight. As discrepancy increases there is more pressure to change, and if change occurs it will be larger. But at large discrepancies, a new element is added—your trust in the communicator is decreased because of the large disagreement. Anyone who disagrees with you that much is usually perceived as unreliable or biased. If you think psychology is awful, how can you trust someone who thinks it is wonderful? So at high discrepancy there is a tendency to reject the source of the communication rather than change your attitude. Your friend says to herself that you must be nuts to believe what you are saying about psychology, and she will not be influenced by anyone who is nuts. Therefore, she changes very little.

The trick is to make the communication as discrepant as possible and still believable. The two factors—trust in the source and strength of the communication—must be balanced in order to produce change; and that usually occurs best at moderate discrepancies (Hovland and Pritzker, 1957; Bochner and Insko, 1966).

Exposure to new opinions Throughout this section we have been describing the factors that affect the amount of attitude change produced by a persuasive communication. This may have given the impression that changing attitudes is fairly simple once these variables are taken into account. The fact of the matter is that changing attitudes in the real world is generally very difficult. As we mentioned earlier, attitudes do not behave as facts. In part because of their emotional component, attitudes about anything that really matters to us are extremely resistant to persuasion. It is possible to alter an opinion about toothpaste, detergents, movies, and perhaps even minor political figures, but attitudes toward religion, morality, and important political issues change slowly and reluctantly if at all. And when they change, it is usually only when they are subjected to a consistent, concerted, powerful attack that includes new and convincing information. Attitudes toward the Vietnam war did change during the 1960s, but it took many years, constant frustrations, horror stories, the enormous effort of the antiwar movement, the pressure of world opinion, and a deteriorating situation both at home and in the war to bring about this change. Even though people did not have a lifelong commitment to that particular war, their attitudes toward it were remarkably resistant to persuasion.

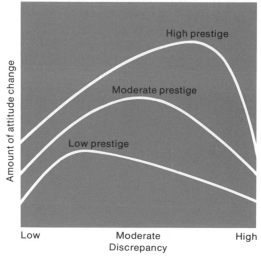

Fig. 18.6
Discrepancy, prestige, and attitude change

As discrepancy increases, attitude change increases to a maximum and then declines. The amount of discrepancy that produces the most change is greater, the higher the prestige of the communicator.

One situation that may produce dramatic attitude change is when people move to a new environment. They are then away from friends and family, who usually support their attitudes, and are sud-

Box 18.2

ATTITUDES AND BEHAVIOR

We tend to behave consistently with our attitudes. Although the relationship is far from perfect, an attitude usually exerts pressure on the individual to behave in a particular way. Other things being equal, someone with Republican attitudes (who likes the Republican party and has relatively conservative views on economics and the role of government) will vote for a Republican candidate, while someone with Democratic attitudes will be more likely to vote for a Democratic candidate. Someone who feels that abortion is morally wrong is much less likely to get an abortion than someone who does not hold this attitude. Someone who holds favorable attitudes toward Catholicism is much more likely to attend Catholic religious services than someone who holds unfavorable attitudes. Many other factors affect behavior so that we do not always behave consistently with our attitudes. We are influenced by practical considerations, by conflicting attitudes, by legal demands, and by our friends. But attitudes are one of the important factors that affect how we behave.

There has been considerable controversy in recent years about the relationship between attitudes and behavior. Several authors (Wicker, 1969; Defleur and Westie, 1963; Fishbein and Ajzen, 1972) have suggested that attitudes have little or no effect on behavior. They offer as evidence for this view the fact that many studies on this topic found very low correlations between attitudes and behavior.

While there is no denying that attitudes and behavior are not perfectly correlated, these authors seem to have placed too much weight on some negative findings and too little on positive ones. Attitudes do affect behavior, but admittedly the effect is often small. It is strongest with relatively unimportant things such as foods, movies, television, and vitamins (see table). But sometimes attitudes have very strong effects on more important behavior, including politics and racial prejudice. The weak relationships between attitudes and behavior tend to occur when there are strong cross-pressures or the attitude is not especially relevant to the behavior. For example, people with positive at-

RELATIONSHIP BETWEEN VALUES AND BEHAVIOR

Attitude	Behavior	Correlation
Vitamins	Taking vitamins	.52
Drugs (marijuana, heroin, etc.)	Taking these drugs	.68
Alcohol	Drinking alcohol	.62
Pornography	Attending pornographic movie or reading porno material	.27

Based on Freedman and Tyler, 1975

denly exposed to all sorts of conflicting ideas. For many people college is one such experience. For the first time, the individual is away from the home and is surrounded by people who come from many different

titudes toward religion do not always attend church; but being religious is not the same thing as having a positive attitude toward church services and thus we would not expect a strong relationship.

The closer the relationships between the attitude and the behavior, the more effect the attitude will have. For example, one study (Weigel, Vernon, and Tognacci, 1974) measured attitudes toward the Sierra Club, an organization that is very active in land conservation. The experimenters also measured attitudes toward conservation, pollution, and the environment in general, and they then measured behavior toward the Sierra Club. As you can see in the figure, they found that attitudes toward the Sierra Club were strongly related to behavior toward the club; attitudes toward conservation and pollution were moderately related to the behavior; and attitudes toward the environment were only slightly related. As the attitude became less and less directly connected with the behavior, it had less and less effect.

In addition, with most behaviors there are many reasons other than attitudes for taking a particular action. The choice of attending or not attending religious services is partly related to your attitudes toward religion and toward services, but there are also other considerations. You may be busy on weekends, you may go to church for social or economic reasons, your spouse may like or dislike church, you may be very tired, you may love golf more than religion. Your attitude toward religion and even toward church is only one element in a complicated decision about whether to attend services.

In contrast, in voting for the presidency there are relatively few cross-

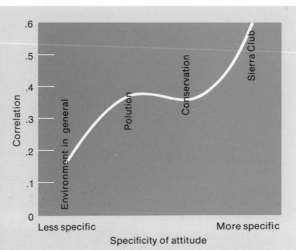

pressures. Your attitude toward the party and the particular candidate are the major factors. Other considerations such as how your spouse is voting and how the rest of the community feels are not very important because your vote is confidential. You can vote as you want, and your voting is determined largely by your attitudes.

To summarize, attitudes cause the individual to lean in a particular direction. Other factors may outweigh the effect of the attitudes, but the pressure remains. And in many cases, the attitude will play a dominant role in how the person acts. The billions of dollars spent on advertising are probably not wasted. People's attitudes do affect their behavior. Indeed, that is why we study them so intensively, and why so much time and effort have been spent trying to understand how attitudes are formed and how they can be changed.

backgrounds and have many different views. Under the onslaught of all these new opinions, there is a general reevaluation and some of the old attitudes do change.

A classic study by Newcomb (1943) produced a dramatic demonstration of this phenomenon. He traced the attitudes of the female students at Bennington College from their freshman term until twenty years after they had graduated. Although most of the students came from wealthy, conservative homes, there was a sharp shift toward liberal attitudes during their time at Bennington. And even twenty years later (Newcomb et al., 1967), most of the women who had left college as liberals were still liberal, while the conservatives were still conservative. Thus, although attitudes are greatly resistant to change, they can be altered if they are exposed to new, conflicting opinions in the absence of any support.

"*They sent her to Bennington to lose her Southern accent, and then she turned her back on every*thing."

Drawing by Saxon; © 1963 The New Yorker Magazine, Inc.

Changing Attitudes Through Behavior

As we have been discussing, a major way to change attitudes is by giving persuasive messages. It is also possible to change an attitude by having the person engage in behavior that is inconsistent with the attitude. If you hate organic chemistry but for some reason go around telling everyone that you love it, you may find that you begin to feel more favorable to the course. If someone who does not believe in abortions decides for some reason she must undergo one, she may find that she is less unfavorable afterwards. The reason is that engaging in the inconsistent behavior arouses dissonance (it is obviously dissonant to have an abortion if you do not believe in them). Because the behavior has already occurred, the simplest way of reducing the dissonance is to change one's attitudes to make them less inconsistent with the behavior. Therefore, according to the theory of cognitive dissonance, whenever a person's behavior conflicts with her attitude, the attitude will tend to change in the direction of the behavior.

The fascinating aspect of this analysis concerns the factors that increase or decrease the amount of attitude change. Contrary to what might be expected intuitively, the theory clearly states that the *more* reason you have for performing the behavior, the *less* attitude change will take place. Any justification for the action serves as a consonant element in the situation, reduces the amount of dissonance that is aroused, and consequently reduces the amount of attitude change caused by dissonance reduction. Thus, to produce the maximum amount of attitude change, you should be given just enough reason so that you will perform the discrepant acts—any less and the discrepant behavior will not occur and there will be no attitude change; any more and the amount of dissonance will be reduced and less attitude change will result.

This means that giving more reasons, greater rewards, or more severe threats should *decrease* the amount of attitude change once you have performed the discrepant act. Festinger and Carlsmith (1959) demonstrated that subjects who were paid twenty dollars for saying that they enjoyed a task that was actually boring changed their opinions of the task much less than subjects who were paid only one dollar. Similarly, Freedman (1965) showed that children who were threatened with severe punishment for playing with a desirable toy

THE EFFECT OF TOO MUCH REWARD

Dissonance theory predicts that there will be more change when rewards for engaging in inconsistent behavior are small rather than large. Recent work by Mark Lepper and others suggests that giving too much reward can sometimes undermine people's interest in a particular behavior. For example, in one study (Lepper, Greene, and Nisbett, 1973), young children were told they would be given rewards for drawing with magic markers, while other children were not told anything about a reward. Some time later, the children were given another opportunity to play with the magic markers, but this time no mention was made of rewards to either group. Those who had expected and been given rewards the first time actually played with the markers less than those who never expected a reward. According to the authors, giving the reward made the children think that drawing was worth doing only to get prizes and thus reduced their interest in doing it when no prizes were available. Other work (Deci, 1975; Lepper and Greene, 1975) has produced similar results.

These findings suggest that it is not always beneficial to give big material rewards (money, prizes, and so on) for behavior if your goal is to get children (and probably adults also) interested in the behavior. Drawing with magic markers is fun for most children, and they do not need any other rewards for doing it. Once you give them prizes, the fun is taken out of the drawing and it becomes a way to win something. This may apply to any kind of activity for which large rewards are available, whether it is tennis, studying psychology, or practicing medicine. If the external rewards are too great, the activity itself may lose its appeal and a person might engage in it only to earn the rewards. Obviously this would make the activity less satisfying in the long run.

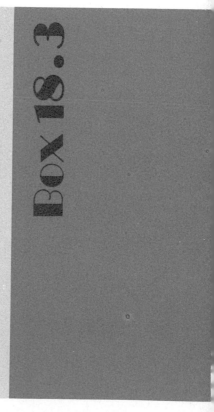

BOX 18·3

BOX 18.4

SELF-PERCEPTION EXPLANATION OF DISSONANCE RESULTS

Working in the general framework of attribution theory (see Chapter 17), Daryl Bem (1967) offered an entirely different interpretation of the results of dissonance research. Bem started with the idea that we judge ourselves much as others judge us. He called this *self-perception*, by which he meant that we look at ourselves and decide what we must be feeling or believing on the basis of what we observe. For example, if you see yourself eating spinach, you decide that you must like spinach; if you see yourself voting for a Democrat, you decide you must believe in the Democratic platform; and so on. Thus, whenever anyone asks you your attitude about an issue, you answer by considering everything you know about how you have acted relevant to that issue.

Now in the dissonance study by Festinger and Carlsmith (1959) (see p. 583), the subject knows he has said that the task was enjoyable. Accordingly, he says to himself (not necessarily literally), "I said it was enjoyable so I must think it was enjoyable," and he then tells that to the experimenter. However, the subject also takes into account other factors in the situation. If he was paid twenty dollars for telling the lie, he concludes that he said it was enjoyable because of the money, not because he really enjoyed it, so he decides that he did not really enjoy the task. If instead he was paid only one dollar, that is a much poorer reason for saying what he did, he assumed that he would not have said anything for so little money alone, and that therefore he must enjoy the task. In other words, there is no feeling of discomfort, no dissonance, no motive to reduce dissonance, but only a cognitive appraisal of the situation.

This seems to be an implausible view of the phenomenon because it is unlikely that people base their attitudes simply on their current behavior and because people do seem to experience discomfort in situations in which dissonance is aroused.

DARYL BEM

Remember for a moment how you felt immediately after a difficult decision. You will probably remember experiencing a feeling of discomfort, uncertainty, and some pressure to relieve this feeling. In fact, there is research that indicates that situations involving dissonance do arouse drive (Pallack and Pittman, 1972), and this finding is clearly contrary to Bem's analysis.

Thus, the self-perception explanation probably does not account for all dissonance effects. However, it does make the important point that just as we interpret the world in terms of what is happening and what people do, so we make the same kinds of interpretations about our own feelings. Dissonance theory appears to be correct in assuming that people prefer cognitive consistency and feel uncomfortable when it does not exist. But self-perception also plays a role and may sometimes be a major determinant of how we feel in a particular situation.

What might be the most effective way to ensure that this child does not play with this gun?

were less affected than children who received only mild threats. Any incentive for performing the act reduces the dissonance and results in less attitude change. In the extreme case when you feel you have no choice because you are forced to perform the act, no dissonance is aroused and no attitude change occurs (Linder, Cooper, and Jones, 1967).

This has important implications for the socialization process. In teaching children how to behave we want them to act correctly not only when we are present but also when no one is around. We want them to obey not only to avoid punishment or get reward, but because they think it is the right thing to do. In order to produce this attitude, we should offer children just enough reasons for acting correctly. Any less, and they will not act correctly; any more, and their own attitudes will be less affected.

For example, if you want a child to avoid fights, you should not punish him too severely when he fights. Strong punishment will probably prevent fights as long as you are around, but will not produce any corresponding attitudes in the child. If he thinks he can get away with fighting, he will still fight. In fact, as we mentioned in Chapter 10, this is exactly what happens. Children who are severely punished in the home for fighting, fight less in the home but actually fight more outside the home. However, if you give only mild punishment for fighting, the child will experience some dissonance—he wants to fight, is not fighting, and the reasons for refraining are barely enough to justify his actions. This dissonance is reduced by deciding that fighting is bad. Once the child forms his opinion, he will be less likely to fight even if no one is around to punish him. The same argument holds for any other behavior or moral value. Severe discipline will influence behavior, but will be less likely than mild discipline to produce internal changes of opinion.

Summary

1. Social influence refers to direct or indirect, overt or subtle attempts to control the social situation in such a way as to affect an individual's thinking or behavior.

2. Although learning principles such as reinforcement and modeling can be used to increase obedience, other, subtler methods are often practical and effective. These include group pressure, situational pressure, the foot-in-the-door technique, and arousal of guilt feelings.

3. Equity theory is based on the premise that in many situations people are motivated by the belief that everyone should be treated according to principles of fairness. While we do not know whether feelings of social justice are stronger than selfish tendencies, equity clearly does affect many kinds of social interactions.

4. Under ambiguous circumstances, people in groups are less likely to intervene in an emergency than individuals who are alone. The explanation is that the other people affect the interpretation of the ambiguous situation.

5. Attitudes combine cognitions (facts) and affect (emotions). Because of the presence of the emotional component, which may be very strong, it is relatively difficult to change an attitude.

6. Learning theory assumes that attitudes are formed by the usual learning processes. New information and experiences are added to existing information, and the attitude will be positive or negative depending on whether the reinforcements, associations, and experiences were positive or negative.

7. Cognitive consistency theory stresses the tendency of individuals to seek agreement among their cognitions, feelings, and behavior. In contrast to the learning view, individuals do not simply add on new information, but interpret and alter it to agree with their existing attitudes.

8. According to Festinger's theory of cognitive dissonance, when individuals perceive inconsistency between their cognitions, a drive-like state called *dissonance* will be aroused. Since this arousal is unpleasant, individuals will try to reduce it and restore a balance. Often the end result is a change in attitudes.

9. An effective way to bring about attitude change is to deliver a persuasive message that the person receiving it will trust. Two elements that affect trust in the message are the prestige of the communicator and the amount of discrepancy between the person's present attitude and the communication.

10. An alternative method of changing attitudes is to have the person behave inconsistently with his or her own attitude. Once the behavior has occurred, the person will tend to change his attitude to agree with the behavior.

RECOMMENDED READING

Bem, D. *Beliefs, Attitudes and Human Affairs.* Belmont, Calif.: Brooks-Cole, 1970. An especially thoughtful though somewhat unusual approach to the general problem of influence and how we form attitudes.

Hovland, C. I., I. L. Janis, and H. H. Kelley. *Communication and Persuasion.* New Haven, Conn.: Yale University Press, 1959. Some of the research is a little dated, but the ideas are still there. One of the books that shaped the field.

Festinger, L. A. *A Theory of Cognitive Dissonance.* Stanford: Stanford University Press, 1957. One of the most influential books in social psychology. Also, a good example of combining theory and research.

Zimbardo, P., and E. Ebbesen. *Influencing Attitudes and Changing Behavior,* 2d ed. Reading, Mass.: Addison-Wesley, 1977. A nicely written, easy introduction to some of the issues in this field.

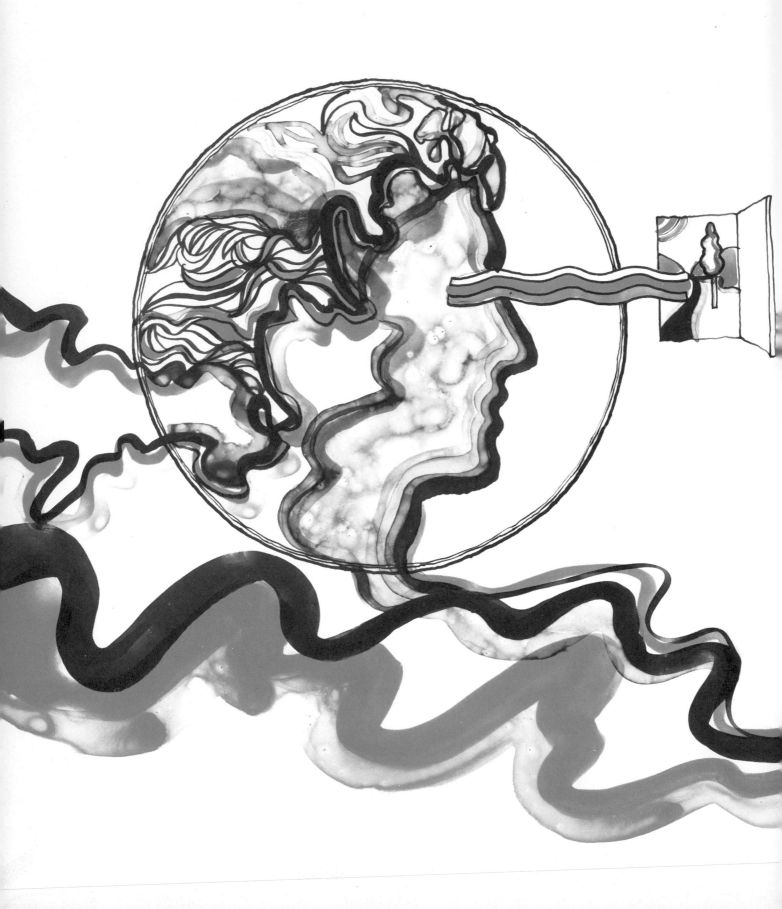

Less is more.
Mies van de Rohe

Clear out 800,000 persons and preserve it as a museum piece.
Frank Lloyd Wright on how to solve Boston's problems

19 Environmental Psychology

Noise ▪ *Personal space* ▪ *Crowding* ▪ *Crowding and humans* ▪ *Life in the city*

Going to college in the country surrounded by lawns, beautiful trees, and the sounds of birds is different from going to college in the city, with concrete walks, highrise buildings, and the honking of horns. Having dinner in a restaurant with bright lights, tables close together, and a rock band playing is a different experience from dinner in a quiet, intimate, uncrowded place. A party with fifty people in a small room is different from one with ten people in a large room. Each of these examples concerns differences in the *environment*, by which we mean the sum total of all parts of the world surrounding us. We know that in each case the environment does change our experience, but how does it change it? Environmental psychologists attempt to answer that question by discovering how various aspects of the environment affect our feelings, thoughts, and behavior.

In a sense, of course, almost all psychology deals with the environment. Perception concerns how we interpret stimuli from the environment; learning involves responding to the environment; social psychology investigates how we interact with other people—obviously an important part of the environment. However, environmental psychology focuses on somewhat different problems from the other fields. In particular, it is concerned with the environment as a background to other activities—with how perception, learning, social interaction, or any other behavior *differs* from one environment to another. For example, we know the basic principles of learning, which are the same regardless of the environment; but we can still ask how well people learn in one environment compared to another. Thus, environmental psychologists study how specific aspects of our world affect a wide variety of behaviors. In particular, work in this field has concentrated on the effects of noise, personal space, crowding, and urban living.

NOISE

One of the most obvious ways in which environments differ is in terms of noise level. Quiet rooms are clearly different from noisy ones; a football game at which the fans sat silently in their seats would be a different experience from one at which the fans yell and shout. Noise is a particularly important factor today because it is an almost inevitable result of modern society. Virtually all of the machinery that technology has produced—cars, planes, washing machines, jackhammers, vacuum cleaners—make more noise than the more primitive implements they replaced. An unspoiled wilderness or meadow is by no means silent; birds, animals, and especially insects generate a lot of noise, and in fact, people who have lived their lives in cities are usually amazed at the racket in the country. But there is no question that in general cities are much noisier than smaller communities, and with more and more of the population living in and around cities, a high level of noise is part of the environment for a great many people. We know that noisy environments are different from quiet ones, but what effect does the noise have on us? The answer is—less than you might think.

Rapid Adaptation

Loud noise does affect us, but we adapt to it very quickly. When people are exposed to short bursts of loud noise, they respond immediately in a variety of ways. In the extreme, we are all familiar with the startle response to a very loud noise—our muscles flex, our stomach gets tense, our eyes blink, and we may even jump. Less loud noises also produce physiological reactions, including a *galvanic skin response* (skin sweating), heightened blood pressure, and other physiological measures of stress or arousal. In addition, loud noise interferes with practically any task. Performance suffers on both complex and simple, creative and rote tasks. People cannot concentrate as well or make decisions as quickly or accurately when they are exposed to loud noise as when it is quiet (Broadbent, 1957).

However, the most important finding of the work on noise is that these negative effects are extremely short-lived. After only a few minutes of noise, both physiological and behavioral effects disappear. People who are subjected to continuous loud noise or to bursts of noise adapt so well that their physiological responses and their behavior return to normal in three or four minutes. On all measures, those who are exposed to loud noise are virtually identical to people who hear moderately loud noise or no noise at all. This is true even when the noise levels are well over one hundred decibels, which is comparable to the noise produced by a huge diesel truck rumbling by a few feet away or a 747 jet aircraft going over your house soon after takeoff.

A study by David Glass and Jerome Singer (1972) showed how rapidly people adapt to noise. They exposed subjects to no noise or very loud noise (108 decibels) at the rate of nine seconds per minute for twenty-three minutes. They found that loud noise did produce physiological and behavioral effects. But as shown in Fig. 19.1, the physiological effects disappeared after three or four minutes. In that short time, those subjects hearing the loud noise adapted perfectly and did not differ from subjects who heard no noise at all.

The same is true of most behavioral measures. After adaptation, noise does not interfere with doing simple arithmetic, matching sets of numbers (such as deciding whether 45126 and 45326 are identical), searching through a list of words and picking out those containing *a*'s, and so on. Even complex tasks such as higher-level mathematics, anagrams, and word problems are largely unaffected. People can perform a wide variety of tasks just as well under loud noise as when it is quiet.

On the other hand, Donald Broadbent (1957) and others have demonstrated that certain kinds of tasks are adversely affected by exposure to extremely intense noise. Some kinds of jobs require the person to monitor one or more dials and to respond whenever they go above a certain level. This kind of constant monitoring is performed less well in a noisy environment. In addition, loud noise seems to make it more difficult to perform two tasks at once. Finkleman and Glass (1970) had subjects track a line by moving a steering wheel and at the same time repeat digits that they had heard. Although noise level had no effect on the tracking task, it did interfere with repeating the digits. It seems as if a person who is already concentrating and

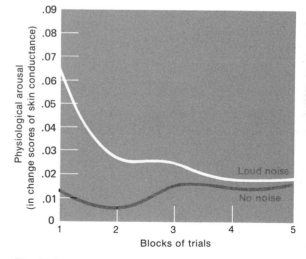

Fig. 19.1
Physiological response to noise

Although loud noise initially has a substantial effect, subjects quickly adapt and after five blocks of trials there is no remaining effect of noise compared to a no-noise control. (After Glass and Singer, 1972)

trying to operate at maximum capacity is adversely affected by loud noise.

This continuing effect of loud noise applies only to special situations that do not occur very often. Most of the time, we concentrate on one task at a time and that task rarely involves constant, close monitoring of many dials. However, we might note that the one obvious situation that fits these criteria is, rather ominously, piloting a plane. The pilot and copilot must continuously check a variety of meters while at the same time controlling the aircraft and perhaps also sending and receiving messages. Moreover, they must do this under fairly noisy conditions. Fortunately, automatic equipment relieves them of some of these duties, and the cockpits of jets are considerably quieter than those of older planes. Nevertheless, it is well to keep in mind that this and probably various other sensitive jobs are the kind that noise makes more difficult.

With these few exceptions, the important point is that noise has little effect on the performance of most tasks. Even when the noise is so loud that it can cause physical pain, people adapt quickly both physiologically and behaviorally.

This result may seem strange, because we all know that loud noise can sometimes be very annoying and that most of us prefer environments that are not too noisy. If noise is irritating, how can it have little lasting effect on us? The answer is that once we adapt to the noise it does not *seem* so loud. In fact, in a short while we barely notice it. People who live in big cities are exposed almost constantly to loud noise. As they walk along the street, they are bombarded with the rumble of cars and trucks and even in their homes the noise level is often very high. People from the country notice the noise immediately and may wonder how city people can stand it. Yet city dwellers really are not aware of how loud the noise is around them. And after a short time in the city, even country people may adapt.

Thus, on a day-to-day basis, people get used to the noise and are generally unaffected. Indeed, a sudden silence can be more distracting than consistently loud noise. City people may even miss the noise when they move to the country. In addition, the type of noise may be more important than its loudness. Crickets keep city people awake but country people hardly notice them; trucks keep country people awake while city people ignore them. Thus, a change in either noise level or type of noise is generally more important than the absolute level of the noise.

Predictability and Control

Yet this is not the whole story. The studies by Glass and Singer (1972) suggest that there are substantial costs in dealing with loud noise. This research went a step beyond most of what had been done before in that subjects were tested not only during the noise but also after it had ceased. They found that under certain circumstances noise that had little effect when it was present produced a sizable decrement on tasks performed after the noise stopped. The most fascinating outcome of this research is that exposure to noise has these negative effects only when the noise is *unpredictable* and *beyond the individual's control*. If subjects know when the noise is going to occur or feel that they can control it in some way, there is no decrement in performance either during or after exposure.

The perception of control over the noise can be based on many different factors. In one study, nine-second noise bursts either occurred at random or were spaced exactly one minute apart during a twenty-three minute session. Table 19.1 shows performance on tasks after the noise sessions. Unpredictable noise caused more errors while predictable noise had little or no effect. Indeed, the unpredictable soft noise produced more errors than the predictable loud noise. This occurred even though subjects rated the predictable and unpredictable noises equally irritating, distracting, and unpleasant. The same effect was produced by giving subjects a button that could stop the noise or even just giving the subject's partner the button and telling the subjects that they could signal their partner if they wanted the noise stopped. Despite the fact that subjects neither pressed the button nor signaled their partner to press it, the availability of this control eliminated the negative effects.

Table 19.1
EFFECTS OF PREDICTABLE AND UNPREDICTABLE NOISE ON PROOFREADING TASK

Condition	Number of errors
Loud unpredictable	40.11
Loud predictable	31.78
Soft unpredictable	36.70
Soft predictable	27.40
No noise control	26.40

Based on Glass and Singer, 1972.

Constant Exposure

There is also evidence that prolonged exposure to loud noise may have detrimental effects under some circumstances. A study of the effects of noise in a natural setting (Cohen, Glass, and Singer, 1973) focused on an apartment house built over a busy highway in New York City. Because of the design of the building, noise levels within the apartments are unusually high. The sound of the cars and trucks on the highway travels through open vents in the building, producing noise levels way above those that most of us are used to in our homes. However, the lower floors are much louder than the higher ones, with readings of sixty-six decibels on the eighth floor and only fifty-five decibels on the thirty-second. According to the loudness scale, that means that it was approximately twice as loud on the eighth floor as on the thirty-second.

The authors reasoned that if the noise had negative effects, they would be worse on lower floors than on higher ones. In addition, whatever effects there were should appear only after someone had lived in the building for a while. Therefore, the authors looked at children who had lived in the building for four years or more and measured their reading achievement and ability to make auditory discriminations. As shown in Fig. 19.2, there was a clear relationship between the floor on which the children lived and both measures of ability. The lower the floor, the poorer the children's ability to make auditory discriminations and to read. In other words, this study suggests that living under conditions of constant loud noise had negative effects on two important behaviors—hearing and reading.

This is, of course, only one study, with relatively few subjects involved. There is no evidence that, in general, children who live in the city have poorer hearing or reading skills than children who live in quieter environments. However, both this study and the work showing negative aftereffects of unpredictable noise should make us aware that at least under some circumstances loud noise may be harmful.

PERSONAL SPACE

Another important factor in the environment is the amount of space around us, especially the distance between us and other people. This space that immediately surrounds us is usually called our *personal space*, and the study of how people use and relate to personal space has been called *proxemics* (Hall, 1959; Sommer, 1969). Research on personal space has revealed that people are quite consistent in how much space they put between themselves and others and that the distance they choose is determined by their relationship to the other

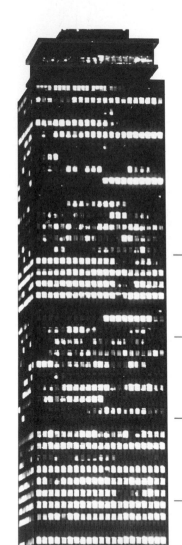

Floor	Noise level (in decibels)	Auditory discrimination	Reading percentile
32 31 30 29 28 27 26	57	25.8	85
25 24 23 22 21 20 19	60	24.9	67
18 17 16 15 14 13 12	63	23.0	63
11 10 9 8 7 6 5	66	22.0	51

Fig. 19.2
Noise, reading, and auditory discrimination. (After Cohen, Glass, and Singer, 1973)

Figure 19.3

Who is friendlier?

person, their national and ethnic background, and their sex. Let us consider each of these variables in turn.

Relationship of the People

Before reading further, look at Fig. 19.3 and indicate your choices. Although very little information is provided, there is probably high agreement in describing the relationships among the people. The closer the relationship between two people, the closer they tend to stand to each other. Friends stand closer than strangers or people who are not friends (Aiello and Cooper, 1972); sexual attraction greatly reduces distance, and if people want to give a friendly impression they sit or stand closer than if they want to appear unfriendly (Lott and Sommer, 1967; Patterson and Sechrest, 1970).

Although most of us may not think about personal space very much, we all know that you can tell a lot about a relationship between two people from how far apart they are standing. At a party, we can probably distinguish those people who are friends from those who are just acquaintances; and even more likely those who are lovers from those who are not. In fact, the choice of personal distance is one way of communicating how you feel about someone. If someone you just met stands closer to you than would ordinarily be appropriate for a stranger, it usually means that he or she is attracted to you, is interested in you, or has positive feelings toward you. Even if the content of your conversation is perfectly ordinary and neutral, standing very close will communicate these feelings. Conversely, if someone stands quite far away, it usually indicates a lack of interest and seems unfriendly.

Personal space is also related to status differences between people. In general, the more equal the status, the closer people tend to stand. In addition, when low-status people approach high-status people, the greater the difference in status, the further away they stand. This was demonstrated in a military setting, where status differences are especially clear (Dean, Willis, and Hewitt, 1975). Officers in the United States Navy were observed in contact with each other. When a petty officer (the lowest rank) approached a captain or commander (highest ranks), the petty officer usually stood further away than when he approached a lieutenant junior grade or ensign (intermediate ranks). This difference held quite well for all ranks—the greater the difference in rank, the greater the distance the subordinate maintained. On the other hand, when the situation was reversed, the difference in rank did not affect distance. A captain stood just as close to a commander as to an ensign. Moreover, the superior officer always chose to stand closer than did the subordinate—rank, apparently, does have its privileges.

Ethnic Differences

The preferred distances for any given relationship appear to differ considerably for various ethnic groups. White Americans, Britons, and Swedes generally stand farther apart than Pakistanis and Arabs

ROBERT SOMMER

(Watson and Graves, 1966; Sommer, 1968). Latin Americans prefer closer distances than North Americans (Hall, 1966), and people in Mediterranean cultures, such as Greeks and Southern Italians, stand closer than Northern Europeans, such as Swedes (Little, 1968). In other words, people in the United States and Northern Europe choose the greatest distance; Southern Europeans, closer; and South Americans, Arabs, and Pakistanis the closest. This is, of course, only a small percentage of all the countries in the world. The important point is that there are cultural differences that seem to be quite consistent.

These differences can often provoke misunderstandings. When a Swede and an Arab talk, the Swede ordinarily would choose a greater distance between them than would the Arab. Obviously they cannot both stand at their preferred distance. If the Swede picks the distance, the Arab may feel that he is being unfriendly and cold; but if the Arab picks the distance, he will seem overly intimate and pushy. Thus, the Swede feels the other is practically stepping on his toes and constantly backs away, while the Arab moves closer in order to establish what he considers a comfortable distance. If they are unaware of their cultural differences, they may perform a little dance around the room while at the same time developing negative views of each other.

Within the United States, there is evidence that pairs of Chicanos stand closer than pairs of either whites or blacks (Baxter, 1970). In general, blacks and whites differ little if at all in the distances they prefer. Middle-class whites do stand further apart than lower-class blacks (Aiello and Jones, 1971), but blacks and whites of the same social class select the same distances (Scherer, 1974). Age seems to play some role. In the first grade, black children stand closer to each other than white children; but by the fifth grade these differences have disappeared (Jones and Aiello, 1973). Thus, social class produces consistent differences—middle class standing further apart than lower class—but blacks and whites of comparable economic levels do not differ in their use of personal space.

Sex Differences

Females generally sit or stand closer than males; and mixed-sex pairs stand closer than same-sex pairs. Regardless of whom they are interacting with, women prefer to stand closer than men (Hartnett, Bailey, and Gibson, 1970; Leibman, 1970). This is especially true with same-sex pairs, in which two women stand closer than two men (Horowitz, Duff, and Stratton, 1970). When a male and female are interacting, they tend to be closer than when the pair is composed of either two males or two females (Kuethe and Weingartner, 1964).

The difference between the sexes also includes preferences for spatial positions. When they like the other person, males tend to sit across a table while females sit side by side or at a corner (Byrne, Baskett, and Hodges, 1971; Sommer, 1959). A study by Fisher and Byrne (1975) shows that this preference is reversed with strangers. Subjects were sitting alone at a library table when a stranger sat down either across from them, one seat away, or right next to them. Various measures indicate that regardless of the sex of the intruder, male subjects were more annoyed when the seat chosen was across from them while females were more annoyed when it was adjacent. In addition, males generally erected barriers between themselves and the seat across the table by placing their books in front of them; while females protected themselves from the side by putting their books and other possessions between themselves and the adjacent chair. Whether this difference would appear in other situations is uncertain, but we should keep these sex differences in mind because they also seem to occur in reactions to crowding, which we will discuss next.

Personal Space and Territoriality

Some people who have investigated the use of personal space believe that humans need a certain amount of space around them, and they will react defensively or aggressively when that space is invaded. This need for space and defense of it is sometimes called *territoriality*. Robert Ardrey (1966), who popularized the use of the term, argues that territoriality is instinctive in humans, that we are born with a built-in mechanism of some kind that makes us desire and defend space. Most psychologists would dispute the instinctive nature of this response, but agree that at least under some circumstances people will defend space they consider their own. Whether or not it is innate, territoriality does seem to exist to some extent in people and is obviously an important element in the use of personal space.

We have already seen that people react negatively to what they consider invasions of their personal space in libraries. If you are sitting alone at a table studying and a stranger sits down right next to or across from you, it is often annoying. Careful observations show that people do become angry and defensive at such invasions, and that the specific location of the invasion makes a difference (Felipe and Sommer, 1966; Fisher and Byrne, 1975). But other circumstances also play a role. If the library is completely full and the seat next to you is the only empty one, someone who sits there is invading your territory much less than if the library is empty. If there are lots of seats, someone who picks one next to you is deliberately choosing to invade

your territory either to be annoying or to get friendly with you. But whatever the motive, it is an invasion. In other words, the act of sitting close to someone must be interpreted in the context of the total situation.

Other factors in the situation also help us interpret and respond to other people's use of personal space. If you are standing on a corner waiting to cross the street, it is inappropriate for someone to stand very close to you unless there is no room. When someone does this, it is seen as an invasion of personal space and as a somewhat aggressive act, and people respond by crossing the street faster to escape (Konečni et al., 1975). However, approaching very close may be entirely appropriate and acceptable in other circumstances, such as a large party. It is expected that people will talk with strangers and a close approach is generally seen as friendly. Naturally, you may move away if you do not want to talk to the particular person; but the approach itself is not an invasion and would be welcomed if you were interested in the person.

Thus, our need for space is not absolute. It depends on many factors, including our feelings toward the other person and the situation. What is seen as an invasion in one context will be perceived as friendly and intimate in another. What might be annoying coming from someone we do not like will be pleasant from someone we like. In fact, standing very close to someone can have two opposite meanings—either friendliness or aggressiveness—depending on the total context. And, as we mentioned above, if there is no choice in where to stand or sit, if the library or bus or room is packed full, where you stand has little significance and is neither friendly nor aggressive.

CROWDING

One of the most active research areas in environmental psychology has been the effects of crowding on people. A great many Americans live in crowded cities, and the whole world is becoming more and more crowded; thus it is extremely important to discover how living under these conditions affects us. As we shall see, the effects are complicated, neither all bad nor all good. As with so many other factors in the environment, the effects of crowding depend largely on the total situation and our interpretation of it.

The Population Problem

Before discussing the effects of crowding, let us put it in the context of the world's population problem. As by now everyone knows, we are having a population explosion completely unprecedented in the history of the world. As you can see in Fig. 19.4, it took tens of

500,000 BC ⟶ 8,000 BC (5 million)

Table 19.2
POPULATION GROWTH RATES AND DOUBLING TIMES

	Growth rate (%)	Doubling time (years)
Industrialized countries		
Canada	1.0	69
United States	1.0	69
France	1.1	63
Italy	0.70	100
United Kingdom	0.60	117
USSR	1.0	69
Japan	1.1	63
Less industrialized		
Costa Rica	3.8	18
Mexico	3.4	21
Brazil	2.9	25
Kenya	3.0	23
UAR	3.0	24
India	2.6	28
China(?)	1.4	50

thousands of years for our population to reach half a billion, two hundred years for it to double to a billion, eighty years to double again, and only forty-five years for its last doubling in 1975. At the present rate of growth, it will double again in thirty-five years. We are now adding people at the rate of one billion every ten years.

The speed of population growth varies enormously from country to country. As shown in Table 19.2, the industrialized countries including all of Western Europe, the United States, Canada, and Japan have slow growth while virtually all of the underdeveloped countries of South America, Africa, and Asia have spectacularly rapid growth. Yet even the United States is adding more than two million people every year—more than the population of Los Angeles every three years. In the last few years the birth rate in the United States has reached the level at which at least theoretically the population will eventually stabilize. Despite this, because of the relatively large number of people of childbearing age, the population will continue to grow until it reaches about three hundred million and then it may level off.

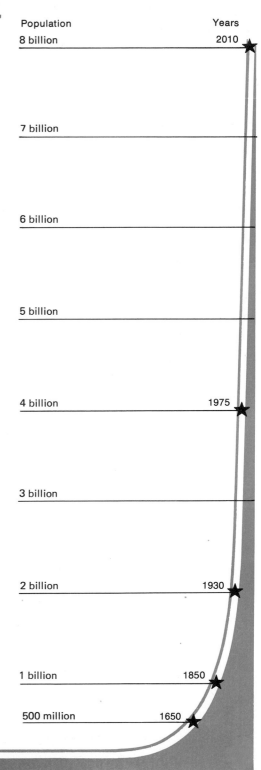

Fig. 19.4
Human population growth

After a slow start, world population has grown very rapidly and is now growing at a rate that will double the total population in about thirty-five years.

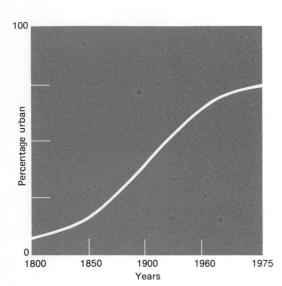

Fig. 19.5
Urbanization of the United States

The United States began as a large rural, agricultural country but has become increasingly urbanized. Now over 70 percent of the population is in or around urban centers.

This population explosion affects practically every aspect of our lives, and its negative consequences are becoming clearer every day. The strain it puts on natural resources is one of the major factors behind the worldwide inflation. Not only fuel, but a wide variety of metals and chemicals are in short supply. Even more basic is the shortage of food. Until recently, there was a great deal of fertile land that was underutilized, and there have been great improvements in agriculture that have greatly increased the yield per acre. Now, however, virtually all of the good land is being used. In addition, the oceans have been over-fished and yields are decreasing at the very time that more and more food is needed. There have already been devastating famines in India, Bangladesh, and parts of Africa, and only the few countries with surpluses have managed to prevent these famines from becoming catastrophes.

In addition to the shortages of power, natural resources, food, and land, the vast population causes pollution of every kind. While the natural processes of the earth can absorb huge amounts of chemical and organic waste, the world's population now consumes such great quantities of resources and produces so much waste that the environment is being damaged.

Finally, in purely human terms, the increase in population interferes with the quality of life of every person. However large and rich the country, the resources are limited. There is just so much good land, just so many lovely beaches, just so much wood for houses, food to eat, and water to drink. The more people there are, the less each one will have. These resources are becoming scarcer even in rich countries such as the United States. And in most parts of the world, with fewer resources and a higher population density, the situation is far graver. Thus, in terms of supplying basic needs, preserving the environment, and maintaining a reasonable quality of life, the population explosion is one of the most serious threats the world's human population faces today.

An Urban World

Within the context of the population problem, psychologists have devoted most of their attention to studying the urban environment. This is partly because all industrial societies and in particular the United States are now primarily urban. The urbanization of the United States occurred gradually during the early nineteenth century and very rapidly during the early part of the twentieth (see Fig. 19.5). By 1975, over 70 percent of the population lived in or near cities, with over 60 percent in just two hundred metropolitan areas. In recent years most of the growth has been not in the cities themselves but in the surrounding suburban areas. This has produced the characteristic structure of a central city surrounded by ever-increasing rings of suburbs.

The pattern of population distribution is similar in most of the other industrialized countries. France, West Germany, Israel, Japan, and Canada are all largely urban. Canada is an interesting example of how industrialization leads to urbanization. It is still primarily an agricultural country, and has a population of only twenty-three million despite the fact that it is the second largest country in the world with almost four million square miles. Nevertheless it is a highly industrialized society, and over 70 percent of its small population lives in or near cities, with 40 percent concentrated in only seven metropolitan areas. In contrast, virtually all the less industrialized countries are still considerably less than 50 percent urban. Burma, India, Ceylon, Haiti, Kenya, and China are all 80 percent non-urban. However, as they have become more industrialized, they too have shown a strong and continuing trend toward becoming urban.

The urbanization of the world means that a great many people are living in very small areas. Although the average population density of the world is still only about sixty people per square mile, the actual densities that occur in limited areas are much higher. Small cities have at least a few hundred people per square mile, and larger cities have densities in the thousands or even tens of thousands. Thus, one of the basic facts of urban life is the high population density, and a very important question is how this affects the people who live under these conditions. Before reading further, look at Fig.

THE PACE OF LIFE

One effect of city life that almost everyone would agree on is that the pace of life is faster. Everything seems to move faster—there are more deadlines, more hurrying, more things to do, and generally a more rapid pace to every activity. While this may not actually be true of all behavior, a recent study shows that it is true of walking speed. Marc and Helen Bornstein (1976) measured walking speed in fifteen communities that ranged in size from Psychro, Greece, a town of 365 people, to Brooklyn, New York, with a population of over two million. As you can see in the figure, there is a clear relationship between size of community and walking speed. The larger the community, the faster people walk. The differences are quite large, from a leisurely pace of about three feet per second to just under six feet per second. Exactly what people do with the time saved is uncertain, nor do we know why people in the city walk faster than those in small towns. But it does seem to be true that the pace of life or at least of walking depends on where you live.

Box 19·1

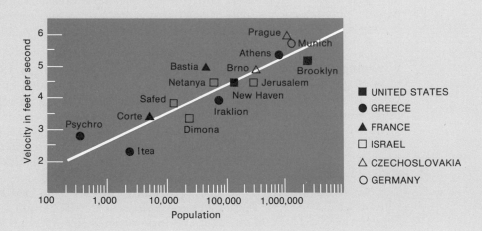

Beer party

Family discussion

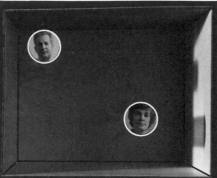

Doctor's waiting room

Fig. 19.6
Crowding and the situation

Using a circle to represent a person, put as many into each room as you think would fit comfortably for the situation described.

19.6 and indicate your preferences. We shall return to this demonstration, but first let us consider how crowding affects other animals and then turn to research on humans.

Crowding and Animals

Living under high density conditions has dramatic effects on many different kinds of animals. In a number of experiments (Calhoun, 1962; Southwick, 1955; and others), a small number of animals have been put in a cage and observed for many generations. Rats, mice, voles (a type of rodent), and various other small creatures have been used as subjects. They are provided with all the food and water they need, the cages are cleaned, and otherwise they are left alone. These are ideal conditions with no shortage of necessary resources, no predators, and a controlled climate. Understandably, the population of the colony grows very rapidly. It does not, however, continue to grow until all of the space is used. On the contrary, the population peaks and then drops sharply. This same pattern of rapid increase and sharp drop in population has also been observed in natural environments among deer who were stranded on an island (Christian, Flyger, and Davis, 1960).

Physiological effects The explanation for this effect must lie in physiological and social changes that occur under crowded conditions. John Christian (1955), Rodgers and Thiessen (1964), and others noted that animals who live under high density had enlarged adrenal glands. The importance of this physiological effect is that an enlarged adrenal gland is evidence of increased adrenal activity, which in turn indicates that the animal is aroused. This means that animals that are crowded with large numbers of other animals are constantly aroused.

Moreover, there is some evidence that crowded male rats have somewhat less active sexual organs (Southwick and Bland, 1959; Snyder, 1968). Their testes and seminal vesicles are smaller than usual, and they may produce fewer sperm than uncrowded animals. This reduced vitality may be due to the constant activity of the adrenal gland, which tends to interfere with normal sexual processes. Or it may be a direct effect of the crowding. Whatever the cause, decreased sexual potency could contribute to a decline in the population of the colony. However, it should be noted that this cannot be a full explanation of the population decline because the effect on the sexual organs is slight and, in any case, the normal number of pregnancies occur even under very crowded conditions (Calhoun, 1962).

Other research has studied the effects of crowding on susceptibility to disease (Friedman, Glascow, and Ader, 1969), formation of ulcers (Ader, 1965), and emotionality (Thiessen, Zolman, and Rodgers, 1962). It is important to note that crowding has no consistent effect in any of these cases, with the possible exception of emotionality, where it has been found that group-reared animals are, if anything, less emotional than those raised by themselves. Thus, the two consistent physiological effects of crowding are increased adrenal activity and somewhat reduced sexual potency.

Social effects Crowding does have major effects on social behavior. As the population of the colonies in closed cages increases, fewer and fewer animals behave normally. A small number of very tough, strong males do manage to lead more or less normal lives. They find nests, collect a small harem, mate, and then protect the nest and offspring. They and their families are healthy, reproduce normally, and have relatively good life expectancy. But animals who are not associated with these few successful males lead lives that are deviant in one way or another. Some males become recluses, staying apart from the other animals, finding a perch far away from the rest of the colony, and venturing forth only to get food and water. John Calhoun (1962) calls these "the beautiful ones" because their coats remain sleek and unbruised. Although they manage to survive, they are severely withdrawn and do not ever mate. The largest group of deviant animals, however, are what might be called "juvenile delinquents." They mill about on the floor of the cage in what Calhoun called a "behavioral sink." They are disorganized, fight continuously, mate indiscriminately, and sometimes roam about the cage intruding upon nests. They do not have nests, families, or permanent mates. They are more aggressive, more destructive, and more promiscuous than most animals under conditions of lower density. And they interfere directly with the process of raising healthy new animals.

Similarly, those females that are not associated with dominant males do not generally perform their maternal functions as well as usual. They try to build nests, but their nests are inadequate (see Fig. 19.7); they try to nurse and protect their young, but they do not give sufficient care. And the result is that most of the young die in infancy. In fact, the most obvious cause for the decline in population in the colony is that few young reach maturity. Whereas under normal conditions about 50 percent of the young live to reproduce, under

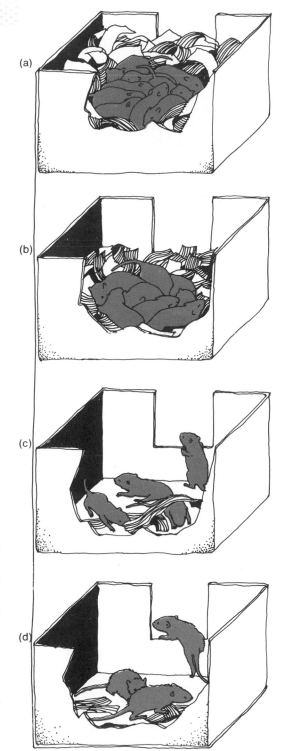

(a)

(b)

(c)

(d)

Fig. 19.7
Crowding and maternal behavior

A newborn litter in a well-shaped nest built by a normal mother is shown in (a) and in (b) about two weeks later. By comparison, (c) shows the inadequate nest made by a disturbed female who has been subjected to crowded conditions. In (d), about two weeks later, the baby rats are already leaving. None can survive alone. (After Calhoun, 1962)

crowded conditions, infant mortality may be as high as 95 percent.

To sum up, crowding is obviously very harmful to many nonhuman animals. When the number of animals in a small area gets very high, there is an almost total breakdown of normal social behavior and the result is disaster for the colony.

Crowding and Humans

Although crowding has negative effects on other animals, and although there is a widespread belief that it also has harmful consequences for humans, this is not supported by the evidence. The research that is currently available indicates that crowding is generally neither harmful nor helpful to people, but rather that the effect depends on a wide variety of factors including characteristics of the people involved, the situation, the quality of the interaction among the people, and probably other considerations.

Definition First, let us be clear what we mean by *crowding*. This is a common term that may not appear to need defining, but unfortunately it has two quite different meanings that can be very confusing. Crowding can refer to a person's *feeling or emotion* that she does not have enough space, is cramped, has no privacy, or is being intruded upon. This feeling is always negative. When anyone says she is crowded, she means she is uncomfortable or unhappy. This feeling is related to the amount of space available, but can occur under many circumstances. If you want to be totally alone, even one other person can make you feel crowded. If you walk ten miles into the forest because you and a friend want to be by yourselves, you will feel crowded if you meet other people camping in your favorite spot. In contrast, twenty people at a party in a small room may not feel crowded if they are having a good time and there is enough room to stand comfortably. In other words, crowding can refer to the psychological state of discomfort associated with wanting more space than is available, regardless of the actual amount of space.

The other meaning of the term crowding is the *physical state of having little space around you*. If there are fifty square feet per person, it is less crowded than if there are ten square feet. This is a purely physical, objective definition, which does not include one's psychological reaction, and it can be measured with precision. Moreover, this physical crowding, which is often called *density*, is not necessarily negative or harmful—it is a neutral situation that may or may not have harmful effects. In fact, the crucial question is what effects it does have. Thus, as Daniel Stokols (1972) and others have pointed out, it is essential to make the distinction between crowding as a psychological feeling and crowding as a physical state. The former depends on many factors and is always negative; the latter is an independent variable whose effect must be determined. From the point of view of environmental psychology, the important question is how the physical fact of density affects people. So keep in mind that when we use the term crowding we are referring to the amount of space available, not to an internal feeling.

Crowding in natural situations—correlational studies Although this will probably come as a surprise to many people, research indicates that living, playing, or working under crowded conditions generally has no harmful effects on us. It does not make us more aggressive,

In certain situations, density can lead to a heightening of good feeling.

does not increase crime, does not increase stress, and does not cause us to become mentally disturbed. This may be difficult to believe and we shall discuss some possible explanations later, but first let us look at some of the evidence.

Pressman and Carol (1971) and Freedman, Heshka, and Levy (1973) compared metropolitan areas in the United States in terms of crime and population density. If high density increases aggressiveness, this should show up in crime statistics. However, when the areas were equated on income and other social factors, there was no remaining relationship between density and crime. Crowded cities had no higher crime rates than uncrowded ones. For example, Los Angeles has one of the lowest densities and one of the highest crime rates.

The same kind of study has been done for individual cities to see if those areas with high density produce more crime, mental disturbance, or any other kind of pathology than those with low density. This has been done in Honolulu, Chicago, and New York. With the exception of Honolulu, where there was a consistent relationship between density and crime (Schmitt, 1957, 1966), the other work has found no substantial relationships between density and any kind of pathology (Winsborough, 1965; Galle, Gove, and McPherson, 1972; Freedman, Heshka, and Levy, 1975). High-density areas do generally produce the most crime, but it must be noted that they are also the poorest areas. When average income is equated, density is shown to have no effect. In other words, it is the poverty in these areas, not the density, that affects the rate of pathology.

Two impressive studies actually interviewed large numbers of people in their homes to assess the effect of crowding on physical and mental health. Mitchell (1971) conducted a study in Hong Kong, where the range of densities was from spacious homes to very cramped quarters with twenty square feet per person or even less (note that a standard single bed takes up more than twenty square feet). Mitchell found that crowding had no effect on the health of the people. Those with little space were no more nervous or tense than those with plenty of space. With less space, the children tended to spend less time in the home, but this was not associated with any negative effects. A similar project conducted in Toronto (Booth and Cowell, 1974) collected a wide variety of measures of physical and mental health and related them to crowding in the home and in the neighborhood. As before, they found that crowding had no consistent effects on any measure of health.

Broad-scale correlational studies of this kind seem to indicate that in the real world population density is not a major factor producing pathology. These are reinforced by changes in crowding and crime rates over the past twenty or so years. As shown in Fig. 19.8, cities are less crowded now but crime rates are much higher. Clearly, it is unlikely that density caused the increase in crime. However, correlational studies are always somewhat difficult to interpret and there remains the possibility that important relationships are obscured or misinterpreted. Accordingly, psychologists have turned to the laboratory to study crowding under controlled conditions.

Experimental research In these experiments, people are put in rooms under high- or low-density conditions and various observations are made. The length of stay in the room is generally only a few hours,

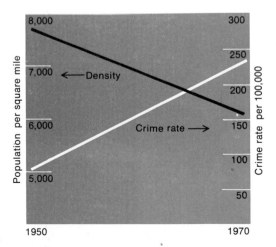

Fig. 19.8
Changes in density and crime rate in United States cities

From 1950 to 1970 the density of most United States cities declined substantially but crime rate more than tripled.

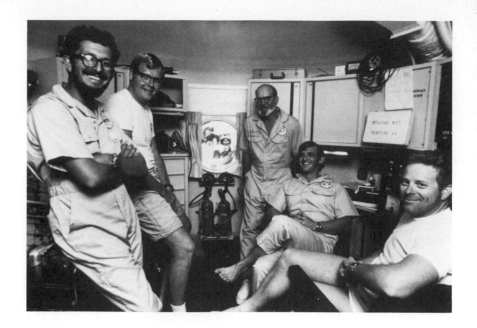

Humans manage to function quite normally even in the extremely cramped quarters of a hydrolab.

but in some isolation studies (such as Smith and Haythorn, 1972) subjects were confined for as long as twenty days. The findings indicate that when heat, odor, and other factors are controlled, crowding does not necessarily produce stress (bodily or mental tension). Crowding itself is not an aversive condition and does not always arouse drive.

Isolation studies conducted in relation to air-raid shelters, submarine warfare, and space flight demonstrated that people could function quite well under extremely high-density conditions for long periods of time. In one study by Smith and Haythorn (1972), men were confined for periods of up to twenty days in tiny quarters. It was found that they performed their tasks efficiently and generally did not break down. Even when they were totally isolated from the outside world and had very little space, they functioned well. They performed complex tasks, got along with each other, and were not especially aggressive or destructive. This should not come as a surprise, since this generation has witnessed men fly to the moon and circle the earth for weeks cooped up in a tiny space craft. The situation may be difficult, but clearly humans can function with little space when they must.

Other research has shown that the density in a room has no effect on task performance (Freedman, Klevansky, and Ehrlich, 1971; Griffitt and Veitch, 1971). Regardless of the type of task, whether it was simple or complex, whether it required creativity or not, the amount of space available per person had no consistent effect. If high density were unpleasant, one would expect it to interfere with complex tasks and perhaps to facilitate simple ones. The lack of effect appears to indicate that high density does not produce stress in the usual sense of the word.

Nor does crowding produce negative effects on social behavior. In a controlled experiment, Judy Price (1972) observed the behavior of children under crowded and uncrowded conditions. She watched first-grade children during their recess periods at school, and provided playrooms that were either quite large or very small. Although the size of the room did affect the kinds of activities and games, it had no effect on aggression—children were no more aggressive under crowded conditions than under less crowded conditions.

INTERVIEW

Philip Johnson is one of the world's foremost architects. He has built many of our outstanding buildings, including the famous "glass house" in which he lives and the Pennzoil building in Houston, which many critics considered the building of the year in 1976. He is a distinguished-looking man who talks with great authority and confidence about architecture. The interview took place in his elegant but spare offices in New York's Seagram's building, perhaps the most completely successful office building in the world from an architectural standpoint.

Q: How do you think architectural design—the design of buildings and of cities—affects the people who live in them and around them?

A: Very, very little. My favorite authority in the field is René Dubos [an eminent biologist and social critic], and his idea is that people are infinitely adaptable. It's hard to believe, but it's certainly been shown in a city like Berlin in 1945 when the city was destroyed and there was no place left standing. I'm sure I would have collapsed, but the people there didn't. So the effects of architecture are highly exaggerated.

Q: Well, what about some specific effects such as making people more productive, more nervous, or less nervous?

A: There you find sometimes in the worst situation, as in a submarine, your health will improve if there is enough danger to keep

PHILIP JOHNSON

People like to be crowded. They get a sense of rubbing together that is absolutely essential to civil life.

the adrenalin flowing. So you can live in a claustrophobic condition that I wouldn't want to be in; but that doesn't bother people. If there is enough danger, their health is fine. Boredom would drive them up a wall. So those things are more important than any spatial considerations—let's get that out of the way.

Now what can architecture do? Making people relax isn't really what one wants. Make them inspired? Maybe. To raise the cultural level of the country? That's hard to say. The history of Greece

shows that conditions in the fifth century in Athens were so appalling because of disease, filth, stench, and so on that they shouldn't have been able to build the monuments. There, architecture was a detriment to the standards of living. I don't care if people do stink as long as they build Parthenons, but you see I'm extreme—it depends on your point of view.

Q: I agree that people have exaggerated the extent to which one design versus another changes people's lives. On the other hand, people do complain about a particular house or building and praise another one—and I mean the people living in them. For example, everyone says the building we are in now is a wonderful building—beautiful to look at and to work in.

A: Now we're on another wave length, which is that aesthetics is much more basic than people will admit. By beauty we can make you physically more comfortable. In Avery Fisher Hall [a concert hall in New York], which we just did over, you hear better now and even the acousticians admit that a good deal of the better acoustics is that the room is visually pleasant to sit in.

Q: But aren't there buildings that look beautiful from the outside or even the inside but people who live or work in them complain that they don't work well?

A: I don't know about that—I doubt it. There are extremes, though. My own glass house. No one wants to live there. And I

Pennzoil Place, Houston, Texas

can't imagine *not* living there. I must have adapted very early.

Q: Do you think living in that house changes your behavior?

A: Not at all. You might think you must live differently in a glass house, but because of the instant adaptability and the beauty you don't mind at all. The Taj Mahal isn't very useful—whether it's good or bad doesn't come into it—you just get a thrill walking through it.

Q: Let me ask you a specific question that concerns a lot of people who are worried about the cities. Many people say they are too crowded and also that people hate high-rise apartments. How do you feel about that?

A: Exactly the opposite in both cases. I used to think that and I was talking to Raymond Hood, who built the first great skyscrapers, and he said people like to be crowded. They get a sense of rubbing together that is absolutely essential to civil life. And as far as high rises go, people in Harlem like to live in the high-rise projects.

Q: Yes, but do you think there are any problems with high-rise housing?

A: Children. I think it's hard to send children down to play with no supervision. Personally I would never build a home that saw over trees. I don't mean to be a sentimentalist, but I don't think you should see out higher than a tree top.

Q: What about the other issue with high-rise housing, which is that there are too many people, you always feel as if you're a stranger, and there is no sense of belonging, of neighborhood community?

A: I went to visit a house in the Near East where the entrance was five feet high, you walked down a 12-percent grade, came into a court the size of this room [about fifteen or twenty feet], where four families lived pretty well. A happier group of people I've never seen. They were a community, which you would not find in the anonymous cities of today.

Q: What do you think about Manhattan. Is it too crowded?

A: No, not at all, but it's badly distributed. I have a simple theory: take a block, tear it down and make a park out of it. Do that in a tic-tac-toe pattern so everybody has a park [in other words, put a park in the middle square of every tic-tac-toe set of blocks]. That's Jefferson's idea, not mine.

Q: Do you think people would really enjoy those parks as much as we would like to think they would?

A: No. I said in Los Angeles, why don't you have any parks? They said, why do we need parks—every house has its own swimming pool. An architect can go along and make lovely speeches and argue about why we don't have the will for handsomer cities, but it isn't so easy. There are social problems involved.

Comment

Johnson's view that architecture has less effect than many people think is consistent with all of the research on crowding and building size. He thinks that people like crowding because it increases social interaction —— an idea quite similar to the density-intensity theory, except that the theory would predict negative effects when the social situation was inherently unpleasant or negative to begin with. Johnson has nothing against high-rise housing (except that it is higher than trees) but does point out, as do many parents, that it is difficult to supervise children when you live on a higher floor and the playgrounds are on the ground. One theme that runs through this interview and also through all of the work on environmental psychology is the great adaptability of people. Things that might seem stressful, such as loud noise and cramped quarters, have little effect because people quickly get used to them and make the best of the situation. As Johnson says, other factors such as the presence of danger (and, we would add, all kinds of social factors such as poverty, discrimination, lack of employment, and so on) play a far greater role than architectural design or any other aspect of the environment. We have seen in the chapter that crowding, personal space, and other features of the environment do affect our behavior and feelings, but these effects are complex, depend on other variables, and are rarely absolute. As in Johnson's example of ancient Greece, it may depend on your point of view —— what you value, what you personally like and dislike —— rather than on any inherent goodness or badness of the environment.

JONATHAN L. FREEDMAN

STANLEY HESHKA

In the isolation study mentioned above (Smith and Haythorn), some groups were provided with more space than others. Rather than making things better, the larger area actually increased the amount of hostility the subjects expressed toward each other. In a series of experiments by Jonathan Freedman, Stanley Heshka, and Alan Levy (Freedman, 1975), no overall negative effects of crowding were observed on aggressiveness, mood, liking for other people, or any other variable. Thus the research shows that high density does not have consistently harmful effects on people's behavior or feelings.

Sex differences On the other hand, density does seem to produce complex effects that sometimes differ for males and females. In one study (Freedman et al., 1972), groups of all males or all females were put in large or small rooms where they played a game that allowed them to be either competitive or cooperative. As shown in Fig. 19.9, the males became more competitive in the small room, while the females were actually slightly less competitive in the smaller room. In another study, subjects pretended they were juries. All-male groups liked each other *less* and gave *more severe* sentences in a small room while all-female groups liked each other *more* and gave *less severe* sentences in the small room. Groups composed of both sexes showed no effect of crowding (see Fig. 19.10). And other experiments also found different reactions by males and females—sometimes females responding more positively to crowding (Ross et al., 1973), sometimes males responding more positively (Loo, 1972).

Since the effects take different directions it seems unlikely that they are due to basic sex differences. It may be that males, because they are larger, are more sensitive to crowding. But under some

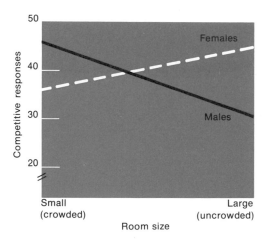

Fig. 19.9
Crowding, sex, and competitiveness

All-male groups compete more in a small room than in a large room; all-female groups show a slight trend in the opposite direction. (After Freedman et al., 1972)

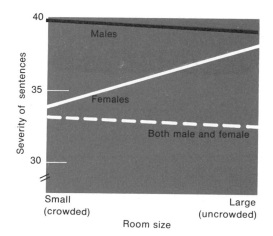

Fig. 19.10
Crowding, sex, and severity

All-female groups give less severe sentences in small rooms; all-male groups show a slight tendency in the other direction; and mixed-sex groups are unaffected by room size. (After Freedman, 1972)

circumstances females are also very sensitive to crowding. Therefore, a more general explanation is necessary. How can we explain the finding that crowding is not harmful, when we know that many people find it uncomfortable to be in a crowded room or crowded city?

Stimulation level and sensory overload One explanation for the negative reaction some people have to crowding is that everyone has a particular level of stimulation that is pleasant, and anything over or under that level produces discomfort. If there is too much stimulation, it may produce what has been called *sensory overload* (more stimulation than the person can handle) and the person may react by shutting out stimulation, responding less well to the world, and becoming upset (Milgram, 1970). A more general version of this idea is that some people like a great deal of stimulation while others like a lower level.

There is evidence that at least under some circumstances crowding can be arousing—that is, stimulating. When people are put into very crowded situations, they do show physiological arousal. For example, in one experiment six subjects in a room only four feet by four feet were more aroused than subjects in a larger room (Aiello, Epstein, and Kralin, 1975). This is, of course, more extreme crowding than almost ever occurs in natural situations. And most other studies, with less severe crowding, do not indicate arousal. Nevertheless, it suggests that crowding can produce arousal. Therefore, living in a city or working in a crowded environment would be fine for those who like a lot of stimulation; indeed, would actually be preferable to an environment with less stimulation. But those who like little stimulation would find cities and crowded environments unpleasant. Considering both kinds of people, crowding would show no effects because it is positive for some and negative for others. Yet it is actually having important effects on everyone—some good, some bad, depending on the amount of stimulation they liked.

Although there is as yet no experimental evidence to support this idea, it could explain some of the sex differences we described. Perhaps men and women differ in the amount of stimulation they like, with women liking more social stimulation than men. The lack of consistency in the effects on men and women could be due to the fact that even those preferences depend in part on the specific situation. That is, men may like a lot of stimulation under some circumstances and very little under others. For the moment this is highly speculative, but the idea that people have varying preferences for levels of stimulation seems plausible and may be a partial explanation of varying reactions to crowding.

Density-intensity Another explanation is that crowding serves to intensify the usual response to any social situation. If people would ordinarily like the other people they are with they will like them more when they are crowded; if they would dislike them, they will dislike them more. Similarly, if they would be afraid, anxious, angry, or aggressive under low density, they will feel these emotions more strongly under high density. Several experiments have demonstrated this effect of crowding. When males or females are placed in pleasant situations, both sexes respond more positively under high density; in unpleasant situations, subjects of both sexes like them less under high density (Freedman, 1975).

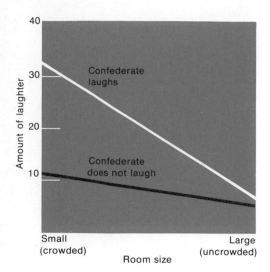

Fig. 19.11
Crowding and laughter

When a confederate laughs in a crowded room, there is a dramatic increase in the amount of laughter. This is consistent with the intensification theory of crowding and also seems to be a contagion effect. (After Freedman and Perlick, 1976)

A recent study (Freedman and Perlick, 1977) demonstrated this intensification effect on laughter. You have probably noticed that things generally seem much funnier when you are with other people than when you are alone. Even a very funny book rarely makes you laugh out loud if you are reading it to yourself, but the same book read out loud to a group of people produces a great deal of laughter. Also, comedy movies usually evoke more laughter if the theater is crowded than if it is half-empty. To test this experimentally, people sat in small or large rooms and listened to tapes by comedian George Carlin. One of the people in the room was a confederate of the experimenter. The confederate in one condition laughed at certain passages on the tapes and in the other condition smiled slightly but did not laugh. Motion pictures were taken of everyone's reactions to the comedy routines. The results are shown in Fig. 19.11, which shows that in the uncrowded rooms there was less laughter and the confederate had little effect; but in the crowded room, when the confederate laughed, there was a great deal more laughter than when she did not laugh. In fact, the one condition in which people were crowded and the confederate laughed caused more than three times as much laughter as any other condition. Apparently, the crowding intensified the effect of both the comedy and the confederate.

This explanation views crowding as similar to other stimuli. For example, if you like a piece of music, you will like it more when it is played louder, and vice versa. In the same way, people become a more important stimulus when the density is higher—you are more aware of them and respond to them more strongly. Whatever your feelings toward the people, those feelings are stronger when you are under high density.

This intensification effect occurs in many social situations. Unpleasant circumstances such as a doctor's waiting room or a subway car are more unpleasant when they are crowded; pleasant situations such as a party or a football game are more exciting and pleasant when the density is high. You may have found in Fig. 19.6 that you were willing to have more people at the party (a positive situation) than at the doctor's waiting room (a negative situation). Indeed, a crowded party is better than an uncrowded one because the positive mood is intensified.

Although this interpretation is consistent with the available research, the investigation of this problem is just beginning. This is an area in which a great deal more work has been done in the past five years than in the ten or twenty years before that. And the next few years will almost certainly see even more attention given to this problem. Accordingly, all of the interpretations given here must be considered tentative. They are based on relatively little research and await further testing. Nevertheless, the work to date does strongly indicate that high density does not ordinarily produce negative effects on humans. It may be negative under some conditions, but will be positive or neutral under others.

LIFE IN THE CITY

As we said earlier, the United States and Canada are largely urban societies, with more than 70 percent of the population living in or very near cities. It is therefore both relevant and important to ask how living in a city differs from living under other conditions. This question is especially appropriate in these times, when our cities seem to be going through a particularly difficult period. In addition to financial problems, the cities are beset by high crime rates, rundown schools, heavy welfare rolls, unemployment, and low morale. Moreover, there appears to be, at least in the United States, a pervasive anti-city feeling among many people. Nevertheless, most of our population is urban and somehow most of us survive. Does living in a city have negative psychological or physical effects on people?

The first point to make is to repeat what we said in the sections on crowding and noise. These two factors, so typical of cities and most often thought to be harmful, have few if any negative effects on people. The next point to make is that people who live in the city do not have any higher rates of mental disturbance than those who live in small towns, or even in rural communities (Dohrenwend and Dohrenwend, 1974; Srole, 1972). It might seem that there would be more stress in the city, but whether or not there is, it does not produce more disturbance. The rates of psychosis are about the same everywhere, including primitive societies; and there are no substantial differences in neurosis. Furthermore, city people do not feel any more anxious or unhappy than other people. In a survey of a large number of Americans (Shaver and Freedman, 1976), those who lived in cities said that they were just as happy and calm as did those who lived in small towns or rural areas. The study found that the particular type of community—urban, suburban, town, or rural—mattered very little in terms of health, psychological wellbeing or anything else.

Drawing by Booth; © 1976 The New Yorker Magazine, Inc.

"*My mother always says that. She always says 'You have to be a little bit crazy to live in New York.' Mother is a little crazy, but she doesn't live in New York. She lives in Nishnabotna, Missouri.*"

On the other hand, we all know that some people hate being in a city. They find the noise unpleasant, the crowds of people upsetting, the pace too fast, and the atmosphere obnoxious. Many people prefer the quieter, more peaceful, slower-paced life in the suburbs or better still a small town or rural area. If they dislike cities so much, how can we say that cities are not harmful?

The answer is that reactions to the city depend on characteristics of the individual. The critical characteristic may be the level of stimulation you prefer. Obviously, if you like a high level, cities are more likely to produce positive feelings than if you like lower levels. In the survey by Shaver and Freedman, many people reported that they were not happy with their community. This was true of all kinds of communities; some people who lived in rural areas were dissatisfied just as were some who lived in urban areas. The amount of dissatisfaction was about the same for all areas. But the important point is that people who did not like their community tended to be the least happy and healthy. Although the type of community in which people lived did not affect happiness, their satisfaction with their community did. Thus, as we have all observed, some people do dislike cities and are unhappy in them; while others like cities and enjoy living there. The research indicates no overall effect of the type of community.

Clearly, every type of community has some advantages and some disadvantages. Cities are exciting, and offer many services and opportunities, many different kinds of people, and a high level of stimulation. But they are noisy, crowded, and certainly not peaceful. In contrast, small towns have what big cities lack—peacefulness, a sense of belonging to a family or neighborhood, and a slower-paced life. It is all a question of what you want and that is an individual decision.

Summary

1. The field of environmental psychology investigates how stimuli from the world around us affect human behavior.

2. Although exposure to loud noise initially causes arousal and interferes with performance on many tasks, for the most part people adapt very rapidly to noise and experience no lasting physiological or psychological effects. However, the effects can be detrimental when the noise is unpredictable and perceived as beyond the individual's control.

3. The study of *proxemics* deals with the personal and cultural spatial needs of people and how they use the space immediately around them. Variations in requirements for personal space depend on the relationship of the people, their ethnic and national background, and their sex.

4. The concept of *territoriality* is that animals and people have an innate tendency to require a certain amount of space and that they react defensively and aggressively to invasions of that space. While some animals may have such an instinct, humans do not. However, depending on the situation, we do sometimes consider certain spaces our property and we then respond negatively if they are invaded.

5. Laboratory experiments have shown that crowding has serious negative effects on animals, including increased adrenal activity, reduced sexual potency, social deviance, and general social breakdown.

6. Studies of the effects of crowding on humans in both natural settings (correlational studies) and experimental settings have shown surprising results. Careful correlational studies have found no consistent relationship between high density and crime, or between crowding and measures of physical or mental health. Similarly, people involved in experiments where they were subjected to high- or low-density conditions did not exhibit higher stress, more aggression, or lowered efficiency in performing tasks. But in several studies, males responded negatively to crowding while females responded positively.

7. One possible explanation for these effects is that people differ in the amount of sensory stimulation that is pleasant for them. Another explanation is that crowding intensifies any response, making a pleasant situation more pleasant but an unpleasant one more unpleasant.

8. The belief that people who live in cities are likely to be less happy, more anxious, and more inclined to suffer from a mental disturbance than those who live in non-urban areas is not supported by the evidence. Rates of psychosis are about the same everywhere, and people who live in cities report that they are as happy and healthy as do those who live in non-urban areas. Probably the most important variable affecting one's reaction to city life is the personal characteristics of the individual.

RECOMMENDED READING

Calhoun, J. B. Population density and social pathology. *Scientific American*, 1962, 206, 139–148. One of the first studies of the effects of crowding on nonhumans.

Freedman, J. *Crowding and Behavior*. San Francisco: Freeman, 1975. An optimistic view of crowding that argues that people are not harmed by living in high-density conditions. Easy reading and comprehensive.

Glass, D. C., and J. E. Singer. *Urban Stress*. New York: Academic, 1972. This book describes in detail most of the work on the effects of noise on people.

Hall, E. T. *The Silent Language*. Garden City, N.Y.: Doubleday, 1959. An interesting book about nonverbal communication via the distance between people. Not especially scientific, but good reading.

Jacobs, J. *Death and Life of Great American Cities*. New York: Random House, 1961. Cities are fine but are being ruined by poor planning. Jane Jacobs is fascinating and thoughtful.

Appendix

STATISTICS

Once you have run a study and collected a lot of numbers, you must use statistics to make sense of them. We use *descriptive statistics* to summarize the data in a form that is easy to deal with and understand. Then we often must use *inferential statistics* to find out how much confidence we should have in the results, and what they mean.

DESCRIPTIVE STATISTICS

It is usually difficult if not impossible to work directly with a large number of separate bits of data. If you have the IQ scores of thirty-five people (see Table A.1), you can make a list of them and perhaps get a general idea of how high they are and how much variation there is among them. But that is the best you can do—a general impression. By using the appropriate statistics, however, you can describe all of your data in a few simple statements that give a precise and mathematically accurate summary of what you have found. The two major characteristics of the data are *average* and *variability*.

Measures of Central Tendency

The first question you should ask is how the average individual scored. There are several different types of averages, all of which are called *measures of central tendency*, which refers simply to the fact that you are describing the middle or typical score. The simplest measure of central tendency is the *mode*, which is the point at which the most scores fall. For example the modal number of years to complete college is four. Although some people take less and quite a few take more, by far the most common number is exactly four. In this case, the mode is a pretty good description of the central tendency because the great majority of students fall at the mode. In other situations, however, there may be a wide distribution of scores and the mode will be less representative. An illustration of this is the publication history of PhD.s in psychology. As you know, many psychologists continue to publish articles or books throughout their

Table A.1

DETERMINING THE AVERAGE

99, 105, 98, 112, 90, 94, 121, 88, 98, 104, 102, 124, 100, 98, 95, 114, 106, 88, 165, 118, 116, 99, 108, 100, 95, 102, 122, 110, 90, 98, 109, 120, 101, 98, 96

A Sample of IQ Scores			
88	98	102	114
88	98	102	116
90	Mode→ 98	104	118
90	98	Mean→105	120
94	99	106	121
95	99	108	122
95	100	109	124
96	100	110	165
98	Median→101	112	

Mode	The most common score. There are five 98s, more than any other score, so the mode is 98.
Median	The middle score. There are thirty-five scores, so the eighteenth score is the middle, meaning that there are as many above it as below it. Counting down eighteen scores, we find the median is 101.
Mean	The average value of all scores, determined by adding them all and dividing by the number of scores. The sum of the scores is 3,683, which, divided by the number of scores (thirty-five), makes the mean 105.23. Note that only the mean is affected by the extreme score of 165.

careers, some producing a great many articles. But the modal number of publications is only one, because a large number of psychologists publish their dissertation and nothing else. Thus, the mode describes a common score, but gives no idea of the wide range of activity and certainly understates the amount of publishing that psychologists in general do. For this reason, we rarely use the mode except for special purposes as a very rough measure of central tendency.

A more useful measure is the *median*—the point at which there are as many scores higher as there are lower. To find this you merely put the scores in order and count off half the scores starting at either the top or the bottom. If there are thirty-one scores, the sixteenth is the median. An interesting point about computing the median is that it is very simple as long as there are a small number of scores, but gets very tedious with many scores. Moreover, although the wonderful new calculators that everyone seems to have can do just about every kind of statistical manipulation with great ease, they are virtually useless when it comes to finding a median.

The median is the midpoint of the scores and completely ignores how much higher or lower other scores fall. If the median income of physicians in this country is $35,000, we know that exactly half make more and half make less than that. We know nothing about the total amount of money all doctors earn, how many make a great deal more, or what the chance is of earning $100,000. Medians are therefore sometimes misleading and can underestimate or overestimate the level of the scores in the group. For example, if 50 percent of the doctors earned between $30,000 and $35,000 and the other half earned between $35,000 and $1,000,000, the median would greatly understate the amount of money doctors are earning. The median always tells you where half the cases fall and that is sometimes just what you want to know, but for many purposes it is an inadequate description of central tendency.

The most useful measure, and the one that conforms to what most people think of as the average, is the *mean*. It is the sum of all of the scores divided by the number of scores. If one hundred doctors earn a total of five million dollars, their mean earning is five million divided by 100, or $50,000. The mean IQ score is 100, the mean grade in a class might be a 75, the mean height of American adult women is 5'5", and so on. As we shall see, the mean is especially important because it is the most appropriate measure when doing inferential statistics.

Just as the median ignores the distribution of the scores, the mean has the opposite problem of giving weight to extreme scores. This can sometimes produce considerable distortion. In our example of doctors' incomes, suppose one of the one hundred doctors earned two million dollars. That would mean that the other ninety-nine earned only three million and had a mean income of about thirty thousand dollars. Adding in the one extreme score changes the mean to fifty thousand dollars and greatly overstates the amount of money most doctors are earning. Thus, when there are a few very extreme scores in either direction, we either use medians instead of means or somehow correct the extreme scores to make them less deviant. For example, in measuring the running times of rats in a maze, we might get scores that ranged from ten seconds up to thirty seconds, and then one score of five minutes because one rat decided to take a snooze or was uninterested in running. This highly deviant score would grossly distort the mean. This problem can be handled by just dropping that score or making it equal to the next lowest score, both reasonable procedures. An even better technique, and one that practically everyone uses in this case, is to use running *speed* instead of time. Speed is simply the reciprocal of time, but it avoids extreme scores because the very long score of 5 minutes (300 seconds) becomes much less important when you compare its reciprocal (.0033) to the next slowest time (.05). Thus, by transforming the data in some legitimate way, we can often control the effect of deviant cases and still use the mean as a measure of central tendency.

Measures of Variation

The second step in describing a set of scores is to find out how much variation there is in them. Are they all grouped closely together or are they spread widely? The IQ scores of college students are usually grouped tightly because the admissions office accepts only highly qualified, bright people. In contrast, the IQ scores of a random sample of people of college age will be more widely spaced because there has been no selection in terms of intelligence. You can get a rough idea of the amount of variation by putting the scores on a graph (a dot for each score), on which a tight distribution clearly would mean less variation. However, we need more precise measures than this for statistical purposes.

One statistic that is rarely used but can be helpful in describing your data is the *range*. This is simply the difference between the highest and lowest scores in your sample. Actors' incomes have a range from a few thousand to over a million; secretaries' incomes have a much smaller range, probably from $5,000 to $20,000. The IQ scores in the population as a whole range from about 30 to 200; in college it would be only from 110 to 200. This is not a complete measure of variation, but it does provide a quick indication of the variability of the scores.

By far the most important measure of variability is the *standard deviation*. This is the average amount that each score deviates from the mean of the sample. It is calculated by subtracting each score from the mean, squaring it, adding the squares, dividing by the number of scores, and taking the square root of the result. The deviations are squared rather than just added because this produces a result that we can use more easily in inferential statistics. It also gives somewhat more weight to scores that deviate a lot from the mean.

Table A.2
MEASURES OF VARIATION

Measure	Description
Range	The difference between the smallest and largest scores. In Table A.1, the range is from 88 to 165, or 77.
Standard deviation	Determined by squaring each deviation from the mean, summing these squares, dividing by the number of scores, and taking the square root. S.D. = 14.17.

Correlations

Another descriptive statistic is the *correlation,* which describes the relationship between two sets of scores. It tells us whether a score on one set is associated in any way with a score on the other set. In particular, if high scores on one measure go along with high scores on the other, they are *positively correlated*; if high scores on one are associated with low scores on the other, they are *negatively correlated. Correlation coefficients,* which indicate the strength of the correlation, range from +1.0 to −1.0. Correlations and correlational research are discussed in more detail in Chapter 1.

INFERENTIAL STATISTICS

Sometimes we collect data purely for descriptive purposes. We want to know the chance of getting enough tall people for a basketball team, the average IQ of incoming college freshmen, or the number of seniors applying to medical school compared to the number of places. In these instances, the mean and standard deviations may give us all the information we need. However, most of the time in psychology we want to do more than just describe one group or one variable. Often we want to compare two groups and see if they are different, or discover whether a particular group differs from some known or theoretical average (for example, is a coin true). Ordinarily, descriptive statistics alone are not sufficient for this purpose because we have no way of knowing whether a difference between two means should be taken seriously. We must assess whether the difference occurred by chance or is a true difference, and to do this we use inferential statistics.

The problem is that groups can have different means and yet, in truth, be identical to each other because the difference was due entirely to chance. For example, suppose you want to compare two coins to see if one comes up heads more often than the other. If you flip each of them once, and one lands on heads and the other on tails, it is doubtful that you would draw any conclusions. If you flip them each ten times, and one gets six heads and the other only four, you probably still would not be likely to decide that they were different. But how about one hundred flips, with one getting sixty and the other forty heads? At some point, it begins to seem as if the coins are different. But you cannot rely on intuition to tell you when that point has been reached. Instead, you use statistics. By using the appropriate test we can calculate precisely what the probability was of any result occurring by chance. If the odds against it are high enough, we assume that the result was due not to chance but to some systematic difference or variation. In psychology, we ordinarily publish or take seriously a result that would occur by chance less than 5 percent of the time, which is written as p (probability) $< .05$ (that is, the odds against it happening by chance are 19 to 1). In practical terms, if we find that one coin produces more heads and with probability = .05, we should be willing to give 19 to 1 odds that on, say, one hundred tosses, that coin will get more heads than the other. It means that we have considerable confidence in our result because it would rarely happen just by accident.

Populations versus Samples

Whenever we have all of the possible cases, we are dealing with *populations.* If you measure the height of everyone in your class, you have the complete population of heights for the class. When the census bureau gathers data, it tries to get information directly about every person in the country. The complete list of stock prices on Wall Street, final batting averages for all major-league baseball players, grades for a whole class, and so on all represent the population of cases. If you have data on the whole population, you usually do not need inferential statistics. You know that steel stocks closed higher than automobile stocks, that ten people in the class got A's, that the women got higher grades than the men, or that the National League teams had higher batting averages than the American League teams. There is no possibility of chance entering into these figures because you have all of the data there are. That is, the National League hitters might have been luckier during the season than the American League hitters, but you know for certain that one set of averages was in fact higher than the other. This is not an inference, it is a fact.

However, very little research in psychology is based on populations. Instead, we deal with only a portion of the possible cases—what we call a *sample* of the population. Pollsters such as Gallup ask only 1,500 people whom they are planning to vote for and these responses are supposed to give some indication of how the total population is likely to vote. Nielsen surveys of television viewing base their estimates of how many people watch a particular program on at most a few thousand cases. It is as if they were sampling a piece of a cake to see how the whole cake tastes, or one apple from a barrel to find out if the rest are good. Manufacturers do spot checks on products, testing every hundredth unit to get an idea of the quality of all units. In our example of the coin tossing, you cannot use the population of all tosses of the coin because you would have to keep tossing it indefinitely. So you toss it a hundred or a thousand times, and assume that its future performance would be similar to your sample. Indeed, we do exactly this in our daily lives all the time. We meet someone for an hour, form an impression from that short sample of the person's behavior, and then assume (often incorrectly) that he or she will behave the same way in future meetings. In all of these instances we want to generalize from a sample to the population.

Basing conclusions on samples rather than populations is a necessary and highly efficient part of psychological research. But unlike populations, where you have all of the cases, samples require us to draw inferences because we want to make a statement about the population based on the sample. The reason this is an inference is that no sample is exactly the same as the whole population. Every sample is somewhat different from every other sample, and this random variation must be taken into account in drawing conclusions. If you toss a coin ten times, you will not get the same result in every set of ten tosses. Even if the coin is perfectly true, sometimes you will get five heads, sometimes four, sometimes nine, and sometimes every other possible number from zero to ten heads. This variation is due entirely to chance. Over a great many sets of ten tosses, the average number of heads should be five, but any particular set of ten may or may not produce five. If Gallup asks 1,500 people chosen at random from the population, their responses will be somewhat different from another group of 1,500 people because every person is different and each sample will have a slightly different mixture of people. However, as with the coins, if Gallup took a hundred sets of 1,500 people each, the average response for all samples should be virtually identical to what he would get if he asked the whole population. Thus, we need statistics to decide how good an estimate we have of the population, and to evaluate our results.

The Normal Distribution

Much of inferential statistics is based on the fact that events that depend on chance or large numbers of cases of any kind tend to fall into a fixed pattern that is called the *normal distribution* (see Fig. A.1). As you would expect, most of the scores fall near the mean of all the scores, the next largest number of scores fall nearby, and the number tapers off as you move further and further from the mean. A great many different kinds of data fall into this pattern. It describes natural events such as the highest temperatures recorded every March 3 for the last one hundred years anywhere in the country, the height of American adult males, the scores on IQ tests, and almost any other physical or psychological characteristic of people. It also applies to chance events such as the scores achieved by throwing two dice, the number of heads gotten by tossing ten coins, and so on. You can verify this for yourself by tossing ten coins at a time and recording the number of heads. Do it fifty times and you will see that the scores fall into a normal distribution.

The characteristic of the normal distribution that makes it so useful for statistical purposes is that it can be described precisely in terms of the mean and standard deviation. As shown in Fig. A.1, theoretically in any group of scores that are normally distributed, exactly 34.13 percent will fall within one standard deviation above the mean and the same percentage below the mean; another 13.59 percent fall between one and two standard deviations above and below; and 2.14 percent between two and three standard deviations from the mean. This is true regardless of the size of the standard deviation, but of course the shape of the distribution will depend on the particular standard deviation. Thus, if you know the standard deviation of the sample, you can specify the probability that a particular score will fall any number of deviations from the mean. For example, if you know that the mean height of American adult males is 5'9" and the standard deviation is two inches, you can calculate the chance of someone being 6', 6'2", 5'3", or any other height. You do this simply by seeing how far the score deviates from the mean, dividing by the standard deviation, and looking in the table to see how likely that score is. A height of 6'1" is four inches or two standard deviations from the mean; the probability of a score that far from the mean or further is shown in Table A.3 as .023, so you know that only 2.3 percent of the population is that tall or taller. In other words, the chance of a randomly chosen man being that tall is about forty to one. You can see that a college basketball coach would have a hard time finding enough tall players if students were admitted to college with no regard to their height. In a class of two thousand undergraduate men you would expect to have about forty-six (.023 × 2,000)

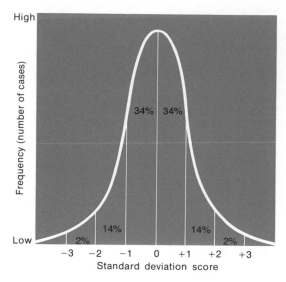

Fig. A.1
Normal distribution

Table A.3
CRITICAL RATIOS

SD from mean	Expected %
−3.0	.1
−2.5	.6
−2.0	2.3
−1.5	6.7
−1.0	15.9
− .5	30.9
0.0	50
+ .5	30.9
+1.0	15.9
+1.5	6.7
+2.0	2.3
+2.5	.6
+3.0	.1

The figures are the percentage of scores that would be expected to fall that far or further from the mean purely by chance. For example, a sample mean drawn from a population would be more than 2 standard deviations below the population mean only about 2.3% of the time, or once in 40; it would fall 3 standard deviations below the mean only one time in 1,000.

men taller than 6'1", but only two taller than 6'3" (because that is three standard deviations from the mean, which has a probability of about .001). Clearly, given the heights of most college teams, the admission procedure is not entirely random with respect to the height of men. Presumably the admissions office looks favorably on tall students who have some athletic ability.

Inference Using the Normal Distribution

The major application of the normal distribution is in deciding whether two samples are different from each other. As we mentioned earlier, if you measure the whole population and find that men and women differ in height, no inference is necessary—you know that on average the two groups differ. But suppose you have scores on only a sample from each group? Imagine you gave IQ tests to one hundred men and one hundred women and found that the men got a mean score of 103 and the women 108. Is this difference big enough for you to conclude that, in general, women have higher scores than men; or is this result likely to be due simply to chance? We answer this question by relying on the normal distribution.

The crucial fact is that the means of samples drawn from a population will always fall into a normal distribution. If you get IQ scores on fifty different samples of women, the fifty different means will be normally distributed. This is true regardless of the standard deviations of the separate samples and regardless of the true mean of the population. It is also true even if the individual scores of each sample are not themselves normally distributed. Sample means always fall into a normal distribution. This basic fact is the basis of much of inferential statistics.

So far we know that the means of the samples are normally distributed. But we do not want to collect all of the samples in order to produce that distribution—that would defeat the whole purpose of using a sample, which is ease and efficiency. Because we do not have the actual normal distribution, we do not know its standard deviation and we must have that in order to interpret our results. In other words, we need the standard deviation of the normal distribution that would have been produced if we actually had a great many samples. This is called the *standard error of the mean,* and fortunately we can estimate this from the standard deviation of one sample. It is equal to the standard deviation of the sample divided by the square root of the number of cases in the sample.

You can understand why the size of the sample is so important. If you have IQ scores on two people, you would not want to conclude that the mean of those two scores was a good estimate of the mean of your whole class. Just as tossing a coin a few times is not a good test of whether it is true, any small number of cases is likely to be affected by chance. If you have ten IQ scores, you would have more confidence that the mean of the ten was close to the mean of the whole class. And as you increase the size of the sample, it becomes less and less likely that chance factors played an important role and more and more likely that the mean of the sample is an accurate estimate of the mean of the whole population. Thus, Gallup is willing to generalize from 1,500 cases to the 200 million people in the country because with that large a sample the standard error of the mean is very small.

Note that the size of the sample is the critical factor—the size of the population is almost irrelevant.

The Difference between Two Samples

Once we have the standard error of the mean and the sample means, we can make decisions about whether two samples differ, or whether a particular sample differs from a known or theoretical mean. The latter is the simpler case. For example, assume that the average IQ of all people is 100 and you have a sample with a mean score of 106 and want to know whether this sample really has a higher IQ than average. If a sample of nine people has a standard deviation of 15, the standard error of the mean is 5 (15 divided by the square root of 9). We then compute how far the sample mean deviates from the known mean in terms of standard errors—this is called the *critical ratio,* and is simply the difference between the two means divided by the standard error or 6/5 = 1.2. Looking in Table A.3, we see that a deviation of 1.2 occurs very often by chance and we conclude that the sample probably differs only by chance from the national average of 100. On the other hand, note what happens if the sample were larger and still had the same mean and standard deviation. With thirty-six cases in the sample, the standard error becomes 15/6 = 2.5 and the critical ratio is 6/2.5 = 2.4. In the table, you see that a deviation of 2.4 occurs very rarely by chance (considerably less than one time in twenty) and so we conclude that the sample does differ from the national average. Thus, even a small difference between the sample mean and the known mean becomes significant if the sample is large enough.

The procedure is very similar when comparing two samples except that the standard error is calculated as a combination of the two, and is called the *standard error of the difference between two means.* To see if two samples differ, you merely find the difference between the two means, divide by the standard error, and look in the table as usual to see the probability of a difference that large occurring by chance. Note that you are trying to choose between two alternatives: (1) the two samples are drawn from the same population and produced different means by chance; or (2) the two samples are drawn from different populations that really have different means. If the critical ratio is greater than 2, we usually accept the second alternative. As in all of our examples, the size of the two samples is very important because even a small difference between means will be significant (that is, critical ratio greater than 2) if the samples are large enough.

Bibliography

Aaronson, B., and H. Osmond (eds.) (1971). *Psychedelics: The Uses and Implications of Hallucinogenic Drugs.* Cambridge, Mass.: Schenkman.

Abramovitch, R., and F. Strayer (1976). Preschool social organization: agnostic, sparing and attentional behaviors. *Erindale Symposium.*

Acord, L. D., and D. D. Barker (1973). Hallucinogenic drugs and cerebral deficit. *J. Nerv. Ment. Dis.* 156:281–3.

Adam, W. R. (1973). Novel diet preferences in potassium-deficient rats. *J. comp. physiol. Psychol.* 84:286–8.

Ader, R. (1965). Effects of early experience and differential housing on behavior and susceptibility to gastric erosions in the rat. *J. comp. physiol. Psychol.* 60:233.

Adorno, J. W., E. Frenkel-Brunswick, D. J. Levinson, and R. N. Sanford (1950). *The Authoritarian Personality.* New York: Harper and Row.

Aiello, J. R., and R. E. Cooper (1972). The use of personal space as a function of social affect. *Proceedings of APA Convention* 7:207–8.

Aiello, J. R., Y. M. Epstein, and R. A. Kralin (1975). Effects of crowding on electrodermal activity. *Sociological Symposium* 14:43–57.

Aiello, J. R., and S. E. Jones (1971). Field study of the proxemic behavior of young school children in three subcultural groups. *J. pers. soc. Psychol.* 19:351–6.

Ainsworth, M. D. S. (1969). Object relations, dependency, and attachment: a theoretical review of the infant-mother relationship. *Child Develpm.* 40:969–1025.

Ainsworth, M. D., and S. M. Bell (1970). Attachment, exploration, and separation. *Child Develpm.* 41:49–67.

Alexander, F. G. (1950). *Psychosomatic Medicine: Its Principles and Applications.* New York: Norton.

Alexander, F. G., T. M. French, and C. L. Bacon (1948). *Studies in Psychosomatic Medicine; An Approach to the Cause and Treatment of Vegetative Disturbances.* New York: Ronald Press.

Allen, V. L. and J. M. Levine (1969). Consensus and conformity. *J. exp. soc. Psychol.* 5:389–99.

Allport, F. H. (1920). The influence of the group upon association and thought. *J. exp. Psychol.* 3:159–82.

Allport, G. W. (1961). *Pattern and Growth in Personality.* New York: Holt, Rinehart and Winston.

Anand, B. K., G. S. Chhina and B. Singh (1961). Some aspects of electroencephalographic studies in Yogis. *EEG clin. Neurophysiol.* 13:452–6.

Anastasi, A. (1968). *Psychological Testing,* 3d ed. New York: Macmillan.

Antrobus, J. S., W. Dement, and C. Fisher (1964). Patterns of dreaming and dream recall: an EEG study. *J. abnorm. soc. Psychol.* 69:341–4.

APA Task Force Report (1975). The current status of lithium therapy. *Amer. J. Psychiat.* 132:997–1001.

Ardrey, R. (1966). *The Territorial Imperative.* New York: Atheneum.

Armentrout, J. A., and G. K. Burger (1972). Children's reports of parental child-rearing behavior at five grade levels. *Developmental Psychol.* 7:44–8.

Arnold, M. B. (1960). *Emotion and Personality.* New York: Columbia University Press, 2 vols.

Aronson, E., and D. Linder (1965). Gain and loss of esteem as determinants of interpersonal attractiveness. *J. exp. soc. Psychol.* 1:156–71.

Aronson, E., and J. Mills (1959). The effect of severity of initiation on liking for a group. *J. abnorm. soc. Psychol.* 59:177–81.

Aronson, E., J. Turner, and J. M. Carlsmith (1963). Communicator credibility and communication discrepancy. *J. abnorm. soc. Psychol.* 67:31-6.

Asch, S. E. (1951). Effects of group pressure upon the modification and distortion of judgments. In Harold Guetzkow (ed.), *Groups, Leadership and Men.* Pittsburgh: Carnegie Press, 177-90.

Aserinsky, E., and N. Kleitman (1953). Regularly occurring periods of eye motility, and concomitant phenomena, during sleep. *Science* 118:273-4.

Athanasiou, R., P. Shaver, and C. Tavris (1970). Sex. *Psychology Today,* 39-52.

Atkinson, K., B. MacWhinney, and C. Stoel (1970). An experiment on recognition of babbling. *Papers and reports on child language development.* Stanford, Calif.: Stanford Univ. Press.

Atkinson, J. W., and G. H. Litwin (1960). Achievement motive and test anxiety conceived as a motive to approach success and to avoid failure. *J. abnorm. soc. Psychol.* 60:52-63.

Attneave, F. (1974). Some informational aspects of visual perception. *Psychol. Rev.* 61:183-93.

Ax, A. F. (1953). The physiological differentiation between fear and anger in humans. *Psychosomatic Med.* 14:433-42.

Axline, V. M. (1947). *Play Therapy; The Inner Dynamics of Childhood.* Boston: Houghton Mifflin.

Ayllon, T., and N. Azrin (1968). *The Token Economy: A Motivational System for Therapy and Rehabilitation.* New York: Appleton.

Backman, M. E. (1972). Patterns of mental abilities: ethnic, socioeconomic, and sex differences. *Amer. Ed. Res. Jour.* 9:1-12.

Bacon, C., and R. M. Lerner (1975). Effects of maternal employment status on the development of vocational role perception in females. *J. genet. Psychol.* 126:187-93.

Bainbridge, L. (1973). Learning in the rat: effect of early experience with an unsolvable problem. *J. comp. physiol. Psychol.* 82:301-7.

Bandura, A. (1965). Vicarious processes: A case of no-trial learning. In L. Berkowitz (ed.), *Advances in Experimental Social Psychology* Vol. 2. New York: Academic Press, 1- 55.

Bandura, A. L. (1969). *Principles of Behavior Modification.* New York: Holt, Rinehart and Winston.

Bandura, A., J. E. Grusec, and F. L. Menlove (1966). Observational learning as a function of symbolization and incentive set. *Child Develpm.* 37:499-506.

Bandura, A., D. Ross, and S. A. Ross (1961). Transmission of aggression through imitation of aggressive models. *J. abnorm. soc. Psychol.* 63:575-82.

Bandura, A., D. Ross, and S. A. Ross (1963). A comparative test of status envy, social power, and secondary reinforcement theories of identificatory learning. *J. abnorm. soc. Psychol.* 67:527-34.

Bandura, A., and R. H. Walters (1963). *Social Learning and Personality Development.* New York: Holt, Rinehart and Winston.

Barber, T. X. (1969). *Hypnosis: A Scientific Approach.* New York: Van Nostrand Reinhold.

Barber, T. X., and L. B. Glass (1962). Significant factors in hypnotic behavior. *J. abnorm. soc. Psychol.* 64:222-8.

Bardwick, J. M. (1973). Her body, the battleground. In *The Female Experience.* Del Mar, California: CRM Publications, 10- 16.

Baron, R. A. (1971). Reducing the influence of an aggressive model: the restraining effects of discrepant modeling cues. *J. pers. soc. Psychol.* 20:240-5.

Barondes, S. H. (1970). Cerebral protein synthesis inhibitors block long term memory. *Int. Rev. Neurobiol.* 12:177-205.

Barron, F. (1958). The psychology of imagination. *Scientific American* 199 (3):150-70.

Bass, M. J., and C. L. Hull (1934). The irradiation of a tactile conditioned reflex in man. *J. comp. physiol. Psychol.* 17:47-65.

Baumrind, D. (1971). Current patterns of parental authority. *Developmental Psychol. Monogr.* 4:1-102

Baumrind, D., and A. E. Black (1967). Socialization practices associated with dimensions of competence in preschool boys and girls. *Child Develpm.* 38:291-327.

Bavelas, A., A. H. Hastorf, A. E. Gross, and W. R. Kite (1965). Experiments on the alteration of group structure. *J. exp. soc. Psychol.* 1:55-70.

Baxter, J. C. (1970). Interpersonal spacing in natural settings. *Sociometry* 33:444-56.

Bayley, N. (1965). Comparisons of mental and motor test scores for ages 1-15 months by sex, birth order, race, geographical location, and education of parents. *Child Develpm.* 36:379-411.

Bayley, N., and E. S. Schaefer (1964). Correlations of maternal and child behaviors with the development of mental abilities. *Monographs of the Society for Research in Child Development* 29:97.

Beach, F. A. (1969). Locks and beagles. *Amer. Psychologist* 24:971-89.

Beck, A. T. (1967). *Depression: Clinical, Experimental and Theoretical Aspects.* New York: Harper and Row.

Beckwith, L. (1972). Relationships between infants' social behavior and their mothers' behavior. *Child Develpm.* 43:397–411.

Bell, D. S. (1965). Comparison of amphetamine psychosis and schizophrenia. *British Journal of Psychiatry:* 701–32.

Bell, R. Q. (1968). A reinterpretation of the direction of effects in studies of socialization. *Psychol. Rev.* 75:81-95.

Bell, R. Q. (1974). Contributions of human infants to caregiving and social interaction. In M. Lewis and L. A. Rosenbaum (eds.), *The Effect of the Infant on Its Caregiver.* New York: Wiley.

Bem, D. (1967). Self-perception: an alternative interpretation of cognitive dissonance phenomena. *Psychol. Rev.* 74:183–200.

Bendig, A. W. (1959). Personality variables related to individual performance on a cognitive task. *J. gen. Psychol.* 60:265-8.

Benedict, R. (1934). *Patterns of Culture.* Boston: Houghton Mifflin.

Benson, H., et al. (1975). Continuous measurement of O_2 consumption and CO_2 elimination during a wakeful hypometabolic state. *J. human stress* 1:37–44.

Berger, F. M., and J. Potterfield (1969). The effect of anti-anxiety tranquilizers on the behavior of normal persons. In W. O. Evans and N. S. Kline (eds.), *The Psychopharmacology of Normal Humans.* Springfield, Ill.: C. Thomas, 38–113.

Bergin, A. E. (1971). The evaluation of therapeutic outcomes. In A. E. Bergin and S. L. Garfield (eds.), *Handbook of Psychotherapy and Behavior Change: An Empirical Analysis.* New York: Wiley, 217–70.

Berkowitz, L., and R. G. Geen (1966). Film violence and the cue properties of available targets. *J. pers. soc. Psychol.* 3:525–30.

Berlyne, D. (1951). Attention to change. *British Journal of Psychology* 42:269–78.

Berscheid, Ellen, and Elaine Walster (1967). When does a harm-doer compensate a victim? *J. pers. soc. Psychol.* 6:435–41.

Bieri, J., W. Bradburn, and M. Galinsky (1958). Sex differences in perceptual behavior. *J. Pers.* 26:1–12.

Binder, A. (1971). An experimental approach to driver evaluation using alcohol drinkers and marihuana smokers. *Accident Analysis and Prevention* 3:237–56.

Birdwhistell, R. L. (1970). *Kinesics and Context.* Philadelphia: Univ. of Pennsylvania Press.

Bloom, Lois (1970). *Language Development: Form and Function in Emerging Grammars.* Cambridge, Mass.: M.I.T. Press.

Bochner, S., and C. A. Insko (1966). Communicator discrepancy, source credibility, and opinion change. *J. pers. soc. Psychol.* 4:614–21.

Booth, A., and J. Cowell (1974). The effects of crowding upon health. Paper presented at the American Population Association Meetings, New York.

Boring, E. G. (1943). The moon illusion. *Amer. J. Physics* 11:55–60.

Boring, E. G., H. S., Langfeld, and H. P. Weld (1948). *Foundations of Psychology.* New York: Wiley.

Bornstein, M., and H. Bornstein (1976). *The New York Times,* Section 2, February 29.

Bourne, L. E., and B. R. Ekstrand (1973). *Psychology: Its Principles and Meanings.* Hinsdale, Ill: Dryden.

Bourne, L. E., Jr., and F. Restle (1959). Mathematical theory of concept identification. *Psychol. Rev.* 66:278–96.

Bower, G. H. (1972). Mental imagery and associative learning. In L. Gregg (ed.), *Cognition in Learning and Memory.* New York: Wiley.

Bower, G. H., and T. Trabasso (1964). Concept identification. In R. C. Atkinson (ed.), *Studies in Mathematical Psychology.* Stanford, California: Stanford University Press.

Bower, T. G. R. (1971). The object in the world of the infant. *Sci. Amer.* 225:30–38.

Bower, T. G. R. (1974). *Development in Infancy.* San Francisco: W. H. Freeman.

Bower, T. G. R., and Paterson, J. G. (1973). The separation of place, movement, and object in the world of the infant. *J. exp. child Psychol.* 15:161–8.

Bowerman, M. (1970). *Early Syntactic Development: A Cross-linguistic Study with Special Reference to Finnish.* Cambridge, England: Cambridge University Press.

Bowlby, J. (1969). *Attachment.* New York: Basic Books.

Brackbill, Y. (1958). Extinction of the smiling response in infants as a function of reinforcement schedule. *Child Develpm.* 29:114–24.

Brady, J. V., R. W. Porter, D. G. Conrad, and J. W. Mason (1958). Avoidance behavior and the development of gastroduodenal ulcers. *J. exp. Anal. Behavior* 1:69–73.

Braine, M. D. S. (1963). The ontogeny of English phrase structure: the first phase. *Language* 39:1–14.

Brecher, E. (1972). *Licit and Illicit Drugs.* Mt. Vernon, N.Y.: Consumers Union.

Broadbent, D. E. (1957). Effects of noise on behavior. In C. M. Harris (ed.), *Handbook of Noise Control.* New York: McGraw-Hill.

Broadbent, D. E. (1958). *Perception and communication.* New York: Pergamon Press.

Broadbent, D. E. (1962). Attention and the perception of speech. *Sci. Amer.* 206(4):143–51.

Brobeck, J. R., J. Tepperman, and C. N. H. Long (1943). Experimental hypothalamic hyperphagia in the albino rat. *Yale Journal of Biological Medicine* 15:831–53.

Brown, J. S., and M. Belloni (1963). Performance as a function of deprivation time following periodic feeding in an isolated environment. *J. comp. physiol. Psychol.* 56:105–10.

Brown, M. (1974). Motivational correlates of academic performance. *Psychol. Rep.* 34:746.

Brown, R. (1973). *A First Language.* Cambridge, Mass.: Harvard University Press.

Brown, R., and U. Bellugi (1964). Three processes in the acquisition of syntax. *Harvard Educational Review* 34:133–51.

Brown, R., and C. Fraser (1963). The acquisition of syntax. In Charles N. Cofer and Barbara Musgrave (eds.), *Verbal Behavior and Learning: Problems and Processes.* New York: McGraw-Hill, 158–201.

Brown, R. W., and D. McNeill (1966). The "tip of the tongue" phenomenon. *J. verb. learn. verb. beh.* 5:325–37.

Bruell, J. H., and G. W. Albee (1955). Notes toward a motor theory of visual egocentric localization. *Psychol. Rev.* 62:391-9.

Bruner, J. S., and C. C. Goodman (1947). Value and need as organizing factors in perception. *J. abnorm. soc. Psychol.* 42:33–44.

Bruner, J. S., J. J. Goodnow, and G. A. Austin (1956). *A Study of Thinking.* New York: Wiley.

Burt, C. (1958). The inheritance of mental ability. *Amer. Psychol.* 13:6–7.

Buss, A. H. (1966). *Psychopathology.* New York: Wiley.

Butler, R. A., and H. F. Harlow (1954). Persistence of visual exploration in monkeys. *J. comp. physiol. Psychol.* 47:258–63.

Byrne, D. (1961). Interpersonal attraction and attitude similarity. *J. abnorm. soc. Psychol.* 62:713–15.

Byrne, D., G. D. Baskett, and L. Hodges (1971). Behavioral indicators of interpersonal attraction. *J. appl. soc. Psychol.* 1:137–49.

Byrne, W. L., et al. (1966). Memory transfer. *Science* 153:658–9.

Calhoun, J. B. (1962). Population density and social pathology. *Sci. Amer.* 206:139–48.

Cameron, N. (1947). *The Psychology of Behavior Disorders.* Boston: Houghton Mifflin.

Campbell, A., P. E. Converse, and W. L. Rodgers (1976). *The Quality of American Life: Perceptions, Evaluations, and Satisfactions.* New York: Russell Sage Foundation.

Cannon, W. B. (1927). The James-Lange theory of emotions: A critical examination and an alternative theory. *Amer. J. Psychol.* 39:106–24.

Cannon, W. B. (1934). Hunger and thirst. In C. Murchison (ed.), *Handbook of General Experimental Psychology.* Worcester, Mass.: Clark University Press.

Carlin, A. S., C. B. Barker, L. Halpern, and R. D. Post (1972). Social facilitation of marijuana intoxication: impact of social set and pharmacological activity. *J. abnorm. Psychol.* 80:132-40.

Carlsmith, J. M., P. Ellsworth, and J. Whiteside (1969). Guilt, confession, and compliance. Unpublished manuscript, Stanford University.

Carlsmith, J. M., and A. E. Gross (1969). Some effects of guilt on compliance. *J. pers. soc. Psychol.* 11:232–9.

Carroll, J. B. and J. B. Casagrande (1958). The function of language classification in behavior. In E. E. Maccoby, T. M. Newcomb, and E. L. Hartley (eds.), *Readings in Social Psychology* (3rd ed.). New York: Holt, Rinehart and Winston.

Carter, L. F., and K. Schooler (1949). Value, need and other factors in perception. *Psychol. Rev.* 56:200–7.

Cartwright, G. M. (1970). Use of a maze habit as a test of the specificity of memory transfer in mice. *J. biol. Psychol.* 12:53–60.

Carver, C. S. (1974). Facilitation of physical aggression through objective self-awareness. *J. exp. soc. Psychol.* 10:365-70.

Cattell, R. B. (1949). *The Culture Free Intelligence Test.* Champaign, Ill.: Institute for Personality and Ability Testing.

Cattell, R. B. (1950). *Personality: A Systematic, Theoretical, and Factual Study.* New York: McGraw-Hill.

Cattell, R. B. (1973). Personality pinned down. *Psychology Today* 7:40–6.

Chen, S. C. (1937). Social modification of the activity of ants in nest-building. *Physiological Zoology* 10:420–36.

Cherkin, A. (1970). Failure to transfer memory by feeding trained brains to naive chicks. *J. biol. Psychol.* 12:83–5.

Chomsky, N. (1968). *Language and Mind.* New York: Harcourt Brace Jovanovich.

Chopra, G. S. (1973). Studies on psycho-clinical aspects of long-term marijuana use in 124 cases. *International Journal of the Addictions* 8:1015–26.

Christian, J. J. (1955). Effect of population size on the adrenal glands and reproductive organs of male white mice. *Amer. J. Physiol.* 181:477–80.

Christian, J. J., V. Flyger, and D. C. Davis (1960). Factors in the mass mortality of a herd of sika deer cervus nippon. *Chesapeake Science* 1:79–95.

Christie, R., and F. L. Geis (eds.) (1970). *Studies in Machiavellianism.* New York: Academic Press.

Cialdini, R. B., J. E. Vincent, S. K. Lewis, J. Catalan, D. Wheeler, and B. L. Darby (1975). Reciprocal concessions procedure for inducing compliance: the door-in-the-face technique. *J. pers. soc. Psychol.* 31:206–15.

Clark, L. D., and E. N. Nakashima (1968). Experimental studies of marihuana. *Amer. J. Psychiat.* 25:379–84.

Clark, R. (1959). Some time correlated schedules and their effects on behavior. *J. exp. Anal. Behav.* 2:1–22.

Clark, R. D. III, and L. E. Word (1974). Where is the apathetic bystander? Situational characteristics of the emergency. *J. pers. soc. Psychol.* 29:279–87.

Clarke-Stewart, K. A. (1973). Interactions between mothers and their young children: Characteristics and consequences. *Monographs of Society for Research in Child Development* 38(153).

Clausen, J. A. and M. L. Kohn (1960). Social relations and schizophrenia: a research report and a perspective. In D. D. Jackson (ed.), *Etiology of Schizophrenia.* New York: Basic Books.

Cleckley, H. M. (1950). *The Mask of Sanity.* St. Louis: Mosby.

Cohen, H. D., and S. H. Barondes (1967). Puromycin effect on memory may be due to occult seizures. *Science* 157(3786):333–4.

Cohen, S., D. C. Glass, and J. E. Singer (1975). Apartment noise, auditory discrimination, and reading ability in children. *J. exp. soc. Psychol.* 9:407–22.

Collins, A. M., and M. R. Quillian (1969). Retrieval time from semantic memory. *J. verb. learn. verb. beh.* 8:240–7.

Condon, W. S., and W. D. Ogston (1967). A segmentation of behavior. *J. Psychiat. res.* 5:221–35.

Cooper, L. M., and P. London (1973). Reactivation of memory by hypnosis and suggestion. *Int. J. clin. exp. Hypnosis* 21:312–23.

Coppen, A., and N. Kessel (1963). Menstruation and personality. *Brit. J. Psychiat.* 109:711–21.

Cotler, S., and R. J. Palmer (1971). Social reinforcement, individual difference factors, and the reading performance of elementary school children. *J. pers. soc. Psychol.* 18:97–104.

Cottrell, N. B., D. L. Wack, G. J. Sekerak, and R. H. Rittle (1968). Social facilitation of dominant responses by the presence of an audience and the mere presence of others. *J. pers. soc. Psychol.* 9:245–50.

Crancer, A., Jr., J. M. Dille, J. C. Delay, J. E. Wallace, and M. D. Haykin (1969). Comparison of the effects of marihuana and alcohol on simulated driving performance. *Science* 164:851–4.

Cronbach, L. J. (1970). *Essentials of Psychological Testing* (3rd ed.). New York: Harper and Row.

Cruze, W. W. (1935). Maturation and learning in chicks. *J. comp. Psychol.* 19:371–409.

Curcio, F., E. Kattef, D. Levine, and O. Robbins (1972). Compensation and susceptibility to conservation training. *Developmental Psychology* 7:259–65.

Darwin, C. (1872). *The Expression of the Emotions in Man and Animals.* London: J. Murray.

Davidoff, L. L. (1976). *Introduction to Psychology.* New York: McGraw-Hill.

Davidson, A. B., and L. Cook (1970). Yeast ribonucleic acid: analysis of effects on pole-climbing avoidance behavior. *Psychopharmacologia* 16:399–408.

Davis, A., and K. Eells (1953). *Davis-Eells Games.* Yonkers, N.Y.: World Book Company.

Davis, J. M. (1976). Overview: maintenance therapy in psychiatry: II. Affective disorders. *Amer. J. Psychiat.* 133:1–13.

Davis, K. (1940). Extreme social isolation of a child. *Amer. J. Sociol.* 45:554–65.

Davis, K. (1947). Final note on a case of extreme isolation. *Amer. J. Sociol.* 52:432–7.

Davis, K. E., W. O. Evans, and J. S. Gillis (1969). The effects of amphetamine and chlorpromazine on cognitive skills and feelings in normal adult males. In W. Evans and N. Line (eds.), *The Psychopharmacology of the Normal Human.* Springfield, Ill.: Charles Thomas, 126–61.

Dean, L. M., F. N. Willis, and J. Hewitt (1975). Initial interaction distance among individuals equal and unequal in military rank. *J. pers. soc. Psychol.* 32:294-9.

Deaux, K. and T. Emswiller (1974). Explanations of successful performance on sex-linked tasks: What is skill for the male is luck for the female. *J. pers. soc. Psychol.* 29(1):80-5.

Deci, E. L. (1975). *Intrinsic Motivation.* New York: Plenum.

DeFleur, M. L., and F. R. Westie (1963). Attitude as a scientific concept. *Social Forces* 42:17-31.

Deikman, A. J. (1963). Experimental meditation. *J. nerv. ment. Dis.* 136:329-73.

DeLucia, L. A. (1963). The toy preference test: a measure of sex-role identification. *Child Develpm.* 34:107-17.

Dement, W. C. (1955). Dream recall and eye movements during sleep in schizophrenics and normals. *J. nerv. ment. Dis.* 122:263-9.

Dement, W. C. (1960). The effect of dream deprivation. *Science* 131:1705-7.

Dement, W. C. (1965). Studies on the function of rapid eye movement (paradoxical) sleep in human subjects. In M. Jouvet (ed.), *Aspects Anatomo—functionnels de la Physiologie du Sommeil,* 571-611. Paris: Centre National de la Recherche Scientifique.

Dement, W. C., and C. Fisher (1963). Experimental interference with the sleep cycle. *Canad. Psychiat. Assoc. J.* 8:395-400.

Dement, W., and N. Kleitman (1957). The relation of eye movements during sleep to dream activity. An objective method for the study of dreaming. *J. exp. Psychol.* 53:339-46.

Dennis, W. (1940). The effect of cradling practices upon the onset of walking in Hopi children. *J. genet. Psychol.* 56:77-86.

Deutsch, M., and R. M. Krauss (1960). The effect of threat on interpersonal bargaining. *J. abnorm. soc. Psychol.* 61:181-9.

Devalois, R. L., and G. H. Jacobs (1968). Primate color vision. *Science,* 162:533-40.

Dion, K. L., R. S. Baron, and N. Miller (1970). Why do groups make riskier decisions than individuals? In L. Berkowitz (ed.), *Advances in Experimental Social Psychology,* Vol. 5 New York: Academic Press, 305-77.

Dohrenwend, B. P., and B. S. Dohrenwend (1974). Social and cultural influences on psychopathology. *Annual Review of Psychology* 25:417-52.

Dollard, J., L. Doob, N. Miller, O. Mowrer, and R. Sears (1939). *Frustration and Aggression.* New Haven: Yale University.

Dollard, J., and N. E. Miller (1950). *Personality and Psychotherapy: An Analysis in Terms of Learning, Thinking and Culture.* New York: McGraw-Hill.

Doob, A. N., and L. E. Wood (1972). Catharsis and aggression: effects of annoyance and retaliation on aggressive behavior. *J. pers. soc. Psychol.* 22:156-62.

Doob, A. N., J. M. Carlsmith, J. L. Freedman, T. K. Landauer, and S. Tom, Jr. (1969). Effect of initial selling price on subsequent sales. *J. pers. soc. Psychol.* 11:345-50.

Droege, R. C. (1967). Sex differences in aptitude maturation during high school. *J. counsel. Psychol.* 14:407-11.

Dubois, P. H. (ed.) (1974). The classification program. *AAF Aviation Psychology Program Research Report,* No. 2.

Duncker, K. (1945). On problem-solving. *Psychol. Monogr.* 58:5 (Whole No. 270).

Durrell, D. E., and D. Weisberg (1973). Imitative play behavior of children: the importance of model distinctiveness and prior imitative training. *J. exp. child Psychol.* 16:23-31.

Duval, S., and R. A. Wicklund (1972). *A Theory of Objective Self-Awareness.* New York: Academic Press.

Ebbesen, E. E., and R. J. Bowers (1974). Proportion of risky to conservative arguments in a group discussion and choice shift. *J. pers. soc. Psychol.* 29:316-27.

Eberhardy, F. (1967). The view from the couch. *J. child psychol. and psychiat. and allied discip.* 8:257-63.

Egozcue, J., and S. Irwin (1970). LSD-25 effects on chromosomes: a review. *J. Psychedelic Drugs* 3.

Ehrlich, P. R. (1968). *The Population Bomb.* New York: Ballantine.

Ekman, P., and W. V. Friesen (1971). Constants across cultures in the face and emotion. *J. pers. soc. Psychol.* 17:124-9.

Ekman, P., W. V. Friesen, and K. Sherer (1977). Body movements and voice pitch in deceptive interaction. *Semiotica,* in press.

Ekman, P., E. R. Sorenson, and W. V. Friesen (1969). Pancultural elements in facial displays of emotions. *Science* 164:86-8.

Elliott, M. H. (1928). The effect of change of reward on the maze performance of rats. *University of California Publications in Psychology* 4:19-30.

Ellsworth, P., J. M. Carlsmith, and A. Henson (1972). The stare as a stimulus to flight in human subjects: a series of field experiments. *J. pers. soc. Psychol.* 21:302–11.

Ellsworth, P., and J. M. Carlsmith (1973). Eye contact and gaze aversion in an aggressive encounter. *J. pers. soc. Psychol.* 28:280–92.

English, D. C. (1961). A comparative study of antidepressants in balanced therapy. *Amer. J. Psychiat.* 11:865.

Erickson, M. H. (1939). Experimental demonstration of the psychopathology of everyday life. *The Psychoanalytic Quarterly* 8:342–4.

Erikson, E. H. (1963). *Childhood and Society* (2nd ed.). New York: Norton.

Erlenmeyer-Kimling, L., and L. F. Jarvik (1963). Genetics and intelligence: a review. *Science* 142:1477–9.

Essig, C. (1970). Drug dependence of the barbiturate type. *Drug Dependence* 5:24–7.

Eyferth, K., U. Brandt, and H. Wolfgang (1960). *Farbige Kinder in Deutschland.* Munich, Germany: Juventa.

Eysenck, H. J. (1953). The effects of psychotherapy. In H. J. Eysenck, *Uses and Abuses of Psychology.* Baltimore: Penguin, pp. 193–208.

Eysenck, H. J. (1959). *The Structure of Human Personality.* London: Methuen.

Fantz, R. L. (1957). Form preferences in newly hatched chicks. *J. Comp. physiol. Psychol.* 50:422–30.

Farley, J. (1974). Coeducation and college women. *Cornell Journal of Social Relations* 9:87–97.

Feldman, M. J., and M. Hersen (1967). Attitudes toward death in nightmare subjects. *J. abn. Psychol.* 72:421–5.

Feldman-Summers, S., and S. B. Kiesler (1974). Those who are number two try harder: the effect of sex on attributions of causality. *J. pers. soc. Psychol.* 30:846–55.

Felipe, N., and R. Sommer (1966). Invasions of personal space. *Social Problems* 14:206–14.

Fenichel, O. (1920–30). *Ten Years of the Berlin Psychoanalytic Institute.*

Feshbach, S., and R. D. Singer (1970). *Television and Aggression.* San Francisco: Jossey-Bass.

Festinger, L. (1954). A theory of social comparison processes. *Hum. Relat.* 7:117–40.

Festinger, L. (1957). *A Theory of Cognitive Dissonance.* Stanford, Calif.: Stanford University Press, Chapters 1–4.

Festinger, L., and J. Carlsmith (1959). Cognitive consequences of forced compliance. *J. abnorm. soc. Psychol.* 58:203–10.

Fieve, R. R., S. R. Platman, and R. R. Plutchik (1968). The use of lithium in affective disorders. *Amer. J. Psychiat.* 125:492–8.

Finkelman, J. M., and D. C. Glass, (1970). Reappraisal of the relationship between noise and human performance by means of a subsidiary task measure. *J. appl. Psychol.* 54:211–13.

Fishbein, M., and I. Ajzen (1972). Attitudes and opinions. *Ann. Rev. Psychol.* 23:487–544.

Fisher, D. J., and D. Byrne (1975). Too close for comfort. Sex differences in response to invasions of personal space. *J. pers. soc. Psychol.* 32:15–20.

Fjerdingstad, E. J., T. L. Nissen, and H. H. Roigaard-Petersen (1965). Effect of ribonucleic acid (RNA) extracted from the brain of trained animals on learning in rats. *Scandanavian J. Psychol.* 6:1–6.

Flexner, L. B., J. B. Flexner, and R. B. Roberts (1967). Memory in mice analyzed with antibiotics. *Science* 155(3768):1377–83.

Fling, S., and M. Manosevitz (1972). Sex typing in nursery school children's play interests. *Developmental Psychol.* 7:146–52.

Fraser, H. F., H. Isbell, A. J. Eisenman, A. Wilker, and F. T. Pescor (1954). Chronic barbiturate intoxification: further studies. *Archives of Internal Med.* 94:34–41.

Freedman, D. X., and E. C. Senay (1973). Methadone treatment of heroin addiction. *Ann. Rev. of Med.* 24:153–64.

Freedman, J. L. (1965). Long-term behavioral effects of cognitive dissonance. *J. exp. soc. Psychol.* 1:145–55.

Freedman, J. L. (1975). *Crowding and Behavior.* New York: Viking Press.

Freedman, J. L., and A. N. Doob (1968). *Deviancy.* New York: Academic Press.

Freedman, J. L., and S. C. Fraser (1966). Compliance without pressure: the foot-in-the-door technique. *J. pers. soc. Psychol.* 4:195–202.

Freedman, J. L., S. Heshka, and A. Levy (1973). Population density and crime in metropolitan U.S. areas. Unpublished.

Freedman, J. L., S. Heshka, and A. Levy, (1975). Population density and pathology: is there a relationship? *J. exp. soc. Psychol.* 11:539–52.

Freedman, J. L., S. Klevansky, and P. Ehrlich (1971). The effect of crowding on human task performance. *J. appl. soc. Psychol.* 1:7–25.

Freedman, J. L., and T. K. Landauer (1966). Retrieval of long-term memory: "Tip-of-the-tongue" phenomenon. *Psychonomic Sci.* 4:309–10.

Freedman, J. L., A. Levy, R. W. Buchanan, and J. Price (1972). Crowding and human aggressiveness. *J. exp. soc. Psychol.* 8:528–48.

Freedman, J. L., and E. F. Loftus (1974). Retrieval of words from well-learned sets: the effect of category size. *J. exp. Psychol.* 102:1085–91.

Freedman, J. L., and D. Perlick (1977). The intensification effect of high density on laughter. Unpublished manuscript, Columbia University.

Freedman, J. L., and P. Shaver (1976). Happiness. *Psychology Today*, July.

Freedman, J. L., and T. Tyler (1975). The relationship between attitudes and behavior. Unpublished manuscript. Columbia University.

Freedman, J. L., S. A. Wallington, and E. Bless (1967). Compliance without pressure: the effect of guilt. *J. pers. soc. Psychol.* 7:117–24.

Freud, S. (1953) (original 1900). The interpretation of dreams. In *The Standard Edition of the Complete Psychological Works of Sigmund Freud.* Vols. IV and V. London: Hogarth.

Friedman, S. B., L. A. Glasgow, and R. Ader (1969). Psychosocial factors modifying host resistance to experimental infections. *Annals of N. Y. Acad. of Sci.* 164:381.

Frijda, N. H. (1968). Intelligence de l'homme et intelligence de la machine: remarques sur la simulation. *Cahiers de Psychologie* 11:1–9.

Funkenstein, D., S. H. King, and M. Drolette (1954). The direction of anger during a laboratory stress-inducing situation. *Psychosomatic Med.* 16:404–13.

Galanter, E. (1962). Contemporary psychophysics. In R. Brown (ed.), *New Directions in Psychology.* New York: Holt, Rinehart and Winston.

Galle, O. R., W. R. Gove, and J. M. McPherson (1972). Population density and pathology: what are the relations for man? *Science* 176:23–30.

Gallo, P., and J. Sheposh (1971). Effects of incentive magnitude on cooperation in the prisoner's dilemma game: a reply to Gumpert, Deutsch, and Epstein. *J. pers. soc. Psychol.* 19:42–6.

Gardner, B. T., and R. A. Gardner (1971). Two-way communication with an infant chimpanzee. In A. M. Schrier and F. Stollnitz (eds.), *Behavior of Nonhuman Primates: Modern Research Trends*, Vol. IV. New York: Academic Press, 117–84.

Gedda, L. (1961). *Twins in History and Science.* Springfield, Ill.: Thomas.

Geller, A., and M. E. Jarvik (1968). The time relations of ECS induced amnesia. *Psychonomic Sci.* 12:169–70.

Gerard, H. B., and G. C. Mathewson (1966). The effects of severity of initiation on liking for a group: a replication. *J. exp. soc. Psychol.* 2:278–87.

Gerard, H. B., and J. M. Rabbie (1961). Fear and social comparison. *J. abn. soc. Psychol.* 62:586–92.

Getzels, J. W., and P. W. Jackson (1962). *Creativity and Intelligence: Explorations with Gifted Students.* New York: Wiley.

Gewirtz, J. L. (1965). The course of infant smiling in four child-rearing environments in Israel. In B. M. Foss (ed.), *Determinants of Infant Behavior*, Vol. III. London: Methuen, 205–60.

Gibson, E. J., and R. D. Walk (1960). The "visual cliff." *Sci. Amer.* 202:64–71.

Glass, D., and J. Singer (1972). *Urban Stress.* New York: Academic Press.

Glassco, J., N. A. Milgram, and J. Youniss (1970). The stability of training effects on intentionality of moral judgment in children. *J. pers. soc. Psychol.* 14:360–5.

Glickman, S. E. (1961). Perseverative neural processes and consolidation of the memory trace. *Psychol. Bull.* 58:218–33.

Glucksberg, S. (1962). The influence of strength of drive on functional fixedness and perceptual recognition. *J. exp. Psychol.* 63:36–51.

Glueck, S., and E. Glueck (1950). *Unraveling Juvenile Delinquency.* New York: The Commonwealth Fund.

Glueck, S., and E. Glueck (1956). *Physique and Delinquency.* New York: Harper.

Glueck, S., and E. Glueck (1964). Potential juvenile delinquents can be identified: what next? *Brit. J. Criminology.* 4:215–26.

Good, E. (1971). Drug use and grades in college. *Nature* 234:225–7.

Goodenough, D. R., H. B. Lewis, A. Shapiro, L. Jaret, and I. Sleser (1965). Dream reporting following abrupt and gradual awakenings from different types of sleep. *J. pers. soc. Psychol.* 2:170–9.

Goodenough, D. R., A. Shapiro, M. Holden, and L. Steinschreiber (1959). A comparison of "dreamers'" and "nondreamers'" eye movements, electroencephalograms, and the recall of dreams. *J. abnorm. soc. Psychol.* 59:295–302.

Goodenough, E. W. (1957). Interest in persons as an aspect of sex difference in the early years. *Genet. Psychol. Monogr.* 55:287–323.

Goodnow, J., and G. Bethod (1966). Piaget's task: the effects of schooling and intelligence. *Child Develpm.* 37:573–82.

Gorfein, D. (1961). Conformity behavior and the "authoritarian personality." *J. soc. Psychol.* 53:121–5.

Gottesman, I. I., and J. Shields (1973). Genetic theorizing and schizophrenia. *Brit. J. Psychiat.* 122:15–30.

Greeley, A. M., and W. C. McCready (1975). Mystics and mysticism. *The New York Times Magazine,* January 26, p. 12.

Greenberg, D. J., D. Hillman, and D. Grice (1973). Infant and stranger variables related to stranger anxiety in the first year of life. *Develpm. Psychol.* 9:207–12.

Greenfield, P. M., and J. S. Bruner (1966). Culture and cognitive growth. *Int. J. Psychol.* 1:89–107.

Griffith, R. M., O. Miyagi, and A. Tago (1958). Universality of typical dreams: Japanese vs. Americans. *Amer. Anthrop.* 60:1173–9.

Griffitt, W., and R. Veitch (1971). Hot and crowded: influences of population density and temperature on interpersonal affective behavior. *J. pers. soc. Psychol.* 17:92–8

Guilford, J. P. (1929). An experiment in learning to read facial expression. *J. abnorm. soc. Psychol.* 24:191–202.

Guilford, J. P. (1954). A factor analytic study across the domains of reasoning, creativity, and evaluation, I: hypothesis and description of tests. *Reports from the Psychology Laboratory.* Los Angeles: Univ. of Southern California.

Guilford, J. P. (1959). *Personality.* New York: McGraw-Hill.

Guilford, J. P. (1967). *The Nature of Human Intelligence.* New York: McGraw-Hill.

Guthrie, E. R. (1959). Association of contiguity. In S. Koch (ed.), *Psychology: A Study of a Science,* Vol. 2. New York: McGraw-Hill.

Haith, M. M. (1966). The response of the human newborn to visual movement. *J. exp. Child Psychol.* 3:235–43.

Hall, C. S., and G. Lindzey (eds.) (1970). *Theories of Personality* (2nd ed.). New York: Wiley.

Hall, E. T. (1959). *The Silent Language.* New York: Doubleday.

Hall, E. T. (1966). *The Hidden Dimension.* New York: Doubleday.

Hansel, C. E. M. (1966). *ESP: A Scientific Evaluation.* New York: Scribners.

Hare, R. D. (1970). *Psychopathy: Theory and Research.* New York: Wiley.

Harlow, H. F. (1949). The formation of learning sets. *Psychol. Rev.* 56:51–65.

Harlow, H. F., and M. K. Harlow (1966). Learning to love. *Amer. Scientist* 54:244–72.

Harlow, H. F., and R. R. Zimmermann (1959). Affectional responses in the infant monkey. *Science* 130:421–32.

Harrell, T. W., and M. S. Harrell (1945). Army General Classification Test scores for civilian occupations. *Educational and Psychological Measurement* 5:229–39.

Harris, G. W., and S. Levine (1962). Sexual differentiation of the brain and its experimental control. *J. Physiol.* 163:42–3.

Hartnett, J. J., K. G. Bailey, and F. W. Gibson, Jr. (1970). Personal space as influenced by sex and type of movement. *J. Psychol.* 76:139–44.

Heath, R. G., S. Martens, B. E. Leach, M. Cohen, and C. Angel (1957). Effect on behavior in humans with the administration of taraxein. *Amer. J. Psychiat.* 114:14–24.

Hebb, D. O. (1949). *The Organization of Behavior.* New York: Wiley.

Heidbreder, E. (1947). The attainment of concepts: III. The problem. *J. Psychol.* 24:93–138.

Heider, F. (1958). *The Psychology of Interpersonal Relations.* New York: Wiley.

Henchy, T., and D. C. Glass (1968). Evaluation apprehension and the social facilitation of dominant and subordinate responses. *J. pers. soc. Psychol.* 10:446–54.

Hess, E. H. (1956). Space perception in the chick. *Sci. Amer.* 71–80.

Hess, E. H. (1958). "Imprinting" in animals. *Sci. Amer.* 198:81–90.

Hess, E. H. (1959). Imprinting. *Science* 130:133–41.

Heston, L. (1970). The genetics of schizophrenia and schizoid disease. *Science* 167:249–56.

Hilgard, E. R. (1965). *Hypnotic Susceptibility.* New York: Harcourt Brace Jovanovich.

Hilgard, E. R., H. MacDonald, G. Marshall, and A. H. Morgan (1974). Anticipation of pain and of pain control under hypnosis: heart rate and blood pressure responses in the cold pressor test. *J. abnorm. Psychol.* 83:561–8.

Hilgard, J. (1932). Learning and maturation in preschool children. *J. genet. Psychol.* 41:36–56.

Hilgard, J. R., and M. F. Newman (1961). Evidence for functional genesis in mental illness: schizophrenia, depressive psychoses, and psychoneuroses. *J. nerv. ment. Dis.* 132:3–16.

Hiroto, D. S., and M. E. P. Seligman (1975). Generality of learned helplessness in man. *J. pers. soc. Psychol.* 31:311–27.

Hobson, J. A., F. Goldfrank, and F. Snyder (1965). Respiration and mental activity in sleep. *J. Psychiat. Res.* 3:79–90.

Hochberg, J. E. (1964). *Perception.* Englewood Cliffs, N.J.: Prentice-Hall, 44.

Hockett, C. F. (1958). *A Course in Modern Linguistics.* New York: Macmillan.

Hoebel, B. G., and P. Teitelbaum (1962). Hypothalamic control of feeding and self-stimulation. *Science* 135:375–7.

Hoebel, B. G., and P. Teitelbaum (1966). Weight regulation in normal and hypothalamic hyperphagic rats. *J. comp. physiol. Psychol.* 61:189–93.

Hoedemaker, F., A. Kales, A. Jacobson, and E. Lichtenstein (1963). Dream deprivation: an experimental reappraisal. Presented to the Association for the Psychophysiological Study of Sleep, Brooklyn. N.Y.

Hoelzel, F. (1927). Central factors in humber. *Amer. J. Physiol.* 82:665–71.

Hogan, H. W. (1975). Time perception and stimulus preference as a function of stimulus complexity. *J. pers. soc. Psychol.* 31:32–5.

Hollander, E. P. (1954). Authoritarianism and leadership choice in a military setting. *J. abnorm. soc. Psychol.* 49:365–70.

Hollingshead, A. B., and F. Redlich (1958). *Social Class and Mental Illness.* New York: Wiley.

Homans, G. C. (1961). *Social Behavior: Its Elementary Forms.* New York: Harcourt Brace.

Horowitz, M. J., D. F. Duff, and L. O. Stratton (1970). Personal space and the body buffer zone. In H. M. Proshansky, W. H. Ittelson, and L. G. Rivilin (eds.), *Environmental Psychology: Man and His Physical Setting.* New York: Holt, Rinehart and Winston.

Hovland, C. I., I. L. Janis, and H. H. Kelley (1953). *Communication and Persuasion.* New Haven: Yale University Press.

Hovland, C. I., and H. A Pritzker (1957). Extent of opinion change as a function of amount of change advocated. *J. abnorm. soc. Psychol.* 54:257–61.

Hovland, C. I., and W. Weiss (1951). The influence of source credibility on communication effectiveness. *Public Opinion Quarterly* 15:635–50.

Howard, K. I., and D. E. Orlinsky (1972). Psychotherapeutic processes. In P. H. Mussen and M. R. Rosenzweig (eds.), *Annual Review of Psychology* 23:615–68. Palo Alto: Annual Reviews.

Hubel, D. H., and T. N. Wiesel (1966). Receptive fields and functional architecture in two non-striate visual areas (18 and 19) of the cat. *J. Neurophysiol.* 28:229–89.

Hughes, B. O., and D. G. Wood-Gush (1971). Investigations into specific appetites for sodium and thiamine in domestic fowls. *Physiol. and Behav.* 6:331–9.

Hull, C. L. (1943). *Principles of Behavior: An Introduction to Behavior Theory.* New York: D. Appleton.

Hull, C. L. (1952). *A Behavior System: An Introduction to Behavior Theory Concerning the Individual Organism.* New Haven: Yale University Press.

Hunt, E. B., and C. I. Hovland (1960). Order of consideration of different types of concepts. *J. exp. Psychol.* 59:220–5.

Hunt, E. B., J. Marin, and P. J. Stone (1966). *Experiments in Induction.* New York: Academic Press.

Hunt, M. (1974). *Sexual Behavior in the 1970's.* New York: Playboy Press.

Hunt, P. J., and J. M. Hillery (1973). Social facilitation in a coaction setting: an examination of the effects over learning trials. *J. exp. soc. Psychol.* 9:563–71.

Hurvich, L. M., and D. Jameson (1957). An opponent-process theory of color vision. *Psychol. Rev.* 64:384–404.

Hydén, H., and P. W. Lange (1970). Brain cell protein synthesis specifically related to learning. *Proceed. Natl. Acad. Science* 65:998–1004.

Inhelder, B., and H. Sinclair (1969). Learning cognitive structures. In P. H. Mussen, J. Langer, and M. Covington (eds.), *Trends and Issues in Developmental Psychology.* New York: Holt, Rinehart and Winston.

Isaacson, R. L. (1964). Relation between *n*-Achievement, test anxiety, and curricular choices. *J. abnorm. soc. Psychol.* 68:447–52.

Iwawaki, S., and E. L. Cowen (1964). The social desirability of trait-descriptive terms: application to a Japanese sample. *J. soc. Psychol.* 63:199–205.

Iwawaki, S., and E. L. Cowen (1964). The social desirability of trait-descriptive terms: further applications to a Japanese sample under a personal set. *J. soc. Psychol.* 63:207–14.

Jacobs, R. A. and P. S. Rosenbaum (1968). *English Transformational Grammar*. Waltham, Mass.: Blaisdell.

Jacobsen, C. F. (1935). Functions of the frontal association area in primates. *Archives of Neurolog. Psychiat.* 33:558–69.

Jacobson, A. L., et al. (1965). Differential approach tendencies produced by injection of RNA from trained rats. *Science* 150:636–7.

Jellinek, E. M. (1959). Estimating the prevalence of alcoholism. Modified values in the Jellinek formula and an alternative approach. *Quart. J. Studies in Alcohol* 20:261–9.

Jenkins, J. G., and K. M. Dallenbach (1924). Oblivescence during sleep and waking. *Amer. J. Psychol.* 35:605–12.

Jensen, A. R. (1973). *Educability and Group Differences*. New York: Harper and Row.

Jones, E. (1937). *Report of the Clinic Work 1926–1936*. London Clinic of Psychoanalysis.

Jones, E. E. (1964). *Ingratiation*. New York: Appleton-Century-Crofts.

Jones, E. E., and V. A. Harris (1967). The attribution of attitudes. *J. exp. soc. Psychol.* 3:1–24.

Jones, E. E., D. E. Kanouse, H. H. Kelley, R. E. Nisbett, S. Valins, and B. Weiner (1971). *Attribution: Perceiving the Causes of Behavior*. Morristown, N.J.: General Learning Press.

Jones, E. E., and R. E. Nisbett (1971). The actor and the observer: divergent perceptions of the causes of behavior. In E. E. Jones, et al. (eds.), *Attribution: Perceiving the Causes of Behavior*. Morristown, N.J.: General Learning Press, 79–94.

Jones, N. B. (1972). Categories of child-child interaction. In N. B. Jones (ed.), *Ethological Studies of Child Behavior*. Cambridge, Eng.: Cambridge University Press.

Jones, S. E., and J. R. Aiello (1973). Proxemic behavior of black and white first-, third-, and fifth-grade children. *J. pers. soc. Psychol.* 25:21–7.

Jordan, H. A., H. Moses, B. V. MacFayden, and S. J. Dudrick (1974). Hunger and satiety in humans during parenteral hyperalimentation. *Psychosomatic Med.* 36:144–55.

Jouvet, M. (1964). Studies on rhombencephalic sleep. Presented to the Association for the Psychophysiological Study of Sleep, Palo Alto, March.

Jouvet, M. (1967). The states of sleep. *Sci. Amer.* 216:62–75.

Julien, R. M. (1975). *A Primer of Drug Action*. San Francisco: W. H. Freeman.

Jung, C. G. (1944). *Psychology and Alchemy*. New York: Pantheon.

Kagan, J. (1971). *Change and Continuity in Infancy*. New York: Wiley (and personal communication).

Kain, S. C., C. H. Klett, and B. Rothfeld (1969). Treatment of the acute alcohol withdrawal state: a comparison of four drugs. *Amer. J. Psychiat.* 125:1640–6.

Kallman, F. J. (1946). The genetic theory of schizophrenia: An analysis of 691 schizophrenic twin index families. *Amer. J. Psychiat.* 103:309–22.

Kamin, L. J. (1974). *The Science and Politics of I. Q.* Potomac, Maryland: L. Erlbaum.

Kamiya, J. (1969). Operant control of the EEG alpha rhythm and some of its reported effects on consciousness. In C. Tart (ed.), *Altered States of Consciousness*. New York: Wiley.

Karaz, V., and D. Perlman (1975). Attribution at the wire: consistency and outcome finish strong. *J. exp. soc. Psychol.* 11:470–7.

Kasamatsu, A., and T. Hirai (1966). An EEG study on the Zen meditation. *Folia Psyckiatria Neurologica Japonica* 20:315–36.

Kastenbaum, R., and P. T. Costa, Jr. (1977). Psychological perspectives on death. *Ann. Rev. Psychol.* 28:225–49.

Kaufman, I., and I. Rock (1962). The moon illusion. *Sci. Amer.* 204:120–30.

Kaufman, I. C., and L. A. Rosenblum (1967). The reaction to separation in infant monkeys: anaclitic depression and conservation-withdrawal. *Psychosomatic Med.* 29:648–75.

Kelley, H. H. (1967). Attribution theory in social psychology. In D. Levine (ed.), *Nebraska Symposium on Motivation, 1967*. Lincoln: University of Nebraska Press.

Kelley, H. H., J. C. Condry, A. E. Dahlke, and A. H. Hill (1965). Collective behavior in a simulated panic situation. *J. exp. soc. Psychol.* 1:20–54.

Kellogg, W. N., and L. A. Kellogg (1933). *The Ape and the Child*. New York: McGraw-Hill.

Kendler, H. H. (1962). Vertical and horizontal processes in problem-solving. *Psychol. Rev.* 69:1–16.

Kendler, H. H., and T. S. Kendler (1962). Vertical and horizontal processes in problem solving. *Psychol. Rev.* 69:1–16.

Kendon, A. (1967). Some functions of gaze-direction in social interaction. *Acta Psychol.* 26:22–63.

Kennedy, B. J. (1973). Effect of massive doses of sex hormones on libido. *Medical Aspects of Human Sexuality* 1:65–78.

Kernan, Keith T. (1969). The acquisition of language by Samoan children. Ph.D. dissertation, University of California, Berkeley.

Kernberg, O. F. (1974). Further contributions to the treatment of narcissistic personalities. *Int. J. Psychoanal.* 55:215–40.

Kessen, W., P. Salapatek, and M. M. Haith (1965). The ocular orientation of newborn infants to visual contours. Paper read at Psychonomic Society, Chicago, October.

Kessler, P., and J. M. Neale (1974). Hippocampal damage and schizophrenia: a critique of Mednick's theory. *J. Abnorm. Psychol.* 83:91–6.

Kiesler, D. J. (1966). Some myths of psychotherapy research and the search for a paradigm. *Psychol. Bull.* 65:110–36.

Kilbey, M. M., J. W. Moore, and M. Hall (1973). Δ 9 -tetrahydrocannabinol induced inhibition of predatory aggression in the rat. *Psychopharmacologica* 31:157–66.

Kinsey, A. C., W. B. Pomeroy, and C. E. Martin (1948). *Sexual Behavior in the Human Male.* Philadelphia: Saunders.

Kinsey, A. C., W. B. Pomcroy, C. E. Martin, and P. H. Gebhard (1953). *Sexual Behavior in the Human Female.* Philadelphia: Saunders.

Klebanoff, L. B. (1959). Parental attitudes of mothers of schizophrenics, brain-injured and retarded, and normal children. *Amer. J. Orthopsychiatry.* 29:445–54.

Klein, G. S., H. J. Schlesinger, and D. E. Meister (1951). The effect of personal values on perception: an experimental critique. *Psychol. Rev.* 58:96–112.

Kleitman, N. (1960). Patterns of dreaming. *Sci. Amer.* 203:82–88.

Kline, M. V. (1972), The production of antisocial behavior through hypnosis: new clinical data. *Int. J. clin. exp. Hypnosis* 20:80–94.

Knight, R. P. (1941). Evaluation of the results of psychoanalytic therapy. *Amer. J. Psychiat.* 98:434–46.

Koffka, K. (1925). *The Growth of the Mind* (R. M. Ogden, trans.). New York: Harcourt Brace.

Kohen-Raz, R. (1968). Mental and motor development of Kibbutz, institutionalized, and home-reared infants in Israel. *Child Develpm.* 39:489–504.

Kohlberg, L. (1969). Stage and sequence: The cognitive-developmental approach to socialization. In D. A. Goslin (ed.), *Handbook of Socialization Theory and Research.* Chicago: Rand McNally.

Kohlberg, L. (1970). Education for justice: A modern statement of the Platonic view. In *Moral Education: Five Lectures.* Cambridge, Mass.: Harvard University Press, 56–83.

Kohler, I. (1962). Experiments with goggles. *Sci. Amer.* 206:62–72.

Kohler, W. (1925). *The Mentality of Apes.* New York: Harcourt Brace Jovanovich.

Kokonis, N. D. (1973). Parental dominance and sex-role identification in schizophrenia. *J. Psychol.* 84:211–18.

Kolansky, H., and W. T. Moore (1972). Clinical effects of marijuana on the young. *Internat. J. Psychiat.* 10:55–67.

Konečni, V. J. (1972). Some effects of guilt on compliance: a field replication. *J. pers. and soc. Psychol.* 23(1):30–2.

Konečni, V. J., L. Libuser, H. Morton, and E. B. Ebbesen (1975). Effects of a violation of personal space on escape and helping responses. *J. exp. soc. Psychol.* 11:288–99.

Krauss, R. M., V. Geller, and C. Olson (1976). Modalities and cues in the detection of deception. Paper given at APA meeting, September.

Kremen, I. (1961). Dream reports and rapid eye movements. Unpublished doctoral dissertation, Harvard University.

Kringlen, E. (1967). *Heredity and Environment in the Functional Psychoses.* London: Heinemann.

Kringlen, E. (1969). Schizophrenia in twins. *Schizophrenia Bull. 1* (December): 27–39.

Krippner, S. (1970). An adventure in psilocybin. In B. Aronson and H. Osmand (eds.), *Psychedelics.* Garden City, N.Y.: Anchor, pp. 35–9.

Kübler-Ross, E. (1969). *On Death and Dying.* New York: Macmillan.

Kuethe, J. L., and N. Weingartner (1964). Male-female schemata of homosexual and nonhomosexual penitentiary inmates. *J. Pers.* 32:23–31.

Landauer, T. K. (1969). Reinforcement as consolidation. *Psychol. Rev.* 76:92–6.

Landauer, T. K., and J. L. Freedman (1968). Information retrieval from long-term memory: category size and recognition time. *J. verb. learn. verb. beh.* 7:291–5.

Langer, J. (1969). *Theories of Development.* New York: Holt, Rinehart and Winston.

Langfeld, H. S. (1918). The judgment of emotions from facial expressions. *J. abnorm. soc. Psychol.* 13:172–84.

Lansky, L. M. (1967). The family structure also affects the model: sex-role attitudes in parents of preschool children. *Merrill-Palmer Quarterly* 13:139–50.

Lashley, K. S. (1950). In search of the engram. In *Physiological Mechanisms in Animal Behavior.* New York: Academic Press.

Latané, B., and J. M. Darley (1968). Group inhibition of bystander intervention in emergencies. *J. pers. soc. Psychol.* 10:215–21.

Latané, B., and J. M. Darley (1970). *The Unresponsive Bystander: Why Doesn't He Help?* New York: Appleton-Century-Crofts.

Latané, B., and J. Rodin (1969). A lady in distress: inhibiting effects of friends and strangers on bystander intervention. *J. exp. soc. Psychol.* 5:189–202.

Lawrence, D. H. (1950). Acquired distinctiveness of cues: II. Selective association in a constant stimulus situation. *J. exp. Psychol.* 40:175–88.

Lazarsfeld, P. F., B. Berelson, and H. Gaudet (1948). *The People's Choice* (2nd ed.) New York: Columbia University Press.

Lazarus, A. A. (1971). *Behavior Therapy and Beyond.* New York: McGraw-Hill.

Lazarus, R. S. (1968). Emotions and adaptation: conceptual and empirical relations. In W. J. Arnold (ed.), *Nebraska Symposium on Motivation,* Vol. 16. Lincoln: University of Nebraska Press. 175–270.

Lazarus, R. S., and E. Alfert (1964). The short-circuiting of threat by experimentally altering cognitive appraisal. *J. abnorm. soc. Psychol.* 69:195–205.

Lazarus, R. S., E. M. Opton, Jr., M. S. Nomikus, and N. O. Rankin (1965). The principle of short-circuiting of threat: further evidence. *J. pers.* 33:622–35.

Leavitt, H. J. (1951). Some effects of certain communication patterns on group performance. *J. abnorm. soc. Psychol.* 46:38–50.

Leibman, M. (1970). The effects of sex and race norms on personal space. *Environment and Behavior* 2:208–46.

Leighton, D. C., J. S. Harding, D. B. Macklin, A. M. Macmillan, and A. H. Leighton (1963). *The Character of Danger: Psychiatric Symptoms in Selected Communities.* New York: Basic Books.

Lepper, M. R., and D. Greene (1975). Turning play into work: effects of adult surveillance and extrinsic rewards on children's intrinsic motivation. *J. pers. soc. Psychol.* 31:479–86.

Lepper, M. R., D. Greene, and R. E. Nisbett (1973). Undermining children's intrinsic interest with extrinsic rewards: a test of the overjustification hypothesis. *J. pers. soc. Psychol.* 28:129–37.

Lerner, M. J. (1974). The justice motive: "equity" and "parity" among children. *J. pers. soc. Psychol.* 29:539–50.

Lerner, R. M. (1976). *Concepts and Theories of Human Development.* Reading, Mass.: Addison-Wesley.

Lesser, G. S., G. Fifer, and D. H. Clark (1965). Mental abilities of children from different social-class and cultural groups. *Monographs of the Society for Research in Child Development* 30:4.

Leukel, F. (1957). A comparison of the effects of ECS and anesthesia on acquisition of the maze habit. *J. comp. physiol. Psychol.* 50:300–6.

Leventhal, H., R. L. Jacobs, and N. Z. Kudirka (1964). Authoritarianism, ideology, and political candidate choice. *J. abnorm. soc. Psychol.* 69:539–49.

Levine, J., and A. Ludwig (1964). The LSD controversy. *Comprehensive Psychiat.* 5:318–19.

Levine, S. (1966). Sex differences in the brain. *Sci. Amer.* 214:84–90.

Lewis, M. (1972). State as an infant-environment interaction: an analysis of mother-infant behavior as a function of sex. *Merrill-Palmer Quarterly* 18:95–121.

Leyens, J. P., L. Camino, R. D. Parke, and L. Berkowitz (1975). The effects of movie violence on aggression in a field setting as a function of group dominance and cohesion. *J. pers. soc. Psychol.* 32:346–60.

Lidz, T., S. Fleck, and A. R. Cornelison (1965). *Schizophrenia and the Family.* New York: International Universities Press.

Lieberman, M. A., I. D. Yalom, and M. B. Miles (1973). *Encounter Groups: First Facts.* New York: Basic Books.

Liebling, B. A., and P. Shaver (1973). Evaluation, self-awareness, and task performance. *J. exp. soc. Psychol.* 9:297–306.

Linder, D. E., J. Cooper, and E. E. Jones (1967). Decision freedom as a determinant of the role of incentive magnitude in attitude change. *J. pers. soc. Psychol.* 6(3):245–54.

Lindsley, D. B. (1951). Emotion. In S. S. Stevens (ed.), *Handbook of Experimental Psychology.* New York: Wiley.

Lindsley, D. B., L. H. Schreiner, W. B. Knowles, and H. W. Magoun (1950). Behavioral and EEG changes following chronic brain-stem lesions in the cat. *Electroencephalography and Clin. Neurophysiol.* 2:483–98.

Littig, L., and C. A. Yeracaris (1963). Academic achievement correlates of achievement and affiliation motivations. *J. Psychol.* 55:115–19.

Little, K. B. (1965). Personal space. *J. exp. soc. Psychol.* 1:237–47.

Little, K. B. (1968). Cultural variations in social schemata. *J. pers. soc. Psychol.* 10:1–7.

Loehlin, J. C., G. Lindzey, and J. N. Spuhler (1975). *Race Differences in Intelligence.* San Francisco: Freeman.

Logan, F. A. (1956). A micromolar approach to behavior theory. *Psychol. Rev.* 63:63–73.

Loo, C. M. (1972). The effects of spatial density on the social behavior of children. *J. appl. soc. Psychol.* 2:372–81.

Lorenz, K. (1966). *On Aggression.* New York: Harcourt, Brace and World.

Lorenz, K. Z. (1952). *King Solomon's Ring.* London: Methuen.

Lott, D. F., and R. Sommer (1967). Seating arrangements and status. *J. pers. soc. Psychol.* 7:90–5.

Lovaas, O. I., and R. L. Koegel (1972). Behavior therapy with autistic children. In C. E. Thoresen (ed.), *Behavior Modification in Education:* I. Chicago: National Society for the Study of Education.

Lowell, E. L. (1952). The effect of need for achievement on learning and speed of performance. *J. Psychol.* 33:31–40.

Luchins, A. (1957). Primacy-recency in impression formation. In C. Hovland, et al., *The Order of Presentation in Persuasion.* New Haven: Yale University Press, 33–61.

Ludwig, A. M., J. M. Brandsma, C. B. Wilbur, F. Bendfeldt, and D. H. Jameson (1972). The objective study of a multiple personality. *Arch. gen. Psychiat.* 26:298–310.

Luria, A. R. (1968). *The Mind of a Mnemonist.* New York: Basic Books.

Lykken, D. T. (1957). A study of anxiety in the sociopathic personality. *J. abnorm. soc. Psychol.* 55:6–10.

Lyon, W. (1954). Justification and command as techniques for hypnotically-induced antisocial behavior. *J. clin. Psychol.* 10:288–94.

MacArthur, L. A. (1972). The how and what of why: some determinants and consequences of causal attribution. *J. pers. soc. Psychol.* 22:171–93.

McCarthy, J. J., and S. A. Kirk (1963). *The Construction, Standardization, and Statistical Characteristics of the Illinois Test of Psycholinguistic Abilities.* Urbana: University of Illinois Press.

McClelland, D. C., J. W. Atkinson, R. A. Clark, and E. L. Lowell (1953). *The Achievement Motive.* New York: Appleton-Century-Crofts.

McClintock, M. K. (1971). Menstrual synchrony and suppression. *Nature* 229:244–5.

Maccoby, E. E., and C. N. Jacklin (1974). *The Psychology of Sex Differences.* Stanford, Calif.: Stanford University Press.

McConnell, J. V. (1962). Memory transfer through cannibalism in planaria. *J. Neuropsychiatry* 3:45.

McGaugh, J. L., and L. F. Petrinovich (1966). Neural consolidation and electroconvulsive shock reexamined. *Psychol. Rev.* 73:382–87.

McGlashin, T. H., F. J. Evans, and M. T. Orne (1969). The nature of hypnotic analgesic and placebo response to experimental pain. *Psychosomatic Med.* 31:227–46.

McGuire, R. J., J. M. Carlisle, and B. G. Young (1965). Sexual deviations as conditioned behaviour: a hypothesis. *Behaviour Research and Therapy* 3:185–90.

McIntyre, A. (1972). Sex differences in children's aggression. Proceedings of the 80th Annual Convention of the APA 7:93–4.

McKenzie, B. E., and R. H. Day (1972). Object distance as a determinant of visual fixation in early infancy. *Science* 178.

MacLean, P. D. (1960). Psychosomatics. In J. Field, H. W. Magoun, and V. E. Hall (eds.), *Handbook of Physiology.* Vol. 3. Washington, D.C.: American Physiological Society.

McNemar, Q. (1942). *The Revision of the Stanford-Binet Scale.* Boston: Houghton Mifflin.

Macnichol, E. F., Jr. (1964). Three-pigment color vision. *Sci. Amer.* 211:48–56.

Maley, R. F., G. L. Feldman, and R. S. Ruskin (1973). Evaluation of patient improvement in a token economy treatment program. *J. abn. Psychol.* 82:141–144.

Mandler, G. and S. B. Sarason (1952). A study of anxiety and learning. *J. abnorm. soc. Psychol.* 47:166–73.

Marinari, K. T., A. I. Lesher, and M. P. Doyle (1976). Menstrual cycle status and adrenocortical reactivity to psychological stress. *Psychoneuroendocrinology* 1:213–8.

Marler, P., and W. J. Hamilton (1966). *Mechanisms of Animal Behavior.* New York: Wiley.

Marquis, D. G. (1962). Individual responsibility and group decisions involving risk. *Industrial Management Rev.* 3:8–23.

Masland, R. L., S. B. Sarason, and T. Gladwyn (1958). *Mental Subnormality.* New York: Basic Books.

Maslow, A. H. (1954). *Motivation and Personality.* New York: Harper and Row.

Masters, W. H., and V. E. Johnson (1966). *Human Sexual Response.* Boston: Little, Brown.

Masters, W. H. and V. E. Johnson (1970). *Human Sexual Inadequacy.* Boston: Little, Brown.

May, P. R. (1971). Psychotherapy and ataraxic drugs. In A. E. Bergin and S. L. Garfield (eds.), *Handbook of Psychotherapy and Behavior Change: An Empirical Analysis.* New York: Wiley, 495–540.

Mayer, J. (1955). Regulation of energy intake and body weight. The glucostatic theory and the lipostatic hypothesis. *Annals of N. Y. Acad. of Sci.* 63:15–43.

Mednick, S. A. (1970). Breakdown in individuals at high risk for schizophrenia: possible predispositional perinatal factors. *Ment. Hygiene* 54:50–65.

Melges, F. T., J. R. Tinklenberg, and L. E. Hollister (1971). Marihuana and the temporal span of awareness. *Archs. gen. Psychiat.* 23:564–7.

Mermelstein, E., and L. S. Shulman (1967). Lack of formal schooling and the acquisition of conservation. *Child Develpm.* 38:39–51.

Meyer, D. E. (1970). On the representation and retrieval of stored semantic information. *Cognitive Psychol.* 1:242–300.

Miczek, K. A., and H. Barry (1974). Δ 9 - tetrahydrocannabinol and aggressive behavior in rats. *Behav. Biol.* 11:261–7.

Miles, H. H. W., E. L. Barabee, and J. E. Finesinger (1951). The problem of evaluation of psychotherapy: with a follow-up study of 62 cases of anxiety neurosis. *J. nerv. ment. Dis.* 114:359–65.

Milgram, S. (1963). Behavioral study of obedience. *J. abnorm. soc. Psychol.* 67:371–8.

Milgram, S. (1970). The experience of living in cities. *Science.* 167:1461–8.

Milgram, S., L. Bickman, and L. Berkowitz, (1969). Note on the drawing power of crowds of different sizes. *J. pers. soc. Psychol.* 13:79–82.

Miller, D. G., and E. F. Loftus (1976). Influencing memory for people and their actions. *Bulletin of the Psychonomic Society,* 7:9–11.

Miller, G. A. (1962). The magical number seven, plus or minus two: some limits on our capacity for processing information. *Psychol. Rev.* 63:81–97.

Miller, N. E. (1948). Theory and experiment relating psychoanalytic displacement to stimulus-response generalization. *J. abnorm. soc. Psychol.* 43:155–78.

Miller, N. E. (1959). Liberalization of basic S-R concepts: extensions to conflict behavior, motivation, and social learning. In S. Koch (ed.) *Psychology: A Study of a Science,* Vol. 2. New York: McGraw, 196–292.

Miller, N. E. (1969). Learning of visceral and glandular responses. *Science* 163:434–45.

Miller, N. E., and A. Banuazizi (1968). Instrumental learning by curarized rats of a specific visceral response, intestinal or cardiac. *J. comp. physiol. Psychol.* 65:1–7.

Miller, N. E., and J. Dollard (1941). *Social Learning and Imitation.* New Haven, Conn.: Yale University Press.

Miller, N. E., and B. R. Dworkin (1973). Visceral learning: recent difficulties with curarized rats and significant programs for human research. In P. A. Obrist, et al. (eds.) *Contemporary Trends in Cardiovascular Psychophysiology.* Chicago: Aldine-Atherton.

Miller, N. E., and M. L. Kessen (1952). Reward effects of food via stomach fistula compared with those of food via mouth. *J. comp. physiol. Psychol.* 45:555–64.

Miller, R. R., and A. D. Springer (1973). Amnesia, consolidation, and retrieval. *Psychol. Bull.* 80:69–79.

Miller, W., and S. Ervin (1964). The development of grammar in child language. In U. Bellugi and R. Brown (eds.), *The Acquisition of Language.* Monographs of the Society for Research in Child Development 29 (Whole Number 92):9–34.

Minton, C., J. Kagan, and J. A. Levine (1971). Maternal control and obedience in the two-year-old. *Child Develpm.* 42:1873–94 (and personal communication).

Mintz, A. (1951). Non-adaptive group behavior. *J. abnorm. soc. Psychol.* 46:150–9.

Mischel, W. (1973). Toward a cognitive social learning reconceptualization of personality. *Psychol. Rev.* 80:252–83.

Mitchell, R. E. (1971). Some social implications of high-density housing. *Amer. sociol. Rev.* 36:18–29.

Moltz, H., and L. J. Stettner (1961). The influence of patterned-light deprivation on the critical period for imprinting. *J. comp. physiol. Psychol.* 54:279–83.

Money, J., J. G. Hampson, and J. L. Hampson (1957). Imprinting and the establishment of gender role. *Archives of Neurological Psychiatry* 77:333–6.

Monroe, L., A. Rechtschaffen, D. Foulkes, and J. Jensen (1965). The discriminability of REM and NREM reports. *J. pers. soc. Psychol.* 2:456–60.

Moray, N. (1959). Attention in dichotic listening: affective cues and the influence of instructions. *Quart. J. exp. Psychol.* 11:56–60

Morgan, C. T., and J. D. Morgan (1940). Studies in hunger: II. The relation of gastric denervation and dietary sugar to the effects of insulin upon food intake in the rat. *J. gen. Psychol.* 57:153–63.

Morris, D. (1967). *The Naked Ape.* New York: McGraw-Hill.

Morris, W. W., and R. S. Miller (1975). The effects of consensus-breaking and consensus-preempting on reduction of conformity. *J. exp. soc. Psychol.* 11:215–23.

Moruzzi, G., and H. W. Magoun (1949). Brain stem reticular formation and activation of the EEG. *Electroencephalography and clin. Neurophysiol.* 1:455–73.

Moss, H. A. (1967). Sex, age, and state as determinants of mother-infant interaction. *Merrill-Palmer Quarterly* 13: 19–36.

Munn, N. L. (1961). *The Fundamentals of Human Adjustment*, 4th Ed. Boston: Hourhton Mifflin.

Myers, J. K., and L. L. Bean (1968). *Social Class and Mental Illness*. New York.

Nash, S. C. (1973). Conceptions and concomitants of sex-role stereotyping. Unpublished doctoral dissertation, Columbia University.

Nelson, K. E. (1971). Accommodation of visual tracking patterns in human infants to object movement patterns. *J. exp. Child Psychol.* 12:182–96.

Neustatter, W. L. (1935). The results of fifty cases treated by psychotherapy. *Lancet* 1:796–9.

Newcomb, T. M. (1943). *Personality and Social Change*. New York: Dryden.

Newcomb, T. M. (1961). *The Acquaintance Process*. New York: Holt, Rinehart and Winston.

Newcomb, T. M., K. E. Koenig, R. Flacks, and D. P. Warwick (1967). *Persistence and Change: Bennington College and Its Students after 25 years*. New York: Wiley.

Newell, A., J. C. Shaw, and H. A. Simon (1960). Report on a general problem-solving program. In *Proceedings of the International Conference on Information Processing*. Paris: UNESCO.

Newell, A., and H. A. Simon (1956). The logic theory machine: a complex information processing system. *Transactions on Information Theory*. Institute of Radio Engineers IT-2(3):61–79.

Newman, H. H., F. N. Freeman, and K. J. Holzinger (1937). *Twins: A Study of Heredity and Environment*. Chicago: University of Chicago Press.

Newson, J., and E. Newson (1968). *Four Years Old in an Urban Community*. Harmondworth, England: Pelican Books.

Nichols, P. L. (1970). The effects of heredity and environment on intelligence test performance in 4- and 7-year white and Negro sibling pairs. Doctoral dissertation, University of Minnesota.

Nisbett, R. E. (1968). Determinants of food intake in human obesity. *Science* 159:1254–5.

Nisbett, R. E., C. Caputo, P. Legant, and J. Marrecek (1973). Behavior as seen by the actor and as seen by the observer, *J. pers. soc. Psychol.* 27:154–64.

Nisbett, R. E., and S. Schachter (1966). Cognitive manipulation of pain. *J. exp. soc. Psychol.* 2:227–36.

Noyes, A. P., and L. C. Kolb (1963). *Modern Clinical Psychiatry*, 6th Ed. Philadelphia: W. B. Saunders.

Oden, M. H. (1968). The fulfillment of promise: 40-year follow-up of the Terman gifted group. *Genet. Psychol. Monogr.* 77:3–93.

Olds, J., and P. M. Milner (1954). Positive reinforcement produced by electrical stimulation of septal areas and other regions of rat brains. *J. comp. physiol. Psychol.* 47:419–27.

Omark, D. R., M. Omark, and M. Edelman (1973). Dominance hierarchies in young children. Paper presented at International Congress of Anthropological and Ethnological Sciences, Chicago.

Orme-Johnson, D. W. (1973). Autonomic stability and transcendental meditation. *Psychosomatic Med.* 35:341–9.

Orne, M. T. (1962). On the social psychology of the psychological experiment: with particular reference to demand characteristics and their implications. *Amer. Psychol.* 17:776–83.

Orne, M. T. (1972). Can a hypnotized subject be compelled to carry out otherwise unacceptable behavior? *Int. J. clin. exp. Hypnosis* 20:101–17.

Ornstein, R. E. (1969). On the experience of duration. *Dissertation Abstracts International.* 29(11-B): 4407–8.

Oskamp, S., and C. Kleinke (1970). Amount of reward a variable in the prisoner's dilemma game. *J. pers. soc. Psychol.* 16:133–40.

Overmier, J. B., and M. E. P. Seligman (1967). Effects of inescapable shock upon subsequent escape and avoidance learning. *J. comp. physiol. Psychol.* 63:23–33.

Paige, K. E. (1971). Effects of oral contraceptives on affective fluctuations associated with the menstrual cycle. *Psychosomatic Med.* 33:515–37.

Pallak, M. S., and T. S. Pittman (1972). General motivational effects of dissonance arousal. *J. pers. soc. Psychol.* 21:349–58.

Parke, R. D., L. Berkowitz, J. P. Leyens, S. G. West, and R. J. Sebastian (1977). Some effects of violent and nonviolent movies on the behavior of juvenile delinquents. In L. Berkowitz (ed.), *Advances in Experimental Social Psychology* 10:136–172.

Parke, R. D., and R. H. Walters (1967). Some factors determining the efficacy of punishment for inducing response inhibition. *Monographs of the Society for Research in Child Development.* 32(109).

Patterson, M. L., and L. B. Sechrest (1970). Interpersonal distance and impression formation. *J. pers.* 38:161–6.

Paul, G. L. (1966). *Insight vs. Desensitization in Psychotherapy.* Stanford: Stanford University Press.

Paulus, P. B., and P. Murdoch (1971). Anticipated evaluation and audience presence in the enhancement of dominant responses. *J. exp. soc. Psychol.* 7:280–91.

Pedersen, F. A., and R. Q. Bell (1970). Sex differences in preschool children without histories of complications of pregnancy and delivery. *Developmental Psychol.* 3:10–15.

Pedersen, F. A., and K. S. Robson (1969). Father participation in infancy. *Amer. J. Orthopsychiatry* 39:466–72.

Penfield, W. (1958). *The Excitable Cortex in Conscious Man.* Liverpool: Liverpool University Press.

Pengelley, E. T. (1974). *Sex and Human Life.* Reading, Mass.: Addison-Wesley.

Perez-Reyes, M., M. C. Timmons, and M. E. Wall (1974). Long-term use of marihuana and the development of tolerance or sensitivity to Δ9 tetrahydrocannabinol. *Archs. gen. Psychiat.* 31:89–91.

Peterson, L. R., and M. J. Peterson (1959). Short-term retention of individual verbal items. *J. exp. Psychol.* 30:93–113.

Phoenix, C. H., A. K. Slob, and R. W. Goy (1973). Effects of castration and replacement therapy on sexual behavior of adult male rhesuses. *J. comp. physiol. Psychol.* 84:472–81.

Piaget, J. (1932). *The Moral Judgment of the Child.* London: Kegan Paul.

Piaget, J. (1953). *The Origins of Intelligence in Children.* London: Routledge and Kegan Paul.

Piliavin, I. M., J. A. Piliavin, and J. Rodin (1975). Costs, diffusion, and the stigmatized victim. *J. pers. soc. Psychol.* 32:429–38.

Pliner, P., H. Heather, J. Kohl, and D. Saari (1974). Compliance without pressure: some further data on the foot-in-the-door technique. *J. exp. soc. Psychol.* 10:17–22.

Posner, M. I. (1969). Abstraction and the process of recognition. In J. T. Spence and G. H. Bower (eds.), *Advances in Learning and Motivation,* Vol. 3. New York: Academic Press.

Posner, M. I., S. J. Boies, W. H. Eichelman, and R. L. Taylor (1969). Retention of visual and name codes of single letters. *J. exp. Psychol.* 79:1–16.

Premack, D. (1971). Language in chimpanzee? *Science* 172:808–22.

Pressman, I., and A. Carol (1971). Crime as a diseconomy of scale. *Review of Social Economy* 29:227–36.

Price, J. M. (1971). The effects of crowding on the social behavior of children. Ph.D. Dissertation, Columbia University.

Price-Williams, D. R. (1961). A study concerning concepts of conservation of quantities among primitive children. *Acta psychol.* 18:293–305.

Rabin, A. I. (1965). *Growing Up in the Kibbutz.* New York: Springer.

Rand, P. (1973). Curvilinear relationship between motive strength and performances: a possible explanation based on J. W. Atkinson's model. *Scandinavian J. Educational Research* 17:83–94.

Raven, B. H., and J. R. P. French, Jr. (1958). Group support, legitimate power, and social influence, *J. Pers.* 26:400–9.

Regan, D. T., and J. Totten (1975). Empathy and attribution: turning observers into actors. *J. pers. soc. Psychol.* 32:850–6.

Regan, J. W. (1971). Guilt, perceived injustice, and altruistic behavior. *J. pers. soc. Psychol.* 18:124–32.

Regula, R. C., and J. W. Julian (1973). The impact of quality and frequency of task contributions on perceived ability. *J. soc. Psychol.* 89:115–22.

Renault, P. F. (1974). Repeat administration of marihuana smoke to humans. *Archives of Gen. Psychiat.* 31:95–102.

Renson, G. J., E. S. Schaefer, and B. I. Levy (1968). Cross-national validity of a spherical conceptual model for parent behavior. *Child Develpm.* 39:1224–35.

Rest, J. (1973). The hierarchical nature of moral judgment: the study of patterns of comprehension and preference with moral stages. *J. Pers.* 41:92–3.

Rest, J., E. E. Turiel, and L. Kohlberg (1969). Level of moral development as a determinant of preference and comprehension of moral judgments made by others. *J. Pers.* 37:225–52.

Restle, F. (1955). A theory of discrimination learning. *Psychol. Rev.* 62:11–19.

Rheingold, H. H., and C. O. Eckerman (1973). The fear of strangers hypothesis: a critical review. In H. Reese (ed.), *Advances in Child Development and Behavior,* Vol. 8. New York: Academic Press, pp. 185–222.

Rhine, J. B., and R. Brier (eds.) (1968). *Parapsychology Today.* New York: Citadel Press.

Robertson, D. (1973). *Survive the Savage Sea.* New York: Praeger.

Rodgers, D. A., and D. D. Thiessen (1964). Effects of population density on adrenal size, behavioral arousal, and alcohol preferences of inbred mice. *Quart. J. Studies on Alcohol* 25:240-7.

Rogers, C. R. (1951). *Client-centered Therapy.* Boston: Houghton Mifflin.

Rogers, C. (1967). *The Therapeutic Relationship and Its Impact: A Study of Psychotherapy with Schizophrenics.* Madison, University of Wisconsin Press.

Rogers, C. R. (1970). *On Becoming a Person: A Therapist's View of Psychotherapy.* Boston: Houghton Mifflin.

Rosen, E., R. E. Fox, and I. Gregory (1972). *Abnormal Psychology,* 2d Ed. Philadelphia: W. B. Saunders.

Rosenkoetter, L. I. (1973). Resistance to temptation: inhibitory and disinhibitory effects of models. *Developmental Psychol.* 8:80-4.

Rosenthal, D., and S. S. Kety (eds.) 1968. *The Transmission of Schizophrenia.* Oxford: Pergamon.

Rosenthal, M. S. (1972). A call for more systematic clinical inquiry. *Internat. J. Psychiat.* 10:75-7.

Rosenthal, R. (1966). *Experimenter Effects in Behavioral Research.* New York: Appleton.

Ross, M., B. Layton, B. Erickson, and J. Schopler (1973). Affect, facial regard and reactions to crowding. *J. pers. soc. Psychol.* 28:68-76.

Ross, T. A. (1936). An enquiry into prognosis in the neuroses. London: Cambridge University Press.

Rowell, T. E., and R. A. Hinde (1962). Vocal communication by the rhesus monkey (Macaca mulatta). *Proc. Zool. Soc. London* 138:379-94.

Rowland, L. W. (1939). Will hypnotized persons try to harm themselves or others? *J. abnorm. soc. Psychol.* 37:114-27.

Rozin, P. (1965). Specific hunger for thiamine: recovery from deficiency and thiamine preference. *J. comp. physiol. Psychol.* 59:98-101.

Rozin, P., and J. W. Kalat (1971). Specific hungers and poison avoidance as adaptive specializations of learning. *Psychol. Rev.* 78:459-86.

Rydin, I. (1971). A Swedish child in the beginning of syntactic development and some cross-linguistic comparisons. Unpublished paper, on file with Roger Brown, Harvard University, Cambridge, Mass.

Saarni, C. I. (1973). Piagetian operations and field independence as factors in children's problem-solving performance. *Child Develpm.* 44:338-45.

Saegert, S., W. Swap, and R. B. Zajonc (1973). Exposure, context, and interpersonal attraction. *J. pers. soc. Psychol.* 25:234-42.

Salapatek, P., and W. Kessen (1966). Visual scanning of triangles by the human newborn. *J. exp. Child Psychol.* 3(2):155-67.

Salapatek, P., and W. Kessen (1973). Infants watching triangles. *J. exp. Child Psychol.* 15:22-9.

Sampson, H. (1965). Deprivation of dreaming sleep by two methods: I. Compensatory REM time. *Archives gen. Psychiat.* 13:79-86.

Samuel, W. (1973). On clarifying some interpretation of social comparison theory. *J. exp. soc. Psychol.* 9:450-65.

Sarnoff, I., and P. G. Zimbardo (1961). Anxiety, fear and social affiliation. *J. abn. soc. Psychol.* 62:356-363.

Sawrey, W. L., J. J. Conger, and E. S. Turrell (1956). An experimental investigation of the role of psychological factors in the production of gastric ulcers of rats. *J. comp. physiol. Psychol.* 49:457-61.

Schachter, J. (1957). Pain, fear and anger in hypertensives and normotensives. *Psychosomatic Med.* 19:17-29.

Schachter, S. (1959). *The Psychology of Affiliation.* Stanford, Calif.: Stanford University.

Schachter, S. (1971). *Emotion, Obesity and Crime.* New York: Academic Press.

Schachter, S., and L. N. Friedman (1974). The effects of work and cue prominence on eating behavior. In S. Schachter and J. Rodin (eds.), *Obese Humans and Rats.* Potomac, Md.: L. Erlbaum.

Schachter, S., and J. E. Singer (1962). Cognitive, social, and physiological determinants of emotional state. *Psychol. Rev.* 69:379-99.

Schachter, S., and L. Wheeler (1962). Epinephrine, chlorpromazine, and amusement. *J. abnorm. soc. Psychol.* 65:121-8.

Schafer, D. (1975). Hypnosis use on a burn unit. *Internat'l J. clin. exp. hypn.* 23:1-14.

Schafer, R. (1948). *The Clinical Application of Psychological Tests.* New York: International Universities Press.

Schaffer, H. R., and P. E. Emerson (1964). The development of social attachments in infancy. *Monographs of the Society for Research in Child Development* 29 (3, Whole No. 94).

Schaie, K., G. Labouvie, and B. Buech (1973). Generational and cohort specific differences in adult cognitive functioning: a fourteen year study of independent samples. *Developmental Psychol.* 9:151-66.

Schaie, K. W., and C. R. Strother (1968). A cross-sequential study of age changes in cognitive behavior. *Psychol. Bull.* 70:671-80.

Scheier, M. F., A. Fenigstein, and A. H. Buss (1974). Self-awareness and physical aggression. *J. exp. soc. Psychol.* 10:264–73.

Schein, E. H. (1956). The Chinese indoctrination program for prisoners of war. *Psychiatry* 19:149–72.

Scherer, S. E. (1974). Proxemic behavior of primary school children as a function of their socioeconomic class and subculture. *J. pers. soc. Psychol.* 29:800–5.

Schjelderup, H. (1955). Lasting effects of psychoanalytic treatment. *Psychiatry* 18:109–33.

Schlesinger, I. M. (1971). Production of utterances and language acquisition. In D. I. Slobin (ed.), *The Ontogenesis of Grammar.* New York: Academic Press, 63–101.

Schlosberg, H. (1952). The description of facial expressions in terms of two dimensions. *J. exp. Psychol.* 44:229–37.

Schmitt, R. C. (1957). Density, delinquency and crime in Honolulu. *Sociology and Social Research* 41:274–6.

Schmitt, R. C. (1966). Density, health, and social disorganization. *J. Amer. Institute of Planners* 32:38–40.

Schreiber, F. R. (1973). *Sybil.* Chicago: Regnery.

Schulman, J. L., R. C. Ford, P. Busk, and J. C. Kaspar (1973). Evaluation of a classroom program to alter friendship practices. *J. educ. res.* 67:99–102.

Schulman, J., P. Shaver, R. Colman, B. Emrich, and R. Christie (1973). Recipe for a jury. *Psychology Today,* May, 37–84.

Sears, R. R., E. E. Maccoby, and H. Levin (1957). *Patterns of Child Rearing.* Evanston, Ill.: Row, Peterson.

Sears, R. R., J. W. M. Whiting, V. Nowlis, and P. S. Sears (1953). Some child-rearing antecedents of aggression and dependency in young children. *Genet. Psychol. Monogr.* 47:135–236.

Segall, M. H., D. T. Campbell, and M. J. Herskovits (1966). *The Influence of Culture on Perception.* New York: Bobbs-Merrill.

Seligman, M. E. P. (1975). *Helplessness.* San Francisco: W. H. Freeman.

Shaver, P., and J. Freedman. Your pursuit of happiness. *Psychology Today,* August 1976, 26.

Sheffield, F. D., and T. B. Roby (1950). Reward value of a non-nutritive sweet taste. *J. comp. physiol. Psychol.* 43:471–81.

Sheffield, F. D., J. J. Wulff, and R. Barker (1951). Reward value of copulation without sex drive reduction. *J. comp. physiol. Psychol.* 44:3–8.

Shepard, R. N. (1967). Recognition memory for words, sentences and pictures. *J. verb. learn. verb. beh.* 6:156–63.

Sherman, J. A. (1963). Reinstatement of verbal behavior in a psychotic by reinforcement methods. *J. Speech and Hearing Disorders* 28:398–401.

Sherman, M. (1927). The differentiation of emotional responses from motion picture views and from actual observations. *J. comp. Psychol.* 7:265–84.

Shikiar, R. (1975). Authoritarianism and political behavior: the 1972 election. *Psychol. Rep.* 36:874.

Shimoyama, T. (1974). A validity study of a scale to measure achievement motivation. *Japanese Psychol. Research* 16:197–204.

Shuck, S. Z., A. Shuck, E. Hallam, F. Mancini, and R. Wells (1971). Sex differences in aggressive behavior subeeet to listening to a radio broadcast of violence. *Psychol. Rep.* 28:921–6.

Siegel, H. I., and G. S. Greenwald (1975). Prepartum onset of maternal behavior in hamsters and the effects of estrogen and progesterone. *Hormones and behav.* 6:237–45.

Siegel, M. G., G. D. Niswander, E. Sachs, Jr., and D. Stavros (1959). Taraxein, fact or artifact? *Amer. J. Psychiat.* 115:819–229

Siegel, R. K. (1967). Yeast ribonucleic acid: effects on avoidance behavior of the neonate domestic chick. *Psychopharmacologia* 12:68–77.

Siegler, R. S., and R. M. Liebert (1972). Effects of presenting relevant rules and complete feedback on the conservation of liquid quantity task. *Developmental Psychol.* 7:133–8.

Simmons, M. W., and L. P. Lipsitt (1961). An operant-discrimination apparatus for infants. *J. exp. Anal. Behav.* 4:233–5.

Simon, H. (1974). How big is a chunk? *Science* 183:482–8.

Singer, J. E., C. Brush, and S. D. Lublin (1965). Some aspects of deindividuation: identification and conformity. *J. exp. soc. Psychol.* 1:356–78.

Sistrunk, F., and J. W. McDavid (1971). Sex variable in conforming behavior. *J. pers. soc. Psychol.* 17:200–7.

Skinner, B. F. (1938). *The Behavior of Organisms.* New York: Appleton-Century-Crofts.

Skinner, B. F. (1948). "Superstition" in the pigeon. *J. exp. Psychol.* 38:168–72.

Skinner, B. F. (1953). *Science and Human Behavior.* New York: Macmillan.

Skinner, B. F. (1957). *Verbal Behavior.* New York: Appleton-Century-Crofts.

Skinner, B. F. (1960). Pigeons in a pelican. *Amer. Psychol.* 15:28–37.

Skinner, wb. F. (1962). Two "synthetic social relations." *J. exp. Anal. Behav.* 5:531–3.

Skinner, B. F. (1971). *Beyond Freedom and Dignity.* New York: Knopf.

Smedslund, J. (1961). The acquisition of conservation of substance and weight in children: VI. Practice in problem situations without external reinforcement. *Scandinavian J. Psychol.* 2:203–10.

Smith, J. C. (1975). Meditation as psychotherapy: A review of the literature. *Psychol. Bull.* 82:558–64.

Smith, S., and W. H. Haythorn (1972). Effects of compatibility, crowding, group size, and leadership seniority on stress, anxiety, hostility, and annoyance in isolated groups. *J. pers. soc. Psychol.* 22:67–79.

Snyder, F., J. A. Hobson, D. F. Morrison, and F. Goldfrank (1964). Changes in respiration, heart rate, and systolic blood pressure in human sleep. *J. appl. Psychol.* 19:417–22.

Snyder, M., and M. R. Cunningham (1975). To comply or not comply: testing the self-perception explanation of the "foot-in-the-door" phenomenon. *J. pers. soc. Psychol.* 31:64–7.

Snyder, R. L. (1968). Reproduction and population pressures. In E. Stellar and J. M. Sprague (eds.), *Progress in Physiological Psychology.* New York: Academic Press, 119–60.

Solomon, R. L., and L. C. Wynne (1954). Traumatic avoidance learning: anxiety conservation and partial irreversibility. *Psychol. Rev.* 61:353–85.

Sommer, R. (1959). Studies in personal space. *Sociometry* 22:247–60.

Sommer, R. (1968). Intimacy ratings in five countries, *Internat. J. Psychol.* 3:109–14.

Sommer, R. (1969). *Personal Space: The Behavioral Basis of Design.* Englewood Cliffs, N.J.: Prentice-Hall.

Sorrentino, R. M., and R. G. Boutillier (1975). The effect of quantity and quality of verbal interaction on ratings of leadership ability. *J. exp. soc. Psychol.* 11:403–11.

Southwick, C. H. (1955). The population dynamics of confined house mice supplied with unlimited food. *Ecology* 36:212–25.

Southwick, C. H., and V. P. Bland (1959). Effect of population density on adrenal glands and reproductive organs of CFW mice. *Amer. J. Physiol.* 197:111–14.

Spence, K. W. (1956). *Behavior Theory and Conditioning.* New Haven: Yale University Press.

Spence, K. W., and E. B. Norris (1950). Eyelid conditioning as a function of the inter-trial interval. *J. exp. Psychol.* 40:716–70.

Spence, K. W., and J. T. Spence (1964). Relation of eyelid conditioning to manifest anxiety, extraversion, and rigidity. *J. abnorm. soc. Psychol.* 68:144–9.

Spence, K. W., J. Taylor, and R. Ketchel (1956). Anxiety (drive) level and degree of competition in paired-associates learning. *J. exp. Psychol.* 52:306–10.

Sperling, G. (1960). The information available in brief visual presentations. *Psychol. Monogr.* 74(11, Whole No. 498).

Sperry, R. W. (1970). Perception in the absence of neocortical commissures. In *Perception and its Disorders.* Association for Research in Nervous and Mental Disease, Vol. 48.

Spitz, R. A., and K. M. Wolf (1946). Anaclitic depression: an inquiry into the genesis of psychiatric conditions in early childhood. In A. Freud (ed.), *The Psychoanalytic Study of the Child,* Vol. II. New York: International Universities Press, 313–42.

Srole, L. (1972). Urbanization and mental health: some reformulations. *Amer. Scientist* 60:576–83.

Srole, L., T. S. Langner, S. T. Michael, M. K. Opler, and T. A. C. Rennie (1962). *Mental Health in the Metropolis: The Midtown Manhattan Study.* New York: McGraw-Hill.

Standing, L., J. Conezio, and R. N. Haber (1970). Perception and memory for pictures: single-trial learning of 2500 visual stimuli. *Psychonomic Sci.* 19:73–4.

Stang, D. J. (1973). Effect of interaction rate on ratings of leadership and liking. *J. pers. soc. Psychol.* 27:405–8.

Stanton, H. E. (1975). Weight loss through hypnosis. *Amer. J. clin. hypn.* 18:94–7.

Steffensmeier, D. J. (1975). Levels of dogmatism and willingness to report "hippie" and "straight" shoplifters. *Sociometry* 38:282–90.

Stokols, D. (1972). On the distinction between density and crowding: some implications for future research. *Psychol. Rev.* 79:275–7.

Stoner, J. A. F. (1961). A comparison of individual and group decisions involving risk. Unpublished Master's thesis, M.I.T.

Stoyva, J. M. (1965). Posthypnotically suggested dreams and the sleep cycle. *Archives gen. Psychiat.* 12:287–94.

Streeter, L. A., R. M. Krauss, V. Geller, C. Olson, and W. Apple (1977). Pitch changes during attempted deception. *J. pers. soc. Psychol.* 33:345–50.

Streib, G. F., and C. J. Schneider (1971). *Retirement in American Society.* Ithaca: Cornell University Press.

Strodtbeck, F. L., R. M. James, and C. Hawkins (1958). Social status in jury deliberations. In E. Maccoby, T. Newcomb, and E. Hartley (eds.), *Readings in Social Psychology.* New York: Holt, 379–87.

Suedfeld, P., S. Glucksberg, and J. Vernon (1967). Sensory deprivation as a drive operation: effects upon problem solving. *J. exp. Psychol.* 75:166–9.

Sullivan, H. S. (1953). *The Interpersonal Theory of Psychiatry.* New York: W. W. Norton.

Svensson, A. (1971). *Relative Achievement. School Performance in Relation to Intelligence, Sex and Home Environment.* Stockholm: Almqvist and Wiksell.

Szasz, T. S. (1974). *The Myth of Mental Illness: Foundations of a Theory of Personal Conduct.* New York: Harper and Row.

Tanner, J. M., R. H. Whitehouse, and M. Takaishi (1966). Standards from birth to maturity for height, weight, height velocity, and weight velocity: British children 1965. *Arch. Childhood* 41:454–71.

Tasch, R. J. (1952). The role of the father in the family. *J. exp. Educ.* 20:319–61.

Taylor, J. A. (1953). A personality scale of manifest anxiety. *J. abnorm. soc. Psychol.* 48:285–90.

Teichman, Y. (1973). Emotional arousal and affiliation. *J. exp. soc. Psychol.* 9:591–605.

Terman, L. M., and M. A. Merrill (1937). Measuring Intelligence. Boston: Houghton Mifflin.

Terman, L. M., and M. H. Oden (1947). *The Gifted Child Grows Up.* Stanford, California: Stanford University Press.

Thibaut, J. W., and H. W. Riecken (1955). Some determinants and consequences of the perception of social causality. *J. Pers.* 24:113–33.

Thiessen, D. D., J. F. Zolman, and D. A. Rodgers (1962). Relation between adrenal weight, brain cholinesterase activity, and hole-in-the-wall behavior of mice under different living conditions. *J. comp. physiol. Psychol.* 55:186–190.

Thigpen, C. H., and H. Cleckley (1957). *The Three Faces of Eve.* New York: McGraw-Hill.

Thompson, D. F., and L. Meltzer (1964). Communication of emotional intent by facial expression. *J. abnorm. soc. Psychol.* 68:129–35.

Thompson, R. F. (1967). *Foundations of Physiological Psychology.* New York: Harper and Row.

Thorndike, E. L. (1898). Animal intelligence, *Psychol. Rev. Monograph Supplement* 2(4, Whole No. 8).

Thurstone, L. L. (1938). Primary mental abilities. *Psychometric Monographs.* No. 1. Chicago: Univ. of Chicago Press.

Thurstone, L. L., and T. G. Thurstone (1941). Factorial studies of intelligence. *Psychometric Monographs,* No. 2. Chicago: Univ. of Chicago Press.

Tienari, P. (1971). Shizofreniya i monosigotnye bliznetsy. *Vestnik Ahademii Meditsinskikh Nauk SSSR* 26:53–57.

Tinklepaugh, O. L. (1928). An experimental study of representational factors in monkeys. *J. comp. Psychol.* 8:197–236.

Titley, R. W., and W. Viney (1969). Expression of aggression toward the physically handicapped. *Percept. mot. Skills* 29:51–6.

Tolbert, K. (1971). Pepe Joy: learning to talk in Mexico. Unpublished paper, on file with Roger Brown, Harvard University, Cambridge, Mass.

Tolman, E. C., and C. H. Honzik (1930). Introduction and removal of reward, and maze performance in rats. *University of California Publications in Psychology* 4:257–75.

Treisman, A. M. (1964). Selective attention in man. *Brit. Med. Bull.* 20:12–16.

Tulving, E. (1972). Episodic and semantic memory. In E. Tulving and W. Donaldson (eds.), *Organization of Memory.* New York: Academic Press.

Turnbull, C. M. (1961). Some observations regarding the experiences and behavior of Bambuti Pygmies. *Amer. J. Psychol.* 74:304–8.

Turner, C. D. (1971). *General Endocrinology* (4th Ed.). Philadelphia: Saunders.

Underwood, B. J. (1957). Interference and forgetting. *Psychol. Rev.* 64:49–60.

Ungar, G. (1973). Molecular mechanisms in central nervous system coding. In G. B. Ansell and P. B. Bradley (eds.), *Macromolecules and Behavior.* Baltimore: University Park Press.

Ungerleider, J. T., et al (1968). A statistical survey of adverse reactions to LSD in Los Angeles County. *Amer. J. Psychiat.* 125:352–7.

Vinokur, A., Y. Trope, and E. Burnstein (1975). A decision-making analysis of persuasive argumentation and the choice-shift effect. *J. exp. soc. Psychol.* 11:127–48.

von Békésy, G., and W. A. Rosenblith (1951). The mechanical properties of the ear. In S. S. Stevens (ed.), *Handbook of Experimental Psychology.* New York: Wiley, 1075–1115.

von Osterman, G. F. (1952). *Manual of Foreign Languages,* 4th ed. New York: Central Book Co.

Wallace, R. K., and H. Benson (1972). The physiology of meditation. *Sci. Amer.* 226:85–90.

Wallach, M. A., and N. Kogan (1965a). *Modes of Thinking in Young Children: A Study of the Creativity-Intelligence Distinction.* New York: Holt, Rinehart and Winston.

Wallach, M. A., and N. Kogan (1965b). The roles of information, discussion, and consensus in group risk taking. *J. exp. soc. Psychol.* 1:1–19.

Wallington, S. A. (1973). Consequences of transgression: self-punishment and depression. *J. pers. and soc. Psychol.* 28:1–7.

Walster, E., E. Aronson, and D. Abrahams (1966). On increasing the persuasiveness of a low prestige communicator. *J. exp. soc. Psychol.* 2:325–42.

Walster, E., E. Berscheid, and G. W. Walster (1975). New directions in equity research. *J. pers. soc. Psychol.* 25:151–76.

Walters, R. H., and D. C. Willows (1968). Imitative behavior of disturbed and nondisturbed children following exposure to aggressive and nonaggressive models. *Child Develpm.* 39:79–89.

Warden, C. J. (1931). *Animal Motivation: Experimental Studies on the Albino Rat.* New York: Columbia University Press.

Watkins, J. G. (1947). Anti-social compulsions induced under hypnotic trance. *J. abnorm. soc. Psychol.* 42:256–70.

Watkins, J. G. (1972). Antisocial behavior under hypnosis: possible or impossible. *Int. J. clin. exp. Hypnosis* 20:95–100.

Watson, J. B., and R. Rayner (1920). Conditioned emotional reactions. *J. exp. Psychol.* 3:1–14.

Watson, O. M., and T. Graves (1966). Quantitative research in proxemic behavior. *Amer. Anthrop.* 68:971–85.

Wechsler, D. (1958). *The Measurement and Appraisal of Adult Intelligence,* 4th ed. Baltimore: Williams & Wilkins.

Weigel, R. H., D. T. A. Vernon, and L. N. Tognacci (1974). Specificity of the attitude as a determinant of attitude-behavior congruence. *J. pers. soc. Psychol.* 30:724–8.

Weiner, B. (1970). New conceptions in the study of achievement motivation. In B. A. Maher (ed.), *Progress in Experimental Personality Research,* Vol. 5. New York: Academic Press, pp. 67–109.

Weisbrod, R. A. (1965). Looking behavior in a discussion group. Unpublished term paper, Cornell University.

Weiss, J. M. (1972). Psychological factors in stress and disease. *Sci. Amer.* 226:106.

Welker, W. I. (1956). Some determinants of play and exploration in chimpanzees. *J. comp. physiol. Psychol.* 49:84–89.

Wells, H. (1963). Effects of transfer and problem structure in disjunctive concept formation. *J. exp.Psychol.* 65:63–9.

Wells, W. D. (1972). Television and aggression: a replication of an experimental field study. Mimeographed abstract, University of Chicago.

Wender, P. H., D. Rosenthal, and S. S. Kety (1968). A psychiatric assessment of the adoptive parents of schizophrenics. In *The Transmission of Schizophrenia.* Oxford: Pergamon, 235–50.

Wenzel, D. G., and C. O. Rutledge (1962). Effects of centrally acting drugs on human motor and psychomotor performance. *J. Pharmacological Sci.* 51:631.

Wertheimer, M. (1912). Experimentelle studien über das sehen von bewegung. *Zeit. Psychol.* 61:161–265.

Wesson, D., and D. E. Smith (1972). Barbiturate toxicity and the treatment of barbiturate dependence. *J. Psychedelic Drugs* 5:159–65.

Wever, E. G. (1949). *Theory of Hearing.* New York: Wiley.

Whalen, R. E. (1964). Hormone-induced changes in the organization of sexual behavior in the male rat. *J. comp. physiol. Psychol.* 57:175–82.

Whalen, R. E., and R. D. Nadler (1963). Suppression of the development of female mating behavior by estrogen administered in infancy. *Science* 141:273–4.

White, R. W. (1956). *The Abnormal Personality,* 2d ed. New York: Ronald Press.

White, R. W. (1964). *The Abnormal Personality,* 3d ed. New York: Ronald Press.

Whorf, B. L. (1956). *Language, Thought and Reality.* Cambridge, Mass.: Technology Press of M.I.T.

Wickelgren, W. A. (1965). Acoustic similarity and retroactive interference in short-term memory. *J. verb. learn. verb. behav.* 4:53–61.

Wicker, A. W. (1969). Attitudes versus action: the relationship of verbal and overt behavior responses to attitude objects. *J. Social Issues* 25(4):41–78.

Williams, H. L., D. I. Tepas, and H. C. Morlock, Jr. (1962). Evoked responses to clicks and electroencephalographic stages of sleep in man. *Science* 138:685–6.

Wilson, P. D., and A. H. Riesen (1966). Visual development in rhesus monkeys neonatally deprived of patterned light. *J. comp. physiol. Psychol.* 61:87–95.

Winsborough, H. H. (1965). The social consequences of high population density. *Law and Contemporary Problems* 30:120–6.

Wise, D. C., B. D. Berger, and L. Stein (1973). Evidence of a-noradrenergic reward receptors and serotonergic punishment receptors in the rat brain. *Biol. Psychiat.* 6:3–21.

Wise, D. C., and L. Stein (1969). Facilitation of brain self-stimulation by central administration of norepinephrine. *Science* 163(3864):299–301.

Witkin, H. A., D. R. Goodenough, and S. A. Karp (1967). Stability of cognitive style from childhood to young adulthood. *J. pers. soc. Psychol.* 7:291–300.

Wolfe, J. B. (1936). Effectiveness of token-rewards for chimpanzees. *Comp. Psychol. Monogr.* 12:(60).

Wolman, B. B. (1965). Family dynamics and schizophrenia. *J. Health and Human Behav.* 6:163–9.

Wolpe, J. (1958). *Psychotherapy by Reciprocal Inhibition.* Stanford, Calif.: Stanford University Press.

Wolpe, J. (1969). *The Practice of Behavior Therapy.* London: Pergamon.

Wolpe, J. (1973). *The Practice of Behavior Therapy* 2nd ed. New York: Pergamon.

Wolpe, J., and A. A. Lazarus (1966). *Behavior Therapy Techniques.* New York: Pergamon.

Wortis, J. (ed.) (1960). *Recent Advances in Biological Psychiatry.* New York: Grune and Stratton.

Wrightsman, L. S. (1960). Effects of waiting with others on changes in level of felt anxiety. *J. abnorm. soc. Psychol.* 61:216–22.

Yarrow, L. J., J. L. Rubenstein, F. A. Pedersen, and J. J. Jankowski (1972). Dimensions of early stimulation and their differential effects on infant development. *Merrill-Palmer Quart.* 18:205–18.

Yates, A. J. (1970). *Behavior Therapy.* New York: Wiley.

Zajonc, R. B. (1965). Social facilitation. *Science* 149:269–74.

Zajonc, R. B. (1968). Attitudinal effects of mere exposure. *J. pers. soc. Psychol.* 9:1–29.

Zajonc, R. B., A. Heingartner, and E. M. Herman (1969). Social enhancement and impairment of performance in the cockroach. *J. pers. soc. Psychol.* 13:83–92.

Zajonc, R. B., R. J. Wolosin, and M. A. Wolosin (1972). Group risk-taking under various group decision schemes. *J. exp. soc. Psychol.* 8:16–30.

Zanna, M. P., G. R. Goethals, and J. F. Hill (1975). Evaluating a sex-related ability: social comparison with similar others and standard setters. *J. exp. soc. Psychol.* 11:86–93.

Zax, M., and G. Stricker (1963). *Patterns of Psychopathology.* New York: Macmillan.

Zegans, L. S., J. C. Pollard, and D. Brown (1967). The effects of LSD-25 on creativity and tolerance to regression. *Arch. gen. Psychiat.* 16:748.

Zelazo, P. R., N. A. Zelazo, and S. Kolb (1972). "Walking" in the newborn. *Science* 176:314–5.

Zillmann, D. (1971). Excitation transfer in communication-mediated aggressive behavior. *J. exp. soc. Psychol.* 7:419–34.

Zillmann, D., A. H. Katcher, and B. Milavsky (1972). Excitation transfer from physical exercise to subsequent aggressive behavior. *J. exp. soc. Psychol.* 8:247–59.

Zimbardo, P. G., C. Rapaport, and J. Baron (1969). Pain control by hypnotic induction of motivational states. In P. Zimbardo (ed.). *The Cognitive Control of Motivation.* Glenview, Ill.: Scott, Foresman.

Zinberg, N. E. (1972). Against hysteria. *Int. J. Psychiat.* 10:69–73.

Continued from page iv

maturity for height, weight, height velocity, and weight velocity: British children 1965. *Archives Childhood* 41:454–71. Reprinted by permission. **14.6** Reproduced by permission from the Minnesota Multiphasic Personality Inventory. Copyright 1943, renewed 1970 by the University of Minnesota. Published by The Psychological Corporation, New York, N.Y. All rights reserved. **B17.1** Adapted from Schachter, S. H. (1959). *The Psychology of Affiliation.* Stanford, Calif.: Stanford University Press with the permission of the publishers, Stanford University Press. © 1959 by the Board of Trustees of the Leland Stanford Junior University. **17.4** Deutsch, M., and R. M. Krauss (1960). The effect of threat on interpersonal bargaining. *J. abnorm soc. Psychol.* 61:181–9. Copyright 1960 by the American Psychological Association. Reprinted by permission. **18.5** Doob, A. N., J. M. Carlsmith, J. L. Freedman, T. K. Landauer, and S. Tom, Jr. (1969). Effect of initial selling price on subsequent sales. *J. pers. soc. Psychol.* 11:345–50. Copyright 1969 by the American Psychological Association. Reprinted by permission. **B19.1** Bornstein, M., and H. Bornstein, (1967). The pace of life. *The New York Times Sunday Supplement*, February 29, 1976. © 1976 by The New York Times Company. Reprinted by permission. **19.7** Calhoun, J. B. (1962). Population density and social pathology. *Sci. Amer.* 206:139–48. Copyright © 1962 by Scientific American, Inc. All rights reserved.

Tables

5.2 Brown, R., and C. Fraser (1963). The acquisition of syntax. In Charles N. Cofer and Barbara Musgrave (eds.), *Verbal Behavior and Learning: Problems and Processes.* New York: McGraw-Hill, pp. 158–201. Used with permission of McGraw-Hill Book Company. **7.2** Wechsler Adult Intelligence Scale Manual. Copyright © 1955 by The Psychological Corporation, New York, N.Y. All rights reserved.

Cases

462 From Davidoff, L. L. (1976). *Introduction to Psychology.* New York: McGraw-Hill. Copyright 1976 McGraw-Hill Book Company. Used with permission of McGraw-Hill. **465** From Zax, M., and G. Stricker (1963). *Patterns of Psychopathology.* New York: Macmillan. Copyright © 1963 by Macmillan Publishing Company, Inc. Reprinted with permission. **466** From Hare, R. D. *Psychopathy: Theory and Research.* New York: Wiley. Reprinted with permission of John Wiley & Sons. **472** From Zax, M., and G. Stricker (1963). *Patterns of Psychopathology.* New York: Macmillan. Copyright © 1963 by Macmillan Publishing Company, Inc. Reprinted with permission. **477** From Davidoff, L. L. (1976). *Introduction to Psychology.* New York: McGraw-Hill. Copyright 1976 McGraw-Hill Book Company. Used with permission of McGraw-Hill. **479** From Eberhardy, F. (1967). The view from "the couch." *J. Child Psychol. Psychiat.* 8:257–63. Reprinted by permission of Pergamon Press, Inc. **514** From Rogers, C. (1967). A silent young man. In C. Rogers (ed.), *The Therapeutic Relationship and Its Impact.* Madison: University of Wisconsin Press. Used by permission of the University of Wisconsin Press and the Tape Library of the American Academy of Psychotherapists. **517** Abridged from Chapter 15 of *Dibs: In Search of Self* by Virginia M. Axline. Copyright © 1964 by Virginia M. Axline. Reprinted by permission of Houghton Mifflin Company.

Photos

6 (top) Mimi Forsyth/Montmeyer; (bottom) Sybil Shelton/Montmeyer 9 Joel Stern 39 Bill Ray/Time-Life Picture Agency © Time Inc. 41 (top) Elliott Erwitt/© Magnum Photos, Inc.; (bottom) The Bettmann Archive, Inc. 42 Philip Jon Bailey 43 Philip Jon Bailey 44 (left) Exploratorium; (right) Exploratorium 45 (left) Marshall Henrichs; (right) Marshall Henrichs 47 (right) Escher Foundation 51 Albert Fenn/Time-Life Picture Agency © Time Inc. 71 Yerkes Regional Primate Research Center of Emory University 75 Peter Vandermark 80 The Boston Globe 85 UPI 86 Albert Bandura 98 (left) Peter Vandermark; (right) Pfizer, Inc. 102 Peter Southwick/Stock, Boston 108 Patricia Hollander Gross/Stock, Boston 128 Bob Peterson/Time-Life Picture Agency © Time Inc. 135 The Boston Globe 148 Ann Kaufman/Stock, Boston 151 Dr. R. A. Gardner, Dr. B. T. Gardner 152 Yerkes Regional Primate Research Center of Emory University 156 William Apple 157 (top) Ken Heyman; (bottom) Robert M. Krauss 165 (top) Peter Vandermark; (middle) Courtesy Wadsworth Atheneum, Hartford; (bottom) The Bettman Archive, Inc. 178 Yerkes Regional Primate Center of Emory University 179 Marshall Henrichs 180 American Antiquarian Society 183 Nancy Pike 188 Floyd Jillson 196 The Bettmann Archive, Inc. 206 Harvard University News Office 209 (left and right) Peter Vandermark 214 AP photos 232 Reproduced with permission of the Literary Executors of Wilder Penfield from Penfield (1958) 245 Leonard Lessin/Photo Researchers 254 Foto Cassin 256 Mark Godfrey/Magnum Photos, Inc. 260 Dr. Neal E. Miller 268 Charles Harbutt/Magnum Photos, Inc. 270 H. F. Harlow, University of Wisconsin Primate Laboratory 277 Ken Heyman 284 The Alvin Ailey City Center Dance Company 287 Dr. José M. R. Delgado 301 Dr. Neal E. Miller 302 The Bettmann Archive, Inc. 304 (bottom) Arthur Tress 307 Lawrence (Mass.) Eagle-Tribune/Photo by Marcia Brockelman 320 News and Publication Service, Stanford University 322 Arthur Tress 329 Julian Wasser/Time Magazine © Time Inc. 382 News and Publication Service, Stanford University 335 (top) Arthur Tress; (right) Ryokain Mandara, Japanese Ashikoga Period, Bigelow Collection 11.7119/Courtesy Museum of Fine Arts, Boston 341 Arthur Tress 343 John Dominis/Time-Life Picture Agency © Time Inc. 349 Lonnie Schlein/NYT Pictures 355 Thomas McAvoy/Life Magazine © Time Inc. 356 Yves de Braine/Black Star 359 (top and bottom) Peter Vandermark 365 University of Wisconsin Primate Laboratory 371 Wide World Photos, Inc. 374 The Boston Globe 382 UPI 385 The Boston Globe 387 Cary Wolinsky/Stock, Boston 389 (top and bottom) UPI 391 (left) Peeter R. Hughes; (right) News and Publications Service, Stanford University 395 Jean-Claude LeJeune/Stock, Boston 398 Peter Vilms/Jeroboam 399 Ken Heyman 414 Wide World Photos 425 Sigmund Freud Copyrights, Ltd. 433 The Bettmann Archive, Inc. 440 (top) Arthur Lavine/Chase Manhattan Bank; (bottom) Ken Heyman 446 Arthur Tress 450 Arthur Tress 458 The Boston Globe 467 Museum of Modern Art/Film Stills Archive 471 John R. Freeman and Co., Ltd. 475 The Washington Post 476 From Silvano Arieti, *Interpretation of Schizophrenia;* Basic Books, 1974. 486 Lorstan Studios 487 (left) Walter Reed Army Institute of Research 494 (top) Museo del Prado; (bottom) The Bettmann Archive, Inc. 497 Murray Suid 507 Don Hogan Charles/NYT Pictures 508 Curt Gunther/Camera 5 513 (left) David Campbell/courtesy Rolf Institute; (right) Bonnie Freer/Photo Trends 514 John T. Wood 518 Alex Webb/Magnum Photos, Inc. 530 Scala New York/Florence 532 Ruth Orkin 540 News and Publications Service, Stanford University 546 Arnold Newman 548 Henri Dauman/Magnum Photos, Inc. 555 UPI 556 Courtesy of Philip G. Zimbardo, Inc. 557 The Bettmann Archive, Inc. 560 Dr. Stanley Milgram 563 Children, Inc. 565 Gary Sherman 567 Wide World Photos, Inc. 574 The American Cancer Society 575 (left) CBS; (right) UPI 584 Paul Fusco 597 Anthony Wolff 602 Marshall Henrichs 604 Peter Vandermark/Stock, Boston 606 Flip Schulke/Black Star 607 William Marlin 608 Architectural Photography/Richard W. Payne Architect 610 (top) Robert M. Krauss

Glossary

Absolute threshold The intensity or frequency at which a stimulus can be reliably perceived or responded to.

Action potential Electrical changes accompanying an impulse along a neuron, produced when neuron is sufficiently stimulated.

Activation theory A theory of emotions that states that the essence of emotion is arousal, and that there is little if any difference among emotional states.

Adaptation Change in the sensitivity of a sense organ. When the organ has been stimulated, sensitivity decreases; when it has not been stimulated, sensitivity increases.

Adaptation level A level of stimulation or arousal to which an organism grows accustomed and then responds to changes or deviations from this level.

Addiction Physiological dependence on a drug so that absence of the drug produces physical symptoms such as sweating or more serious effects.

Adrenal glands Endocrine glands that secrete the hormones epinephrine and norepinephrine, which by a complex mechanism produce the response we know as fear.

Affiliation Association with others. There appears to be universal tendency among human beings to affiliate with other human beings.

Afterimage The sensory image that remains when external stimulation is withdrawn; for example, the circle of light one sees after staring at a bright light.

Age regression In hypnosis, a phenomenon whereby people act as if they are much younger than they are, sometimes apparently having memories from their actual childhood.

Aggression Behavior intended to hurt another person.

All-or-none rule A law in the activation of neurons that states that a neuron either does fire and produce an action potential or it does not—there is no partial degree of firing.

Alpha rhythm One of the wave forms found in EEG's of the brain. A high level seems to be associated with calm and detached feelings.

Altruism Cooperative, helping behavior when nothing is expected in return; doing good for its own reward.

Ambivalence Positive and negative feelings toward the same object at the same time.

Anal stage The second of Freud's psychosexual stages of development, characterized by concern with the control of one's bodily functions.

Antidepressants Any of a group of drugs, such as lithium, that reduce manic symptoms and relieve depression, and are therefore useful in the treatment of psychopathology.

Anxiety In Freudian theory, a particular kind of discomfort, nervousness, and psychological pain, without a real object or logical cause, arising from conflicts between the id and the superego.

Anxiety neurosis A form of neurosis characterized by free floating anxiety and sometimes accompanied by physical symptoms such as shortness of breath, dizziness, pounding of the heart, nausea, and fainting.

Approach-avoidance conflict The simultaneous existence of both positive and negative motives produced by the same stimulus.

Ascending reticular activating systems (ARAS) A structure in the brain stem, forming the central core of the medulla, pons, and midbrain, that determines the particular level of arousal experienced at any moment of time.

Association theory A theory of concept formation as a more or less random process of discrimination learning, in which we learn the essential elements of a stimulus or class of stimuli through the selective strengthening of associations common to those stimuli.

Attachment The combination of positive feelings, dependence, trust, and the desire to be physically close, developed because of innate or intrinsic tendencies in infants, that characterizes a child's relationship with the parent.

Attitude A combination of cognitions (knowledge) about an object and affect (emotions) toward it.

Attribution theory A theory dealing with the process by which individuals decide what motivated a particular act or behavior.

Authoritarianism An alleged personality trait characterized by conventional thinking, rigidity, aggressiveness toward those who deviate from the norms, a preoccupation with power, and an overall cynicism about human nature.

Autism A form of schizophrenia, usually referred to as infantile autism, that occurs early in life and is characterized by almost total lack of contact with or response to other people.

Autokinetic phenomenon The illusion of erratic movement of a light that occurs when the light is presented in a totally dark room.

Autonomic nervous system That part of the peripheral nervous system that controls the internal functions and organs of the body. *See also* Sympathetic nervous system, Parasympathetic nervous system, and Somatic nervous system.

Aversive conditioning A technique used in behavior therapy in which the patient is punished for a maladaptive behavior until he or she no longer performs the behavior.

Avoidance training Teaching an animal to perform an act by presenting an unpleasant stimulus that can be terminated by that act. The animal is allowed to prevent the unpleasant stimulus from occurring by performing the act before a set time or in response to a warning signal.

Axon That part of the neuron that transmits information to other neurons or to an effector such as a muscle or gland.

Balance model A theory dealing with attitudes toward other people that says that your likes and dislikes should be similar to those of someone you like and dissimilar to those of someone you dislike; imbalance will lead to attitude change about either the person or the object involved.

Barbiturates A class of highly addictive drugs with strong sedative effects.

Basilar membrane Part of the cochlea in the inner ear. The vibration of the membrane is important in hearing.

Behavior genetics The study of the genetic inheritance of traits affecting behavior.

Behavior modification *See* Behavior therapy.

Behavior therapy A technique of psychotherapy based on the theory that since maladaptive behaviors are learned, they can be unlearned by means of teaching methods based on learning theory and research.

Behavioral sink A condition appearing in animals who have been subjected to crowding, characterized by aimless milling about and indiscriminate aggression and sexuality.

Behaviorism An approach to psychology that focuses on observable (external) activities of an organism, especially learning. Also called stimulus response (SR) psychology.

Binocular cues Cues used in judging depth and distance that involve the use of two eyes, such as convergence and retinal disparity.

Biofeedback A procedure for enabling people to control the alpha rhythms of their brain for the purpose of achieving a relaxed state.

Brainwashing The use of coercive persuasion techniques.

Brightness The psychological perception of the intensity of light.

Broca's speech area An area in the left hemisphere of the brain that plays a major role in controlling speech.

Bystander intervention The spontaneous helping of a stranger who is in distress. When the situation is ambiguous, the presence of others reduces the likelihood of intervention.

Catharsis The reduction or elimination of the aggression drive—and therefore aggressive behavior—through the expression of that aggression.

Central nervous system That part of the nervous system that includes the spinal cord and the brain. *See also* Peripheral nervous system.

Cerebral cortex The highest level of the brain. It controls perception, thought, speech, memory, and all of the most complex cognitive processes.

Chemical therapy (chemotherapy) The use of drugs and chemicals, such as tranquilizers and antidepressants, in the treatment of mental illness.

Chlorpromazine The most important antipsychotic drug; one of the major tranquilizers.

Chromosomes Strands of specialized chemicals in the nucleus of the cell that along their length carry the genes that determine the characteristics passed from one generation to another. Humans have twenty-three pairs (forty-six chromosomes in all).

Chunking Combining information into larger units to make memory easier (for example, the letters t, c, a combined into one chunk—"cat").

Circadian rhythms Daily patterns or cycles of the bodily processes of most animals. More active at certain times of the day than others, they control our daily rhythms of sleeping, walking, eating, and so on.

Classical conditioning The learning of a new response to a stimulus, caused by pairing a conditioned stimulus (CS), which initially produces no response, with an unconditioned stimulus (US), which automatically produces the unconditioned response (UR). Eventually the CS alone produces the CR, which is similar or identical to the UR.

Client-centered therapy *See* Person-centered therapy.

Clinical psychologist A psychologist, usually with a Ph.D. in psychology but not generally a physician, who has taken part in a clinical internship that consists of practical training in a treatment center.

Clinical psychology The field of psychology devoted to treatment, testing, and research dealing with mental disturbance.

Cochlea A part of the inner ear, shaped like a snail, that is involved in hearing.

Coefficient of correlation A statement of the relationship between two variables. It ranges from -1.0 to $+1.0$, a perfectly negative to perfectly positive relationship.

Cognitions A term referring to thoughts, beliefs, connections among events, memories, expectations, and other mental activity.

Cognitive approach An approach to psychology that emphasizes the role of thought in determining behavior.

Cognitive consistency theory The theory that people tend to seek agreement or balance among their cognitions, feelings, and behavior, and that they will do what they can to minimize conflict among the various elements.

Cognitive learning The processes by which we acquire and recall beliefs, connections among events, expectations, and information in general.

Collective unconscious In Jungian theory, the unconscious memories and beliefs common to all humanity. Usually inaccessible to the conscious or waking mind, it appears in our dreams and gives us insight and knowledge we cannot get in any other way.

Color constancy The perception of familiar objects as being of consistent color despite different intensities of the light falling on them.

Complementarity The tendency to like someone with very different characteristics from oneself because those traits complement and satisfy certain needs in oneself.

Complementary colors Colors opposite each other on the color spectrum;

when mixed, they will cancel and produce gray.

Compliance Doing what you are asked to do, especially if you would rather not perform the behavior.

Computer simulation A computer program designed to make the computer approximate human thought processes or any other system.

Computer-assisted instruction (CAI) Using a computer to help teach various subjects. Especially useful in early grades.

Concept A notion or idea, generalized from particular instances, that identifies the similarities among different stimuli or situations and enables us to discriminate this class of stimuli from another; it may be simple or complex, concrete or theoretical.

Concept formation The process of learning that certain objects belong to the same group and then learning to discriminate one class of objects from another.

Concrete operations A developmental stage between ages seven and eleven when children begin to understand the relationships among numbers and also arithmetic, to form concepts, to master the principle of conservation, to classify objects into hierarchies, and to produce an ordered series in terms of size or number.

Conditioned response (CR) In classical conditioning, a learned, or conditioned, response—similar or identical to the unconditioned response—to a conditioned stimulus.

Conditioned stimulus (CS) In classical conditioning, a stimulus that, when paired often enough with an unconditioned stimulus, produces a conditioned response similar or identical to the unconditioned response.

Cones Receptors for vision in the retina, concentrated in the fovea, and requiring considerable light to respond. Color vision depends on them. *See also* Rods.

Conformity The tendency to do what others do simply because they do it.

Conjunctive concept A concept that demands that several characteristics be present for an object or stimulus to fit a particular class. *See also* Disjunctive concept.

Conservation The principle that a given quantity, weight, or volume of a substance remains the same regardless of its shape or configuration.

Conservative focusing A technique in problem solving or concept formation in which we compare a positive instance of the concept with a similar but negative instance of the concept in order to identify the crucial elements.

Consolidation A process by which memories are made permanent or relatively permanent; may involve chemical changes in the brain.

Constitutional theories of personality Theories of personality that suggest that personality is determined in large part by the biological constitution of the individual. Particular theories concentrate on the role of physique and reactivity in the brain.

Contiguity In cognitive learning, the law that once stimuli have appeared together, an association is formed and one stimulus will make us think of the other.

Contrast effect Perception of the same stimulus differently when it is contrasted with other stimuli; for example, a white circle appears lighter against a black background than against a white background.

Convergence The angle at which the images seen by the left eye and the right eye fuse; an important binocular cue for judging distance.

Convergent thinking The ability to solve problems, learn material, remember, and think logically; generally refers to so-called intellectual abilities rather than creativity. *See also* Divergent thinking.

Conversion neurosis *See* Hysterical neurosis.

Corpus callosum A large bundle of axons that connects the two hemispheres of the cerebral cortex and transmits information from one to the other. *See also* Split-brain phenomenon.

Correlation In statistics, the relationship between two sets of scores. In particular, a measure of whether scores in one set go up when those in the other do, go down, or are not related.

Correlational research A research method that seeks to establish associations among variables. When two factors vary together (both increasing or one increasing when the other decreases), we say they are correlated.

Creativity The ability to perceive the world, interpret experiences, and solve problems in new and original ways.

Cretinism A form of mental retardation caused by a thyroid gland deficiency.

Criterion A standard on which a judgment can be based; some trustworthy measure against which to judge the validity of a test.

Critical period A crucial, finite stage in the development process during which a behavior such as imprinting must appear if it is to develop normally.

Critical ratio In inferential statistics, the difference between the means of two samples, or a correlation coefficient divided by the standard error.

Crowding A term used to refer to an individual's feeling or emotion that he or she does not have enough space, is cramped, has no privacy, or is being intruded upon. Also used to refer to the physical amount of space available per person, usually called population density.

Deep structure In transformational grammar, the underlying or intended meaning of a sentence, as opposed to surface structure, which is simply the sequence and form of the morphemes.

Defense mechanism Various techniques, including denial, repression, projection, displacement, reaction formation, and rationalization and intellectualization, that are specifically designed to reduce or avoid anxiety by distorting the source of the conflict or obscuring the conflict entirely.

Deindividuation The tendency of people in a group to submerge their own personalities in the group and as a result feel less responsible for their own behavior.

Delta waves The large, slow brain waves, recorded by an EEG, that characterize mental activity in Stage 4 of sleep.

Delusion Unrealistic beliefs characteristic of schizophrenia and paranoia, often consisting of individuals thinking they are famous people or that they are being persecuted and attacked.

Dendrite An area of the neuron, consisting of several nerve fibers, that receives information from other neurons.

Denial A defense mechanism in which the individual seeks to reduce anxiety by pretending that the source of the anxiety does not exist.

Density The amount of space available per person; sometimes referred to as the degree of crowding.

Deoxyribonucleic acid (DNA) A system of molecules that is largely responsible for genetic inheritance and therefore determines the makeup of the entire organism.

Depressant Any of a large group of drugs that reduce the activity of the central nervous system by slowing down reactions, reducing the strength of responses, and producing drowsiness, sleep, or even death depending on dosage. *See also* Stimulant.

Depression A mental state characterized by sadness, low self-esteem, and negative feelings about the world. Its extreme form is manic-depressive psychosis.

Depth perception Perception of the distance of an object from the observer.

Descriptive statistics The summarizing and simplifying of a number of separate bits of data into a form that is easy to deal with and understand.

Developmental psychology A broad area of psychology that focuses on behavioral changes that occur during the process of maturation. Some of the major developmental topics are language development, thinking, personality, and social behavior.

Difference threshold The point at which a person can reliably distinguish between two stimuli.

Differential reinforcement A learning technique in which responses to one stimulus, called the discriminative stimulus, are reinforced while responses to another are not, until the subject can distinguish between the two stimuli.

Discrimination The ability, essential to the learning process, to distinguish among stimuli and to give the appropriate response to each.

Discriminative stimulus A stimulus or event that signals that reinforcement will occur if the appropriate response is made.

Disjunctive concept A concept defined in terms of one *or* another characteristic. *See also* Conjunctive concept.

Displacement The tendency to find a substitute object for aggression if the source is inappropriate or unavailable for aggression. Also, a defense mechanism in which the individual seeks to reduce anxiety by directing his or her feelings or actions not toward their primary object but toward some substitute.

Distributed practice *See* Spaced practice.

Divergent thinking The ability to form unusual associations, construct original arguments, and reach new conclusions, as measured by creativity tests. *See also* Convergent thinking.

Dominant gene A gene whose characteristic will be expressed even if the other member of the gene pair is different. *See also* Recessive gene.

Down's syndrome A form of mental retardation caused by a chromosome deficiency. Sometimes called Mongolism because of the characteristic facial features that accompany it.

Drive A state of arousal produced by physiological needs. More generally, any aroused state.

Drive-reduction theory A theory of reinforcement and motivation that states that all arousal is unpleasant, that we seek to reduce the arousal, and that this reduction is positively reinforcing.

Eardrum A membrane between the outer and middle ears. Its vibration in response to sound waves is the first step in the process of hearing.

Ectomorph One of three body types designated by Sheldon, characterized by a thin, lightly muscled, slim build. *See also* Endomorph, Mesomorph.

Effector In the nervous system, those parts of the body, such as the muscles and glands, that cause responses.

Ego In Freudian theory, the individual's aware, conscious, deliberately functioning mind; it follows the reality principle, is by and large logical, and is able to delay gratification in order to achieve greater satisfaction later. *See also* Id, Superego.

Ego ideal In Freudian theory, the image of ourself that we would like to achieve; part of the superego.

Ego psychology A major trend in neo-Freudian psychoanalytic thinking that emphasizes how the ego—the conscious process of thinking, planning, perceiving, and problem-solving—deals with the conflicts it faces, rather than emphasizing the conflicts themselves.

Eidetic imagery The ability to look briefly at a picture or page of type and retain a clear image of it in the mind; sometimes called photographic memory.

Electroconvulsive shock (ECS) A procedure used to treat severe depression in which a powerful electric current is passed through a person's head, producing a convulsion.

Electroencephalograph (EGG) A technique for measuring and recording activity in the brain.

Emotion An internal state that involves either physiological arousal or depression and is composed of either positive or negative feelings.

Encounter group A type of group therapy in which major emphasis is an open expression of feelings. Encounter groups vary greatly in size, focus, type of leader, and even purpose.

Endocrine system A system composed of ductless glands that secrete hormones carrying information throughout the body; it works in conjunction with the nervous system, which operates much faster but cannot affect as many cells simultaneously.

Endomorph One of three body types designated by Sheldon, characterized by a soft, rounded, unmuscled body. *See also* Mesomorph, Ectomorph.

Engram A hypothetical structure in the brain constituting a memory. *See also* Memory trace.

Environmental psychology A recent field of psychology that studies the relationship between people and their environment.

Equity *See* Social justice.

Escape training Teaching a response by presenting an unpleasant stimulus that is terminated when the desired response is made. The termination reinforces the response. Also called negative reinforcement.

Estrogen The "female" sex hormone. Although females have a much higher level of estrogen, it is also present in men.

Estrus The cyclical period of sexual receptivity and fertility in most female mammals. Human females do not have estrus periods.

Ethologist A scientist who studies the behavior of animals in natural settings, relying largely on observational research.

Evolution The process by which the average genetic composition of a group of animals changes over time.

Excitatory chemical In the nervous system, a chemical released at the synapse by the axon terminal that will activate the second cell. *See also* Inhibitory chemical.

Experimental design A research method that seeks to establish a causative relationship between two variables. Conditions are controlled so that extraneous variables do not affect the results.

Experimental psychology A broad area of psychology that concentrates on discovering rules and principles of learning, memory, concept formation, problem solving, motivation, and emotions. Psycholinguistics is sometimes also included.

Extinction In classical conditioning, the disappearance of a conditioned response after the conditioned stimulus is presented a number of times without the reinforcement of the unconditioned stimulus. In operant conditioning, the disappearance of the learned response when reinforcement is withheld. Also refers to the procedure of omitting the unconditioned stimulus or reinforcement.

Extrasensory perception (ESP) A controversial class of supernormal powers that supposedly enable us to read other people's minds or predict the future.

Figure-ground In perception, a rule of organization in which part of the visual field (figure) is seen as standing out against a background (ground).

Fixation In Freudian theory, arrested progress at one of the psychosexual steps of development, as a result of which the individual will always have problems relating to the original conflict arising at that stage.

Flow chart   A chart outlining all of the steps and choices involved in the working out of a problem; often translated into computer language.

Foot-in-the-door technique   The technique of starting with a small request in order to get people to comply with a much larger request.

Forebrain   That portion of the brain, consisting of the thalamus, hypothalamus, and cerebral cortex, that controls our higher mental processes, such as language, problem solving, and memory, as well as our emotions and many of our motivations.

Formal operations   The last stage of cognitive development, occurring between the ages of eleven and fifteen and marking the development of abstract thought, higher-level conceptualization, the systematic forming and testing of hypotheses, and the development of formal, logical reasoning.

Fovea   A recessed portion of the retina where millions of cones are concentrated.

Fraternal twins   Twins who developed from separate eggs and are no more alike genetically than ordinary siblings. Also called dizygotic (DZ) twins.

Free association   A method used in psychoanalytic psychotherapy in which the patient is encouraged to say anything that comes to mind on the theory that this will reveal unconscious conflicts.

Free floating anxiety   A form of extreme neurotic anxiety that is entirely unfocused and has no connection with particular objects or situations.

Frequency theory   A theory of hearing that states that our ability to hear pitch is determined by the frequency of impulses within the auditory nerve. *See also* Place theory, Volley theory.

Freudian slip   In Freudian theory, a slip of the tongue that actually is an expression of our unconscious feelings.

Frustration-aggression hypothesis   The principle of behavior that states that preventing someone from reaching a goal will tend to arouse aggressive feelings in that person.

Functional fixedness   The tendency to try to apply problem-solving techniques that have been successful in the past to all similar problems regardless of whether thay are appropriate; rigid thinking.

Gene   The basic unit controlling heredity. Composed of DNA, it controls the exact chemical nature of the particular proteins within a cell, thus controlling how the cell functions. *See also* Chromosomes.

Generalization gradient   Responses learned to one stimulus are also made to other, similar stimuli, but the less similar, the less likely the response is to occur. The generalization gradient describes this relationship, being highest for the original stimulus and declining as stimuli are less similar.

Gestalt psychology   A school of psychology that stresses the tendency to perceive the world in terms of whole structures rather than separate pieces; from the German word meaning "shape" or "whole."

Gradients of texture   In the texture of objects or the visual field, variations that affect perception of distance; finer textures appear to be farther away and coarser ones closer.

Grammar   The set of rules that govern construction and allow us to understand the meaning of a sentence.

Group therapy   A therapeutic technique based on the assumption that many of people's problems involve relationships with other people and that discussing one's problems with other people can produce the same positive effects as individual therapy.

Hallucinogen   Any of a group of drugs that alter the perceptions, thoughts, and feelings of the people who use them.

Heredity   The transmission of traits from parents to offspring and from previous to future generations.

Heuristics   Problem-solving strategies, including focusing, scanning, and exercising preferences over certain types of material, that enable us to solve problems and form concepts more easily than by random processes.

Hindbrain   That portion of the brain, consisting of the medulla, the pons, and the cerebellum, that controls those bodily activities that are largely automatic, such as heart rate, breathing, nausea, and so on.

Homeostatic theory   A theory of motivation that states that motivation is produced by the natural tendency of the body to maintain a constant level. Any deviation from this level motivates individuals to take actions that will return them to the optimal level.

Homosexuality   Sexual preference by either a man or a woman for people of the same sex.

Hormone   Chemicals that are manufactured and secreted into the bloodstream by the endocrine glands and produce wide-ranging physical and behavioral effects.

Humanistic psychology   An approach to psychology that emphasizes the individual as a unique person rather than merely as a representative of the species; according to humanists, people are free to act and must take responsibility for their actions.

Humanistic therapy   Any one of a group of therapeutic techniques based on the assumption that people have within them the ability to solve their problems and to grow, and that therapists must be especially careful not to impose their standards on patients.

Hypnosis   A state of consciousness produced by entrusting oneself to another person, and characterized by heightened suggestibility, acceptance of distortion, selective attention, and similar symptoms.

Hypothalamus A region of the fore-brain just below the thalamus that plays a role in controlling eating, aggression, sexuality, and emotionality in general. Part of the limbic system.

Hypothesis-testing theory A theory that concept formation and problem solving involve a systematic process of focusing on a specific characteristic of a stimulus or group of stimuli and then testing to see if the characteristic is essential to that concept.

Hysterical neurosis The most dramatic form of neurosis, also known as conversion neurosis, in which the individual develops an actual physical disability for no apparent physical reason.

Id In Freudian theory, the basic source of energy and motivations; it is composed of our primitive, innate physiological needs collected together and operates according to the pleasure principle—with seeking maximum satisfaction of our needs and desires. The most important of these needs make up the libido, which consists of the positive, sexual, loving impulses, and thanatos, which includes destructive, aggressive impulses. *See also* Ego, Superego.

Identical twins Twins who developed from the same egg and therefore have identical genes. Also called monozygotic (MZ) twins.

Identification The strong tendency for children to imitate the behavior, mannerisms, and beliefs of significant adults in their lives.

Identity crisis A crisis involving a questioning of one's role in one's life, values, goals, and even who one is. Typical during adolescence but can occur at other times also.

Idiot-savant A mentally retarded or defective individual who exhibits extraordinary skill or ability in one particular area, typically mathematical calculation.

Imagery A technique of learning and memorization that involves the visualization in one's mind of the material to be learned.

Imitation Behavior that copies the behavior of another; a major process by which learning occurs.

Imprinting The rapid development of a response to a stimulus, during a brief period of an animal's life. Once developed, the response is usually very resistant to change. Especially common among birds.

Inappropriate affect The expression of emotion inappropriate to the situation; a common symptom of schizophrenia.

Incentive theory A theory of motivation that states that motives are produced by the interaction between the internal state and the external situation; for example, a juicy steak may be motivating if you are hungry, but would not be particularly motivating if you are very thirsty.

Inferential statistics Mathematical procedures by which it is possible to draw conclusions from a body of data; for example, to decide if two means or correlations are different from each other.

Inflection That aspect of grammar involving changes in the form of words to indicate certain meanings, such as number, tense, case, gender.

Information processing A general approach to many areas of psychology—especially perception, concept formation, and problem solving—that views the phenomena in terms of interpreting and responding to information.

Inhibitory chemical In the nervous system, a chemical released at the synapse by the axon terminal that will prevent the second cell from being activated. *See also* Excitatory chemical.

Innate characteristics Inherited features of an organism that affect its behavior, such as types of sense organs and size limitations.

Insight The sudden discovery of the essential elements necessary in the solution of a problem; a critical phenomenon in human problem-solving ability.

Instincts Innate patterns of behavior, usually triggered by a particular stimulus or situation, but not requiring learning or experience in order to appear.

Intellectualization A defense mechanism in which the individual puts an anxiety-arousing or conflict-producing situation entirely into intellectual terms and ignores or avoids the emotions that ordinarily go with the situation.

Intelligence Intellectual ability; the ability to solve problems, master concepts, and deal rationally with the environment.

Intelligence quotient (IQ) A widely used measurement of intelligence, calculated by dividing mental age by chronological age and multiplying by one hundred. Also obtained directly from scores on many intelligence tests.

Intensification effect The tendency for the usual responses to any social situation to be intensified by high-density conditions.

Interference In our memory system, the substitution of one item for another, or the confusion of one item with another, tending to weaken or even remove the memory of the original item. A major cause of forgetting. *See also* Proactive interference, Retroactive interference.

Interpretation In psychoanalytic therapy, suggestion by the therapist of the meaning or explanation of certain problems, behaviors, or acts of resistance by the patient in order to help the patient.

Introversion-extroversion One of three personality dimensions in Eysenck's theory, supposedly produced by differences in neural reactivity.

Involutional melancholia A depressive reaction characterized by loss of interest in life and thoughts of suicide. Typically occurs after age forty, around menopause in women or somewhat later in men. May be caused in part by hormonal changes in the body.

James-Lange theory A theory of emotions that states that emotions are caused and preceded by physiological reactions, and that emotions are, in fact, our awareness of these physiological reactions.

Just noticeable difference (j.n.d.) The point at which the difference between two stimuli (for example, light bulbs of different intensity) is just barely noticeable.

Kinesthetic sense The sense that receives sensory data from the muscles and tells us our body's position in space and its movement. *See also* Proprioceptive sense.

Kleptomania A condition in which a person constantly steals objects that he or she does not need yet does not sell for gain. More common among women than men.

Latent content In Freudian theory, those aspects of our dreams that represent our unconscious impulses and conflicts, usually in disguised form; the true meaning of a dream. *See also* Manifest content.

Latent learning Learning that does not affect behavior until the appropriate situation occurs.

Law of contiguity *See* Contiguity

Lens The part of the eye that focuses light.

Lesion Cut or other damage to a part of the body, usually in the nervous system, especially the brain.

Libido That part of the id consisting of the positive, sexual, loving impulses.

Light adaptation The process by which the visual system, especially the cones in the retina, changes in sensitivity in the presence of strong light so that it can deal with higher levels of light energy.

Limbic system A region of the brain, lying beneath the cortex and surrounding the thalamus, and usually thought to involve the hypothalamus, hippocampus, and amygdala. It is significant in many activities including emotions, learning, and memory, and includes reward centers that can be activiated by electrical stimulation.

Linear perspective A monocular cue of depth perception in which equally spaced objects appear closer together as they become more distant.

Lithium A chemical element that has been found to be effective in the treatment of manic-depressive psychosis.

Long-term memory In the memory system, information that becomes consolidated and can remain indefinitely—lasting memory. *See also* Short-term memory.

Loudness Magnitude or intensity of a sound.

Lysergic acid diethylamide (LSD) A psychedelic drug that produces distortions of perception, thought, and emotion. It is extremely powerful, and very small doses are sufficient to produce dramatic effects.

Machiavellianism A personality trait involving the ability and tendency to manipulate other people and characterized by a relative lack of affect in personal relations, a lack of concern with conventional morality, and weak or nonexistent commitment to any ideology.

Mandala A graphic, often symbolic, pattern used as a subject of concentration during meditation.

Manic-depressive psychosis A form of psychosis characterized by extreme sadness, lowered self-esteem, and feelings of worthlessness and pessimism (depressive phase), sometimes vacillating with inappropriate, fragile elation (manic phase).

Manifest content In Freudian theory, those aspects of our dreams that relate to the activities of the day and current concerns of the dreamer. *See also* Latent content.

Mantra A mystical phrase or invocation repeated over and over again during meditation.

Massed practice Learning in which the material is studied intensively for a short period of time, as in cramming for an exam. *See also* Spaced practice.

Maternal motivation The innate, often instinctive, drive in female animals to care for their young. It may also be felt by male parents, especially human fathers.

Maturation Those patterns of individual growth that are largely independent of experience and learning, but that appear more or less automatically as the individual gets older.

Mean In a collection of data, the sum of the scores divided by the number of scores; the average; the most useful measure of central tendency.

Measure of central tendency Any of several different types of average, including the mode, the median, and the mean.

Median That point in a collection of data at which there are as many scores higher as there are lower.

Meditation A state of consciousness produced by intense concentration on a repetitive act and characterized by relaxation, peace, calm, and sometimes by perceptual or temporal distortions.

Memory drum A machine that automatically displays a series of stimuli for memory experiments.

Memory trace A hypothetical trace in the brain that is the physical means of storing a piece of information. *See also* Engram.

Menopause That stage in the adult woman when the ovaries cease to produce egg cells, menstruation stops, and the ability to have children ceases.

Mental age A concept introduced by Alfred Binet in the assessment of intelligence in children, based on the average ability of children of a certain age to perform certain specified tasks; used in the Stanford-Binet intelligence test to compute IQ.

Mental retardation A condition of subnormal intelligence, usually applied to people whose IQ is below 70.

Mental telepathy The ability to read other people's minds.

Mesomorph One of three body types designated by Sheldon, characterized by a tough, muscled, angular structure. *See also* Endomorph, Ectomorph.

Methadone A synthetic drug used in the treatment of heroin addiction. It produces many of the same effects as heroin, including addiction.

Microcephalism A quite rare form of mental retardation characterized by impaired development of the brain—both head and brain are abnormally small.

Midbrain That portion of the brain that coordinates reflex movements of the head and neck and acts as a receiving center for the output of the cerebellum.

Middle ear That part of the ear containing the ossicles (anvil, hammer, stirrup). It connects the eardrum of the outer ear to the oval window, which leads to the inner ear.

Minnesota Multiphasic Personality Inventory (MMPI) A widely used test designed to give a general picture of someone's personality, particularly an overall assessment of adjustment and neuroticism.

Mnemonic trick Any procedure for improving memory by transforming coding, or visualizing information so as to make recall easier.

Mode The point in a collection of data at which the most scores fall.

Monocular cues Cues used in judging depth and distance that depend on only one eye, such as clearness, brightness, and linear perspective.

Monogenic trait A hereditary trait that is fully determined by one pair of genes; for example, eye color.

Morpheme The smallest meaningful unit of a language, which can either stand alone or be combined with other morphemes to make words.

Motivation An internal state involving arousal toward a specific goal.

Motive An internal condition, usually stemming from a need, that causes us to act in a manner to satisfy that need.

Mutation In evolution, a change in a gene that can potentially produce a change in a characteristic of the organism.

Mystical experience A powerful spiritual, often religious, experience, occurring more or less unexpectedly, that gives the individual an overwhelming sense of understanding and a feeling of ecstasy, warmth, and joy.

Narcissism A form of personality disorder in which the individual is totally self-absorbed and can think about and care for only himself or herself. Characterized by grandiosity and selfishness, but also moments of extreme self-doubt and feelings that life is meaningless and unrewarding.

Narcotics A class of drugs that produce a slowdown in physical and mental processes and reduction in pain. They are highly addictive, and include heroin, morphine, opium, codeine, and many others.

Natural selection The process of the survival of the fittest working in a natural population.

Need for achievement (*n*-ach) A learned motive, widely studied, that involves the need for success and the fear of failure.

Negative reinforcement A type of reinforcement that involves the termination of an unpleasant, undesirable, or negative stimulus after a response. *See also* Positive reinforcement, Punishment.

Neuron The individual nerve cell, consisting of a cell body and nerve fibers.

Neurosis A form of psychopathology in which the individual is in touch with reality and can generally function reasonably well in society but has developed anxiety, fears, and behavior patterns that interfere substantially with his or her freedom of action.

Nonreversal shift In concept formation, a change in the solution to a problem that involves changing the critical dimension; for example, from color to shape. *See also* Reversal shift.

Normal distribution The bell-shaped frequency distribution that is produced (approximately) by many natural events and observations, especially successive samples from the same population. Very useful in statistics.

Norms Typical patterns of behavior in a society or group; accepted ways of behaving and thinking.

Obedience Doing what one is told, especially if one would rather not.

Object constancy The perception of an object as retaining its identity even if it is hidden from view.

Objective self-awareness The tendency or ability to look at ourselves as others would. A state in which this tendency is increased.

Obsessive-compulsive neurosis A form of neurosis involving the constant repetition of certain acts or thoughts.

Oedipal stage *See* Phallic stage.

Oedipus complex In Freudian theory a young boy's sexual attraction to his mother and hatred of his father, resulting in feelings of guilt and fear of his father. Occurs during the phallic stage of psychosexual development, ages four to six.

Operant conditioning A type of conditioning in which a response is made to a stimulus, a reinforcement occurs, and the response to that stimulus becomes more likely in the future (that is, the S-R connection is strengthened). *See also* Classical conditioning.

Opium A narcotic from which many others such as morphine and heroin are derived.

Opponent-process theory The theory that color vision is due to two types of cones, each producing two color experiences—red-green and yellow-blue—while a third produces only white.

Oral stage The first stage of Freud's psychosexual stages of development, characterized by dependence on the mother and the nipple.

Organ of Corti In the auditory system, a structure on the cochlea in the inner ear.

Paired-associate learning A form of learning in which pairs of words are presented and the individual must learn to give the second half of the pair when the first half is shown.

Paralanguage That form of nonverbal communication that involves aspects of speech other than the actual words, such as pitch, tempo, loudness, and pauses.

Paranoia A relatively rare form of psychosis in which the individual has persistent delusions of importance and persecution.

Parasympathetic nervous system That part of the autonomic nervous system that slows down our bodily processes and returns them to a normal state. *See also* Sympathetic nervous system.

Partial reinforcement The reinforcement of a response only a portion of the times the response occurs.

Perceptual constancy The perception of familiar objects, shapes, and the like as relatively unchanging despite variations in the stimuli reaching our sense organs; for example, size, shape, brightness and color constancies.

Performance test A nonverbal intelligence test, generally less likely to be biased than verbal tests.

Peripheral nervous system That part of the nervous system other than the spinal cord and brain (the central nervous system). It consists of the neurons that carry information from other parts of the body to the central nervous system and messages from the central nervous system back to the rest of the body; divided into the somatic nervous system and the autonomic nervous system.

Personal space The space that immediately surrounds us; research has revealed that the amount of space people put between themselves and others is determined by their relationship to the other person, their national background, and their sex.

Personality A personal style involving how a person differs from other people, how he or she acts under various circumstances, and how he or she responds to other people.

Personality disorder A form of psychopathology, including the psychopathic personality and narcissism, in which the individual develops a set of behaviors or personal characteristics that are harmful to either the individual or to other people in society, but without the specific symptoms that are present in neuroses or psychoses.

Person-centered therapy A form of humanistic therapy developed by Carl Rogers that emphasizes allowing the patient to discover his or her own problems, at the same time allowing the therapist to make comments that reflect the therapist's personal views and feelings rather than his or her professional theories.

Phallic stage The third of Freud's psychosexual stages of development, characterized in part by the child's sexual attraction to the parent of the opposite sex. *See also* Oedipus complex.

Phi phenomenon The perception of apparent movement when two identical or similar objects appear successively with only a brief interval between their appearances, and a small distance between their locations.

Phobia A type of neurosis in which the individual becomes abnormally afraid of a particular situation or object.

Phonemes The distinct sounds out of which a language is constructed. They generally carry no meaning of their own but combine with others to make meaningful units, or morphemes.

Physiological-biological approach A broad approach to psychology that studies the physiological and genetic mechanisms that affect behavior.

Pitch The psychological dimension of hearing corresponding to frequency of the sound waves.

Pituitary gland The "master" endocrine gland, consisting of the anterior pituitary and the posterior pituitary; controls growth, skin-color alterations, the production of eggs and sperm, and many other bodily functions, as well as the behavior of several other glands.

Pivot grammar A theory of childhood grammar, according to which children select certain words that represent basic concepts in their world and use them constantly in connection with all other words. It is no longer considered an adequate description of children's speech.

Place theory A theory of hearing that states that pitch is determined by the part of the basilar membrane that is stimulated. *See also* Frequency theory, Volley theory.

Placebo An inactive substance given as a control to research subjects in place of an active drug.

Plateaus Periods in learning during which no apparent progress occurs—especially common in the learning of motor skills.

Play theory A therapeutic technique, used primarily with children, in which the therapist gives the patient a game to play, hoping the patient will make revealing statements and act out his or her feelings during the course of the play.

Pleasure principle Concern solely with the seeking of maximum satisfaction of our needs and desires without regard to planning, rules, or the future. Characteristic of the id. *See also* Reality principle.

Population In statistics, the total of all possible cases, as opposed to a sample, which is a subset of the population. *See also* Sample.

Positive reinforcement A type of reinforcement that involves giving a pleasant, desirable, or positive stimulus after a response. *See also* Negative reinforcement, Punishment.

Post-hypnotic amnesia Amnesia, or forgetting, produced by a command given during hypnosis to take effect after the subject is out of the hypnotic state.

Prefrontal lobotomy An operation in which a small part of the frontal lobes is surgically disconnected from the rest of the brain. Once used as a method of treating extreme emotional disorders, but now no longer employed.

Preoperational stage The period between ages two and seven, during which children develop the ability to understand language and communicate, to form concepts, and to use objects symbolically rather than only literally.

Primacy effect The tendency of people to weigh first impressions or primary information more heavily than information received subsequently.

Primary reinforcer Stimuli or events that satisfy basic physiological needs such as the needs for food, water, oxygen, and sex. *See also* Secondary reinforcer.

Proactive interference A type of memory interference in which new material is harder to learn because of its similarity to old information. *See also* Retroactive interference.

Programmed learning or instruction A system of teaching consisting of a carefully prepared sequence of questions, exercises, and bits of information designed to minimize errors and provide maximum immediate reinforcement and feedback on accuracy.

Projection A defense mechanism in which the individual seeks to reduce anxiety by assuming that someone else has the individual's own, unacceptable, feelings.

Projective test A form of indirect test of personality in which the subject is asked to respond to an ambiguous stimulus, and in which the responses are presumed to reveal something about the subject.

Prolactin A pituitary hormone that produces maternal behavior in females.

Proprioceptive sense The sense that receives information from the body's skeletal joints and from which we can determine our body's position in space. *See also* Kinesthetic sense.

Proxemics The study of how people use and relate to personal space.

Psychiatrist A medical doctor who specializes in the treatment of mental disorders.

Psychoactive drugs Any drugs that affect the emotional, perceptual, or cognitive state of the user; that is, have psychological effects.

Psychoanalysis A system of therapy for mental disorders based on Freud's theories. Relies on free association and interpretations by the therapist in order to discover and work through unconscious conflicts.

Psychoanalyst A therapist, usually a medical doctor, who has received specialized training at an institute for psychoanalysis.

Psychoanalytic theories of personality A group of personality theories based on Freud that stress the interaction between the individual's innate needs and characteristics and the environment, with particular emphasis on the role of unconscious conflicts and the effects of experiences in early childhood.

Psychopathic personality A type of personality disorder in which the individual has little control of his or her impulses, cannot delay gratification, shows little or no emotion about anything or anyone, has no moral sense, and experiences no anxiety or guilt about his or her actions.

Psychopathology Mental disturbance or disorder, including neuroses, personality disorders, and psychoses; the study of mental disturbance and disorder.

Psychophysics The study of the relationship between physical stimuli and psychological experience.

Psychosexual stages The Freudian notion that children go through a series of stages—oral, anal, and then phallic—and that during each stage the conflicts among the various parts of the personality and society focus on that area of the body and events connected with it. If conflicts at each stage are not resolved, the individual will become fixated at that stage and will always have problems relating to the original conflict.

Psychosis The most severe class of mental disorders, including manic-depression, paranoia, and schizophrenia. Psychoses always involve a significant break with reality, and may have specific physiological or genetic causes.

Psychosomatic condition Physical illness or damage produced by a mental condition.

Psychosurgery The use of surgery on the brain as a treatment for mental illness.

Psychotherapy The treatment of mental illness through psychological means.

Puberty The period during which we physically change from children into adults, characterized by a sudden spurt in growth, rapid development of the reproductive organs, and marked by the beginning of menstruation in women and roughly by the appearance of sperm in the urine of men. *See also* Adolescence.

Punishment The use of an unpleasant stimulus following a response in order to decrease the likelihood of that response.

Random search A process of memory retrieval, beginning at some point in the memory store and proceeding with no particular order, from one item to another until the correct piece of information is found. *See also* Directed search.

Range In statistics, the difference between the highest and lowest scores in a collection of data.

Rapid eye movement (REM) sleep The dreaming stage of sleep, characterized by heightened activity in terms of eye movement, brain waves, and other physiological indicators, but extreme muscle relaxation. Also known as paradoxical sleep.

Rationalization A defense mechanism in which the individual makes up complex, seemingly rational arguments to explain an anxiety-arousing or conflict-producing event.

Reaction formation A defense mechanism in which the individual tries to cover up an anxiety-arousing feeling by expressing its exact opposite.

Reality principle Concern with planning, obeying rules, dealing with the world while trying to maximize the satisfaction of needs on a long-term basis. Characteristic of the ego. *See also* Pleasure principle.

Recall Memory by the production of the required piece of information, as opposed to recognition, which requires only choosing the correct item from a list that is provided.

Recessive gene A gene whose characteristic will be expressed only if both members of a gene pair are identical. *See also* Dominant gene.

Recognition Memory by selection of the correct item from a list that is provided. *See also* Recall.

Refractory period A period immediately after the production of an action potential in which a neuron will not fire no matter how much excitatory chemical it receives.

Rehearsal Repeating an item out loud or to oneself in order to increase memory.

Reinforcement Any stimulus or event that increases the likelihood that a response will occur again in the future. *See also* Positive reinforcement, Negative reinforcement.

Reliability The extent to which a test consistently produces the same result for the same person, as measured by the correlation between scores on one occasion and scores on another, or between the score on one half of the test and the score on the other half. *See also* Validity.

Repression A defense mechanism consisting of pushing unacceptable feelings or emotions into the unconscious.

Resistance A phenomenon in psychoanalytic psychotherapy in which the patient is reluctant to deal with certain topics and issues, and avoids them by not free associating, or by missing or being late for sessions, talking about irrelevant items, and so on. *See also* Interpretation.

Retina The part of the eye on which light is focused and which contains visual receptors. *See also* Cones, Rods.

Retinal disparity The difference between the images seen by the right eye and those seen by the left eye; an important binocular cue for judging distance.

Retrieval The ability to call back from our long-term memory diverse bits of information.

Retroactive interference A type of memory interference in which old information is harder to remember because of new information. *See also* Proactive interference.

Reversal shift In concept formation, a change in the correct solution to a problem that does not involve changing the critical dimension but merely reverses the meaning of that dimension; for example, learning that a green light meant stop and a red meant go, instead of the reverse. The frequency (hue) of the color is still the relevant dimension. *See also* Nonreversal shift.

Ribonucleic acid (RNA) A chemical that is present in the brain and may be involved in the storage of memories.

Risky shift The tendency for individuals in a group to favor riskier decisions than they would make by themselves.

Rods Structures in the retina of the eye that register light intensity but not color; functioning mainly in dim light. *See also* Cones.

Rorschach Inkblot Test A widely used projective personality test in which an inkblot is used as a stimulus for individualized response.

Sample In statistics, a portion of all possible cases, or population, whose properties are studied to gain information about the whole. *See also* Population.

Scapegoat A group, person, or object against whom aggression is expressed when the real cause of the anger is unacceptable or unavailable as a target. One cause of prejudice.

Schedule of reinforcement A procedure in which a response is reinforced only part of the time, according to a prearranged schedule.

Schizophrenia An extreme form of psychosis characterized by a break with reality, inappropriate affect, strange and illogical thought patterns, and withdrawal from social interaction.

Secondary reinforcer A stimulus that an individual learns through experience to associate with either positive or negative outcomes, occurring when some initially neutral stimulus is paired with a primary reinforcer and eventually takes on the quality of the reinforcer. *See also* Primary reinforcer.

Self-actualization According to Abraham Maslow's personality theory, the goal of each person, which is the full and complete expression of his or her greatest potential.

Semicircular canals Canals in the inner ear that are concerned with the perception of equilibrium and motion.

Sensitivity group Another name for an encounter group or T-group.

Sensorimotor stage The first eighteen months to two years of life, during which children's dealings with the world consist mainly of sensation and physical interaction and during which children become aware that there is an outside world entirely separate from themselves.

Sensory homunculus In the cerebral cortex, an imaginary representation of the surface of the human body, or "little man," whose parts are proportional in size to the degree of sensitivity of the parts of the body they represent.

Sensory neuron A neuron associated with one of the sensory receptors, such as the retina of the eye.

Sensory overload More stimulation than an individual can handle, resulting in the individual responding less well to the world, ignoring some stimulation, or becoming upset.

Sensory register In the memory system, the mechanism by which we receive perceptual information, which stays in memory only momentarily unless it is transferred to short-term memory.

Serial learning Learning a list of items successively, usually with the requirement that the order be memorized (for example, learning the months of the year in order).

Set The tendency or expectation of responding to certain stimuli in a specific way.

Sex hormones The so-called male and female hormones, named androgen and estrogen respectively, that control the development of sexual characteristics, to some extent the strength of the sex motive, and possibly emotional reactions as well.

Sex role The behavior, thought patterns, and attitudes that a society generally considers appropriate to one sex and not the other. Accepting this picture or acting in line with it would be to fit into the traditional sex role.

Shape constancy The perception of familiar objects as always having the same shape even though viewed from different angles.

Shaping A technique, also called successive approximation, in operant conditioning that involves reinforcing behaviors that gradually approximate the desired behavior until the animal is performing the desired behavior.

Short-term memory In the memory system, a mechanism by which we retain a small amount of information

for a short period of time. *See also* Long-term memory.

Situational pressure The pressure on individuals to become extremely compliant in situations where they feel they have little or no choice about their behavior.

Size constancy The perception of familiar objects as being their actual size regardless of how big or small their image may be on the retina.

Skinner box An experimental chamber devised by B. F. Skinner to provide a way to present stimuli, give reinforcements, and allow the animal to make a specified response. Often fully automatic.

Social facilitation A term used to describe the fact that the presence of other people often improves our performance on a variety of tasks. Now we know that the reverse may occur, depending on the nature of the task.

Social justice A term used to describe the feeling of most people that all people should get what they deserve according to their needs and efforts; equity.

Social learning theory A theory that explains the development of personality and other processes almost entirely in terms of experience, rather than innate or biological factors. It assumes that personality is learned just as is anything else.

Social psychology A field of psychology that studies how individuals behave in social situations, how they are affected by groups, and how groups themselves function.

Socialization The process by which children are taught the rules and conventions of society.

Somatic nervous system Part of the peripheral nervous system, consisting of those neurons that are connected with the muscles, sense organs, and skin and deal with sensory information, body movement, and spinal reflexes.

Spaced practice A system of learning, also known as distributed practice, in which the material is studied

for short intervals over a long period of time. *See also* Massed practice.

Spinal cord A cord of nervous tissue, descending from the brain down the backbone, that carries messages from the brain to the rest of the body and vice versa.

Spinal reflex Physical responses that involve only the spinal cord without involving the brain, such as the knee-jerk.

Split-brain phenomenon A phenomenon caused by severing the corpus callosum, thereby separating the two hemispheres of the brain; experiments with split-brain individuals lend support to the theory that the two hemispheres have different functions.

Split-half reliability The correlation between the scores obtained by individuals on two halves of a test. *See also* Reliability.

Spontaneous recovery In conditioning, the reappearance of a response after a rest period following a period during which the response appeared to have extinguished fully. Also, as used in psychotherapy, the recovery rate of untreated control subjects.

Standard deviation A statistical measurement of variability.

Standard error of the mean An estimate of the standard deviation of the normal distribution that would have been produced by many samples from the same population.

Stanford-Binet test A test for measuring intelligence in children.

Statistics A method of dealing mathematically with a set of numbers or scores, describing and drawing inferences from them.

Stereotype A picture or set of assumptions about the characteristics of a whole group of people, a situation, or even an object. A major factor in prejudice.

Stimulant Any of a group of drugs that increase the activity of the body and/or the central nervous system, speeding up reactions and producing a feeling of lightheadedness, alertness, or euphoria. *See also* Depressant.

Stimulus generalization The tendency, essential to the learning process, to respond to stimuli similar to the one to which learning occurred.

Stranger anxiety The tendency among infants at a certain age to respond with fear or hesitation to an unfamiliar face.

Subject A person participating in an experiment.

Successive approximations *See* Shaping.

Successive scanning In memory retrieval, a process by which items are considered one at a time until the correct one is found.

Superego In Freudian theory, the conscience of the individual, containing the rules, values, and morals that tell us what is right and wrong, and also containing our ego ideal, the image of ourself that we would like to achieve. *See also* Id, Ego.

Superstitious behavior Behavior performed because of a chance reinforcement of an act even though there is no actual connection between that act and the delivery of reinforcement.

Surface structure In transformational grammar, the sequence and form of a sentence, as opposed to the deep structure, which is the underlying meaning of a sentence.

Sympathetic nervous system That part of the autonomic nervous system that activates and speeds up our bodily processes in response to an external threat or stimulation. *See also* Parasympathetic nervous system.

Symptom substitution The idea in psychoanalytic theory that a symptom is the result of an underlying conflict, and that removing it without dealing with the conflict will result in some other symptom appearing.

Synapse In the nervous system, a minute space between the axon terminal of one nerve cell and a second cell, through which information is passed.

Systematic desensitization A technique used in behavior therapy in which the patient progresses through an imaginary or real hierarchy of anxiety-producing situations while remaining completely relaxed until he or she can face the actual situation without being afraid.

Tachistoscope A mechanism for presenting visual stimuli for very brief exposures.

Taylor Manifest Anxiety Scale (TMAS) A test of anxiety based on the theory that anxiety is evident in a person's physical behavior and responses.

Telegraphic speech The simplified speech used by young children, which eliminates the unnecessary descriptive words, prepositions, articles, conjunctions, most pronouns, and auxiliary verbs, much as an adult would do when sending a telegram.

Territoriality The need for personal space and the tendency, possibly instinctive, to react defensively or aggressively when that space is invaded.

Thalamus A large area of the forebrain that relays sensory information from all sources to the cerebral cortex.

Thanatos That part of the id consisting of destructive, aggressive impulses. *See also* Libido.

Thematic Apperception Test (TAT) A projective personality test that uses an ambiguous picture as a stimulus for individualized response.

Theory of cognitive dissonance The theory that inconsistency, or dissonance, exists whenever a person holds two cognitions and the opposite of one follows psychologically from the other, and that people will try to reduce this dissonance.

Threshold A measure of perceptual sensitivity; the point at which an increasing stimulus not previously perceived becomes perceptible.

Timbre Tonal quality of a sound; for example, the tone of a violin versus that of a trumpet.

Tip-of-the-tongue phenomenon A phenomenon of retrieval failure where we know we have a particular piece of information but cannot quite recall it.

Token economy A behavioral technique used in some mental hospitals and jails that consists of rewarding people for certain acts in order to make the operation systematic and explicit.

Training group (T-group) Another name for an encounter group or therapy group.

Transference A common occurrence in psychoanalytic therapy in which the patient forms a strong emotional attachment to the therapist, who comes to symbolize a variety of crucial relationships in the patient's life.

Transformational grammar A complete set of grammatical rules that allow us to transform the surface structure of a sentence—that is, the sequence or form of the morphemes—into the deep structure, which is the underlying meaning of a sentence.

Transsexuality Holding an image of oneself that is appropriate for the opposite sex; for example, a man who considers himself a woman. Also hormonal and surgical procedures for giving a person of one sex the physical characteristics of the other sex.

Unconditioned response In classical conditioning, the automatic response to an unconditioned stimulus, such as salivation at the sight of food.

Unconditioned stimulus In classical conditioning, a stimulus, such as food, that automatically and without any learning produces an unconditioned response, such as salivation.

Unconscious In Freudian theory, those motives, feelings, memories, and thoughts that we are not aware of and that are assumed to affect our behavior.

Validity The extent to which a test measures what it is supposed to measure. Judged in part by the correlation between the scores on the test and information provided by some trustworthy criterion. *See also* Reliability.

Variable A characteristic or condition measured in an experiment that is subject to change.

Vestibular sacs Sacs in the inner ear that enable us to perceive when we are upright or how far we are leaning.

Visual cliff A device used to study depth perception in infants, consisting of a glass floor that appears to drop off. The infant is observed to see if he or she will crawl over the edge of the "cliff."

Volley theory A theory of hearing that states that nerve fibers are divided into groups that "fire" at different times. *See also* Place theory, Frequency theory.

Weber-Fechner law The basic law of psychophysics stating that for any sensory dimension (for example, brightness or sound frequency), the just noticeable difference between two stimuli is always the same proportion of the existing stimulus.

Wechsler scales Two sets of subtests, the Wechsler Intelligence Scale for Children (WISC) and the Wechsler Adult Intelligence Scale (WAIS), designed to measure intelligence in children and adults by measuring several different kinds of abilities.

Whorf hypothesis A hypothesis proposed by Benjamin Whorf that contends that the words in any given language to some extent limit and shape the thoughts of the people who speak that language.

Wish fulfillment The expression in our dreams of an unconscious desire or wish. In Freudian theory, all dreams represent wish fulfillment.

Working through A part of psychoanalytic psychotherapy in which the patient is helped to resolve underlying conflicts by talking about them, understanding their source, reliving early experiences, and confronting similar conflicts in day-to-day life.

Yerkes-Dodson law The general rule that there seems to be an optimal (best) level of motivation for every task, and that the more complex the task, the lower the optimal level of motivation.

Young-Helmholtz theory The theory of color vision that assumes the existence of three different types of cones, each of which produces one color—red, green, or blue. *See also* Opponent-process theory.

Zygote A single cell formed by the union of a sperm and an egg.

Author Index

Abrahams, D., 575
Abramovitch, R., 16
Acord, L. D., 342
Adam, W. R., 255
Ader, R., 603
Adler, A., 5, 433–434, 452
Adorno, J. W., 448
Aiello, J. R., 595, 596, 611
Ainsworth, M. D. S., 365
Ajzen, I., 580
Albee, G. W., 44
Alexander, F. G., 486
Allen, V. L., 552, 553
Allport, F. H., 542
Allport, G. W., 420
American Psychological Association, 21
Anand, B. K., 336
Anastasi, A., 204
Angel, C., 482
Antrobus, J. S., 322
Apple, W., 156
Ardrey, R., 597
Armentrout, J. A., 370
Arnold, M. B., 292
Aronson, E., 278, 557, 573, 575
Asch, S. E., 550, 551, 552
Aserinsky, E., 319
Athanasiou, R., 383, 384
Atkinson, J. W., 272
Atkinson, K., 142
Attneave, F., 50
Austin, G. A., 169
Ax, A. F., 288
Axline, V. M., 516, 517, 525
Ayllon, T., 510
Azrin, N., 510

Backman, M. E., 392
Bacon, C. L., 390
Bailey, K. G., 596
Bainbridge, L., 84
Bandura, A. L., 2, 6, 86, 94, 303, 373, 392, 434, 435, 485, 506, 508
Banuazizi, A., 82
Barabee, E. L., 523

Barber, T. X., 331
Bardwick, J. M., 238
Barker, D. D., 342
Barker, R., 72
Baron, J., 187, 332
Baron, R. A., 373
Baron, R. S., 553
Barondes, S. H., 117
Barron, F., 182
Baskett, G. D., 596
Bass, M. J., 87
Baumrind, D., 369, 397
Bavelas, A., 548
Baxter, J. C., 596
Bayley, N., 204, 214
Beach, F. A., 274
Bean, L. L., 488
Beck, A. T., 471, 491
Beckwith, L., 397
Bell, R. Q., 370, 391
Bellugi, U., 142, 144
Bem, D., 584, 586
Bendfeldt, F., 475
Bendig, A. W., 449
Benedict, R., 373, 458
Benson, H., 335, 336
Bergin, A. E., 520, 521, 523
Berkowitz, L., 304, 305, 550
Berlyne, D., 54
Berscheid, E., 280, 565, 566
Bickman, L., 550
Bidder, G., 186
Bieri, J., 393
Binder, A., 343
Binet, A., 200
Birdwhistell, R. L., 156
Black, A. E., 369, 397
Bland, V. P., 602
Bless, E., 565
Bloom, L., 142, 145
Bochner, S., 579
Boies, S. J., 111
Booth, A., 605
Boring, E. G., 21, 38, 43
Bourne, L. E., Jr., 27, 167
Boutiller, R. G., 548

Bower, G., 10, 167
Bower, G. H., 94, 106, 107
Bower, J. G. R., 357, 358
Bowerman, M., 145
Bowers, R. J., 554
Bowlby, J., 5, 364
Brackbill, Y., 363
Bradburn, W., 393
Brady, J. V., 486
Braine, M. D. S., 144
Brandsma, J. M., 475
Brandt, U., 212
Brecher, E., 340
Brier, R., 190
Broadbent, D. E., 54, 115, 591
Brobeck, J. R., 260
Brown, D., 341
Brown, M., 449
Brown, R., 142, 144, 145, 147, 159
Brown, R. W., 121
Bruell, J. H., 44
Bruner, J. S., 55, 169
Brush, C., 556
Buchanan, R. W., 610
Buech, B., 412
Burger, G. K., 370
Burnstein, E., 554
Burt, C., 213
Busk, P., 447
Buss, A. H., 468, 541
Butler, R. A., 270
Byrne, D., 277, 596, 597
Byrne, W. L., 117

Calhoun, J. B., 2, 602, 603, 615
Cameron, N., 478
Camino, L., 305
Campbell, A., 408
Campbell, D. T., 52
Cannon, W. B., 257, 258, 288
Caputo, C., 536
Carlsmith, J. M., 157, 557, 565, 575, 583, 584
Carol, A., 605
Carter, L. F., 55
Cartwright, G. M., 118

Carver, C. S., 541
Catalan, J., 564
Cattell, R. B., 211, 420, 442
Chen, S. C., 542
Cherkin, A., 118
Chhina, G. S., 336
Chomsky, N., 10, 139, 146, 148, 150, 159
Chopra, N. S., 343
Christian, J. J., 602
Christie, R., 447, 448
Cialdini, R. B., 564
Clark, D. H., 212
Clark, L. D., 343
Clark, R., 257
Clark, R. A., 272
Clark, R. D., III, 567
Clarke-Stewart, K. A., 392
Clausen, J. A., 485
Cleckley, H. M., 467, 475
Cohen, H. D., 117
Cohen, M., 482
Cohen, S., 593
Colburn, Z., 186
Coleman, J., 491
Colman, R., 447
Collins, A. M., 124, 126
Condon, W. S., 156
Condry, J. C., 555
Conezio, J., 107
Conger, J. J., 82, 417
Conrad, D. G., 486
Converse, P. E., 408
Cook, L., 117
Cooper, J., 585
Cooper, R. E., 595
Coppen, A., 238
Cornelison, A. R., 485
Costa, P. T., Jr., 415
Cotler, S., 392
Cottrell, N. B., 543
Cowell, J., 605
Cowen, E. L., 423
Crancer, A., Jr., 343
Cronbach, L. J., 219, 445
Cruze, W. W., 351, 352
Cunningham, M. R., 564

Dahlke, A. E., 555
Dallenbach, K. M., 120
Darby, B. L., 564
Darley, J. M., 567
Darwin, C., 295
Dase, J., 186
Davidoff, L. L., 462, 477
Davidson, A. B., 117
Davis, A., 211
Davis, D. C., 602
Davis, J. M., 501
Davis, K., 149
Davison, C. C., 491
Day, R. H., 51
Dean, L. M., 595
Deaux, K., 390

Deci, E. L., 583
Deese, J., 21
De Fleur, M. L., 580
Deikman, A. J., 336
Delay, J. C., 343
DeLucia, L. A., 399
Dement, W., 2, 318, 320, 321, 322, 345
Dennis, W., 353
Deutsch, M., 543, 544
DeValois, R. L., 32
Dille, J. M., 343
Dion, K. L., 553
Dohrenwend, B. P., 489, 613
Dohrenwend, B. S., 489, 613
Dollard, J., 86, 299, 434
Doob, A. N., 302, 303, 530, 573
Dove, A., 208
Doyle, M. P., 238
Droege, R. C., 393
Drolette, M., 300
DuBois, P. H., 206
Dudrick, S. J., 258
Duff, D. F., 596
Duncker, K., 174
Durrell, D. E., 87
Duval, S., 541

Ebbesen, E. B., 554, 587, 598
Eberhardy, F., 479
Eckerman, C. O., 363
Edelman, M., 391
Eells, K., 211
Egozcue, J., 341
Ehrlich, P. R., 606
Eichelman, W. H., 111
Ekman, P., 156, 298, 312
Ekstrand, B. R., 27
Elliott, M. H., 99
Ellsworth, P., 157, 312, 565
Emerson, P. E., 365
Emrich, B., 447
Emswiller, T., 390
English, D. C., 501
Epstein, Y. M., 611
Erickson, B., 610
Erickson, M. H., 330
Erikson, E. H., 5, 88, 274, 362, 363, 370, 371, 377, 400, 483, 484
Erlenmeyer-Kimling, L., 213
Ervin, S., 144
Evans, F. J., 331, 332
Eyferth, K., 212
Eysenck, H. J., 5, 423, 442, 450, 451, 520, 524

Fajone, R., 276
Fantz, R. L., 51
Farley, J., 390
Feldman, G. L., 510
Feldman, M. J., 326
Feldman-Summers, S., 390
Felipe, N., 597
Fenigstein, A., 541

Feshbach, S., 305
Festinger, L., 6, 531, 540, 556, 572, 583, 584, 587
Fieve, R. R., 501
Fifer, G., 212
Finesinger, J. E., 523
Finkelman, J. M., 591
Fishbein, M., 580
Fisher, C., 320, 322
Fisher, D. J., 596, 597
Fjerdingstad, E. J., 117
Flacks, R., 582
Flavell, J. H., 377
Fleck, S., 485
Flexner, J. B., 117
Flexner, L. B., 117
Fling, S., 398
Flyger, V., 602
Ford, R. C., 447
Foulkes, D., 322
Fox, R. E., 464
Fraser, C., 143, 144
Fraser, S. C., 564
Freedman, D. X., 340
Freedman, J. L., 121, 126, 302, 370, 408, 409, 411, 530, 557, 564, 565, 573, 580, 582, 583, 605, 606, 610, 611, 612, 613, 614, 615
Freeman, F. N., 213
French, J. R. P., Jr., 549
Frenkel-Brunswick, E., 448
Freud, A., 425, 434, 452, 504
Freud, S., 5, 323, 324, 325, 326, 327, 424, 425, 430, 431, 432, 433, 451, 452, 484, 491, 505
Friedan, B., 417
Friedman, L. N., 265
Friedman, S. B., 603
Friesen, W. V., 156, 298, 312
Frijda, N. H., 297
Fromm, E., 437
Funkenstein, D., 300

Galanter, E., 26, 37
Galinsky, M., 393
Galle, O. R., 605
Gallo, P., 544
Gardner, B. J., 2, 150
Gardner, R. A., 2, 150
Gedda, L., 352
Geen, R. G., 304
Geis, F. L., 448
Geller, A., 116
Geller, V., 156
Gerard, H. B., 540, 573
Getzels, J. W., 181
Gewirtz, J. L., 363
Gibson, E. J., 51, 59
Gibson, F. W., Jr., 596
Gladwyn, T., 214
Glasgow, L. A., 603
Glass, D., 591, 592, 593
Glass, D. C., 543, 615
Glassco, J., 375

Glickman, S. E., 116, 281
Glucksberg, S., 174, 259
Glueck, E., 368
Glueck, S., 368
Goethals, G. R., 531
Goffman, E., 557
Goldfrank, F., 318
Good, E., 343
Goodenough, D. R., 322, 393
Goodenough, E. W., 398
Goodman, C. C., 55
Goodnow, J. J., 169
Gorfein, D., 448
Gove, W. R., 605
Goy, R. W., 269
Graves, T., 596
Greeley, A. M., 337
Green, H., 477, 525
Greenberg, D. J., 363
Greene, D., 583
Gregory, I., 464
Gregory, R. L., 59
Grice, D., 363
Griffith, R. M., 324
Griffitt, W., 606
Gross, A. E., 548, 565
Grusec, J. E., 392
Guilford, J. P., 181, 182, 203, 295

Haith, M. M., 51, 354
Hall, C. S., 21, 421, 453
Hall, E. T., 594, 596, 615
Hallam, E., 391
Hamilton, W. J., 134
Hampson, J. G., 388
Hampson, J. L., 388
Hansel, C. E. M., 190
Harding, J. S., 488
Hare, R. D., 466, 468
Harlow, H. F., 176, 177, 192, 270, 365
Harlow, M. K., 365
Harrell, M. S., 207
Harrell, T. W., 207
Harris, G. W., 267
Harris, V. A., 534
Hartnett, J. J., 596
Hastorf, A. H., 548
Hawkins, C., 548
Haykin, M. D., 343
Haythorn, W. H., 606, 610
Heath, R. G., 482
Heather, H., 564
Hebb, D. O., 253
Heidbreder, E., 170
Heider, F., 534, 571
Heingartner, A., 542
Held, R., 59
Henchy, T., 543
Henson, A., 157
Hering, W., 31, 32
Herman, E. M., 542
Hersen, M., 326
Herskovits, M. J., 52
Heshka, S., 605, 610

Hess, E. H., 53, 356
Heston, L., 481
Hewitt, J., 595
Hilgard, E. R., 94, 329, 332, 345
Hilgard, J., 353, 354
Hilgard, J. R., 485
Hill, A. H., 555
Hill, J. F., 531
Hillery, J. M., 542
Hillman, D., 363
Hinde, R. A., 21, 134, 159
Hirai, T., 335
Hiroto, D. S., 84
Hobson, J. A., 318
Hochberg, J. E., 31, 36, 59
Hodges, L., 596
Hoebel, B. G., 260
Hoedemaker, F., 321
Hoelzel, F., 257
Hogan, H. W., 54
Holden, M., 322
Hollander, E. P., 448
Hollingshead, A. B., 485, 488
Hollister, L. E., 343
Holzinger, K. J., 213
Homans, G. C., 565
Honzik, C. H., 99
Horowitz, M. J., 596
Hovland, C. I., 6, 166, 570, 575, 579, 587
Howard, K. I., 523
Hubel, D. H., 30
Hughes, B. O., 255
Hull, C. L., 4, 10, 72, 87, 253
Hunt, E. B., 166, 168
Hunt, P. J., 542
Hurvich, L. M., 31
Hyden, H. P., 117

Inhelder, B., 359, 360
Insko, C. A., 579
Irwin, S., 341
Isaacson, R. L., 272, 449
Iwawaki, S., 423

Jacklin, C. N., 391, 417
Jackson, P. W., 181
Jacobs, G. H., 32
Jacobs, J., 615
Jacobs, R. A., 141
Jacobs, R. L., 448
Jacobsen, C. F., 288
Jacobson, A. L., 117, 321
James, R. M., 548
James, W., 285, 287–289, 337
Jameson, D., 31, 475
Janis, I. L., 570, 587
Jankowski, J. J., 397
Jarvik, L. F., 213
Jarvik, M. E., 116
Jenkins, J. G., 120
Jensen, A. R., 204
Jensen, J., 322
Johnson, V. E., 384, 385, 413, 417

Jones, E. E., 10, 278, 534, 536, 585
Jones, N. B., 16–17
Jones, S. E., 596
Jordan, H. A., 258
Jouvet, M., 321
Julian, J. W., 548
Julien, R. M., 341, 345
Jung, C. G., 5, 327, 328, 433, 452

Kagan, J., 397
Kahneman, D., 59
Kalat, J. W., 255
Kales, A., 321, 323
Kallman, F. J., 481
Kamin, L. J., 213, 219
Kamiya, J., 188
Karaz, V., 535
Karp, S. A., 393
Kasamatsu, A., 335
Kasper, J. C., 447
Kastenbaum, R., 415
Katcher, A. H., 292
Kaufman, I., 42
Kaufman, I. C., 371
Kelley, H. H., 534, 555, 587
Kellogg, L. A., 150
Kellogg, W. N., 150
Kendler, H. H., 176
Kendler, T. S., 176
Kendon, A., 157
Kennedy, B. J., 269
Kernan, K. T., 142
Kernberg, O. F., 469
Kesey, K., 525
Kessel, N., 238
Kessen, M. L., 260
Kessen, W., 51, 354
Kessler, P., 482
Ketchel, R., 450
Kety, S. S., 481
Kiesler, S. B., 390, 520
King, S. H., 300
Kinsey, A. C., 383
Kirk, S. A., 392
Kite, W. R., 548
Klatsky, R., 131
Klebanoff, L. B., 485
Klein, G. S., 55
Kleinke, C., 544
Kleitman, N., 318, 319
Klevansky, S., 606
Kline, M. V., 333
Knight, R. P., 523
Knowles, W. B., 229
Koegel, R. L., 510
Koenig, K. E., 582
Koffka, K., 46
Kogan, N., 181, 182, 553
Kohen-Raz, R., 372
Kohl, J., 564
Kohlberg, L., 374, 375
Kohler, J., 53
Kohler, W., 178, 192
Kohn, M. L., 485

Kokonis, N. D., 485
Kolansky, H., 343
Kolb, L. C., 354, 498
Konečni, V. J., 566, 598
Kralin, R. A., 611
Krauss, R. M., 156, 543, 544
Kremen, I., 322
Kringlen, E., 481
Kübler-Ross, E., 415
Kudinka, N. Z., 448
Kuethe, J. L., 596

Labouvie, G., 412
Landauer, T. K., 109, 121, 126, 573
Lange, C., 285, 287–289
Lange, P. W., 117
Langer, J., 356
Langfeld, H. S., 38, 295
Langner, T. S., 488
Lansky, L. M., 398
Lashley, K. S., 232
Latané, B., 567
Lawrence, D. H., 176
Layton, B., 610
Lazarus, A. A., 506, 508, 523
Lazarus, R. S., 292
Leach, B. E., 482
Leavitt, H. J., 548, 549
Legant, P., 536
Leibman, M., 596
Leighton, A. H., 488
Leighton, D. C., 488
Lepper, M. R., 2, 583
Lerner, M. J., 566
Lerner, R. M., 355, 377, 390
Lesher, A. I., 238
Lesser, G. S., 212
Leukel, F., 499
Leventhal, H., 448
Levin, H., 373, 397
Levine, J. A., 397
Levine, J. M., 552, 553
Levine, S., 267
Levinson, D. J., 448
Levy, A., 605, 610
Levy, B. J., 370
Lewin, K., 6
Lewis, M., 397
Lewis, S. K., 564
Leyens, J. P., 305
Libuser, L., 598
Lichtenstein, E., 321
Lidz, T., 485
Lieberman, M. A., 519, 525
Liebert, R. M., 360
Liebling, B. A., 541
Linder, D. E., 278, 585
Lindsley, D. B., 229, 288
Lindzey, G., 212, 219, 421, 453
Lipsitt, L. P., 89
Littig, L., 449
Little, K. B., 596
Litwin, G. H., 272
Loehlin, J. C., 212, 219

Loftus, E. F., 56, 126, 131
Loftus, G. R., 131
Logan, F. A., 84
Long, C. N. H., 260
Loo, C. M., 610
Lorenz, K., 300, 312, 355
Lott, D. F., 595
Lovaas, O. I., 510
Lowell, E. L., 272
Lublin, S. D., 556
Luchins, A., 574
Ludwig, A. M., 475
Luria, A. R., 111, 131
Lykken, D. T., 468
Lyon, W., 333

MacArthur, L. A., 535
Maccoby, E. E., 5, 373, 391, 397, 417
MacDonald, H., 329
MacFayden, B. V., 258
Macklin, D. B., 488
MacLean, P. D., 286
Macmillan, A. M., 488
Macnichol, E. F., Jr., 31, 32
MacWhinney, B., 142
Magoun, H. W., 229
Maley, R. F., 510
Mancini, F., 391
Mandler, G., 259, 450
Manosevitz, M., 398
Marin, J., 168
Marinari, K. T., 238
Marler, P., 134
Marrecek, J., 536
Marshall, G., 329
Martens, S., 482
Masland, R. L., 214
Maslow, A. H., 11, 274, 281, 437, 438, 513
Mason, J. W., 486
Masters, W. H., 384, 385, 413, 417
Mathewson, G. C., 573
May, P. R., 500
Mayer, J., 258
McCarthy, J. J., 392
McClelland, D. C., 272
McClintock, M. K., 239
McConnell, J. V., 117
McCready, W. C., 337
McDavid, J. W., 392
McGaugh, J. L., 116
McGlashin, T. H., 331, 332
McIntyre, A., 391
McKenzie, B. E., 51
McNeill, D., 121
McNemar, Q., 213
McPherson, J. M., 605
Mednick, S. A., 181, 481
Meister, D. E., 55
Melges, F. T., 343
Meltzer, L., 295, 297
Menlove, F. L., 392
Merrill, M. A., 201
Meyer, D. E., 126

Michael, S. T., 488
Michaelson, W., 2
Milavsky, B., 292
Miles, H. H. W., 523
Miles, M. B., 519, 525
Milgram, N. A., 375
Milgram, S., 2, 550, 560, 561, 563, 611
Miller, D. G., 56
Miller, G. A., 10, 103
Miller, N., 6, 9, 553
Miller, N. E., 72, 82, 86, 260, 269, 271, 301, 434
Miller, R. R., 116
Miller, R. S., 552
Miller, W., 144
Mills, J., 573
Milner, P. M., 73, 281
Minton, C., 397
Mischel, W., 5, 438, 439, 453
Mitchell, R. E., 605
Miyagi, O., 324
Moltz, H., 356
Money, J., 388
Monroe, L., 322
Moore, W. T., 343
Moray, N., 55
Morgan, A. H., 329
Morgan, C. T., 258
Morgan, J. D., 258
Morlock, H. C., Jr., 318
Morris, D., 386
Morris, W. W., 552
Morrison, D. F., 318
Morton, H., 598
Moruzzi, G., 229
Moses, H., 258
Moss, H. A., 397
Mullahy, P., 453
Munn, N. L., 420
Murdoch, P., 543
Myers, J. K., 488

Nadler, R. D., 267
Nakashima, E. N., 343
Nash, J., 377
Nash, S. C., 393
Neale, J. M., 482, 491
Neisser, U., 25, 59
Nelson, K. E., 357
Neustatter, W. L., 523
Newcomb, T. M., 582
Newell, A., 175, 192
Newman, H. H., 213
Newman, M. F., 485
Newson, E., 397
Newson, J., 397
Nichols, P. L., 213
Nisbett, R. E., 187, 261, 536, 583
Nissen, T. L., 117
Niswander, G. D., 482
Nomikus, M. S., 292
Nordby, V. J., 21
Norman, D. A., 131
Norris, E. B., 109

Nowlis, V., 301
Noyes, A. P., 498

Oden, M. H., 216
Ogston, W. D., 156
Olds, J., 2, 8, 73
O'Leary, K., 525
Olson, C., 156
Omark, D. R., 391
Omark, M., 391
Opler, M. K., 488
Opton, E. M., Jr., 292
Orlinsky, D. E., 523
Orme-Johnson, D. W., 336
Orne, M. T., 331, 332, 333
Ornstein, R. E., 54
Oskamp, S., 544
Overmier, J. B., 84

Paige, K. E., 238–239
Pallak, M. S., 584
Palmer, R. J., 392
Parkc, R. D., 70, 305
Paterson, J. G., 357
Patterson, M. L., 595
Paul, G. L., 522, 523
Paulus, P. B., 543
Pavlov, I., 63–64
Pedersen, F. A., 391, 397
Penfield, W., 232
Pengelley, E. T., 243
Perez-Reyes, M., 343
Perlick, D., 612
Perlman, D., 535
Perls, F., 6, 437, 452, 513, 518
Peterson, L. R., 114
Peterson, M. J., 114
Phoenix, C. H., 269
Piaget, J., 5, 356, 360, 361, 374, 377
Piliavin, I. M., 567
Piliavin, J. A., 567
Pittman, T. S., 584
Pliner, P., 564
Plutchik, R. R., 501
Pollard, J. C., 341
Porter, R. W., 486
Posner, M. I., 111, 114, 131
Premack, D., 152
Pressman, I., 605
Price, J., 606, 610
Pritzker, H. A., 579

Quillian, M. R., 124, 126

Rabbie, J. M., 540
Rabin, A. I., 372
Rachlin, H., 76–77, 94
Rand, P., 449
Rankin, N. O., 292
Rapaport, C., 187, 332
Rapaport, D., 6, 434, 504
Raven, B. H., 549
Ray, O. S., 345
Rayner, R., 64

Rechtschaffen, A., 322
Redlich, F., 485, 488
Regan, J. W., 536, 565
Regula, R. C., 548
Renault, P. F., 343
Rennie, T. A. C., 488
Renson, G. J., 370
Rest, J., 375
Restle, F., 166, 167
Rheingold, H. H., 363
Rhine, J. B., 190
Richards, W. R., 59
Riecken, H. W., 535
Riesen, A. H., 355
Rittle, R. H., 543
Robertson, D., 162
Robson, K. S., 397
Roby, T. B., 72
Rock, I., 43
Rodgers, D. A., 602, 603
Rodgers, W. L., 408
Rodin, J., 567
Rogers, C. R., 6, 437, 452, 513,
    514–515, 525
Roigaard-Petersen, H. H., 117
Rosen, E., 464
Rosenbaum, P. S., 141
Rosenblith, W. A., 32
Rosenblum, L. A., 371
Rosenkoetter, L. I., 373
Rosenthal, D., 481
Rosenthal, M. S., 343
Rosenthal, R., 206
Ross, D., 86, 87, 373, 435
Ross, M., 610
Ross, S. A., 86, 87, 373, 435
Rowell, T. E., 134
Rowland, L. W., 333
Rozin, P., 255
Rubenstein, J. L., 397
Ruskin, R. S., 510
Rydin, I., 142

Saari, D., 564
Saarni, C. I., 393
Sachs, E., Jr., 482
Saegert, S., 276
Salapatek, P., 51, 354
Sampson, H., 321
Samuels, W., 531
Sanford, R. N., 448
Sarason, S. B., 214, 259, 450
Sarnoff, I., 540
Sawrey, W. L., 82
Schachter, J., 288
Schachter, S., 2, 6, 10, 14, 187, 261,
    264, 265, 290, 291, 292, 313, 530,
    535, 538, 539, 540
Schaefer, E. S., 204, 370
Schafer, D., 333
Schaffer, H. R., 365
Schaie, K. W., 205, 412
Scheier, M. F., 541
Schein, E. H., 569

Scherer, S. E., 596
Schjelderup, H., 521
Schlesinger, H. J., 55
Schlesinger, I. M., 145
Schlosberg, H., 296
Schmitt, R. C., 605
Schooler, K., 55
Schopler, J., 610
Schreiber, F. R., 475
Schreiner, L. H., 229
Schulman, J. L., 447
Schultz, D. P., 21
Sears, D. O., 557
Sears, P. S., 301
Sears, R., 5
Sears, R. R., 301, 373, 397
Sebastian, R. J., 305
Sechrest, L. B., 595
Segall, M. H., 52
Sekerak, G. J., 543
Seligman, M. E. P., 84
Senay, E. C., 340
Shapiro, A., 322
Shaver, P., 370, 383, 384, 408, 409,
    411, 447, 541, 613, 614
Shaw, J. C., 175
Sheffield, F. D., 72
Sheldon, W., 421, 422, 442, 451
Shepard, R. N., 123
Sheposh, J., 544
Sherer, K., 156
Sherman, J. A., 508
Sherman, M., 295
Shikiar, R., 448
Shimoyama, T., 449
Shuck, A., 391
Shuck, S. Z., 391
Siegel, M. G., 482
Siegel, R. K., 117
Siegler, R. S., 360
Simmons, M. W., 89
Simon, H., 103
Simon, H. A., 175, 192
Sinclair, H., 359, 360
Singer, J. E., 290, 291, 535, 536, 591,
    592, 593, 615
Singer, R. D., 305
Singh, B., 336
Sistrunk, F., 392
Skinner, B. F., 4, 9, 68–69, 70, 80, 94,
    146, 434
Slob, A. K., 269
Slobin, D. I., 159
Smedslund, J., 360
Smith, J. C., 336
Smith, P., 16
Smith, S., 606, 610
Snyder, F., 318
Snyder, M., 564
Snyder, R. L., 602
Solomon, R. L., 66
Sommer, R., 594, 595, 596, 597
Sorenson, E. R., 298
Sorrentino, R. M., 548

Southwick, C. H., 602
Spence, J. T., 423
Spence, K. W., 109, 253, 423, 450
Sperling, G., 55, 110
Sperry, R. W., 2, 234
Spielberger, C. D., 313
Spitz, R. A., 371
Springer, A. D., 116
Spuhler, J. N., 212, 219
Srole, L., 488, 613
Stang, D. J., 548
Stanton, H. E., 334
Stavros, D., 482
Steffensmeier, D. J., 448
Stein, L., 482
Steinschreiber, L., 322
Stettner, L. J., 356
Stoel, C., 142
Stokols, D., 604
Stone, P. J., 168
Stoner, J. A. F., 553
Stoyva, J. M., 322
Stratton, L. O., 596
Strayer, F., 16
Streeter, L. A., 156
Streib, G. F., 414
Stricker, G., 465, 472, 478
Strodtbeck, F. L., 548
Strother, C. R., 205, 412
Suedfeld, P., 259
Sullivan, H. S., 430
Svensson, A., 392
Swap, W., 276
Szasz, T. S., 491, 495

Tago, A., 324
Takaishi, M., 381
Tanner, J. M., 381
Tart, C. T., 345
Tasch, R. J., 397
Tavris, C., 383, 384
Taylor, J., 450
Taylor, J. A., 450
Taylor, R. L., 111
Teichman, Y., 540
Teitelbaum, P., 260
Tepas, D. I., 318
Tepperman, J., 260
Terman, J. M., 200, 201, 216
Teyler, T. J., 249, 345
Thibaut, J. W., 535
Thiessen, D. D., 602, 603
Thigpen, C. H., 475
Thompson, D. F., 295, 297
Thompson, R. F., 32, 249
Thompson, R. T., 249
Thorndike, E. L., 171
Thurstone, L. L., 203
Timmons, M. C., 343

Tinklenberg, J. R., 343
Tinklepaugh, O. L., 99
Titley, R. W., 391
Tognacci, L. N., 581
Tolbert, K., 142
Tolman, E. C., 4, 10, 99
Tom, S., 573
Totten, J., 536
Trabasso, T., 167
Treisman, A. M., 55
Tropc, Y., 554
Tulving, E., 100
Turiel, E. E., 375
Turnbull, C. M., 52
Turner, C. D., 267
Turner, J., 575
Turrell, E. S., 82
Tyler, T., 580

Underwood, B. J., 120
Ungar, G., 117
Ungerleider, J. T., 342

Veitch, R., 606
Vernon, D. T. A., 581
Vernon, J., 259
Vincent, J. E., 564
Viney, W., 391
Vinokur, A., 554
Von Békésy, G., 32
von Osterman, G. F., 136

Wack, D. L., 543
Walk, R. D., 51
Wall, M. E., 343
Wallace, J. E., 343
Wallace, R. K., 335
Wallach, M. A., 181, 182, 553
Wallington, S. A., 565
Walster, E., 280, 565, 566, 575
Walster, G. W., 565, 566
Walters, R. H., 70, 303, 373
Warden, C. J., 266
Warwick, D. P., 582
Watkins, J. G., 333
Watson, J. B., 64
Watson, O. M., 596
Wechsler, D., 201, 202, 204
Weigel, R. H., 581
Weiner, B., 273, 281
Weingartner, N., 596
Weisberg, D., 87
Weisbrod, R. A., 157
Weiss, J. M., 487
Weiss, W., 575
Weld, H. P., 38
Welker, W. I., 270
Wells, H., 166
Wells, R., 391

Wells, W. D., 305
Wender, P. H., 481
Wertheimer, M., 44
West, S. G., 305
Westie, F. R., 580
Wever, E. G., 33
Whalen, R. E., 267, 268
Wheeler, D., 564
Wheeler, L., 291
White, R. W., 464, 465, 476
Whitehouse, R. H., 381
Whiteside, J., 565
Whiting, J. W. M., 301
Whorf, B. L., 152
Wickelgren, W. A., 120
Wicker, A. W., 580
Wicklund, R. A., 541
Wiesel, T. N., 30
Wilbur, C. B., 475
Williams, H. L., 318
Willis, F. N., 595
Willows, D. C., 303
Wilson, G., 525
Wilson, P. D., 355
Winsborough, H. H., 605
Wise, D. C., 482
Witkin, H. A., 393
Wolf, K. M., 371
Wolfe, J. B., 71
Wolfgang, H., 212
Wolman, B. B., 485
Wolpe, J., 485, 506, 508, 521, 523, 525
Wood, L. E., 303
Wood-Gush, D. G., 255
Word, L. E., 567
Wortis, J., 498
Wrightsman, L. S., 539
Wulff, J. J., 72
Wynne, L. C., 66

Yalom, J. D., 519, 525
Yarrow, L. J., 397
Yates, A. J., 510
Yeracaris, C. A., 449
Youniss, J., 375

Zajonc, R. B., 275, 276, 542
Zanna, M. P., 531
Zax, M., 465, 472, 478
Zegans, L. S., 341
Zelazo, N. A., 354
Zelazo, P. R., 354
Zillmann, D., 291, 292, 293, 304
Zimbardo, P. G., 187, 332, 540, 556, 587
Zimmermann, R. R., 365
Zinberg, N. E., 343
Zolman, J. F., 603
Zuckerman, M., 313

Subject Index

Page numbers in italic refer to illustrations.

Absolute threshold, 36
Acceptance, need for, 529
Achievement need, 272-273, 449
Acrophobia, 462
Action potential, in neuron, 223
Activation theory of emotions, 288-289, 311
Adaptation, and perception, 38-40
Adolescence
    and identity search, 400-401
    and peer group, influence of, 401
    sexual behavior during, 380-381
Adrenal cortex, 241, 242
Adrenal medulla, 241
Adrenalin, 241
Adult development, 400-415
    middle age, 408-412
    old age, 412-415
Affiliation, 536-541
    and birth order, 538
    and fear reduction, 539-541
    instinctive drive for, 537-539
    and social comparison, need for, 540-541
Afterimage, 30-31. See also Color Plate C.
Age regression, under hypnosis, 329
Aggression, 298-310
    anonymity, effect of, 555-556, 556
    arousal of, 299-300
    catharsis, 302-304, 312
    and discipline in childhood, effect of, 368
    displacement of, 301-302, 301, 312
    in dreams, 327
    and frustration, 299-300
    imitation of by children, 86, 86, 300
    and instinct, 300
    neural control of, 287
    television, effects of, 304-305, 310, 312

Aggressiveness, and sex differences, 391-392
Agoraphobia, 462
Alcohol, 339
Alcoholism, 339
    and aversive learning, in treatment of, 508, 508
All-or-none rule, 224
Alpha rhythm, 188-189
Altruism, 565-566
American Sign Language, 150-151
Ames room, 44
Amnesia, post-hypnotic, 330-331
Amniocentesis, 243
Amphetamines, 501
Amygdala
    lesions of, 286
    as part of limbic system, 286
Anal personality, 431
Analytic psychology, 433
Androgens, 241, 267
Animal husbandry, 247
Anonymity, and aggression, 555-556, 556
Anterior pituitary gland, 240
Antidepressants, 501
Anvil, of ear, 33
Anxiety
    and affiliation, 540
    in childhood, 363
    and defense mechanisms, 427-430
    versus fear, 427-428
    free-floating, 461
    Freudian meaning of, 427
    as personality trait, 449-451
    See also Neuroses.
Anxiety mechanisms, 427-430
Anxiety neurosis, 461-462
Appetite, 271. See also Hunger.
Approach-avoidance conflict, 268-269, 436
Armed Forces Qualification Test (AFQT), 203
Army Alpha and Beta Tests, 203

Army General Classification Tests (AGCT), 203
Arousal
    adaptation level, 253-255
    of aggressive feelings, 299-300
    and autonomic nervous system, 238
    crowding, effect of, 611
    by drugs, 340
    and homeostasis, 253-255
    interpretation of, 290-293
    problem solving, effect on, 259
    and reinforcement, 72-73
    and reticular formation, 229
    sexual, 270
    See also Emotions; Motivation.
Ascending reticular activating system, 229
Association cortex, 231, 233
Association theory of concept formation, 166-167, 171-172
Associations, in learning, 104-105
    nonverbal, 105
Attachment, in childhood, 364-366
Attention
    and ascending reticular activating system, 229
    in human attachment, 365-366
    and perception, 53-55
Attitude change, 574-585
    through behavior, 582-585
    and discrepancy of communication, 579
    and exposure to new opinions, 579-582
    prestige of communicator, effect of, 575
Attitudes, 569-585
    changing, see Attitude change
    and cognitive consistency theory, 571-574
    and learning theory, 570-571
    and primacy effect, 574
Attribution theory, 534-536
Auditory canal, 33

Authoritarianism, as personality trait, 448
Autism, 478, 479
Autonomic nervous system, 225, 236-238, *237*
Average, determining the, 616-617
Avoidance training, 68
Axon, 223
Axon terminal, 223

Babinski reflex, 350
Backward conditioning, 66
Balance model of liking, 571-572, *571*
Basilar membrane of cochlea, 33
Bedwetting, and classical conditioning, 64
Behavior control, 511
Behavior genetics, 242-247
Behavior therapy, 485-488, 506-512
    aversive techniques, 508
    modeling, 508
    and positive reinforcement, 508
    and psychoanalytic therapy, compared, 508-512
    systematic desensitization, 506-508, *507*
Behaviorism, 9
Bias, in intelligence testing, 207-211, *210*, *211*
Binocular cues to depth, 40-41
Biofeedback, 188-189
Biological "clocks," 317
Birth control
    contraceptive pills as related to hormones, 238
    and effect on sex roles, 397
Birth order, and affiliation, 538
Birth rate, changes in, 407-408
Blind spot, in vision, 28
Body types, Sheldon's theory of, 421-422, *422*
Brain, 227-235, *227*
    corpus callosum, 234-235
    damage to, 214-215, 482
    electrical stimulation of, 222, 229, 232, 260, 286
    electroshock therapy, 498-499
    electroencephalogram (EEG), 188
    and emotions, 286-287
    forebrain, 229-233
    and hearing, 33
    hindbrain, 228-229
    and hunger sensations, 257-258
    learning as chemical changes in, 116-117
    limbic system, 233, 286-287
    midbrain, 229
    and motor activity, 231
    pleasure centers, stimulation of, 73
    prefrontal lobotomies, 288, 499
    split-brain phenomenon, 234-235, *235*

and vision, 30
    See also Memory.
Brain teasers, *179*
Brain waves
    control of, 188-189
    during sleep, 318, *318*
Brainwashing, 568-569
Brightness constancy, 45
Broca's speech area, 231
Bystander intervention, 567-569

Camouflage, 46. *See also Color Plate D.*
Career choice, 401-403
    changes in during middle age, 410
    and sex-role typing, 390, 400
Catatonia, 478
Catharsis, 302-304, 312
Cattell's personality traits, *442*
Cell body of neuron, 223. *See also Color Plate E.*
Central nervous system, 225-235
    spinal cord, 225-226, *225*
    See also Brain.
Central tendency, measures of, 616-618
Cerebellum, 229
Cerebral cortex, 230-233
    and memory storage, 232
    structure of, *231*
    visual area of, 28
    See also Color Plate F.
Charisma, 545
Childrearing methods
    on kibbutz, 371-372
    Skinner's ideas on, 68-69
Children
    and affiliation, need for, 537
    aggression in, 86, *86*, 300
    attachment, parental, 364-366
    concept formation in, 166, 167
    and conservation concept, 359-360
    disturbed, treatment for, 516, 517
    identification in, 371-372
    independence, development of, 366-367
    mentally gifted, 216-217
    mentally retarded, 214-216
    and operant conditioning, 69-70, 75, 79
    and sex, interest in, 380, 430-432
    and sex-role typing, 397-399
    television, effects of, 304-305, 310, 312
    trust, development of, 363-366
    See also Cognitive development; Infancy; Language development; Moral development; Personality development.
Chimpanzees
    cognitive learning in, 99
    curiosity in, 270

insight in, 178-179
    language development in, 149-152
    and operant conditioning, 71
    perceptual development in, 354-355
    prefrontal lobotomy in, 288
    and trial-and-error learning, 176-178
Chlorpromazine, 291, 499
Chromosomes, 243, *245*
    sex, 244-245
Chunking, and memory, 103, *103*
Circadian rhythms, 317
Classical conditioning, 63-67, *66*
    extinction, 66-67
    versus operant conditioning, 83-84
    Pavlov's experiments in, 63-64
    spontaneous recovery, 66-67
    steps in, 64-65
Claustrophobia, 462
Clinical psychologists, 496, 497
Cochlea, 33
Cognitive consistency theory, 571-574
    contributions of, 573-574
Cognitive control over body functions, 187-188
Cognitive development, Piaget's stages of, 356-361
    concrete operations stage, 360-361
    formal operations stage, 361
    preoperational stage, 359-360
    sensorimotor stage, 357-359
Cognitive dissonance, theory of, 572-573
Cognitive learning
    in animals, 99
    contiguity, 100-101
    factors affecting, 101-109
Cognitive psychology, 10
Cohabitation, 406
Collective unconscious, 328, 433
Colorblindness, 222. *See also Color Plate B.*
Color circle, 30. *See also Color Plate A.*
Color constancy, 45
Communication
    and leadership, 548-549, *549*
    nonverbal, 154-157
Competition, versus cooperation, 543-545
Complementarity, and liking, 277
Compliance, socially induced, 562-565
    through guilt feelings, 564-565
    and situational pressure, 563-564
    See also Conformity.
Computer models, in information processing, 174-176
Computer-assisted instruction, 128-129
Concept formation
    association theory of, 166-167, 171-172
    Gestalt approach to, 167-168, 173-174

and grammar, 148–149
heuristics, 169–170
hypothesis-testing theory of, 167, 172–173
importance of, 164
information-processing approach to, 168–169
problems, *163*
See also Problem solving.
Concepts, types of, 164–166
Concrete operations stage of cognitive development, 360–361
Conditioned response, 64
Conditioned stimulus, 64
Conditioning, *see* Backward conditioning; Classical conditioning; Operant conditioning
Cones of retina, 28, 30, 31–32
Conflicts
  and defense mechanisms, 428–430
  Erikson's theories on, 362
  and mental disorders, 483–485
  and psychosomatic conditions, 486
  sexual, during adolescence, 381
  unconscious, 505, 509
Conformity, socially induced, 562–565
  blind, 561–562
  and group pressure, 563
  through guilt feelings, 564–565
  and situational pressure, 563–564
Conformity in groups, 550–553
  Asch's experiment on, 550–552, *551*
  and group pressure, 563
Conjunctive concept, *163*, 164
Consciousness, states of
  dreams, 322–328
  hypnosis, 328–334
  meditation, 334–337
  mystical experiences, 337
  sleep, 317–322
Conservation, concept of, 359–360
  effect of training on, 359–360
  lack of, *359*
Constancy, 42–45
  brightness, 45
  color, 45
  object, 52, 357–359
  shape, 45, *45*
  size, 42–44
Contiguity, 100–101
Contrast effects, 38–40
Convergence, 40–41
Convergent thinking, 181
Conversion neurosis, 464–465
Cooperation, versus competition, 543–545
Cornea, 27
Corpus callosum, 230, 234–235
  and split-brain phenomenon, 234–235

Correlation, 15–16, 197, 619
  of IQ scores, 204–205, *204*, 213
Correlation coefficients, 619
Cortex, 229
Creativity, 180–182
  in dreams, 328
  and drugs, 341
  in preoperational stage of cognitive development, 359
  tests of, 181–182
Cretinism, 215
Criminal behavior
  crowding, effects of, 605, *605*
  and extroversion-introversion, 423
  of psychopaths, 467–468
Critical periods, 355–356
  in language acquisition, 149
Critical ratios, 621, 623
Crowding, 598–612
  animals, effects on, 602–604
  crime, relation to, 605, *605*
  definition of, 604
  and intensification, theory of, 612
  laughter, effects on, 612, *612*
  mental health, effects on, 605
  and population growth, 598–600
  and sex differences, 610–611
  and stimulation level, 611
  task performance, effects on, 606
Crowds, as attention-getters, 550
Cuder Preference Test, 403
Culture
  and expression of emotions, 298, 311–312
  and "normal" behavior, 458–459
  and sexual behavior, 382
Curiosity, 270

Darwinian reflex, 350
Death, 415
Decay, and loss of memory, 119
  versus interference, 120
Defense mechanisms, 427–430, *427*
  as reaction to anxiety, 427–430
  as resistance to therapy, 504
Deindividuation, 555–556
Delayed reinforcement, 74–75, *74*
Delta waves, 318
Delusions, paranoid, 473
Dendrites, 223
Denial, as anxiety mechanism, 428
Depressants, 338–340, *338*, 345
Depression
  and antidepressant drugs, 501
  and electroshock therapy, 498–499
  and learned helplessness, 84
  manic, 471–473
  in middle age, 410–411
  organic causes, 482
  post-partum, 482
  treatment of, *see* Psychopathology, treatment of

Depth perception, 40–41, 51
Descriptive statistics, 616–619
Development
  adult, 400–408
  cognitive, 356–361
  moral, 372–375
  of motor skills, 351–354, *351*
  perceptual, 354–356
  personality, Erikson's stages of, 362–371
  physical, 348–354
  prenatal, 348–349, *349*
Developmental psychology, 5. *See also* Development.
Deviance, 529–531. *See also* Psychopathology.
  sexual, 385–388
Difference threshold, 36
Differential reinforcement, 89
Discipline, in childhood, 367–369
  styles of, 369
Discrimination learning, 87, *89*, 89–91, 167
Discriminative stimulus, 89
Disjunctive concept, *163*, 165–166
Displacement
  of aggression, 301–302, *301*, 312
  as defense mechanism, 429
  in dreams, 324–325
  and prejudice, 302
Dissonance reduction, 573, 583–585
Distance, and communication, 157
Distance perception, 40–41, *41*
Distortions, of perceptions, 25–26
  through drugs, 340–341
  under hypnosis, 329–330, 333
Divergent thinking, 181, 204
Divorce, 403–405, 408
  rates of, *403*
DNA (deoxyribonucleic acid), 116, 117, 243
Dove Counterbalance General Intelligence Test, *208*
Down's syndrome, 215
Dreams, 322–328, 503–504
  aggression in, 327
  content of, 324–325
  Freud's theory of, 323–327, 344
  Jung's ideas on, 327–328, 344
  purpose of, 325–326
  recalling, 322–323
  and REM sleep, 322
  and wish fulfillment, 325
Drive, 72. *See also* Hunger; Sex drive.
Drive-reduction theory, 72–73, 253
Drugs
  and arousal, 291
  depressants, 338–340, *338*
  hallucinogens, 340–342
  and hunger, control of, 261
  marijuana, 342–343
  prenatal development, effects on, 349

psychoactive, 338–343
and psychotherapy, treatment of, 499–501
and schizophrenic-like symptoms, 482
stimulants, 340

Ear, 26, 32–33, 33
and perception of uprightness and motion, 35–36
Eardrum, 33
Eating center (hypothalamus), 260
Ecstasy, 337
Ectomorph, 421
Effectors, 224
Ego, 426–427, 426
Ego functioning, 434
Ego ideal, 427
Ego states, 512
Eidetic imagery, 108
Electric shock therapy, 498–499
and memory loss, 116, 498
Electroconvulsive shock (ECS), 498
Electroencephalogram (EEG), 188, 318
Embryo, human, 349. *See also Color Plates G, H.*
Emotions
activation theory of, 288–289, 289, 311
brain function and, 286–287
cognitive appraisal of, 292–293, 311
control of, 297
defined, 284–285
effects of, 310–311
and epinephrine, 242
expression of, 294–298, 299
identifying, 295–298
inappropriate, 293–294
James-Lange theory of, 285–288, 286, 311
during menstrual cycle, 238–239
and motivation, 284–285
physiological/cognitive theory of, 289–294, 289, 311
Schlosberg emotion circle, 296–297, 296
and sex roles, 299
universality of, 298, 311–312
See also Aggression.
Encounter groups, 517–519
Endocrine glands, 238–242, 240
Endomorph, 421
Engram, 116
Environment
adaptation to, 256
and intelligence, effects on, 213–214
Environmental psychology, 6
crowding, 598–612
noise, effects of, 590–594
personal space, 594–598
urban living, 600–601, 612–614 '
Enzymes, 243

Epinephrine, 241, 290–291
and control of emotions, 242
Episodic memory, 100–101
Equity theory, 566
Erikson's stages of personality development, 362–368
EST (Erhard Seminar Training), 513
Estrogens, 238–239, 241, 267
"Eureka" phenomenon, 178–179
Evolution, 245–247
Excitatory chemicals, in neurons, 224
Experimental psychology, 4, 13–15
Extinction
in classical conditioning, 66–67, 67
in operant conditioning, 77–79
Extramarital sexual experience, 383–384, 407
Extrasensory perception, 189–190
Extroversion, 423
Eye, 26, 27–28, 27. *See also* Color vision; Vision.
Eye color, genetic determination of, 243–244, 244
Eye contact, and communication, 157
Eysenck's three-factor theory of personality, 423

Familiarity
learning, effect on, 101–102, 102
and liking, 275–276, 276
Father, and Oedipus complex, 431–432, 505–506
Fear, 310
and adrenal glands, 242
versus anxiety, 427–428
and anxiety mechanisms, 427–428
of being deviant, 529–531
desensitization of, 506–508
generalization of, 88
in infancy, 363
learned, 271
phobias, 462–463
Fear reduction, and affiliation, 539–540
Femininity, images of, 387–388, 397–399. *See also* Sex roles.
Feminist movement, *see* Women's movement
Fertilization of human egg, 244–245
Fetus, human, 349
Figure-ground relationship, 46, 47, 47
in social behavior, 50
Fixation, 431
Fixed interval schedule of reinforcement, 76
Fixed ratio schedule of reinforcement, 76
Flow charts, and problem solving, 175, 175
Focusing, conservative, 169
Food deprivation in rats, 257
Forebrain, 229–233
Forgetting, 118–122
and decay, 119

and interference, effects of, 119–120
motivated, 121–122
See also Memory.
Formal operations stage of cognitive development, 361
Fovea, 28
Free association, 503–504
Free-floating anxiety, 461
Freud's theory of dreams, 323–327, 344
criticism of, 326–327
Freud's theory of psychoanalysis, *see* Psychoanalytic theory
Frontal lobes, 230
Frustration, 299–300
Frustration-aggression hypothesis, 299
Functional fixedness, 174, 174, 259

Galvanic skin response, 591
Games
non-zero-sum, 543
psychological, 512–513
zero-sum, 543
Generalization gradient, 87, 87, 89
See also Stimulus generalization.
Genes, 243
mutations in, 245
Genetics
and behavior, 242–247
and intelligence, 213–214
and psychopathology, 480–481
Gestalt approach to concept formation, 167–168, 173–174
Gestalt psychology, 46
Gestalt therapy, 512
Gestures, in communication, 156
Glucagon, 241
Grammar, 137–140
acquisition of, 147–148
children's, 142–143, 143, 147
concept formation of, 148–149
early, 145–146
pivot, 144–145, 144
transformational, 139–140
See also Language.
Group marriage, 407
Group pressure, 563
Group therapy, 516–517
Groups, 545–556
conformity in, 550–553
deindividuation in, 555–556
leadership in, 545–550
as mobs, 554–555
risk taking in, 553–554
Growth, physical, in puberty, 380–381
Growth curves, 381
Gua (chimpanzee), 150
Guilt, feelings of
as cause of homosexuality, 388
in childhood, 367–369
in inducing compliance, 564–565
in psychopathic personality, lack of, 466–467
sexual, during adolescence, 381

Halfway houses, 521
Hallucinogens, *338*, 340–342, 345
  dangers of, 341–342
  effects of, 340–341
Hammer, of ear, 33
Harlow's artificial mothers, 365
Hearing
  effects of noise on, 590–592
  effects of on intelligence testing, 209
Hebephrenia, 478–479
Hemispheres of brain, 234–235
  corpus callosum, 234–235
  split-brain phenomenon, 234–235
Heredity, 242–247, 349–350
  intelligence, effects on, 211–213
  and psychopathology, 480–481
Hering illusion, 25
Heroin addiction, 340
Heuristics, 169–170
Hindbrain, 228–229
Hippocampus, 233
Homeostasis, 253–255
Homosexuality, 383, 386–388
  causes of, 387–388
Hormones, 239, 240–241
  and maternal behavior, 266–267
  in menstrual cycle, 238–239
Humanistic movement, 299
Humanistic psychology, 10–11,
  437–440
  therapies based on, 512–516
Hunger, 255, 257–265
  food deprivation in rats, *257*
  and nutritional state of body, 258
  social factors, 261
  stomach contractions, 257–258, *258*
  and tasting, 258–260
Hydrocephalus, 215
Hypnosis, 328–334, 344
  and antisocial behavior, 332–333
  and cooperation, necessity of,
  332–333
  distortions under, 329–330, 333
  effect on pain, 331–332, 333–334
  post-hypnotic suggestion, 330–331
  and psychopathology, treatment of,
  503
  skepticism concerning, 331
  uses of, 333–334
Hypothalamus, 230, 240
  electrical stimulation of, 260
  and hunger, 260–261
  and limbic system, 286
  and obesity, 260
Hypothesis-testing theory of concept
  formation, 167, 172–173
Hysterical neurosis, 464–465

Id, 425–426, *426*
Identification, 371–372, 373
  sexual, 372, 388, 397–399
Identity crisis, during adolescence, 401
Idiot-savants, 187

Illusions, optical, 25
  moon, 42–43
  of movement, 44
  Mueller-Lyer, *25*, 44
Imagery, effect on learning, 106–107,
  107
  eidetic, 108
Imitation, 85–87
  and aggressive behavior, 300–301
  and behavior therapy, 508
  in language development, 143, 147
  and learning, 85–87
  and personality development,
  435–436
Imprinting, 355–356
  and age, *356*
  See also Identification.
Inappropriate affect, in schizophrenics,
  476
Incentive theory of motivation, 253
Independence, development of in
  childhood, 366–367
Individual psychology, 433–434
Infancy
  innate behavior in, 92, 350
  object constancy in, 357–359, *358*
  and perceptual preferences, 51, *354*,
  354–355
  reflexes in, 350
  and sexuality, Freudian theory,
  430–431
  speech, appearance of, 142
  trust, development of, 363–366
  vision in, 354–355
Infantile autism, 478, 479
Inferential statistics, 619–623
Inferiority, feelings of in childhood,
  369–370, 434
Information-processing approach to
  concept formation, 168–169
  and computer models, 174–176
Inhibitory chemicals, in neuron, 224
Insanity, legal definition of, 468–469
  See also Psychopathology.
Insight, in problem solving, 178–179
Instincts
  for affiliation, 537–539
  aggressive, 300
  maternal, 265–266
Instrumental conditioning, *see*
  Operant conditioning
Insulin, 241
Intellectualization, as defense
  mechanism, 430
Intelligence
  age, effects of, 205, *205*
  environmental factors, 213–214
  genetic factors in, 213
  Guilford's model of, 203–204
  measures of, *see* Intelligence tests
  racial differences in, 212
Intelligence quotient (IQ)
  computation of, 200

  in the mentally retarded, 214–215
  occupation and, 206–207, *207*
  scores, distribution of, *203*, *204*
  in twins, correlation of scores,
  213–214
Intelligence tests
  bias in, 207–211, *210*, *211*
  complex, 203–204
  group, 203
  individual, 200–203
  reliability of, 204–205
  scoring of, 202–203
  validity of, 205–207
Interference
  versus decay, 120
  effects of on memory, 119–120
  proactive, 120
  retroactive, 120
Introversion, 423
Involutional melancholia, 471
Iris, 27
Isolation, studies on, 606

James-Lange theory of emotions,
  285–288, *286*, 311
  criticism of, 287–288
Just noticeable difference (j.n.d.), 36

Kibbutz, childrearing in, 371–372
Kinesthetic sense, 27, 35–36
Kleptomania, 469
Koans, 334
Kohlberg's stages of moral
  development, 374–375

Lana (chimpanzee), 152, *152*
Language
  acquisition of, 146–152
  ambiguous sentences, *140*, 141
  in animals, 149–152
  context, social and cognitive, of
  sentences, 138–139
  and memory, 154
  morphemes, 136–137, *137*
  nonverbal communication, 154–157
  phonemes, 135–136, *136*
  and sex differences, 392
  sexual stereotypes in, 153
  sign, 150–151
  and thought, 152–154
  See also Grammar; Language
  development; Speech.
Language development
  in animals, 149–152
  childhood grammar, 142–146
  critical periods, 149
  by imitation, 85, 143, 147
  and learning, role of, 147–148
  in preoperational stage of cognitive
  development, 359
  and reinforcement, 79–80
  speech, appearance of, 142
Latent learning, 99

Lateral geniculate body, 28, 32
Leadership, 545–550
   communication networks and, 548–549, *549*
   legitimacy of, 549–550
Learned helplessness, 84
Learning
   and aggression, 300–301
   aversive, in behavior therapy, 508
   chemical transfer of, 117–118
   computer-assisted instruction, 128–129
   by contiguity, 100–101
   critical periods, 355–356
   definition of, 62–63
   and delayed reinforcement, 75
   discrimination, 87, *89*, 89–91, 167
   extinction of, 66–67, 77–79
   imitation, 85–87
   imprinting, 355–356
   insight, 178–179
   latent, 99
   to learn, 176–178
   maladaptive, 90
   and mental disorders, applications to, 90–91
   and moral development, 373
   noise, effects of, 593–594
   paired-associate, 104
   and perception, 51–53
   versus performance, 252
   of personality, 434–437
   plateaus in, 83
   and positive reinforcement, 69–70
   programmed instruction, 127–128
   and punishment, 69–70
   stimulus generalization, 87–89, *87*
   storage of, 116–118; *see also* Memory
   See also Classical conditioning;
      Cognitive learning; Concept
      formation; Development;
      Memory; Operant conditioning;
      Problem solving.
Learning theory approach to attitudes, 570–571
Lens, of eye, 28
Lesions
   of hypothalamus, 260, 286
   of limbic system in animals, 286–287
Libido, 425
Librium, 500
Lie detection, 156
Life expectancy, 412
Light waves, and eye, 27–28. *See also* Vision.
Liking, 273–279, 529
   balance model of, 571–572, *571*
   and complementarity, 277
   and familiarity, 275–276
   and social perception, 533–534
   and reinforcement, 278–279
   and similarity, 276–277

Limbic system, 233, *233*, 286–287
   and emotions, 286–287
Lithium, in treatment of manic-depressive psychosis, 501
Lobotomy, *see* Prefrontal lobotomy
Long-term memory, 115
Loudness, 32
LSD, 340–342

Machiavellianism, as personality trait, 448–449
Maladaptive learning, 90–91
Mandalas, 335
Manic depression, 471–473. *See also* Depression.
Mantra, 334
Marijuana, 342–343, 345
Marriage, 403–410
   contracts, 406–407
   group, 407
   and happiness, 409
   open, 407
   trial, 406
Masculinity, images of, 387–388, 397–399
   See also Sex roles.
Maslow's hierarchy of needs and motives, 274–275, 439–440
Maternal behavior
   in animals, 265–267, *266*, 603
   crowding, effects of, 603–604, *603*
   and Harlow's artificial mothers, 365
   and hormones, 266
   human, 267
   and post-partum depression, 482
   See also Mothers.
Maturation, and development of motor skills, 352–353
Mean, 617
Median, 617
Meditation, 334–336, 344
   effect on pain, 366
   transcendental, 334
Medulla (oblongata), 228, 242
Memory
   biological effects on, 222
   and cerebral cortex, role of, 232
   and chunking, 103, *103*
   electric shock studies of, 116
   episodic, 100–101
   and forgetting, nature of, 118–122
   and language, 154
   localization of, 232
   long-term, 115
   loss of, 330–331, 498
   meaningfulness, effect of, 105–106, *106*
   mnemonics, use of, 111
   organization of, 123–125
   process of, *110*
   semantic, 100–101
   and sensory register, 110–114

   short-term, 114
   See also Forgetting; Memory retrieval.
Memory consolidation, 116
Memory retrieval, 121–127
   directed search, 125–126
   failure of, 121–122
   recall versus recognition, 122–123
   sequential processing, 125
   simultaneous processing, 126–127
Menstrual cycle, 238–239
Mental age, 200
Mental arithmetic tricks, 186
Mental disorders
   applications of learning to, 90–91
   and drugs, 342, 343
   prevalence of, 488–489
   psychoanalytic theory of, 483–485
   treatment of, *see* Psychopathology, treatment of
   See also Personality disorders;
      Psychopathology; Psychoses.
Mental health, definition of, 456–460
Mental illness, concept of, 495
Mental retardation, 214–216
   causes of, 214–215
   treatment of, 215–216
Mentally gifted, 216–217
Meprobromate, 500
Mesomorph, 421
Methadone, 340
Microcephalus, 215
Midbrain, 229
Middle age, 408–412
Minnesota Multiphasic Personality Inventory (MMPI), 443, *443*
Mnemonics, 111
Mob behavior, 554–555
Mode, 616
Mongolism, 215
Monocular cues to depth, 41
Monogenic traits, 243–244
Moon illusion, 42–43
Moral development, 372–375
   in psychopathic personality, 467–468
Moro reflex, 350
Morphemes, 136–137, *137*
Mothers
   artificial, monkeys' response to, 365
   and Oedipus conflict, 431, 505
   schizophrenogenic, 485
   substitute, effect of on children, 371–372
Motivation
   achievement, 272–273, 449
   adaptation level, 253–255
   approach-avoidance conflict, 268–269
   curiosity, 270
   defined, 252–253
   drive-reduction theory, 253
   and emotions, 284–285

homeostatic theory, 253-255
and hunger, 255
incentive theory, 253
learned, 270-279
Maslow's hierarchy, 274-275
maternal behavior, 265-267
versus needs, 255-256
and perception, 55
and performance, 259
self-actualization, 274-275
sex drive, 267-270
social, 528-531
unconscious, 424-425
as warnings, 256
Motor activity, and brain, 231
Motor neurons, 224
Motor skills, development of, 351-354, 351
Movement, perception of, 44
Mueller-Lyer illusion, 25, 44
Multiple births, 352, See also Twins.
Multiple personalities, 475
Mutations, genetic, 245
Mystical experiences, 337, 344

Narcissism, 468-470
Natural selection, 246-247
Needs
Maslow's hierarchy of, 274-275
versus motivation, 255-256
Negative reinforcement, 67-68
Nerve fibers of neuron, 223
Nervous breakdowns, 461
Nervous system
divisions of, 224-225, 225
and endocrine glands, 239
See also Central nervous system;
Peripheral nervous system.
Neurons, 222-224, 223
and auditory nerve, 32-33
functions of, 224
in peripheral nervous system, 235
and visual stimulation, 30
See also Color Plate E.
Neuroses, 460-465
anxiety, 461-462
hysterical-conversion, 464-465
obsessive-compulsive, 463-464
phobias, 462-463
spontaneous recovery from, 520-521
Nine-circle problem, 173
Noise, effects of, 590-594
adaptation to, 591-592
control over, 592-593
physiological response to, 591, 591
Nonreversal shift, in learning, 176
Nonverbal communication, 154-157
Norepinephrine, 242
Normal distribution, 621-623
Nyctophobia, 462

Obedience, socially induced, see
Compliance; Conformity
Obesity, 261-265
and hypothalamus, 260
in rats, 260
Object constancy, 52, 357-359, 358
Obsessive-compulsive neurosis, 463-464
Occipital lobe, 230
and vision, 28
Oedipus complex, 431-432, 431, 505-506
Old age, 412-415
Open marriage, 407
Operant conditioning, 67-83
in animals, 70, 71
versus classical conditioning, 83-84
extinction of, 77-79
factors affecting, 74-81
of heart rate, 82
positive reinforcement versus punishment, 69-70
Skinner box, 68-69
theories of reinforcement, 72-74
See also Reinforcement.
Opponent-process theory of color vision, 31
Optic nerve, 28
Oral personality, 431
Organ of Corti, 32, 33
Oval window, of ear, 33
Ovulation, 238-239

Pain
cognitive control over, 187
hypnosis, effects of, 331-332, 333-334
meditation, effects of, 336
Paired-associate learning, 104, 104
Pancreas, 241
Panic behavior, 554-555
Paradoxical sleep, see REM sleep
Paralanguage, 155-156
Paranoia, 473, 478
Paranoid schizophrenia, 477
Parasympathetic nervous system, 236, 237
Parathyroid glands, 241
Parents
and attachment, development of, 364-366
child's identification with, 371-372
discipline of children, 367-369
effect of children on, 370-371
and personality development, effect on, 435-436
of schizophrenic children, 485
and sex-role typing, 397-398
Parietal lobes, 231
Partial reinforcement, 77-79
See also Schedules of reinforcement.

Pavlov's experiments on classical conditioning, 63-64
Perception, 36-57
adaptation, 38-40, 53
and attention, 53-55
camouflage, 46
of causality, 534-536
constancies, 42-45, 52
contrast effects, 38-40
culture differences in, 52
of depth, 40-41
of distance, 40-41
distortions of, 25-26, 42-43
figure-ground relationship, 47, 47
Gestalt rules of organization, 47-50
and learning, 51-53
motivation and set, 55
of movement, 44
prejudice, influence of, 56
psychophysics, 36-38
of time, 54
visual cliff, 51, 51
See also Social perception.
Perceptual development, 354-356
Performance
crowding, effects of, 606
versus learning, 252
motivation, effects of, 259
noise, effects of, 591-592
and social facilitation effect, 542-543
Peripheral nervous system, 225, 235-238
Personal space, 594-598
and ethnic differences, 595-596
and personal relationship as criterion of, 595
sex differences, 596-597
and territoriality, 597-598
Personality, 5-6
comparison of theories of, 440-441
definitions of, 420
existence of, questioning, 438-439
Freud's theory of, 424-433
multiple, 475
neo-Freudian theories of, 433-434
physiological theories of, 421-423
social learning theory of, 434-437
Personality assessment, 442-447
direct tests, 443-444
problems in, 442-443
projective tests, 444-446
status of, 446
Personality development, 362-371
Freudian theory, 430-432
social learning theory, 434-437
Personality disorders, 465-470
narcissism, 468-470
psychopathology, 466-468
Personality traits, 448-451
Person-centered therapy, 513-516
Phenylketonuria, 216
Phi phenomenon, 44

Phobias, 90, 462–463
Phonemes, 135–136, *136*
Physical development, 348–354
  acceleration of, 351–354
  delaying, 351–354
Piaget's stages of cognitive
    development, 356–361
Pineal organ, 241
Pitch, of sound, 32
Pituitary gland, 230, 240, 241
Pivot grammar, 144–145, *144*
Place theory of sound, 32
Placebos, 14, 82, 331–332
Plateaus in learning, 83
Play therapy, 516, 517
Pleasure centers, stimulation of, 73
Pleasure principle, 425–426
Pons, 229
Population growth, 598–600, *599*
Populations, in statistics, 620–621
Positive reinforcement, 67
  attitude change, effect on, 584–585
  behavior therapy, as method of, 508
  versus punishment, 69–70
  See also Discipline.
Post-hypnotic suggestion, 330–331
Post-partum depression, 482
Practice
  motor skills, effect on, 354
  spaced versus massed, 109
Precognition, 189
Preferences, in concept formation, 170
Prefrontal lobotomies, 288, 499
Prejudice
  and displacement, 302, 312
  through generalization, 88
  and perceptual distortions, 56
  and projection, 429
  and stereotyping, 532–533
Premarital sexual experience, 383
Prenatal development, 348–349, *349.*
    See also Color Plates G, H.
Preoperational stage of cognitive
    development, 359–360
Primal therapy, 512
Primary reinforcers, 70
Proactive interference, 120
Probability, 619
Problem solving, 170–176
  association theory, 171–172
  and computer models, 174–176
  functional fixedness, 174, *174*
  Gestalt approach, 173–174
  hypothesis-testing theory, 172–173
  insight, 178–179
  and motivation, 259
Prodigies, mathematical, 182, 186–187
Programmed instruction, 127–128
Progesterone, 238–239, 241
Projection, as defense mechanism,
    429
Projective personality tests, 444–446
Prolactin, 266

Proprioceptive sense, 35–36
Proxemics, *see* Personal space
Psychiatrists, 496–497
Psychoactive drugs, 338–343, 344
Psychoanalysts, 496, 497
Psychoanalytic theory of personality,
    423–435
  and anxiety, 427–431
  criticisms of, 432–433
  defense mechanisms, 428–430
  and motivation, 424–425
Psychoanalytic theory of mental
    disorder, 483–485
Psychoanalytic therapy, 502–506
  and behavior therapy, compared,
    508–512
  duration of, 506
  effects of, 520–523
  free association, 503–504
  interpretations, 504
  resistance to, 504
  transference, 504–505
  "working through," process of,
    505–506
Psychokinesis, 189
Psychology
  analytic, 433
  behavioral approach to, 9
  cognitive approach to, 10
  ego, 434
  humanistic approach to, 10–11,
    437–440
  individual, 433–434
  major fields of, 3–6
  physiological-biological approach to,
    8–9
  research methods in, 13–18
Psychopathic personality, 466–468
Psychopathology, 6
  attitudes toward, 494–496
  genetic factors, 480–481
  neuroses, 460–465
  personality disorders, 465–470
  physiological causes, 481–482
  prevalence of, 488–489
  psychoanalytic theory of, 483–485
  psychoses, 470–479
  social learning theory of, 485–488
Psychopathology, treatment of
  behavior therapy, 506–512
  chemical therapy, 499–501
  electroshock therapy, 498–499
  encounter groups, 517–519
  Gestalt therapy, 512
  group therapy, 516–517
  person-centered therapy, 513–516
  play therapy, 516, 517
  primal therapy, 512
  psychoanalytic therapy, 502–506
  psychosurgery, 499
  reality therapy, 512
  specialists in, 496–497
  transactional analysis, 512–513

Psychophysics, 36–38
  of airplane noise, 37
  Weber-Fechner law of, 37–38
Psychoses, 470–479
  manic depression, 471–473
  paranoia, 473
  schizophrenia, 474–479
Psychosomatic conditions, 486–487
Psychosurgery, 499. *See also* Prefrontal
    lobotomy.
Psychotherapy, *see* Psychopathology,
    treatment of
Puberty, 380–381
Punishment
  for aggressive behavior, 301
  in learning, 68
  versus positive reinforcement, 69–70
  See also Discipline.
Pupil of eye, 27

Race, and intelligence differences, 212
Range, in statistics, 618
Rationalization, 429–430
Reaction formation, 429
Reality principle, 426–427
Reality therapy, 512
Recall versus recognition, and memory
    retrieval, 122–123
Reflexes, 226, 229
  in infants, 350
Refractory period, in neuron, 224
Reinforcement, 67–81
  amount of, 75–76
  and behavior control, 511
  delayed, 74–75, *74*
  differential, 89
  and liking, effect on, 278–279
  negative, 67–68
  partial, 77–79
  positive, 67
  primary, 70, 72
  schedules of, 76–77
  secondary, 70–72
  and sex-role typing, effect on,
    297–298
  theories of, 72–74
  and token economies, 510
  See also Motivation.
Reliability, of tests, 197–198, 204–205
REM (rapid eye movement) sleep,
    319–322, 344
  in relation to age, *323*
  after deprivation, *321*
  dreams during, 322
  function of, 320–322
Remarriage, 409–411
Remote Association Test (RAT), 181,
    181
Repetition, effect of on learning,
    108–109
Repression, as defense mechanism, 429
Research methods, 13–18
Reserpine, 499

Retina, 28
  and size constancy, 43-44
Retinal disparity, 40, *40*
Retirement, psychological effects of, 414-415
Retroactive interference, 120
Reversal shift, in learning, 176
Reward, *see* Positive reinforcement
Rhesus calls, language of, 134, 136
Rigid thinking, 173-174
Risk taking, in groups, 553-554
Risky shift, concept of, 553
RNA (ribonucleic acid), and role in memory, 117
Rods and cones of retina, 28, 30, 31-32
"Rolfing," *513*
Rorschach Inkblot Test, 445, *445*
Rooting reflex, 350

Salmon, evolution in, 245-246
Samples, in statistics, 620-621
Sara (chimpanzee), 152
Satiety center (hypothalamus), 260
Scanning, 169-170
Scapegoats, 302
Scatter plot, 15
Schachter-Singer experiment on arousal of emotions, 290-291
Schizophrenia, 337, 474-479
  and drugs, use of in treatment, 500
  genetic factors, 480-481
  and mother-child relationship, 484-485
  physiological causes, 481-482
  symptoms, 474-477, *474*
  types of, 477-479
Schlosberg emotion circle, 296-297, *296*
Scholastic Aptitude Tests, 203, 205
Secondary reinforcers, 70-72
Self-actualization, 11, 274-275, 437-440
Self-awareness, objective, 541
Self-esteem, need for, 274
Self-evaluation, 531
Self-perception, 573
Semantic memory, 100-101
Semicircular canals of ear, 35
Sensation, 26-36
  and adaptation, 38-40
  hearing, 32-33
  kinesthesis, 35-36
  smell, 33-34
  taste, 34
  touch, 34-35
  vision, 27-32
  See also Perception.
Sensorimotor stage of cognitive development, 357-359
Sensory homunculus, 231
Sensory neurons, 224
Sensory overload, 611
Sensory register in memory, 110-114

Sentences
  ambiguous, *140* 141
  children's, 145-146
  context of, 138-139
  deep and surface structures of, 139-140
  meaning of, 138-139
  See also Grammar.
Separation, psychological effect of on children, 371-372
Set
  and effect on perception, 55-57
  and problem solving, 173
Sex, determination of, 244-245
Sex differences, 391-393
  in aggressiveness, 391-392
  in amount of personal space, 596-597, 610-611
  in quantitative and spatial ability, 392-393
  in verbal ability, 392
Sex drive, 267-270
Sex hormones, 238-239, 267-269
Sex roles, 388-400
  and career choice, 390, 400
  changes in, 400
  and emotions, expression of, 299
  origin of, 393-399
  and social factors, 397-399
  and women's movement, 394-396
Sex therapy, 384-385
Sexual behavior, 267-270
  during adolescence, 380-381
  in childhood, Freudian theory, 430-432
  current attitudes, 382-385
  extramarital, 383-384, 407
  Freudian theory, 430-433
  homosexuality, 383, 386-388
  and limbic system, 286
  in middle age, 410-411
  in old age, 413-414
  premarital, 383
  surveys on, 383-384
  transsexualism, 389
Sexual deviance, 385-388
Sexual feelings, repression of, 430, 484
Sexual identification, 372, 397-399
Shape constancy, 45, *45*
Sheldon's body types, 421-422, *422*
Short-term memory, 114
Similarity
  and concept formation, 164
  and liking, effect on, 276-277
  and stimulus generalization, 88
Size constancy, 42-44
Skin sensors, 35
Skinner box, 68-69
Sleep, 317-322, 344
  deprivation, 320-322
  and effects on memory, 120
  function of, 320-322
  patterns of, 317

REM, 319-322
  stages of, 317-318
  See also Dreams.
Smell, sense of, 33-34
Smiling, in infancy, 363
Social behavior
  affiliation, 536-541
  and attribution theory, 534-536
  competition versus cooperation, 543-545
  and perception of others, 532-536
  See also Crowding; Groups.
Social comparison, theory of, 39, 531, 540-541
Social evaluation, 542-543
Social facilitation, 542-543
Social influence
  and attitude change, 574-585
  bystander intervention, 567-569
  in increasing compliance, 562-565
Social justice, 565-567
Social learning theory of personality, 434-437
  implications of, 436-437
Social learning theory of psychopathology, 485-488
Social motives
  acceptance and liking, need for, 529
  fear of being deviant, 529-531
  fear reduction, 539-540
  social comparison, 531
Social perception, 532-536
  and attribution theory, 534-536
  and liking, 533-534
  stereotypes and prejudice, 532-533
Social pressure, *see* Social influence
Somatic nervous system, 225, 236
Speech
  appearance of, 142
  manic, 472
  schizophrenic, 476
  telegraphic, 143-144
Spinal cord, 225-226, *225*
Spinal reflexes, 226
Split-brain phenomenon, 234-235, *235*
Split-half reliability, of tests, 198
Spontaneous recovery
  in classical conditioning, 67, *67*
  from neurosis, 520-522
Standard deviation, 618, 621
  on Wechsler scales, 202
Standard error of the difference between two means, 623
Standard error of the mean, 622
Stanford-Binet, 200-201, *201*
Statistics, 616-623
  central tendency, measures of, 616-619
  correlation, 619
  descriptive, 616-619
  inferential, 619-623
  normal distribution, 621-623
  populations, 620-621

samples, 620-621
  and variation, measures of, 618-619
Stereotypes, 532-533
  in language, 153
  sexual, 389-390; *see also* Sex roles
Steroids, 241, 242
Stimulants, *338*, 340
Stimulus generalization, 87-89, *87*, 164, 301
  and basic trust, 88
  generalization gradient, 87
  and learning, 88
  and prejudice, 88
Stimulus-response psychology, 9
Stirrup, of ear, 33
Stomach contractions, from hunger, 257-258, *258*
Stranger anxiety, 363
Strong Vocational Guidance Test, 403
Successive approximations, process of, 79
Sultan (chimpanzee), 178-179
Superego, *426*, 427
Superstitious behavior, 80-81
Survey research, 17
"Survival of the fittest," 246
Swimming reflex, 350
"Swinging," 383
Sympathetic nervous system, 236, *237*
Symptom substitution, 488, 509
Synapse, 223-224
Systematic desensitization, 506-508, *507*

Tarexin, 482
Taste, 34
  and hunger motive, 258-260
Taste receptor cells, 34
Taylor Manifest Anxiety Scale (TMAS), 450
Telegraphic speech, 143-144
Telepathy, 189
Television, effects of on aggression, 304-305, 310, 312
Temporal lobes, 230
Territoriality, 597-598
Test anxiety, 450
Testes, 241
Testosterone, 241, 267
Tests
  creativity, 181-182
  motivation, effects of, 259
Tests, personality
  direct, 443-444
  problems in, 442-443
  projective, 444-446
Tests, psychological
  reliability of, 197-198
  theory of, 197
  validity of, 198-199
  See also Intelligence tests.
Thalamus, 230

Thalidomide, 349
Thanatos, 425
Thematic Apperception Test (TAT), 272, 446, *446*
Therapist-patient relationship, 511
Therapy
  behavior, 485-488, 506-512
  chemical, 499-501
  eclectic, 520
  electroshock, 498-499
  encounter groups, 517-519
  EST, 513
  evaluation of different types of, 519-523
  Gestalt, 512
  group, 516-517
  person-centered, 513-516
  play, 516, 517
  primal, 512
  psychoanalytic, 502-506
  reality, 512
  sex, 384-385
  specialists in, 496-497
  transactional analysis, 512-513
Thinking
  convergent, 181
  creative, 180-182
  defined, 162-163
  divergent, 181
  heuristics, 169-170
  insight, 178-179
  obsessive, 464
  schizophrenic, 476-477
  See also Concept formation; Problem solving.
Thorndike's puzzle box, 171-172, *171*
Three-factor theory of personality, 423
Thyroid gland, 241
Tickling, 35
Timbre, of sound, 32
Time perception, 54
Tip-of-the-tongue phenomenon, 121
Toilet training, 366-367
Token economies, 91, 510
Touch, 34-35
Traits, genetic, 243-244
Tranquilizers, 499-501
Transactional analysis, 512-513
Transference, in psychoanalytic therapy, 504-505
Transsexualism, 389
Trial-and-error approach to problem solving, 171-172, 176
Tropic hormones, 240-241
Trust
  development of in infancy, 363-366
  lack of as cause of mental disorder, 483-484
Twins, 352
  and correlation of IQ scores, 213-214, *213*
  and studies on schizophrenia, 480

Unconditioned response, 64
Unconditioned stimulus, 64
Unconscious, concept of, 424-425
Unemployment, and effect on career choice, 402
Universal unconscious, 328
Urban living, 600-601, 612-614

Validity, of tests, 198-199, 205-207
Valium, 500
Values, during adolescence, 401
Variable interval schedule of reinforcement, 77
Variable ratio schedule of reinforcement, 77
Variation, measures of, 618-619
Vestibular sacs in ear, 35
Vision
  color, 29-32
  convergence, 40-41
  effects on intelligence testing, 209
  in infants, 354-355
  physiology of, 27-28
  retinal disparity, 40
  See also Eye; Illusion; Perception.
Visual cliff, 51, *51*
Visual field, 29, *29*
  and figure-ground relationship, 47
  position of objects in, 41
Vocational guidance tests, 403, *403*
Volley theory of hearing, 33

Walking reflex, 350
Washoe (chimpanzee), 150-151, *151*
Water-jar problems, *173*
Weaning, 366
Weber-Fechner law of psychophysics, 37-38
Wechsler Adult Intelligence Scale (WAIS), 201-202, *202*
Wechsler Intelligence Scale for Children (WISC), 201-202
Whorf hypothesis, 152
Wish fulfillment, in dreams, 325, 326-327
Women's movement, 299, 394-396

Xenophobia, 462

Yerkes-Dodson law, 259, *259*
Yoga, 334-335
Young-Helmholtz theory of color vision, 31

Zen Buddhism, and meditation, 334
Zygote, 245